Discovering
Generic CADD® 6.0/6.1

Discovering
Generic CADD® 6.0/6.1

Derik J. White
Janice L. White

Delmar Publishers Inc. ™

I(T)P™

NOTICE TO THE READER

Publisher does not warrant or guarantee any of the products described herein or perform any independent analysis in connection with any of the product information contained herein. Publisher does not assume, and expressly disclaims, any obligation to obtain and include information other than that provided to it by the manufacturer.

The reader is expressly warned to consider and adopt all safety precautions that might be indicated by the activities described herein and to avoid all potential hazards. By following the instructions contained herein, the reader willingly assumes all risks in connection with such instructions.

The publisher makes no representations or warranties of any kind, including but not limited to, the warranties of fitness for particular purpose or merchantability, nor are any such representations implied with respect to the material set forth herein, and the publisher takes no responsibility with respect to such material. The publisher shall not be liable for any special, consequential or exemplary damages resulting, in whole or in part, from the readers' use of, or reliance upon, this material.

Delmar staff:

Publisher: Michael McDermott
Project Development Editor: Mary Beth Ray
Art and Design Coordinator: Lisa Bower

Associate Editor: Pamela Graul
Production Coordinator: Andrew Crouth

For information, address

Delmar Publishers Inc.
3 Columbia Circle, Box 15015,
Albany, NY 12212-5015

COPYRIGHT © 1994 BY DELMAR PUBLISHERS INC.
The trademark ITP is used under license.

Generic CADD is a registered trademark of Autodesk Retail Products.

All rights reserved. No part of this work may be reproduced or used in any form, or by any means—graphic, electronic, or mechanical, including photocopying, recording, taping, or information storage and retrieval systems—without written permission of the publisher.

Printed in the United States of America
Published simultaneously in Canada by Nelson Canada,
a division of The Thomson Corporation

1 2 3 4 5 6 7 8 9 10 XXX 00 99 98 97 96 95 94

Library of Congress Cataloging-in-Publication Data
White, Derik.
    Discovering generic Cadd 6.0/6.1/Derik J. White, Janice L. White.
        p. cm.
    Includes index.
    ISBN 0-8273-5571-8
    1. Computer graphics. 2. Generic CADD. I. White, Janice L.
II. Title
T385.W537   1994
620'.0042'02855369—dc20

93—34249
CIP

Contents

Introduction I-1
    Generic CADD Then and Now I-1
    Making a Smart Investment I-2
    What's in Store for You I-2

Chapter 1 Basic CADD Concepts 1-1
    Introduction 1-1
    CAD Versus Paint Programs 1-2
    Drawing Scale and Driving to the Mountains 1-2
    CAD Objects 1-3
    Revising and Reusing Drawings 1-4
    2D or 3D CAD? 1-4
    Chapter Summary 1-6

Chapter 2 Nothing but the Kitchen Sink 2-1
    Introduction 2-1
    Conventions Used Here 2-1
        Mouse Conventions 2-2
        Command Conventions 2-2
    Start Generic CADD 6 2-3
    The CADD 6 Screen 2-3
    Drawing the Kitchen Sink 2-5
        What To Do If You Get Into Trouble 2-6
        Draw the Left-Side Basin 2-7
        Draw the Drain 2-11
        Draw the Right-Side Basin 2-12
        Draw the Faucet 2-15
        Draw the Faucet Handles 2-19
        Adding Text 2-21
    Saving, Erasing, and Loading Your Drawing 2-22
    Chapter Summary 2-23

Chapter 3 Speaking the Language 3-1
    Interfacing with CADD 6 3-1
    Basic CADD 6 Concepts 3-1
        Building Blocks 3-1
        Primitives Are Not Enough 3-2
        A Picture Is Worth 1000 Words 3-4
        Managing Your Drawings 3-5
        Not for the Weak of Heart 3-6
    Special Keys and Pointing Devices 3-7

Enter Key	3-7
Backspace Key	3-8
Delete Key	3-8
Insert Key	3-8
Arrow Keys	3-8
Home Key	3-9
Space Bar	3-9
Escape Key	3-9
Control Key	3-9
Pointing Devices	3-10
When You Need Help	3-11
Selecting Commands	3-11
Using the Video Menu	3-12
Two-Letter Commands	3-13
Three-Letter Commands	3-14
Nested Commands	3-15
What Does CADD 6 Want?	3-16
Four Types of Input	3-16
Identifying Points	3-17
Command Line Input	3-18
Choosing from a List	3-18
No Input	3-19
Selecting Points	3-21
Selecting with the Mouse	3-21
Snapping to a Point	3-21
Selection with Direct Distance	3-21
Entering Coordinates	3-22
Chapter Summary	3-24
Chapter 4 Creating	**4-1**
Using the DRAW and CONSTRAINTS Menus	4-1
Draw	4-1
Constraints	4-2
Using the Draw Commands	4-2
Point (PO)	4-2
Line (LI)	4-3
Individual Line (L1)	4-3
Rectangle (RE)	4-3
Regular Polygon (RP)	4-3
Center Construction	4-3
Side Construction	4-4
Circles	4-4
Circle 2-Point (C2)	4-4
Circle 3-Point (C3)	4-4

Arcs	4-5
Arc 2-Point (A2)	4-5
Arc 3-Point (A3)	4-5
Ellipses and Curves	4-6
Ellipse (EP)	4-6
Bezier Curve (BV)	4-7
Individual Bezier Curve (BW)	4-8
Spline or Complex Curve (CV)	4-9
Double Lines (L2)	4-9
Double Line Settings (DB)	4-10
Left Offset and Right Offset	4-10
Solid	4-10
Autofillet	4-11
Fillet radius	4-11
Multidraw (MU)	4-11
Multidraw Settings (MS)	4-11
Line and Of	4-11
Layer	4-12
Color	4-12
Type	4-12
Width	4-12
Offset from Cursor	4-12
Using the Constraint Commands	4-14
Ortho Mode (OR) and Ortho Angle (OA)	4-14
Grid ON/OFF (GR)	4-14
Snap To Grid (SG)	4-15
Grid Size (GS)	4-15
Grid Re-Origin (GO)	4-15
Cursor Movement (CM)	4-16
Tutorial — Kitchen Layout, Part I	4-16
Initial Drawing Parameters	4-17
Drawing Walls	4-19
Drawing the Counter Tops	4-21
Inserting the Kitchen Sink	4-23
Drawing the Trash Compactor	4-27
Drawing the Dishwasher	4-29
Drawing the Refrigerator	4-31
Drawing the Stove	4-33
Chapter Summary	4-37
Sample Exercises	4-38
Chapter 5 Modifying with SHORTCUTS and EDITS	**5-1**
Using the SHORTCUTS and EDITS Menus	5-1
Shortcuts	5-1

Object Copy (OC)	5-2
Object Erase (OE)	5-3
Object Move (OM)	5-4
Object Change (OG)	5-4
Using the Window Feature	5-5
Window Change (WG)	5-6
Window Copy (WC)	5-6
Window Erase (WE)	5-7
Window Move (WM)	5-7
Window Stretch (WS)	5-8
Window Rotate (WR)	5-9
Using the Scale Feature	5-9
Window Scale (WZ)	5-13
Drawing Scale (DZ)	5-13
Drawing Rotate (DR)	5-14
Drawing Change (DG)	5-14
Shortcut Summary	5-15
Using the EDITS Commands	5-15
Selection Sets	5-16
Window	5-16
Object	5-17
Layer	5-17
Drawing	5-17
Crossing	5-17
Last	5-18
Filter	5-18
Components	5-18
Hatches, Fills, and Dimensions	5-19
Text	5-19
Some Filter Examples	5-19
Highlight	5-20
More EDITS Commands	5-20
Move Point (MP)	5-21
Mirror Copy (MI)	5-22
Radial Copy (RC)	5-23
Object Break (OB)	5-23
Stretch (SS)	5-24
Bezier Edit (BE)	5-25
Unerase (UE)	5-27
Undo (OO)	5-27
Redo (UU)	5-27
Chapter Summary	5-27
Sample Exercises	5-28

Chapter 6 Modifying with Snaps and Trims 6-1
Using the SNAPS and TRIMS Menus 6-1
  SNAPS 6-1
    Snap Nearest Point (NP) and Closest Point (SC) 6-2
      Snap Nearest Point (NP) 6-2
      Snap Closest Point (SC) 6-3
    Snap All Visible Layers (SY) 6-3
    Snap Object (SO) 6-3
    Snap Midpoint (SM) 6-3
    Snap Percentage (SR) 6-3
    Snap Intersection (SI) 6-6
    Snap Perpendicular (SP) 6-7
    Snap Parallel (SL) 6-7
      Snap Parallel to Lines 6-7
      Snap Parallel to Arcs and Circles 6-9
    Snap Arc Center (SN) 6-9
    Snap Arc Tangent (ST) 6-10
    Snap Grid (SG) and Component Snap (GC) 6-11
    Tolerance (TO) and Quick Pick (QP) 6-12
      Tolerance (TO) 6-12
      Quick Pick (QP) 6-12
Using TRIM Commands 6-13
  TRIMS 6-13
  Trim (RM) 6-14
  Extend (XT) 6-15
  Fillet (FI), Fillet Radius (RF), and Autofillet (AF) 6-16
  Chamfer (CH) and Chamfer Distance (CA) 6-17
  Intersection Trim (IT) 6-18
  Multiple Trim (MT) 6-19
  Multiple Extend (MX) 6-20
CADD Tutorial — Kitchen Layout, Part II 6-20
  Insert a Kitchen Window 6-21
  Modify the Sink 6-22
  Drawing the Drains 6-26
Chapter Summary 6-33
Sample Exercises 6-33

Chapter 7 Viewing Your Drawing 7-1
Using the ZOOM and DISPLAY Commands 7-1
  ZOOMS 7-1
  Zoom All (ZA) 7-2
  Zoom Window (ZW) 7-2
  Zoom In (ZI) 7-2
  Zoom Out (ZO) 7-3

Pan (PA)	7-4
Zoom Previous (ZP)	7-4
Multiview (VP)	7-4
Multiview Settings (VS)	7-5
Multiple views	7-5
Active view	7-5
Layer management	7-5
Redraw (RD)	7-5
Backwards Redraw (BR)	7-6
Redraw Window (WD)	7-6
Zoom Limits (ZL)	7-6
Zoom Value (ZM)	7-6
DISPLAY	7-8
Line Color (LC)	7-8
Line Type (LT)	7-8
Line Scale (LZ)	7-9
Line Width (LW)	7-9
Color Settings (CS)	7-10
Units (UN)	7-11
Display Coordinates (DC)	7-11
Coordinates	7-11
Absolute	7-11
Relative	7-11
Basepoint	7-12
Numeric Display Format (NF)	7-12
Angular	7-12
Linear	7-12
Decimal value	7-12
Fractional value	7-12
Leading zeros	7-13
Show units	7-13
Display Settings (DI)	7-13
Display color	7-13
Cursor color	7-13
Cursor size	7-13
Status line	7-13
Tandem cursor	7-14
Reference Points (PR)	7-14
Construction Points (PC)	7-14
Standard Points (PS)	7-14
Object Drag (OD)	7-14
Rubberband (RB)	7-15
Fast Redraw (FA)	7-15
Fast Text	7-15

Fast Arcs and Arc Sides	7-15
Disable Line Widths and Line Types	7-16
Fills and Hatching	7-16
Layer update	7-16
Highlight (HI)	7-16
Chapter Summary	7-17
Sample Exercise	7-18

Chapter 8 Adding Text 8-1

Using the TEXT Menu	8-1
TEXT	8-1
Setting Text Parameters	8-2
Text Settings (TS)	8-2
Font	8-3
Size	8-5
Filled	8-6
Justification	8-6
Slant	8-6
Aspect	8-7
Rotation	8-8
Color	8-8
Spacing	8-9
Between Character	8-9
Between Line	8-9
Proportional	8-10
Entering and Editing Text	8-11
Text Place (TP)	8-12
Text Line (TL)	8-12
Text Insert (TI)	8-14
Text Delete (TD)	8-14
Text Replace (TX)	8-14
Text Append (TA)	8-14
Text Change (TG)	8-15
Text Edit (TE)	8-15
Creating and Editing Text Fonts	8-15
Chapter Summary	8-16

Chapter 9 Using Symbols 9-1

Using the COMPONENTS and ATTRIBUTES Menus	9-1
COMPONENTS	9-2
ATTRIBUTES	9-2
Creating and Saving Components	9-3
Component Create (CC)	9-3
Component Create Window (CW)	9-6

    Save Component (SAC) 9-7
    Component Dump (CD) 9-7
  Using Components in Your Drawings 9-8
    Load Component (LOC) 9-8
    Component Place (CP) 9-8
    Insertion Point (IP) 9-10
    Component Explode (CE) 9-11
    Explode Destination Layer (XY) 9-11
    Component Image (CI) 9-12
    Component Replace (CN) 9-12
    Component Remove (CX) 9-13
    Component Scale (CZ) 9-14
    Component Rotate (CR) 9-15
    Component Snaps (GC) 9-15
  Introduction to Attributes 9-17
    Attribute Create (AC) 9-17
    Save Attribute (SAT) 9-18
    Load Attribute (LOT) 9-19
    Attribute Attach (AT) 9-19
    Attribute Detach (DE) 9-21
    Attribute Edit (AE) 9-21
      To Edit a Definition 9-22
      To Edit a Placement 9-22
    Attribute Settings (AS) 9-24
      Font 9-24
      Size 9-25
      Color 9-25
      Display 9-25
      Label 9-25
      At Placement 9-26
      Direction 9-26
      Auto placement 9-26
    Export Attribute (XA) 9-26
  Electronic Schematic Tutorial 9-29
    Creating the Components and Attributes 9-29
    Creating the Schematic Drawing 9-38
  Chapter Summary 9-46

Chapter 10 Hatching and Filling **10-1**
  Using the HATCH/FILL Menu 10-1
    HATCH/FILL 10-2
  Hatching and Selecting Boundaries 10-2
    Window Hatch (WH) 10-2
    Object Hatch (OH) 10-3

Fitted Hatch (FH)	10-4
Boundary Hatch (BH)	10-5
Selecting, Changing, and Displaying Hatch Patterns	10-6
Hatch Settings (HS)	10-6
Pattern	10-6
Scale	10-7
Rotate	10-7
Color	10-7
Display	10-9
Boundary	10-10
Choosing and Displaying Fills	10-10
Fill Color (FC)	10-10
Identifying Boundaries for Fills	10-11
Window Fill (WF)	10-11
Object Fill (OF)	10-11
Fitted Fill (FF)	10-11
Boundary Fill (BF)	10-12
Chapter Summary	10-14
Chapter 11 Dimensioning	**11-1**
Using the DIMENSIONS Menu	11-1
DIMENSIONS	11-2
Choosing Dimensioning Variables	11-2
Dimension Settings (US)	11-3
Text	11-3
Placement	11-3
Direction	11-3
Centered	11-4
Size	11-4
Offset	11-4
Tolerance	11-4
Display	11-5
Extensions	11-5
Offset	11-6
Length Above and Length Below	11-6
Stretch	11-6
Display 1 and Display 2	11-7
Arrows	11-7
Type	11-7
Angle	11-7
Length	11-8
Location	11-8
Display 1 and Display 2	11-8
Dim line	11-8

Proximity fixed	11-8
Direction	11-8
Display	11-9
Font	11-9
Layer	11-10
Color	11-11
Dimension Mode (UM)	11-11
Single	11-11
Partitioned	11-12
Cumulative	11-12
Proximity Fixed (PF)	11-12
Placing Dimensions in a Drawing	11-12
Linear Dimension (LX)	11-12
Angular Dimension (AX)	11-14
Radial Dimension (RX)	11-15
Diameter Dimension (IX)	11-16
Dimension Leader (LE)	11-17
Shoulder Length (LL)	11-18
Dimension Move (UV)	11-18
Linear	11-18
Angular	11-18
Radial and Diameter	11-18
Leader	11-18
Dimension Change (UG)	11-21
Arrows	11-21
Dimension Lines	11-22
Dimension Text	11-22
Extension Lines	11-22
Dimensioning Tutorial	11-23
Part I — Setting Up Initial Dimensioning Variables	11-23
Part II — Creating the Drawing to Dimension	11-25
Part III — Dimensioning the Drawing	11-26
Chapter Summary	11-31
Sample Exercises	11-32
Chapter 12 Organizing	**12-1**
Using the LAYERS Menu and Named Views	12-1
LAYERS	12-2
ZOOMS	12-2
Introduction to Layers	12-2
Layer Selection Methods	12-3
All Layers Edit (AL)	12-4
Set Current Layer (YC)	12-5
Layer Display (YD)	12-5

Layer Name (YN) 12-6
Layer Hide (YH) 12-6
Layer Erase (YX) 12-7
Layer Rotate (YR) 12-7
Layer Re-scale (YZ) 12-7
Layer Change (YG) 12-8
Layer Dimension (UL) 12-8
Layer Load (YL) 12-8
Layer Save (YS) 12-9
Using Named Views (ZOOMS) 12-10
Name View (NV) 12-10
Zoom View (ZV) 12-10
Delete Named View (NX) 12-10
Kitchen Tutorial for Layers and Named Views 12-11
Chapter Summary 12-16

Chapter 13 Input and Output 13-1
Using the FILE and CONVERT Menus 13-1
FILE 13-1
CONVERT 13-2
Using the File Commands 13-2
Print Manager (Print Mgr) 13-2
Select GCDs 13-2
Prt Cfg 13-3
Print 13-4
Start Printing 13-4
Set Timer 13-4
Job Delete 13-4
Troubleshooting 13-5
Plot/Print/Postscript (DP) 13-5
1) Send To 13-6
2) Port 13-7
3) Page Size 13-8
4) Options 13-8
Options: Printer 13-8
Options: Plotter 13-9
Options: Postscript 13-12
Select View Type 13-13
Page Setup 13-14
Origin 13-15
Scale 13-16
Rotate90 13-16
Fit 13-17
Center 13-17

xv

Start Plot 13-17
Select Plot (PL) 13-17
Upgrade Environment (EN) 13-18
Pack Data (PD) 13-18
Definition Unload (DU) 13-18
Select Saved Drawing (SV) 13-19
Drawing Rename (DN) 13-19
Drawing Remove (DX) 13-20
Load (LO) 13-20
    Drawing 13-20
    Component 13-22
    Batch file 13-22
    Attribute 13-22
    Ascii 13-22
    Image 13-23
    AutoCAD drawing 13-23
    DXF 13-23
Save (SA) 13-23
    Drawing 13-24
    Component 13-25
    Batch file 13-25
    Attribute 13-25
    Level 3 Drawing File 13-25
    Image file 13-26
    AutoCAD File 13-26
    DXF 13-26
File Paths (FP) 13-26
Quit (QU) 13-27
Using the CONVERT Commands 13-28
Drawing In (LOA) 13-28
Dxfin (LOX) 13-28
Dxfout (SAX) 13-28
Exchange Setup (XG) 13-28
HPGL to GCD 13-28
Load ASCII File (LA) 13-29
Chapter Summary 13-29

Chapter 14 Utility Commands **14-1**
Using the UTILITY Menu 14-1
    UTILITIES 14-1
    Explode (EX) 14-2
    Measure (ME) 14-2
        Distance 14-2
        Area 14-4

2-Point Angle	14-7
3-Point Angle	14-7
Screen Flip (SF)	14-9
Display Drawing Status	14-10
Drawing Extents	14-11
Point Records	14-11
Entities	14-11
Definitions	14-11
List Objects in Drawing	14-12
View	14-12
Drawing	14-13
Selected List	14-13
Display Assigned Macros	14-13
File Selector	14-13
Object Information (OI)	14-15
Entity Filter (EF)	14-16
Selection (SE)	14-16
Match (MH)	14-17
Shell Exe (SH)	14-17
Fast Text View (TV)	14-18
Set Limits (LS)	14-18
Drawing Origin (DO)	14-19
Macros and Batch Files	14-19
Save Batch (SB)	14-20
Selection Batch Save (BS)	14-20
Macro Assign (MA)	14-20
Bill of Materials (BI)	14-21
Shell to BOM	14-21
Chapter Summary	14-21
Chapter 15 Menus, Macros, and Batch Files	**15-1**
Customizing CADD 6	15-1
Keyboard Macros	15-1
Menu Macros	15-2
Batch Files	15-3
Special Characters Used in Macros and Batch Files	15-4
Comma (,)	15-4
Tilde (~)	15-4
At Sign (@)	15-4
Pound Sign (#)	15-5
Semicolon (;)	15-5
Exclamation Point (!)	15-5
Forward Slash (/)	15-6
Forces Toggle ON (++)	15-6

Forces Toggle OFF (--)	15-6
More on Batch Files	15-6
Slide Shows	15-8
Advanced Programming	15-9
Algebraic Functions	15-10
Square and Square Root Functions	15-11
System Variable ($VAL)	15-12
Using Manual Entry Modes with Macros	15-13
Example Macros	15-13
Automatic Component Rotate (45° Intervals)	15-13
Component Scale (Step-Up by Increments of 0.5)	15-14
Component Scale (Step-Down by Increments of 0.5)	15-14
Drawing a Parabola	15-15
Circle and Spiral—Using Polar Coordinates	15-18
Trigonometric Functions	15-20
Natural Log and the Exponential Function	15-23
Creating Video Menus	15-24
MENUS	15-24
Menu File Format	15-25
The Root Menu and Submenus	15-25
Menu Page Command	15-26
Video Menu Macros	15-27
Prompting for User Input	15-28
Modifying Menus	15-29
Linking Menus	15-30
Starting Batch Files from Video Menus	15-31
Symbol Library Menus	15-31
Creating Digitizer Menus	15-32
Creating a Template Overlay	15-32
Creating the Digitizer .MNU File	15-33
Load Digitizer Menu (LD)	15-35
Select Digitizer Menu (DM)	15-35
Drawing Align (DA)	15-36
Active Area (AA)	15-37
Trace Mode (TM)	15-37
Trace Scale (RZ)	15-37
Chapter Summary	15-37
Appendix A Using Coordinates	A-1
Coordinate Systems	A-1
Using Rectangular and Polar Coordinates	A-2
The Drawing Origin, Coordinate Display, and Cursor	A-6
Using the Drawing Modes	A-6
Changing the Coordinate Display	A-9

Using Polar Coordinates to Enter Bearings A-11
Summary A-12

Appendix B Using Generic CADD 6.1 and AutoCAD Together **B-1**
   The Same, Yet Different B-1
      Interface Similarities and the New AutoCAD-Style Menu B-1
      Drawing file translation B-2
   Using The AutoCAD-Style Menu B-2
   Using The Command Cross Reference Table B-3
   Drawing File Translation B-4

Index **I-1**

About the Authors

Derik J. White is founder and president of The CAD Zone of Beaverton, Oregon. For more than seven years he has provided mechanical and architectural design and drafting services, CAD training, and consulting. Since early 1991, he has worked closely with Autodesk Retail Products to develop their Home Series for "do-it-yourselfers" and their Office Series products. He specializes in customizing Generic CADD and developing easy-to-use, CADD-based applications for clients such as AutoDesk, Toyota, American Property Management, Serious Weightlifting, Portland Fire Bureau, and many others.

Janice L. White has more than 12 years of experience in engineering and software development. She was previously Manager of Research and Development for Generic Software, now Autodesk Retail Products, and a Product Manager for PC-Kwik Corporation, a developer of performance utility software for PCs. She also contributed to the development of Autodesk's Home Series and Office Series products, with Derik. She has a Master of Science in Engineering from the University of Washington and a Bachelor of Science from Michigan Technological University.

Trademark Acknowledgments

AutoCAD is a registered trademark of Autodesk Inc.
Generic CADD and Generic 3D are registered trademarks of Autodesk Retail Products.
Hewlett-Packard and LaserJet are registered trademarks of Hewlett-Packard Company.
WordPerfect is a registered trademark of WordPerfect Corporation.
Lotus 1-2-3 is a registered trademark of Lotus Development Corporation.
Trademarks of other products mentioned in this book are held by the companies producing them.

Introduction

GENERIC CADD THEN AND NOW

In 1985, Generic Software introduced Generic CADD, billed as "Real CADD for $99." They gave the personal computer market its first taste of an affordable, simple to use, yet versatile CAD program. The first version of Generic CADD possessed only the most basic drafting features, but users could see it's potential. It was the first time a CAD program was commercially available for a reasonable price.

Version 2.0 of Generic CADD was introduced as a modular CAD program. Users could save money by purchasing only the particular feature modules they needed. Separate modules were offered for "Auto-Dimensioning" and "Snaps and Trims." At that time, they continued to market the original Generic CADD as "First CADD."

Generic CADD Version 3.0 was later introduced as a much improved upgrade. This product incorporated the advanced feature modules and added other features that were commonly available only in programs that cost thousands of dollars.

Their later strategy changed to marketing different levels of Generic CADD, following a good, better, and best philosophy. Version 3.0 was dropped, and Level 1, Level 2, and Level 3 Generic CADD products were introduced. Level 1 replaced First CADD, Level 3 (Version 4.0) replaced version 3.0, and Level 2 stood in the middle.

A significant leap in program power and versatility came about with CADD 5.0, introduced in 1990. In turn, Levels 1, 2, and 3 were dropped. Over two years in the making, Generic CADD 5.0 added 150 enhancements to 25 major aspects of the previous version.

Generic CADD 6.0 added even more power and versatility to the earlier CADD 5.0. Newcomers to Generic CADD will find this latest version to be more intuitive, easier to learn, and faster, allowing users to be more productive than ever. During its growth, Generic CADD has increased in overall power and sophistication, while remaining a low cost alternative to most CAD software available today.

In 1989, Generic Software was bought by Autodesk, the makers of the largest selling CAD program, AutoCAD. Generic Software became a division of Autodesk and is now known as Autodesk Retail Products, which still maintains and develops Generic CADD today. In addition to Generic CADD, they now offer many other products including drawing and drafting application products for professionals and "do-it-yourselfers."

Today, Generic CADD 6.1 offers two-way compatibility with AutoCAD. CADD 6.1 users can import drawings from and export drawings directly to AutoCAD's native .DWG format. This makes for a strong partnership between the two programs, since CADD 6.1 users can easily share drawings with others in their company who use AutoCAD.

MAKING A SMART INVESTMENT

Generic CADD is an excellent investment because it helps you reduce and eliminate many repetitive tasks. CADD lets you make changes to existing drawings and easily create clean, new masters without redoing the entire drawing. It also allows you to design and draft in real world units, so there is no need to convert dimensions to a scale as you do when you draw manually.

All the time you invest now to become proficient at using CADD will pay off in the long run. If you have been doing manual drafting for some time, you may not be able to initially produce drawings as fast in CADD. However, keep in mind that the real power of CADD is in its accuracy and editing capabilities. When you begin to modify drawings, then you truly see what a good investment CADD is.

WHAT'S IN STORE FOR YOU

This book is a good place for you to start learning about computer-aided design and drafting. It is a valuable resource tool for those beginning and also for expert users.

If you have little or no experience with personal computers or with design and drafting, concentrate on becoming comfortable and productive with general CAD concepts and CADD 6.0's features. Don't become discouraged by trying to create a complicated drawing before you have had some practice. The best way to get started is to complete the "Quick Start Tutorial" in Chapter 2. This teaches many of the essential commands you need to become a proficient CADD 6.0 user. The concepts introduced in the Quick Start tutorial are the building blocks needed to complete the tutorials in later chapters.

If you already have experience in drafting and design on personal computers, this book can help you enhance your skills and knowledge. You will especially benefit from the many tips and practical examples given throughout.

Here is a summary of the topics in each chapter:

CHAPTER 1, "Basic Concepts," includes a brief overview of general CAD concepts and CADD 6.0. This chapter describes scale, primitive elements, revising drawings, and 2D versus 3D CAD programs.

CHAPTER 2, "Nothing But the Kitchen Sink (Quick Start Tutorial)," is where you start drawing. First, the basic functions of the CADD 6.0 screen, video menu, and commands are described. Then the "Quick Start Tutorial" shows you how to create your first drawing. You learn to start CAD, draw basic objects, and save your drawing to a file on disk. The commands and methods introduced in this chapter are some of the most frequently used features of CADD 6.0.

CHAPTER 3, "Speaking Generic CADD 6.0's Language," introduces additional CAD concepts and methods. Now that you have some experience drawing in CADD 6.0, you are ready to learn more about how to communicate with the program and how things work. This chapter explains the command structure, the basic drawing building blocks, the importance of visual feedback, and many other details which make CADD such a powerful tool.

Chapters 4 - 12 contain tutorials for drawing a kitchen floor plan, an electronic schematic, and a mechanical detail part, with different concepts introduced in each tutorial. This combination of drawings gives you a wide range of applications to learn from. The other commands available on the CADD 6.0 menus are discussed within these chapters, regardless of whether or not they are used in the tutorials.

CHAPTER 4, "Creating," starts with the essentials for creating a drawing in CADD 6.0. This includes the accurate placement of "drawing primitives" or basic objects. This chapter focuses on commands from the DRAW and CONSTRAINTS menus.

CHAPTER 5, "Modifying with Edits and Shortcuts," covers the concepts of changing your drawings, such as scaling, moving, copying, stretching, and rotating. This chapter focuses on the EDIT and SHORTCUT menus.

CHAPTER 6, "Modifying with Snaps and Trims," additional editing commands are introduced that help ensure the accuracy of your drawings. Snaps and trims allow you to select exact points, connect objects together accurately, and trim and extend objects so they end exactly at another object.

CHAPTER 7, "Viewing and the Display," describes use of the zoom commands and the many settings for customizing the video display such as choosing units, decimal value, coordinate modes, and numeric display. This chapter focuses on commands from the ZOOMS and DISPLAY menus.

CHAPTER 8, "Adding Text," explains how to add words, notes, and labels to your drawings. Commands from the TEXT menu and concepts related to CADD text are described.

CHAPTER 9, "Symbols and Grids," describes creating, placing and modifying symbols, called components, with their attributes. Attributes are data that can be added to symbols and extracted later for use in lists and bills of materials. Grids are also discussed here, as this drawing constraint is commonly used for placing components. Commands discussed in this chapter are from the COMPONENTS, ATTRIBUTES, and CONSTRAINTS menus.

CHAPTER 10, "Hatching and Filling," covers creating solid color fills and hatch patterns for making objects or drawing sections stand out. This chapter explains commands on the HATCH AND FILL menus.

CHAPTER 11, "Dimensioning," explains how to add dimensions to your drawings. Dimensioning is fast and easy because CADD 6.0 calculates the measurements and automates much of the process. These commands are found on the DIMENSIONS menu.

CHAPTER 12, "Organizing," looks at features that separate portions of your drawing into layers and specific views. You learn how layers can be established at the start of creating a drawing or added when it is complete. The commands in this chapter are from the LAYER and ZOOM (for Named View) menus.

CHAPTER 13, "Input and Output," discusses commands to load, save, and print your drawings. Other commands allow you to update your drawing environment, change file paths and names, load ASCII files, and convert your drawings to other file formats. These commands are found on the FILE and CONVERT menus.

CHAPTER 14, "Utility Commands," are a grab bag of features related to drawing setup, batch files, macros, measuring, and more. This chapter discusses commands found on the UTILITIES menu.

CHAPTER 15, "Menus, Macros, and Batch Files," describes how to create custom video menus, digitizer menus, macros, and batch files. These concepts allow you to customize CADD 6.0 to automate tedious or slow tasks.

APPENDIX A, "Coordinate Systems," this appendix contains additional information about coordinate systems and using coordinates to locate points in CADD 6.0.

APPENDIX B, "Generic CADD 6.1 and AutoCAD," this appendix explains the details of using Generic CADD 6.1 and AutoCAD together. It describes the ACAD Menu that was introduced in CADD 6.1 and what you need to understand to translate files between the two programs.

CHAPTER 1

Basic CADD Concepts

INTRODUCTION

CADD (Computer-Aided Design and Drafting), or simply CAD, is an automated graphics system that eliminates many of the redundant tasks performed in manual drafting. In traditional drafting, you have to redraw an object each time it is used in a drawing. In CAD, you draw an object once and reuse it as often as you want in the current drawing and in any future drawings.

The CAD program replaces conventional drafting tools like the T-square, templates, and drafting machine. If you think of your computer as a toolbox, then CAD certainly represents a powerful set of custom tools. As any craftsman knows, the more you use your tools, the more proficient and productive you will become.

Ivan Sutherland can be credited for bringing together many of the tools used in CAD systems today. In 1962, Sutherland described a sketch pad program that included a graphics system, a CRT (Cathode Ray Tube) display, a pointing device, and many concepts the industry still uses.

Since then, CAD has become available on a variety of computer systems, ranging in price from a few hundred dollars to more than $500,000. With the acceptance of personal computers came the advent of CAD software for PCs. Even on the PC, a broad range of CAD capabilities are available, ranging in price from $50 to more than $10,000 for many specialized CAD applications.

Generic CADD was developed as a low-cost, easy-to-learn CAD program that can run on a large variety of personal computer systems. While CAD systems were available

1-1

only to engineers and architects, Generic CADD also appeals to many nontraditional computer users such as home builders, landscapers, and interior decorators. Because of its low cost and ease of use, Generic CADD is ideal for producing accurate and professional drawings.

CAD VERSUS PAINT PROGRAMS

You may be familiar with other computer graphics programs, called paint or drawing programs. These programs can be used for creating graphics or drawing with a computer, but they are conceptually very different from a CAD program. The major differences are in drawing accuracy and the way objects are defined.

With Generic CADD, you can draw objects and select points with an accuracy of up to 6 places to the right of the decimal point. When you draw a 10-foot, 6-inch line, CAD actually stores, or remembers, the length as 10 feet, 6.000000 inches. This kind of accuracy is impossible to obtain with a paint program.

With paint programs, objects shown on-screen are defined by a number of dots, or pixels, of a specified color that make up the objects. If you draw a circle and then change the display so the circle appears larger, the pixels also become larger. The circle will no longer be smooth but will obviously be made up of individual dots.

Alternatively, CAD programs define all objects with their true mathematical definition. The program keeps a database of the definition and location of each object in the drawing. A circle may be defined by the exact location of its center and the size of its radius. CAD then uses a mathematical equation to create the circle so it looks the same regardless of how large or small it is displayed. This is called vector-based graphics rather than raster (or pixel-based) graphics.

Because all true CAD programs are vector based, you can display CAD drawings accurately and with full detail, at whatever graphics resolution you have available. On high resolution printers, such as laser printers, you can produce prints of a drawing that have an even higher resolution than what you see on screen.

DRAWING SCALE AND DRIVING TO THE MOUNTAINS

Unlike those in manual drafting, the entities in a CAD drawing can be drawn in actual size and stored in the size drawn. You can think of CAD as giving you an unlimited-size sheet of paper to draw on. You don't need to convert each drawing to a specific scale for it to fit. If you draw a house, it can be stored as a full-size house. A 20-foot wall can be stored as a 20-foot wall. Only when you want to create a hardcopy (plot or print) of the drawing do you need to specify a scale so the drawing will fit on the paper.

Actually, you could "scale" every object in a drawing as you draw them in CAD, but this is not recommended. For example, to produce a 1/4-scale drawing, a 20-foot wall would be drawn as 5 feet long. To draw this way, you would first need to calculate the scaled size of each object. Obviously, this extra step is time consuming and prone to errors. It is really better to draw everything in your CADD drawings at real world scale, or actual size. If you want to change the scale of certain detailed views, CADD 6.1 has features for doing just that.

You may ask "How can an object 20 feet long fit on a video screen that's less than 2 feet in length without scaling down the object first?" As explained earlier, if you enter an object that's 20 feet long, CAD saves this object with the 20-foot value. To view it on your video screen, CAD is equipped with viewing tools or *zoom* commands. These features let you zoom in and out on the drawing displayed, similar to using a zoom lens on a camera.

Zoom commands do not change the actual size of objects created in CAD; they merely change your perspective. To help you understand zooming, imagine taking a Sunday drive to the mountains. The closer you get to the mountains, the larger they appear. A foot away from the mountains you won't see much more than a patch of dirt or a few blades of grass. No matter where you were in respect to the mountains, whether it was 20 miles away or 1 foot, the mountains' physical dimensions did not change. If a mountain was 5000 feet tall when you started your drive, it was 5000 feet tall when you reached your destination.

CADD 6.1 works much the same way. You can zoom in on tiny details until they look huge on your screen. The size of the object is not changed, only how it is displayed.

CAD OBJECTS

To create a CAD drawing, you use a specific set of basic geometric objects or *primitives*. The primitives available in CADD 6.1 include points, arcs, circles, lines, curves, and ellipses. CADD 6.1 provides you with many commands used to select and manipulate (move, erase, connect, enlarge, reduce, etc.) these objects. Even the most complex drawings are created from combinations of these simple objects.

CADD 6.1 also has commands for placing and editing complex items like dimensions, text, and symbols; but these objects are not primitives. Each of these items can be "exploded" back to the basic objects from which they are composed (lines, arcs, curves, and so on).

There are different ways of selecting primitives that you want to change or edit. You can select a single object, any group of objects that can be enclosed in a box (called a window), or pick objects with a selection set. Selection sets allow you to use several methods to select all the objects you want to edit. Sometimes it requires some extra steps to use a selection set, but it gives you the greatest flexibility in object selection. You will learn many ways of selecting objects throughout the tutorials that follow.

REVISING AND REUSING DRAWINGS

Your CAD drawings and any portion of them can be stored on disk and reused. You save your drawings to disk as files and assign them a meaningful file name. Once saved, you can recall any drawing file to revise it or to incorporate it into another drawing.

You can also store drawings (or portions of drawings) as symbols, called *components*. Components can then be reused in all your other drawings and manipulated like single objects. It is often helpful to create whole sets of components commonly used in your types of drawings, such as electronic symbols, furniture, fasteners, welding symbols, and so on.

Your CADD 6.1 drawing and component files can also be converted to a number of other file formats. This makes it possible to use your drawings in other software programs like presentation graphics, word processors, desktop publishers, and other CAD programs.

2D OR 3D CAD?

Upon introduction to CAD you may find the difference between 2D (two-dimensional) and 3D (three-dimensional) drawing capabilities to be somewhat confusing. Generic CADD 6.1 is a 2D drafting program. All drawings created in version 6.1, regardless of their appearance, are two-dimensional. As easily as you can sketch a drawing on paper with the appearance of having three dimensions, you can create a similar drawing in your 2D CAD program; but it's obvious there is no depth to the drawing. Figure 1.1 shows what would happen to a 2D drawing if you tried to rotate it to see the objects from another direction.

A true 3D CAD package gives you the power to create and view an object from any side and angle in 3D space, as shown in Figure 1.2. You can rotate objects about any axis and see what they look like from any side. If you need 3D drafting capabilities, then consider Generic 3D, available from Autodesk Retail Products. Drawings can be created in Generic CADD 6.1 and imported into Generic 3D so that you can add depth to them. Similarly, a drawing created in Generic 3D and brought into CADD 6.1 (the 2D program) will look identical to the view sent from 3D, but it will lack the 3rd-axis information.

Although 3D CAD drawings are impressive, they are generally more difficult to create and edit. Many architectural, electronic, and mechanical drafters find that 2D CAD is adequate to meet their needs.

Chapter 1: Basic CADD Concepts ■ 1-5

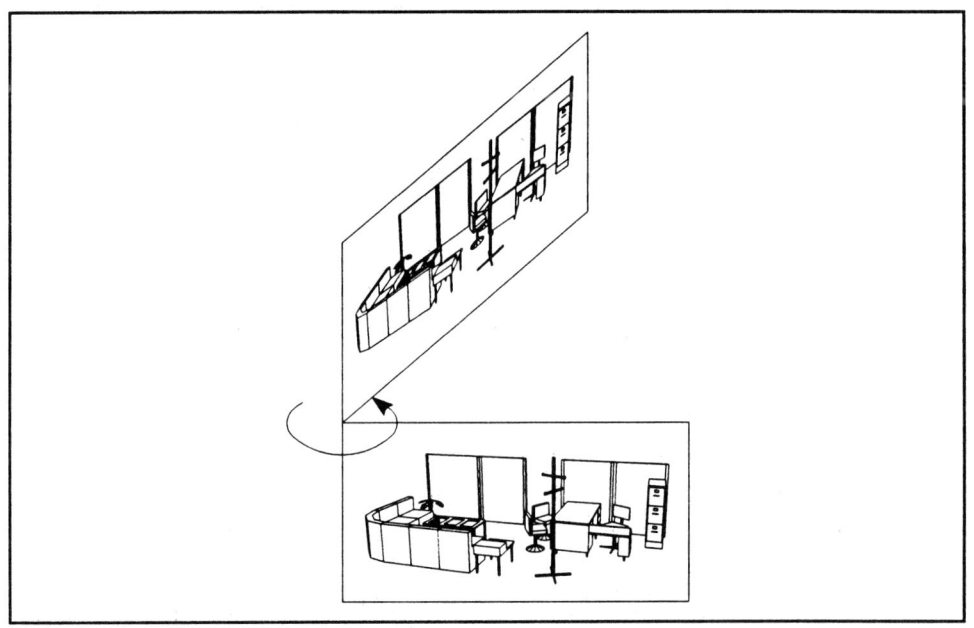

Figure 1.1 2D drawings cannot be rotated in space.

Figure 1.2 Four views from a 3D CADD program.

CHAPTER SUMMARY

In this chapter, you received an overview of some basic CADD concepts. You learned that CAD uses precise lines, not the dots used in many paint programs, and you learned that lines are electronically stored by CAD with precise measurements and locations that result in more accurate drawings.

The biggest advantage of using CAD is that your drawings can be reused and modified quickly and easily. CAD drawings can also be imported into other programs such as word processors and other CAD programs.

While 2D CAD programs and 3D programs can produce drawings on paper that look similar, 2D drawings lack any information about depth. Many drafters do not need full 3D capabilities and Generic CADD 6.1 should meet their needs.

CHAPTER 2

Nothing but the Kitchen Sink

INTRODUCTION

You've done plenty of reading about CADD 6. Now it's time to start drawing. This chapter includes instructions for starting CADD 6, introductions to the CADD 6 screen, and use of the command menus. The rest you "learn by doing" as you create your first drawing of a kitchen sink. This "quick-start" tutorial is a good place to start because it introduces many of the most commonly used drawing commands. Also, the kitchen sink you draw here becomes a part of a kitchen floor plan that is completed in a later tutorial.

CONVENTIONS USED HERE

The tutorials in this book provide the step-by-step instructions and figures you need to create each of the drawings. The first time a particular command is used, each step needed to complete it will be described in detail. Later in the book, after you have had more practice, many of the instructions will be shortened. If you cannot remember how a particular command works, refer to the Contents to find the chapter that describes it in detail.

An explanation is usually given that describes the result of performing each group of commands, although you may not always understand *why* you are doing something. Just continue through the exercise and the "method to the madness" should become obvious. There are many tricks to using CADD 6 that are just easier to show on the screen than to explain with words.

Mouse Conventions

For simplicity we assume you are using a mouse, so you commonly see instructions like this:

> Click on the desired point...

For this step, you would move your mouse around until the cursor (crosshair) is at the desired position on the drawing. Click the first button. The first button is on the left side; the second button is on the right side of a two-button mouse and in the middle of a three-button mouse.

If you don't have a pointing device (a mouse or digitizer) you can still perform all the CADD 6 commands. When the tutorial instructs you to click, use the arrow keys on your keyboard to move the cursor; then press the Enter key to select the point.

Command Conventions

Throughout the tutorials, you will see instructions like:

> Select the DRAW menu

In this case, move your cursor to highlight the DRAW menu name, found on the ROOT MENU, and click the second button of your mouse or digitizer puck (if you are using a puck like a mouse) to select the menu. If you do not have a pointing device, use the arrow keys to highlight the desired menu, then press the Home key.

To select a command from a menu, you will be instructed this way:

> Select Rectangle (from the DRAW menu)

You would first select the DRAW menu, if it is not already on the screen, then click with the second mouse button on the command called Rectangle. Then look at the bottom of the screen, CADD 6 gives you a "prompt" or an instruction that tells you what to do next.

Commands can also be selected by simply typing a two-letter abbreviation for the command name, as follows:

> Type: DN

This instruction means to type the letters DN at the CADD 6 command prompt. It doesn't matter if you use upper- or lower- case letters. You do not have to press the Enter key. The command is executed as soon as you type the second letter. In this example, typing DN starts the Drawing Rename command. Refer to Chapter 3 for more information on the ways to execute commands.

You will be instructed to enter values and measurements, as follows:

>   Type: 20'
>   Press Enter

or:

>   Type: 20' (and press Enter)

In both cases, it means you should type in the value exactly as shown, including the foot mark in this case, then press the Enter key. Unlike the two letter commands, CADD always waits for you to press the Enter key before it accepts any numbers or values that you type. This gives you the chance to change your mind or correct mistakes before completing the command.

START GENERIC CADD 6

The first step to drawing is to start up the CADD 6 program. From the DOS prompt, C:\> (or the drive where your CADD 6 is located):

>   Type: CD\CADD6
>   Press Enter

This changes you to the subdirectory \CADD6 where CADD 6 is normally located. If your copy of CADD 6 is located elsewhere, substitute the name of that subdirectory. Then:

>   Type: CADD
>   Press Enter

To start the program, type the word CADD and then press the Enter key. The CADD 6 opening screen appears for a moment and then the program starts.

THE CADD 6 SCREEN

Figure 2.1 shows the CADD 6 screen with all of the major areas labeled, including the drawing area, menu area, command prompt, cursor, and coordinate readout. Notice the menu is on the right side of the screen, a command prompt and status information are on the bottom left, and the x,y coordinate readout is on the top. The drawing area is the blank area covering most of the screen. This is where your drawing is displayed; think of it as an electronic piece of paper.

2-4 ■ Chapter 2: Nothing But the Kitchen Sink

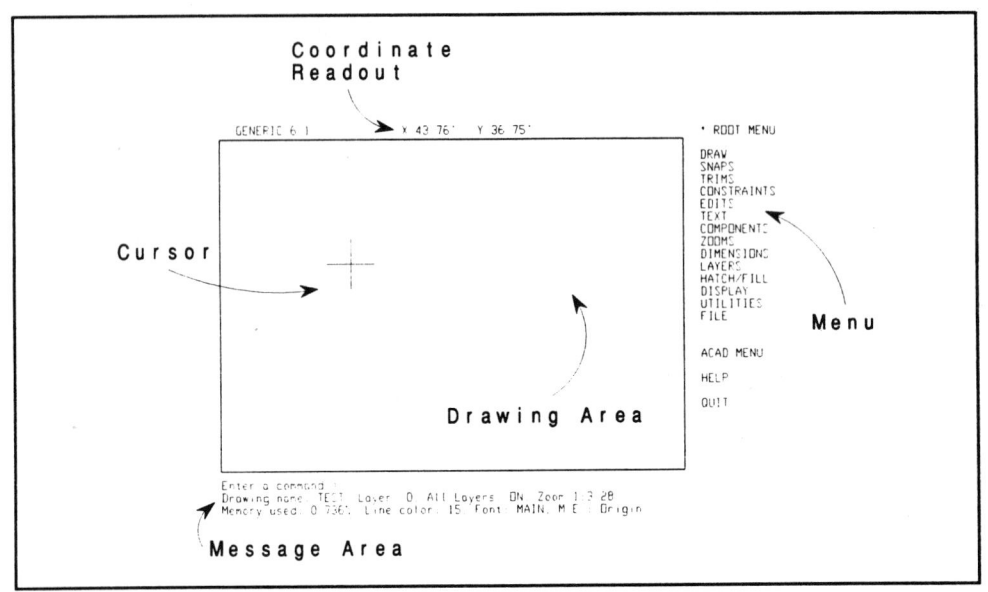

Figure 2.1 The CADD 6.1 screen.

The cursor, or crosshair, shows your actual position on the drawing. In manual drafting, the cursor would be analogous to the point of your pencil. Use your mouse, digitizer puck, or keyboard arrow keys to move the cursor around your drawing. As you move the cursor, notice that the numerical readout at the top of the screen changes. This readout displays the instantaneous X and Y coordinates of the cursor's position. This information can be displayed in several different formats, as explained in Chapter 7. Appendix A provides a general discussion of coordinate systems and how they are applied in CAD, if you want some additional background information.

The menu on the right side of the screen is really a hierarchical set of menu pages that list the CADD 6 commands. A folded card is included in your CADD 6 package that lists every menu page with their relationships to the other pages. The name of the each menu page is listed at the top in capital letters. For example, the first menu page is the ROOT MENU. This is a special menu, because it doesn't list any commands, only the names of other menu pages. Other menu pages contain the names of commands found in that menu category; the DRAW menu contains drawing commands; the DIMENSIONS menu contains dimensioning commands, and so on.

To select items from the video menu, move your cursor so the desired item is highlighted and click your right mouse button. For example, the Rectangle command is found on the DRAW menu, so to draw a rectangle:

    Select the DRAW menu
    Select Rectangle (RE)

Highlight the word DRAW on the ROOT MENU and click your second mouse button (the right button of a two-button mouse or the middle button of a three-button mouse). Then, highlight the word Rectangle on the DRAW menu and click your second mouse button again. If you have been following along in CADD, press the Esc key now to cancel the Rectangle command, since this was just an example.

> **TIP:** The Esc key (or Escape key) cancels the last command given. Use it to abort a command if you make a mistake or if you aren't sure what to do next and want to start over.

You can select commands from the video menu (as in the previous example) or by entering an abbreviation or command code from the keyboard. In this first tutorial you will be instructed to select commands from the menus since that is the easier way to get started using CADD. However, it really is much faster to use the command codes once you learn them. Later tutorials will use that approach. Either method gives the same results; use whatever works best for you. Refer to Chapter 3 for more information on the different types of CADD 6 commands.

In addition to using the menus, you also communicate with CADD 6 from the command line below the drawing area. The characters you enter from the keyboard are printed on this command line, so you can verify information before pressing the Enter key. CADD 6 also talks to you through this line. When a command is entered or selected from the menu, CADD 6 gives you a prompt, or message, that tells what to do next. CADD 6 may ask you to select a point on the drawing, select some objects to change, enter a value, or choose from a list of command options.

Below the command lines are two status lines, which give you information about the drawing on-screen. Become familiar with this information and get in the habit of referring to it as you are drawing.

DRAWING THE KITCHEN SINK

Now that you know how to use the menus to tell CADD 6 what to do, it's time to start drawing your sink. A kitchen sink may not seem like a very glamorous item for your first drawing, but it is perfect to introduce many of the basic CADD 6 drawing techniques. The completed sink is shown in Figure 2.2.

The step-by-step instructions and the illustrations show you how to draw the sink. AT first you may not understand exactly how each command works or why each command is used. All the commands are explained in detail throughout the rest of this book. This quick-start lessons shows you just how easy it can be to create a practical drawing.

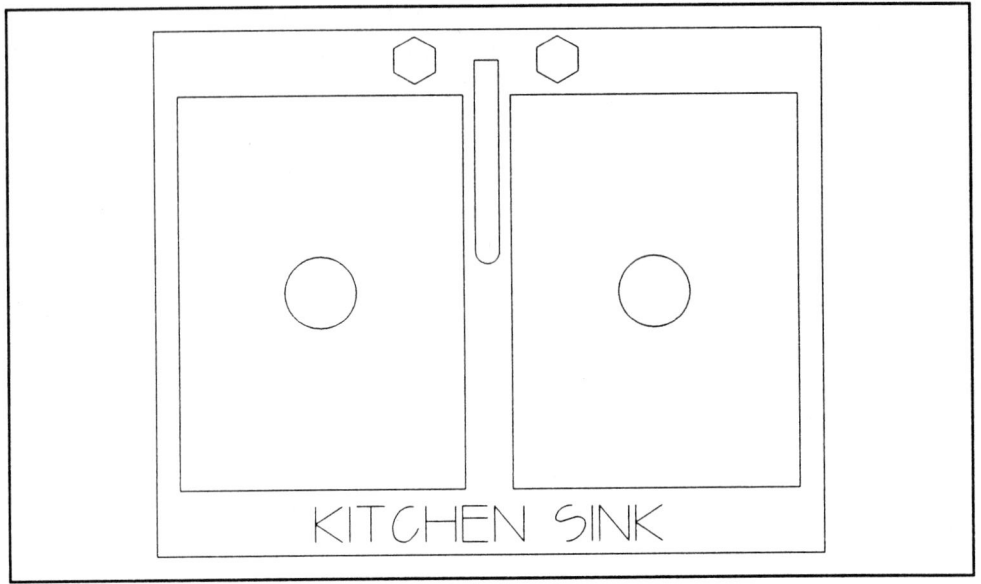

Figure 2.2 The completed kitchen sink drawing.

The commands used in this tutorial are listed below, in order of appearance:

1. Ortho Mode (OR)
2. Zoom All (ZA)
3. Manual Entry Offset Relative (MR)
4. Snap Close Point (SC)
5. Zoom Out (ZO)
6. Rectangle (RE)
7. 2-Point Circle (C2)
8. Copy, Window (CO W)
9. Highlight (HI)
10. Object Drag (OD)
11. Move, Window (MV W)
12. Snap Midpoint (SM)
13. Regular Polygon (RP)
14. Text Settings (TS)
15. Place Text Line (TL)
16. Save, Drawing (SA D)

What To Do If You Get Into Trouble

If you make a mistake or you aren't sure what to do next, you can abort or cancel any command by pressing the Escape (Esc) key. You may have to press Esc more than once to cancel some commands, so keep trying until you are back to the normal prompt.

If you complete a command but don't get the results you want, select the Undo command (or type OO) from the EDITS menu. This feature puts things back the way they were before the last operation. Continuing to select Undo steps backwards through the last commands executed. If you go back too far, select Redo to perform the last operation again.

> **TIP:** The two-letter command code for Undo is easy to remember. Whenever the results of a command cause you to say "Oops," just type OO until things are back the way they were.

Draw the Left-Side Basin

These first steps explain how to draw a 22" X 28" rectangle for the basic shape of the sink, then draw the left basin inside it. A rectangle is made up of four lines. First, make sure you can only draw horizontal and vertical lines by turning ON the Ortho Mode.

> Select the CONSTRAINTS menu (from the ROOT MENU)
> Select Ortho Mode
> Select ROOT MENU (from the bottom of the CONSTRAINTS menu)

Remember that you must click your second mouse button (from the left side) to select items from the CADD 6 video menu (as previously explained in the "Conventions Used Here" section).

Look at the bottom of your screen and make sure that CADD 6 says "Ortho Mode is ON." If it says that Ortho Mode is OFF, select it again from the menu to turn it ON. (This feature is a *toggle*, it is either ON or OFF. You will learn more about Ortho Mode in Chapter 4.)

Now you are ready to start drawing. To draw lines in CADD 6, you simply have to move the cursor to the desired point on the screen and click your first (or left) mouse button. There is a special Line command on the DRAW menu, but you only need to use it in special circumstances.

Use your mouse to move the cursor (crosshair) near the lower left corner of the screen.

> Click the first mouse button

This places the first point of the first line, as shown in Figure 2.3.

2-8 ■ Chapter 2: Nothing But the Kitchen Sink

Move your mouse to the right, away from the first point. You should see a line take shape between the starting point and the cursor. As you move your mouse, the line changes in length to reflect the instantaneous position of the cursor. You could simply click your mouse to arbitrarily place the other end of the line, but we want to be more exact.

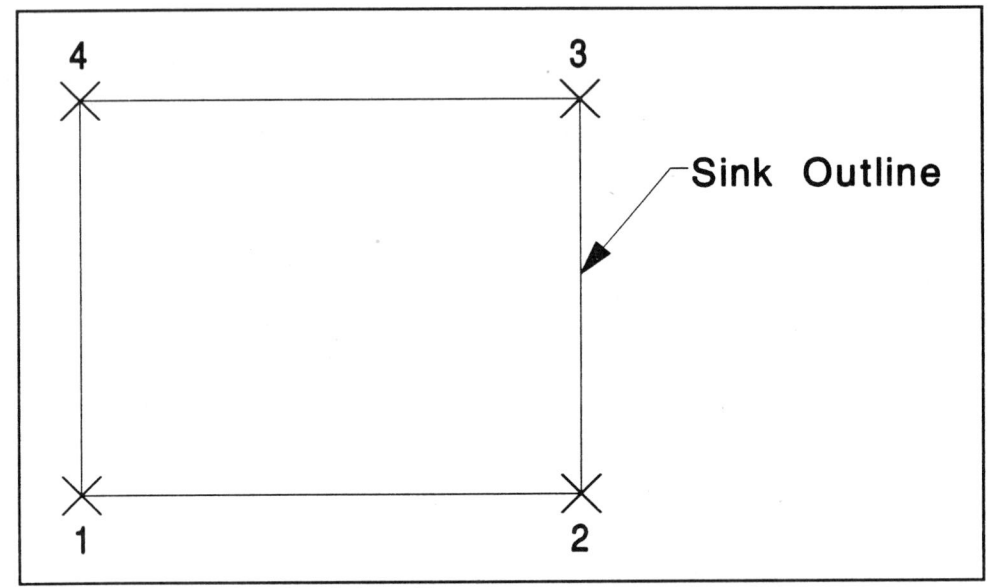

```
     4                      3
     ✗──────────────────────✗
     │                      │
     │              ┌─Sink Outline
     │              ↙       │
     │                      │
     │                      │
     │                      │
     ✗──────────────────────✗
     1                      2
```

Figure 2.3 Drawing the sink outline.

First, make sure the *rubberbanding* (stretching and contracting) line is horizontal and to the right, then:

    Type: 28 (and press Enter)

This means type the value 28 (the width of the sink) and then press the Enter key. This tells CADD 6 to draw a line 28" long in the direction the cursor was moving, horizontal and to the right in this case. By default, CADD 6 interprets numbers as being in inches. There is no need to enter units for distances in inches. Now draw a 22" line for the right side of the rectangle. There should still be a line rubberbanding between the cursor and the right end of the first line drawn.

    Move the cursor up toward the top of the screen
    Type: 22 (and press Enter)

Again, this means type the number 22 and then press the Enter key. The cursor jumps to a point 22" above the first line. A vertical line is drawn for the right side of the rectangle. If the vertical lines appear to go off the screen, you can just tell CADD 6 to show more on the screen, as follows:

Chapter 2: Nothing But the Kitchen Sink ■ 2-9

>   Select the ZOOMS menu (from the ROOT MENU)
>   Select All
>   Select the ROOT MENU (from the ZOOMS menu)

This executes the Zoom All command, one of the most commonly used of all the CADD 6 commands. Both lines should now appear on the screen. The cursor should be rubberbanding from the end of the vertical line.

TIP: Use Zoom commands to adjust the view of your drawing. Whenever you can't see all of an object on the screen, or if you want to see some details close up, Zooms are the answer.

Now, draw the last two sides of the rectangle:

>   Move the cursor horizontally to the left
>   Type: 28 (and press Enter)
>   Move the cursor vertically toward the bottom of the screen
>   Type: 22 (and press Enter)
>   Press Esc (the Escape key) to finish drawing lines

The last line drawn should end exactly at the starting point of the first line. This completes the outline of the sink, although this wasn't the easiest way to draw a rectangle! You can use the Rectangle command on the DRAW menu to draw the left basin. But first, you must establish a framework for CADD to interpret the distances you are about to enter.

>   Type: MR

MR is the command code for Manual Entry Offset Relative. This tells CADD 6 to interpret all the distances you enter as being measured from (or relative to) the last point entered. In Chapter 3 and Appendix A you learn all about using coordinates and CADD 6's various drawing modes.

Figure 2.4 shows that the rectangle for the left-sink basin is 1" over and 2.75" up from the lower left corner of the sink outline.

To draw the basin accurately, you must first locate this exact starting point. CADD 6 has commands called *snaps* that are used to locate points accurately. You can use your mouse to click near a point, but you will never be able to select it exactly. To select any exact point you must snap to it.

2-10 ■ Chapter 2: Nothing But the Kitchen Sink

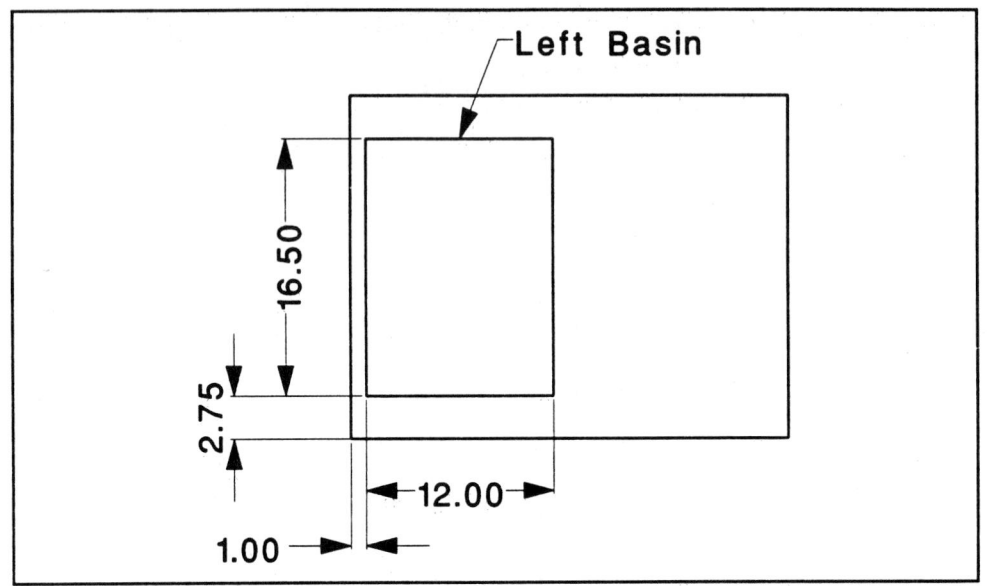

Figure 2.4 Location and size of the left-sink basin.

>   Type: SC (for Snap Close Point)
>   Move your cursor so it is close to the lower left-hand corner of the rectangle
>   Click your first mouse button

This snaps to the lower left-hand corner of the rectangle. The next distances entered will be measured from that corner. Now:

>   Select the DRAW menu (from the ROOT MENU)
>   Select Rectangle (the Rectangle command)

Look at the command prompt at the bottom of the screen. CADD 6 asks you to:

>   Enter one corner of the rectangle >

Do not click with your mouse; instead, enter the next set of numbers just as they appear, including the comma.

>   Type: 1,2.75
>   Press Enter

The cursor jumps to a point that is 1" to the right and 2.75" above the lower corner of the rectangle. CADD 6 then prompts you to enter the opposite corner of the rectangle. Move the cursor up and to the right to see the rubberbanding rectangle, then:

Type: 12,16.5
Press Enter

This establishes the upper-right corner of the basin as 12" to the right and 16.5" above the first corner. In other words, the plan view of this sink basin is exactly 12" wide and 16.5" tall.

Draw the Drain

To place a drain hole in the sink, you must first locate a circle at the exact center of the sink basin rectangle. To do this, use the same method used to locate the starting corner of the left basin, except enter values that will position the cursor at the center of the rectangle.

Type: SC (for Snap Closest Point)
Move your cursor so it is close to the lower left-hand corner of the rectangle
Click your first mouse button

This snaps to the lower left-hand corner of the basin, as shown in Figure 2.5. The next distances entered will be measured from that corner.

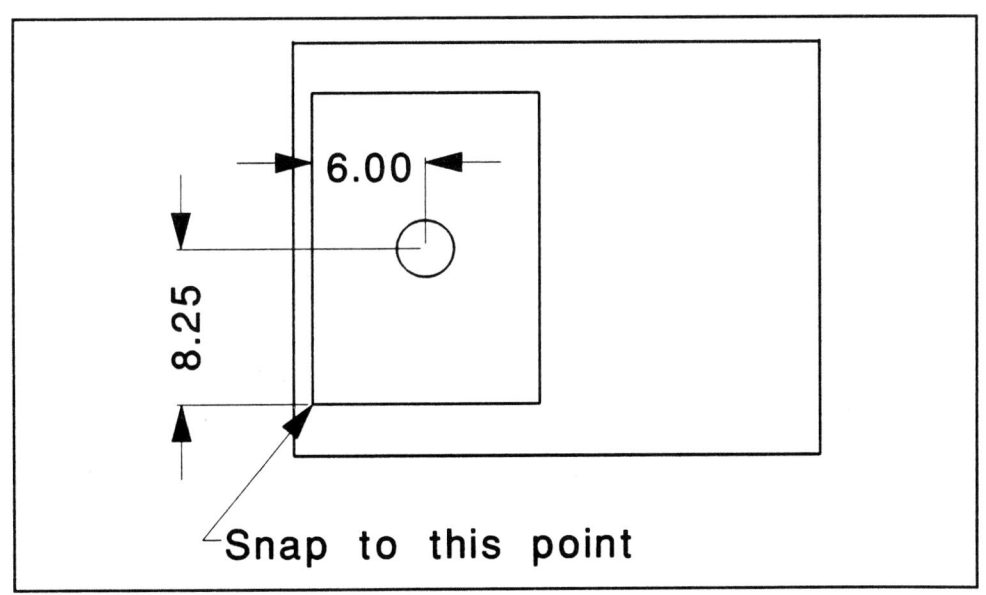

Figure 2.5 Positioning the sink drain.

Now use the Two-Point Circle command to draw the circle. To define the size and location of the circle, you must locate its center point and another point on the circle itself.

Select Circle 2 (C2)

2-12 ■ Chapter 2: Nothing But the Kitchen Sink

CADD 6 then asks you to locate the circle's center point:

> Type: 6,8.25
> Press Enter

This tells CADD 6 to put the center of the circle 6" to the right and 8.25" up from the basin's corner. Where did those number come from? We drew the basin to be 12" wide, so it's midpoint is over 6". Likewise, the basin was drawn 16.5" tall, so 8.25" is half way up.

Next, CADD 6 asks you to enter a point on the circle. The radius of the circle is the distance between the center of the circle and this point. Move the cursor and you should see a circle, centered in the basin, that changes size with the cursor movement. Make a circle that has a 1.5" radius (3.0" diameter), as follows:

> Move the cursor horizontally to the right
> Type: 1.5 (and press Enter)

This completes the drain. Your drawing should now have a circle that is exactly 3" in diameter, centered in the left basin.

Draw the Right-Side Basin

Now that you've created the first basin, it's easy to make a copy of it for the right-side basin. Copying is one of the features that makes CADD 6 so fast and powerful.

> Select the EDITS menu (from the ROOT menu)
> Select Copy (CO)

A list of Copy command options show up on the command prompt at the bottom of the screen. Each of these options represents a different way of selecting the objects you want to copy. You learn more about these in Chapter 5. For now, use the Window option:

> Type: W

CADD 6 prompts you to place a *window*. A window is an imaginary rectangle that you draw on the screen, any objects that are completely enclosed in the window are selected for the command. Objects that cross the window or are outside of it are not selected. Start the window by clicking its lower-left corner, near point 1 in Figure 2.6.

> Click on a point that is below and to the left of the lower corner of the basin
> Move the cursor up and to the right until the basin is enclosed in the window
> Click near point 2 in Figure 2.6

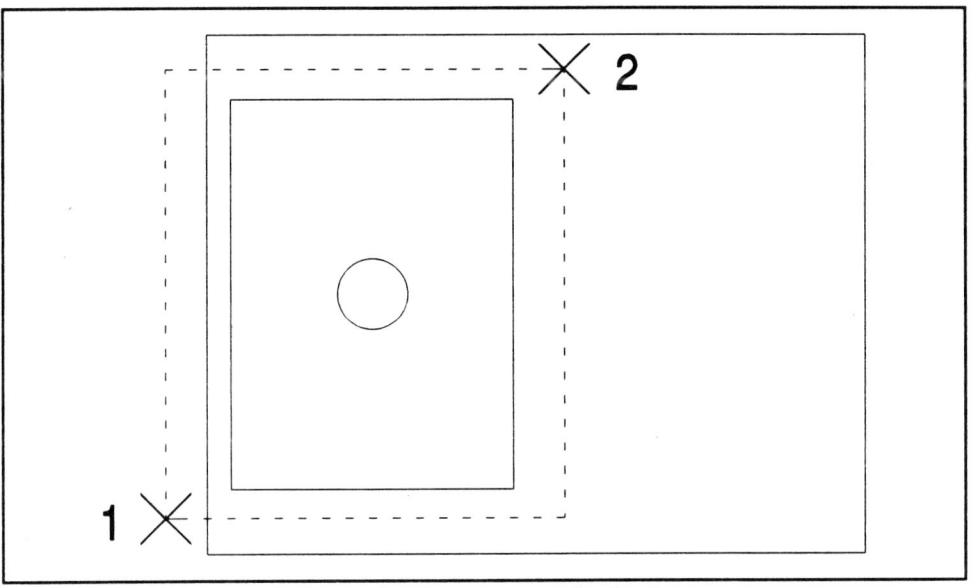

Figure 2.6 Using a window selection to copy the basin.

> **TIP:** If you place the first point of the selection window poorly, just press the Esc key. This puts you back at the selection options and you can press W for Window and start the selection again.

This completes the selection window, everything inside of it will be copied. All the items that are selected are highlighted on the screen by showing them as dashed.

   Press the Enter key or click on the word <RET>

This tells CADD 6 to accept the selection.

> **TIP:** If no objects are highlighted on the screen, check to make sure Highlight is turned ON. At the bottom of the screen on the command line the status of the Highlight feature is shown. If it says OFF, click on the word Highlight to turn it ON. Turning Highlight ON and OFF in the middle of the Copy command will not change the current display; you must press Esc to abort the command and start it over.

The next prompt asks for a reference point. This is simply a point you select to help tell CADD how to complete the command, in this case where to place the copy of the

2-14 ■ Chapter 2: Nothing But the Kitchen Sink

basin. Snap to the lower left-hand corner of the now highlighted sink basin for the reference point, which is point 1 in Figure 2.7.

Type: SC
Click near the lower-left corner of the basin

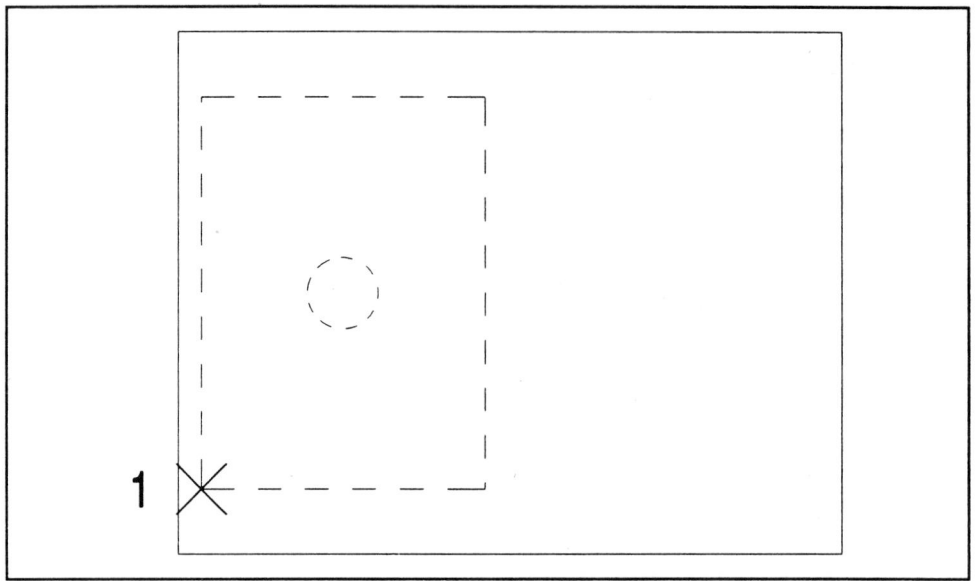

Figure 2.7 The objects selected to copy are highlighted.

Move your cursor around and you should see a ghost image of the sink basin that moves with the cursor. This image is attached to the cursor at the basin's lower-left corner, the point you selected as the reference point. (If you don't see the ghost image, type OD to turn ON Object Drag and a ghost image should appear with the cursor.)

CADD 6 now prompts you to:

   Enter new reference point or offset >

This is really asking "Where should the copy of the objects be placed?" You must give a location for the new reference point and all the copied objects are placed relative to that point. You can either click on a point or enter an exact distance. Here, make the copy of the basin exactly 14" to the right of the first basin, as follows:

Move the cursor horizontally to the right
Type: 14 (and press Enter)

Chapter 2: Nothing But the Kitchen Sink ■ 2-15

You are then prompted for the number of copies to create.

    Type: 1 (and press Enter)

Figure 2.8 shows the result; an exact copy of the left-sink basin is placed 14" to the right of the left one.

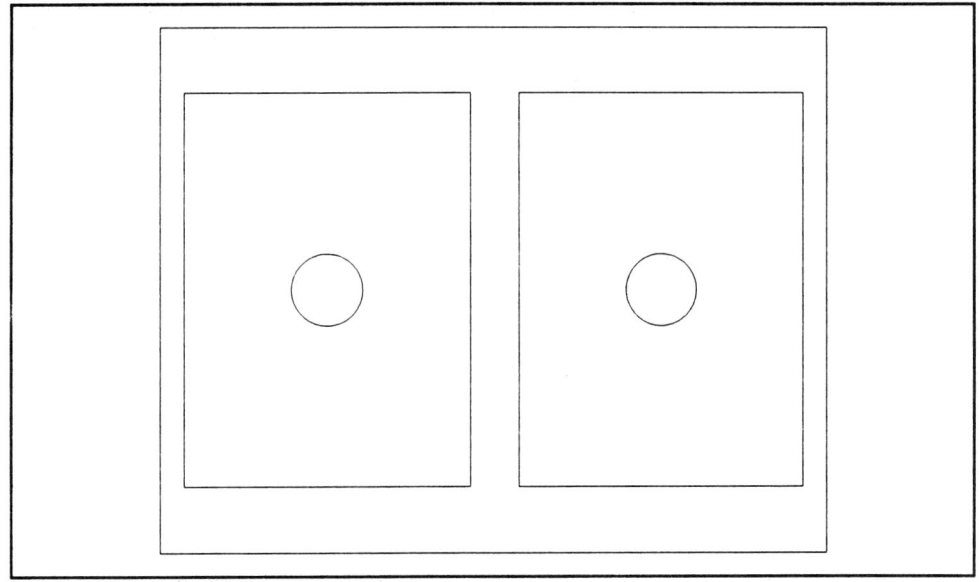

Figure 2.8 The first sink basin is copied.

Draw the Faucet

The last step in drawing this sink is to create the faucet. To make it as easy as possible, the faucet is drawn beside the sink and then moved into the correct position. You will draw a 1" X 8" rectangle to the right of the sink, as shown in Figure 2.9.

First, change your display to make room to draw the faucet:

    Select the ZOOMS menu (from the ROOT MENU)
    Select Zoom Out

CADD prompts you to pick a point for the center of the zoom.

    Click near the right-sink drain

Your sink should now appear smaller on the screen and there should be more blank space around it. Zoom commands, like Zoom Out, do not actually change the size of objects in your drawing. Your sink is still 22" X 28", it simply appears smaller on the screen.

2-16 ■ Chapter 2: Nothing But the Kitchen Sink

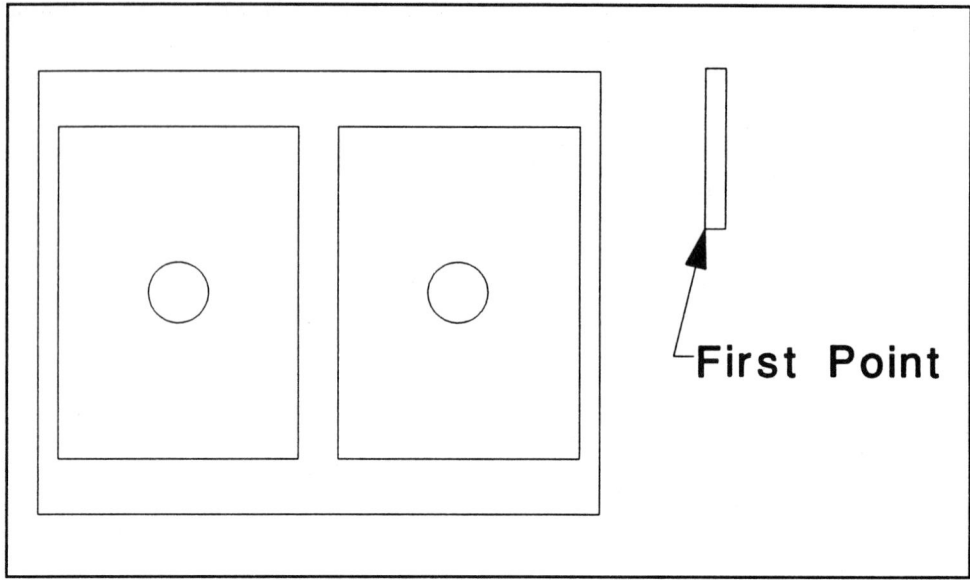

Figure 2.9 Use RE to draw the faucet.

Now you are ready to draw a rectangle for the faucet.

> Select Rectangle (from the DRAW menu)
> Click to place the first corner point (as shown in Figure 2.9)
> Type: 1,8 (and press Enter)

You should now have a rectangle 1" X 8" inches on the screen, as shown in Figure 2.9. Use the Move command to move the rectangle into its proper position.

> Select the EDITS menu (from the ROOT MENU)
> Select Move
> Type: W

This starts the Move command with the Window selection option, just as was done earlier for the Copy command.

> Place a window around the faucet to select it

To do this, click slightly below and to the left of the rectangle that represents the faucet. Move the cursor up and to the right until the entire faucet is enclosed in the selection window, as shown in Figure 2.10. Click again to establish the upper corner of the window. This causes the faucet to be highlighted on the screen. When the command line options return, press the Enter key to tell CADD 6 that you accept the selection.

Chapter 2: Nothing But the Kitchen Sink ■ 2-17

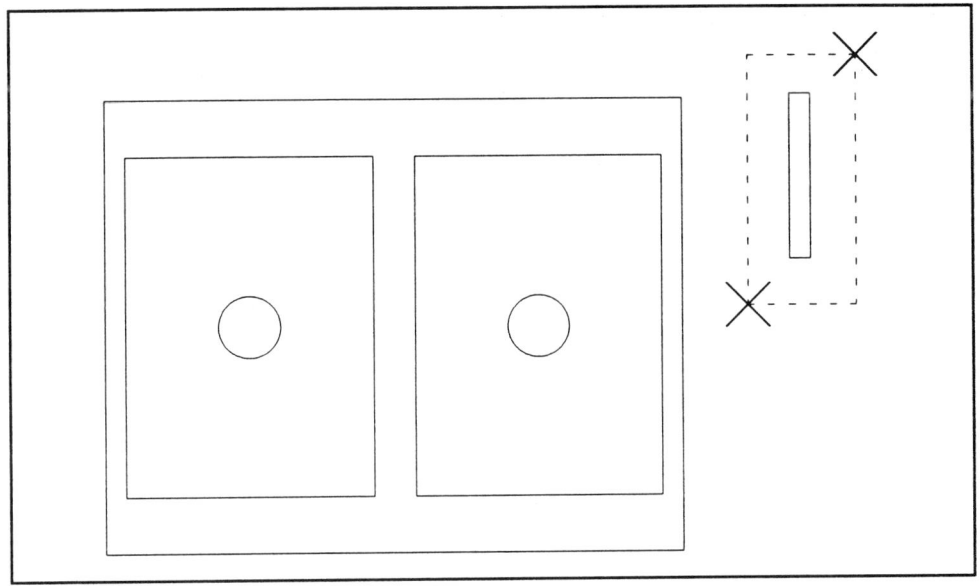

Figure 2.10 Use a Window to select the faucet.

To center the faucet perfectly on the sink you use another snap command called Snap Midpoint (SM). This command tells CADD 6 to snap to the exact midpoint, or center, of a line. At the prompt for a reference point:

    Type: SM (for Snap Midpoint)
    Click on the top line of the faucet

Be sure you click on the top line and not at an end point of the line. This could cause CADD 6 to select the side line of the faucet instead of the line you want.

Next, CADD 6 asks for the location of the new reference point. This is where the faucet will be moved to. You can think of picking up the faucet by the point you first selected (the midpoint of the top line) and moving it to the new reference point. In this case, you want to move the faucet to the midpoint of the top of the sink.

    Type: SM

Move the mouse and notice that the cursor's movement is restrained to only move horizontally and vertically. This means you won't be able to place the faucet exactly on top of the sink since the two objects are not perfectly aligned. The Ortho command, used at the beginning of this tutorial, causes the cursor movement to be restrained, so turn it off temporarily.

    Hold down the Ctrl key (the control key)

2-18 ■ Chapter 2: Nothing But the Kitchen Sink

Notice that the cursor is now free to move in any direction. When you release the Ctrl key, Ortho mode goes back into effect.

    Click on the top line of the sink
    Release the Ctrl key

Figure 2.11 shows the faucet moved to its new position at the top of the sink. It would be more realistic if the faucet were positioned away from the top edge of the sink, so let's move it down 1.25".

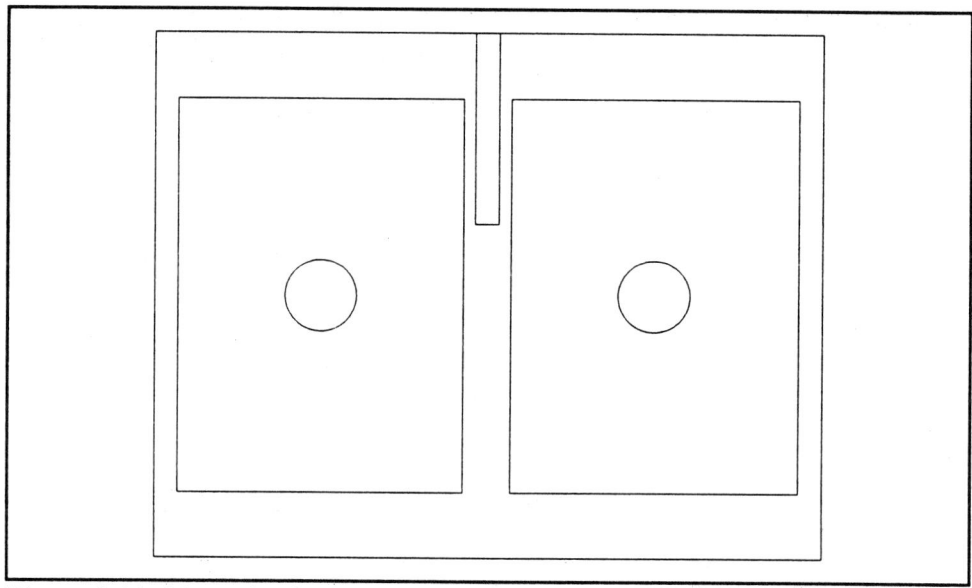

Figure 2.11 Move the faucet to a temporary position.

    Select Move
    Type: W
    Select the faucet by enclosing it in a selection window
    Press Enter (to accept the selection)
    Click on any point of the faucet for the reference point

The new reference point is to be 1.25" straight down. To instruct CADD 6, you move the mouse to establish the desired direction then enter the distance to move in that direction.

    Move the cursor vertically downward
    Type: 1.25 (and press Enter)

The result is shown in Figure 2.12.

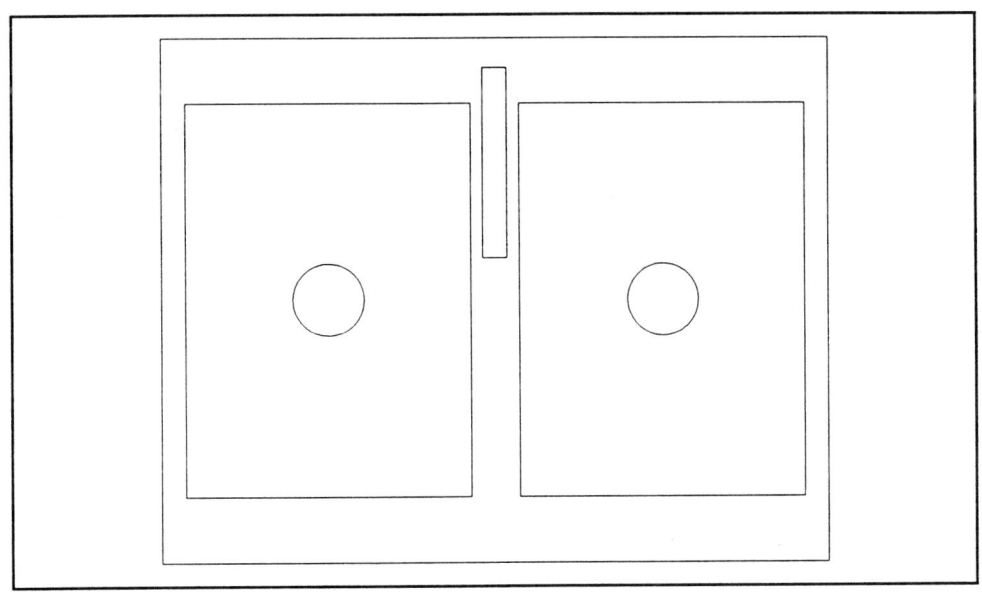

Figure 2.12 Move the faucet to its final position.

In later chapters, you will learn a faster way to move the faucet in one step instead of two. This tutorial is meant to show that it is easy to create an accurate drawing in CADD 6. Later you can focus on being faster and more efficient.

Draw the Faucet Handles

The faucet handles are drawn with six-sided polygons using the Regular Polygon (RP) command. To draw a polygon, the first point located is its center. To find this point, use the same method used to locate the left-sink basin, but reference the faucet from the midpoint of the faucet top.

>   Type: SM (for the Snap Midpoint command)
>   Move your cursor so it is on the top line of the faucet
>   Click your first mouse button

This snaps to the midpoint and causes the next distances entered to be measured from there.

>   Select the Draw Menu (from the ROOT MENU)
>   Select Regular Polygon (RP)

First, you are prompted for the number of sides of the polygon.

>   Type: 6 (and press Enter)

2-20 ■ Chapter 2: Nothing But the Kitchen Sink

This polygon is to be drawn from its center point, so when CADD 6 asks if you want center or side construction:

>Type: C (for center construction)
>Type: -3,0
>Press Enter

This places the center of the handle 3" (in the negative X direction) to the left of the faucet center. Then, you're prompted to enter a point on the side of the polygon, which establishes its size.

>Move the cursor in any direction (left, right, up, or down)
>Type: 1 (and press Enter)

Your sink should now have a six-sided faucet handle that is 2" in diameter, as shown in Figure 2.13.

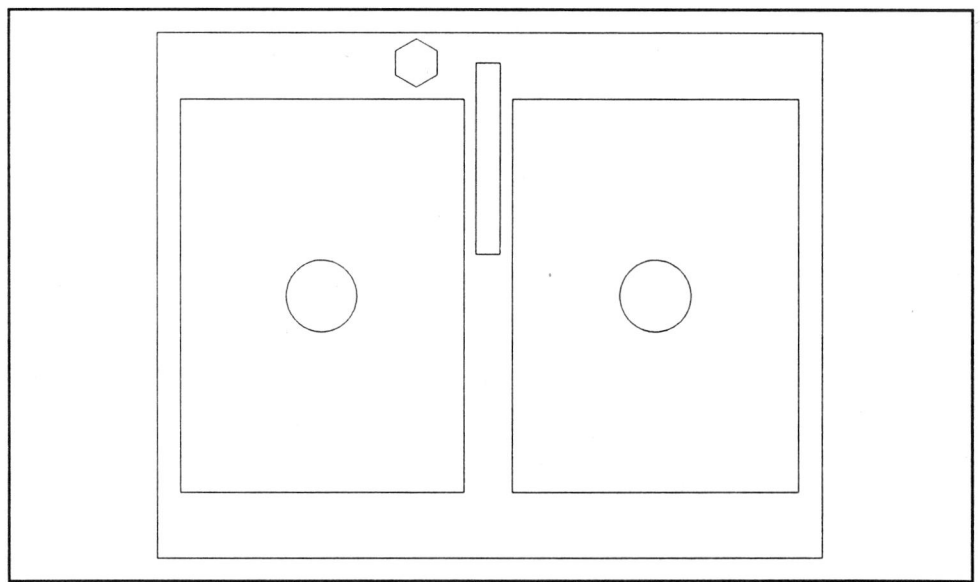

Figure 2.13 Drawing the left-side faucet handle.

To create another faucet handle like the first, you could draw a second one, or just make a copy of the first handle. It is usually faster to copy objects, like you did to make the second sink basin. Since you have used the Copy command before, the instructions will be given without any further explanation.

>Select the EDITS menu (from the ROOT MENU)
>Select Copy (CO)
>Type: W

Chapter 2: Nothing But the Kitchen Sink ■ 2-21

    Place a window around the existing faucet handle (press Enter to finish the window)
    Click a reference point anywhere on the handle
    Move the cursor to the right
    Type: 6 (and press Enter)
    Type: 1 (and press Enter)

This results in one copy of the handle being placed 6" to the right of the first handle. The two handles should be perfectly centered about the faucet.

Adding Text

Now that the basic drawing is complete, you can add text to label items in the drawing. In this case, just label the sink "KITCHEN SINK." Text is easy to place in CADD, but you have to set up some parameters to make sure you get what you want.

    Select the TEXT menu (from the ROOT MENU)
    Select Txt Settings (TS)

A list of text options shows up in the command prompt area. From here you can select a font, choose the size (or height) of the text letters, the justification mode, and other characteristics of the text in your drawing. For this drawing, set the size to 1.5" and the justification to "center."

    Type: Z (for text size)
    Type: 1.5 (and press Enter)
    Type: J (for justification)
    Type: C (for center)
    Press Enter to finish the command

To actually draw the text, use the Place Text Line (TL) command. You will learn about the other ways to place text in Chapter 8.

    Select Place Text Line (from the TEXT menu)

CADD 6 prompts you for the starting point of the text line. The starting point is always at the bottom of the text letters. Since the text justification was set to "center," the starting point will also be at the center of the text line.

    Click near the text starting point in Figure 2.14
    Type: KITCHEN SINK (and press Enter)
    Press the Esc key to finish the command

As you type, you see the letters displayed on the command line and a box is drawn on the sink that represents the text being typed in. This text box rubberbands from the starting point and grows as you enter more letters.

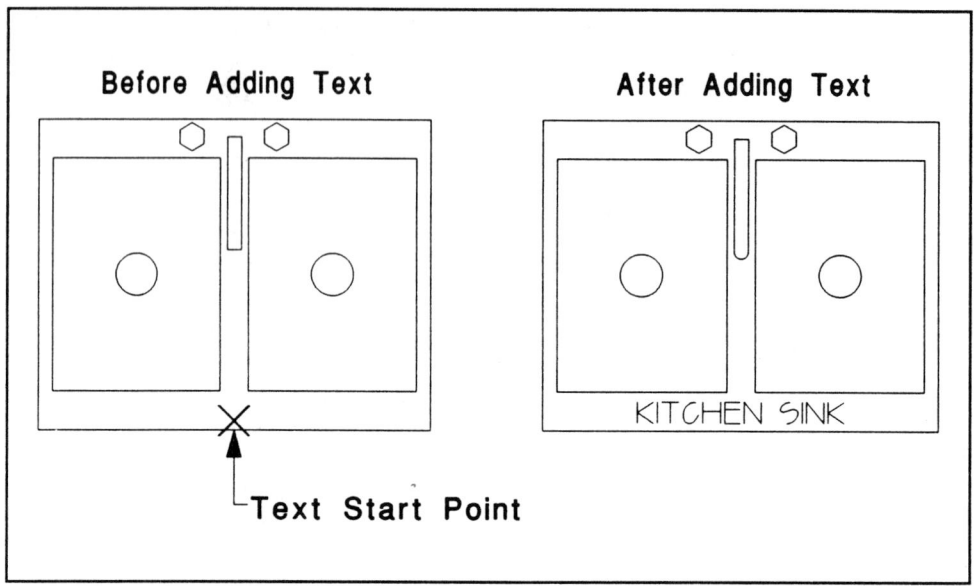

Figure 2.14 Adding text to your drawing.

SAVING, ERASING, AND LOADING YOUR DRAWING

The drawing is complete! Don't worry if it doesn't look like a very fancy sink, you will learn many techniques later for making your drawings more attractive and complex.

This sink drawing is needed for a tutorial later, so you should save it as a file on your hard disk. To be on the safe side, you should save any drawing you're working on at regular intervals, at least every half hour. It is not unusual for something to happen that causes the drawing in memory to be lost. For example, a power loss could occur. Whenever you are working on a drawing that you will want later, be sure to save it often!

To save your drawing:

    Select the FILE menu (from the ROOT MENU)
    Select Save (SA)

A list of options are given for you to select the type of file to save. In this case, you want to save the entire drawing, so:

    Type: D (for Drawing)

Next, CADD 6 prompts to enter the name of the drawing to save. Drawing file names in CADD 6 must follow the same rules that apply to any other DOS file name. They

> **TIP:** Here is a trick to help you remember the three letters SAD needed for the Save Drawing command. If you ever forget to save a drawing that you need later, just think of how "SAD" you will be!

can have up to eight characters (no spaces), and the following characters cannot be used:

" * + , . / : ; < = > ? [\ ] |

For this drawing:

Type: **KSINK** (and press Enter)

CADD 6 saves the file as "KSINK.GCD" so you can identify it as a Generic CADD drawing file.

When you save a drawing for the second time, or if another drawing exists with the same name, CADD 6 asks if you want to overwrite the old file or rename this drawing before saving it. If you are just updating a drawing, you want to select the overwrite option. If you get this message the first time you save a particular drawing, be careful about choosing "overwrite." You may have previously saved a different drawing with the same file name and it will be lost if you overwrite.

CHAPTER SUMMARY

In this chapter you learned about the CADD 6 screen and video menu, then you put them to work to create your first real CADD drawing. To create a basic kitchen sink you learned to draw primitive objects, move them, copy them, change the drawing view, and save drawings to disk. These commands are among the most frequently used in CADD 6. As you become more proficient with CADD 6, you will use them over and over.

CHAPTER 3

Speaking the Language

INTERFACING WITH CADD 6

You had some hands-on experience with CADD 6 in the last chapter, now some explanation of what you did is in order. This chapter will introduce some fundamental CAD concepts and the ways you communicate with CADD 6. These concepts should make more sense now that you used many of them in the kitchen sink tutorial. Take the time now to develop a good understanding of the basics, and you will be a faster, more productive CADD 6 user.

BASIC CADD 6 CONCEPTS

Building Blocks

The basic features of CADD 6 are essentially the same as those offered in any professional CAD program. You create a drawing from various lines, circles, arcs, ellipses, and curves, similar to those shown in Figure 3.1. Then you manipulate those basic objects until you have the desired result. These basic objects are often called entities or "primitives." They are the simplest building blocks of any CADD 6 drawing.

All objects in a drawing are composed of primitives. Rectangles, polygons, and multiple parallel lines are drawn with one command, but they are really composed of individual lines. Even seemingly complex shapes, like text, dimensions, hatches, and components (symbols) can be broken down into the primitives that compose them.

These complex items are often treated like a single object, so it is easy to select them for commands like move, copy, scale, and rotate. That is why you want to create components from objects that you use over and over. However, when you want to modify complex objects, they can be broken down into individual primitives with the Explode command on the UTILITIES menu.

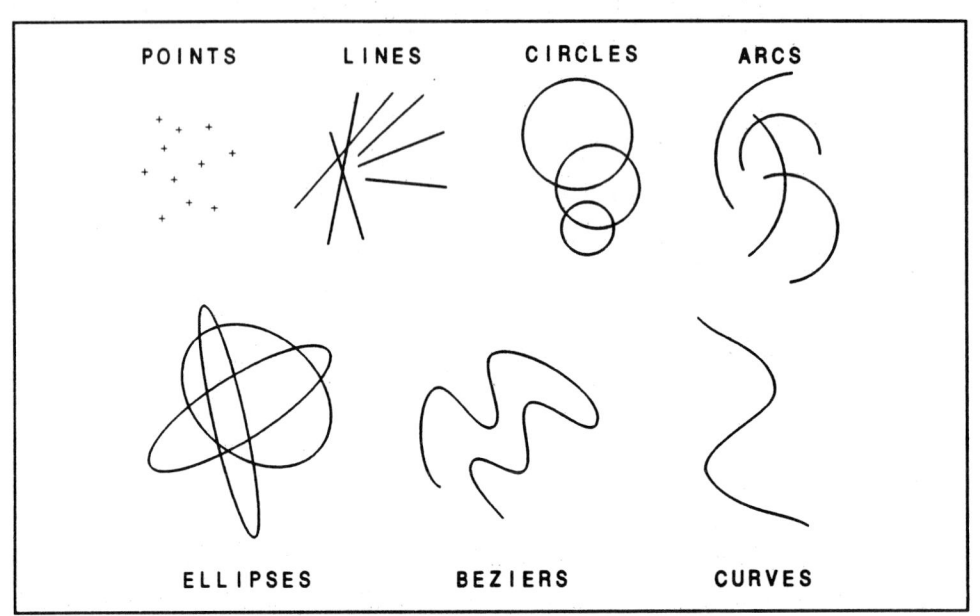

Figure 3.1 Primitive CADD objects.

The kitchen sink drawing you created in Chapter 2 is completely composed of lines and circles. The drains were drawn with circles, but everything else is made of lines. Even though the faucet was drawn with the Rectangle command, rectangles are really just four lines. Likewise, the faucet handles are made from lines, even though they were drawn with the Polygon command.

Primitives Are Not Enough

The ability to draw with primitive objects is not what makes CADD 6 a powerful drafting tool. You could just as easily do that with a pencil and paper! The power of CADD 6 becomes obvious when you see what you can do with those primitives.

Once placed in a drawing, primitives are combined and modified with the use of commands from the EDITS menu, as discussed in Chapter 5. These commands let you easily transform the basic drawing entities to any complex shape with complete accuracy. You can quickly move and copy groups of objects, like you did to create your kitchen sink. CADD 6 also has editing features to break, rotate, scale, and stretch entities.

Snap and Trim commands, covered in Chapter 6, help ensure that your drawings are an accurate representation of the real thing. These features are used to connect primitives together exactly, and to determine specific points on primitives. You used the Snap Closest and Snap Midpoint commands in the kitchen sink tutorial. Without them, you would not have been able to locate the exact endpoint or midpoint of lines in your drawing.

If you want to create professional quality drawings, don't ever try to just "eyeball" points. You can click on a point that looks like the endpoint of a line, but when you print the drawing or zoom-in on it, you see that it was not really on the endpoint. Remember that CADD 6 locates every point with six decimal place accuracy; no one can manually get that close without using snaps. Figure 3.2 shows a simple shape that was drawn once with snaps and once without.

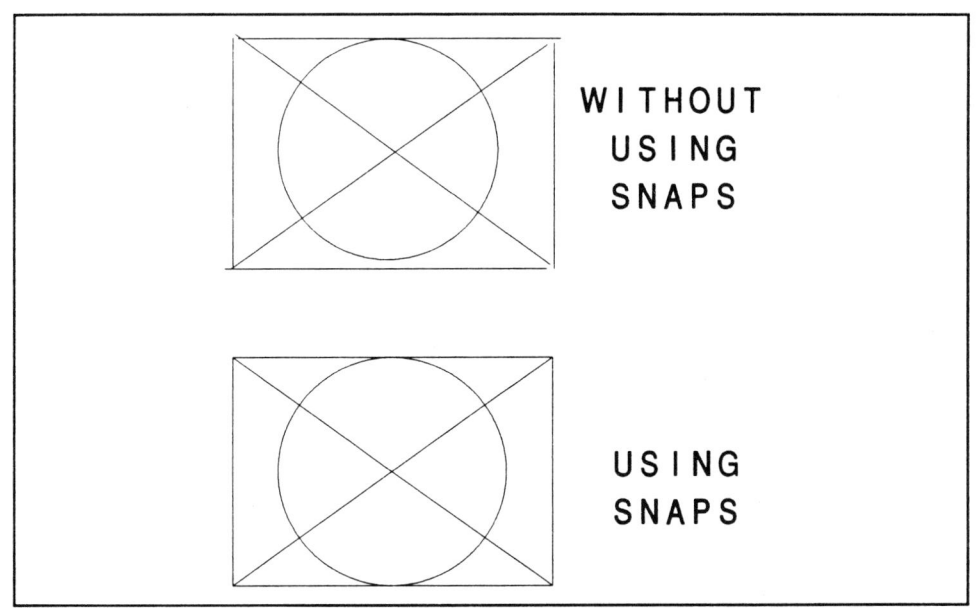

Figure 3.2 Using Snaps to ensure accuracy.

You will want to add lettering to most drawings, such as notes, labels, a parts list, and title block. CADD 6 calls all lettering *text* and has many commands for placing and modifying it, as you saw in Chapter 2. Chapter 8 discusses all the text commands. Text can be placed as "lines," like you did in the kitchen sink drawing, or as individual characters. CADD 6 lets you adjust the text size, adjust spacing between characters and lines, select the justification mode, and select the font. Once text is placed in the drawing, it can be modified with the text-editing commands. Even the font style of previously placed text can be changed.

Architectural and mechanical drawings typically include dimensions that show the sizes of objects. CADD 6 offers a wide variety of ways to dimension your drawing. You can create virtually any style of linear dimensioning (single line, partitioned, and cumulative), as well as angular, radial, and diameter dimensioning. In any of these modes, various tolerance styles can automatically be placed with the dimension. You can also select the text font, location, and size, and change arrow types. All of these features are explained in Chapter 11.

Dimensioning in CADD 6 is *associative*, meaning the numerical values in the dimensions are linked to the actual objects in the drawing. If you decide to change the size of an object, the dimension is automatically updated to reflect that change, as shown in Figure 3.3.

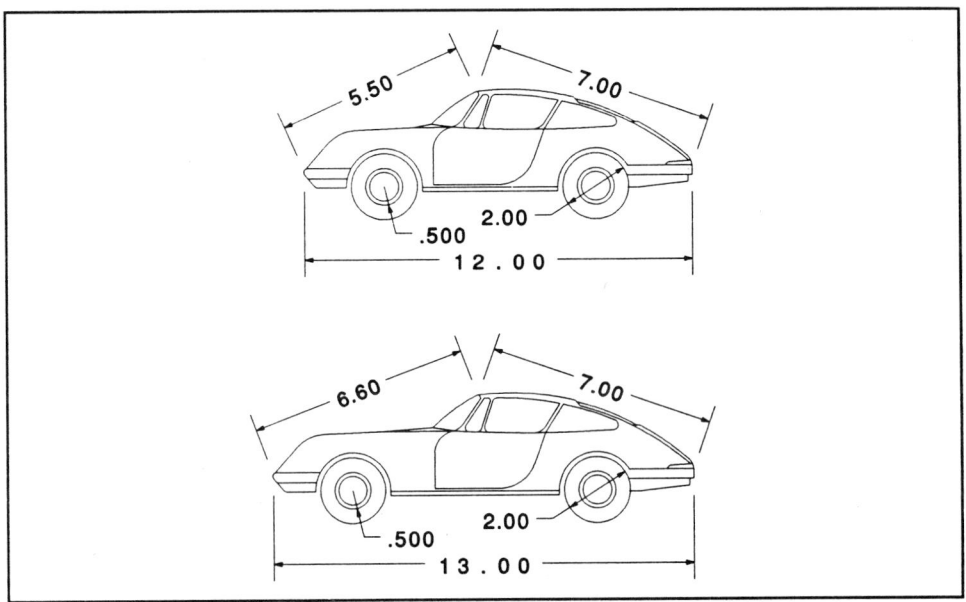

Figure 3.3 Dimensions are related to the objects in the drawing.

A Picture Is Worth 1000 Words

One of the main reasons CADD 6 is easy to use is because it constantly gives dynamic visual feedback as you draw and modify drawings. Most commands show you what things are going to look like before you have to commit to finishing the command. This feedback causes drawing and editing features to come alive on the screen, providing a very intuitive feel for what you are doing.

You already experienced this in the kitchen sink tutorial. When you placed the first point of a line, you saw what the line was going to look like as you moved your mouse. The line was rubberbanding between the first point and the instantaneous position of the cursor. Dynamic visual feedback also made it easier for you to draw circles and rectangles. In both cases, the object being drawn dynamically changed size with the movement of the cursor. Even when you draw accurately with snaps and exact dimensions, visual feedback makes CADD 6 easier to learn and use.

Dimensioning provides another example of CADD 6's dynamic visual feedback. Dimension settings (like arrows, text characteristics, and color) can be altered in the middle of placing a dimension, and the changes are shown on the screen as they are made. You can continue to change settings until the particular dimension is just what you want. To place a dimension, you point and click on the objects you want to dimension, then move your cursor to see what it is going to look like. First, you make sure that the dimension is positioned just where you want it; then you click to complete the placement.

You saw other examples of CADD 6's visual feedback when you copied and moved objects in the kitchen sink tutorial. The features for editing and modifying drawings have two kinds of visual feedback, *highlighting* and *drag image*. For example, in the tutorial you used a window to select the left sink basin. CADD 6 showed you exactly which objects were to be copied by highlighting them on the screen. This gives you the chance to add or delete objects from the chosen selection set. Once you accept the group of selected objects, they are shown on the screen as a "ghost" or drag image, like that in Figure 3.4. When you move your cursor, the image of the selected objects moves with it to the new position. This lets you see just what the objects will look like before you actually move them.

In the beginning, CADD 6's visual feedback saves you plenty of time, since you can see the result of each command before you actually execute it. Even so, you will still make some mistakes and not quite get the results you want. Don't worry, there are also ways of "undoing" commands that are completed by mistake!

As you become a more proficient user, you may want to reduce the amount of visual feedback CADD 6 provides. While it is very helpful, it also slows down the drawing process. In a large drawing, you may find yourself waiting several seconds for a drag image to be generated. If this happens, CADD 6 provides commands that turn off many of the feedback features.

Managing Your Drawings

As your drawings become complex, it gets harder to differentiate objects and see everything clearly. This can even slow you down, since you may have to continuously zoom-in to see details. CADD 6 has plenty of features to help you manage large drawings, such as layers, colors, and views.

Large drawings can be managed by separating objects with *layers* and colors. Creating objects with various colors can greatly help you distinguish parts of your drawing. Layers, discussed in Chapter 12, are also excellent for managing your large drawings. Layers are like transparencies that you stack on top of each other. When the layers are all stacked up, you can see through them to see every object drawn on every sheet. You can also remove layers from the stack if you don't want to display the objects on that particular layer.

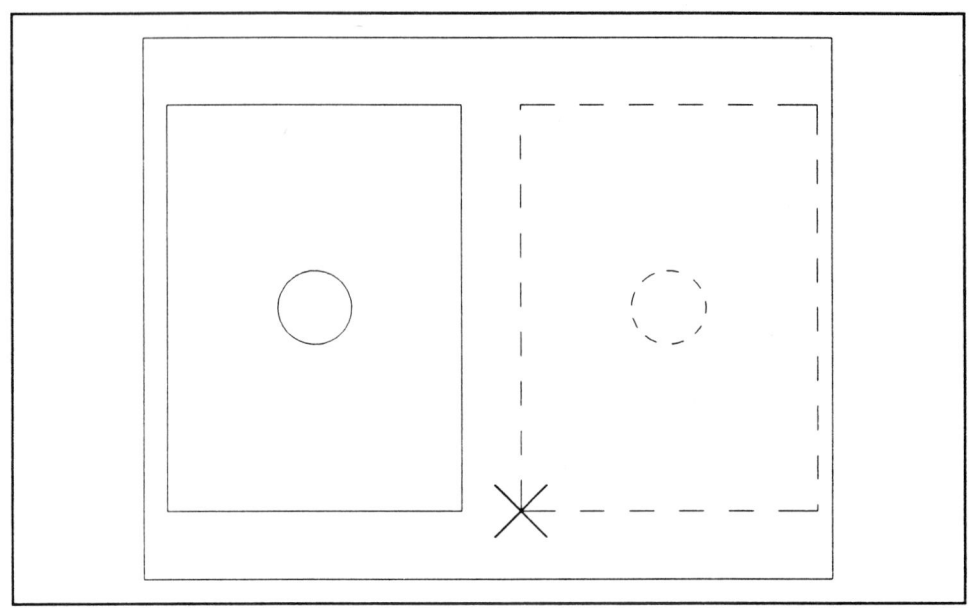

Figure 3.4 CADD 6.0 shows you changes before you commit to them.

CADD 6 has 256 layers available for you to use. You can draw objects on particular layers, then display any combination of those layers on the screen. For example, a detailed drawing of your new car could use one layer for the geometric entities (lines, arcs, and so on), another layer for the dimensions, and a third layer for notes, specifications, and the title block, as shown in Figure 3.5. Then, you could easily create a drawing that displays only the car design or just the notes. You can even assign names to the layers so it is easy to remember what is drawn on every layer.

Multiviews are also available to help you manage your drawings. Multiviews let you divide the screen to show different views of the drawing at the same time. For example, you could show a complete mechanical assembly in one view, then show a zoomed-in view of one detail part in another view. With multiviews, you can work in the detail view and the changes are updated in the view of the complete assembly. This is discussed in Chapter 7, along with other commands for viewing drawings.

Not for the Weak of Heart

Your kitchen sink was drawn using the easiest possible methods, not necessarily the fastest. You will find that there are more efficient ways to perform many of the basic tasks you frequently use.

Once you master the standard CADD 6 functions, the next step is to customize them to your specific needs. Creating your own macros and menus lets you easily automate many of the tasks you do everyday. There is even a complete programming language for users who want to develop complicated application programs and new commands.

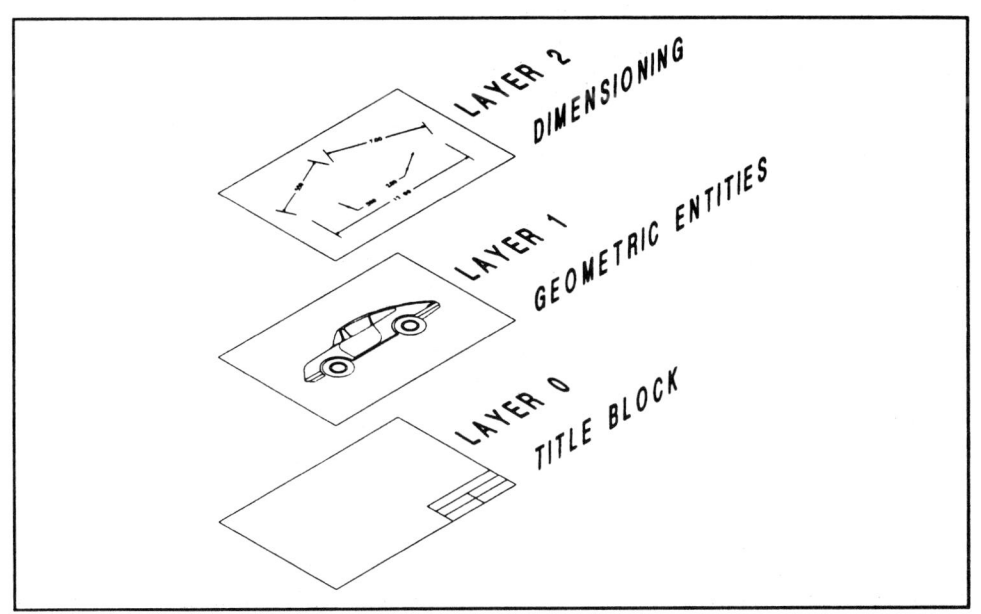

Figure 3.5 Layers help you manage large drawings.

Macros are created by combining the standard two-letter commands just as you would use them in the program. They can be used to automate repetitive drafting functions, giving you more time to concentrate on complex tasks. You can assign macros to your function keys or put them on a special video menu. For example, macros can automatically rotate and scale components, reset text and dimensioning variables, and even create an opening in a wall for a door.

You can use various math functions and variables in your macros. These allow you to add, subtract, multiply, and divide numbers within a macro. You can also calculate absolute value, natural log, exponent, square and square root, and the sine, cosine, and arctangent of angles within macros.

SPECIAL KEYS AND POINTING DEVICES

The keyboard and pointing device are used to talk to CADD 6 — to select commands, pick points, enter values, distances, and coordinates. Many keys and buttons have preset functions, and others allow you to assign commands or strings of commands to them.

Enter Key

The Enter key is used to select points on the screen. Just move the cursor to the desired point and press Enter. Beware, however, that this is not the best way to pick points on an existing line, like an endpoint or midpoint. It may look like you are exactly on a point, but looks are seldom good enough for CADD 6's accuracy; you must use snap commands.

Pressing Enter is also the way to tell CADD 6 when you are finished typing information. Prior to pressing Enter you can change values that you have typed on the command line. When you press Enter, it tells CADD 6 to act on that information.

Some items, like two-letter commands, are accepted by CADD 6 immediately and do not require pressing the Enter key to activate them.

Backspace Key

The Backspace key (or left arrow) is used to move left over a line of text and erase each character. Backspace can be used this way to erase text on the command line or when placing text in your drawing. When you placed the text "KITCHEN SINK" in Chapter 2, instead of pressing the Enter key, you could have pressed the Backspace key to erase the letters and put in something else.

The Backspace key can only be used to change the command line until you press the Enter key. Pressing Enter tells CADD 6 that the text is finalized and is ready to place in the drawing.

Delete Key

The Delete key (Del) has two functions. The most common usage is for editing text, similar to the Backspace key. When entering text on the command line, or editing text in your drawing, press the Del key to erase the character that the cursor is currently on.

Del is also used to adjust the cursor movement that results from using the keyboard arrow keys. Pressing Del causes the cursor to move in smaller increments across the screen for each press of an arrow key. This is really only necessary if you do not have a mouse or other pointing device.

Insert Key

The Insert key is used to make the cursor move in larger increments for each press of the keyboard arrow keys. This does exactly the opposite of the Delete key.

Arrow Keys

There are four arrow keys on the keyboard pointing in different directions. These keys move the cursor across the drawing screen in whichever direction they point. The up and down arrow keys can also be used to move the cursor (or highlight bar) through the commands on a video menu page. The cursor moves in increments that are adjusted by pressing the Insert and Delete keys.

Home Key

The Home key is used to select items from the video menu. If you do not have a pointing device (mouse or digitizer), position the highlight bar on the desired menu command and press Home to select it.

Space Bar

Pressing the Space Bar causes the previous command to be executed again. For example, if you complete a Move command and then want to move something again, press the Space Bar at the CADD 6 command prompt. This causes the Move command to be started again, just as if you had typed MV or selected it from the menu. You have the chance to select the same objects moved before, or select new objects.

> **TIP:** Toggle commands, like Ortho (OR) cannot be repeated by pressing the Space Bar. Component Image (CI) is the only exception to this rule.

Escape Key

The Escape (Esc) key is used to abort commands that are in process. Any time CADD 6 is waiting for some kind of input, you can press Esc instead, and exit the command before any changes are made to your drawing.

Since you must press Esc at each of CADD 6's prompts, some commands require you to use Esc multiple times before the command aborts. Just watch the command line, and continue to press Esc until you are back to the prompt for a new command.

> **TIP:** Both the Space Bar and Escape keys can be used when selecting objects for the various EDITS commands, like Move (MV), Copy (CO), and Rotate (RO). For example, if you have just used the Object selection method to select an object to move, and you want to select another object, just press the Space Bar. This is equivalent to typing O for Object again, and you will be prompted to select another object in the drawing. Use Esc to change the selection method. If you press O to select an Object, but decide that the Window method would be better, press Esc one time. The prompt to select an Object will be canceled and you will be returned to the list of selection methods, where you can then choose Window.

Control Key

Holding down the Control (Ctrl) key temporarily toggles Ortho Mode ON or OFF. If Ortho Mode is currently ON, holding down the Ctrl key turns it OFF; if Ortho Mode is OFF, holding down the Ctrl key turns it ON. The new mode is only in effect as long as the Ctrl key is held down. As soon as you stop pressing the Ctrl key, Ortho Mode reverts back to its previous setting. You used this method in the kitchen sink tutorial of Chapter 2.

This is very convenient if most of your work is done with Ortho Mode turned ON, but you occasionally need to move the cursor at some angle other than the Ortho Angle. Simply press Ctrl and your cursor is free to move in any direction. Lift Ctrl and the Ortho Mode constraint is back ON.

Pointing Devices

The most useful device you can use with CADD 6 is a pointing device — a mouse, trackball, or digitizer. It is possible to execute every function from the keyboard, using the arrow keys and other special keys, like Home, Insert, and Delete. However, if you tried to use CADD 6 just from the keyboard, you probably found it to be a frustrating and time-consuming experience! A pointing device makes it fast and easy to move the cursor around the graphics screen and to select commands from the menu.

Mouse devices and trackballs are relatively inexpensive pointing devices with either two or three buttons used to select objects and commands. You move a mouse around on a small area of your desk and the cursor moves with it on the screen. The trackball device is stationary. You control the cursor by using your thumb to rotate the ball within its housing. There are many brands of pointing devices available, and you must tell CADD 6 exactly which one you are using. This is done in the CADD 6 Configuration program, explained in the *CADD 6 User's Guide*.

Digitizers can also be used with CADD 6, although a mouse is adequate for most users. Digitizers consist of a *puck* (similar to a mouse) or *stylus* (like a pen) and an *electronic tablet*. You control the cursor by moving the puck or stylus across the tablet. The puck usually contains 4 to 16 buttons.

Regardless of which pointing device you choose, the first two buttons (from the left) have preassigned functions and cannot be changed. The first button of your pointing device is the button used to select points and objects on the drawing screen. The second button is used to select menu items. If your pointing device has more than two buttons, you can assign the remaining buttons to issue any command or string of commands.

The first button has another function. If you hold down the Shift key and press the first button simultaneously, it issues the Snap Nearest Point (NP) command. This causes the cursor to snap to the closest point it can find on an existing object in the drawing. (This command is not found on the video menu because the cursor must be close to the point to which you intend to snap. If you tried to select this command from the menu, you would invariably move the cursor away from the intended snap point.)

If you have a three-button mouse, Snap Nearest Point (NP) is automatically assigned to the third (or right) button. You can change this assignment if you prefer to use some other button or key. The Snap Nearest Point (NP) command is one of the most often used commands in CADD 6. To be a productive user, you should determine which button or key works best for you and get in the habit of using that method to select NP.

WHEN YOU NEED HELP

CADD 6 has a new online help system that provides information about each of the commands. To access the help system, just select HELP from the ROOT MENU, or type HE. You can also access Help with the Alt-H "hot key." Just hold down the Alt key and then press H. This brings up an alphabetical index of all the topics for which help is available.

The topics are divided according to their starting letters, like "A,B," "C," "D," and "E,F." The A,B category is shown on the screen when you start Help. Use your mouse or keyboard arrow keys to move the cursor to another category, and select it by clicking your first mouse button or pressing the Enter key. For example, to learn about the Component Place command, click on "Alphabetical Contents C," and the list of commands starting with C will display. Click on "Component Place" to see instructions for the command.

Most of the help screens have some words or phrases in bold or bright text that are related to the chosen topic. When you pass the cursor over these words they are highlighted, signifying that additional help is available for that topic. Position the cursor on one of these words or phrases and press Enter, or click your first mouse button to bring up help on that topic. For example, from the Component Place help screen, you can use this method to get additional help on topics like Component, Like (=), Object Drag, and other related commands.

The help screens themselves give you instructions on how to maneuver through the help topics and indices. The bottom and top of the screen show which function keys move you back to the last subject, the main index, exit help, and give you "help on help." When in the help system, you can press F1 to get additional help and instructions on using help, like how to "turn pages," change the help window size, print the help message for a topic, and other functions.

SELECTING COMMANDS

In the kitchen sink tutorial, you used two different methods to give commands to CADD 6, the video menu and "command codes" entered from the keyboard. Both of these methods work equally well. It may be easier for a new user to click commands from the menu, since all the commands are listed there in logical categories. However, if you plan to use CADD 6 often, take the time to learn the two-letter codes for all the

3-12 ■ Chapter 3: Speaking the Language

commands you use regularly. This shortcut method of issuing commands is one of CADD 6's greatest assets, and provides a big boost in productivity.

Using the Video Menu

You have already learned the basic organization of the video menu. You practiced selecting commands from it by clicking on them with the second mouse button (from the left), or pressing the Home key if you do not have a pointing device. This section gives some additional tips for understanding the menus and moving quickly through them.

The video menu pages are arranged *hierarchically*, meaning one page leads to another page, which leads to another. For example, from the ROOT MENU you can select the EDITS menu, and from EDITS you can move another step down the hierarchy to the SHORTCUTS menu. You can always move back up the hierarchy in the same path. Figure 3.6 shows the structure of this particular example. The CADD 6 package includes a folded card that shows all the menus and the relationships between them.

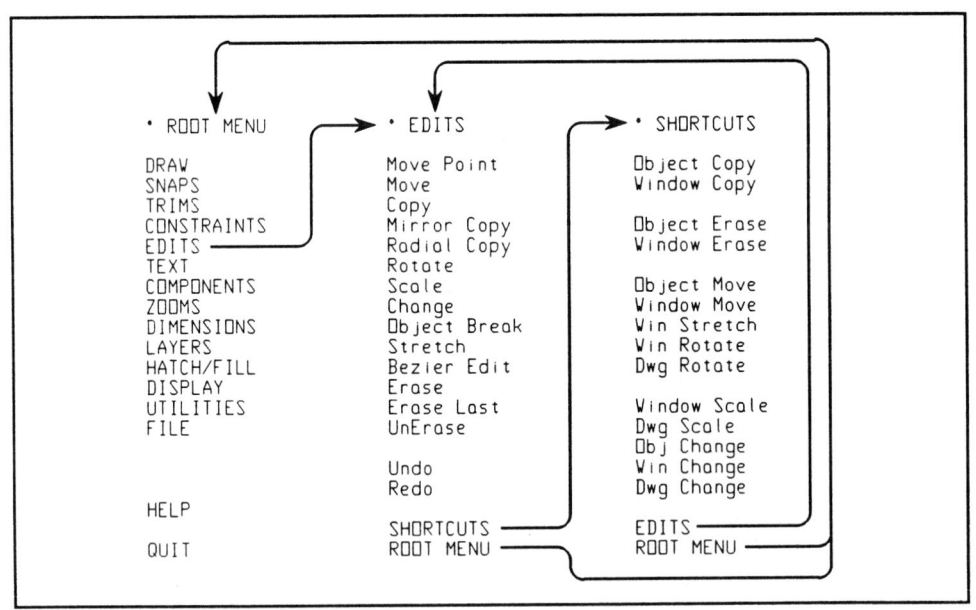

```
• ROOT MENU    ➤ • EDITS        ➤ • SHORTCUTS

DRAW             Move Point        Object Copy
SNAPS            Move              Window Copy
TRIMS            Copy
CONSTRAINTS      Mirror Copy       Object Erase
EDITS            Radial Copy       Window Erase
TEXT             Rotate
COMPONENTS       Scale             Object Move
ZOOMS            Change            Window Move
DIMENSIONS       Object Break      Vin Stretch
LAYERS           Stretch           Vin Rotate
HATCH/FILL       Bezier Edit       Dwg Rotate
DISPLAY          Erase
UTILITIES        Erase Last        Window Scale
FILE             UnErase           Dwg Scale
                                   Obj Change
                 Undo              Vin Change
                 Redo              Dwg Change

HELP             SHORTCUTS         EDITS
QUIT             ROOT MENU         ROOT MENU
```

Figure 3.6 The Video Menu hierarchy.

You can move between menu pages by clicking (with the second mouse button) on the name of the desired page. The titles of menu pages are always listed in all capital letters, so it is easy to distinguish them from command names. You can also use the Page Up and Page Down keys on your keyboard to move between pages of the menu, in the order they appear on the ROOT MENU. For example, with the ROOT MENU displayed, press Page Down to move to the DRAW menu; press Page Down again to move to the SNAPS menu, and so on.

There are faster ways to issue commands than using the video menu, but you won't want to turn the menu OFF. The menu provides the best way to load drawings, components, ASCII files, and other files. Once you select a type of file to load, the menu lists all of that type of file found on your hard disk in the selected path (directory). Then you simply click on the desired file name to select it. This is generally much easier than remembering and typing in exact file names.

The video menu also lets you visually select many other settings, like line widths, line types, colors, layers, and hatch patterns. Each of these can be entered as a particular number, but it is much easier to see them on the menu and click on the one you want. With layers, you can determine which layer is current, what the layer names are, and turn layers ON and OFF from the video menu.

Two-Letter Commands

While there are advantages to using the video menu, in most cases it is faster to enter the two-letter command code to execute a command. This saves time because you don't have to move between pages of the video menu every time you want to execute a command. Every command has a two-letter code and you at least want to learn the codes for the commands you use most frequently, like zooms, draw commands, edits, and snaps.

When using two-letter command codes, you don't press the enter key. As soon as the second letter of the command is typed, the command is set into motion.

Most of the two-letter codes are mnemonic, so they are easy to remember. For example, the two-letter command for Move is MV; for Zoom Window it's ZW. The Snap commands start with S, so Snap Midpoint is SM (as you saw in Chapter 2). All of the layer commands begin with a "Y". Once you remember that, then the layer commands are relatively easy to remember. To hide a layer, type YH; to display a layer type YD.

Unfortunately, CADD 6 has many more commands than the 26 letters of the English alphabet, so some of the codes are not that intuitive. The letter L, for example, is used for line commands; so it can't be used for layers. Instead, Y (the next consonant in the word layer) is used for all the layer commands.

> **TIP:** The command codes are consistent, even if they don't seem to be! Here are some rules that apply to the less intuitive codes:
>
> G is used for Change, as in Drawing Change (DG)
> X is used for Erase and Remove, as in Remove Video Menu (VX)
> Z is used for Scale or Size, as in Component Scale (CZ)
> N is used for Replace or Rename, as in Drawing Rename (DN)

Three-Letter Commands

Many CADD 6 commands can actually be thought of as requiring a three letter command code, because you must choose from a list of options before the command is executed. All of the EDITS commands which require you to pick the selection method work this way.

You saw this in the kitchen sink tutorial when the COPY (CO) command was used with the Window (W) method of selecting objects. When you typed CO, you were given a list of selection methods to choose from: Window, Object, laYer, Drawing, and so on. You had to first pick one of these methods before continuing the command. You were instructed to type W for the Window method, then you went on to select and copy the desired objects. If you knew that you wanted the COpy — Window command, you could have just typed the three letters COW without stopping to look at the list of options.

Versions of Generic CADD previous to version 5.0 did not have selection sets, so two-letter codes were used to specify both the command (like copy or move) and the selection type (like a window or object). The introduction of selection sets resulted in new editing commands and new two-letter codes. These commands have only one code to remember, but they provide six different ways to perform the command. However, many of the original two-letter commands (without selection sets) are still available as SHORTCUTS, and are discussed in Chapter 5.

The CADD 6 package includes a card that lists all of the commands with their two-letter codes. Get in the habit of using the codes for all commands you use regularly. Try to figure out the right code first. If that doesn't work, look it up on the list. Don't worry about entering a wrong code, you can press Esc anytime to cancel unwanted commands before any damage is done.

There is another tool to help you learn the command codes, a special video menu called HELP6. This menu is identical to the normal CADD6 menu except it also shows every command's two-letter code. When you have to use the menu for a command, type in the command code listed instead of clicking on the menu. This will help you quickly memorize the codes you use most often.

To load the HELP6 video menu do the following:

>   Type: VX (Remove Menu) to erase the current video menu
>   Type: LV (Load Menu) to load the new video menu
>   Click on HELP6 from the list of names in the menu area

The new menu should load immediately. Click on the menu names to move through the menu pages and you will see the command codes listed for each command.

Nested Commands

Many of the CADD 6 commands can be *nested*, meaning you can execute one command while you are in the middle of another. Nested commands give you the capability to change the drawing view or many of the settings, without having to abort the command. Not having to interrupt a command in order to adjust a setting is a real time saver.

Zooms are a perfect candidate for nesting, since changing the view often makes it easier to complete a command. For example, suppose you want to move an object from one area to another, as shown in Figure 3.7. Start the Move (MV) command, select the desired objects and pick the first reference point (the point to move the objects from). While still in the Move command, type ZW (Zoom Window) and zoom-in around the area you are moving the objects to, then pick the final point to complete the move.

Other commands that can be nested are Ortho Mode and Ortho Angle. You used Ortho Mode in the kitchen sink tutorial so lines could be drawn at exactly 90 degrees to each other. The Ortho Angle allows you to change the angle of the lines in relation to the drawing. You can toggle the Ortho Mode and adjust the Ortho Angle "on-the-fly," in the middle of drawing and editing commands.

Placing components is faster and more convenient because of nested commands. When you place a component, its "ghost image" is shown on the screen so you can check for the proper scale and rotation. If you don't like what you see, change the rotation and scale values on-the-fly. You can execute the desired commands to make the changes without affecting the Component Place function. Once the component looks right, click to finish placing it. The component's image changes size and rotation as you execute the nested commands, so you can make all of the necessary adjustments before placing the component in your drawing.

Dimension settings can also be changed on-the-fly. If you don't like the arrow size, text placement, text size, or extension line length and placement, you can change these values and see the changes on the screen. Keep making changes until the dimension looks just the way you want it, then finish placing it. Without nested commands, you would have to place the dimension to see it, then erase it, change the settings and place it again to see the effect of your adjustments. Obviously, nesting commands to change your dimension settings saves you a tremendous amount of time.

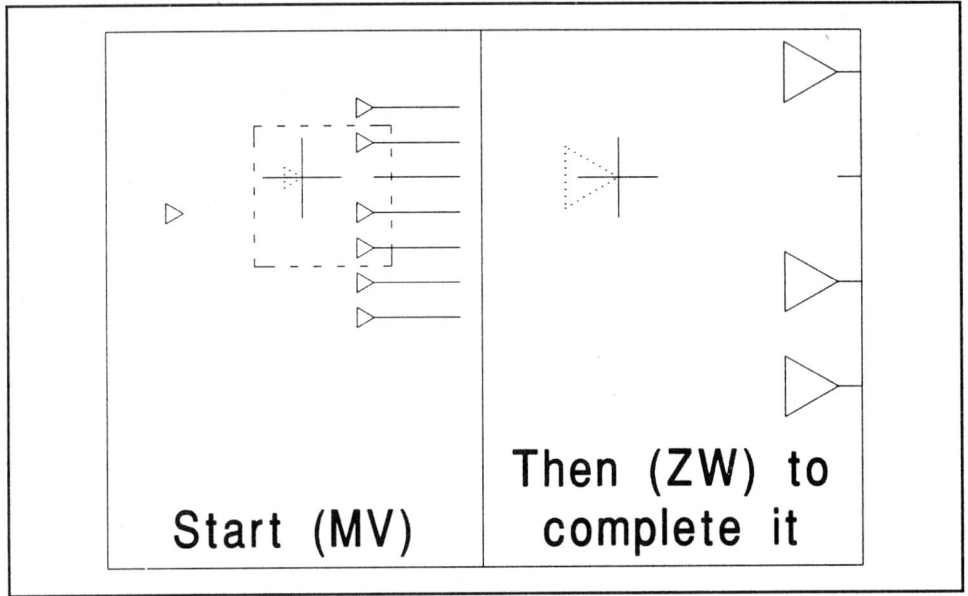

Figure 3.7 Completing one command while in the middle of another.

WHAT DOES CADD 6 WANT?

This section explains the CADD 6 commands in terms of how you implement them and what type of information you have to provide. You already experienced most of the command types when you completed the kitchen sink tutorial, although you may not have recognized the similarities. Understanding the types of commands helps you easily know what CADD 6 expects you to do in almost every situation.

Four Types of Input

Since CADD 6 can't read your mind, almost all commands require you to provide some kind of information. This input falls into one of four categories, depending on exactly what CADD needs to complete the task:

1. Identification of points
2. Input entered on the command line
3. Options chosen from a list
4. No input, simply ON or OFF

Chapter 3: Speaking the Language ■ 3-17

It is helpful to examine the commands that require these types of input and the way CADD 6 asks for it. Keep in mind, however, that most of the commands actually require more than one of these types of input. You will find that you usually must select an option from a list, then identify one or more points in the drawing that are related to that option.

Identifying Points. Almost all commands require the first type of information, where you must identify one or more points in the drawing. You can either do this by clicking with your mouse, snapping to an existing point, or entering exact coordinates or distances. In this case, by "point" we don't mean the point primitive that can be drawn in CADD 6. Rather, we mean any specific location in the drawing that may or may not be part of some existing object, like a point on a line or circle.

All commands on the DRAW menu (except settings commands) require this type of input; you select what to draw from the menu, then CADD 6 prompts you for where and how large to make the object. When you used the Rectangle command in Chapter 2, CADD prompted you to identify the location of each corner of the rectangle, as shown in Figure 3.8. To draw the sink drain with the Circle 2 command, you first identified a point that became the center of the circle, then gave a second point that defined how large the circle was to be.

Rectangle (RE) Prompts

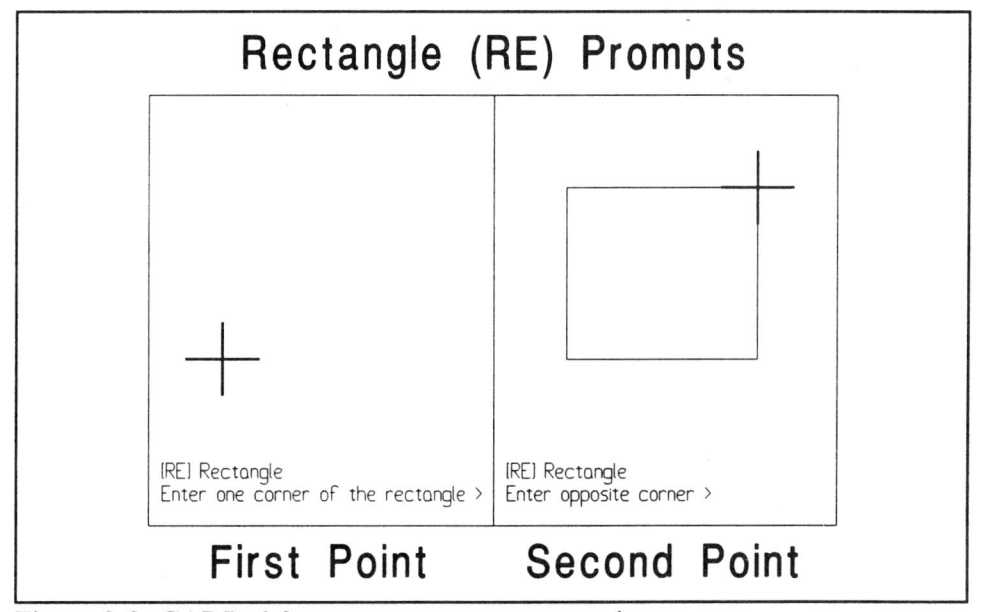

First Point	Second Point
[RE] Rectangle Enter one corner of the rectangle >	[RE] Rectangle Enter opposite corner >

Figure 3.8 CADD 6.0 prompts you to enter a point.

Also in this category, are the text and dimension commands. You saw this when you used the text Line Place command and CADD 6's first prompt was to ask for the starting point of the text line. Dimension commands ask you to identify the objects or distance to be dimensioned. Often a dimension is placed between two edges of a part to show its size, but they can actually be drawn between any two points clicked.

Command Line Input. The second category of input is information you type on the command line (or pick from a special menu) that does not locate points. These commands are mostly used to define settings, like Color Settings (CS), Hatch Settings (HS), Text Settings (TS), Grid Size (GS), and so on. Settings that are a numeric value, like text size and grid size, require you to type in the number. Other settings have particular choices, which you select from a special video menu, like those used for colors and hatch pattern names.

Figure 3.9 shows an example of CADD 6 asking for command line input, for Text Size in this case. You used this command before placing text in Chapter 2. You first chose the Text Size option from the list of settings. Then you entered 1.5 (inch) for the height of the letters.

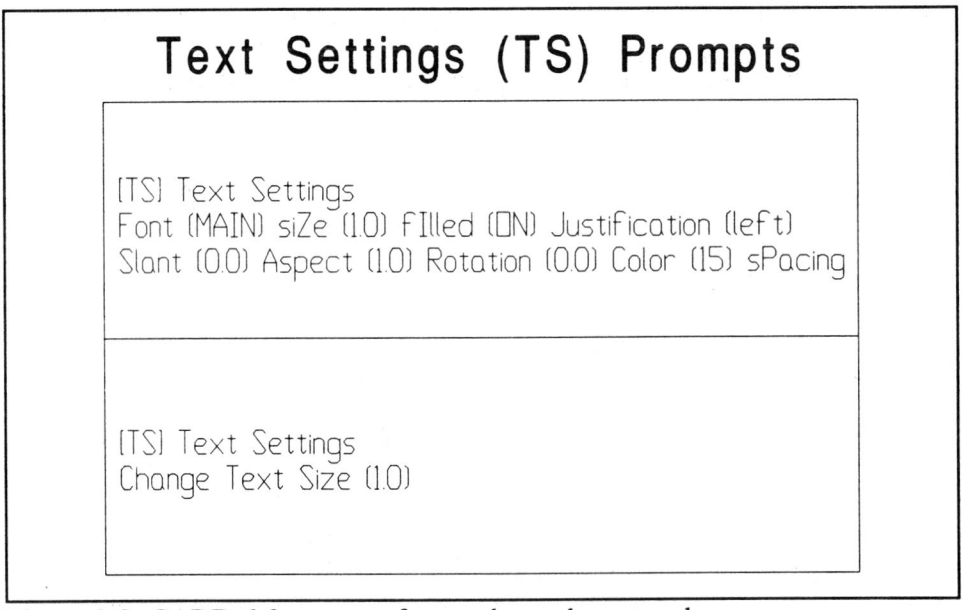

```
            Text Settings (TS) Prompts

   [TS] Text Settings
   Font (MAIN) siZe (1.0) fIlled (ON) Justification (left)
   Slant (0.0) Aspect (1.0) Rotation (0.0) Color (15) sPacing



   [TS] Text Settings
   Change Text Size (1.0)


```

Figure 3.9 CADD 6.0 prompts for a value to be entered.

Choosing from a List. Many commands are so flexible, they actually have several different ways of doing the same task. You must first select from a list of options so CADD 6 knows exactly how you want to perform the command. In the case of the various settings commands, you select from a list of options that tells which setting you want to change.

Most commands from the EDITS menu first prompt you to choose from a list of selection options. Each one represents a different way of selecting the objects to edit.

For example, in Chapter 2 you used Copy to create a second sink basin. You first chose W for the Window selection method, as shown in Figure 3.10. Then you clicked on two corners of a window that enclosed the objects to copy (the basin).

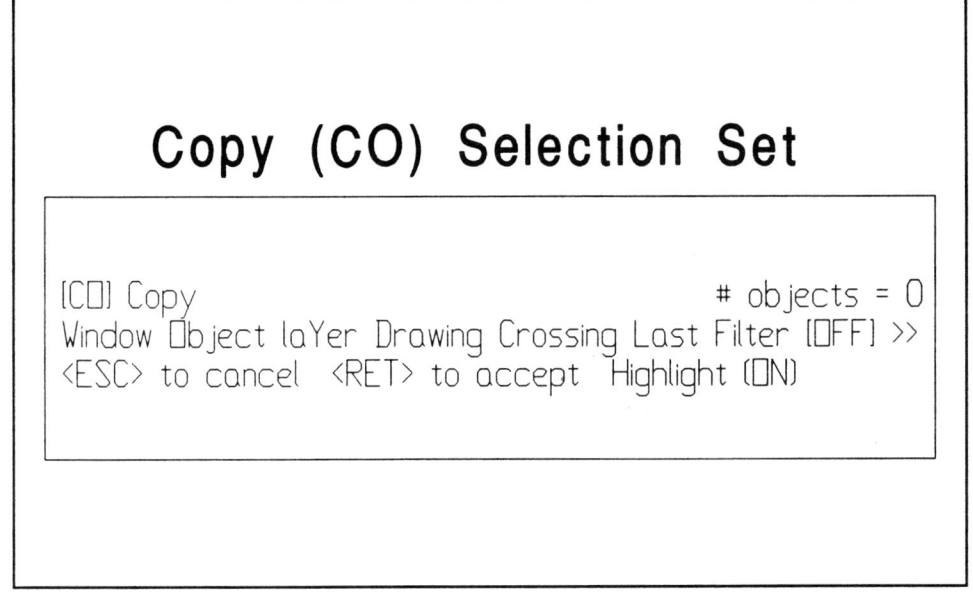

```
           Copy (CO) Selection Set

 [CO] Copy                                    # objects = 0
 Window Object laYer Drawing Crossing Last Filter [OFF] >>
 <ESC> to cancel  <RET> to accept  Highlight [ON]
```

Figure 3.10 Edit commands commonly require an option to be chosen.

Commands like Print, Plot, and Screen Flip, provide more than a simple list of options. They actually open up a whole new menu of related features. For example, when you select the Print or Plot features, a special menu is displayed with all the choices that control the look and size of your output. The Screen Flip (SF) function, on the UTILITIES menu, also provides a new menu of choices where you can get information about your drawing and the objects in it.

Many of the settings commands, like Text Settings, Dimension Settings, Attribute Settings, and so on, also start with a list of options from which to choose. In these cases, the options represent the various types of settings that can be modified. For example, the options for Text Settings are Font, Size, Filled, Justification, Slant, Aspect, Rotation, Color, and Spacing. These are all the characteristics of text that can be controlled with this one command.

No Input. Several commands require no input. When you select the command, it either turns it ON, or turns it OFF. These commands are commonly called toggles. If a toggle is currently ON, issuing the command turns it OFF. If it is currently OFF, issuing the command turns it ON. No other user input is required.

You used a toggle in the kitchen sink tutorial when you turned ON the Ortho Mode of drawing. This command allowed you to only draw lines that were perfectly horizontal or vertical. You simply clicked Ortho Mode on the CONSTRAINTS menu to turn it ON (or type OR). To turn it OFF, just select the Ortho Mode command again.

> **TIP:** Whenever you select a toggle command, be sure to check the message that CADD 6.0 displays on the command line. As Figure 3.11 shows, this message tells whether you turned the toggle ON or OFF. If the result isn't what you had in mind, just click the command again to toggle it to the opposite state.

Ortho Mode (OR) Toggle

```
Enter a command >
* [OR] Ortho Mode is OFF
```

Figure 3.11 Toggle Commands do not require additional input.

There are other commands, which don't require any input, that either set a particular drawing parameter or perform a one-step operation. You used an example of a drawing parameter in Chapter 2 when you typed MR for the Manual Entry Relative command. Issuing this command tells CADD 6 to interpret the distances you enter in a particular way. No other input is needed. The commands for correcting mistakes (like Undo, Redo, Unerase, and Erase Last) also do not require any other input. They just perform the selected operation.

SELECTING POINTS

Almost all CADD 6 commands require you to pick points, so it is important to know the best method to use. There are at least four methods of telling CADD 6 exactly what point to select:

1. Use the *point-and-click* method; move your mouse (or the keyboard arrow keys) to position the cursor on the desired point, then click to select that point.
2. Use a Snap command so CADD 6 snaps to an exact point on an existing object, like the end of a line or center of a circle.
3. Use the *direct-distance* method; move the cursor in the desired direction and enter the exact distance that the point is in that direction.
4. Enter the exact coordinates of the point, in absolute or relative mode, as *(X, Y)* or polar coordinates.

Selecting with the Mouse

The easiest way to select points is to just point and click. Move the cursor to the desired point, and click the first (the left) mouse button to select the point. Whatever point the cursor was on is picked. The problem is, CADD's six-decimal-place accuracy makes it nearly impossible to pick a specific point in the drawing. Even if it looks like you are on some point, like the endpoint of a line, you can not visually pick that specific point with CADD 6's accuracy.

Snapping to a Point

When point and click is not accurate enough, how do you select a specific point? The Snap commands are ideal for selecting an exact point on some existing object, like the endpoint of a line or arc, center of a circle, or the closest point on a particular object.

You used snaps in Chapter 2 to position the sink basin and move the faucet into position so it was centered on the sink. These and the other Snap commands are discussed in Chapter 6.

It is also important to use snaps when selecting objects to dimension, or else the text of the dimension will not be correct. If you just point and click to place a dimension, you are really dimensioning to arbitrary points, not to a specific object.

Snaps are among the most useful tools that CADD 6 has to offer. Get into the habit of always snapping, and your drawings will be clean and professional. Without using snaps, objects don't connect where they are supposed to. They overhang, and it is hard to center them where you want them to be.

Selection with Direct Distance

A very intuitive method of locating exact points is with direct distance input. Once you start a line or other operation, move the cursor to establish a direction and enter the distance to move in that direction to get to the desired point. The value you enter defines the distance between the starting point and the next point CADD 6 selects.

You used direct distance to draw the first lines that made up your sink outline. You clicked to start the first line, moved the cursor horizontally to the right, then entered the distance of 28". The value 28 was the distance from the starting point to the desired point (the other end of the line), in the established direction. In this case, the distance defined the length of a line, but direct distance could also be used to select a reference point for a Move, Copy, or other editing function.

You do not have to be in Ortho Mode for direct distance to work. With Ortho Mode set to OFF, you could move the cursor in any arbitrary direction and enter the distance to the next point. This is not very accurate, since it is very hard to estimate a direction on the screen, even horizontal or vertical. It is usually better to use Ortho Mode or polar coordinates in order to establish accurate angles in your drawing.

Direct distance entry becomes even more powerful when used in combination with Tracking (TK). Tracking lets you precisely position the cursor anywhere in the drawing by entering distances from some other object or point. The idea is to move in horizontal and vertical increments until you get the cursor where you want it. You do this by entering distances and using snaps. Chapter 4 discusses more about how to use Tracking. While you can draw in CADD 6 without the use of Tracking, it can make drawing and positioning objects much more convenient, saving you time in the process.

You could have used Tracking in the kitchen sink tutorial to move the faucet into position with one step. Figure 3.12 shows the faucet where it was drawn to the right of the sink, and how you would track to move it to its desired position.

Entering Coordinates

Another common method of locating exact points is to enter their rectangular coordinates in the form *X,Y*. If you are not familiar with the concept of coordinates, review Appendix A for more information.

Figure 3.13 shows the *X* and *Y* coordinate axes. Every point in a drawing has *X* (horizontal) and *Y* (vertical) coordinates that are measured relative to these axes. The point where the *X* and *Y* axes intersect is called the *origin* or the point with coordinates (0,0). Coordinates are always specified so the positive *X* values are horizontal to the right and positive *Y* values are vertical and upward. Similarly, negative *X* values are horizontal to the left and negative *Y* values are vertical downward.

If you want to start a line at point A in Figure 3.14, simply enter its *X,Y* coordinates at the command line prompt:

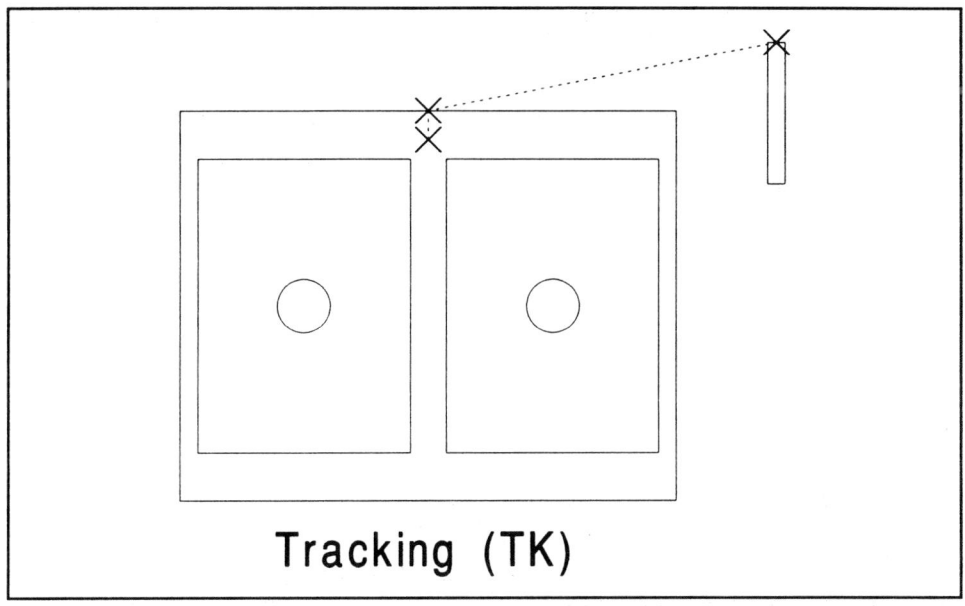

Figure 3.12 Tracking helps you precisely position objects.

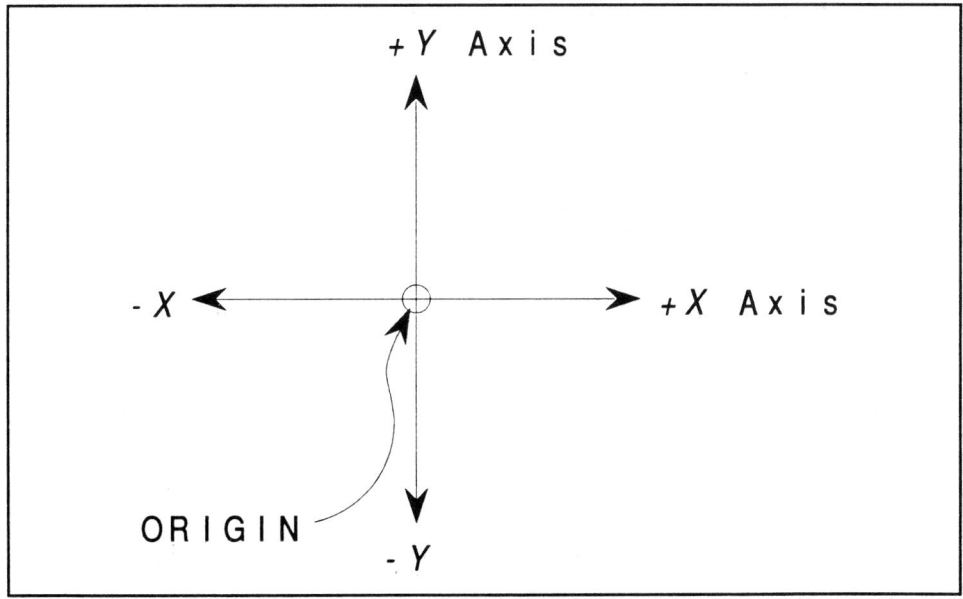

Figure 3.13 The basic components of the Cartesian coordinate system.

Type: 3,5
Press Enter

Be sure to include the comma when you enter the coordinates. When you press the Enter key, the cursor jumps to the point 3,5, even if it is off the screen. That point is

```
                    + Y   A x i s
                         ↑
             Y = 5 ┈┈┈┈┈•( 3 , 5 )
                      ⁄ ┊
                    ⁄   ┊
     - X ←─────────────┼─────────→ + X   A x i s
                    X = 3
     P o i n t   A
                         ↓
                    - Y
```

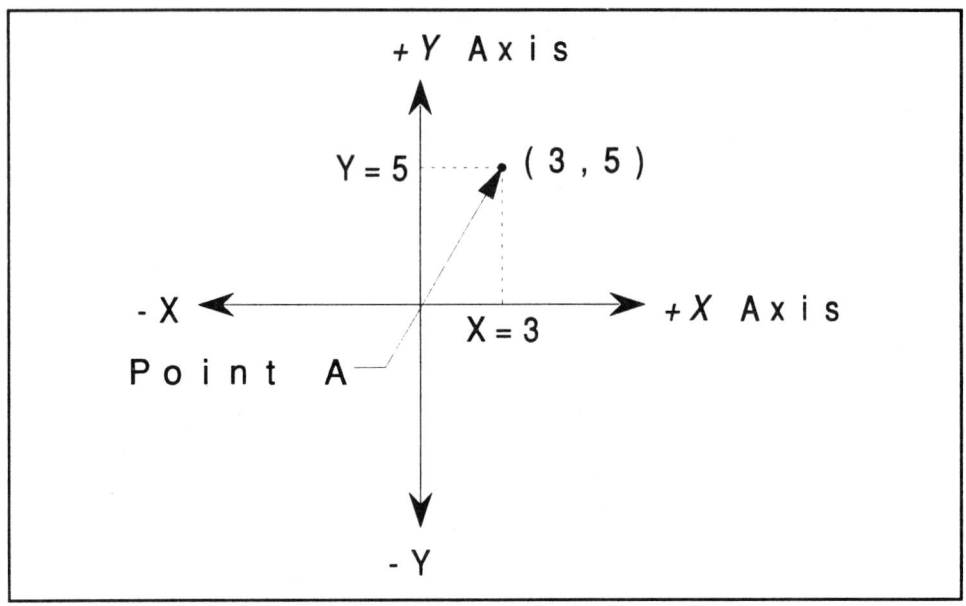

Figure 3.14 Using coordinates to locate points.

3 units in the positive X direction (right of the origin point) and 5 units in the positive Y direction (above the origin).

It is not always convenient to use coordinates that are relative to the origin point, since it is a somewhat arbitrary point. It is often easier to enter coordinates relative to other objects in the drawing. You did this in the kitchen sink tutorial when you initiated the Manual entry Relative command. The MR mode of coordinate entry causes CADD 6 to interpret all coordinate entry as being relative to the previous point entered. The coordinates still represent distances in the X and Y directions, they are just no longer measured from the origin point, but rather from the last point clicked or selected.

CHAPTER SUMMARY

This chapter introduced many of the fundamental concepts you need to understand to become a proficient CADD 6 user. It also further explained many of the methods used to create the kitchen sink drawing in Chapter 2. In that tutorial, you were told what to do, but not why you were doing it. The reasons should become clear once you have a good understanding of the fundamentals covered here.

You now know more about how to communicate with CADD 6, select commands from the menus, use special keys and buttons, and use commands. The different types of input that CADD 6 expects for each command were also explained.

To create professional quality drawings, it is important that you understand the many ways to select points. It is seldom accurate enough to just point and click on a drawing location. This chapter introduced you to three methods of accurate point entry — direct distances, snaps, and using coordinates.

CHAPTER 4

Creating

USING THE DRAW AND CONSTRAINTS MENUS

When you start CADD 6 and you're staring at a blank drawing screen, you probably are wondering "What do I do first?" Just how do you begin the process of creating a CADD drawing? The first thing you should do is place a basic drawing entity, or primitive, on your screen. This will be the first of many primitive entities in your drawing that provide a basis to build on. Your finished drawing could consist of hundreds of these primitives combined together to form complex entities. Other commands in CADD 6 are used to help you place entities in the drawing and modify them. Some commands allow you to establish drawing parameters that help the drawing process go faster.

When placing drawing primitives on screen, you can expect to see them rubberbanding after the first or second point has been placed (depending on the entity). This "dynamic visual feedback" is a great aid in CADD 6 drafting. If you don't see the entity rubberbanding, check to make sure the Rubberbanding (RB) toggle is ON.

You use the commands on the DRAW menu to select and draw the CADD 6 primitives. The following commands are found on the DRAW menu. (Their two-letter codes are in parentheses.)

DRAW

Point (PO)
Line (LI)
Individual Line (L1)
Rectangle (RE)

Regular Polygon (RP)
Circle 2-Point (C2)
Circle 3-Point (C3)
Arc 2-Point (A2)
Arc 3-Point (A3)
Ellipse (EP)
Bezier Curve (BV)
Individual Bezier Curve (BW)
Spline Curve (CV)

Double Lines (L2)
Double Line Settings (DB)
MultiDraw (MU)
MultiDraw Settings (MS)

Placing entities in a drawing, whether lines, circles, or arcs, is easier and more accurate when you use coordinates and the various CONSTRAINTS commands. The Constraint commands help you control cursor movement and place entities uniformly with the use of grids. The following are some items found on the CONSTRAINTS menu:

CONSTRAINTS

Ortho Mode (OR)
Ortho Angle (OA)
Grid ON/OFF (GR)
Snap to Grid (SG)
Grid Size (GS)
Grid Re-origin (GO)
Cursor Movement (CM)

All of the DRAW and CONSTRAINTS commands are discussed here. You have a chance to try many of them for yourself when you complete the first part of a kitchen layout drawing later in this chapter.

USING THE DRAW COMMANDS

All of these commands can be executed by their two-letter command code, or selected from the DRAW menu.

Point (PO)

The Point (PO) command allows you to place a standard point in a drawing. A single point is the simplest of the CADD 6 primitives. Execute the Point (PO) command by using the two-character command code PO or select Point (PO) from the DRAW menu.

Then, simply click on the drawing screen where you want the point to be placed (or use a Snap command).

Line (LI)

Another simple object is the line. You define a line by telling CADD 6 where to place its two endpoints. Select Line (LI) from the menu or use the command code LI. Think of "Line Insert" to make this command code easier to remember.

To insert a line, position the cursor at the desired location of the line's first endpoint and press Enter or click your first mouse button. Then move your cursor to the location of the second endpoint and press Enter again.

This command actually starts a line drawing mode. You can continue to draw connected lines by clicking to the next endpoint. Press Esc, or select another command from the menu to stop drawing lines.

Individual Line (L1)

The Individual Line (L1) command works just like the Line (LI) command with one exception. Once you've specified the second point on the line, the line command is completed, with no new line rubberbanding from the cursor.

Rectangle (RE)

To draw a rectangle, select the Rectangle (RE) from the DRAW menu or type RE and position the cursor on the first point of your rectangle. Press Enter to place the point, and then move your cursor across the screen. Notice that the rectangle rubberbands between the first point and the cursor. Click or press Enter to place the second point when you're satisfied with the size and shape of the rectangle.

Regular Polygon (RP)

A regular polygon is a geometric figure with sides of equal length and with equal angles between each of the sides. Triangles, octagons, and hexagons with equal-length sides are all regular polygons.

To draw a regular polygon, select the Regular Polygon (RP) command from the DRAW menu or use the command code RP. You will first be prompted to change the number of sides. A default number is displayed in brackets. You can select anywhere from 3 to 255 sides. The next prompt asks you if you want Center or Side construction.

Center Construction. Center construction is similar to the Circle 2-Point (C2) command. Figure 4.1 shows that you specify a center point and a corner point on the polygon, just as you selected a point on the radius of the circle.

X = Pick Point

Center Construction

Side Construction

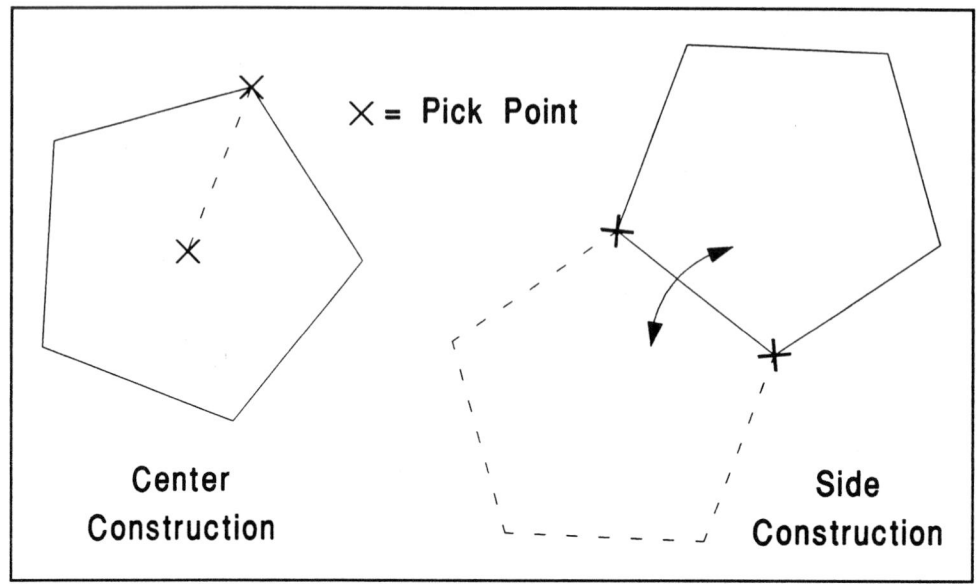

Figure 4.1 Different Polygon Construction methods.

Side Construction. The Side method prompts you to enter one corner of the polygon's side, then the adjacent corner point. Next, you are prompted to enter the location of the polygon with respect to the polygon's side you just specified. A "ghost" image of the polygon flips about the specified side. Pressing Enter freezes the polygon's position and completes the command. (See Figure 4.1.)

Circles

In CADD 6, you can draw two different types of circles depending on the number of points you use to define the size and location of the circle. (There are actually three types, since an ellipse drawn with equal major and minor axes appears to be a circle.)

Circle 2-Point (C2). A Circle 2-Point (C2) can be specified by a center point and a point on the circumference (radius). To execute the Circle 2-Point (C2) command, use the command code C2. Move the cursor to the place where you want your circle centered. When the cursor is positioned at the proper place, set the center point by pressing Enter. Move the cursor to a location on the circumference of the circle and press Enter again. The circle is displayed, as shown in Figure 4.2.

Circle 3-Point (C3). A Circle 3-Point (C3) is drawn by defining three points on the circle's circumference. Select the Circle 3-Point (C3) command by using the command code C3. Answer the first prompt by placing the cursor where you want to set the first point on the circumference, and press Enter. Select a second and third point on the circumference, and press Enter after selecting each. CADD 6 draws a circle through the three selected points, as shown in Figure 4.2. Be careful not to select three points

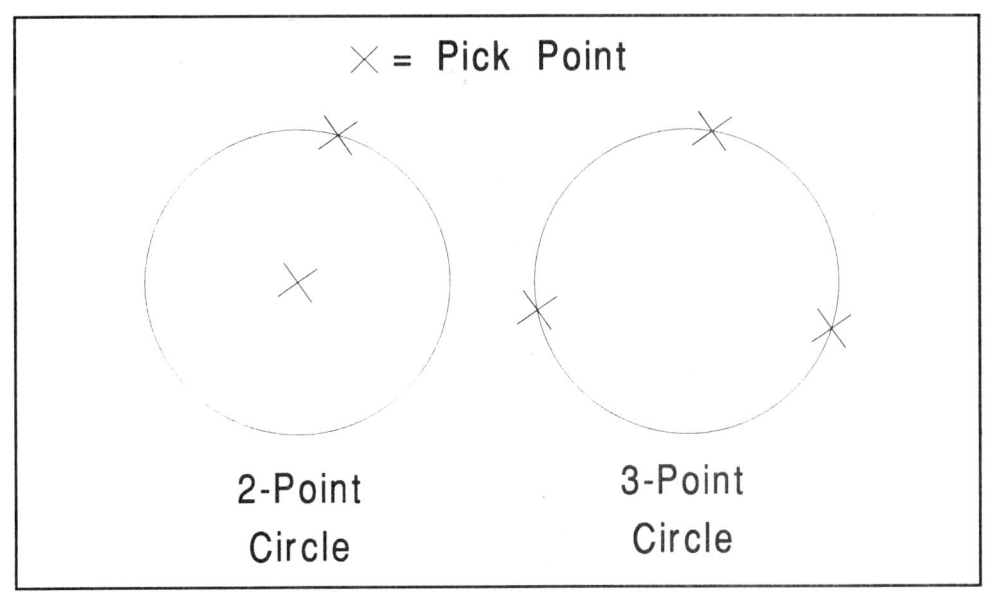

Figure 4.2 Constructing 2-Point and 3-Point circles.

in a straight line; CADD 6 will interpret those points as an infinitely large circle, and the results may be unpredictable.

Arcs

There are two ways to draw arcs in CADD 6. One command creates a two-point arc by defining a specified center point and points on the arc. You define a three-point arc by selecting any three points that the arc passes through.

Arc 2-Point (A2). A Arc 2-Point (A2) can be specified by a center point, a starting point, and an endpoint. To draw this arc, use the command code A2 to select the Arc 2-Point (A2) command from the menu. Move your cursor to the point you want to pick as the arc center, then press Enter. A new prompt appears, asking you to select an endpoint. Move your cursor to the point you want to select for the endpoint, and press Enter. By moving your cursor, you will see a continually changing outline of an arc. When you are satisfied with the size of the arc, press Enter to freeze the arc and complete the command. (See Figure 4.3.)

Arc 3-Point (A3). You can specify an Arc 3-Point (A3) by defining three points that the arc passes through. To draw this kind of arc, use the command code A3 or select the Arc 3-Point (A3) command from the menu. At the first prompt, move your cursor to the point where you want to start the arc. Press Enter to set your starting point. At the next prompt, move the cursor to the midpoint of the arc and press Enter. Position the cursor where you want to select the last endpoint and press Enter. Your arc should be displayed, as shown in Figure 4.3.

4-6 ■ Chapter 4: Creating

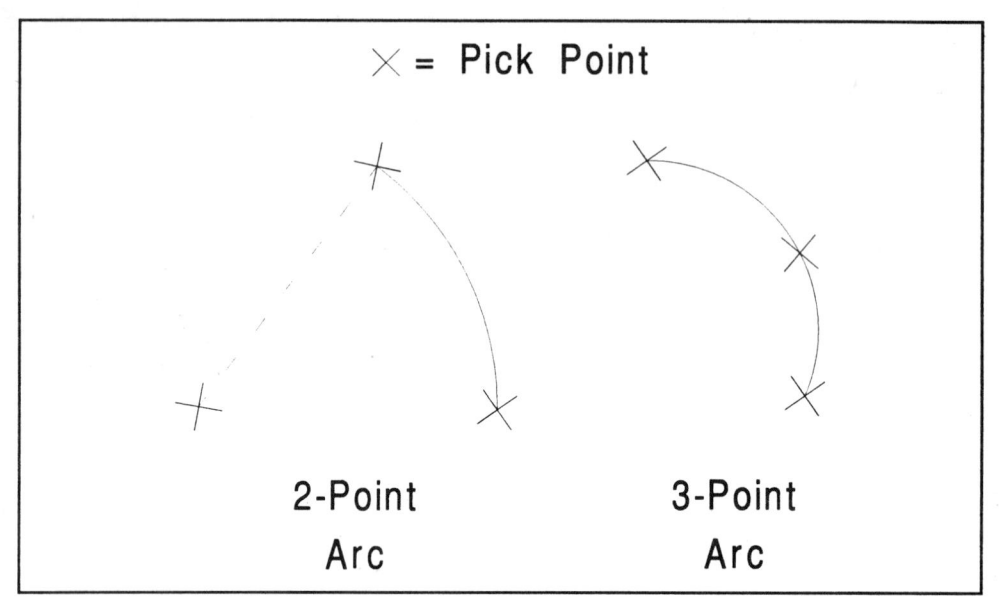

Figure 4.3 Constructing 2-Point and 3-Point arcs.

Ellipses and Curves

Ellipses and curves come in handy when creating isometric drawings, or drawing smooth curves that vary too much to be drawn with arcs.

Ellipse (EP). An ellipse is an oval-shaped object defined by two points on its major axis and two points on its minor axis, shown in Figure 4.4. The major axis is a line from one end of the ellipse to the other end and determines its length, location, and rotation. The minor axis is perpendicular to the major axis and *bisects* it (passes through its midpoint). The minor axis determines the width of the ellipse.

Begin by selecting the Ellipse (EP) command. Move the cursor to where you want to set the first major axis point and press Enter. Move the cursor to where you want to set the second major axis point and press Enter again. Once the major axis has been defined, you see the minor axis rubberbanding perpendicular to the major axis, about the center point. The minor axis rubberbands symmetrically about the major axis. You will be prompted to enter the endpoint of the minor axis.

Next, a prompt asks whether the ellipse is "true" or "construction." A true ellipse is a perfect representation of an ellipse, but cannot be broken with the Object Break (OB) command. A construction ellipse is an approximation of an ellipse that is actually drawn with four arcs, each positioned by their apexes at the ends of the major and minor axes. Arcs can be broken, so it is possible to edit a construction ellipse. After you press either T or C (for True or Construction), the command is complete and the ellipse is drawn, as shown in Figure 4.5.

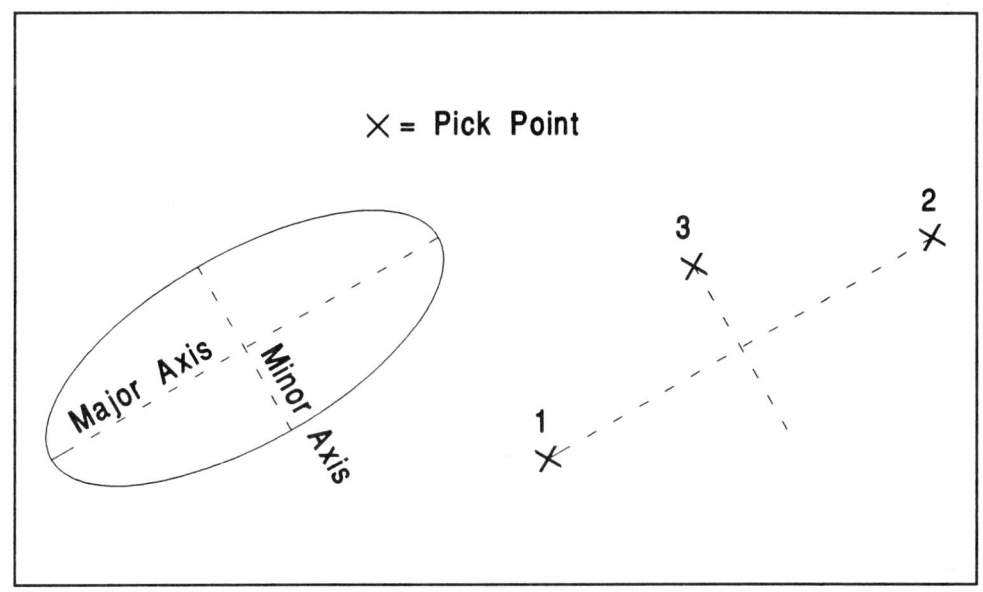

Figure 4.4 Constructing an Ellipse.

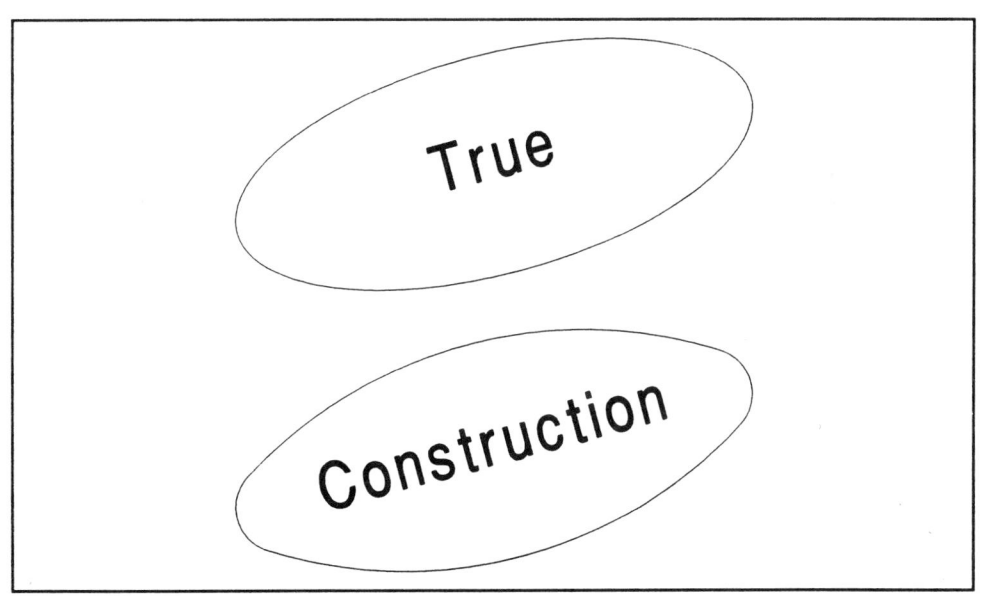

Figure 4.5 A true ellipse versus a construction ellipse.

Bezier Curve (BV). A bezier curve is a type of curve that can be edited after it is created. To draw this curve, use the command code BV. Then move the cursor and click to set each point on the curve. As you enter a series of points, notice the bezier curve forming on the screen. This curve takes a little practice to learn to place the points exactly where you want them, but it allows you to draw very complex shapes, as shown in Figure 4.6. Once drawn, you can edit, or modify, the curves with the Bezier Edit (BE) command.

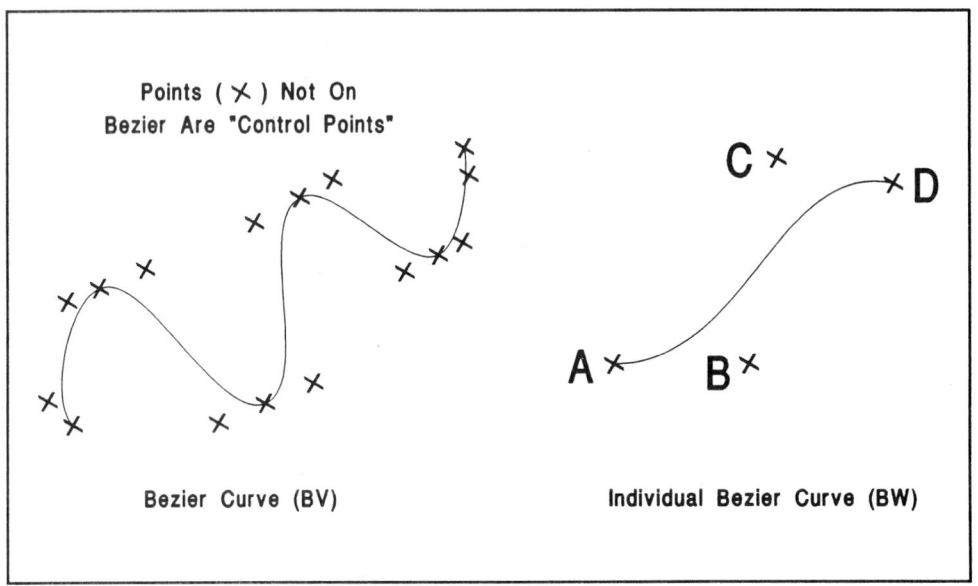

Figure 4.6 Drawing bezier curves.

Individual Bezier Curve (BW). The Individual Bezier Curve (BW) command provides an alternate way of drawing individual bezier curves. To understand the difference between BW and BV, consider how bezier curves are constructed with the BV command code. With the BV command code, the bezier curve is drawn as smoothly as possible between specified endpoints. If you keep entering points, you add more sections to the bezier curve. Entering three points in the bezier mode produces a curve consisting of two connected, but separate bezier sections. Each section can be erased, moved, or copied with the standard CADD 6 object editing commands.

To edit a bezier curve, you need at least two bezier sections, not necessarily connected. When you edit a bezier curve, you are relocating control points (two per section) because they determine the shape of the curve. To view these control points, turn construction points on with the Construction Points (PC) command by typing the command code PC.

With the BW command code, only one bezier section is constructed. You are prompted to place the start point, the two control points, and the endpoint of the curve. Control points are the endpoints of lines tangent to the curve that determine its direction and curvature. With the BW command code, you select the location of the control points so that your curve can be constructed tangent to existing lines in the drawing. Figure 4.6 shows an example. Point A is the starting point, points B and C are the first and second control points, and point D is the end of the curve.

Chapter 4: Creating ■ 4-9

Spline or Complex Curve (CV). You can create a complex curve from a minimum of three points. CADD 6 then creates a curve passing through the points. To draw a Curve (CV), use the command code CV. Two prompts appear together. For now, ignore the second prompt, and instead respond to the first prompt by setting at least three points that will form the curve. Set these points by positioning the cursor where desired, and then press Enter, as shown in Figure 4.7. After you set the points, use the Pen Up (PU) command to complete the curve.

> **TIP:** If you don't establish at least three points before using the Pen Up (PU) command, the command is aborted and you will see the message:
>
> NEED AT LEAST 3 PNTS FOR A CURVE!
>
> You then must execute the command again.

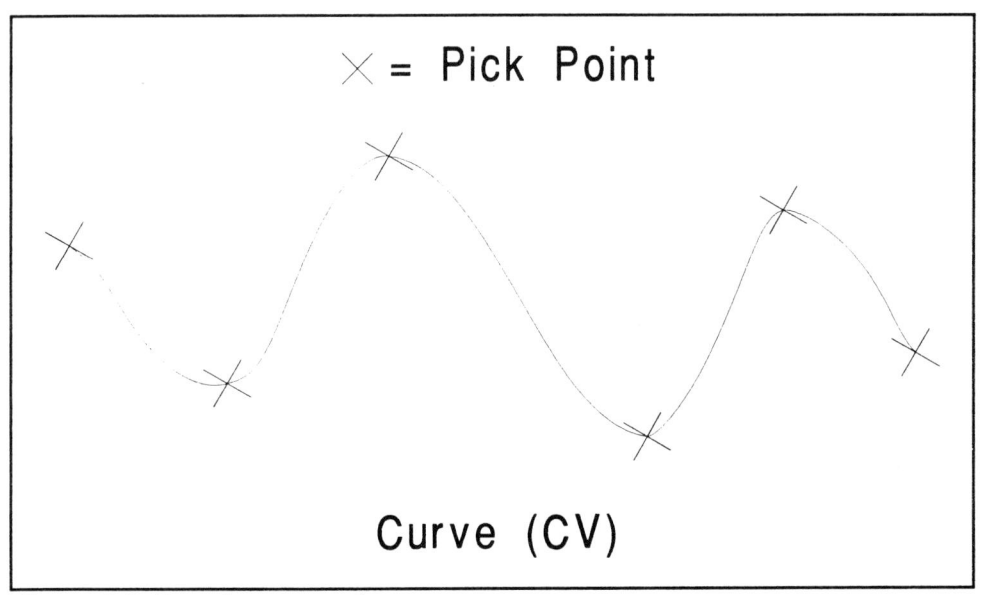

```
                    × = Pick Point


                    Curve (CV)
```

Figure 4.7 Drawing a complex curve.

Double Lines (L2)

The Double Lines (L2) command is used to automatically draw parallel lines. This command works exactly like the Line (LI) command, except a second, parallel line is drawn at the same time. When you are finished with this command, either press Escape, or enter PU. The spacing between the two lines is determined by the Double Line Settings (DB).

4-10 ■ Chapter 4: Creating

To draw double lines, type L2 and draw a line as you normally would in CADD 6. When you move in different directions, the lines are automatically trimmed to accommodate the angle. Figure 4.8 shows an example.

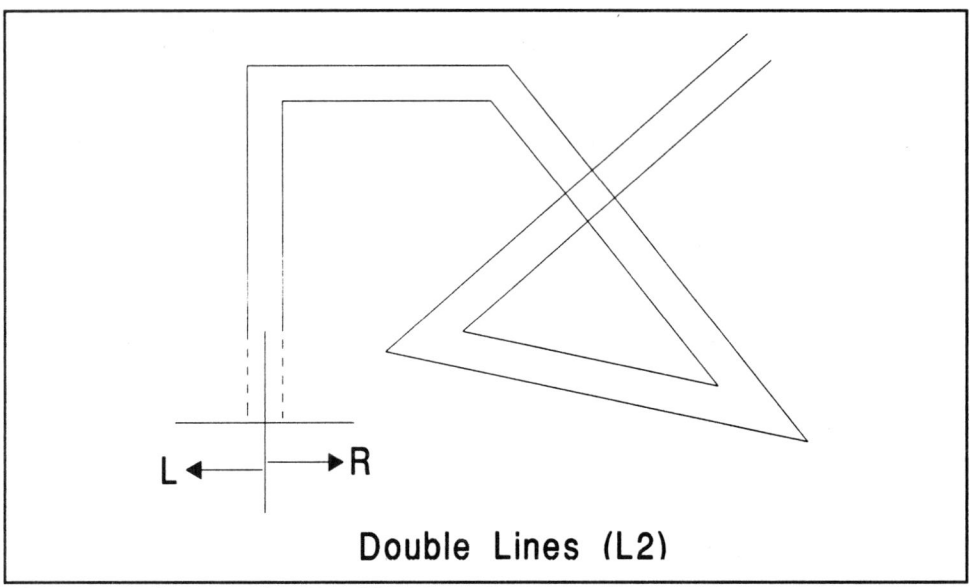

Figure 4.8 Constructing Double Lines.

Double Line Settings (DB)

When you type in DB, a submenu appears prompting you to choose from five variable settings: Left offset, Right offset, Solid, Auto fillet, and Fillet radius.

Left offset and Right offset. The first two settings are the Left and Right line offsets. These settings control where the two lines will be drawn in relation to your cursor. The lines are offset from the center of the cursor crosshair. The Left offset is measured to the left of the cursor when the cursor points horizontal and vertical. Similarly, the Right offset is measured to the right of the cursor. Select L to set the Left offset, and select R to set the Right offset.

If you start a double line from the bottom of your screen and move up, the offsets are relative to the left and right side of your cursor. If you then move the cursor to the right, the left side of the cursor is the side toward the top of the screen, the right side is toward the bottom of the screen.

Solid. Solid is a toggle that, when turned ON, automatically causes the space between the double lines to be filled as they are placed on the drawing.

Autofillet. Autofillet is a toggle that, when turned ON, causes an automatic filleting of the double lines every time the lines are drawn in a new direction. Autofillet also affects lines drawn using the Line (LI) command.

Fillet radius. Fillet radius is the variable setting that defines the radius of the fillet that's created when Autofillet is ON or when the Fillet (FI) command is used.

Multidraw (MU)

The Multidraw (MU) command, like the Double Line (L2) command, is used to automatically draw parallel lines. This command works very much like the Double Line (L2) command, except you have the option of drawing up to 16 parallel lines, bezier curves, or spline curves at the same time. When you are finished with this command, either press Escape, or enter PU. The spacing between any two lines or curves is determined by the Multidraw Settings (MS) command.

In addition to the spacing (offset) between each of the lines or curves, each line or curve can have an independent setting of:

> Line\Curve Type
> Line\Curve Width
> Line\Curve Color
> Line\Curve Layer

To draw multiple lines or curves, type MU and draw a line or curve as you normally would in CADD 6. When you move in different directions, lines are automatically trimmed to accommodate the angle, as shown in Figure 4.9.

Multidraw Settings (MS)

When you type in MS, a submenu appears prompting you with a choice of five variable settings: Lines, Beziers, Curves, Rubberbanding, and Auto Fillet.

> **TIP:** Auto Fillet does not apply to Beziers or Curves.

Choose between Lines, Beziers, or Curves and press Enter. Next, you are prompted with the following settings for each individual line or curve: Line, Of, laYer, Color, Type, Width, and Offset from cursor. The following is an explanation of these settings.

Line and Of. The Line and Of settings work hand-in-hand. When you select the Line option, you are choosing which line's (or curve's) parameters to set out of the total number of lines selected. The total number of lines or curves drawn is established with the Of option. If Of is set to 7, then only seven lines or curves are drawn. In turn, you

4-12 ■ Chapter 4: Creating

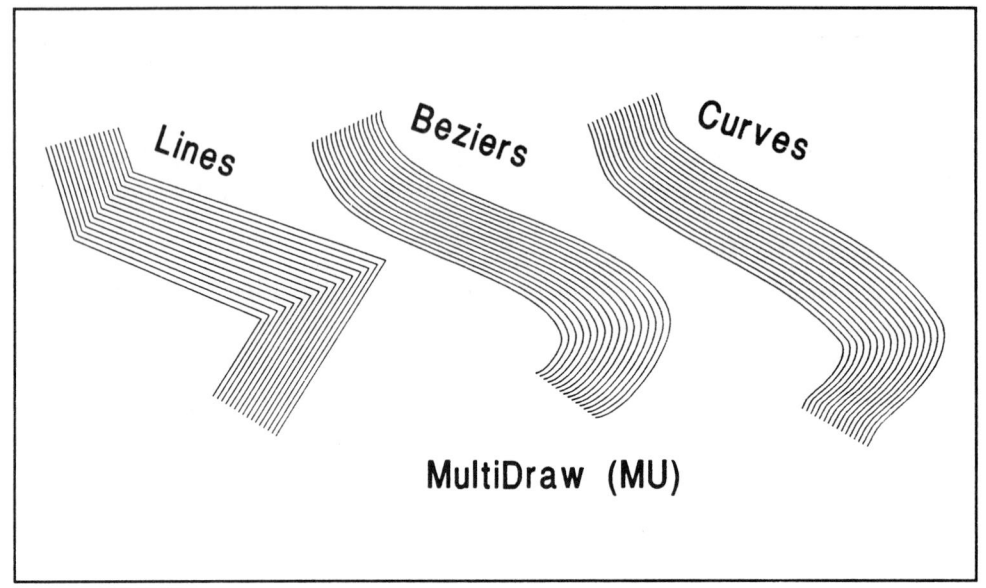

Figure 4.9 Using Multidraw with lines, beziers, and complex curves.

will only be able to change the parameters of lines 1 to 7. The Of setting accepts a value no greater than 16.

If you entered 1 from the Line option with Of set to 7, you would be setting the first line of 7. Once this line is set and you press Enter, the settings automatically move to Line 2 of 7. This goes on until all of the lines or curves have been drawn. Press Enter to accept the default settings of any line or curve. Figure 4.10 shows an example of multiple lines, Bezier curves, and spline curves drawn with different settings.

Layer. Establishes the layer of the line or curve selected.

Color. Establishes the color of the line or curve selected.

Type. Establishes the line type of the line or curve selected.

Width. Establishes the width of the line or curve selected.

Offset from Cursor. This option controls where a line or curve is drawn in relation to the cursor. The lines or curves are offset from the sides of the cursor crosshair (the point where the two cursor lines intersect). The side of the cursor where the lines or curves are drawn depends on whether the Offset value is positive or negative. If you start a multiple line from the bottom of your screen and move up, a positive offset will be drawn to the left side of the cursor. A negative offset will be drawn to the right side of the cursor. An offset of zero is drawn from the center of the cursor.

Chapter 4: Creating ■ 4-13

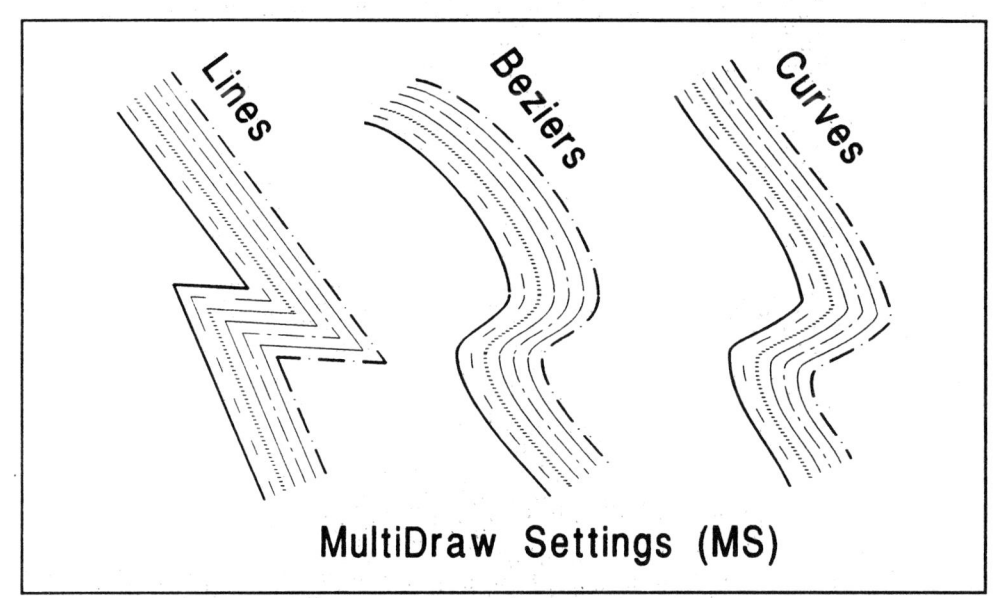

Figure 4.10 Changing the characteristics of multidraw objects.

If you move the cursor to the right, the left side of the cursor is the side toward the top of the screen and the right side is toward the bottom of the screen. Figure 4.11 shows examples of positive, negative, and zero offsets in relation to the cursor.

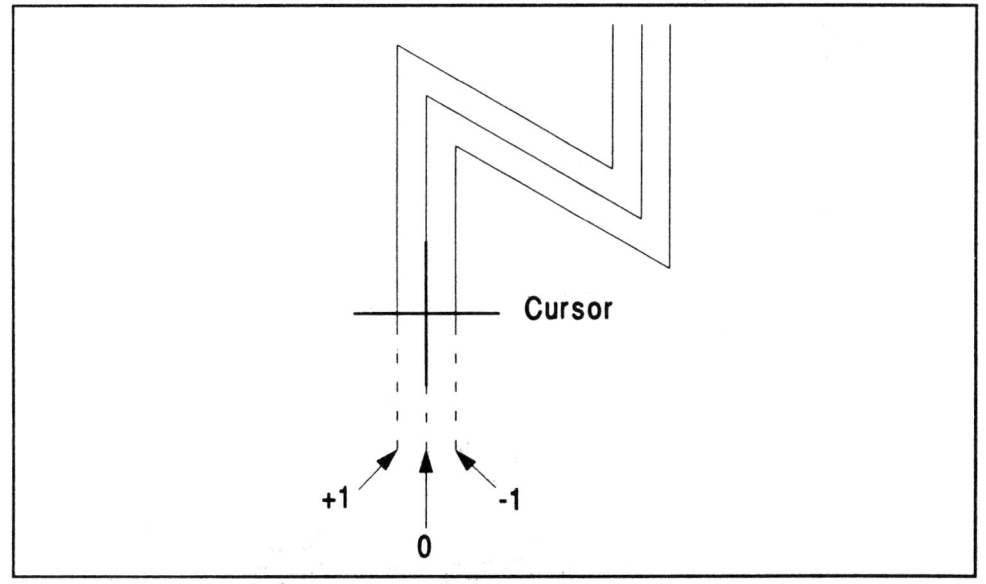

Figure 4.11 Adjusting the offset relative to the cursor.

USING THE CONSTRAINT COMMANDS

All of the commands in this section can be executed by their two-letter command code, or they can be selected from the CONSTRAINTS menu.

Ortho Mode (OR) and Ortho Angle (OA)

The Ortho Mode (OR) command is a toggle. When it's ON, your cursor is restricted to move (when drawing a line or dragging an object) at 90-degree increments of its starting position. To set this offset, or angle of movement, use the Ortho Angle (OA) command. If the angle is set to 0, the cursor is restricted to horizontal or vertical movement. If it's set to 30 degrees, the cursor can either move at 30, 120, 210, or 300 degrees, as shown in Figure 4.12. These angles are offset by 90-degree increments.

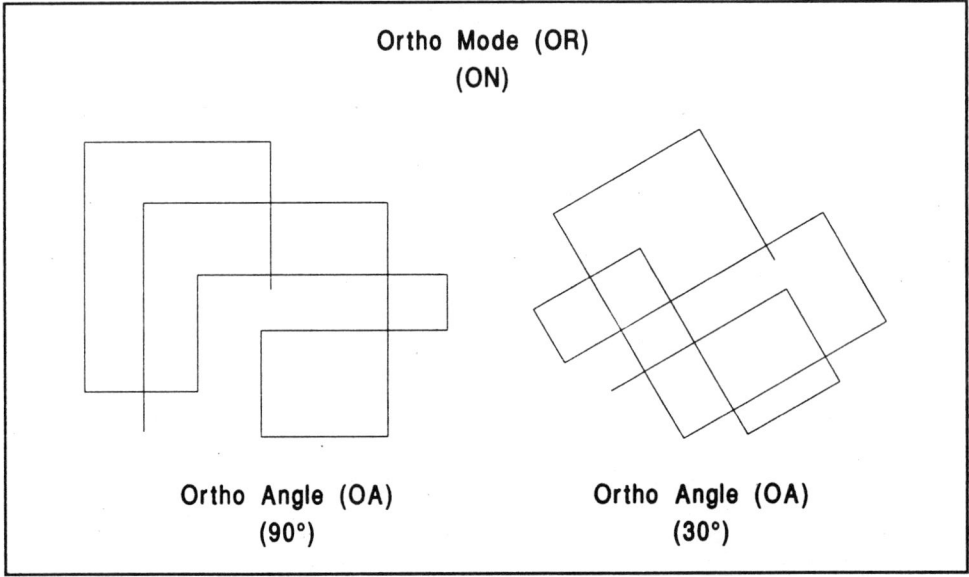

Figure 4.12 Constraining the cursor with Ortho Mode and Ortho Angle.

The Ortho Mode (OR) command is a very valuable tool in CADD 6. If you want to draw lines that are always at right angles to each other, or drag an object on the screen at a set angle, turn Ortho Mode ON. You can type in OR, or select Ortho Mode (OR) from the CONSTRAINTS menu. The Ortho Mode (OR) can also be changed by holding down the Control (Ctrl) key during an operation. The Ortho Mode (OR) toggles ON or OFF depending on its initial setting. When you let up on the Ctrl key, it reverts back to its initial setting.

Grid On/Off (GR)

This command toggles the screen grid ON or OFF. A grid can be a very helpful tool for positioning and aligning objects in your drawing. It is simply a set of evenly spaced dots that cover the screen, and are used only for reference. The grid points are never printed and are not really a part of your drawing. Grids are available to make drawing easier. Use them if you want, but they are never mandatory.

Once you establish the parameters that control the grid, select the Grid (GR) command to see the grid on the screen.

Snap To Grid (SG)

The Snap To Grid (SG) command is also a toggle command. If this command has been turned ON, the cursor moves between grid points on the screen. Even if the Grid (GR) has been turned OFF, the cursor still snaps to the grid points, even though they are not shown on the screen.

Grid Size (GS)

Grid Size (GS) determines how close or far apart the dots are on your screen when you turn ON a grid. The grid size is the distance between each grid point; it is defined independently for the X (horizontal) and Y (vertical) directions. Use the command code GS, and answer the prompt either by pressing Enter twice to accept the current grid size, or supplying new sizes for the X and Y prompts before pressing Enter. The distance between the points along the X- axis do not have to be equal to the distance between the points along the Y- axis. Because you can vary these values, you could offset the X and Y values to aid in isometric drawings.

Some preset grid sizes are listed on the video menu. These are commonly used sizes listed for convenience; you are in no way limited to just those choices.

You should choose a Grid Size (GS) that is appropriate to the size of objects in your drawing. Grid Size (GS) is not at all related to screen size. A very large grid may be good for drawing a subdivision plan, and a very small grid is appropriate for drawing the components of an electronic schematic.

You will also notice that the grid points appear closer together as you Zoom Out (ZO). At some zooms you should see the message "Only every XXX grid point shown" (where XXX is 2nd or 3rd or some other number). This message indicates that CADD 6 decided the grid points were too close together for all of them to be shown clearly on the screen. The points are all still there, and they can be snapped to (with Snap Grid [SG] ON), but some of the points are invisible. If some of the points were not hidden, the screen would be covered with grid points and you wouldn't be able to see your drawing.

Grid Re-Origin (GO)

If you want part of your drawing to be aligned with the current grid settings, you can use the Grid Re-origin (GO) command instead of moving your drawing. When you execute this command, you will be asked to enter a new point of origin for the grid. Snap to a point on your drawing, and you'll see the grid align to that point.

Cursor Movement (CM)

This command comes in handy if you are using your arrow keys to move your cursor and the Snap Grid command is currently ON. When moving the cursor with the arrow keys, while in the snap-to-grid mode, you may find that the cursor either skips grid points or gets stuck on a grid point. If the Cursor Movement (CM) command is turned ON, the cursor will snap to the individual grid points with each press of an arrow key. This works regardless of the grid size. This command is not needed if you are using a mouse or other pointing device.

TUTORIAL — KITCHEN LAYOUT, PART I

Now that you have examined the commands in this chapter, an exercise will help you put them to practical use to draw the kitchen layout shown in Figure 4.13. Actually creating a drawing is the only way to understand the many commands that have been discussed. You use the DRAW and CONSTRAINT commands covered in this chapter as the starting point for the exercise. The tutorial is then continued in Chapter 6, so you can add the new ideas presented there to your CADD knowledge.

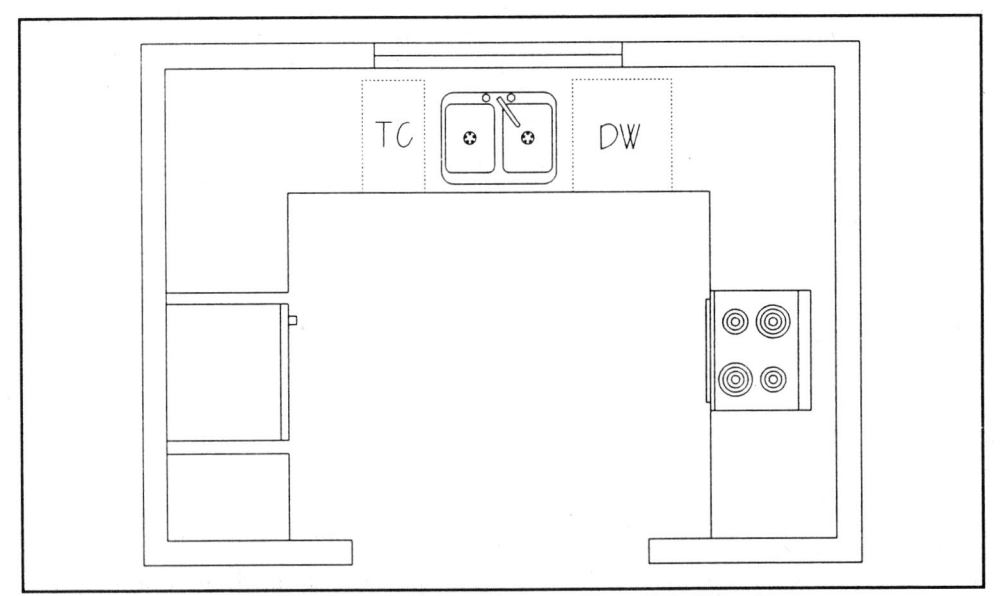

Figure 4.13 The result of the Kitchen Layout Tutorial, Part I.

Keep in mind that not every command discussed in these chapters will be used to construct the tutorial drawing. Commands from other sections are also used where necessary. Just as in Chapter 2, if you do not understand one of the commands used to create the kitchen drawing, refer to your CADD 6 manual or the other sections of this book for more information. As commands are repeated in the tutorials, only limited instructions are given. For this drawing, you may want to refer to the kitchen sink tutorial where more details are provided for the commands used there.

Often, more than one method can be used in CADD 6 to get the same result. There is not always a right or wrong way to draw or edit something. Some procedures, however, are more efficient when done in a certain way. Feel free to experiment with different commands during this exercise.

When working through the kitchen drawing, you create one section of the drawing at a time. Don't be surprised if something is left incomplete at the end of this chapter's tutorial. When more commands are introduced in the following two chapters, you will return to finish these portions of the drawing.

Throughout this tutorial, you are instructed to use the two-letter command codes discussed in Chapter 3. Feel free to use the video menu if you are more comfortable issuing commands that way. You can become a proficient CADD 6 user with either method.

Initial Drawing Parameters

Begin by setting up your drawing parameters. If you know the parameters you need to set, you can do them right away, before you start drawing. Of course, you can also change any parameters as you draw, if that is easier. For this drawing, initially set the following parameters:

Type: PC to turn Construction Points ON
Type: DC (for Display Coordinates) or select it from the menu
Type: R (or select it from the menu) to turn Relative Coordinates ON
Press Enter to finish the command
Type: MR to turn Manual Entry Offset Relative ON

Type: YC (for Current Layer)
For the current layer, type: 0 (or select it from the sidebar menu)

Type: LC (for Line Color)
Select color 13 from the color bar menu (or type 13 and press Enter)

Type: UN for Units
Select Feet/inches for the drawing units

Type: LZ (for Line Scale)
Type: 3 (and press Enter) for the line scale

Now, select the text font and text size with the Text Settings command.

Type: TS
Type: F (for Font)
Select the ARCHITEK font from the command line menu

4-18 ■ Chapter 4: Creating

>Type: Z (for size)
>Type: 6 (and press Enter)
>
>Press Enter to finish the command

This selects the font called "architek," and establishes a text height of 6".

You will use CADD 6's Double Line command to draw the walls of the kitchen. Establish the parameters that affect the look of double lines with the Double Line Settings (DB) command.

>Type: DB (Double Line Settings)
>Type: L to set the Left offset
>Type: 3 (and press Enter) to set the offset to 3"
>Type: R to set the Right offset
>Type: 3 (and press Enter) to set the offset to 3"

Verify the state of some of the other variables listed on the Double Line Settings command line menu.

>Verify that the Solids toggle is OFF (or click to turn it OFF)
>Verify that the Autofillet toggle is OFF (or click to turn it OFF)

Set these toggles, and watch the command line prompt to verify that they are in the desired state:

>Type: RB (to turn the Rubberbanding toggle ON)
>Type: HI (to turn the Highlight toggle ON)
>Type: OD (to turn the Object Drag toggle ON)

Remember that many of the settings, such as Construction Points (PC) and Rubberbanding, are toggles. Be sure to read the command line response after you execute a toggle command to verify that it has been set correctly. You may have to execute the command more than once to get the desired state of ON or OFF.

If you are still new to CADD 6, you will probably make some mistakes during this drawing exercise. Just as you learned in the kitchen sink tutorial of Chapter 2, there are some commands especially for correcting mistakes and putting the drawing back to where it was. If you perform an operation like scale, stretch, or move incorrectly, use the Undo (OO) command to correct it and put the drawing back the way it was. This feature has the widest application and can correct most mistakes. You can also use the Erase Last (EL) command to remove an object that was drawn in error. If you erase a line or object accidentally, use the Unerase (UE) command to bring it back. If the screen looks a little cluttered after all the erasing, unerasing, line placing, and so on, use the Redraw (RD) command to refresh the screen.

When drawing objects in this tutorial, you will be instructed to enter coordinates of points manually and use snap commands. This is the best way to ensure that all points are placed exactly as shown in the dimensioned figures. Remember that it is not accurate enough to simply point and click, you must specify points exactly. If you are not familiar with coordinates, you may want to review Appendix A before continuing with the exercise.

Drawing Walls

Start by drawing the walls of the kitchen, as shown in Figure 4.14. The walls are drawn with the Double Lines (L2) feature.

Figure 4.14 Drawing walls with the Double Lines feature.

```
Type: L2
Click on a point to start drawing, somewhere near the bottom left part of your screen
```

Move your cursor after placing the first point and you should see the double line rubberbanding between the cursor and the starting point. Next, use coordinates to establish the second endpoint of the lines:

```
Type: -4',0
Press Enter
```

Since Manual Entry Relative (MR) is ON, these coordinates are distances measured from the first point. The coordinates place the second endpoint 4' in the negative X direction and 0' in the Y direction from the first point.

Be sure to use the foot sign (') after the 4 or CADD 6 will interpret the distance as inches. Inches are the default distance and can be entered without the use of the inch mark (").

Now, continue drawing lines by entering the coordinates of each endpoint:

> Type: 0,10' (and press Enter)
> Type: 14',0 (and press Enter)
> Type: 0,-10' (and press Enter)
> Type: -4',0 (and press Enter)
> Press the Escape (Esc) key to finish drawing lines

You probably can't see all the lines you drew on the screen, so perform a zoom to make the whole drawing fit on the screen.

> Type ZA: (Zoom All)

This will cause your entire drawing to be displayed on the screen. You should see all of the walls shown in Figure 4.14. You could just as easily have used the direct distance method of entering distances that was used in the kitchen sink tutorial. Coordinates were used here, instead, to introduce this alternate method.

Next, cap off the ends of the walls at locations A and B in Figure 4.15. Draw lines between the endpoints to connect them and close each wall segment.

> Snap to one endpoint in area A
> Snap to the other endpoint of the wall to cap it off
> Press Esc to end the first line
> Repeat the process to cap off the wall in area B

Be sure to use Snap Nearest Point (NP) or Snap Closest Point (SC) to snap to each of the endpoints. This is the only way to accurately connect lines to existing points, like the ends of the walls. If you have a three-button mouse, NP is probably programmed onto the third (or right) button. You just get near the point and click the third button. If you have a two-button mouse, press the Shift key and the first (left) button to snap NP. If you are not using a pointing device button, use the command SC (Snap Closest Point), as you did in the kitchen sink tutorial of Chapter 2.

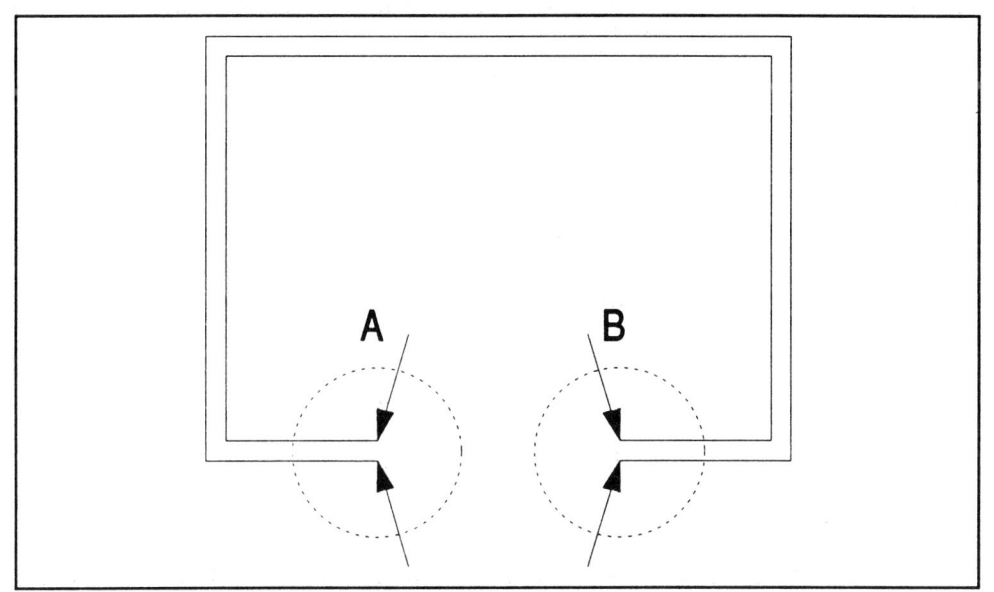

Figure 4.15 Finishing the ends of the walls.

From now on, it is assumed that you understand how to use NP or SC to snap to an existing point, so the instructions will be simplified.

This completes the kitchen walls. If you can't see the entire drawing on the screen, use the ZA (Zoom All) command to fill the screen with the entire drawing. From now on, you will not always be prompted to adjust the drawing view with zooms. Just use Zoom All (ZA) and Zoom Window (ZW) whenever you want to change the display.

Drawing the Counter Tops

Now that the walls are complete, the next step is to draw the outline of the kitchen counter tops. This drawing is a "plan view," so it is drawn as if you are looking straight down at the floor. Only the tops of items show in the drawing. You can't see the cabinets, only the counter that is on top of them. Start the counter by connecting to an existing corner of a wall:

>   Snap NP to point A in Figure 4.16
>   Type: LI (to start a line)

CADD 6 prompts you for the starting point of the line. Since you're in Manual Entry Offset Relative mode (you entered the MR command at the start of the tutorial), any coordinates you enter are interpreted as being measured from the last point selected. In this case, the last point selected is point A. Next, enter coordinates for the endpoints of the line:

4-22 ■ Chapter 4: Creating

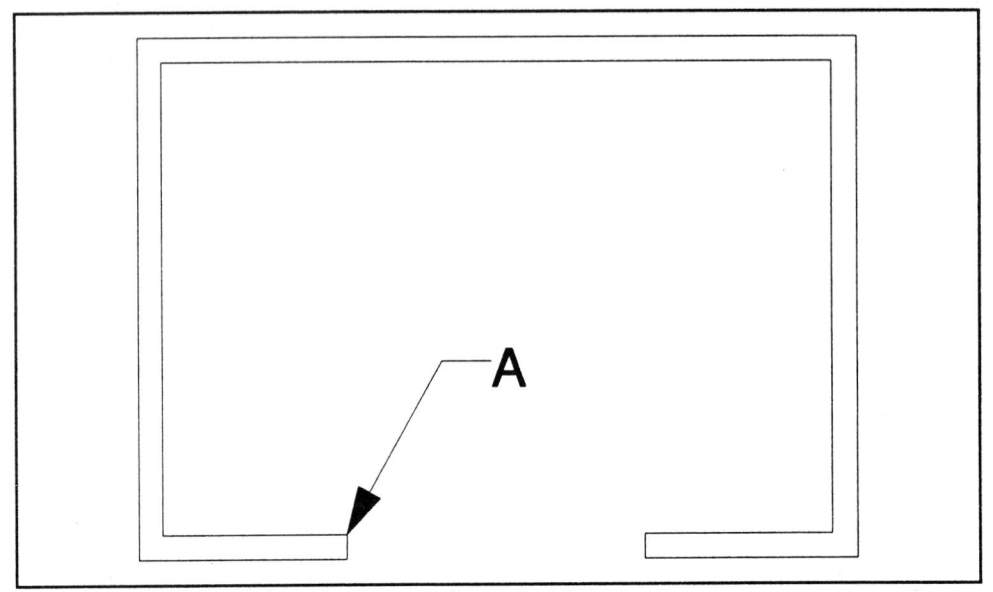

Figure 4.16 Pick point to measure from for the counter tops.

    Type: -15,0 (and press Enter)
    Type: 0,21 (and press Enter)

If your OR (Ortho Mode) is not ON, type OR to turn it ON (remember, it's a toggle) and verify it by the command line message. Then:

    Move your cursor to the left until it is near the wall
    Type: SO (Snap Object)

The Snap Object command causes the closest point to be selected that is exactly on an existing object, on the wall in this case. This finishes the first counter top and your drawing should now look like Figure 4.17.

    Type: LI
    Type: 0,3'3 (and press Enter)

This starts the next line 3'3" up from the first counter top. It is not necessary to include an inch mark ("), but you must include the foot mark (') for CADD 6 to interpret the value correctly. Do not enter any spaces between the coordinates or the comma.

    Type: CF (Cursor Free) and verify that it is turned ON

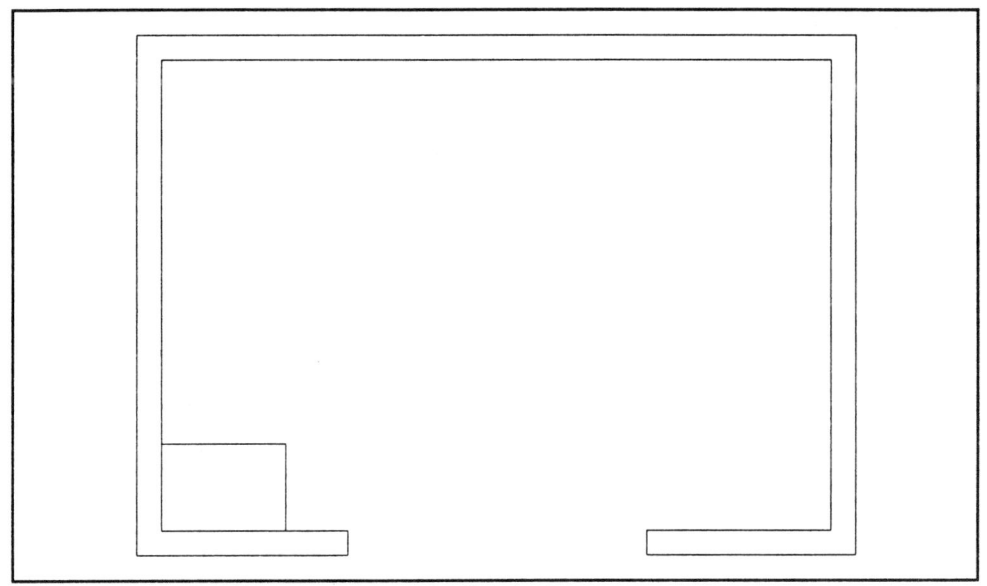

Figure 4.17 The first counter top is finished.

Since Ortho Mode is ON, you should be able to move your cursor to the right and see the horizontal line rubberbanding. The difference now is that the cursor is free to move anywhere on the screen, away from the line. This is the result of the Cursor Free (CF) toggle.

> Move the cursor to start the line going to the right
> Move your cursor down and snap to the corner of the previous counter top, point A in Figure 4.18

Now enter coordinates to draw the other edges of this counter top:

> Type: 0,2' (and press Enter)
> Type: 8'6,0 (and press Enter)
> Type: CF to turn Cursor Free OFF
> Move the cursor down toward the bottom wall
> Snap SO to that wall
> Press Esc to end the line

This completes the counter tops, as shown in Figure 4.19.

Inserting the Kitchen Sink

Every kitchen has a kitchen sink. You don't need to draw one here if you saved the sink you drew in Chapter 2. You can save time by loading the sink drawing you created previously and placing it where you want it in this drawing.

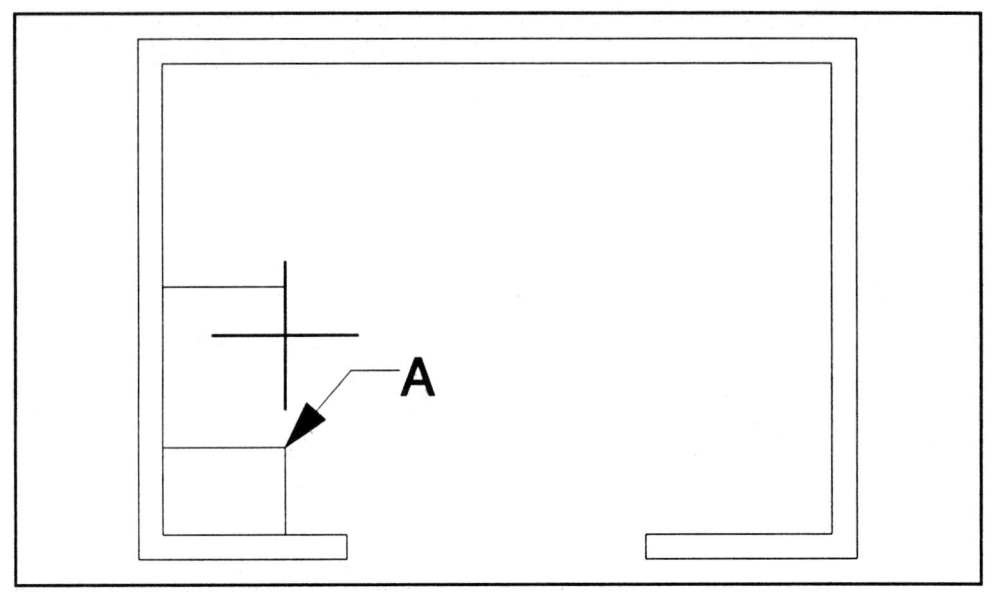

Figure 4.18 Continuing to draw the other counter tops.

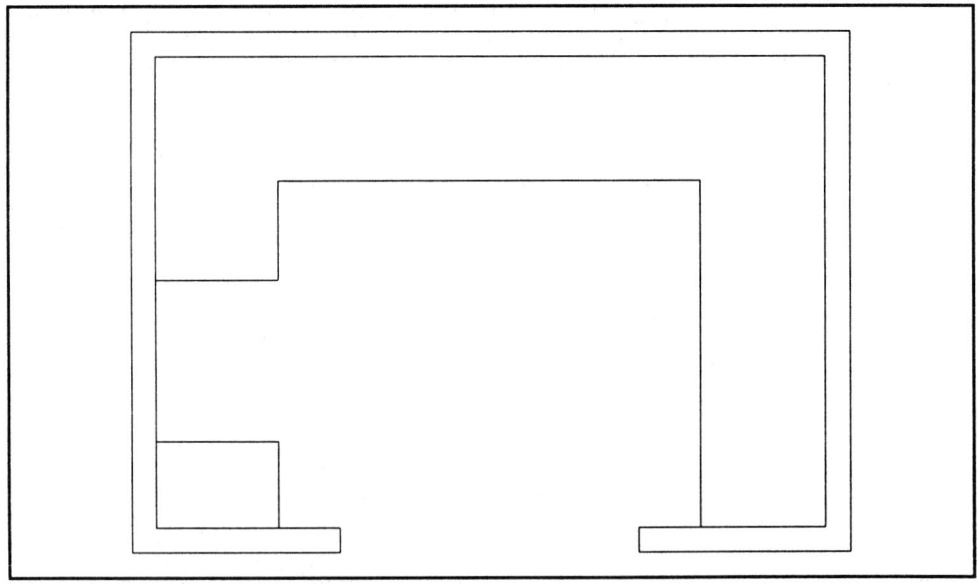

Figure 4.19 The finished counter tops.

    Type: LO (Load)
    Type: D for Drawing

CADD 6 prints a list of drawing names to pick from in the sidebar menu area. These are all of the drawing files in the current drawing path (directory).

Click on the drawing name KSINK

The outline of the sink drawing is displayed as a rectangle with an X through it so you can see just how large it is relative to your current view. This rectangle is attached to the cursor, so it moves when you move the cursor. This is how you position the drawing being loaded where you want it, in the current drawing. For this example, you place the sink temporarily in the drawing and then move it to its final position.

Move the sink image to be near the center of your drawing, as shown in Figure 4.20
Press Enter or click your first mouse button to place the sink as shown in Figure 4.21

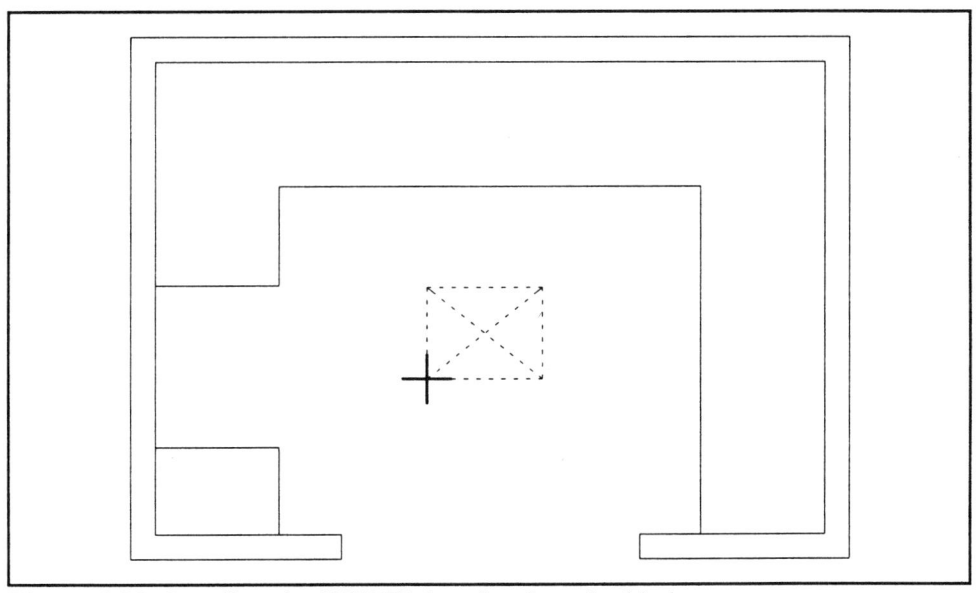

Figure 4.20 Loading the KSINK drawing into the kitchen.

Use the SHORTCUT command WM (Window Move) to move the sink into its proper position. This is similar to the Move (MV) command used in the kitchen sink tutorial, except it is restricted to the window method of selecting the objects to be moved.

Type: WM, and enclose the sink in a selection window
For the reference point, type: SM (Snap Midpoint)
Click near the midpoint of the top line of the sink

At this point, the cursor is attached to the midpoint of the top of the sink and you can visibly drag the sink around the screen. You can use Tracking (TK) to move the sink into its final position, relative to the top wall of the kitchen. Tracking is just a method for moving the cursor through the drawing by specifying incremental distances. It is like moving along reference lines of known length and direction, without actually drawing any lines.

4-26 ■ Chapter 4: Creating

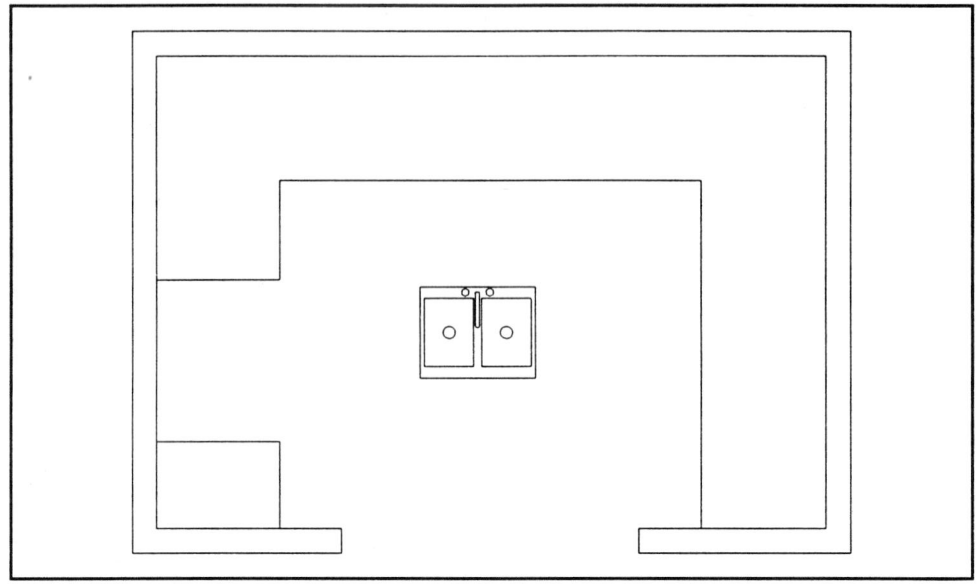

Figure 4.21 Temporary position of the sink.

CADD 6 is waiting for the next reference point, the location to which the sink will be moved:

 Type: TK (Tracking)
 Snap midpoint (SM) to the bottom line of the top wall

You are now tracking, as the command line prompt implies. Notice that the cursor can only move in horizontal and vertical directions from the starting point.

 Type: 0,-6 (and press Enter)

The cursor jumps to a point 6" below the wall.

 Type: PU (Pen Up) to complete Tracking

Your drawing should now look like Figure 4.22. You simply used tracking to find the point where the sink was to be placed, exactly 6" below the top wall.

Be sure to save your drawing periodically to make sure none of your work is lost.

 Type: SA (Save) and type D to select Drawing
 Type: KITCHEN (and press Enter) for the drawing filename

This establishes KITCHEN.GCD as the name of the file on the disk (remember that CADD 6 adds the .GCD extension automatically). Now, rename the drawing in

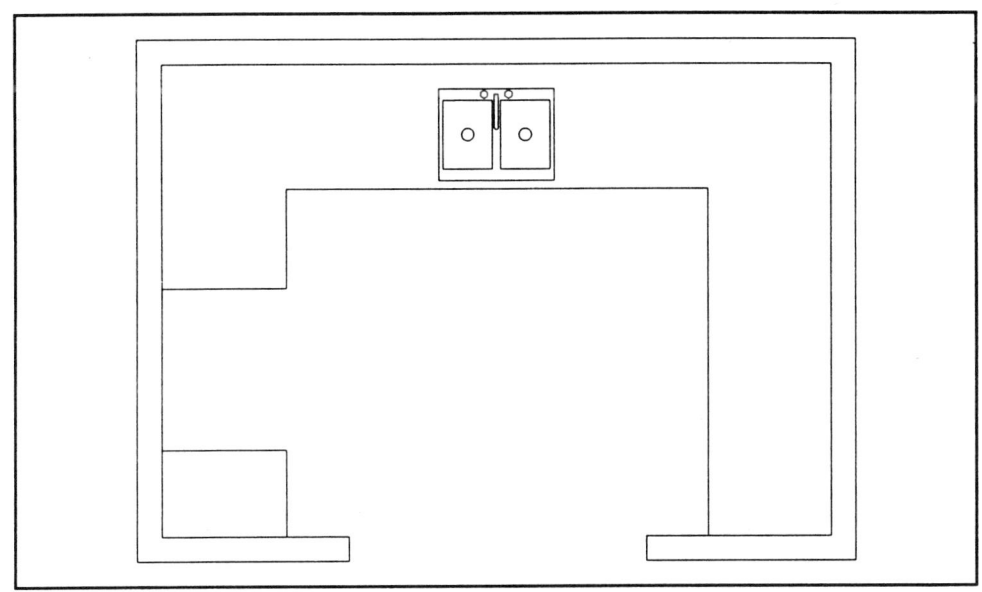

Figure 4.22 Moving the sink into its final position.

memory (the one you are currently working on) to also have the name KITCHEN. Then, you do not have to type in the name each time you save it, you simply tell CADD 6 that you want to overwrite the file on the disk.

    Type: DN (for Drawing Rename)
    Type: KITCHEN (and press Enter) for the new name for the drawing

Drawing the Trash Compactor

Next, you will draw and position the appliances in the kitchen. The first appliance to draw is the trash compactor. First, change the line type to 14 in order to draw the trash compactor with dashed lines, signifying it is hidden underneath the counter top. Then, change the color to 15 so it is easy to differentiate the appliances from the walls and counters.

    Type: LT (for Line Type)
    Type: 14 (and press Enter) for the new line type

    Type: LC (for Line Color)
    Type: 15 (and press Enter) or click color 15 from the sidebar menu

Draw the trash compactor near the center of the kitchen floor, as shown in Figure 4.23. Then move it into its final position.

    Type: RE (for Rectangle)
    Click to place the lower left corner of the rectangle

4-28 ■ Chapter 4: Creating

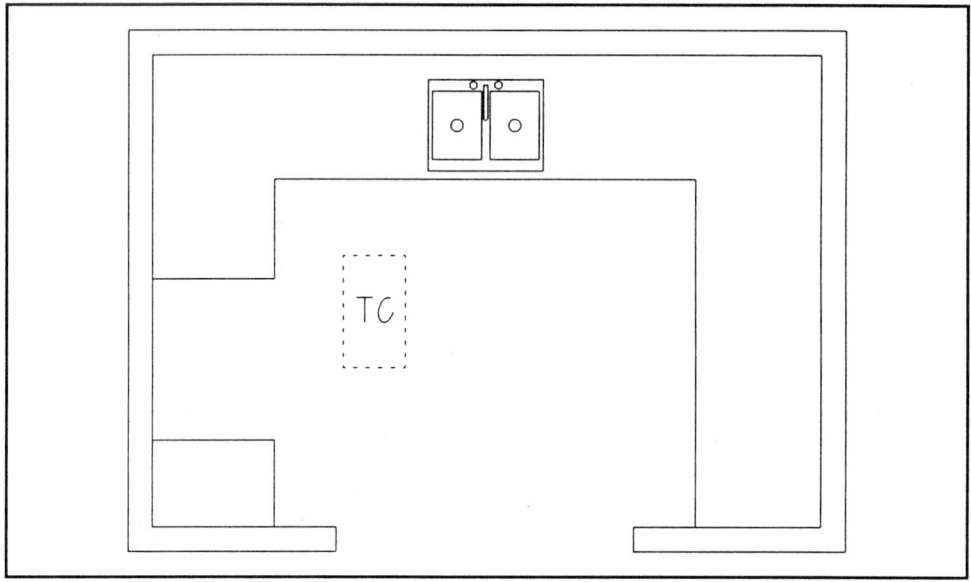

Figure 4.23 Drawing the trash compactor.

> For the opposite corner, type: **1'3,2'3**
> Press Enter

Change the Line Type back to 0 so you can label the trash compactor.

> Type: **LT** (for Line Type)
> Type: **0** (and press Enter)

Use the Place Text Line command to label the compactor, as you did in Chapter 2.

> Type: **TL** (for Place Text Line)
> Click inside the rectangle to start the text (this point will become the lower left corner of the text)
> Type: **TC** (for trash compactor)
> Press the Esc key to stop placing text

If you don't like the position of the label, move the characters with the WM (Window Move) command. Your drawing should now look like Figure 4.23. Now, move the trash compactor to its final position.

> Type: **WM** (for Window Move)
> Place a window around the entire trash compactor to select it
> For the first reference point, snap (NP) to the lower left-hand corner of the compactor

Use Tracking to find the second reference point:

Chapter 4: Creating ■ 4-29

    Type: OR (to turn Ortho Mode OFF)
    Type: TK (for Tracking)
    Snap (NP) to corner A in Figure 4.24
    Type: 1',0 (and press Enter)
    Type: PU (Pen Up) to finish tracking

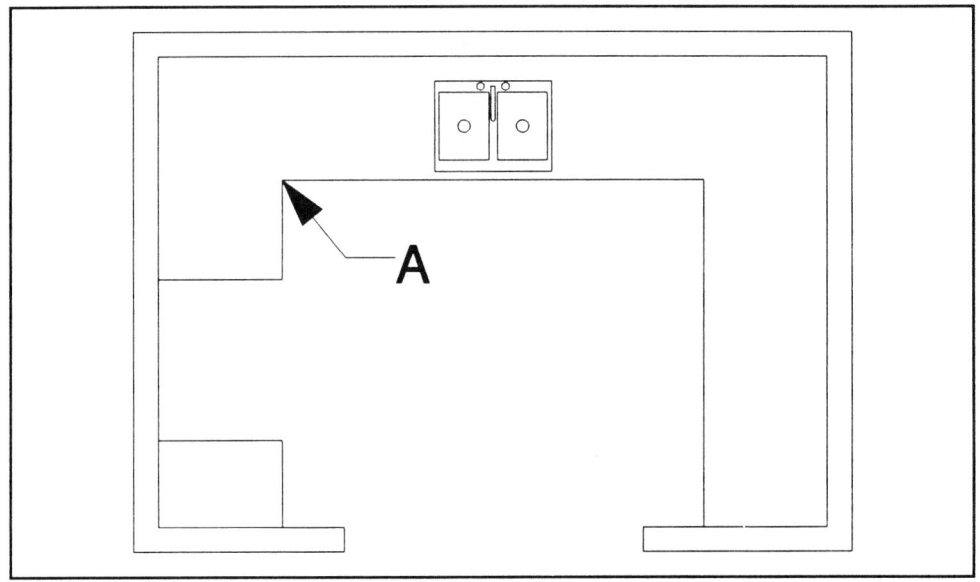

Figure 4.24 Pick point to start tracking.

Your drawing should look like Figure 4.25.

Drawing the Dishwasher

You can create and position the dishwasher using the same methods you used with the trash compactor. Of course, the dimensions and the position of the dishwasher will not be the same as the trash compactor.

    Type: LT (for Line Type)
    Type: 14 (and press Enter) for the new Line Type
    Type: LC (for Line Color)
    Type: 15 (and press Enter), or select 15 from the side bar menu

Just as you did for the trash compactor, draw the dishwasher in the center of the kitchen floor and them move it into position.

    Type: RE (for Rectangle)
    Click to place the first corner in the drawing area

4-30 ■ Chapter 4: Creating

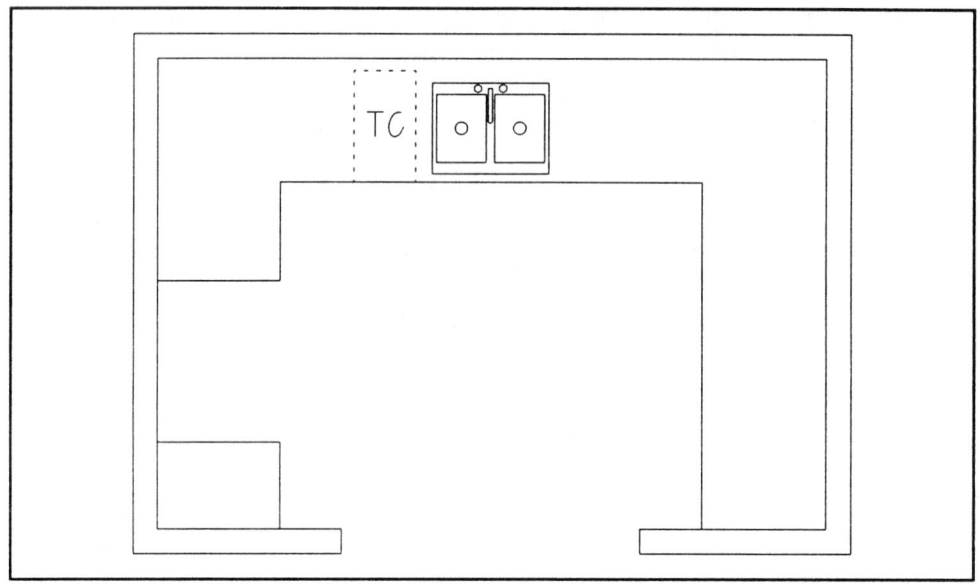

Figure 4.25 The final position of the trash compactor.

>   Type: 2',2'3 (and press Enter) for the opposite corner of the rectangle

Now switch to line type 0 and label the dishwasher.

>   Type: LT (for Line Type) and set the line type to 0
>   Type: TL (Place Text Line)
>   Click inside the rectangle to start placing the text
>   Type: DW (and press Enter) for dishwasher
>   Press the Esc key to stop placing text

If you don't like the position of the label, move the characters with the WM (Window Move) command. Now move the dishwasher into its final place under the counter.

>   Type: WM (for Window Move)
>   Place a window around the entire dishwasher
>   Snap (NP) to the lower right-hand corner of the dishwasher
>   Type: TK (for Tracking)
>   Snap (NP) to corner A, as shown in Figure 4.26
>
>   Type: -9,0 (and press Enter)
>   Type PU (Pen Up) to finish tracking

Your dishwasher should now look like that shown in Figure 4.27.

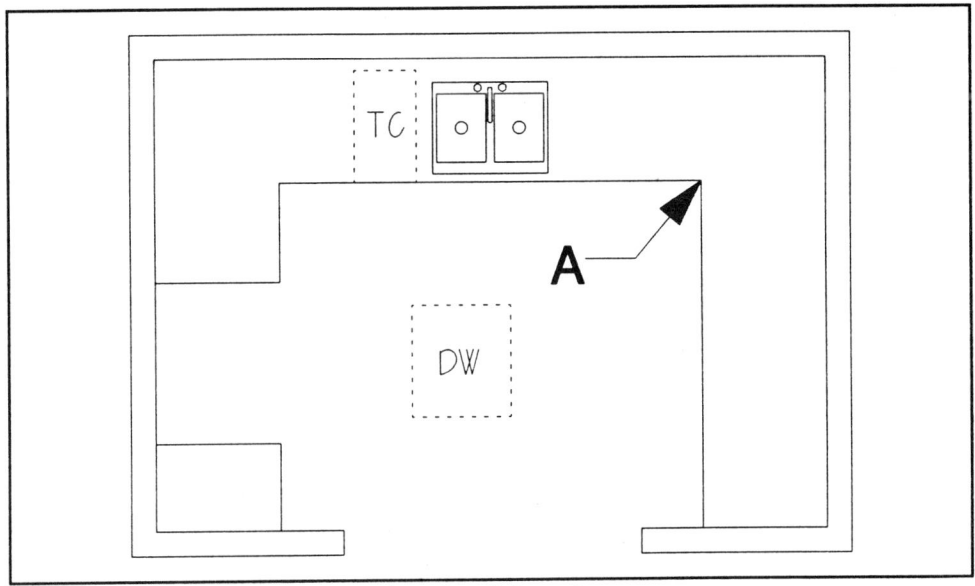

Figure 4.26 Drawing and moving the dishwasher.

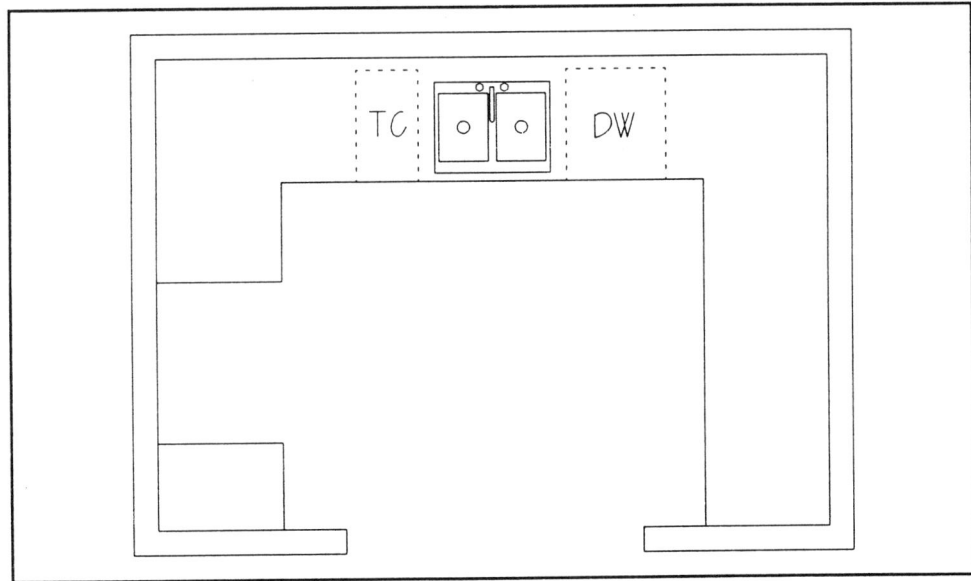

Figure 4.27 Final position of the dishwasher.

Drawing the Refrigerator

The next appliance to create is the refrigerator. After creating the refrigerator, you can move it into position near the wall. Before starting, you may want to check that LT is set to 0 and LC is set to 15.

4-32 ■ Chapter 4: Creating

    Type: RE (for Rectangle)
    Click on a point in an open area of the kitchen floor
    Type: 2'6,2'9 (and press Enter) to place the opposite corner of the rectangle
    Type: LI (for Line)
    Type: -2,0 (and press Enter)
    Type: 0,-2'9 (and press Enter)

This draws a refrigerator that is 2'6" X 2'9". You can use other dimensions, if desired. Now draw the refrigerator handle, as would be seen from above.

    Type: RE (for Rectangle)
    Type: TK (for Tracking)
    Snap to the upper right-hand corner of the rectangle, corner A in Figure 4.28
    Type: 0,-3 (and press Enter)
    Type: PU (for Pen Up) to end Tracking and place the first corner of the rectangle
    Type: 2,-2 (and press Enter) to place the opposite corner of the rectangle

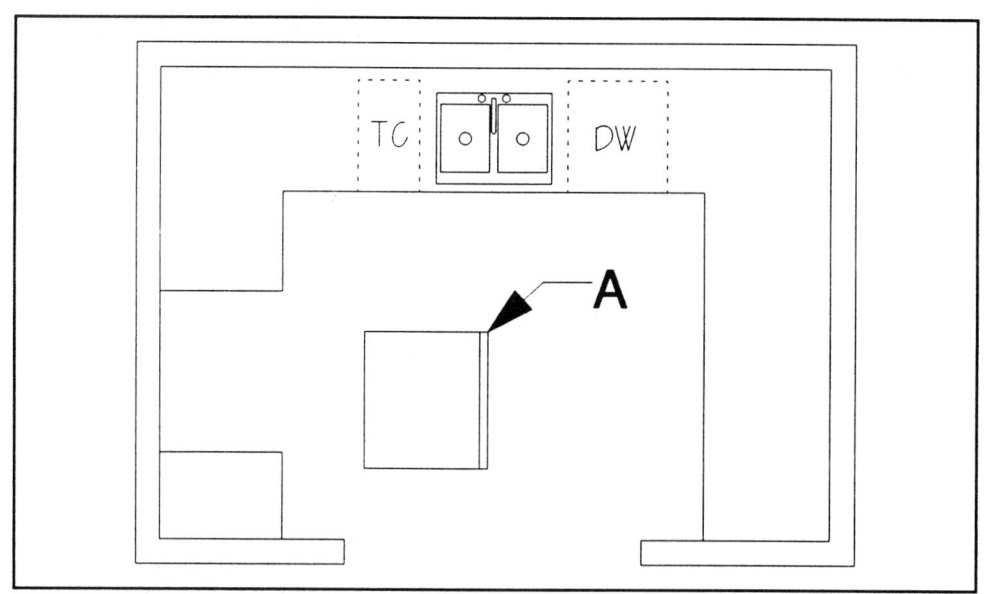

Figure 4.28 Drawing the refrigerator.

Now that the refrigerator is drawn, you can use WM (Window Move) to move it into position.

    Type: WM (for Window Move) and enclose the refrigerator with a selection window
    Type: SM (for Snap Midpoint) to snap to the back of the refrigerator

Move the refrigerator into position against the wall, as shown in Figure 4.29.

Type: SO (Snap Object) and click on the wall to finish placing the refrigerator

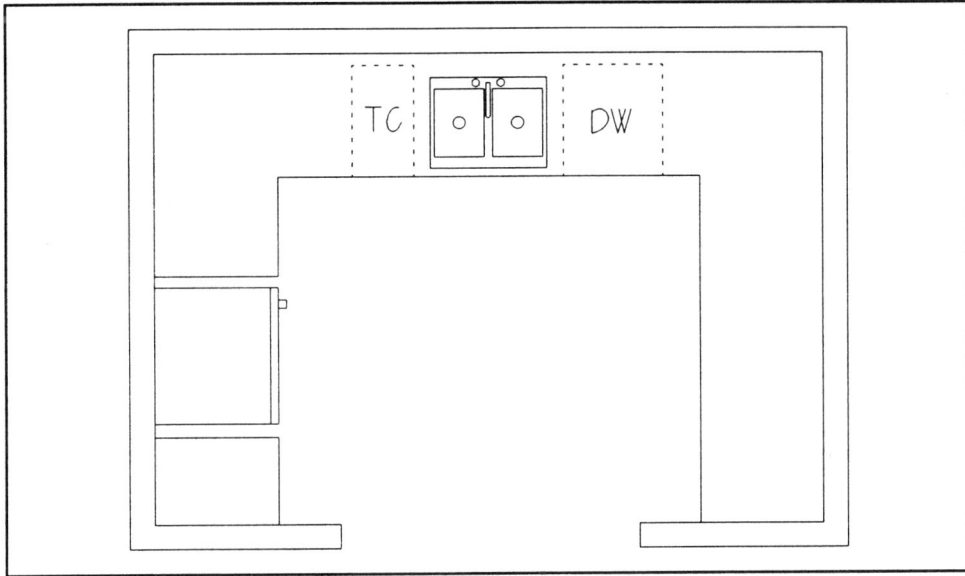

Figure 4.29 Moving the refrigerator into position.

Drawing the Stove

The stove will be drawn in its final position, not moved into position as the other appliances were. To start the stove, draw the first line on the counter-top, as follows:

> Snap NP (for Nearest Point) to corner A, as shown in Figure 4.30
> Type: RE (for Rectangle)
> Type: 0,-2' (and press Enter)
> Type: 2',-2'5 (and press Enter)
> Type: -3,0 (and press Enter)
> Move the cursor up (make sure Ortho Mode (OR) is ON) and snap to the top line of the stove
> Press Esc to end the line

Use Zoom Window (ZW) to zoom up on the stove, as shown in Figure 4.31.

Your display should now look like Figure 4.32. If you are not satisfied with the current display, type ZA (Zoom All), and repeat the last procedure to adjust move stove.

> Snap NP (Nearest Point) to the corner closest to point B in Figure 4.33

Next, create the first burner on the stove by drawing concentric circles with the Circle 2 (C2) command.

4-34 ■ Chapter 4: Creating

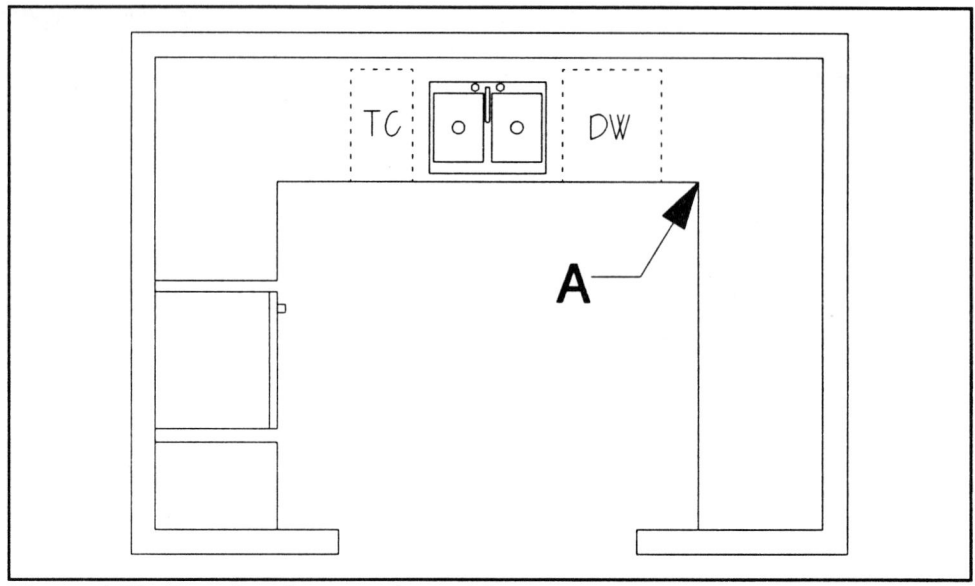

Figure 4.30 Drawing the stove in position.

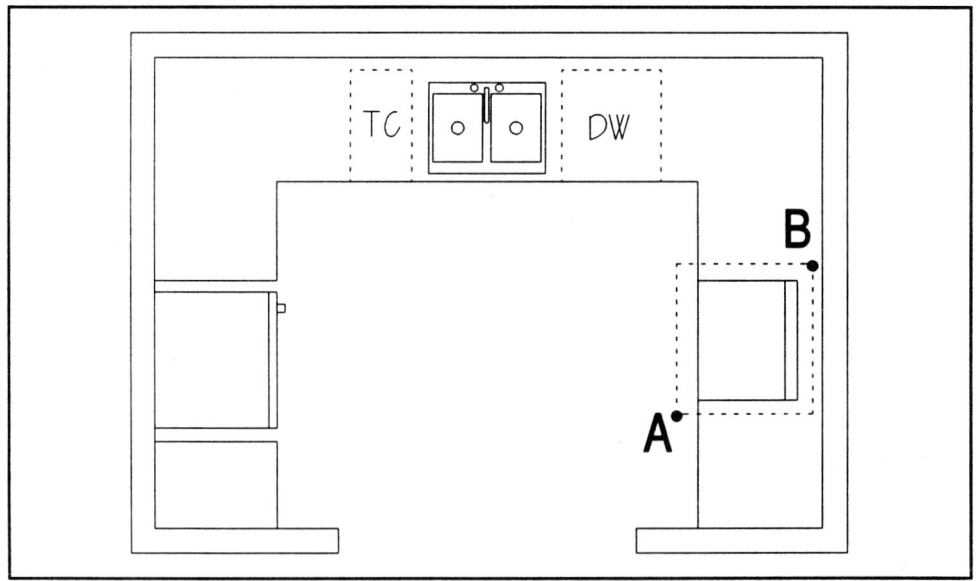

Figure 4.31 Zooming-up on the stove to view the details.

    Type: C2 (for 2-Point Circle)
    Type: -9,-7.5 (and press Enter)
    Type: 0,1 (and press Enter)
    Type: C2
    Snap NP to the center of the last circle created
    Type: 0,2 (and press Enter)

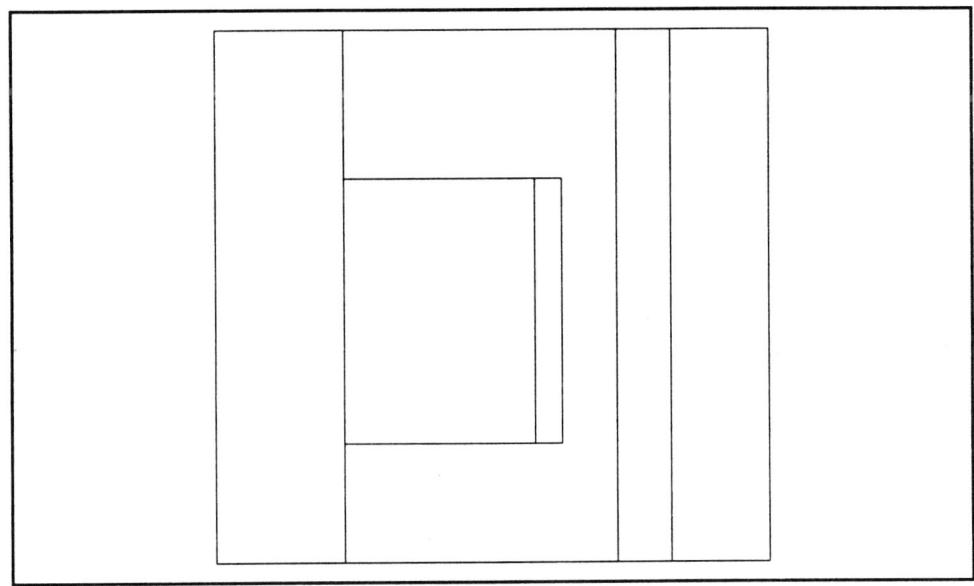

Figure 4.32 The zoomed view of the stove.

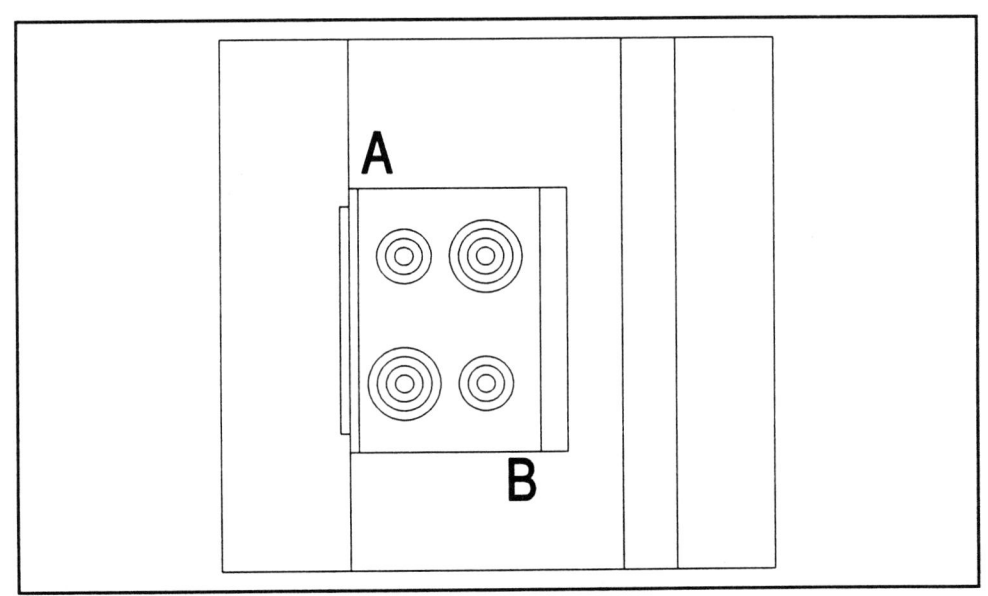

Figure 4.33 Drawing the stove burners.

    Type: C2
    Snap NP to the common center of the two circles
    Type: 0,3 (and press Enter)
    Type: C2
    Snap NP to the circle's center
    Type: 0,4 (and press Enter)

Now make a copy of this burner:

> Type: WC (for Window Copy)
> Place a window around the group of four circles just created
> Snap to the circle's common centers to specify the reference point
> Type: -9,0 (and press Enter)
> At the prompt, type: 1 (to specify 1 copy)
> Press Enter

Copy the two burners to the other side of the stove:

> Type: WC (Window Copy) and place a window around both sets of circles (burners)
> Snap to the center of either burner to specify the reference point
> Type: 0,1'2 (and press Enter)
> Type: 1 (to make 1 copy)
> Press Enter

Two of the burners should be smaller than the other two. To erase the outer circle and create the small burners:

> Type: OE (Object Erase)
> Pick the outer-most circle on burner A to erase it
> Repeat the command and erase the outer-most circle on burner B

Your drawing should start looking more like a stove now. To complete it, draw the handle shown in Figure 4.34.

> Snap (NP) to the upper left-hand corner of the stove
> Type: LI (for Line)
> Type: 1,0 (and press Enter)
> In Ortho Mode (OR), pull the line down the screen
> Snap SO to the bottom line of the stove
> Type: LI (for Line)
> Type: -1,2 (and press Enter)
> Type: -1,0 (and press Enter)
> Type: 0,2'1 (and press Enter)
> Type: 1,0 (and press Enter)
> Press the Esc key
> Type: ZA (Zoom All)

Your drawing should now look like Figure 4.34.

This ends part I of the Kitchen Layout Tutorial. In Part II, you will add a window and modify the kitchen sink. Be sure to save your final drawing so you can continue the Kitchen Layout Tutorial in later chapters.

    Type: SA (for Save)
    Type: D (to select Drawing)
    Type: KITCHEN for the drawing filename (and press Enter)

If you saved the drawing previously, type O so CADD 6 knows to overwrite the old file with your final drawing.

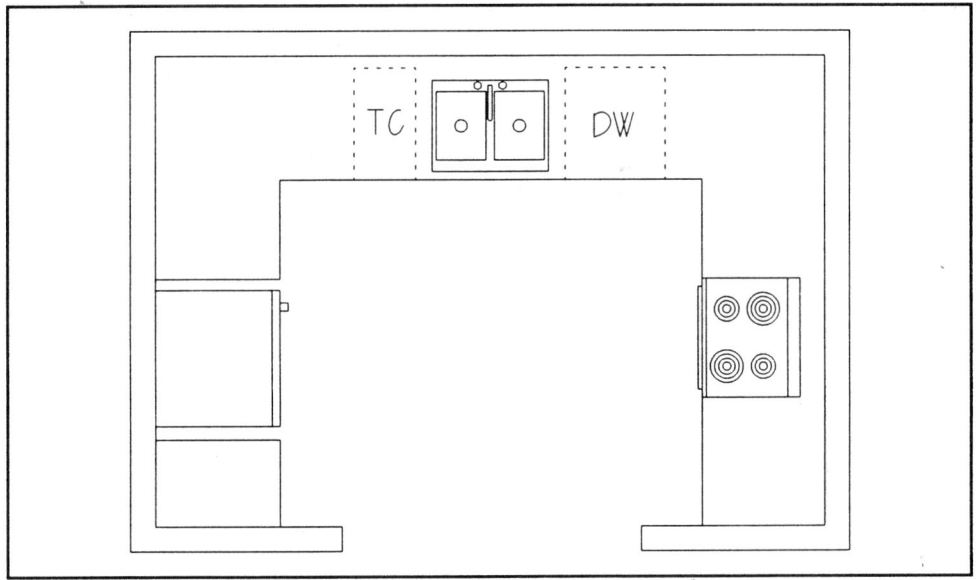

Figure 4.34 The final kitchen drawing from Part I of the Tutorial.

CHAPTER SUMMARY

In this chapter you learned about the various drawing primitives used to create your CADD 6 drawings. You also learned how Constraint commands make drawing creation easier. At the end of the chapter, you put many of the commands from the DRAW menu and CONSTRAINTS menu into practice to create the first part of a kitchen layout drawing. This Tutorial also applied many of the fundamentals and concepts introduced in Chapter 3. The kitchen layout drawing is continued in Chapter 6.

Some of the other commands discussed here are used in tutorials later in this book. For example, the grid commands are a powerful tool for creating schematic-type drawings. In Chapter 9, the grid commands are further discussed and used to create an electronic schematic drawing.

SAMPLE EXERCISES

Use the commands you have learned thus far to complete the following sample exercises. Use the dimensions shown to draw the parts to full-scale. Do not try to draw in the dimensions, unless you want to skip ahead to Chapter 11 and apply those commands.

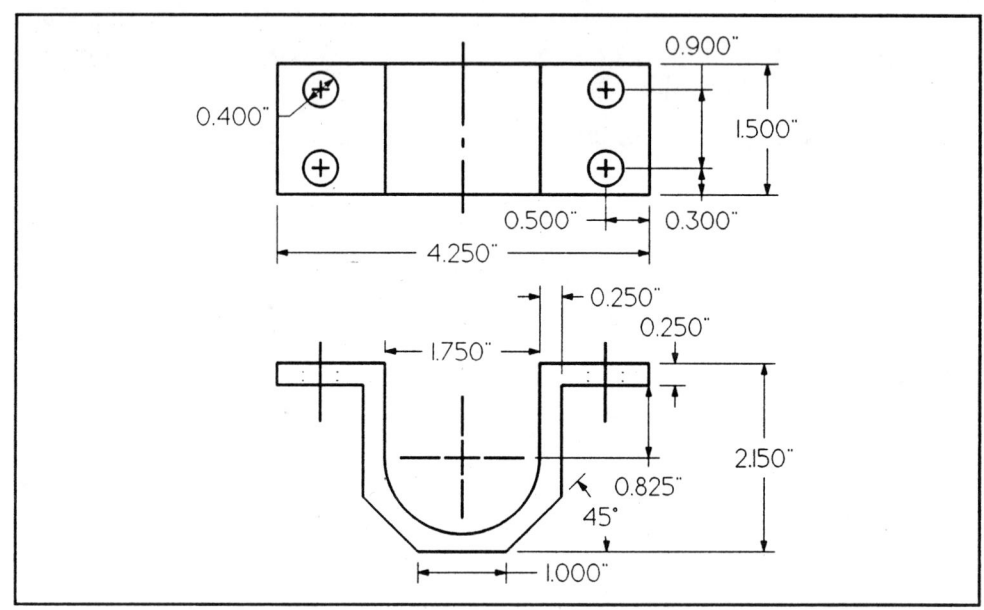

Figure 4.35 Sample exercise for the DRAW commands.

Chapter 4: Creating ■ 4-39

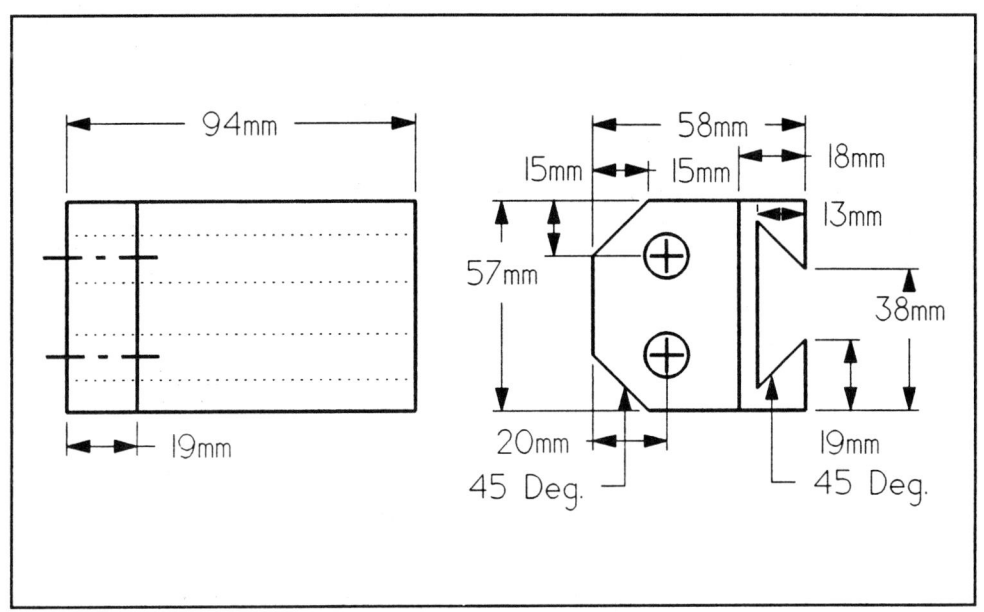

Figure 4.36 Sample exercise for the DRAW commands.

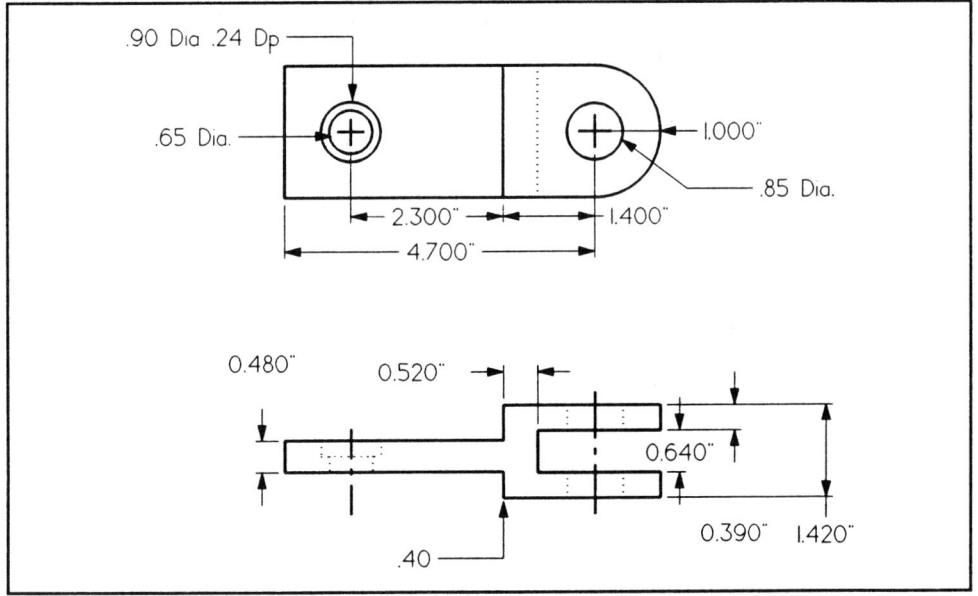

Figure 4.37 Sample exercise for the DRAW commands.

CHAPTER 5

Modifying with Shortcuts and Edits

USING THE SHORTCUTS AND EDITS MENUS

Commands on the EDIT and SHORTCUT menus, discussed in this chapter, are used to modify objects in your drawing. Chapter 6 discusses additional commands used to enhance the accuracy of your drawings.

You will find that the majority of the commands used during drawing creation are the modifying commands. Without these commands, CADD 6 work would become a long, tedious, and sloppy process. When you become familiar with these commands, you will find that you have an arsenal of time-saving CADD 6 tools to work with.

The SHORTCUT commands serve the same purpose as the EDIT commands, but do not have selection set capabilities, so they are not as flexible. The operations the SHORTCUT and EDIT commands perform are copying, erasing, moving, stretching, rotating, scaling, and changing. The first part of this chapter discusses the concepts of these modifying operations. The second part reviews the EDIT commands. The concepts are the same, with the exception of selection set capabilities.

SHORTCUTS

The SHORTCUTS menu is accessed from the EDITS menu page of the video menu. The following commands are found on the SHORTCUTS menu page:

Object Copy (OC)
Window Copy (WC)
Object Erase (OE)
Window Erase (WE)

Object Move (OM)
Window Move (WM)
Window Stretch (WS)
Window Rotate (WR)
Drawing Rotate (DR)

Window Scale (WZ)
Drawing Scale (DZ)
Object Change (OG)
Window Change (WG)
Drawing Change (DG)

Along with the commands, this section also covers the fundamentals of using a window to enclose more than one object on the screen, object scaling, and changing object characteristics.

The SHORTCUT menu commands are referred to as shortcuts because they lack a selection prompt. The type of selection these commands use is evident from the command's name. For example, the Object Erase (OE) command requires you to select an object to erase. This is a shortcut to using the Erase (ER) command and selecting "Object" from the selection prompt. The analogous EDIT commands that use a selection set are Copy (CO), Erase (ER), Move (MV), Rotate (RO), Scale (SZ), Change (CG), and Stretch (SS).

Using a shortcut command can save you two steps, as seen with the Erase (ER) command. To erase an object using the Erase (ER) command, you must first type (ER) or select Erase (ER) from the EDITS menu. Second, you have to select "Object" from the selection set. Third, you must select the object to erase. Fourth and last, you have to press Enter to complete the command. Using the shortcut Object Erase (OE), you must first type (OE) or select "Obj Erase" from the SHORTCUTS menu. Second and last, select the object to erase. The object is erased without any further prompting.

The next part of this section on SHORTCUT commands names and explains each of the commands found on the SHORTCUTS menu. During the explanation and use of commands, you are prompted to enter the command's two-letter command code to initiate the command sequence. Feel free to select commands from the menus, if you prefer. The result is the same.

Object Copy (OC)

The Object Copy (OC) command allows you to make one or multiple copies of an object. Use the command code OC to select this command. Place the cursor anywhere on an object on the screen. Click with your pointing device or press Enter to select the object. Now, select a reference point on the object. The reference point is the handle used to mark the next position for the object or copies of the object. The new copies of the object will be located relative to the reference point. Place the next point where you want the copied object to be placed, and click with your pointing device or press Enter. (See Figure 5.1.)

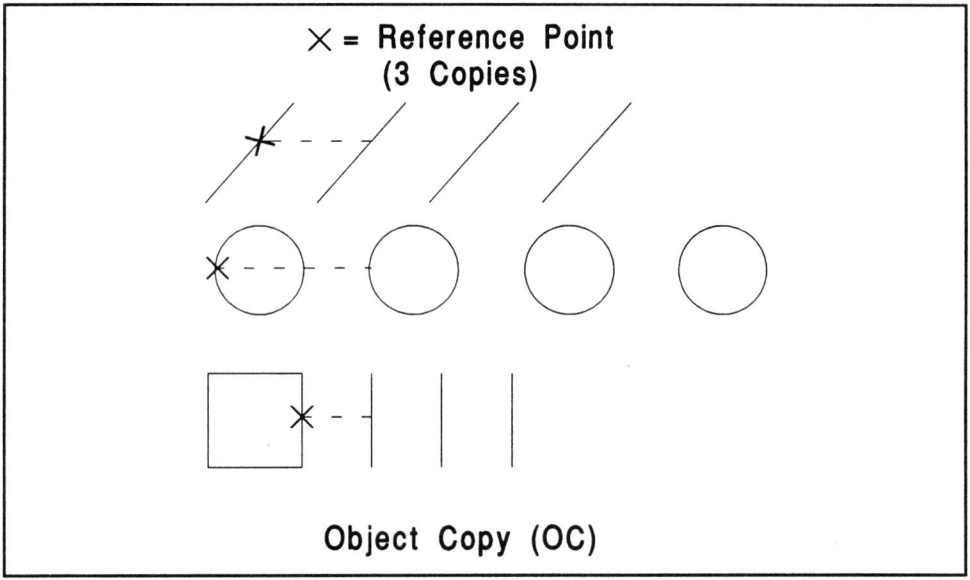

Figure 5.1 Using the Object Copy command.

> **TIP:** You will notice at the prompt for the new reference or offset point, that a ghost image of the object can be moved around with your pointing device. If you don't see this ghost image, make sure that Object Drag (OD) is ON. Object Drag (OD) will work as a nested command, so you can toggle it ON or OFF during the editing process.

You will be prompted for the number of copies to create. Enter the number of copies in addition to the original object. The distance between multiple copies is equal to the distance between the original and the first copy made.

Object Erase (OE)

The Object Erase (OE) command is a simple way to remove a single object from your drawing. Type the command code OE to initiate Object Erase (OE). Place your cursor on the object to erase and click with your pointing device or press Enter. The object should disappear.

Object Move (OM)

To move a single object on the screen from one point to another, use the Object Move (OM) command. Type the command code OM and you will be prompted to select an object. Pick an object on the screen with your cursor, and click with your pointing device or press Enter. Next, you will be prompted to enter a reference point. Choose a point on the object for reference and click to select it. You will then be prompted to enter a new location for the reference point. Move your cursor to the desired location, and press Enter or click with your pointing device. The ghost image that was attached to the cursor solidifies at the object's new location. (See Figure 5.2.)

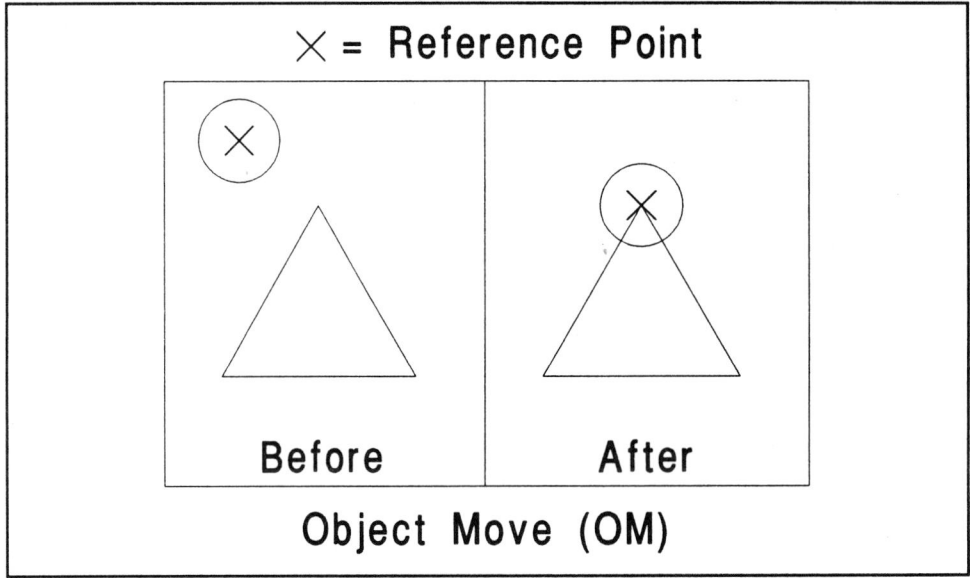

Figure 5.2 Using the Object Move command.

Object Change (OG)

Changing an object means changing its characteristics, such as layer, color, type, and width. To start the change process for a single object, type the command code OG. Place your cursor on the object to be changed and click with your pointer or press Enter. You will be prompted to select which characteristic(s) to change from a sub-menu on the command line. You can either select the characteristic to change with your pointing device, or type in the bold letter of the characteristic. For example, to select laYer type in Y, to select Color, type in C, to select Type, type in T, and to select Width, type in W.

The sub-menu selections list the current setting of each characteristic. Any combination of the four settings can be changed during the command. When a characteristic setting is selected, a list of choices for that setting is displayed on the sidebar menu. For example, to change the line type of the object to 4, type in T and enter a 4, or select

Line Type 4 from the sidebar menu. The number (4) is then displayed next to the Type setting on the status line sub-menu. To change the line width of the object to 3, type in W and enter a 3, or select Line Width 3 from the sidebar menu. The number (3) is then displayed next to the Width setting on the status line sub-menu. Press Enter to accept the changes made to the object, or click on the <RET> icon on the status line sub-menu. (See Figure 5.3.)

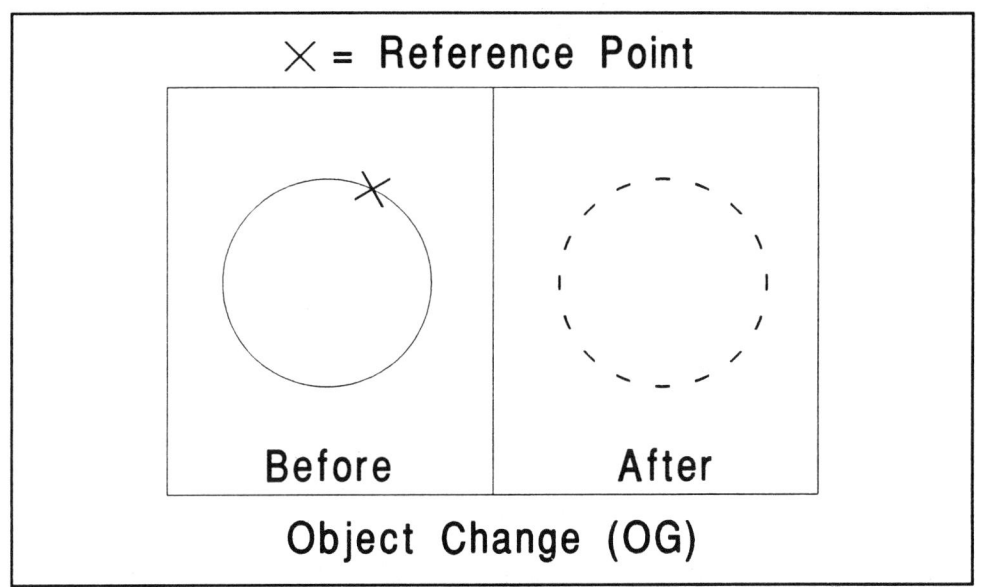

Figure 5.3 Using the Object Change command.

USING THE WINDOW FEATURE

Often you want to select more than one object at a time to be changed or edited. Window edit commands prompt you to enclose the objects to be modified within a window. If an object is completely enclosed within the boundaries of the window, then the object is affected by the command. If any part of the object crosses the boundaries of the window, the object is not selected for editing.

You define the location and size of the selection window every time you use a window command. It is defined by placing either of the two diagonal corner points. Start the window by placing a point below and to the left of the objects you want to select. Move the cursor up and to the right to define the top corner at the other end of the diagonal. Alternatively, you can start the window at any of the four corners, as long as the rectangular window on-screen completely surrounds the objects to be selected.

5-6 ■ Chapter 5: Modifying With Shortcuts and Edits

Window Change (WG)

As with the Object Change (OG) command, the Window Change (WG) command lets you change object's characteristics, except that you can change multiple objects at once. With the change feature you can change an object's layer, color, type, and width. To start the change process for an object, or group of objects, type the command code WG. Place a selection window entirely around the object(s) to be changed. You will then be prompted with the characteristics to change from a sub-menu on the command line. You can either select the characteristic to change with your pointing device, or type in the bold letter of the characteristic. For example, to select laYer type in Y, to select Color, type in C, to select Type, type in T, and to select Width, type in W.

The sub-menu selections list the current setting of each characteristic. Any combination of the four settings can be changed during the command. When a characteristic setting is selected, a list of choices for that setting is displayed on the sidebar menu. For example, to change the line type of the object(s). Type in T and enter the value; to change the line width of the object(s), type in W and enter that value. The new values for each characteristic will be displayed on the status line. Press Enter to accept the changes made to the objects, or click on the <RET> icon. (See Figure 5.4.)

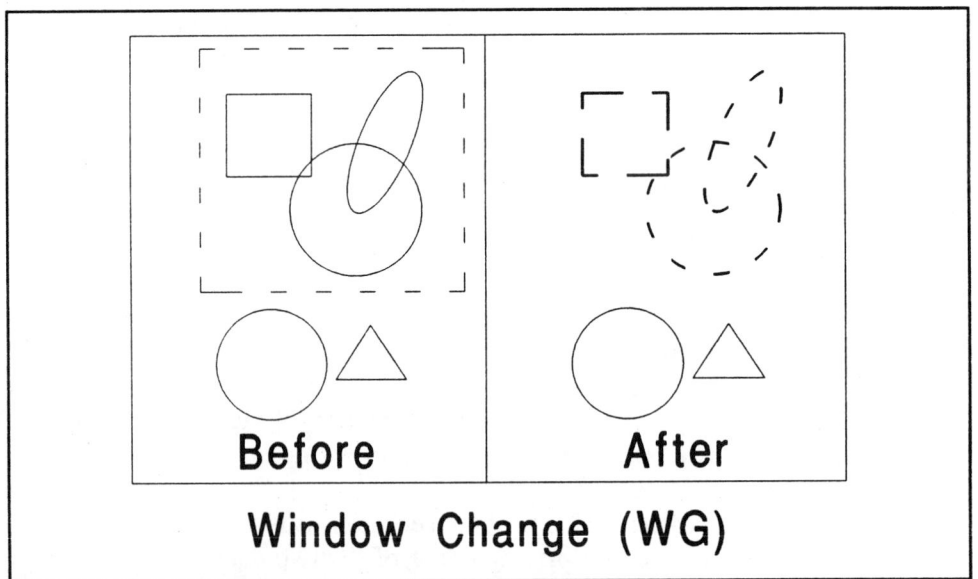

Figure 5.4 Changing a group of objects with Window Change.

Window Copy (WC)

Window Copy (WC) works like Object Copy (OC), but Window Copy (WC) can copy single or multiple objects, which you select by enclosing in a window. To select Window Copy (WC), use the command code WC. Place a selection window completely around all objects to copy (as described above). When prompted, select the first reference point — the point the objects are being copied from. You will then be prompted for a new reference point location. Move the cursor to the location where you want the group of objects copied and press Enter. While moving the cursor to the destination reference point, you should see a ghost image of the selected objects. Answer the final prompt with the number of copies you want and press Enter. Your objects are copied. (See Figure 5.5.)

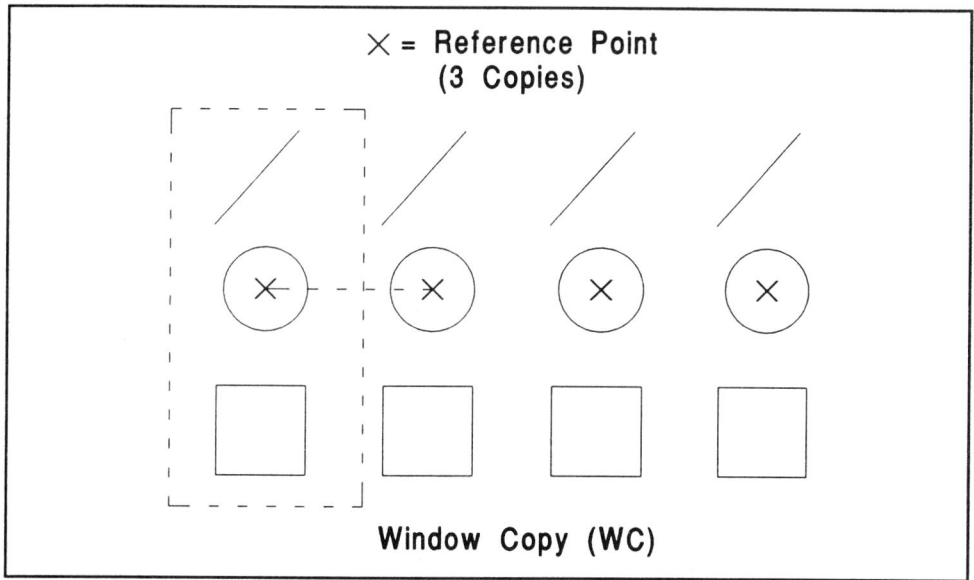

Figure 5.5 Copying groups of objects with Window Copy.

Window Erase (WE)

Use the Window Erase (WE) command to remove one object, or a group of objects, from your drawing. To select this command, use the command code WE. When you are prompted for the first corner of the window, place a selection window completely around all objects to erase. When you click to place the second corner of the window, the objects should be removed.

Window Move (WM)

The Window Move (WM) command allows you to enclose an object, or group of objects, in a window, and then move the object(s) to a new location in the drawing. To select this command, use the command code WM. When you are prompted for the first corner of the window, place a selection window completely around all the objects to move. Answer the next prompt by selecting a reference point, the point the objects are being moved from. Pick a conveniently located reference point, possibly on one of the objects being moved. You will then be asked to enter a new location for the reference point. Select the location to which you want the reference point moved, and then press Enter or click with your pointing device. The object is moved relative to its chosen reference point. As with all copy and move commands, you should see a ghost image of the objects selected as you move the cursor to the final location. (See Figure 5.6.)

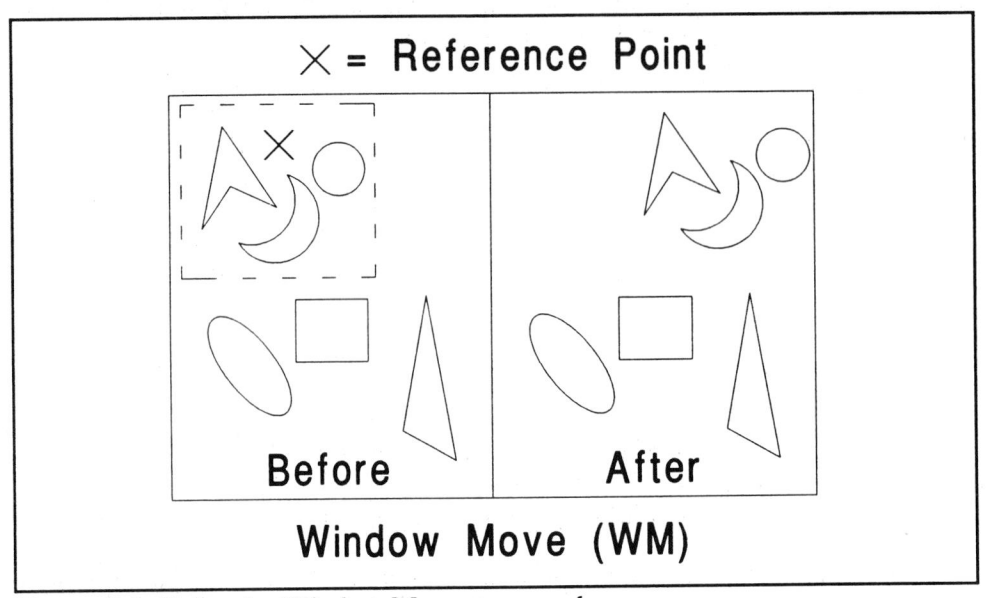

Figure 5.6 Using the Window Move command.

Window Stretch (WS)

The Window Stretch (WS) command allows you to stretch or shorten objects by moving one endpoint to a new location. If an entire object is enclosed by the Window Stretch (WS) window, the object will only be moved, and not stretched. The Stretch Window must cross over any lines to be stretched.

> **TIP:** Entities other than lines, such as arcs, circles, curves, text, components, and so on, are not stretched, but merely react to stretching as they would to having the selected points moved with the Move Point (MP) command. MP is explained later in this chapter. The only difference with Window Stretch is that more than one point can be selected at once. Test the possibilities by stretching various drawing entities.

To select this command, use the command code WS. Enclose the objects to modify in a selection window, being sure to cross any lines that are to be stretched. Answer the next prompt by selecting a reference point and move the cursor in the direction the objects are to be stretched. Select the location where you want to move the reference point, and press Enter or click with your pointing device. The object is stretched relative to its chosen reference point. As with all copy and move commands, you should see a ghost image of the objects selected when moving the cursor on the screen. (See Figure 5.7.)

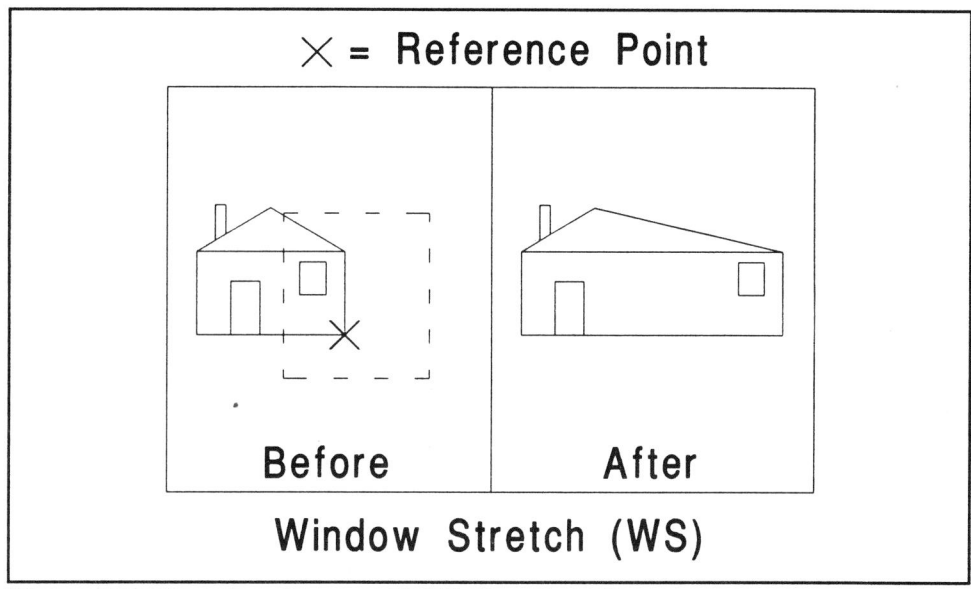

Figure 5.7 Changing shapes with Window Stretch.

Window Rotate (WR)

Window Rotate (WR) lets you enclose objects in a window and rotate them about a common axis. To Window Rotate (WR), enter the command code WR. Use a selection window to enclose all objects to be rotated. You will be prompted for an axis point. Select a point on the screen about which you wish the object(s) to be rotated. This point does not have to be within the area enclosed in the initial selection window. The next prompt will ask you to enter an angle of rotation. Type in a value for the rotation, and press Enter. (See Figure 5.8.)

The angle entered can be either positive or negative, and can be greater than 360°. Angles are measured positive in the counterclockwise direction, with the three o'clock position being 0° (horizontal to the right). An angle of -90° is equivalent to an angle of +270°, an angle of 720° is equal to 0°, -360°, or +360°, and so on.

USING THE SCALE FEATURE

Scale commands such as Window Scale (WZ) and Drawing Scale (DZ) can be used to change an object's size and proportion. During a scale command, you are prompted to enter an X and Y scale factor. These factors determine the object's new size along the X and Y axes. If the scale factors are set at 1 for both axes, then no change is made to

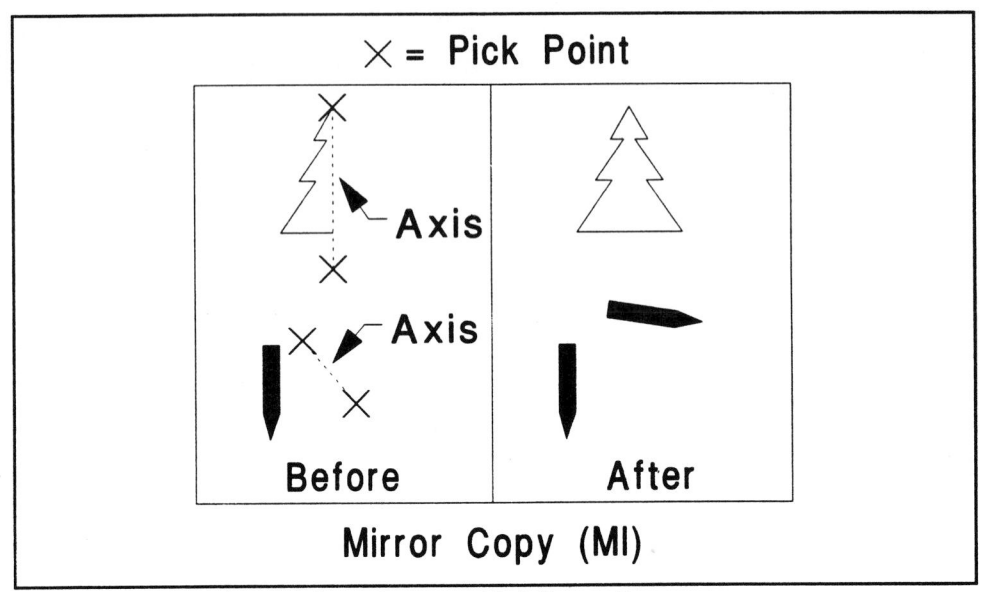

5-10 ■ Chapter 5: Modifying With Shortcuts and Edits

Figure 5.8 Creating a mirror image with Mirror Copy.

the existing object(s). If the scale factors for both axes are changed to 2, the object(s) will increase in size and proportion by a factor of 2. A 1" x 1" square would change in size to a 2" X 2" square. (See Figure 5.9.)

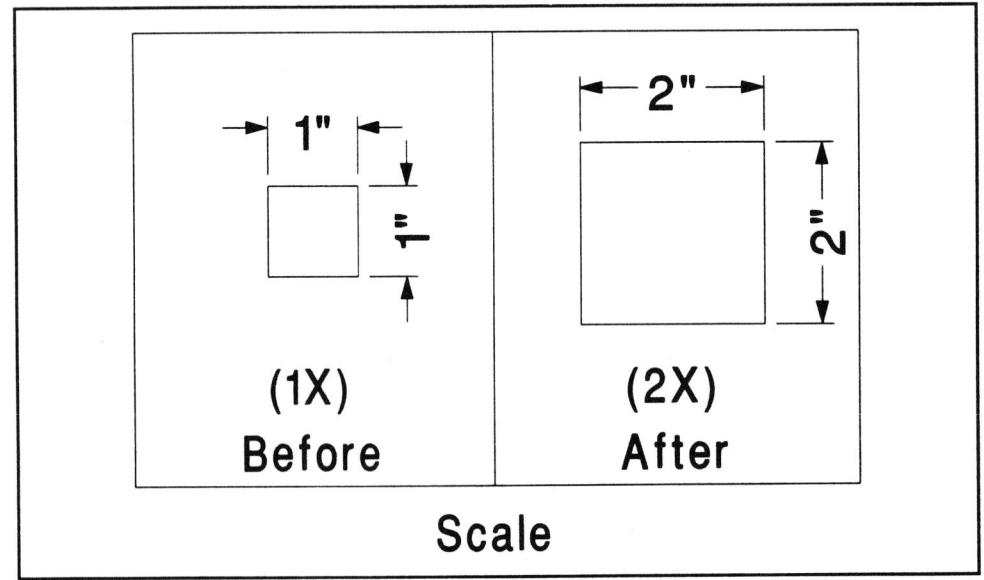

Figure 5.9 Changing size with the Scale command.

Chapter 5: Modifying With Shortcuts and Edits ■ 5-11

The proportion of an entity changes if the *X* and *Y* scale factors are not set at values equal to each other. For instance, if you change the scale of a 1" x 1" square using scale factors of X=2 and Y=1, the square will change to a rectangle, with a length of 2" along the X-axis and will remain at a 1" height on the Y-axis. To make an object 50% larger, use scale factors of 1.5, which makes a 1" object 1.5" after scaling. Similarly, a 4" object would increase to 6" (1.5 X 4" = 6"). (See Figure 5.10.)

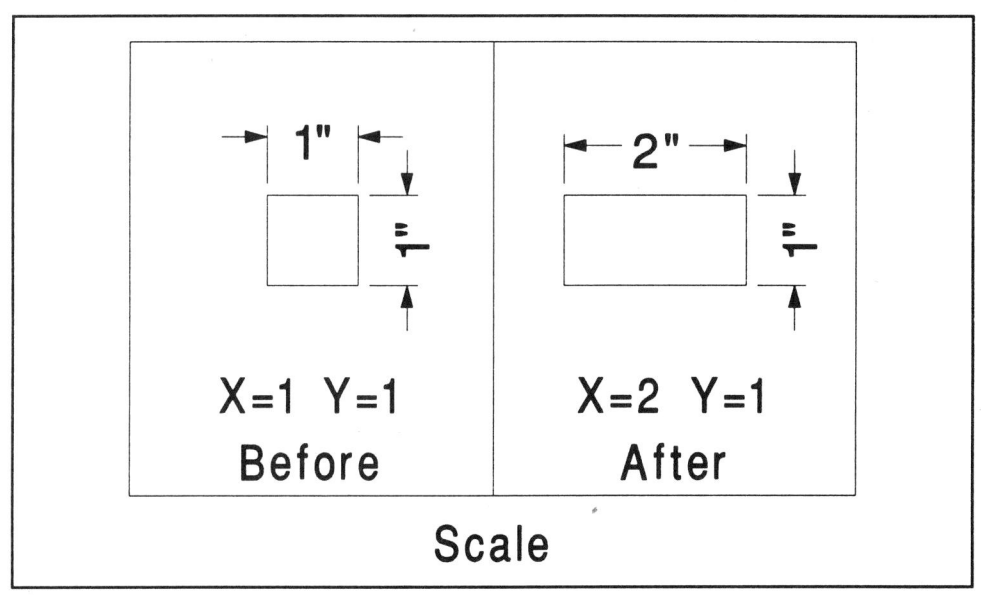

Figure 5.10 Using different *X* and *Y* scales.

As you can see, values greater than 1 increase the overall size and proportion of the scaled object(s). Any value with up to 6 places to the right of the decimal point can be used for a scale factor. A scale factor of 2.038 would be an acceptable value to the program. Any value less than 1 decreases the overall size and proportion of the scaled object(s). A scale factor of X=0.5 and Y=0.5 would change a 1" X 1" square to a 0.5" X 0.5" square. (See Figure 5.11.)

Negative scale factors can also be used and can be very helpful. A negative scale factor mirrors the scaled object(s) about the opposite axis. Suppose an arrow is pointing toward the positive X-axis, and is scaled with an *X* factor of -1 and a *Y* factor of 1. The arrow will not change in size or proportion. Instead, it will be mirrored about the Y-axis to point toward the negative direction of the X-axis.

If two negative scale factors are used, the object(s) are mirrored about both axes. Proportion and size can also be changed with negative scale factors. The larger the negative factor, the greater the size increases along the affected axis. A scale factor of -2 on the X-axis and a scale factor of -4 on the Y-axis changes a 1" X 1" square to a 2" X 4" square, and mirrors it about both the X- and Y- axes. (See Figure 5.12.)

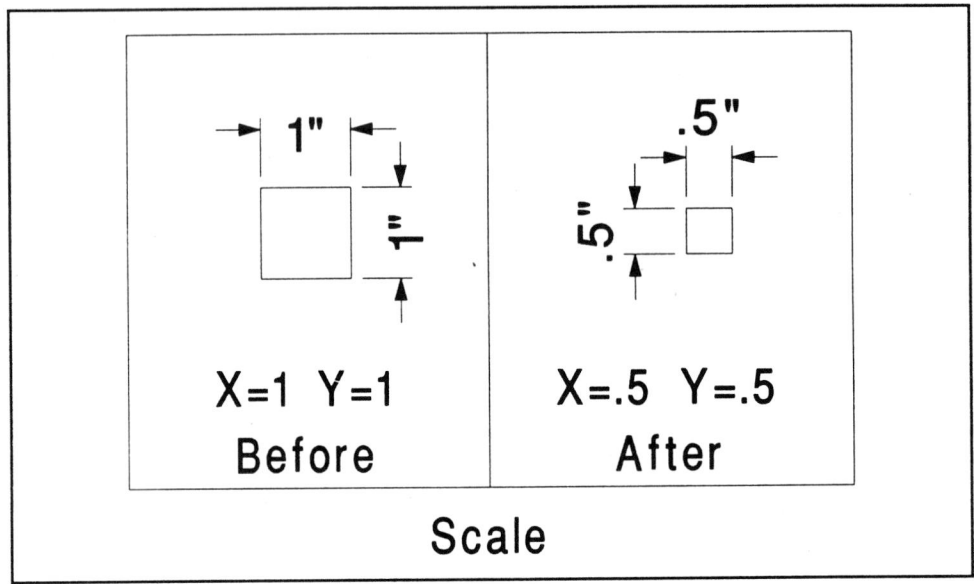

5-12 ■ Chapter 5: Modifying With Shortcuts and Edits

Figure 5.11 Reducing the size with a Scale Value less than one.

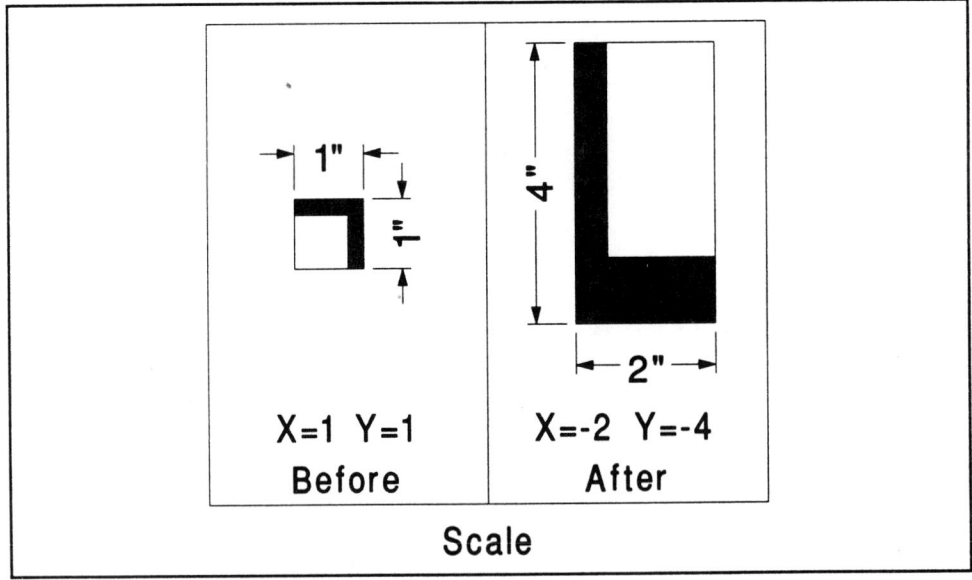

Figure 5.12 Using a Negative Scale factor.

The main advantage to using negative scale factors, as opposed to using a mirror command, is that you have the power to scale and mirror an object with one command. Scale commands are like two commands in one.

All objects, except circles and arcs, can be scaled using unequal X and Y scale factors with predictable results. If a circle or arc is scaled using unequal scale factors, it may change in size relative to one of the scale factors. A circle does not change into an ellipse unless it is used in a component. Circles contained in a component that are scaled using different X and Y scale factors appear to be transformed into ellipses. This holds true until the component is exploded, and these "ellipses" are converted back to circles.

Window Scale (WZ)

The Window Scale (WZ) command lets you enclose an object or group of objects in a selection window and scale them. Type WZ, and place a window about the object or objects to scale. You will be prompted for a reference point. The objects that are scaled change in a direct relationship to this reference point. If the reference point is placed at the center of the objects, the scaling will occur equally about the reference point. You will be prompted for a new X and Y scale value. When these values are entered, the objects are scaled. Enter a 1 if you do not want to change the scale for a particular direction. (See Figure 5.13.)

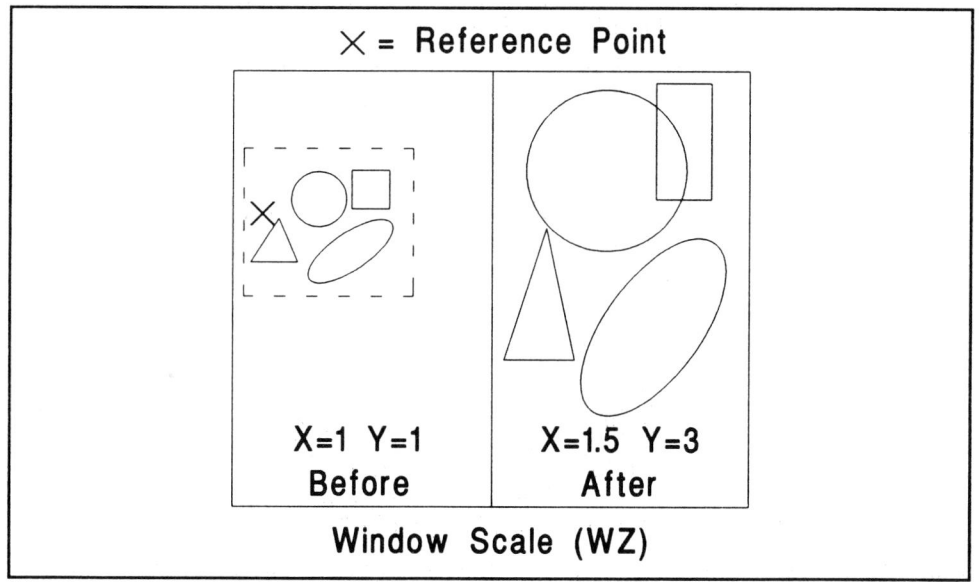

Figure 5.13 Using the Window Scale command.

Drawing Scale (DZ)

The Drawing Scale (DZ) command works the same way as the Window Scale (WZ) command, except every object in the drawing is scaled, not just one object. Type DZ to start the Drawing Scale (DZ) command. You will be prompted for a reference point on the drawing relative to which the scale is performed. After specifying the reference point, you will be prompted to enter new X- and Y- axis scale values. Once the Y value has been entered, the entire drawing is scaled.

Drawing Rotate (DR)

Drawing Rotate (DR) allows you to rotate an entire drawing about a common axis. Enter the command code DR, and CADD 6 will prompt you for an axis point. Select the point on the screen about which you wish to rotate the drawing. The next prompt will ask you to enter an angle of rotation. Type in the desired rotation value, and press Enter. (See Figure 5.14.)

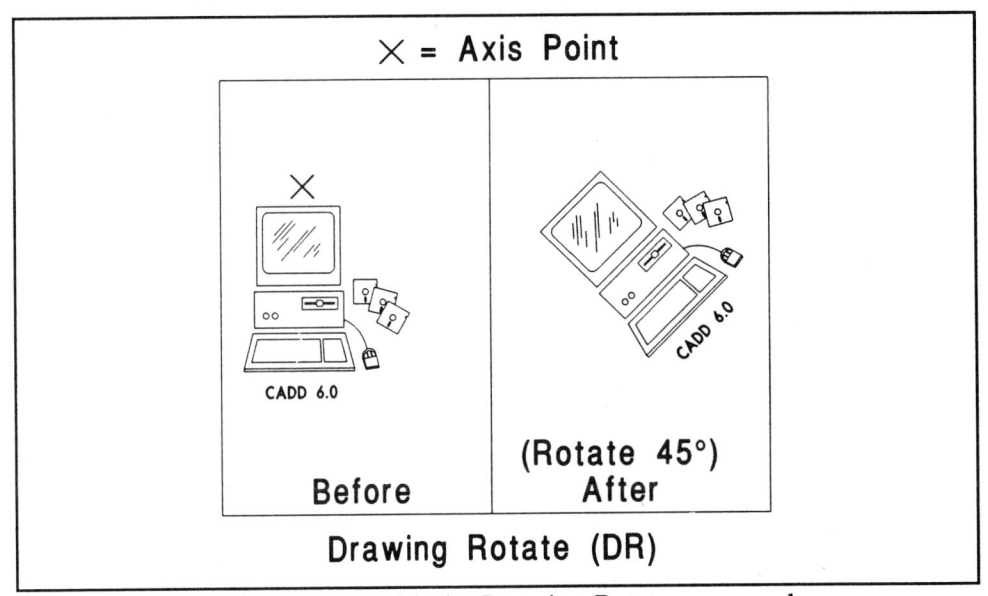

Figure 5.14 Rotating objects with the Drawing Rotate command.

The rotation angle can be either positive or negative, and can be greater than 360°. Angles are measured positive in the counterclockwise direction, with the three o'clock position being 0° (horizontal to the right). An angle of -90° is equivalent to an angle of +270°. An angle of 720° is equal to 0, -360, or +360°.

Drawing Change (DG)

The Drawing Change (DG) command is very similar to Window Change (WG), except that it affects all objects in the drawing. Using the Drawing Change (DG) command, you can change an entire drawing's characteristics at once, including the layer, color, line type, and width. To start the change process for a drawing, type the command code DG. You will be prompted to select characteristics from a sub-menu on the command line. You can either select the characteristic to change with your pointing device, or type in the bold letter of the characteristic. For example, to select layer, type in Y, to select Color, type in C, to select Type, type in T, and to select Width, type in W.

The sub-menu selections list the current setting of each characteristic. Any combination of the four settings can be changed during the command. When a characteristic setting is selected, a list of that setting's choices are displayed on the sidebar menu. For example, to change the line type of all objects in the drawing to 4, type in T and enter a 4, or select Line Type 4 from the sidebar menu. The number (4) is then displayed next to the Type setting on the status line sub-menu. Press Enter to accept all the changes made to the drawing, or click on the <RET> icon on the status line sub-menu. (See Figure 5.15.)

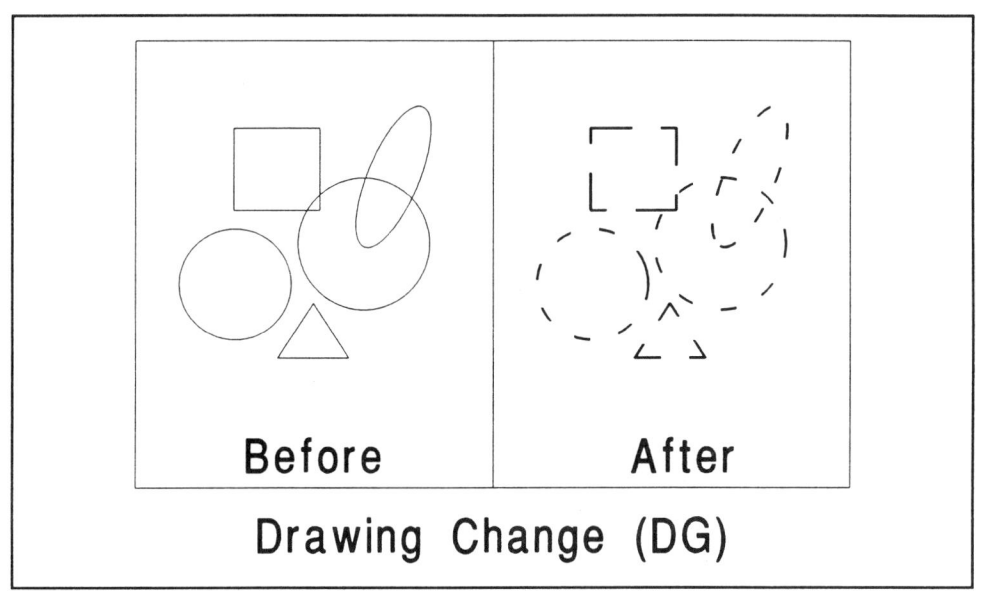

Figure 5.15 Changing All Objects with Drawing Change.

SHORTCUT SUMMARY

The commands on the SHORTCUT menu are worth remembering and adding to your arsenal of editing commands. Selection sets (as used in the EDITS commands) are a very powerful feature; however, for common editing, they are often not necessary and can slow you down. Be sure to practice using the most common SHORTCUT commands whenever possible to increase your productivity.

USING THE EDITS COMMANDS

Some of the commands found on the EDITS menu work according to the same concepts as the SHORTCUTS commands. These commands perform the tasks of moving, copying, rotating, scaling, changing, and erasing. The only difference is their method of object selection. Before moving on to the rest of the EDIT commands, selection sets are explained. The following commands prompt with a selection set, but otherwise work the same way as the SHORTCUT commands:

Move (MV)
Copy (CO)
Rotate (RO)
Scale (SZ)
Change (CG)
Erase (ER)
Mirror Copy (MI)
Radial Copy (RC)
Object Break (OB)
Stretch (SS)

The following commands are also included to help you correct mistakes:

Unerase (UE)
Undo (OO)
Redo (UU)

Selection Sets

General purpose editing commands such as Copy (CO), Change (CG), Move (MV), Scale (SZ), Erase (ER), and Rotate (RO) prompt you with the following selection set:

Window Object laYer Drawing Crossing Last Filter (ON/OFF)
<ESC> to cancel <RET> to accept Highlight (ON/OFF)

The selection set options allow you to select any combination of objects in your drawing by choosing either a single Object, multiple objects enclosed by a Window, the entire Drawing, or a specific laYer on which to perform the selected edit. You can choose to highlight the selected objects in the drawing, allowing for visual feedback of your selections. Any unwanted object selections can be de-selected simply by holding down the control key while repeating the selection process for the object. There is no limit to the number of objects that can be selected when using selection sets. Any combination of selection set options can be used during the selection process.

The following is an explanation of the different selection set options:

Window. Often you may want to concurrently select more than one object to be changed or edited. You can do this by selecting Window from a selection set, which changes any group of objects totally enclosed by the boundaries of a selection window.

> **TIP:** If the All Layer Edit (AL) toggle is currently in the OFF mode, the selection type used will only affect the current layer set. To ensure that all of the layers will be affected, be sure that AL is toggled ON. This can be set anytime you are prompted for a point. If you need to set it during the selection process, choose the Object or Window selection options, which prompt for a point. To exit a selection mode before executing it, press the Escape (Esc) key. This cancels the current selection mode, and returns you to the selection options.

In other words, any object inside the selection window will be affected by the command. If any part of an object crosses the boundaries of the window, the object will not be selected for editing.

You define the location and size of the selection window each time you use the Window selection method. Define the selection window by placing two corner points on either diagonal to construct the window. Place a point below and to the left of the objects you want to select. Move the cursor up and to the right to define the top point or other corner of the diagonal. Alternatively, you can start the window at any of the four corners, as long as the rectangular window on-screen completely surrounds the objects to be selected.

Object. Select the Object method, and point and click on an individual object to select it. Objects include all primitives, single-text characters, single-text lines, hatches, fills, and dimensions.

laYer. Use the laYer prompt to select all entities on a particular layer.

> **TIP:** The All Layers Edit (AL) toggle, whether ON or OFF, will not affect the laYer option. Even hidden layers can be selected with the laYer option.

Drawing. Use the Drawing prompt to select all of the entities in the drawing.

If the Drawing option is chosen, all the entities in the drawing are selected. This includes all entities on hidden layers. The Drawing option ignores the All Layers Edit (AL) command, whether it is ON or OFF.

Crossing. Similar to the Window option, the Crossing option also uses a window selection. Only objects that cross over the selection window are chosen.

> **TIP:** When selecting objects such as polygons, which are made up of multiple lines, make sure the Crossing window comes in contact with a portion of every line you intend to select.

Last. The Last option selects whatever entity or entities were selected for modification the last time a selection set was chosen.

The Last option only works if it is the first selection set option picked. A new selection set list is created as soon as any other selection set option is chosen.

Filter. To trap more specific entities during the selection process, you can use the Filter selection. This allows you to single-out an entity type and characteristics in a drawing, window, or layer selection. This includes primitives, hatches, fills, text, and dimensions. For example, one could select all circles of line type 4, select all lines of line width 3, line type 7, and color 12. The Filter selection also allows you to select ALL entities of a certain color, type, layer, or width. Once the edit command using the defined Filter has been performed, that Filter is turned OFF. During the Filter process, you are prompted to select the type of object you want to Filter. The Filter prompt is:

Point **L**ine **C**irc a**R**c **E**lips cur**V** **B**ez **T**ext co**M**p **F**ill **H**atch **D**imen **A**ll
<ESC> to cancel <RET> to accept f**I**lter (ON/OFF) = like

Once you have selected the type of entity to Filter, you are prompted with the entity characteristics appropriate to that entity. Highlighted entity characteristic selection letters and names are listed below:

Primitives (Point, Line, Circle, aRc, Elips, curV, Bez)

la**Y**er **C**olor **T**ype **W**idth **A**ll

LaYer, Color, line Type, and line Width can either be entered on the command line through the keyboard, or selected from the video menu on the right side of your screen. When the All feature is selected, you filter by the entity type only. The characteristics by which to filter can also be defined using the All feature. The "= like" feature also works when setting entity characteristics.

Components. Characteristics appropriate for components include component layer and name, plus the unique characteristic of attributes.

la**Y**er **N**ame attribut**E** **A**ll

Chapter 5: Modifying With Shortcuts and Edits ■ 5-19

Hatches, Fills, and Dimensions. The characteristics appropriate for hatches, fills, and dimensions are layer and color.

laYer Color All

> **TIP:** Hatch and dimension widths can be modified, but are not part of the characteristic selection set.

Text. Text has the same characteristics as the primitive objects, except for the font. Fonts are a unique characteristic of text. Text's characteristics include:

laYer Color Type Width Font All

Some Filter Examples. The following examples use filters to simplify the modification of complex drawings:

Example: Erase all circles of line type 14 and line width 3 from your drawing.

    Type: ER (for Erase)
    Type: F for filter
    Type: C for circles
    Press Enter to accept the selection
    Type: T (for line type)
    Type: 14 (and press Enter) to select line type 14
    Type: W (for line width)
    Type: 3 (and press Enter) to select line width 3
    Press Enter after the appropriate characteristic has been selected to confirm the filter settings
    Type: D (for drawing) to highlight all the filtered items in the drawing
    Press Enter to erase the highlighted items (See Figure 5.16.)

Entities can also be filtered for de-selection from a selection set. This process makes more sense if you actually run through the procedure several times.

Example: All circles of line type 14 and line width 3 are to remain on the screen, while the rest of the drawing is erased.

    Type: ER (for Erase)
    Type: D for drawing to highlight all the entities in the drawing
    Type: F (for filter)
    Type: C (for circles)

Erase Circles (LT=14 and LW=3)

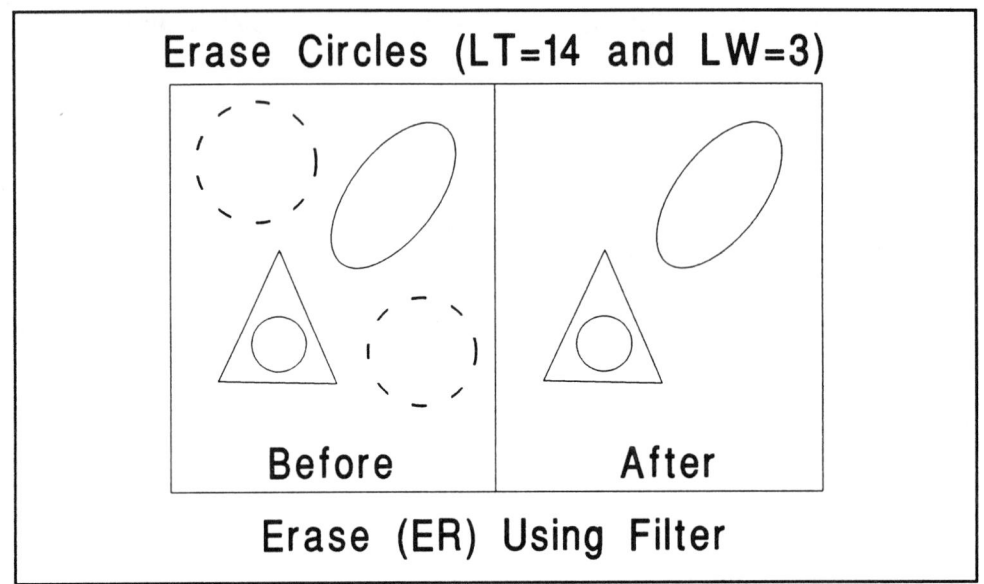

Figure 5.16 Using Filters to Define a Selection Set.

       Press Enter to accept the selection
       Type: T (for line type) then type 14 (and press Enter)
       Type: W (for line width) then type 3 (and press Enter)
       Press Enter after each entity characteristic has been selected to confirm the filter settings
       Press CTRL D to de-select the entire drawing

Since a filter has been defined, only the filtered entities are de-selected in the drawing.

       Press Enter and all but the filtered entities are erased

Highlight. The Highlight feature is a toggle. When it is turned ON, selected entities are displayed with dotted lines. This differentiates them from non-selected items.

MORE EDITS COMMANDS

The commands that remain to be discussed from the EDITS menu are listed below. Some of these commands prompt for a selection set. The Object Break (OB) and Move Point (MP) commands do not prompt for a selection set. They are designed to modify only a single point or entity.

Move Point (MP)
Mirror Copy (MI)
Radial Copy (RC)
Object Break (OB)
Stretch (SS)

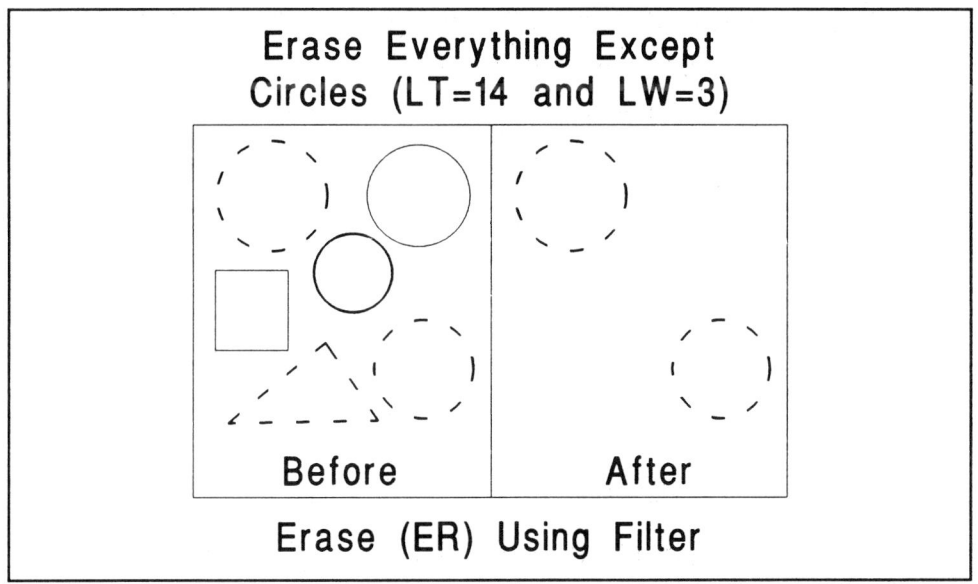

Figure 5.17 An example of using a selection filter.

Bezier Edit (BE)
Erase Last (EL)
UnErase (UE)

Undo (OO)
Redo (UU)

Move Point (MP)

The Move Point (MP) command can be used to move any point on any object. Primitive objects, such as the Standard Point (PO), Lines, Circles, Arcs, Ellipses, and Curves can have their size, shape, and location changed with the Move Point (MP) command. You can use the MP command to move their construction points (the points used to define the geometry of the object). Construction points can be seen if the Construction Point (PC) toggle is ON (you may have to redraw the display).

Defined objects, such as Components, Text, Fills, Hatches, Dimensions, and Leaders are moved by selecting their Reference Points with the MP command. To display their Reference Points, make sure the Reference Point Display (PR) toggle is ON. If the MP command is used on Components, Text, Hatches, or Fills, the whole object moves. On Dimensions and Leaders, the point on the end selected moves.

Some objects share the same point. The corners of a rectangle consist of two lines intersecting at a common point. If you only want to move the endpoint of one of the sides of a rectangle, you would type MP, click on the line you want to move, then point or snap on the endpoint to move. When you move your cursor around, the line attached to the selected point rubberbands from the cursor. If you want both lines that form the corner to be moved simultaneously, type MP, snap NP to the corner endpoint, then point or snap to the same corner endpoint. When you move your cursor around, the two sides of the rectangle should be rubberbanding simultaneously from the point attached to the cursor.

Mirror Copy (MI)

Type MI to execute the Mirror Copy (MI) command. The Mirror Copy (MI) command initially prompts you to select objects to mirror with a selection set. Select the objects you wish to mirror. You will be prompted to:

> Enter the starting point of the axis line

The Mirror Copy (MI) command makes a copy of the object(s) selected, while mirroring them about the user-specified axis line. The mirrored copy is placed symmetrically about the axis line.

The next prompt asks you to "Enter the ending point of the axis line." Once this point is entered, a mirrored copy of the selected objects appears in your drawing. The axis line is only temporary, and disappears when its second point has been defined. (See Figure 5.18.)

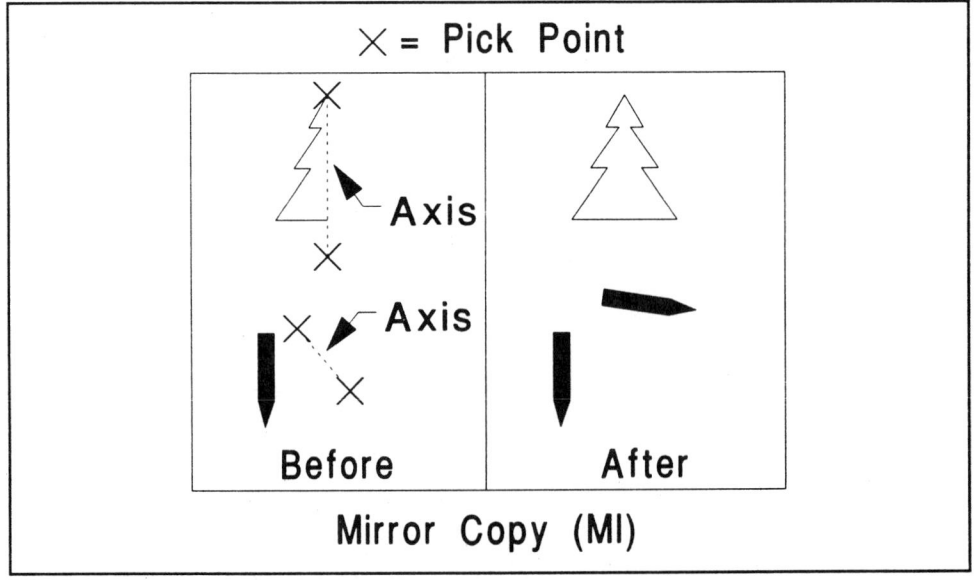

Figure 5.18 Using the Mirror Copy command.

Radial Copy (RC)

Type RC to execute the Radial Copy (RC) command. This command prompts you to select the objects to Radial Copy (RC) with a selection set. Select the objects you wish to copy in a radial manner, then you will be prompted to:

> Enter an axis point

The axis point is the point about which the objects are copied. Think of this point as the axle of a wheel. Spokes on the wheel can signify items radially copied about the axle. The next prompt will ask you to specify:

> Total number of degrees to span

If you want the object(s) to be equally spaced about a complete circle, specify 360°. If you specify 90°, the objects will be equally spaced about a section equal to a quarter circle. The next prompt will ask you for:

> Total number of items in the span

This number includes the object(s) selected for copying. (See Figure 5.19.)

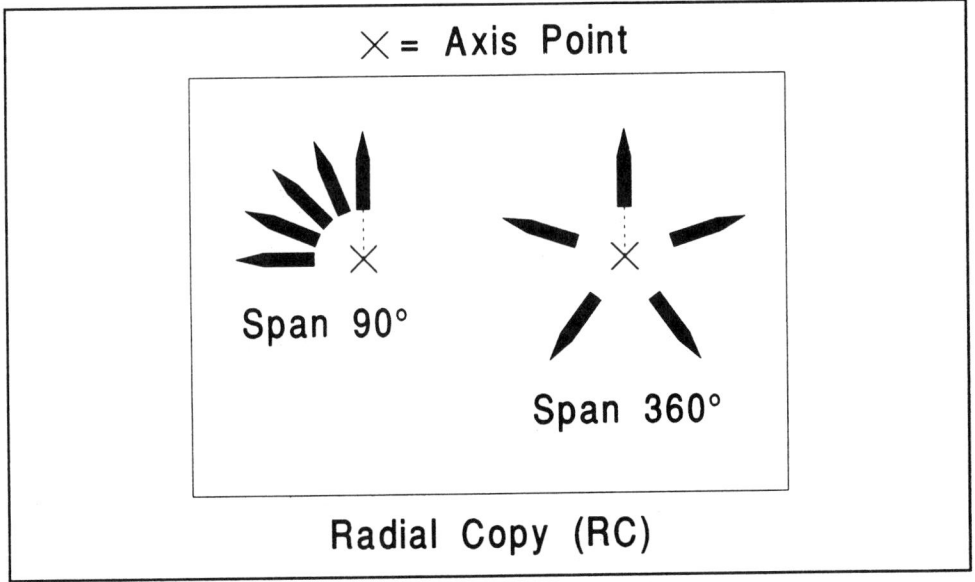

Figure 5.19 Copying objects with Radial Copy.

Object Break (OB)

The Object Break (OB) command is used to break a section out of an object. Type OB to execute the Object Break (OB) command. The first prompt will ask you to:

Enter a point on the object to break

In other words, click on the object you wish to break. The next prompt will ask you to:

Enter the first break point

You should click or snap on the point where the break in the object is to start. The next prompt will ask you to:

Enter the second break point

Before entering the second point, move your cursor to different sides of the object. Notice how the display changes dynamically, showing the possible breaks. You can see the break before actually accepting it. When you are satisfied with the display, click to select the second break point. (See Figure 5.20.)

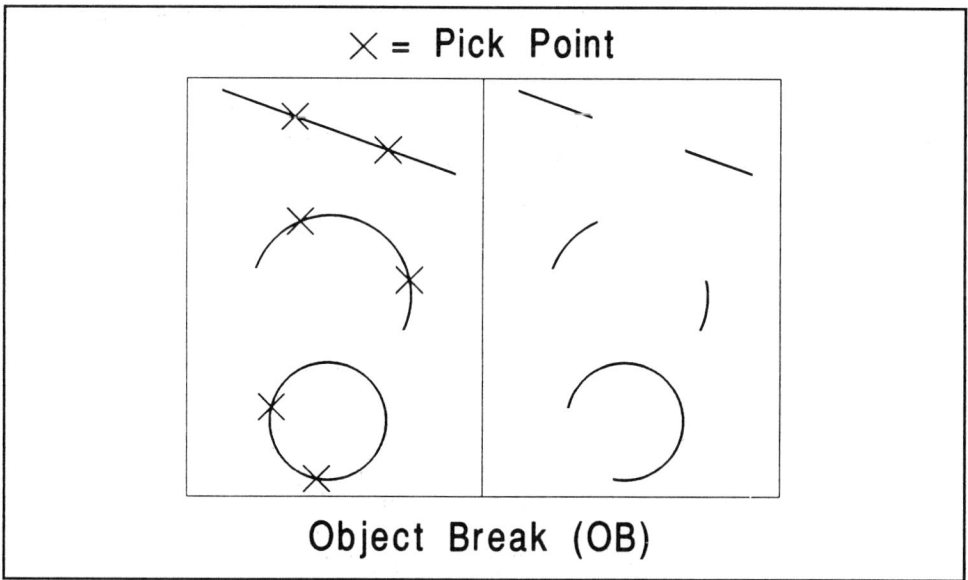

Figure 5.20 Creating Breaks in objects with Object Break.

Stretch (SS)

The Stretch (SS) command initially prompts you to select the objects to stretch using the selection set feature. Type SS to execute the Stretch (SS) command and select the objects to stretch. You will then be prompted to:

Place a window around the points to be moved

Before placing this window, be sure that every object you wish to stretch has been selected and highlighted. Sometimes, it is easier to select the entire set of objects, even objects you don't wish to stretch, using the Window select method. Once you are satisfied that the objects to stretch have been selected, place the window around the points to be moved. Next, you are asked to:

   Enter a reference point

Pick an object you want to move from its origin to a new location. The next prompt will ask you to:

   Enter a new location of the reference point

Before you specify this point, move your cursor and watch the dynamic stretching performed on your objects. (See Figure 5.21.)

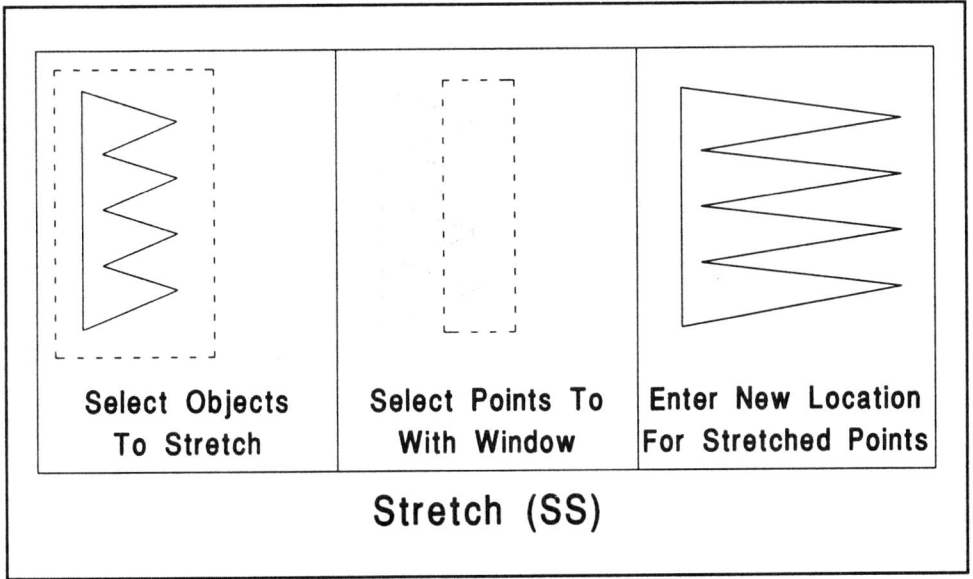

Figure 5.21 Stretching Objects with the Stretch command.

Bezier Edit (BE)

The Bezier Edit (BE) command can only be used to edit an existing bezier curve. The Bezier Edit (BE) command allows you to simultaneously edit two sections of a bezier curve, not necessarily adjoining, by repositioning control points used to define Bezier curves.

Type BE to execute the Bezier Edit (BE) command. First, you are prompted to:

5-26 ■ Chapter 5: Modifying With Shortcuts and Edits

> Enter a point on the object to edit

Select a section of the bezier curve. It may be easier to edit a bezier if the construction points (PC) are turned ON. Dashed lines automatically appear on the bezier, showing the location of the two control points for the section of curve selected. Next, you will be prompted to:

> Enter a point of the second object to edit

Select another section of the bezier. You will be prompted to:

> Enter a point to be moved

Select one of the control points to move. If you are within the set tolerance, the cursor automatically jumps to the closest control point. Most of the time, the control points are not positioned directly on the bezier curve. Once you have selected a point to move, the bezier dynamically change shape on the screen with the movement of your cursor. (See Figure 5.22.)

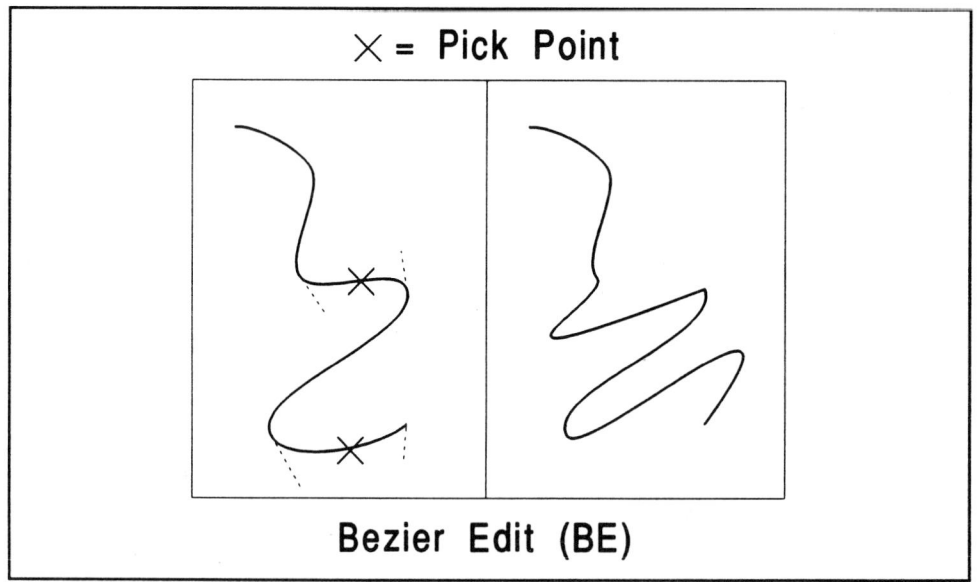

Figure 5.22 Editing Bezier Curves with Bezier Edit.

Even if you don't immediately see a need for bezier curves, try them out anyway. The dynamic changing of the curve is very impressive to watch. You can produce the impression of a three-dimensional jump rope moving on your screen.

Unerase (UE)

The Unerase (UE) feature works as it sounds. This command brings back the last object or objects erased. Draw a line, erase the line, type UE, and the line reappears. Use the Window Erase (WE) command to erase an entire section of a drawing. Type UE, and the erased portion of the drawing reappears. If you want to move a portion of your drawing, leaving a small section behind, you can erase the portion to leave behind, move the remaining drawing, type UE, and the erased portion will reappear in its original location.

Undo (OO)

The Undo (OO), or "oops" command reverses the last action performed, for up to 25 actions back. This is true for all changes except zoom or settings commands. Move an object, type OO, and the object will be placed back in its previous location. Change the color of a line, type OO, and the line will change back to its previous color. Undo (OO) also Unerases (UE) objects. If you zoom-in or out of your drawing, or change any variable settings such as turning ON ortho mode, the Undo (OO) feature has no affect on these changes. Remember, only changes to the screen entities themselves can be undone. Variable settings or zoom values do not affect the characteristics of drawing entities.

> **TIP:** Unerase (UE), as with the Undo (OO) and Redo (UU) commands, will not work on actions executed *before* the Pack Data (PD), Definition Unload (DU), or Drawing Remove (DX) commands are executed. These commands clean out the portion of CADD 6.0 that retains entity types and values, even if changed or erased.

Redo (UU)

The Redo (UU) command reverses the last action undone with the Undo (OO) command. The Redo (UU) feature is merely an "Un-Undo" command, hence the mnemonic (UU).

CHAPTER SUMMARY

In this chapter you learned to use the commands designed to modify entities in your drawing. Step saving modifications can be made using SHORTCUT commands. By using EDIT commands that prompt with selection set options, you have the power to fine-tune the selection of entities to be modified.

Without these commands, you might think that you would be better off drafting manually. It is because of these powerful CADD commands that using CADD is more productive and inviting than manual design and drafting.

SAMPLE EXERCISES

Use the commands you have learned thus far to complete the following sample exercises. Use the dimensions shown to draw the parts to full-scale. Do not try to draw in the dimensions, unless you want to skip ahead to Chapter 11 for instructions.

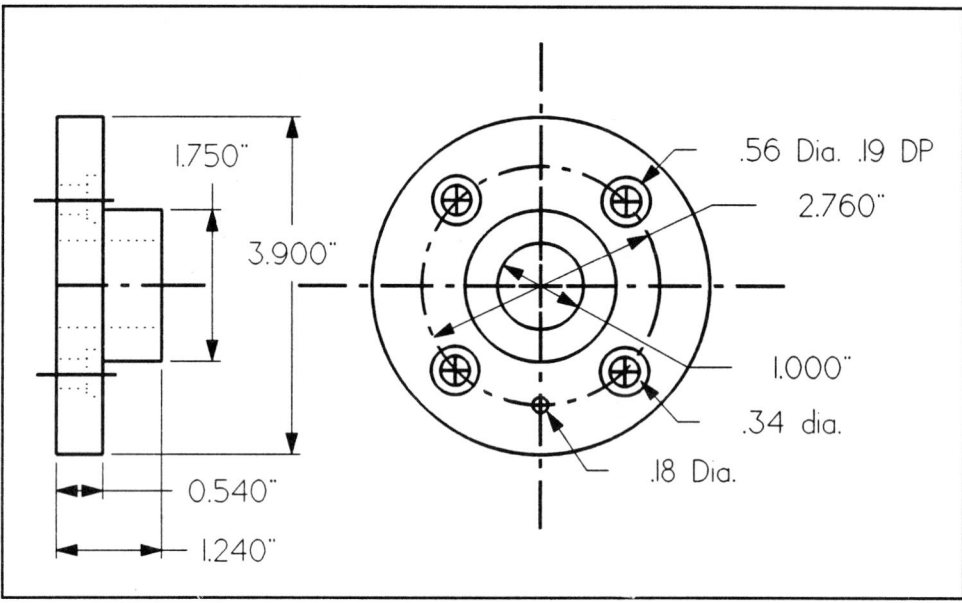

Figure 5.23 Sample exercise for the EDITS commands.

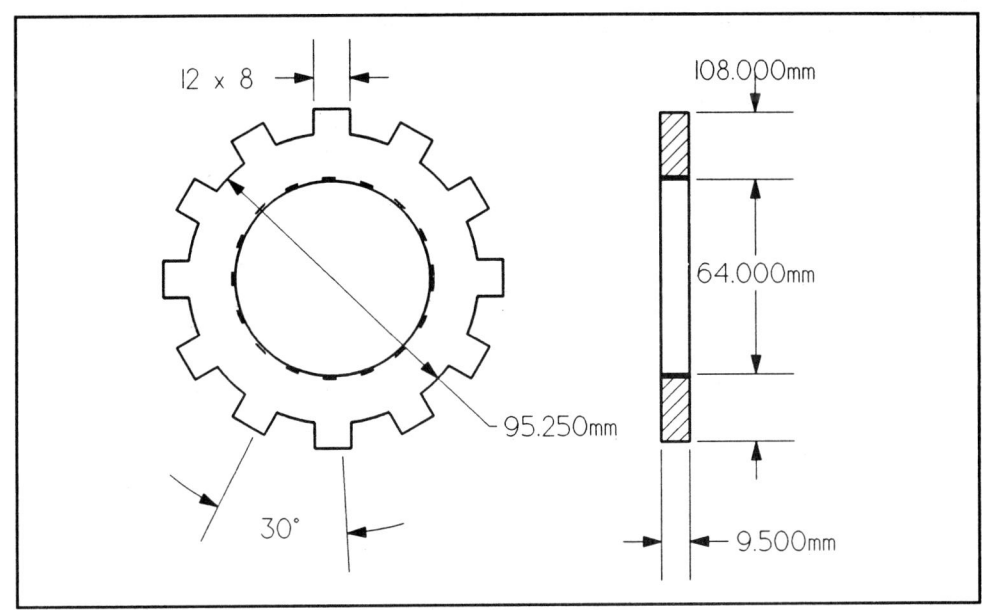

Figure 5.24 Sample exercise for the EDITS commands.

CHAPTER 6

Modifying with Snaps and Trims

USING THE SNAPS AND TRIMS MENUS

Snap and Trim commands let you improve the accuracy and quality of your CADD 6 drawings. Snap commands control the accuracy of point placement on the screen allowing you to exactly place and connect lines, circles, arcs, components, and so on. Trim commands permit you to trim and extend entities to start or end exactly at another entity.

You can produce drawings without using any Snap or Trim commands, but accuracy and clarity will suffer. Creating clean corners, parallel lines, perpendicular lines, and connecting one entity exactly to the end of another would be difficult tasks if you did not have CADD 6's Snap and Trim features.

At the end of this chapter, Part II of the Kitchen Layout tutorial will show you how to continue your kitchen drawing. The existing drawing (created in Chapter 5) is modified using commands from this chapter and from Chapter 5.

The first part of this section covers the SNAP commands:

SNAPS

Snap Nearest Point (NP)
Snap Close Point (SC)
Snap Object (SO)
Snap Midpoint (SM)
Snap Percentage (SR)

Snap Intersection (SI)
Snap Parallel (SL)
Snap Perpendicular (SP)

Snap Tangent (ST)
Snap To Arc Center (SN)

Snap To Grid (SG)
Component Snaps (GC)
Snap To All Visible Layers (SY)

Tolerance (TO)
Quick Pick (QP)

Use snaps to accurately control the selection of points on the screen. A snap can be used whenever CADD 6 asks you to specify a point (when drawing entities, editing, dimensioning, measuring, and so on). You can get close to an existing point with the cursor, but you are never able to exactly select it unless you snap to it.

Snap Nearest Point (NP) and Closest Point (SC)

If you do not have the Snap Nearest Point (NP) command programmed on your mouse or puck, rely on the Snap Close (SC) command, which functions like Snap Nearest Point (NP). NP (Near Point) is not on the video menu because the cursor automatically snaps to the nearest point the moment NP is entered. To select NP from the menu, you would be forced to move the cursor away from the desired point.

Snap Nearest Point (NP). You can snap to any construction point of an object with the Snap Nearest Point (NP) command. Use this command to snap to the endpoints of lines, the centers and radii points of circles, reference points of components, and standard points. Since you will use this command frequently, assign it to one of the buttons on your mouse or digitizer puck, or to a function key. CADD 6's default configuration assigns NP to the third button of a three-button mouse.

> **TIP:** To see all the possible snap points, you may want to display the construction points that make up existing objects in the drawing. Use the command code PC (Construction Points). Be sure the command line shows that the construction points are turned ON, and then use the command code RD (Redraw) to redraw the objects with the points visible.

Snap Closest Point (SC). Another option is to enter the SC (Snap Closest) command code, which gives you the chance to move your cursor to the desired snap point after entering the command. Type SC, then move the cursor close to the desired point. Press Enter to snap to the point or click on it with your mouse.

Snap to All Visible Layers (SY)

To ensure that you can snap to objects on visible, but non-editable layers, turn Snap All Visible Layers (SY) ON. (Layers are explained in detail in Chapter 12.)

Drawing entities on different layers can be hidden, erased, changed, and so forth, using various commands found on the LAYERS menu. If you are working on Layer 1, and there are objects visible on Layer 5, you may want to snap to objects on Layer 5, without accidentally editing them. To set this up correctly, you must:

> Make sure All Layers Edit (AL) is OFF
> Make sure Snap to All Visible Layers (SY) is ON

If All Layers Edit (AL) is ON, the objects on any layer, including the current layer, can be snapped to and modified.

Snap Object (SO)

The Snap Object (SO) command is similar to Snap Closest (SC), but it snaps the cursor to the closest point on the selected object. To use Snap Object (SO), enter the command code SO. At the prompt, move your cursor to a point near a line, circle, or arc where you want to connect a new entity, and click to select it. The entity or object you were drawing should connect exactly to the selected entity. For example, suppose you want to draw a line that ends precisely on another line, but is not connected to one of its endpoints. Start a line at point A of Figure 6.1 and select the Snap Object (SO) command. Position the cursor near point B on line C and click your first mouse button. The line AB is drawn to end exactly at the vertical line marked C.

Snap Midpoint (SM)

To select the exact midpoint of an existing line in a drawing, use the Snap Midpoint (SM) command. After you enter the command code SM, respond to the prompt by moving your cursor along the line of which you want to find the midpoint. When you press Enter, the cursor moves to the exact midpoint of the line. Suppose, for example, you want to draw a line that ends at the midpoint of another line. Start the line at point A of Figure 6.2 and select the Snap Midpoint (SM) command. Position the cursor anywhere along line C (at point B, for example) and press Enter. Line AB is drawn to end exactly at the midpoint of line C.

Snap Percentage (SR)

Use the Snap Percentage (SR) command to snap to a point located a certain percentage along a line, arc, or circle. This command works only with line, arc, and circle

6-4 ■ Chapter 6: Modifying With Snaps and Trims

✕ = Pick Point

Snap Object (SO)

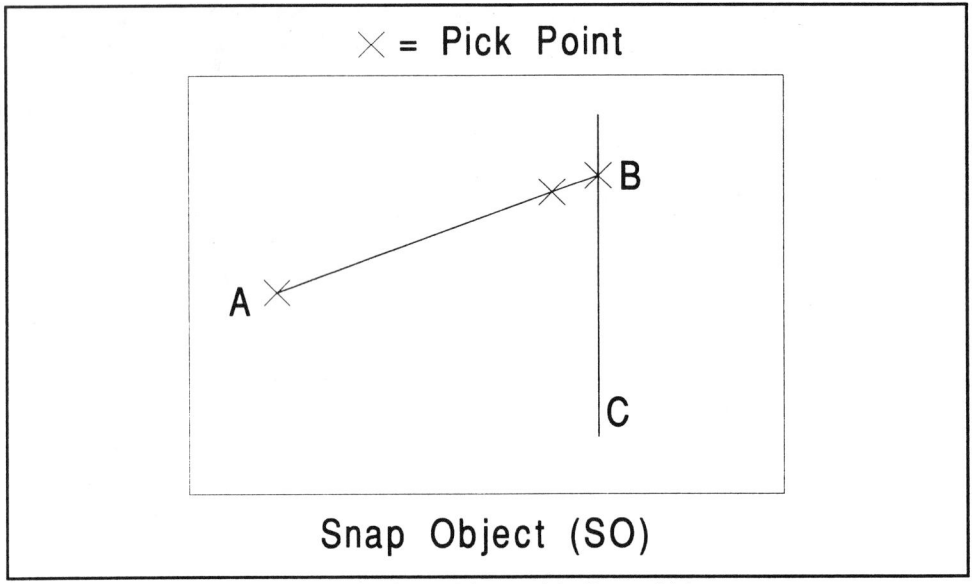

Figure 6.1 Snapping to an existing object with Snap Object.

✕ = Pick Point

Snap Midpoint (SM)

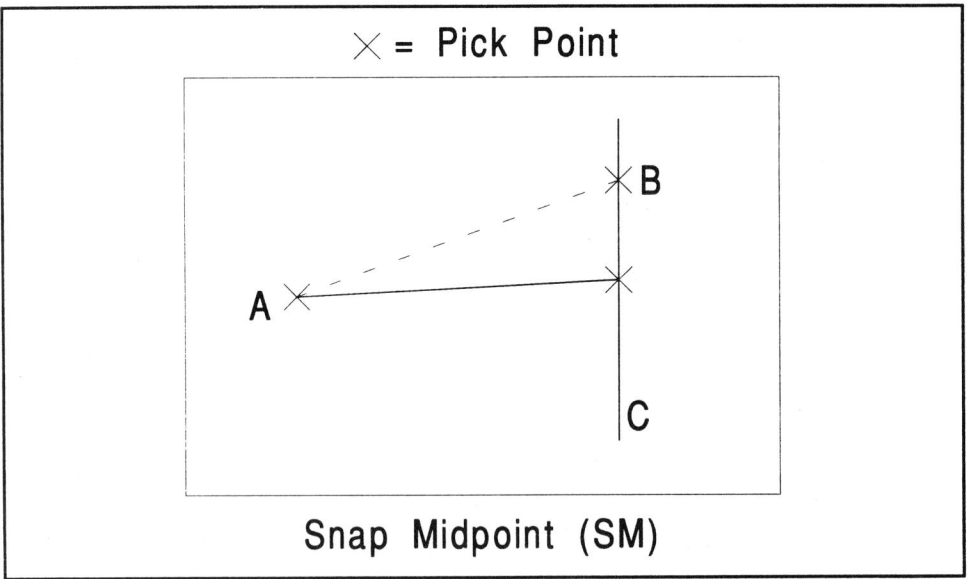

Figure 6.2 Snapping to the midpoint of a line with Snap Midpoint.

entities. To use this command, type SR. Select the object to snap to. Enter the percentage of snap. The default percentage will be displayed. The default is the last percentage entered. To use the default value, press Enter without entering any values.

For a line, the percentage is measured from the endpoint closest to the point initially selected on the line.

For arcs, the percentage is always measured in a counter-clockwise direction on the arc. The 0% point is the beginning point of the arc as it is traced in a counter-clockwise direction.

Figure 6.3 shows an example of the Snap Percentage (SR) command, used to snap to a point 25% along a line and an arc.

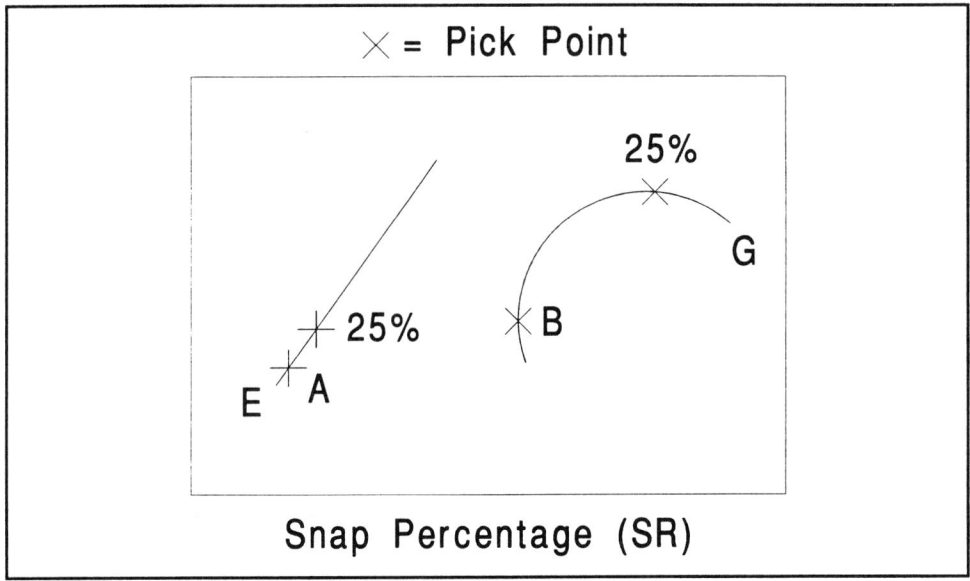

```
                    X = Pick Point

                                    25%
                                     X

                                          G
                      25%     X B
                    +
                    X
                  E  A

              Snap Percentage (SR)
```

Figure 6.3 Using Snap Percentage on a line and an arc.

To use Snap Percentage (SR) to snap to a particular point along a line:

    Type: SR
    Select the line at point A
    Type: 25 (and press Enter) for the percentage

A point on the line is selected that is 25% of the distance along the line from endpoint E, where endpoint E is closest to point A.

To use Snap Percentage (SR) to snap to a point along an arc:

    Type: SR
    Select the arc at point B
    Type: 25 (and press Enter) for the percentage, or just press Enter if the default shows 25 from the last example

6-6 ■ Chapter 6: Modifying With Snaps and Trims

This selects a point on the arc that is at 25% of the distance along the arc from endpoint G. The point is measured from Endpoint G since it is the first point on the arc that starts a path in the counter-clockwise direction.

Snap Intersection (SI)

Use the Snap Intersection (SI) command to select the point where two objects cross, or *intersect*. If you want to connect a line to some point where two other lines intersect, for example, enter the command code SI. At the prompt, move your cursor near the point of intersection and click. The second end of the diagonal line is then snapped to the intersection of the two existing lines.

Figure 6.4 provides two examples of the Snap Intersection (SI) command. In drawing 1, a line has been drawn that ends at the intersection of two lines. The procedure to follow is:

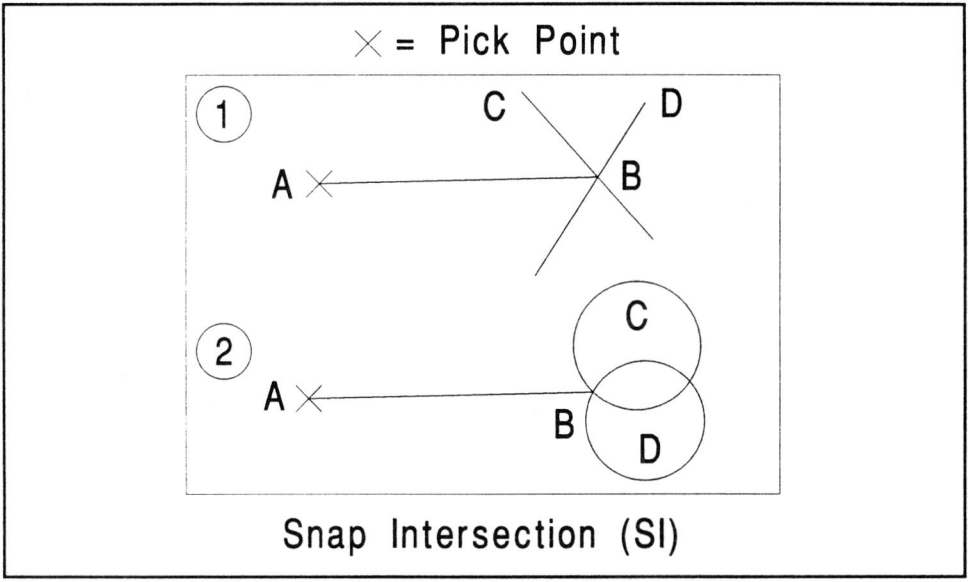

Figure 6.4 Snapping to an existing intersection with Snap Intersection.

```
Start a line at point A
Type: SI (for Snap Intersection)
Position the cursor near the intersection of lines C and D (point B)
Click or press Enter to select the point
```

The endpoint of line AB is placed at the exact intersection point of lines C and D.

In drawing 2 of Figure 6.4, a line has been drawn that ends at the intersection of two circles. The procedure to accomplish this is:

Start a line at point A
Type: SI (for Snap Intersection)
Position the cursor near the intersection of circles C and D (point B)
Click to select the point

The endpoint of line AB is at the exact intersection of the two circles.

Snap Perpendicular (SP)

With the Snap Perpendicular (SP) command, you can create one line exactly perpendicular to another line. You can also snap lines perpendicular to a circle or arc. To place a perpendicular line, start drawing a line by placing its first endpoint. When you are asked for a second point, enter the command code SP, and move your cursor near or on an existing line to which you want the new line to be perpendicular. Click to select the line. (Figure 6.5.)

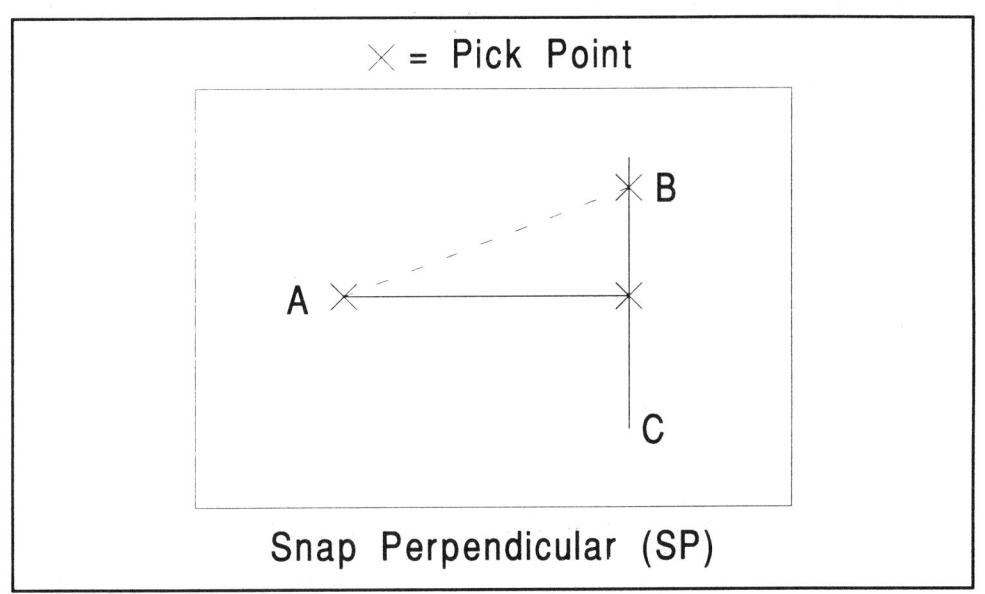

Figure 6.5 Drawing Perpendicular Lines with Snap Perpendicular.

Snap Parallel (SL)

Use the Snap Parallel (SL) command to draw lines, arcs, and circles parallel to existing lines, arcs, and circles.

Snap Parallel To Lines. You can use this command in two ways: when you have already entered the first point of a line, and before you begin to draw a line.

To use this command when you have already entered the first point of a line, enter the command code SL, identify the existing line you want to parallel, and place the second point of the line. It will be snapped parallel, even if the first line is a curved surface.

6-8 ■ Chapter 6: Modifying With Snaps and Trims

Suppose, for example, that you want to draw a line parallel to another line. Do the following (See drawing 1 in Figure 6.6.):

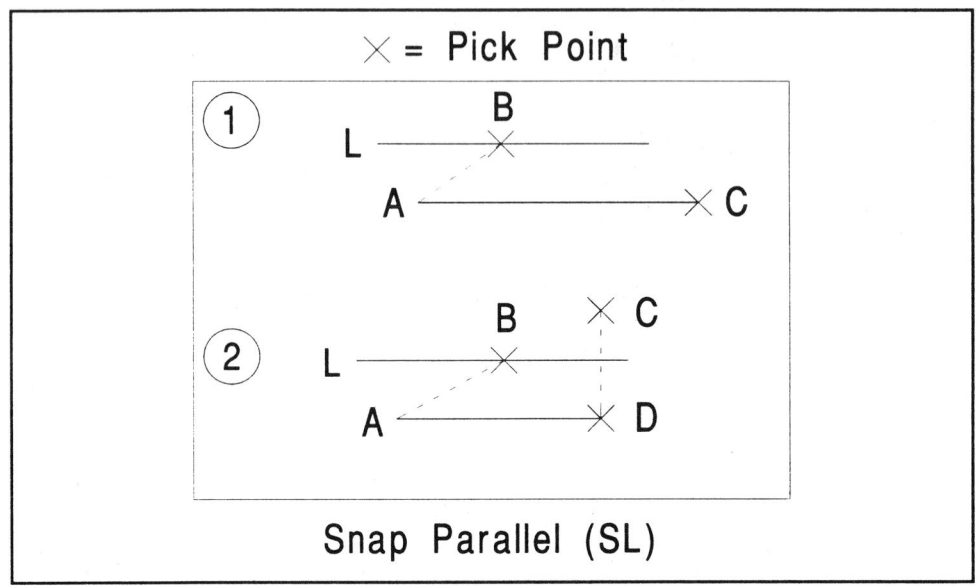

```
                    × = Pick Point
  ┌─────────────────────────────────────────────┐
  │                        B                    │
  │  ①      L ─────────×─────────               │
  │                                             │
  │         A ──────────────────× C             │
  │                                             │
  │                                             │
  │                        B    × C             │
  │  ②      L ─────────×─────                   │
  │                                             │
  │         A ──────────────× D                 │
  │                                             │
  └─────────────────────────────────────────────┘
                 Snap Parallel (SL)
```

Figure 6.6 Drawing parallel lines with Snap Parallel.

> Place the cursor at point A (and press Enter) to start a line (The line labeled L already exists.)
> Type: SL (for Snap Parallel)
> Click to select a point anywhere on line L (at point B, for example)
> Click to place the other endpoint of line A (point C)

Drawing 2 in Figure 6.6 shows that no matter where you place point C, the new line (AD in this case) is always drawn parallel to the existing line. CADD 6 uses the location of the second point (point C, in the example) only to determine the length of line AD.

You also can use the Snap Parallel (SL) command to specify an offset distance from an existing line. Use the command codes LI and SL. At the prompt, select a point on the existing line parallel to the new line. The next prompt will ask you for an offset distance, or the perpendicular distance between the new and old lines. A negative value places the new line *below* the old line. A positive value positions the new line *above* the old line. Type in a number and press Enter. After you enter the offset distance, the next prompt will ask for the starting point of the new line. Move your cursor to the desired location of the first point, and click to select it. Pick a second point and click again. The new parallel line will then be drawn at the exact offset distance specified.

Snap Parallel To Arcs and Circles. To snap parallel to an arc or circle, you must select the Snap Parallel (SL) command before placing the first point of the arc or circle, as shown in Figure 6.7. You can use any of these arcs or circles; A2, A3, C2, or C3.

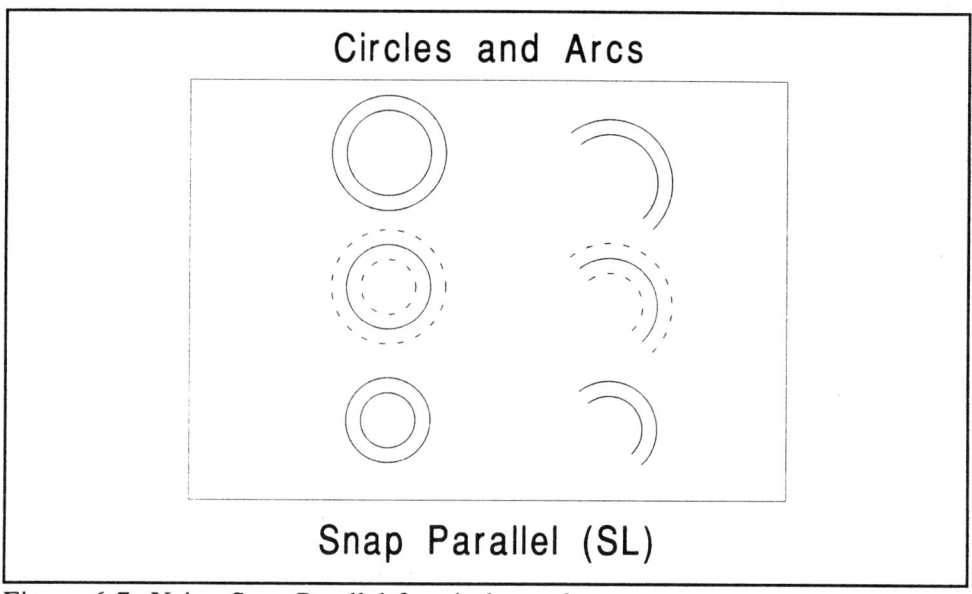

Figure 6.7 Using Snap Parallel for circles and arcs.

Example: Create an arc parallel to an existing arc.

> Type: A3 (for 3 Point Arc)
> Type: SL (for Snap Parallel)
> Click on the arc to which you want to snap parallel
> Type an exact value for the offset (the distance from the existing arc) and press Enter, or move the cursor and click when the new arc is positioned properly.

The new arc is dynamically displayed on the screen. By moving your cursor, you position the arc to the inside or outside of the existing arc, at a distance specified by the offset prompt.

Snap Arc Center (SN)

The Snap Arc Center (SN) command snaps to a point at the center of an existing arc or circle. To use this command, first enter the command code SN. At the prompt, select the existing circle or arc to which you want to snap to the center. When you press Enter, the center is located and you can continue drawing from this point. Figure 6.8 shows an example of Snap Arc Center (SN) used on a circle and arc.

6-10 ■ Chapter 6: Modifying With Snaps and Trims

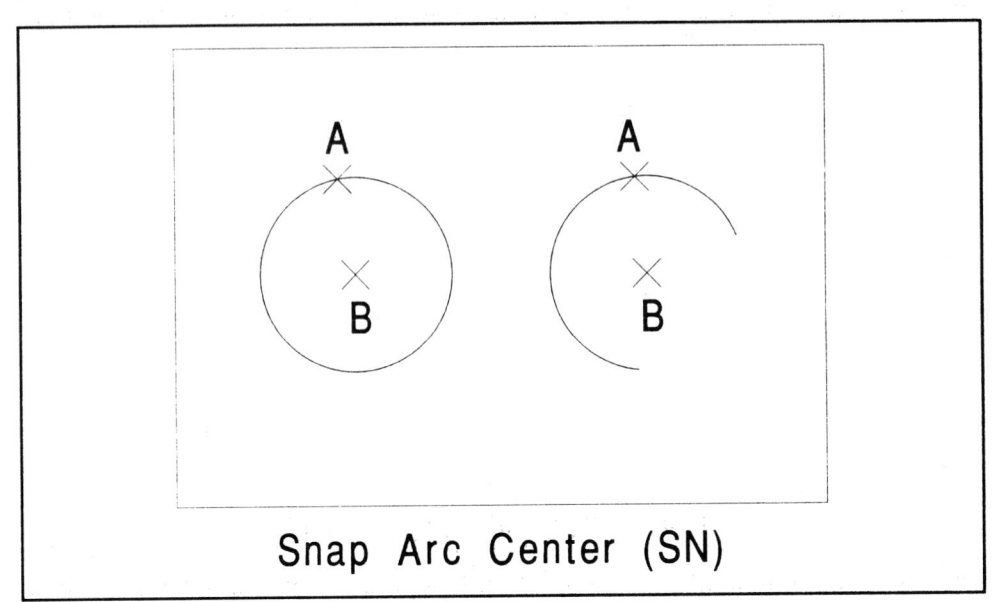

Figure 6.8 Snapping to the center of an arc.

Snap Arc Tangent (ST)

The Snap Tangent (ST) command is used for snapping to a point that is tangent to a circle or arc. Use this command to draw a line that is tangent between two circles or two arcs, or a circle and an arc.

Figure 6.9 shows two examples using the Snap Tangent (ST) command. Drawing 1 shows a line drawn tangent to a circle. To accomplish this task, do the following:

> Click to start a line at point A
> Type: ST (for Snap Tangent)
> Position the cursor on circle C at point B and click to select the point

The line is drawn to the tangent point nearest to where you selected point B.

Drawing 2 shows a line drawn tangent to two circles. To accomplish this, follow these steps:

> Type: ST (for Snap Tangent)
> Position the cursor near point A and click to select the first circle

The construction line is shown tangent to the circle. The tangent point changes dynamically as you move the cursor. To complete the definition of the line, you must place the second endpoint. Use Snap Tangent again to place the second end of the line, making it tangent to circle C.

× = Pick Point

Snap Arc Tangent (ST)

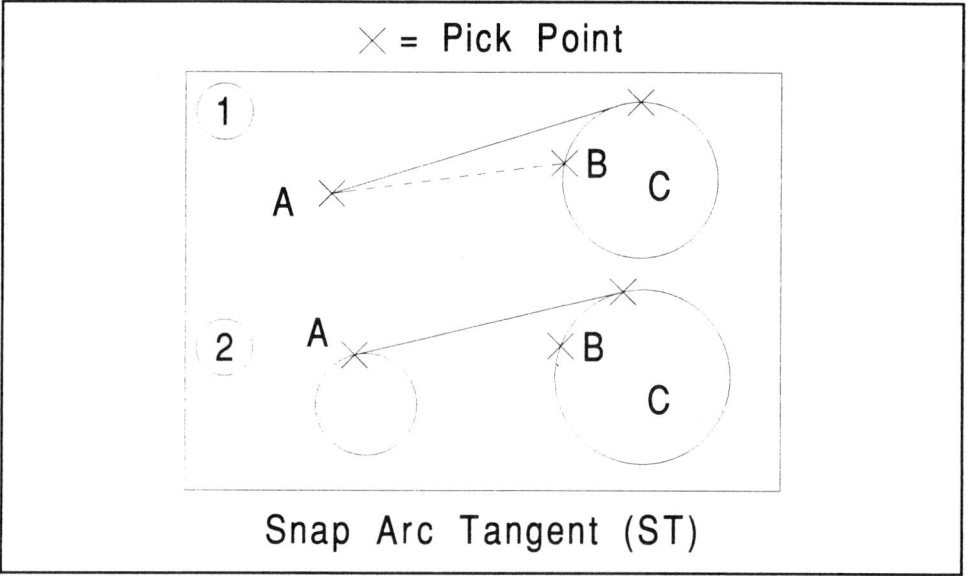

Figure 6.9 Creating tangent lines with Snap Arc Tangent.

TIP: This works similarly with arcs. If you want the line facing a different direction from the initial circle selected, drag your cursor through the center of the circle (or arc) to the other side. The orientation of the line will change automatically.

    Type: ST (for Snap Tangent)
    Position the cursor on circle C near point B and click

The completed line is drawn so it is tangent to both circles, as near to the points you selected as possible.

Snap Grid (SG) and Component Snap (GC)

The Snap Grid (SG) command is a toggle command. When it is set to ON, the cursor snaps to individual grid points on the screen, whether they are displayed or not. This command is covered in Chapter 4 with the other Constraint commands.

The Component Snap (GC) command is also a toggle command. When this command is set to ON, you can snap to the endpoints of objects that make up a component. Other snap commands, such as the snap to midpoint, perpendicular, parallel, and so on, are not effective on components.

Tolerance (TO) and Quick Pick (QP)

Tolerance and Quick Pick are especially useful in very large drawings to reduce the time it takes CADD 6 to find exact points.

Tolerance (TO). If you receive a message indicating that an object was not found, you may need to increase the size of the area where CADD 6 searches for selected objects. Enter the command code TO for the Tolerance (TO) command, and respond to the prompt with a larger tolerance value. You may wish to try selecting the object again by getting closer to it before clicking.

The Tolerance (TO) command sets the size of the search area around the cursor intersection in which a snap may occur. The Snap Nearest Point (NP) and Snap Closest Point (SC) are not affected by the TO command. These commands snap to the nearest point in the drawing regardless of the Tolerance (TO) setting.

The Tolerance command also comes into play when selecting objects on the screen. If you are not within the tolerance or pick area when selecting an object, you may get the messages "Object not found!" or "Point could not be located."

The tolerance does not depend upon the scale of the drawing, but remains a constant area on the video monitor. If you set the Tolerance (TO) to 0.25, you must be within a quarter-of-an-inch diameter circle, in real world measurements, of the object you are selecting. Tolerance (TO) cannot be set to a value greater than 1 inch.

Quick Pick (QP). Every time you select an object in your drawing, the program searches through the entire drawing database until it finds the point you are clicking on. The more complex the drawing, the longer the search. The Quick Pick (QP) command can help speed up this process by limiting the search area.

The Quick Pick (QP) command is a toggle. It defines a visual search area to speed up object selection in complex drawings. The search area is a circle defined at the center of the cursor no greater than 1 inch in diameter. The size of the search region is directly related to the Tolerance (TO) setting.

Quick Pick (QP) is applied during the execution of other commands, such as Snap Object (SO). QP searches for the first relative point it finds in the specified tolerance. Don't confuse searching for the first point with finding the Nearest Point (NP), though this can sometimes be the case. If the object selected does not fall within the search area, no point is selected.

> **TIP:** If Backwards Redraw (BR) is toggled ON, the first point that QP finds is actually the most recent point placed within the search area. This feature often helps speed up the process of finding points.

USING TRIM COMMANDS

The commands covered in this section are listed below:

TRIMS

Trim   (RM)
Extend (XT)

Fillet (FI)
Fillet Radius (FR)
Autofillet (AF)

Chamfer (CH)
Chamfer Distance (CA)

Intersection Trim (IT)
Multiple Line Trim (MT)
Multiple Extend (MX)

Trims are a set of editing features that accurately define the ends of lines, circles, and arcs, and the way they connect or intersect other entities. The commands Trim (RM) and Extend (XT) allow you to do just what their names imply; either trim or extend objects to a new point. You can trim to another object or to any point in the drawing you select. Also included in the set of commands are features for inserting a specified *fillet radius* or *chamfer* between two previously drawn entities.

> **TIP:** Trims do not work on components unless you explode them and return them to the original objects of which they are composed. To explode a component, enter the command code CE for the Component Explode (CE) command and respond to the prompts.

TRIM (RM)

The Trim (RM) command trims off a line or arc so that it exactly meets another line, arc, or circle. The objects must intersect visually on the screen in order to be trimmed. If two objects intersect at an imaginary point in space, they can be trimmed to one another.

The Trim (RM) command is especially useful when you want to trim one line to the point where it intersects another. Use the command code RM to begin a Trim (RM). Select a line to trim by placing your cursor on the side of the line you want to remain and clicking to select it. A new prompt will ask you to select a second object. Move your cursor to a second line or entity that you want the first one trimmed to. After you press Enter again, you see the first line clipped-off (trimmed) at the intersection of the two lines. If the two entities don't actually meet on the drawing, the line being trimmed is trimmed to a projection of the second one.

Look at Figure 6.10 for an example. The desired result is line A trimmed to the end exactly at line C. The procedure is as follows:

```
Type:  RM (for Trim)
Position the cursor on line A near point B and click to select it
Position the cursor anywhere along line C and click to select it
```

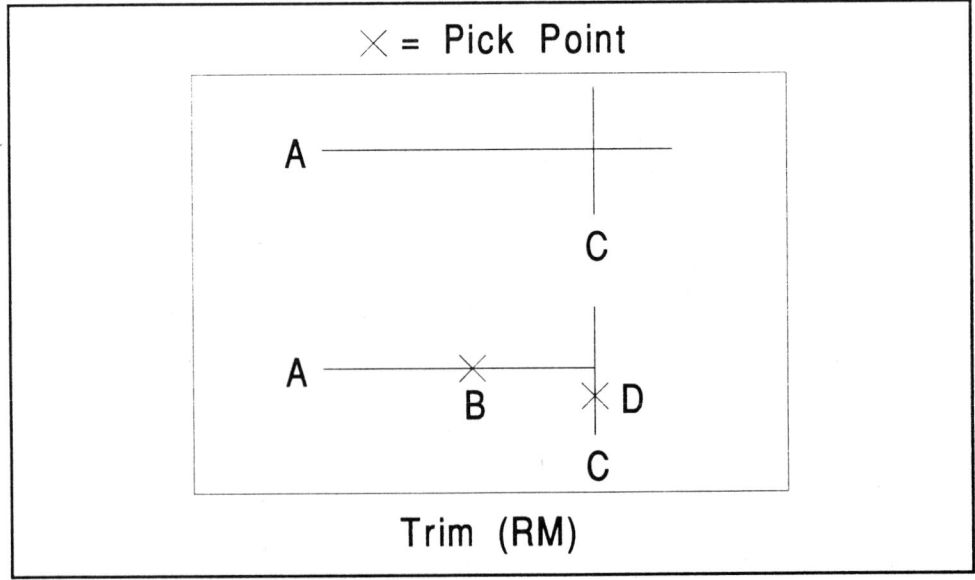

Figure 6.10 Using the Trim command.

> **TIP:** If you don't have a second entity near the line you want to trim, you can still use the Trim (RM) command to shorten your existing line to any selected point. Use the command code RM, and place the cursor on the line to trim. Click to select the line and then move your cursor to any point to which you want the line trimmed. Click again and you should have a new, trimmed line.

Extend (XT)

The Extend (XT) command lengthens one line or arc to meet another line, arc, or circle. The objects need to intersect visually on the screen to be extended. If two objects intersect at an imaginary point in space, they can be extended to one another.

This command can also function like Trim (RM) to lengthen an existing line to the projection of any point you select. To use this command, enter the command code XT. At the prompt, move your cursor to a point on or near the line you want to extend, and click to select it. Then move your cursor to where the extended line should reach. This destination can be any point on the screen, or a point on another object. Click again to select this second point, and the line is extended.

Figure 6.11 shows an example of extending a line to the boundary of another line. Follow these steps:

    Type: XT (for Extend)
    Position the cursor on line A near point B and click
    Position the cursor anywhere along line C and click

> **TIP:** Trim (RM) and Extend (XT) can sometimes perform the same operations. For example, if you accidentally use the Trim (RM) command on a line that has to be made longer before it intersects the second point, the line is extended instead. You often find, however, that using Trim (RM) to trim, and Extend (XT) to extend is better. In some instances, interchanging these commands can cause unpredictable results.

```
                    × = Pick Point

         A ─────────────
                            │
                            C
                            │

         A ────────×────────┤ ×D
                   B        │
                            C

              Extend (XT)
```

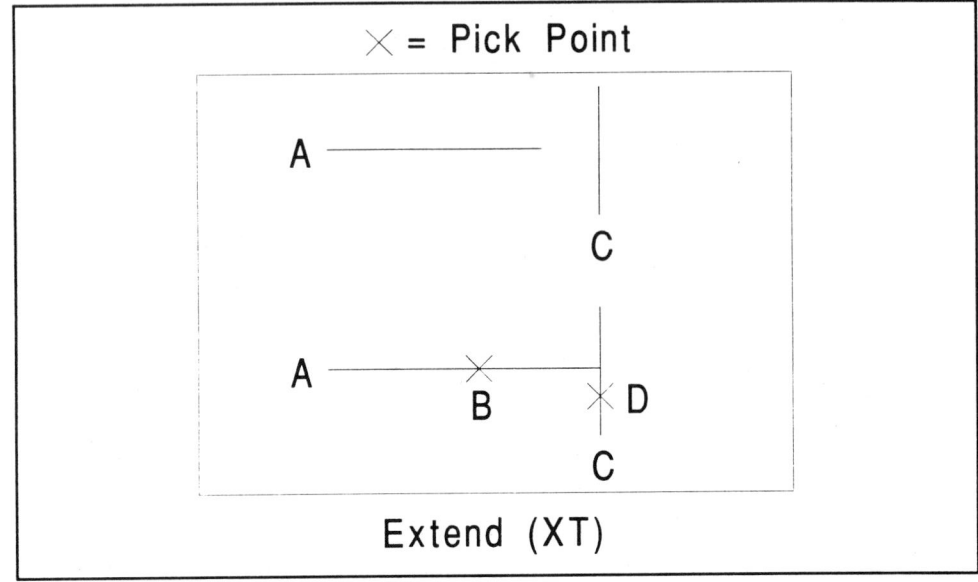

Figure 6.11 Using the Extend command.

Fillet (FI), Fillet Radius (RF), and Autofillet (AF)

You can round-off corners between non-parallel lines or arcs by inserting an arc between them with the Fillet (FI) command. This command inserts an arc of a predefined radius between the two objects, and trims them off to end exactly at the arc. Use this command in conjunction with the Fillet Radius (FR) command, which sets the size of the radius. With the fillet radius set to 0, the two lines you fillet form a sharp, 90° corner. Using this procedure is much faster than using the TRIM command to shape a corner.

To use Fillet (FI), first set the radius size. Enter the command code FR and enter a radius value at the prompt. After a fillet radius is specified, it stays in effect until changed again.

Next, Enter the command code FI, and respond to the prompt by placing your cursor on one of the lines you want to fillet. Make sure that your cursor is on the side of the line you want to save and then click to select it. Move your cursor to the second line, again on the side of the corner you want to keep, and click. An arc is drawn at the intersection of the two lines, and the existing lines are trimmed or extended to end at the arc endpoints. If you fillet between an arc and a line, or between two arcs, you sometimes have to trim-off the excess as a separate step.

Figure 6.12 shows an example of inserting a fillet between two intersecting lines. Follow these steps:

Chapter 6: Modifying With Snaps and Trims ■ 6-17

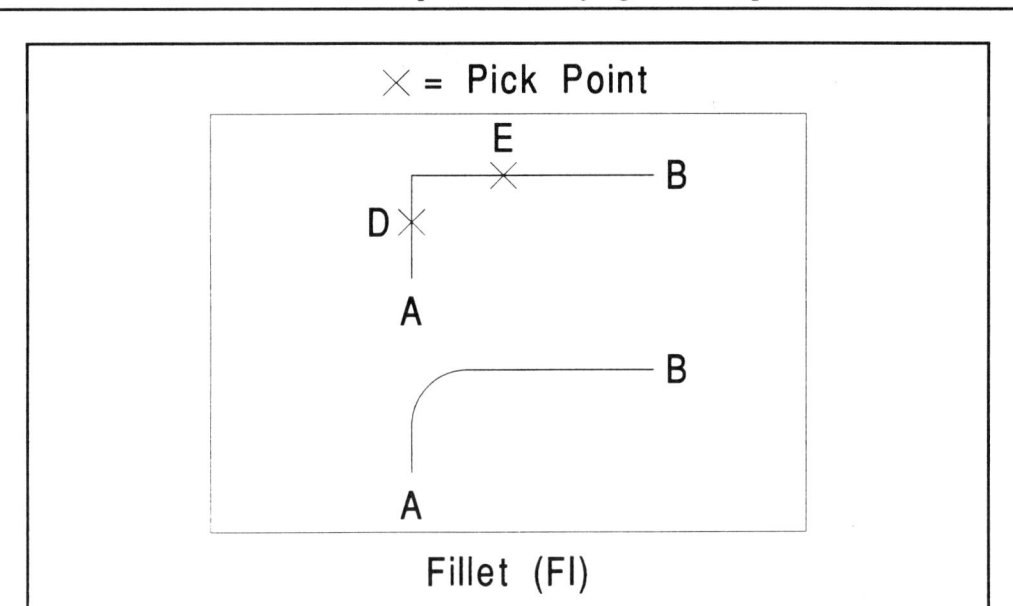

Figure 6.12 Filleting a corner with the Fillet command.

Type: FR (for Fillet Radius)
Type in the desired radius value and press Enter
Type: FI (for Fillet)
Place the cursor on line A near point D and click to select it
Place the cursor on line B near point E and click

The resulting fillet is inserted, as shown in Figure 6.12.

Autofillet (AF) is a toggle command. If Autofillet has been set to ON, the corners between lines drawn are automatically filleted. The fillets change dynamically on the screen at corners made by placing lines. The fillets freeze in position when the endpoint of the line adjoining the fillet has been placed.

Chamfer (CH) and Chamfer Distance (CA)

With the Chamfer (CH) command, you can place a line at a specified slope between two other nonparallel lines, giving the effect of a cutoff, or beveled corner. You must first define some parameters with the Chamfer Distance (CA) command so CADD 6 knows how to construct the chamfer. Use the Chamfer Distance (CA) command to specify the two distances that define the slope of the chamfer line. Chamfer Distance (CA) is similar to Fillet Radius (FR), because it requires you to enter the proper parameters to get the result you want. Also, as with the Fillet (FI) command, setting the chamfer distance to 0 creates a sharp corner when Chamfer (CH) is used.

To use the Chamfer (CH) command, begin by setting the two values for chamfer distance (these define the slope of the line to be inserted between the two existing lines). Use the command code CA and enter values at the prompts. With the chamfer distances set, type CH, move your cursor on or near one of the two lines you want to chamfer, and click to select it. Remember to place your cursor on the side of the corner you want to remain. Then move your cursor on or near the second line on the side of the corner you want to keep. Click again to complete the process.

Figure 6.13 shows four examples of the effect of chamfer distances. Chamfer distance 1 (labeled CA1 in Figure 6.13), is the amount to be cut-off the first line selected. Similarly, chamfer distance 2 (CA2), is the amount to be cut-off the second line selected. This value is always the distance along the existing line. It is not necessarily a horizontal or vertical distance.

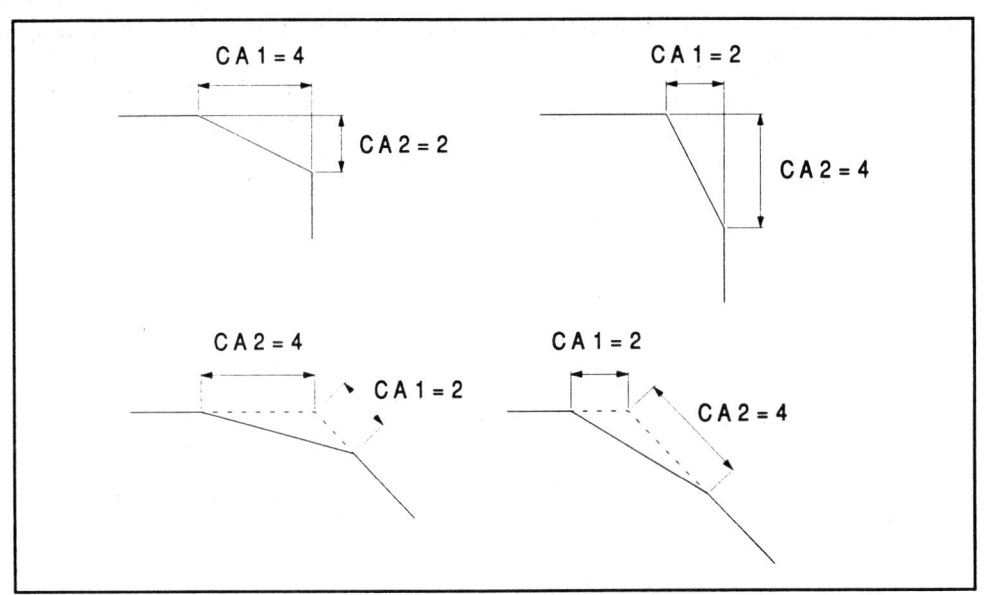

Figure 6.13 Examples of changing the Chamfer Distance.

Figure 6.14 shows an example of beveling, or chamfering, a corner of two intersecting lines:

    Type: CA (for Chamfer Distance)
    Type in the desired distances (and press Enter) at each prompt
    Type: CH (for Chamfer)
    Place the cursor on line A near point D and click to select it
    Place the cursor on line B near point E and click to select it

Intersection Trim (IT)

This command works with multiple lines as a trim, extend, and break command in-one. The easiest way to learn this command is to draw an intersection on your screen and practice trimming it. (See Figure 6.15, ignore Point A for now.)

```
                            × = Pick Point
                          E
                          ×————— B
                     D ×
                       |
                       A


                              ————— B
                          /
                         /
                        A
                     Chamfer (CH)
```

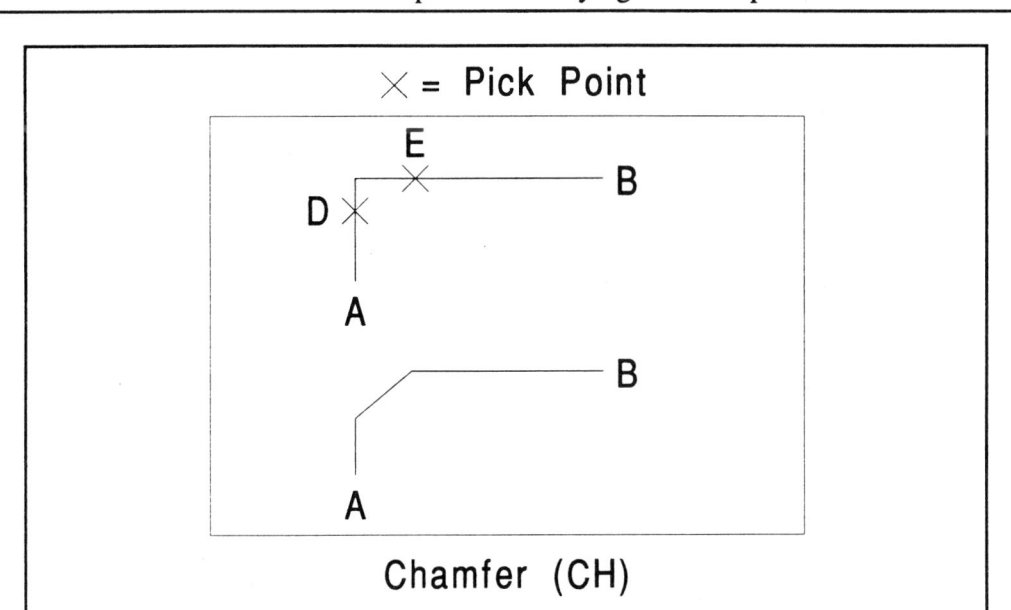

Figure 6.14 Chamfering a corner with the Chamfer command.

> Type: IT (for Intersection Trim)

You are first prompted to:

> Enter a point inside the intersection

Click to place this point approximately in the center of the intersection. (See Point A, Figure 6.15.) The next prompt asks you to:

> Enter an outside corner point

Before entering this next point, move your cursor in different directions. You should see the lines of the intersection changing dynamically on your screen into different configurations. When the configuration you want is displayed, press Enter or click with your mouse.

Multiple Trim (MT)

The Multiple Trim (MT) command is used to trim multiple lines (not arcs) about a single entity (line, arc, or circle). This command works only as a Trim command and not as a Multiple Extend command, unlike the standard Trim (RM) and Extend (XT) commands, which can be used for both functions.

When the Multiple Trim (MT) command is executed, you will be prompted with a selection set. Use the selection set to pick the objects you wish to trim. Once the objects have been selected, you are prompted to select the object to which to trim them.

Intersection Trim (RM)

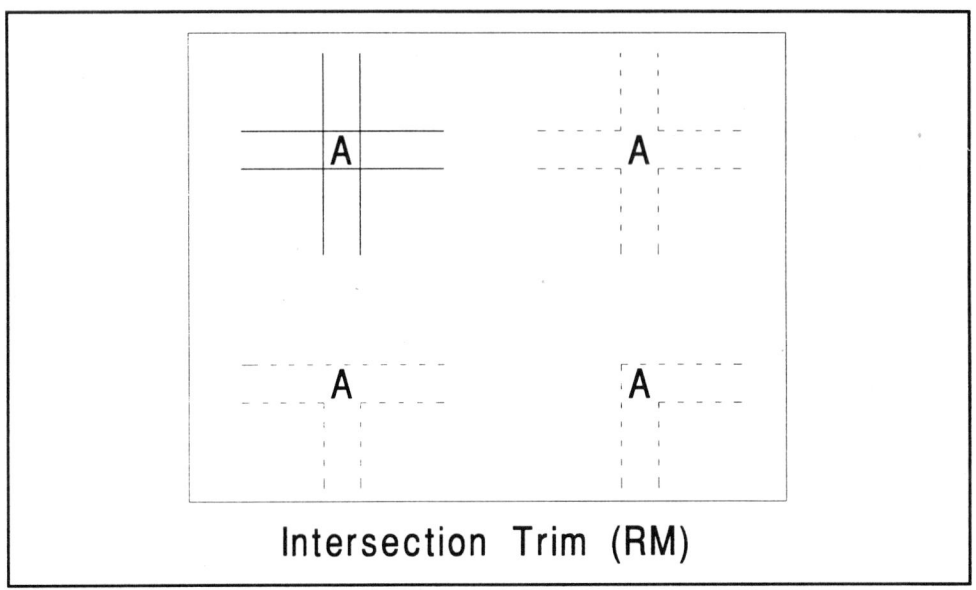

Figure 6.15 Different ways to Trim Intersections.

Once you have selected the object to trim to, you will see the objects to be trimmed displayed about the reference object in a highlighted state. By moving your cursor about the reference object, you will be able to see how the objects would look trimmed about either side. The display dynamically changes as the cursor is moved. When you are satisfied with the display, press Enter or click with your mouse. The result is shown in Figure 6.16.

Unlike Trim (RM) and Extend (XT), the Multiple Trim (MT) command only trims objects to a line, arc, or circle if they actually intersect. If you try to trim a line to an object it doesn't actually intersect, the line will not be trimmed.

Multiple Extend (MX)

Use the Multiple Extend (MX) command to simultaneously extend several lines (not arcs) to the intersection of another object (line, arc, or circle).

The same rules that apply to Multiple Trim (MT) also apply to Multiple Extend (MX). See the above explanation of Multiple Trim (MT).

CADD TUTORIAL — KITCHEN LAYOUT, PART II

In this section of the kitchen layout tutorial, you will break a section of wall near the sink area, and insert a window. The window is centered on the wall closest to the sink. The window is drawn to be 6" X 60". You will then modify the kitchen sink with some of the commands that have been discussed.

Multiple Trim (MT)

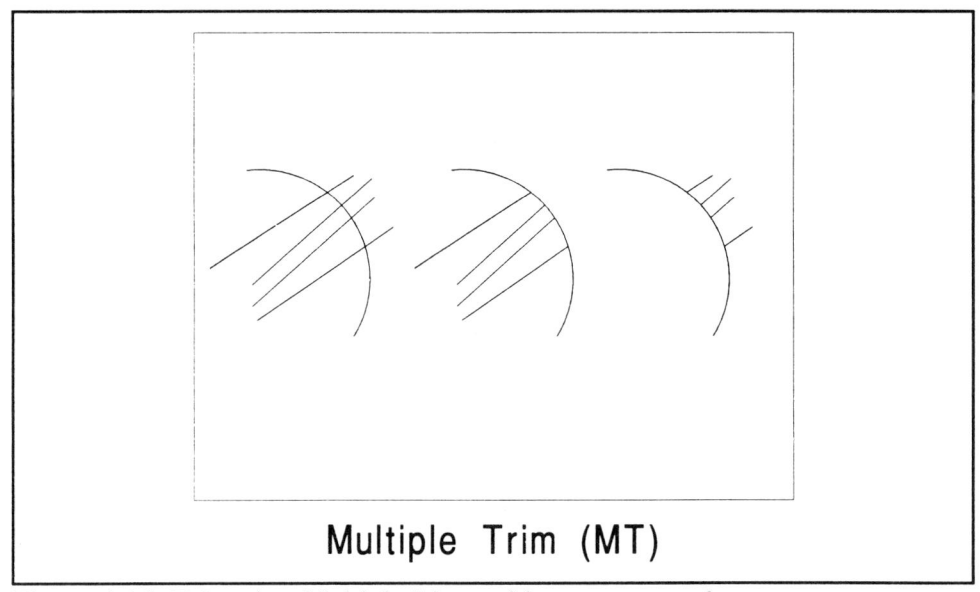

Figure 6.16 Trimming Multiple Lines with one command.

First, call up the "KITCHEN" drawing you created in Chapter 4.

>Type: LO (for Load)
>Select D for drawing
>Click on KITCHEN from the sidebar listing of drawing names
>Press Enter to place the drawing at the origin point

Insert a Kitchen Window

The first step to inserting a kitchen window is to break a hole in the wall where the window is to be placed

>Use Zoom Window (ZW) to zoom-up on the sink and wall area. (Shown in Figure 6.17.)
>
>Type: MR (for Manual Entry Offset Relative)

Now, use the Object Break (OB) command to break a hole in the wall. Since the wall is really just two parallel lines, you must break both of the lines.

>Type: OB (for Object Break)
>Click on the top line of the wall above the sink to select it
>At the prompt "Enter first break point," type: TK (for Tracking)
>Type: SM (for Snap Midpoint) and click on the top line of the wall above the sink
>Type: -2'6,0 (and press Enter)
>Type: PU (for Pen Up) to end tracking

6-22 ■ Chapter 6: Modifying With Snaps and Trims

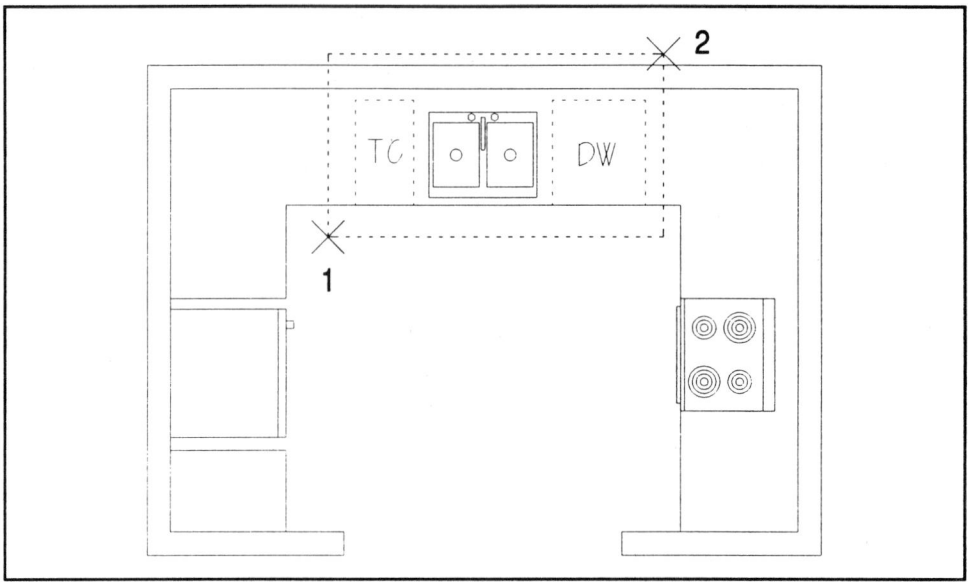

Figure 6.17 Zoom-up on the sink area to place the window.

If you move your cursor to the right, you'll see the break in the line dynamically changes size on the screen. Create a break, or hole, for the window that is 5' wide.

    Type: 5',0 (and press Enter)

Repeat the above steps for the other line of the wall. After completing these steps, your drawing should look like Figure 6.18. Next, draw the window in the opening.

    Type: LC (for Line Color)
    Type: 14 (and press Enter) to change your Line Color to 14
    Type: RE (for Rectangle)
    Snap NP (Nearest Point) to point A in Figure 6.19
    Snap NP to point B to complete the window

Windows are normally symbolized with a line drawn through their center, as shown in Figure 6.20. To do this:

    Snap to the midpoint (SM) of the left side of the window
    Snap Midpoint (SM) to the window's right side
    Press the Esc key to finish the line command

Modify the Sink

Now that you have had more experience with CADD 6, the kitchen sink you created in Chapter 2 just isn't good enough. The first step is to zoom-up on the sink so you can modify it.

Chapter 6: Modifying With Snaps and Trims ■ 6-23

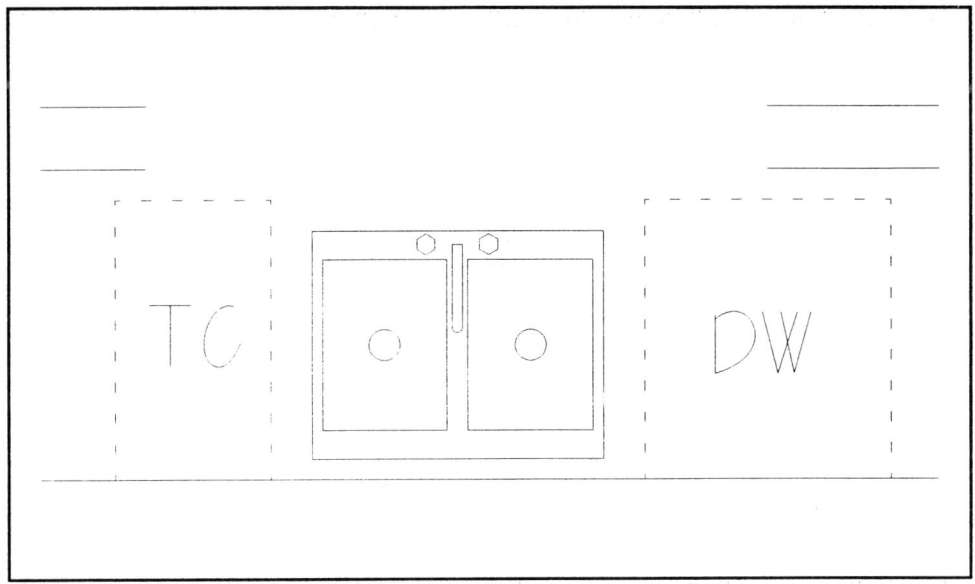

Figure 6.18 Breaking a hole in the wall for the window.

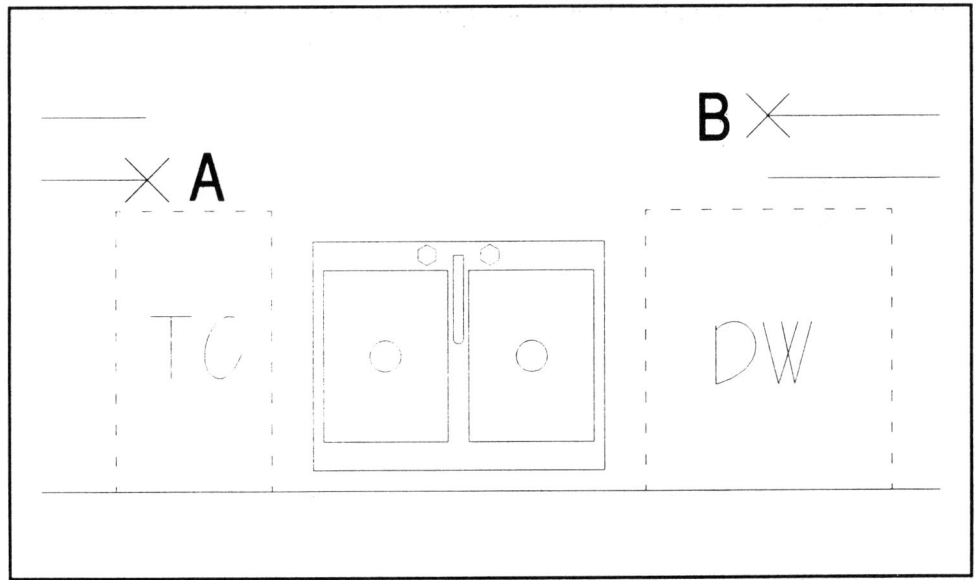

Figure 6.19 Drawing the outline of the window.

Type: ZI (for Zoom In)

At the prompt "Enter center of zoom," place your cursor as close possible to the sink's center (see Figure 6.21) and press Enter or click your first mouse button. Your display should change to look like Figure 6.22.

6-24 ■ Chapter 6: Modifying With Snaps and Trims

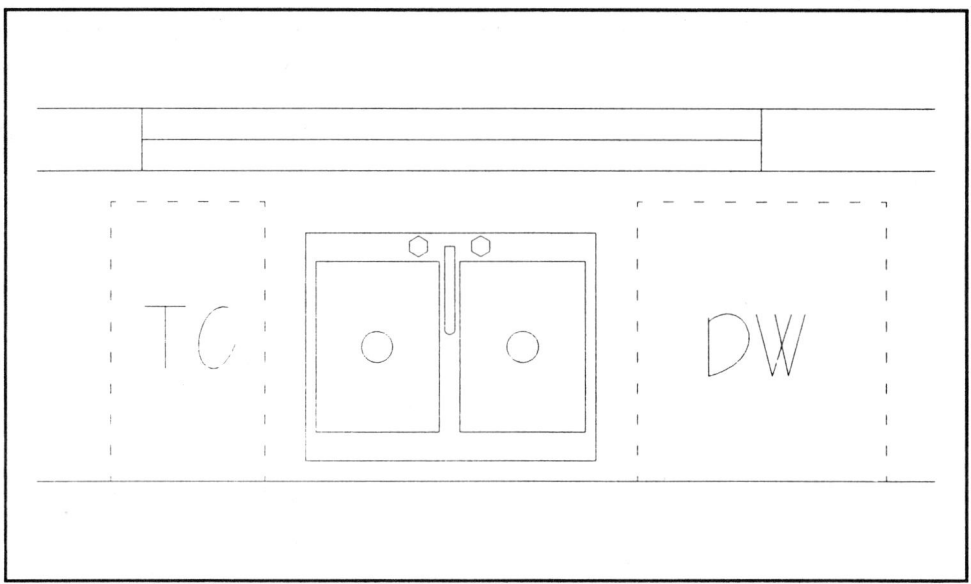

Figure 6.20 Complete the window.

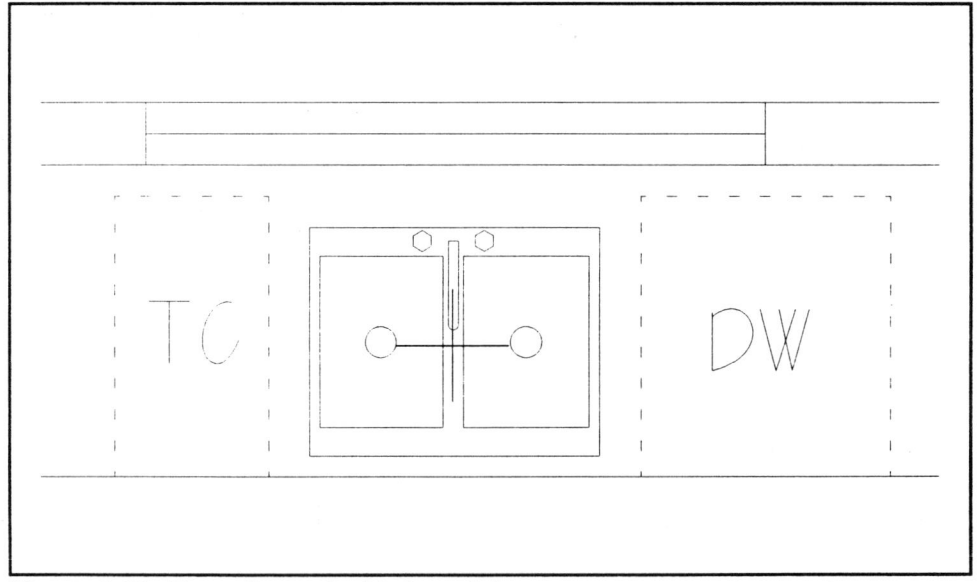

Figure 6.21 Zoom In on the kitchen sink.

In the next set of steps, you will round-off the corners of the sink with the Fillet (FI) command. First, set the fillet radius to 1.5".

Type: FR (for Fillet Radius)
Type: 1.5 (and press Enter)

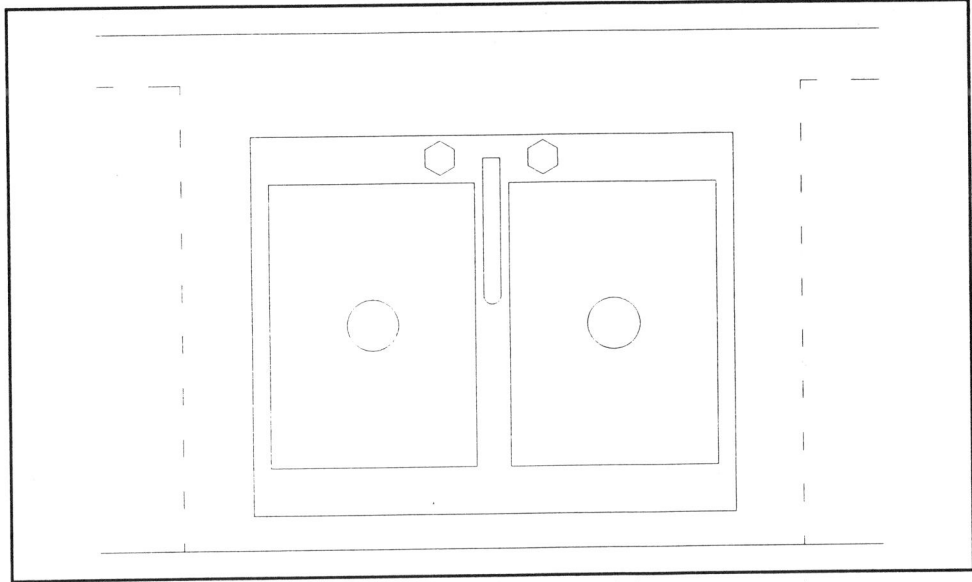

Figure 6.22 The resulting Zoom In view of the sink.

Now, fillet the inside corners of the sink basins, as marked by X's in Figure 6.23.

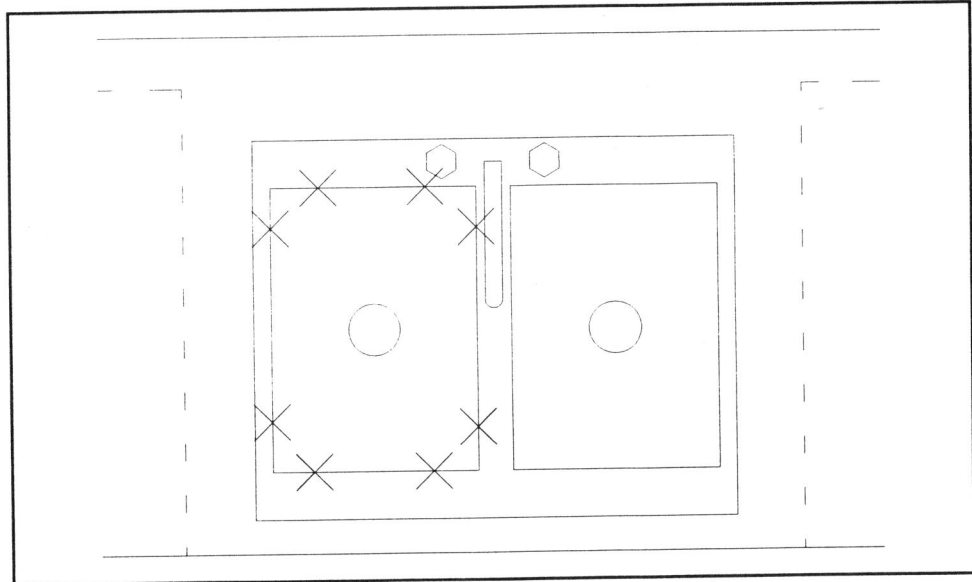

Figure 6.23 Add a Fillet Radius to the corners of the sink.

    Type: Fl (for Fillet)
    Click on one side of the sink basin near a corner to fillet it
    Click on the other line that makes up that corner
    Press the spacebar to repeat the Fl command

Move around the sink basins, selecting the lines that make up each of the corners, in turn. Your drawing should look like Figure 6.24.

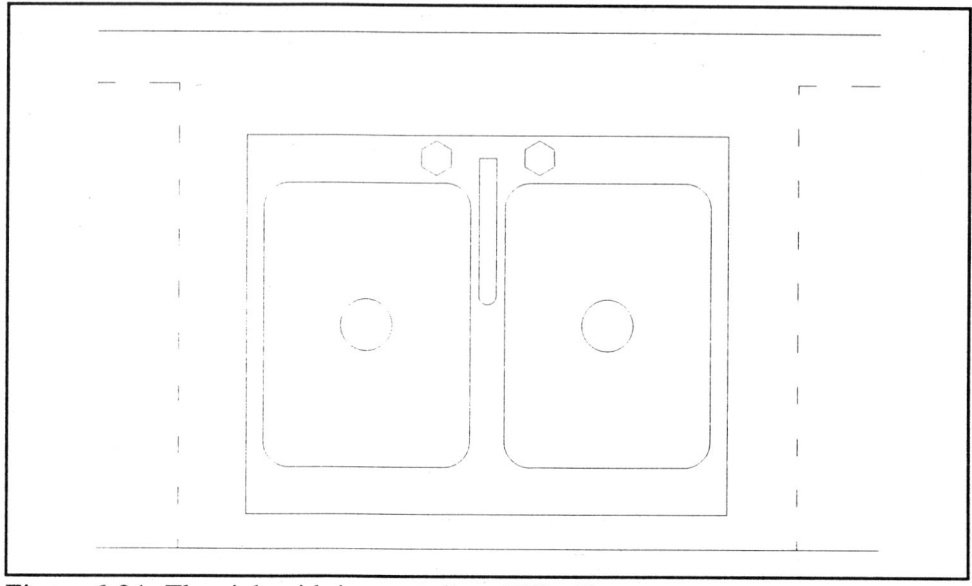

Figure 6.24 The sink with inner corners Filleted.

Change the fillet radius to 3" so you can round the outside corners of the sink, as shown in Figure 6.25.

>   Type: FR (for Fillet Radius)
>   Type: 3 (and press Enter) for the radius
>   Type: FI (for Fillet) and round each of the sink's outer corners, just as you did for the inner corners

Drawing the Drains

The Radial Copy (RC) command, introduced in Chapter 5, can be used to draw more realistic drains in the sink. First, Zoom In (ZI) on the left drain and change to the proper line color.

>   Type: ZI (for Zoom In)
>   Click near the center of the left basin's circular drain
>   Type: LC (for Line Color)
>   Type: 15 (and press Enter) to select color 15

Draw the first drain hole so it is centered 1" above the large circle and 0.50" in diameter, as shown in Figure 6.26.

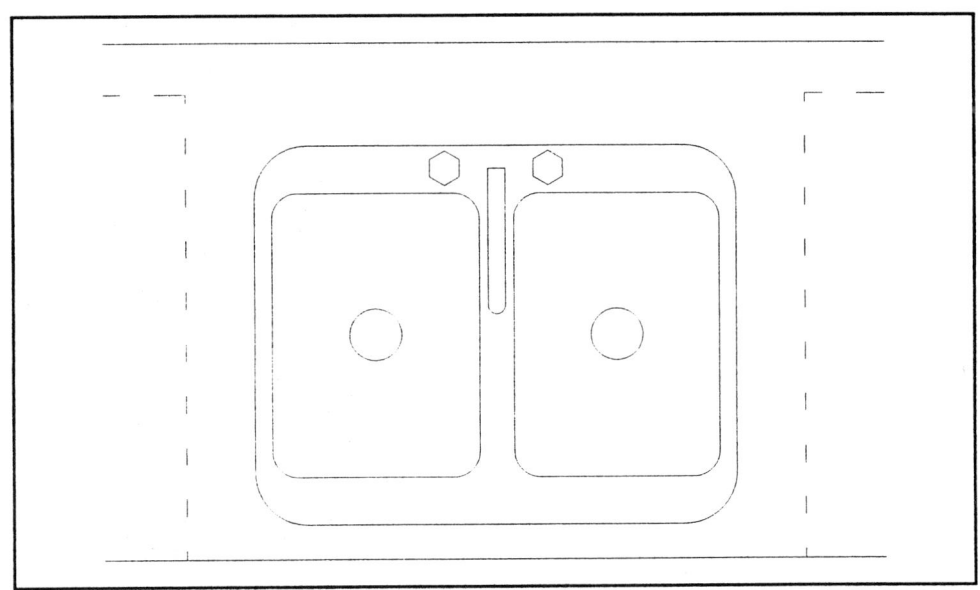

Figure 6.25 The resulting sink with all corners Filleted.

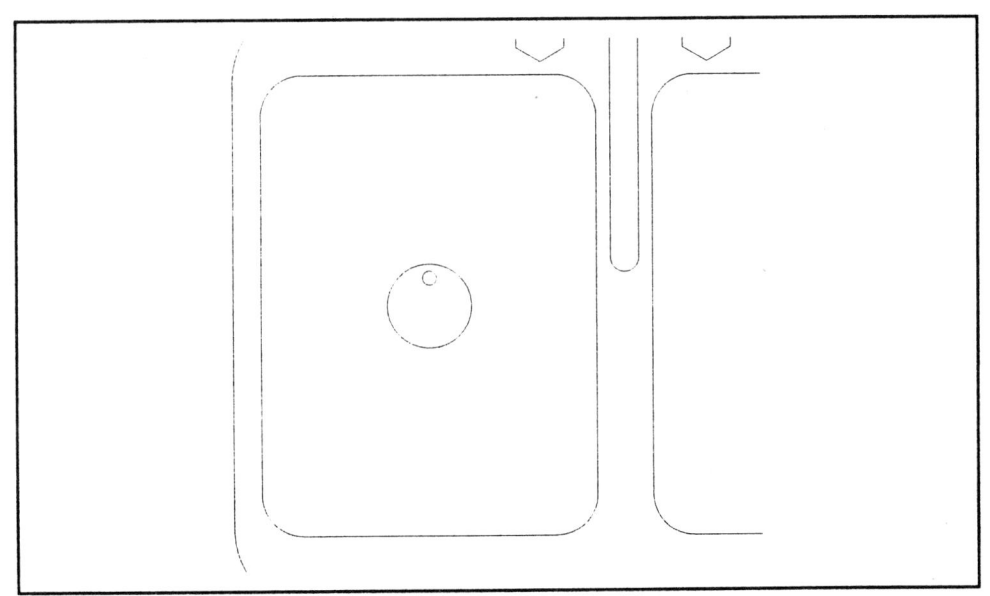

Figure 6.26 Placing the first drain hole.

Snap NP to the drain's center
Type: C2 (for Circle 2)
Type: 0,1 (and press Enter)
Type: 0,.25 (and press Enter)

Your display should look like Figure 6.26. Now create four copies of the first drain hole, equally-spaced around the center of the large circle.

> Type: RC (for Radial Copy)
> Type: O for Object or select Object from the command line menu
> Click on the small circle within the drain that you want to copy
> Press Enter to complete the selection

The Radial Copy command requires you to specify an axis point around which the objects are to be copied. In this case, you want the six drain holes to be equally-spaced about the center of the large circle.

> Snap to the center of the drain, (the larger circle), to specify an axis point
> Type: 360 (and press Enter) for the "total degrees to span"
> Type: 5 (and press Enter) for the "total number of items to span"

These steps create four copies of the original drain hole, creating five holes equally-spaced around the drain, as shown in Figure 6.27.

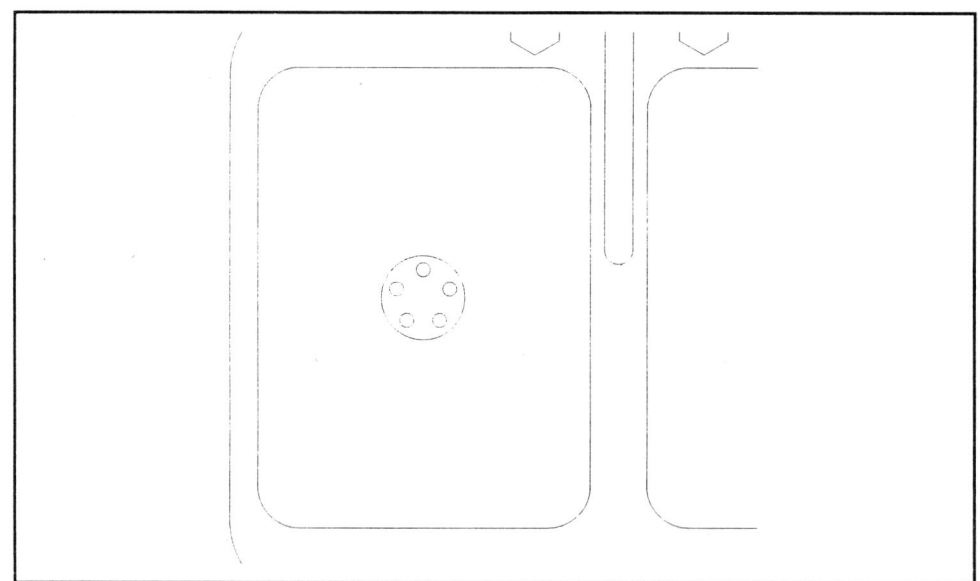

Figure 6.27 Using Radial Copy to create the other drain holes.

Now change the display so you can work on the right-side drain.

> Type: ZO (Zoom Out) and click near the center of the sink
> Type: ZI (Zoom In) and click near the center of the right-side drain

Use Radial Copy (RC) again to add holes to this drain, as shown in Figure 6.28

Chapter 6: Modifying With Snaps and Trims ■ 6-29

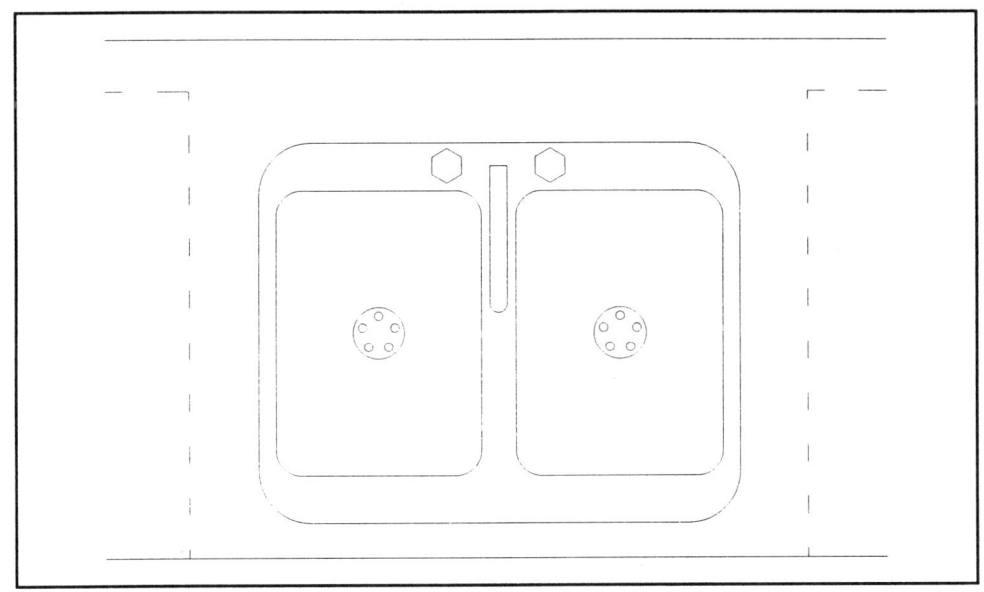

Figure 6.28 Completing the right-side drain holes.

Now, make some modifications to the faucet to make it more realistic. Rotate it 35 degrees to the side, and break the side of the sink basin to accommodate it.

>Type: ZO (Zoom Out) and click near the center of the faucet
>Type: ZW (Zoom Window) and place a window around the faucet

The corners of the window should be placed approximately at points A and B, as shown in Figure 6.29.

>Type: RO (Rotate)
>Type: W to choose the Window selection method
>Place a window around the faucet, as shown in Figure 6.30
>
>Snap to the midpoint (SM) of the top line of the faucet
>Type: 35 (and press Enter) for the rotation angle

The faucet should be rotated as shown in Figure 6.31.

>Type: OB (Object Break)
>Select the arc that runs through the faucet, as shown in Figure 6.32
>
>At the prompt, "Enter first break point," type SI (for Snap Intersection) and click on point A in Figure 6.33
>For the second break point, SI (Snap Intersection) to point B

6-30 ■ Chapter 6: Modifying With Snaps and Trims

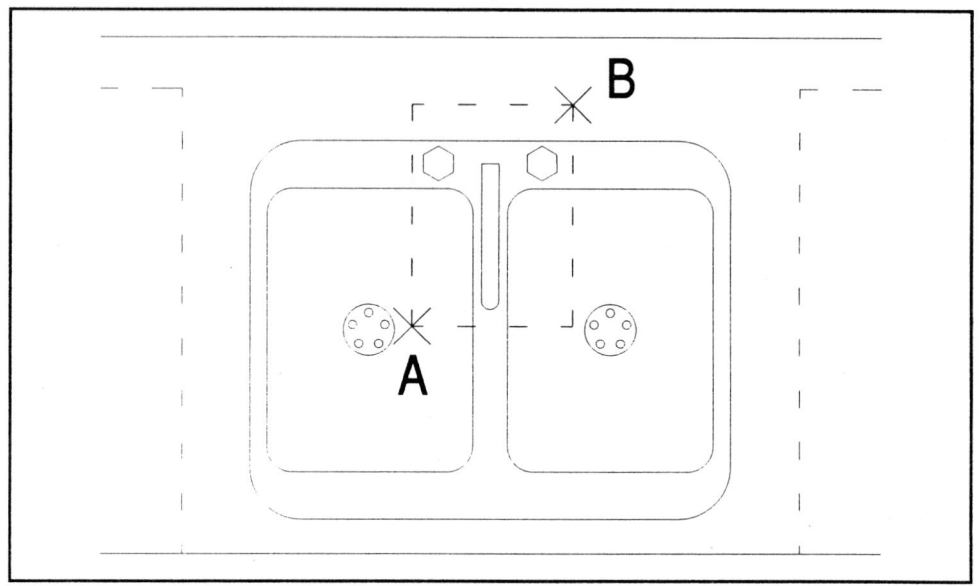

Figure 6.29 Zoom Window around the faucet.

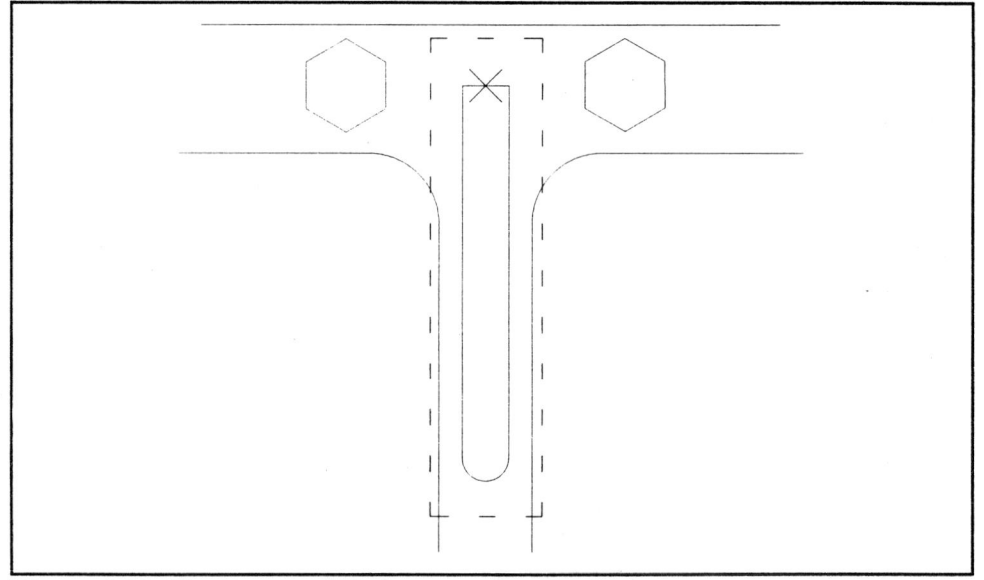

Figure 6.30 Use Rotate - Window to select the faucet.

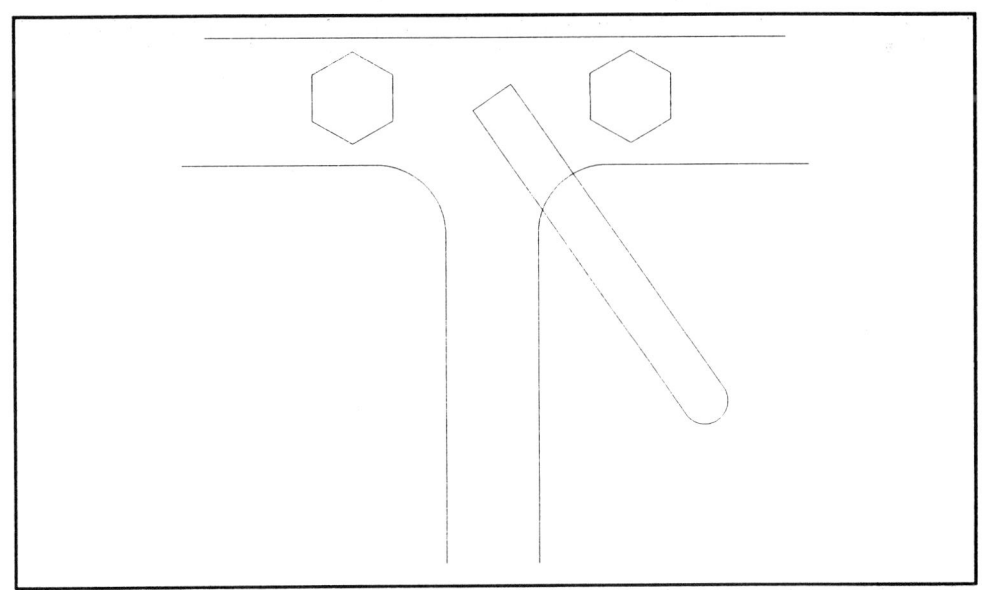

Figure 6.31 The result of rotating the faucet.

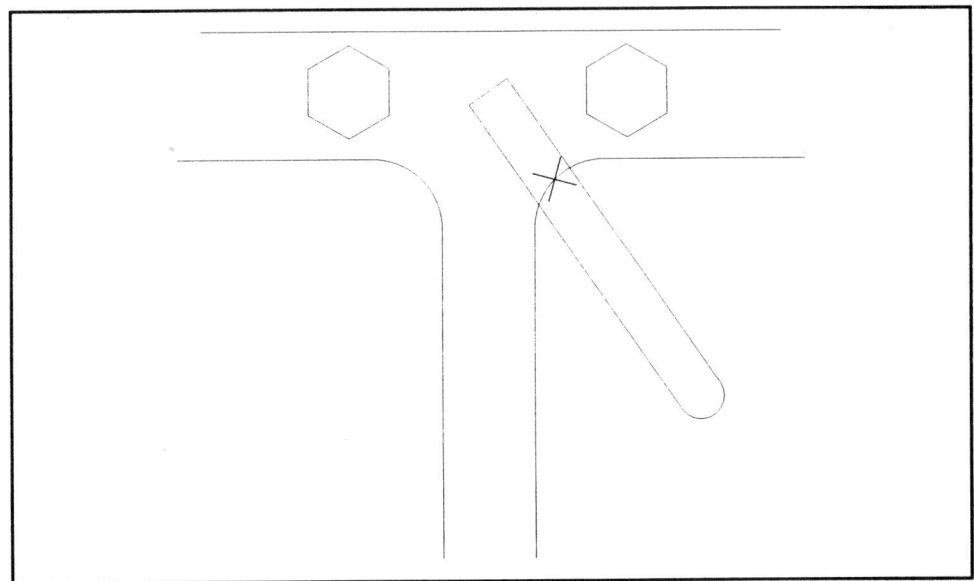

Figure 6.32 Select the corner of the basin to break it.

6-32 ■ Chapter 6: Modifying With Snaps and Trims

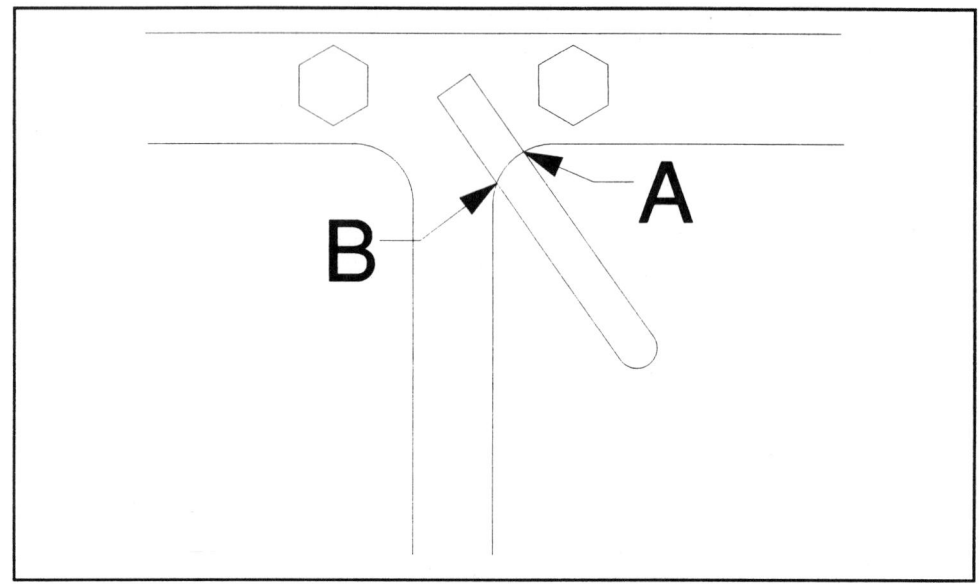

Figure 6.33 Select the intersections of the arc and the faucet.

Your display should look like Figure 6.34.

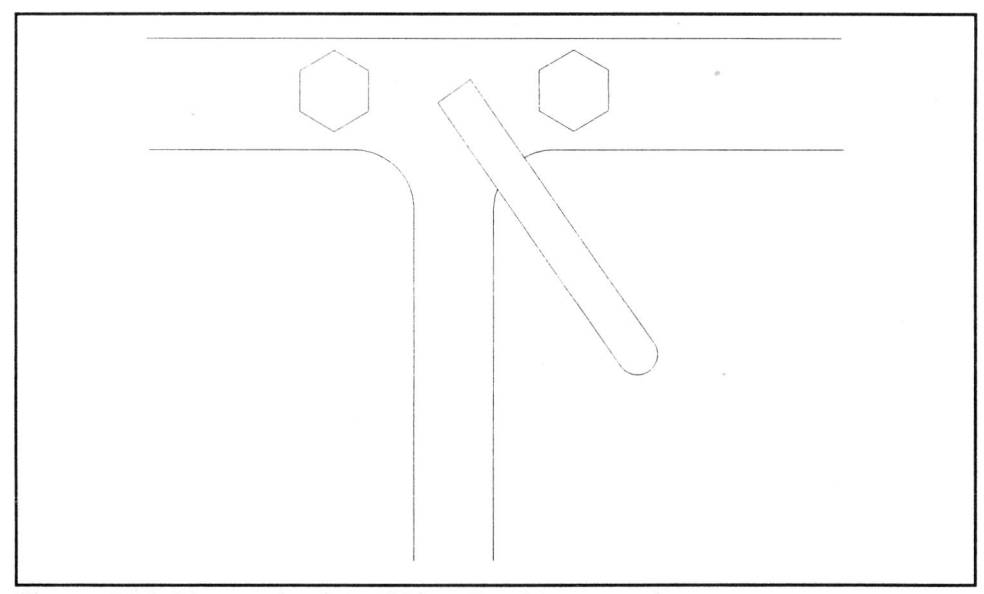

Figure 6.34 The result of the Object Break command.

Type: ZA (Zoom All) to view the entire drawing

This completes the modifications to your kitchen layout. Your drawing should look like Figure 6.35. Save your drawing with the SA (Save) command. You will need this

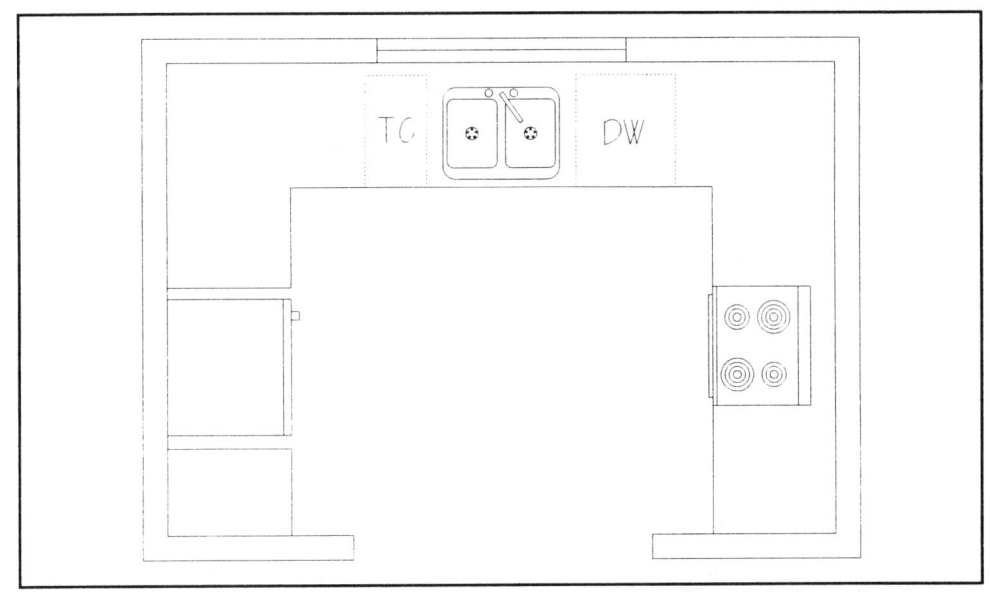

Figure 6.35 The final drawing of the Kitchen Layout Tutorial, Part II.

drawing for Part III of the Kitchen Layout tutorial, found at the end of the next chapter.

CHAPTER SUMMARY

In this chapter, you learned to use commands that ensure your drawings are accurate and clean. With SNAPS and TRIMS in your tool box of CADD 6 commands, operations that may have been complex and time-consuming are now fast and easy.

Snaps let you exactly select points in order to place and connect objects with complete accuracy. Trims are used to trim and extend objects to exact points, as well as insert fillets and chamfers on parts.

SAMPLE EXERCISES

Use the commands you have learned thus far to complete the following sample exercises. Use the dimensions shown to draw the parts to full-scale. Do not try to draw in the dimensions, unless you want to skip ahead to Chapter 11, for more instructions.

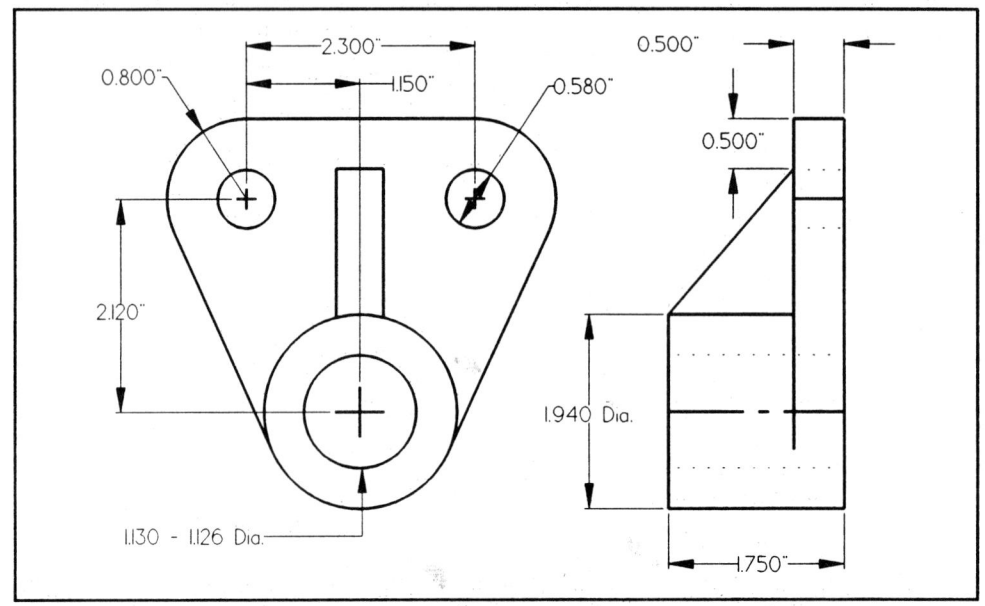

Figure 6.36 Sample exercise for the SNAPS and TRIMS commands.

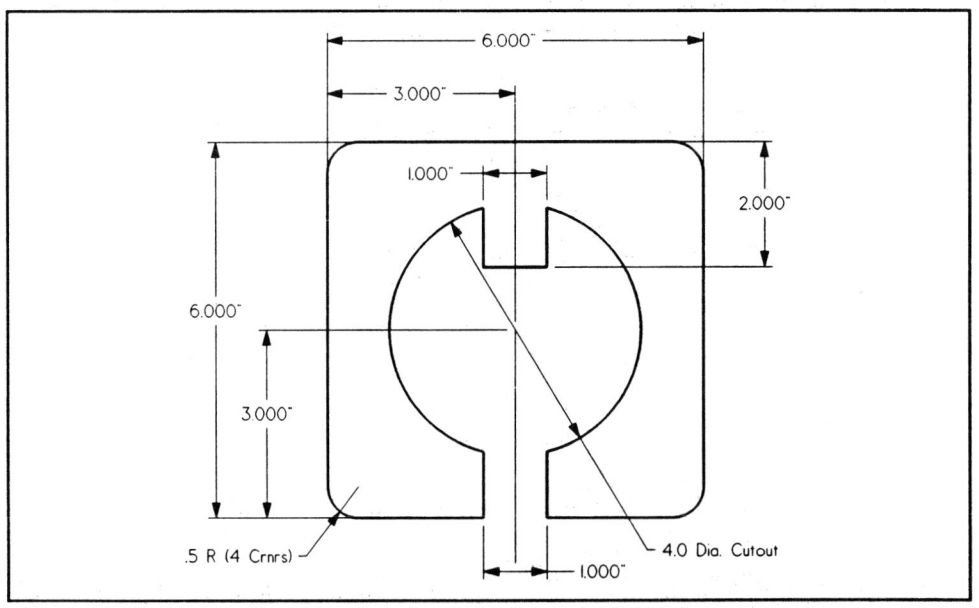

Figure 6.37 Sample exercise for the SNAPS and TRIMS commands.

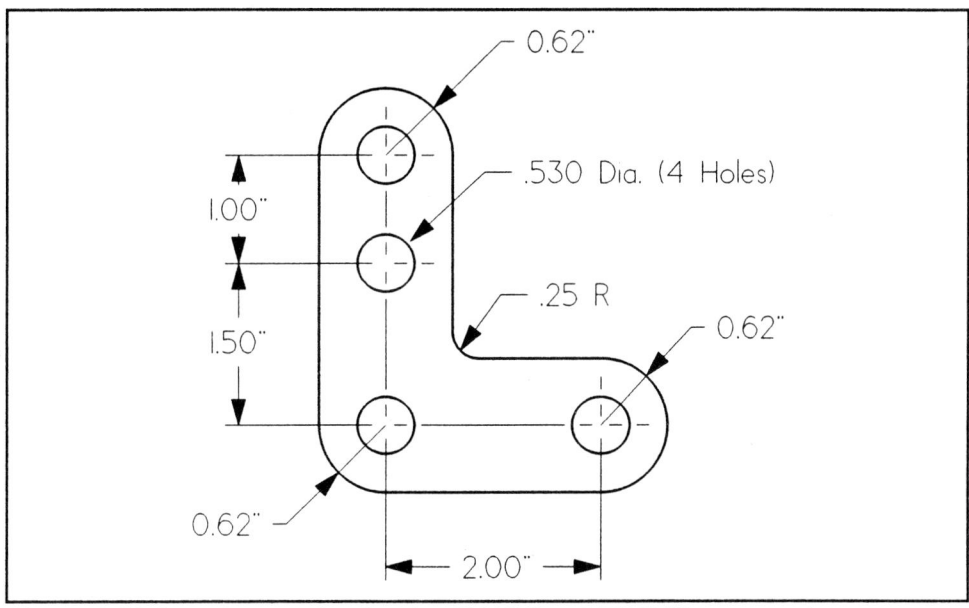

Figure 6.38 Sample exercise for the SNAPS and TRIMS commands.

CHAPTER
7

Viewing Your Drawing

USING THE ZOOM AND DISPLAY COMMANDS

The commands discussed in this section can be found under the ZOOMS and DISPLAY menus. The ZOOM commands offer a variety of commands used to control the amount of drawing displayed on your screen at any given time. In CADD 6, you can use ZOOM commands to clearly display the most detailed parts of a drawing or zoom-back until it's only a dot on your screen. With zooms, you can even control the exact scale in which the drawing appears on your display. You have already had a lot of practice using Zooms in the kitchen drawing tutorials.

The DISPLAY commands give you control over the visual features associated with CADD 6. This includes such items as coordinate displays, line color, type, and width, as well as construction and reference points. Essentially, the DISPLAY commands are used to configure the visual part of your CADD 6 program.

ZOOMS

Zoom All (ZA)
Zoom Window (ZW)
Zoom In (ZI)
Zoom Out (ZO)
Pan (PA)
Zoom Previous (ZP)

Multiview (VP)
Multiview Settings (VS)

Redraw (RD)
Backwards Redraw (BR)
Redraw Window (WD)
Zoom Limits (ZL)
Zoom Value (ZM)

The commands Zoom View (ZV), Name View (NV), and Delete Named View (NX) are found on the ZOOMS menu, but are covered in Chapter 12 since they are used to organize your drawing data.

The commands on the ZOOMS menu change how a drawing is displayed, similar to a zoom lens on a camera. These commands enlarge or reduce the size of your drawing as it is displayed on-screen. The dimensions of your drawing, however, are not changed. The Zoom Out (ZO) command, for example, makes objects look smaller relative to the size of the screen, but a 2-foot line still measures 2 feet long, regardless of how you zoom.

Zoom All (ZA)

Zoom All (ZA) re-sizes your entire drawing (up or down) to fill the screen. Again, note that you are not changing the dimensions or scale of objects in the drawing, but rather the way your drawing is displayed. To select this command, use the command code ZA and then press Enter. A prompt indicates that the program is checking the size. Then the drawing is redrawn, and everything is displayed in the new size.

Zoom Window (ZW)

The Zoom Window (ZW) command is similar to using a magnifying glass. This command allows you to enlarge a specific area of a drawing. To select Zoom Window (ZW), use the command code ZW. You will be prompted to enclose the area to zoom with a window. Whatever is enclosed by the window is zoomed to fill the entire drawing screen. The larger the zoom window, the less the increase in magnification, and vice versa. (See Figures 7.1 and 7.2.)

Zoom In (ZI)

As the name implies, Zoom In (ZI) moves in on the drawing display, making objects appear larger on-screen. To select this command, use the command code ZI. Place the cursor at the center-point of the portion you want displayed after the drawing is enlarged. Then click or press Enter. Zoom In (ZI) can be repeated. Repeat this command until you see only a small, magnified portion of your drawing. Zoom In (ZI) doubles the drawing size relative to the screen each time the command is invoked.

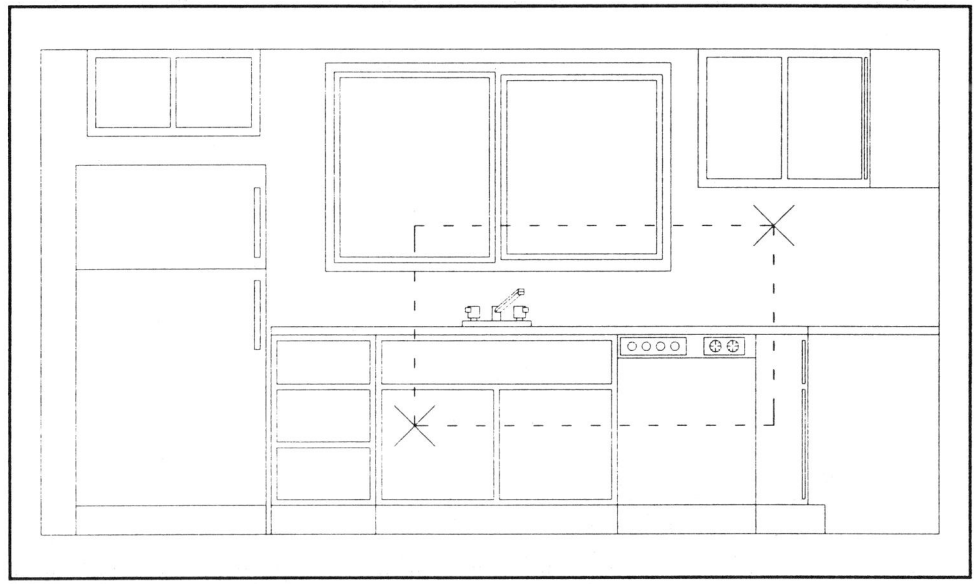

Figure 7.1 Selecting an area with Zoom Window.

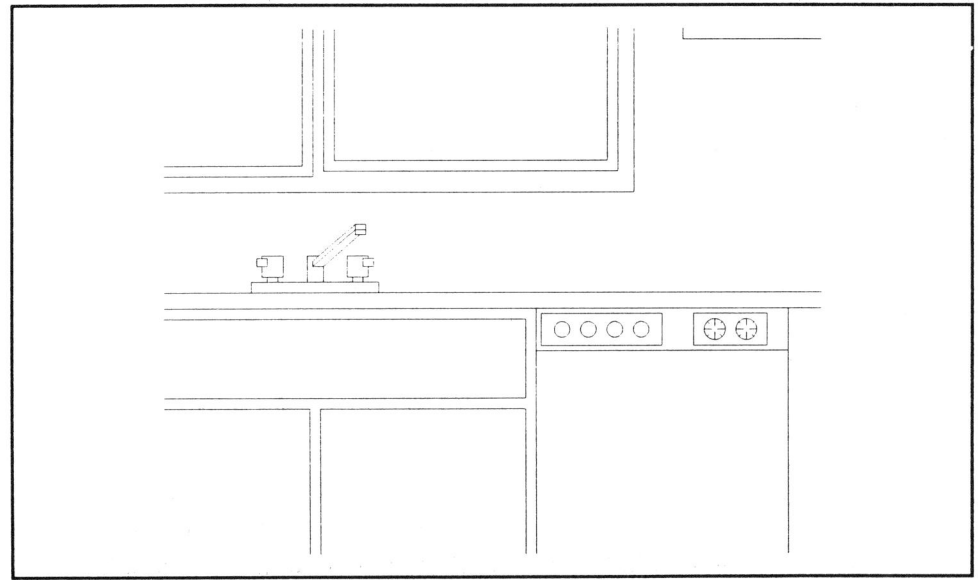

Figure 7.2 The result of Zoom Window.

Zoom Out (ZO)

Select Zoom Out (ZO), and place the cursor at the center-point of the portion you want displayed after the drawing is reduced. Then click or press Enter. The drawing is re-displayed in a smaller format. If you want, you can continue to reduce the drawing by repeating the command. Zoom Out (ZO) halves the drawing size relative to the screen each time the command is invoked.

Pan (PA)

You can use the Pan (PA) command to move your drawing around on-screen. Suppose, for example, that you have a drawing printed on a very long piece of paper, and you can look at only one portion of it at a time. Using the Pan (PA) command is like picking up the drawing and sliding it over (a maximum of one screen width) to view another section. This command is particularly useful when you have zoomed-up on a particular section, and you need to move the drawing to view a small portion in another section. To select the command, use the command code PA. Then select the center-point of the location you want to see after the command is invoked. Press Enter, and the center-point you have picked will be re-displayed at the center of the screen. The zoom factor of your current screen remains constant while you're using the Pan (PA) command.

Zoom Previous (ZP)

The Zoom Previous (ZP) command brings up the view you were working with before the current view was selected. Suppose, for example, that you have a detailed area of the drawing zoomed-up on the screen. Then you execute Zoom All (ZA) to see the entire drawing. If you next execute the Zoom Previous command by entering the command code ZP, the screen display switches back to the zoomed-up, previous view.

Multiview (VP)

With the Multiview (VP) command, you can see several views of your drawing simultaneously. There are twelve different viewport variations, the first selection being the whole, undivided screen. The last selection divides the screen into six equal viewports. There are also multiple variations of two, three, four, and five viewports. Each viewport can have a different view of the drawing, whether it's of a different drawing section, zoom, layer, or any combination of these.

You can change viewport configurations anytime. Type VP to turn on the display of viewport configurations. Enter the selected number by keyboard entry, or choose it from the screen with your pointing device. If there are any objects on the screen when a new viewport configuration is selected, the full extent of the drawing is displayed in each viewport. It would look the same if you executed Zoom All (ZA) in each viewport.

To change the zoom of a viewport, just move your cursor on the viewport to change, and use the zoom commands as you normally would. None of the other viewports are affected. Move the cursor to the viewport you wish to add to or modify. As changes are made, each viewport is instantly updated.

You can start a command in one viewport, such as drawing a line or circle, and move to another viewport to finish it. Rubberbanding only works in the current viewport, so you won't see the object being created or modified in any but the current viewport until the task is completed. As you move to different viewports during an operation, dragging or rubberbanding moves with you.

Multiview Settings (VS)

When Multiview Settings (VS) is selected, you will be prompted with three options: Multiple views, Active view, and Layer management. The following is an explanation of these options.

Multiple views. Select the Multiple views option to toggle between a single viewport (the whole screen) and the previously selected viewport. If this toggle is ON, the Active view and Layer management options are displayed. If it is OFF, then only the Multiple views option is displayed. If Multiple views are OFF, you have no need for the other two options.

Active view. The Active view option is a toggle command, and can also be selected by entering the command AV (Active View). Active view lets you single-out one viewport in a multiple viewport configuration. When turning Active view on, you are prompted to pick the Active view with your cursor. The chosen viewport's boundary is highlighted to distinguish it from the others. The ZOOM commands ZL, ZP, ZV, ZA, and Redraw (RD) will only affect the Active view when one of these commands is executed (even if the cursor is in another viewport).

If the TAB key is pressed, the Active view moves to the next viewport in a clockwise direction. The Active view changes every time the TAB key is pressed.

Layer management. The Layer management option lets you select between "viewport," and "global." The following is a list of different Layer management possibilities.

1. If "viewport" is selected and Active view is ON, the Layer Display (YD) and Layer Hide (YH) commands only work within the Active viewport.
2. If "viewport" is selected and Active view is OFF, you are prompted for the viewport Layer Display (YD) and Layer Hide (YH) affects.
3. If "global" is selected, YH and YD affects all of the viewports. It doesn't matter whether Active view is ON or OFF.
4. If Multiple views is ON, and Active view is OFF, then the ZOOM commands ZL, ZP, ZV, ZA, and Redraw (RD) prompt you for the viewport to change, or you can press Enter to perform the operation on all the viewports simultaneously.

Redraw (RD)

Redraw (RD) is not a zoom. It is used anytime you want to refresh the screen image. Sometimes CADD 6 leaves construction points on the screen, or otherwise does not clearly update the drawing display. Suppose, for example, you have made many drawing changes and you are not certain that your screen display has captured all the work you have done. You can use Redraw (RD) to clean up the screen and make sure that all changes were executed properly.

Backwards Redraw (BR)

Backwards Redraw (BR) is a toggle command that causes screen redraws to be executed, starting with the most recent entity drawn and working toward the first. This is the opposite order in which drawings are normally redrawn. To use this command, type the command code BR. A prompt tells you whether the command is turned ON or OFF. Repeat the command code to toggle it again.

If you are working on a large drawing, you may need to redraw many times while editing. With Backwards Redraw (BR) turned ON, you can stop the redraw as soon as enough of the drawing is redrawn. (Remember that you can interrupt the redraw process at any time by pressing any key.) You save time by not having to redraw the entire drawing each time. You only have to redraw the area you are currently working on, not everything that was drawn earlier.

Redraw Window (WD)

The Redraw Window (WD) command functions just like the Redraw (RD) command, but only redraws what is enclosed by a selection window. This command can save you time if you have a large drawing. With the Redraw Window (WD) command, you can refresh the particular area you are currently working in instead of refreshing the entire drawing. To execute this command, type WD and place a window around the drawing area to refresh.

Zoom Limits (ZL)

You can use Zoom Limits (ZL) to display the extent of the drawing limits that were specified earlier with the Limits (LS) command. Suppose, for example, that you set the drawing limits for a 100-foot area and then draw a 25-foot room that is zoomed-up on-screen. When you use the Zoom Limits (ZL) command, the drawing is redrawn so that the room is displayed relative to the 100-foot limits.

Zoom Value (ZM)

With Zoom Value (ZM), you specify a numerical value that causes the drawing to be displayed at that proportion of its actual size. To select Zoom Value (ZM), use the command code ZM. Respond to the prompt by selecting a zoom factor and then press Enter. Answer the next prompt by choosing the point that you want to be the new center of the screen. To enlarge an object to twice its size, for example, you need to specify a zoom value of 0.5. To reduce that object to half its size, you must specify a zoom value of 2. Entering whole-number values reduces an object's size, and entering decimal values enlarges an object's size. (See Figures 7.3 and 7.4.)

Chapter 7: Viewing Your Drawing ■ 7-7

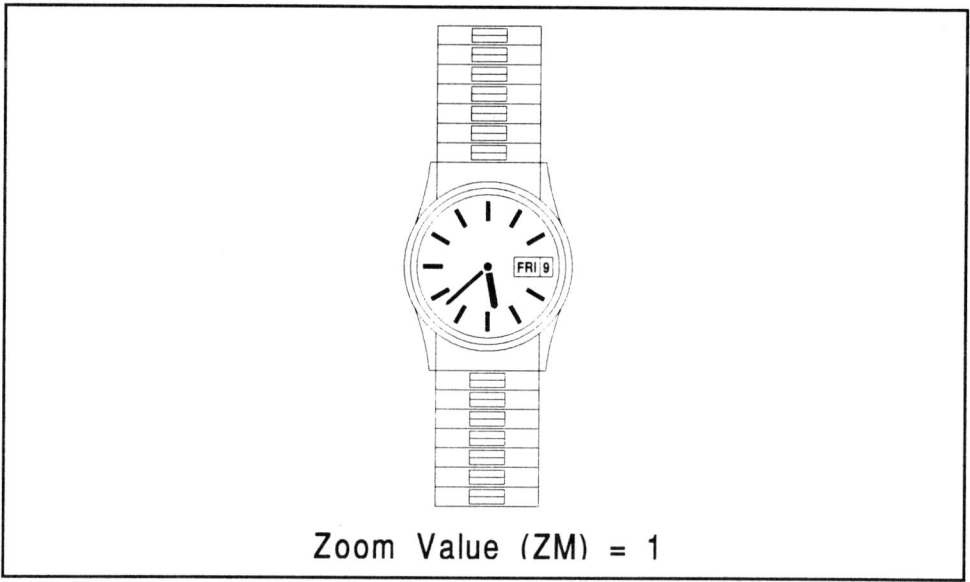

Figure 7.3 Setting Zoom Value to 1.

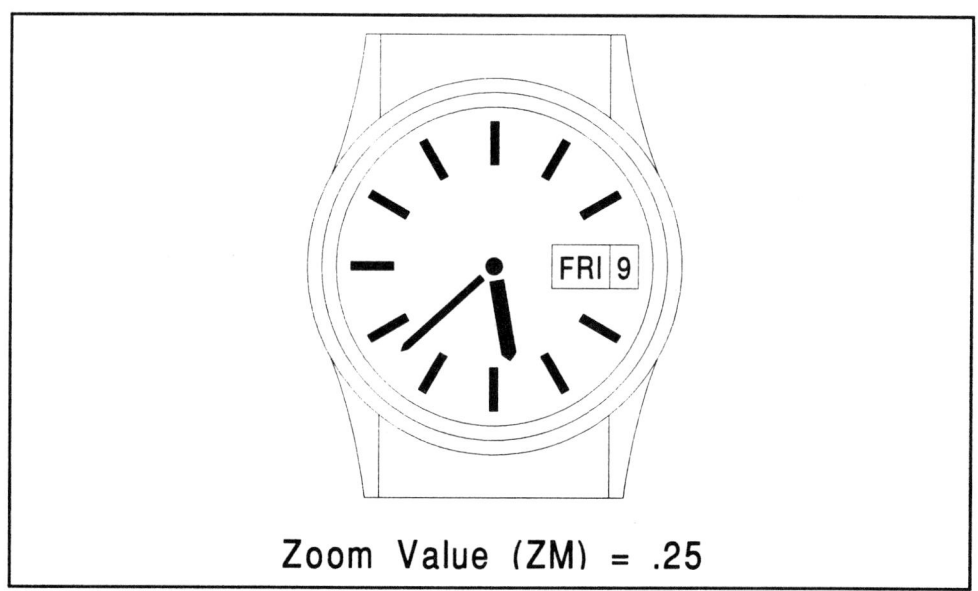

Figure 7.4 Setting Zoom Value to .25.

These values appear to be the opposite of the effect they have on the object's size. Think of the zoom value as a proportion, or ratio, of the object's actual size to its displayed size. The formula for Zoom Value (ZM) is: ZM = 1:n. For example:

If n = 0.5 then ZM = 2
1:0.5 = 1/0.5 = 1/(1/2) = 2

Negative zoom values act both absolutely and inversely when applied to the Zoom Value (ZM) command. A zoom value of -2, for example, is the same as a zoom value of 0.5.

DISPLAY

Line Color (LC)
Line Type (LT)
Line Width (LW)
Line Scale (LZ)
Color Set (CS)

Units (UN)
Display Coordinate (DC)
Numeric Format (NF)
Screen Display (DI)
Reference Points (PR)
Construction Points (PC)
Standard Points (PS)

Object Drag (OD)
Rubberbanding (RB)
Fast Redraw (FA)
Highlight (HI)

Line Color (LC)

With the Line Color (LC) command, you can select the color of all basic entities to be added to your drawing. This command applies to entities drawn *after* the color is selected, not to anything currently displayed. This command is affected by the type of video card you have in your system. If your graphic card supports it, you can select from any of 256 colors. (Color 0 is black. It doesn't show up on the black background, but it can be selected.) Begin this command with the command code LC. The prompt shows the current color setting and asks you to select a new one. If you enter a new color number and press Enter, the color is changed. You also can choose colors from the video menu by highlighting a particular color bar and selecting the option with the second mouse button.

Line Type (LT)

Choose a solid, dashed, or dotted line for a drawing with the Line Type (LT) command. (See Figure 7.5.) When you type LT, the basic patterns available are displayed on the sidebar menu with numbers 0 through 9, but you can actually select Line Types from 0 to 255.

Line Types 0, 10, 20, and so on, up to 250 are always continuous (solid). Types 1 through 9 are scaled to the screen. This means that no matter how you zoom or change

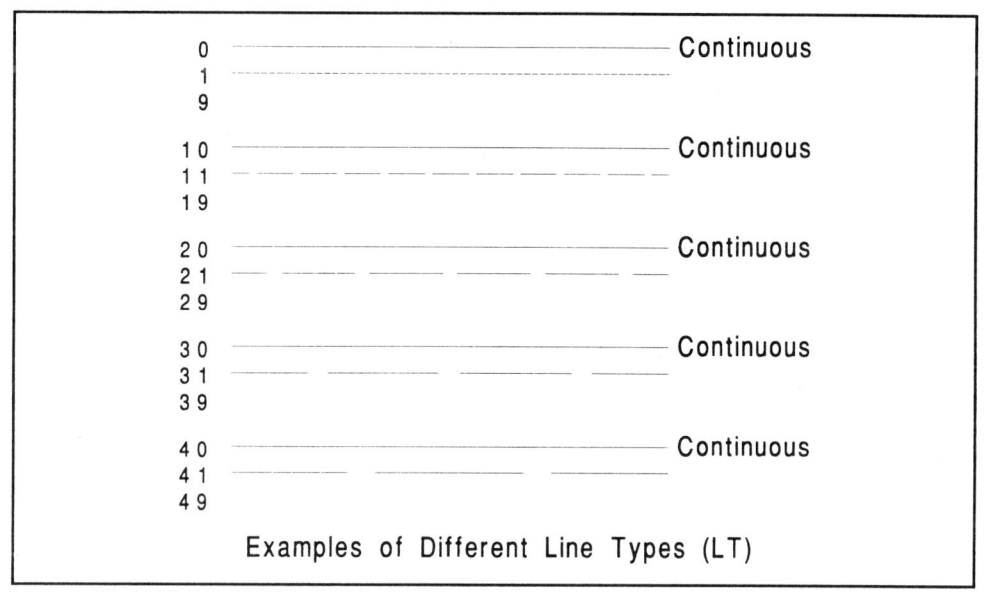

Figure 7.5 Using different line types.

the way the drawing is displayed, the dashes appear to have the same length.

The basic line type patterns are repeated with every 10 Line Types, as shown in Figure 7.5. Type 11 is the same pattern as type 1, type 21, type 31, and so on. The difference is in the length of the repeating pattern. The dashes in Line Type 21 are twice as long as those in type 11. Similarly, the dashes in Line Type 31 are three times the size.

Line Scale (LZ)

Line Types 11 to 255 are affected by the value for Line Scale. The Line Scale (LZ) command changes the distance between the patterns of dots and dashes for all noncontinuous Line Types from 11 to 255. LZ cannot be set for individual lines but affects every line in the entire drawing. The value set for the Line Scale determines the interval on which the Line Type pattern repeats. A Line Scale of 1 causes the patterns to be repeated every 1 unit (inch or centimeter, for example). A Line Scale of 0.25 results in a repetition every 1/4 inch. Figure 7.6 gives examples of the effect of changing the Line Scale.

To use this command, enter the command code LZ, and enter a multiplier at the prompt. Redraw the drawing to see the effect on existing lines.

Line Width (LW)

To set the width of the lines in a drawing, use the Line Width (LW) command. Use the command code LW and answer the prompt with a number between 0 (thinnest) and 255 (widest), or select a Line Width from the sidebar menu. (See Figure 7.7.)

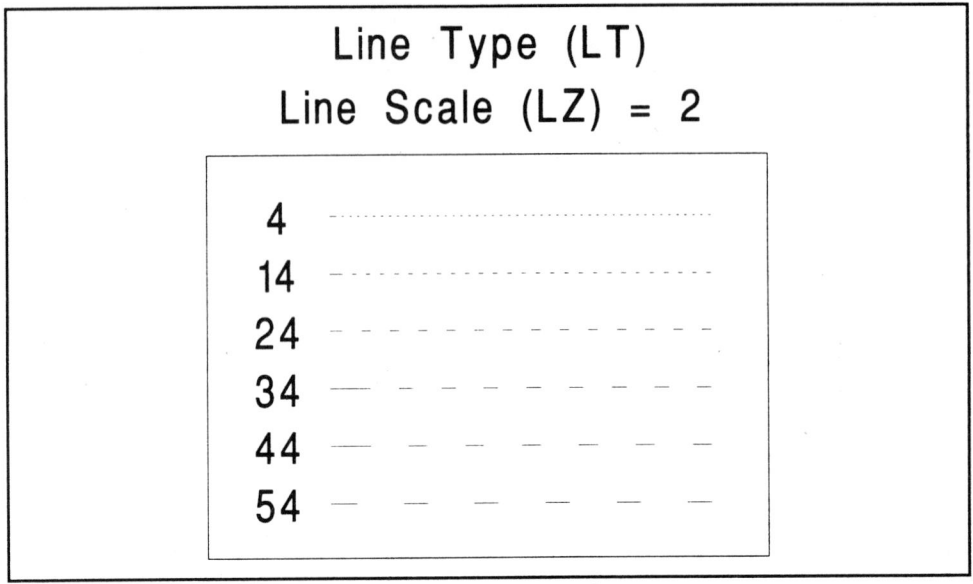

Figure 7.6 Combining Line Type with Line Scale.

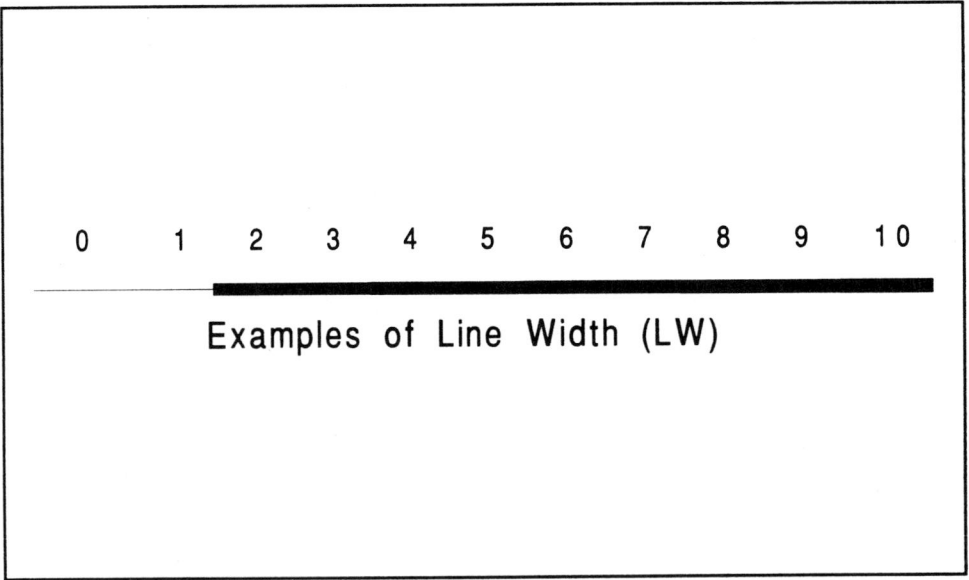

Figure 7.7 Adjusting the Line Width.

Color Settings (CS)

The Color Settings (CS) command contains six object types for which to set the color: Lines, Text, Dimensions, Attributes, Hatches, and Fills. This command is the "one stop shopping" color selection center for all on-screen entities.

For example, to establish a color for new text entities:

Type: CS (for Color Settings)
Type: T (for Text) or select it from the command line sub-menu
Click to select a color from the sidebar menu.

All new text entities placed in the drawing will be drawn with the new color.

Units (UN)

The Units (UN) command is nested with a selection of six different unit types. This selection includes settings for: Inches, Feet/Inches, Feet, Millimeters, Centimeters, and Meters. Depending on what units your drawing is in, you can use this command to select the current drawing units. These units will appear in the coordinate display and in any dimensions created using the programs auto-dimensioning.

> **TIP:** It is recommended that you do not mix English and Metric units. If you have configured units in your CADD 6.0 database to English units, set your display units to English as well. The same recommendation applies to Metric units.

Display Coordinates (DC)

The Display Coordinates (DC) command is nested with four coordinate display settings options: Coordinates, Absolute, Relative, and Basepoint. These settings can be selected by entering the highlighted letter of the selection (usually the first letter), or clicking on the selection with your pointing device. The following is an explanation of these settings:

Coordinates. The Coordinates selection lets you change your coordinate display to show X, Y coordinates, or polar coordinates. The polar coordinates display is a distance and angle instead of a display of X- axis and Y- axis distances.

Absolute. The Absolute setting is a toggle. If it's ON, the coordinates display the cursor's position relative to the drawing's origin point. This setting, when ON, directly reflects the same values entered when in the MO (Manual Entry Offset Origin) mode. If you are using the MO mode, it is recommended that you also set Absolute to ON.

Relative. The Relative setting is a toggle. If it's ON, the coordinates display the cursor's position relative to the last position selected on-screen. This setting, when ON, directly reflects the same values entered when in the MR (Manual Entry Offset Relative) mode. If you are using the MR mode, it is recommended that you also set Relative to ON.

Basepoint. The Basepoint setting is a toggle. If it's ON, the coordinates display the cursor's position relative to the user-set basepoint. This setting, when ON, directly reflects the same values entered when in the MB (Manual Entry Offset Basepoint) mode. If you are using the MB mode, you should definitely set Basepoint to ON.

> **TIP:** If either the Absolute, Relative, or Basepoint settings are ON, the other two are automatically shut OFF.

Numeric Display Format (NF)

The Numeric Display Format (NF) command is nested with six numeric format settings. They are: Angular, Linear, Decimal value, Fractional value, leading Zeros, and Show units.

> **TIP:** These settings do not affect the accuracy of the values you enter into CADD 6, they are simply available for the user's convenience. They do however, affect the format of any values calculated with the dimensioning features. For example, if your numeric display is set to show fractions, then any dimensioning is also in fractions.

Angular. With the Angular selection, you can toggle between Degrees, and Deg:Min:Sec. This is evident if Polar coordinates is ON. Polar coordinates are turned ON with the Display Coordinates (DC) command.

Linear. If your Display Coordinates (DC) are set to X,Y coordinates, you can use the Linear selection to toggle the linear format between Decimal or Fractions.

Decimal value. The Decimal value setting only appears if the Linear selection is set to decimal. The Decimal value can be set to a value from 0 to 6. If it is set to 3, then your display shows all values with 3 places to the right of the decimal point.

Fractional value. The Fractional value setting only appears if the Linear selection is set to decimal. The Fractional value setting is used to set the value of the denominator in a fractional display. You are given a selection of: (2,4,8,16,32,64) If you set this value to 2, the most accurate numeric display would be to the half inch. As you move your cursor on the screen, you would see the numeric display changing by halves. For greater display accuracy, increase the size of the denominator setting.

leading Zeros. The leading Zeros selection toggles the leading Zeros display ON or OFF. This affects numbers between 1 and -1. When leading Zeros is displayed, you would have a display that looks like this:

X 0.203 Y 0.538

When leading Zeros is not displayed, your numeric display looks like this:

X .203 Y .538

Show units. The Show units selection is a toggle which controls whether units are displayed in the coordinate display at the top of the screen. If Show units is set to ON, units are displayed. If Show units is set to OFF, the units are not displayed.

Display Settings (DI)

The Display Settings (DI) command contains five display settings options; Display color, Cursor color, cursor SiZe, Status line, and Tandem cursor. These settings can be selected by entering the highlighted letter of the selection (usually the first letter), or clicking on the selection with your mouse. The following is an explanation of these settings:

Display color. The Display color selection lets you set the color of the display. The display includes the status line, menu, and coordinate display. These colors cannot be changed individually.

Cursor color. This selection lets you change the color of the cursor.

cursor siZe. Cursor siZe allows you to change the size of the cursor displayed on the screen. The upper value displayed depends on the current screen resolution of your system. The larger the value you select, the larger the cursor becomes. At the largest value, the cursor crosshair stretches across the entire screen.

> **TIP:** A setting of 0 does not turn OFF the cursor display. Rather, a setting of 0 gives you the maximum cursor size.

Status line. Use the Status line toggle selection to turn ON the status line, displayed below the command line at the bottom of the screen. The status line displays the drawing name, current layer, zoom factor, coordinate entry mode, and other status information. This command is a toggle, so repeating it turns the status line ON or OFF. Turning the status line OFF does not give you any more drawing room on your screen. (Turning your video menu OFF with the VM command will give you move drawing space.)

Tandem cursor. The Tandem cursor option toggles the cursor display between being visible in both the drawing area and the video menu area, or in just one at a time.

If ON, you will see the cursor on the drawing screen and the menu highlight bar in the video menu at the same time. You may find the flash of the menu highlight bar distracting while working within the drawing area. In this mode, the first button on your mouse is for clicking points within the drawing area, and the second button is for clicking items from the menu area.

If OFF, the cursor is visible while working within the drawing area, and the menu highlight bar becomes visible if the cursor is moved into the video menu area. This may be less distracting, but you always have to move from your drawing to the video menu area if you want to select a command from the menu. With the single cursor, you only have to select the first button on your pointing device to click on items in either the drawing area or the menu area.

Reference Points (PR)
The Reference Points (PR) command is a toggle that turns ON or OFF the display of the reference points within an object. To turn the reference points ON or OFF, use the command code PR, and then use the Redraw (RD) command to reset your display. This also turns the drawing origin point ON or OFF.

Construction Points (PC)
The Construction Points can be turned on by using the command code PC. PC is also a toggle command. With this option turned ON, any time you draw an object, an X appears at the points used to construct the object (the points where the object starts, takes new directions, and ends).

Standard Points (PS)
Just as with reference points and construction points, you can toggle ON or OFF the display of points drawn with the Standard Points (PS) command. Often you may use Standard Points as your own reference or locator points, so you don't want them to show up on the final drawing. To turn OFF the display of standard points, enter the command code PS. Use PS again to toggle this display back ON. You do not actually see any change on the screen until the drawing is redrawn.

Object Drag (OD)
When the Object Drag (OD) toggle is ON, objects being moved, or components being placed are displayed as a ghost image and are dynamically moved on screen in conjunction with the cursor. During component placement, the component's rotation and scale values can be changed dynamically (on-the-fly). If Object Drag (OD) is ON,

you are able to see this change before the component is placed. This gives you a chance to make the proper scale and rotation adjustments before committing the component to the drawing.

> **TIP:** If you are manipulating complicated or large amounts of objects that take a long time to drag, you may want Object Drag (OD) turned OFF. This may also help if you have a slower computer.

Rubberband (RB)

Rubberband (RB) is a toggle command that turns ON or OFF a feature that drags a line from one point to another on-screen when you draw. To stop the placement of the rubberbanding line that drags behind your cursor, press Esc. To turn OFF the Rubberband (RB) feature completely, use the command code RB. Rubberbanding is a helpful visual aid while you are drawing. It is recommended that you leave this command turned ON, especially when first learning CADD 6.

Fast Redraw (FA)

The Fast Redraw (FA) command contains seven options to speed-up the screen regeneration time. These settings include: fast Text, fast Arcs, disabling line wiDths and line types, Fill display, Hatch display, and Layer updates. Generally, these features can be temporarily turned OFF during drawing creation to speed-up redraw times.

Each one of these features, when ON, adds a little more time to the regeneration (refresh) speed of CADD 6. Turning these items ON or OFF, or changing their display complexity is not permanent, and can be reversed any time during the drawing process. To see the changes made by the variable settings, the screen must initially be redrawn or refreshed. Any objects drawn later are affected by the Fast Redraw (FA) settings.

fast Text. Fast Text, when set to ON, displays any text placed with the Text Place (TP) command as Standard Points (PO). (See Figure 7.8.) Any text placed with the Text Line (TL) command will be displayed as a line if fast Text is toggled ON. Standard points and lines redraw much faster than actual text characters, especially text created with a lot of detail such as the Chancery font. Fast Text can be viewed in its normal state without turning the fast Text toggle OFF, using the View Fast Text (TV) command found in the UTILITIES menu. This command, along with fast Text is discussed further in Chapter 14.

fast Arcs and arc Sides. The fast Arcs selection is a toggle that works in conjunction with the arc Sides command. It allows you to set the number of sides used to display arcs as a value between 3 and 12. If you set the arc Sides to 3, any arcs or circles will be displayed with 3 sides. The circles will be displayed as triangles. It's easier and

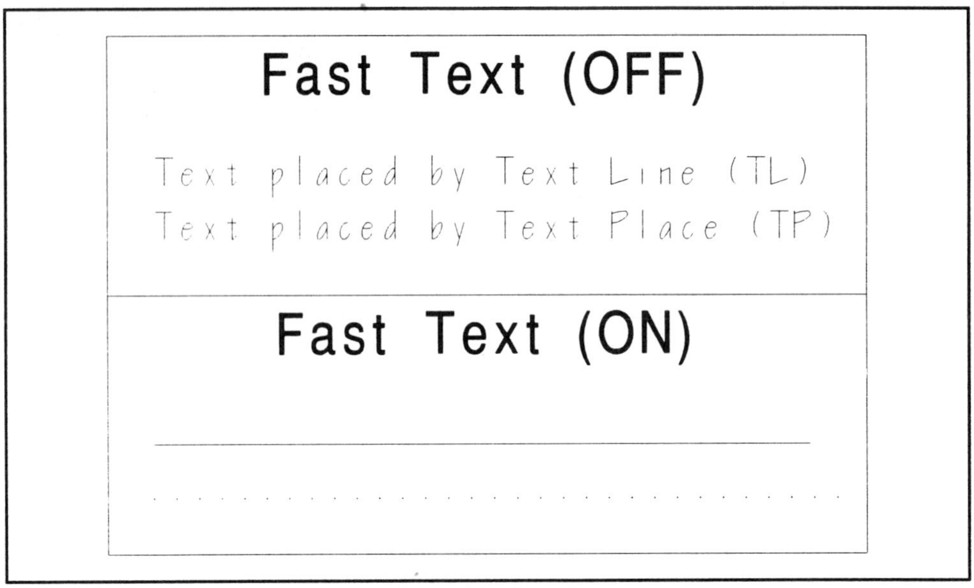

```
┌─────────────────────────────────────────────┐
│                                             │
│          Fast Text (OFF)                    │
│                                             │
│   Text placed by Text Line (TL)             │
│   Text placed by Text Place (TP)            │
│                                             │
├─────────────────────────────────────────────┤
│                                             │
│          Fast Text (ON)                     │
│                                             │
│   ─────────────────────────                 │
│                                             │
│   . . . . . . . . . . . . . . . .           │
│                                             │
└─────────────────────────────────────────────┘
```

Figure 7.8 Speeding up the display with Fast Text.

faster for the program to generate straight lines on the display instead of the smooth curves of arcs and circles. This selection does not affect the display of curves or ellipses. (See Figure 7.9.)

Disable line wiDths and line types. The disable line wiDths and line types selection is a toggle. If it's ON, all line types are displayed as continuous, and all line widths are displayed as having a line width of 0.

Fills and Hatching. The Fill display and Hatch display settings are both toggles. If they're set to OFF, any fills or hatches will not be displayed when the display is redrawn or refreshed.

Layer update. When Layer update is turned OFF, layers do not redraw when selected during a Layer Display (YD) or Layer Hide (YH) command. When this option is OFF, you must refresh the screen with Redraw (RD) or a zoom command to display the newest layer display. When Layer update is ON, the YD and YH commands automatically update the Layer Display as it is changed.

Highlight (HI)

The Highlight (HI) command is a toggle used to turn CADD 6's object highlighting feature ON and OFF. If Highlight (HI) is ON, an object selected for modification changes to a dotted image on the screen. Only the EDITS commands that prompt with a selection set take advantage of the Highlight (HI) feature. This is to help you keep track of the selected items, making sure you didn't select the wrong object, or just miss the targeted object all together.

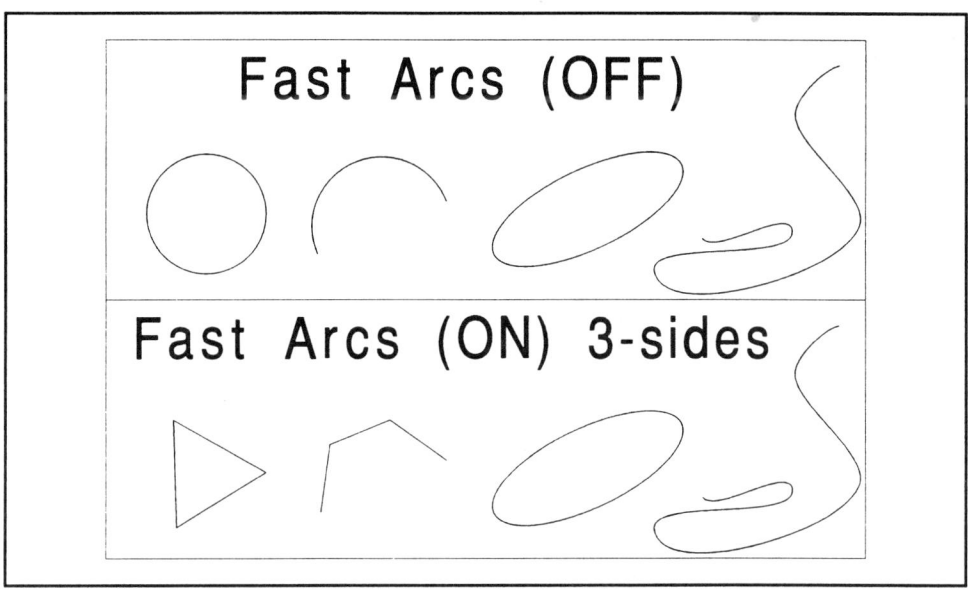

Figure 7.9 Using the Fast Arcs command.

> **TIP:** If your computer is slow, selection can be made quicker if the Highlight (HI) toggle is OFF.

CHAPTER SUMMARY

In this chapter, you reviewed different ways to view your drawing and configure the display. Without Zoom commands, drawing creation would be next to impossible in CADD 6. Only small-scale and minimum-detail drawings could be created. You will use Zoom commands often and in every project you work on in CADD 6.

To enhance your program and aid you in drawing creation, you have a multitude of display commands at your disposal. Commands are available to modify colors, numeric displays, coordinate readouts, and much more. CADD 6 also provides many features to help you speed-up the drawing process by simplifying the display of text, arcs, and circles, eliminating highlighting, and so on. Use these commands to tailor CADD 6 to suit your needs.

SAMPLE EXERCISE

Use the commands you have learned thus far to complete the following sample exercises. Use the dimensions shown to draw the parts to full-scale. Do not try to draw in the dimensions, unless you want to skip ahead to Chapter 11.

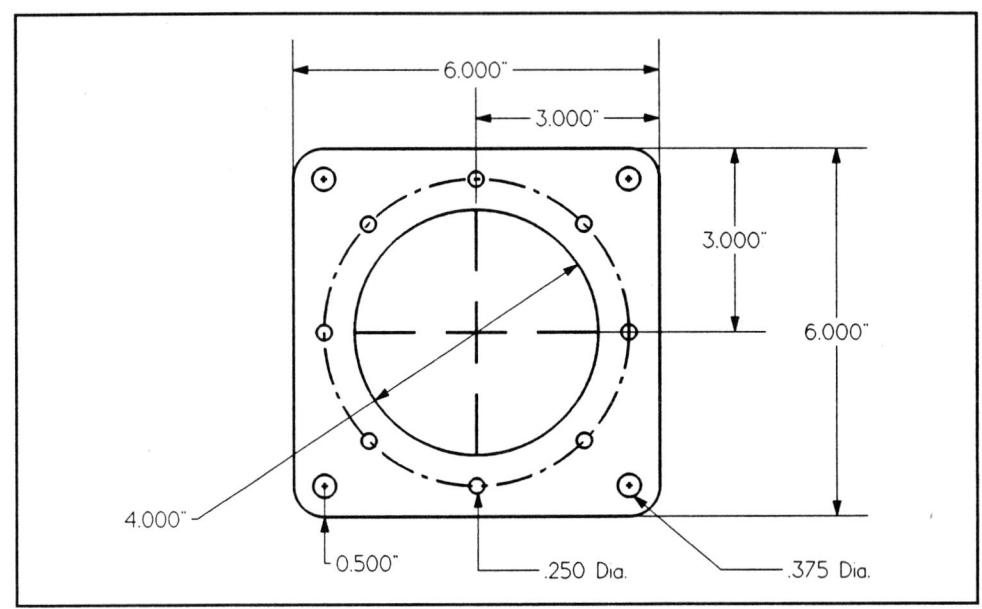

Figure 7.10 Sample exercise for the DISPLAY commands.

CHAPTER 8

Adding Text

USING THE TEXT MENU

Thus far, you have been introduced to commands for drawing objects (lines, arcs, circles, and so on), and editing drawings. Some lettering (text) was placed as part of the Quick Start tutorial in Chapter 2, but very little was discussed about text.

More than likely, you will want to add more text to your drawings in the form of notes, labels, and title block information. In this chapter, you will find information about creating and changing text in your drawings. Methods of creating, placing, changing previously placed text, and setting the appearance of text within CADD 6 are discussed as well. This chapter discusses the following text commands, all found on the TEXT menu:

TEXT

Line Place (TL)
Append (TA)
Change (TG)
Edit   (TE)

Character Place (TP)
Insert (TI)
Delete (TD)
Replace (TX)

Create Font (WT)
Text Settings (TS)

Load ASCII (LA) and Match Parameters (MH) can be found on more than one menu, including the TEXT menu, but will not be discussed in this chapter. Refer to Chapter 13 for information regarding the Load ASCII (LA) command. Match Parameters (MH) can be found in Chapter 14.

In CADD 6, there are two basic ways of entering text. Text can be entered as individual characters, or in string form. The following is an explanation of some important facts to keep in mind when deciding which type of text to enter.

Text placed in line or string form, with the Line Place (TL) command, can be automatically justified and proportionally spaced during placement. Justification and Proportion are set with the Text Settings (TS) command. Text placed in single-character form with the Character Place (TP) command must be moved, letter by letter, with the EDITS commands. Single-character text can be mirrored, while line text can not. A text line can be exploded into single-text characters and then mirrored. All single-text characters can be exploded into their component parts. The characters can then be modified like any other basic objects such as lines, arcs, circles, and curves.

A line of text is treated as a single entity in CADD 6, and can be selected by a reference point found at the placement point of the text line. If you plan to export a CADD 6 drawing into another CADD program, place text in line form. The line form transfers to other programs more reliably than individual characters.

SETTING TEXT PARAMETERS

The Text Settings (TS) command on the TEXT menu controls the features of your text. Choose from a wide selection of text characteristics and styles before you first place your text. You can change text characteristics at any time, but it affects only text entered *after* the change.

> **TIP:** If you change the font for Dimensions or Attributes, the existing Dimensions or Attributes are changed to the new font. This rule does *not* apply to the Text font. If you change the style of the Text font, the previously placed Text remains unchanged. Any text placed after the change is in the newly selected font.

Text Settings (TS)

This command is used to set the text Font (style), siZe, fIlled (if a fillable font is used), Justification, Slant, Aspect (ratio of width to height), Rotation, Color, and sPacing.

The Text Settings (TS) command is executed by typing TS. You will then be prompted with a selection set. The following is an explanation of the text settings commands.

Font. Choose and load one of the fonts included with CADD 6 by entering the command code TS and entering F. A font is a typeface, or group of characters assigned to the keys on the keyboard. They may be letters in a particular style or some other kinds of characters. There are 37 available fonts shipped with CADD 6, categorized as non-fillable, fillable, and AutoCAD-converted fonts.

Non-fillable: These fonts are made up of lines, arcs, circles, and curves (bezier and complex):

1	ARCHITEK
2	COMPLEX
3	DECO
4	ENGINEER
5	ITALICS
6	MAIN
7	SIMPLEX
8	TEXT

Fillable: These fonts are designed to visually mimic Postscript typefaces. These fonts can be set to either filled or unfilled in CADD 6:

1	BOOK
2	CHANCERY
3	COURI
4	FUTURE
5	GARAMOND
6	HELVET
7	OPTIM
8	PALATIN
9	SYMBOL
10	TIMESRMN

AutoCAD: These fonts include 19 of the 25 AutoCAD fonts, and are made up entirely of line segments with no arcs, circles, or curves:

1	CYRILLIC
2	CYRILTLC
3	GOTHICE
4	GOTHICG
5	GOTHICI
6	GREEKC

8-4 ■ Chapter 8: Adding Text

7	GREEKS
8	ITALIC
9	ITALICC
10	ITALICT
11	ROMANC
12	ROMAND
13	ROMANS
14	ROMANT
15	SCRIPTC
16	SCRIPTS
17	SYASTRO
18	SYMAP
19	SYMATH

Figure 8.1, "The Font Wheel," shows an example of each font supplied with CADD 6. The numbers on the Font Wheel correspond to the previous list of non-fillable, fillable, and AutoCAD-converted fonts. To view complete samples of each, see the figures in Appendix A of the CADD 6 Reference Guide. The simplest font included with CADD 6 is MAIN. This font is also the fastest and takes up the least amount of memory.

Your choice of font affects the amount of memory and time you need for redraws. Fancy, detailed fonts require more drawing time and memory than simpler fonts. To see this more clearly, compare the MAIN and COMPLEX fonts in your CADD 6 Reference Guide. Some people use simpler fonts for labels and dimensions, and save the more complex fonts for the title block. You will find that if you have a drawing with large amounts of text, the drawing is significantly slower to redraw if a font like COMPLEX is used. This becomes a bigger problem if you have a drawing full of filled fonts instead of un-fillable fonts. Choose fonts wisely when placing text characters with the TP command; no automatic method is available to replace letters in one font with letters from another font. If you are placing text lines, the font can be changed in the existing text lines placed on your screen.

Select Font, and type the name of the font style you want to load. You can also select a font from the compiled list of fonts which appears on the sidebar menu.

> **TIP:** To load a font, you may have to specify its correct file path (the subdirectory where the font file is located). The selected font is then loaded which, depending on the complexity of the font, may take a few seconds.

Chapter 8: Adding Text ■ 8-5

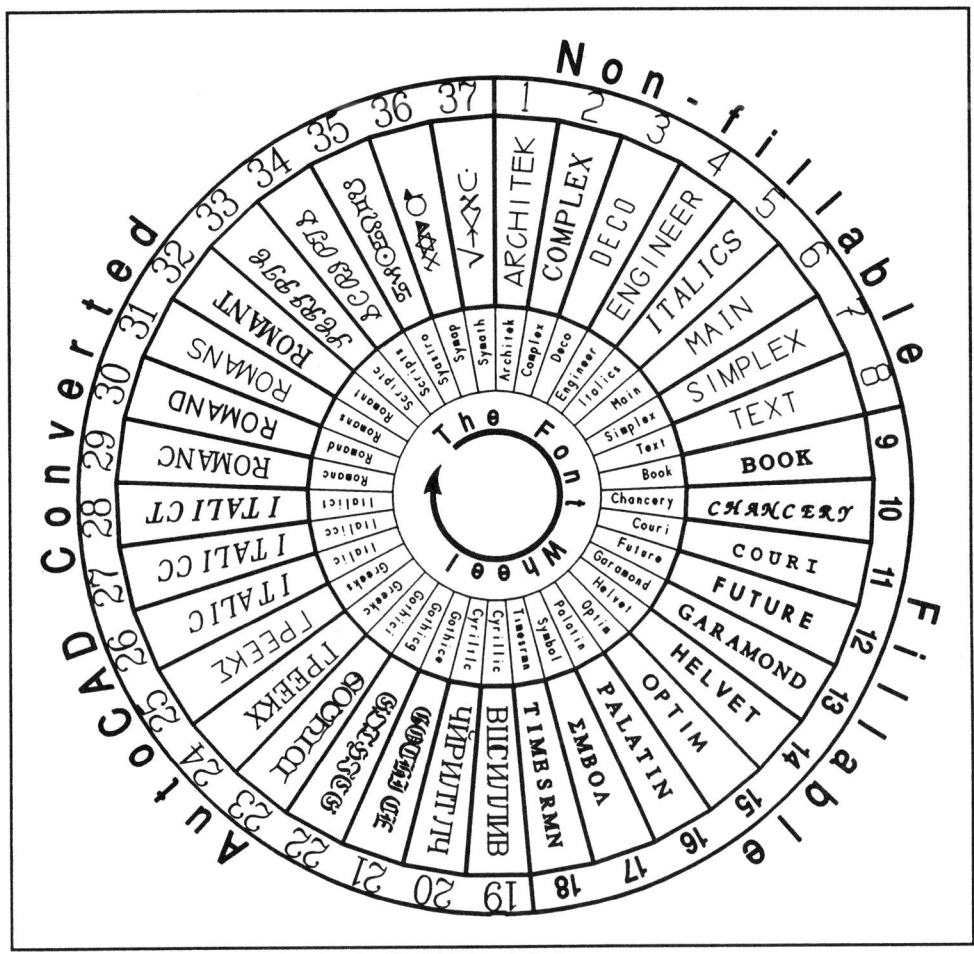

Figure 8.1 A Font Wheel of all CADD 6.0 fonts.

If you enter a font name that is not defined, you are asked whether this is a new font. Answer NO if you didn't mean to make this selection. Answer YES if you want to create a new font. Before trying to create a font, be sure to refer to the discussion of the Font Create (WT) command, described later in this chapter.

siZe. Set the height of your text with the siZe feature. Make sure that you set it appropriately for your drawing. If you are working in a 50-foot area, 1-inch high text height is barely visible. To change the text height, enter the command code TS and Z, then type in the new height and press Enter. As with other values you entered, the unit associated with the height (inches, centimeters, etc.) is the default unit unless you specify something different (by adding a foot mark ('), for example.)

fIlled. The fIlled feature is an ON/OFF toggle. When set to ON, it displays fillable fonts as filled and when set to OFF, it displays them as open. To change the fIlled feature, enter the command code TS and enter I to toggle it ON or OFF.

Justification. The Justification feature lets you set text that is aligned to the left, the right, or centered on the text insertion point. (See Figure 8.2.) The Justification feature contains three selections; Left, Center, and Right.

```
╳ = Text Start Point

              ╳Left Justification

         Center Ju╳tification

    Right Justification╳

         Justification (TSJ)
```

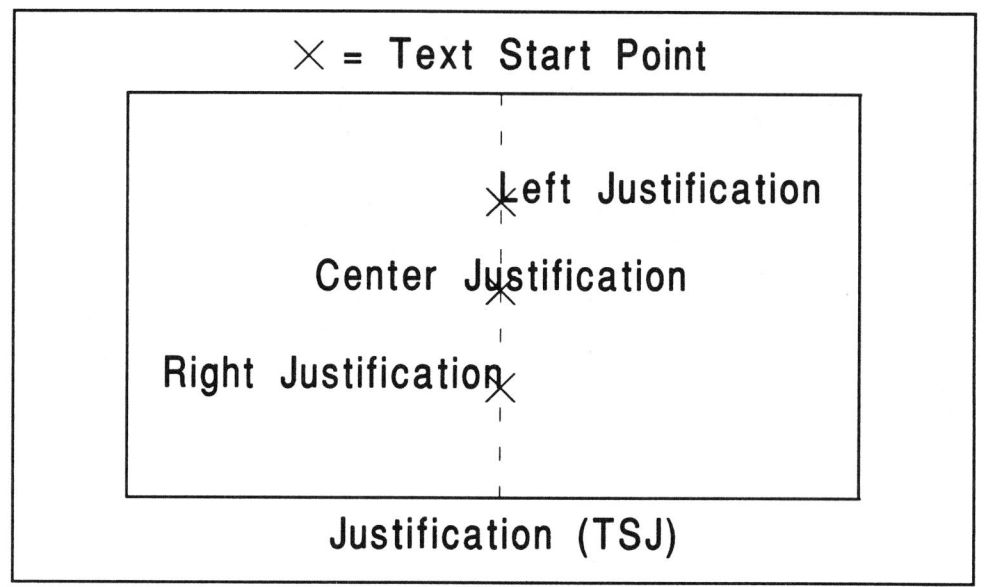

Figure 8.2 Adjusting the Text Justification with Text Settings.

Slant. The Slant feature defines how much the letters are slanted away from an imaginary vertical line running through the center of the letters. To ensure legibility, maximum slant values are 45° to the left (negative) or right (positive.) With this command, you can change any font from its standard vertical appearance (default of 0) to italic. A slant of 14° is a good moderate slant for special text. Figure 8.3 shows examples of text at a slant of 0°, 45°, and -45°.

> If you are creating isometric drawings with lines running 30 degrees from the horizontal, you can create the illusion of isometric text. Experiment by setting the Slant feature to 45° and the Rotation feature to 30°. (see Figure 8.4). These settings work on side 1. For side 2, set the slant to -45°, keeping the rotation at 30°. For side 3, set the rotation to 330° or -30°, and keep the slant set to -45°.

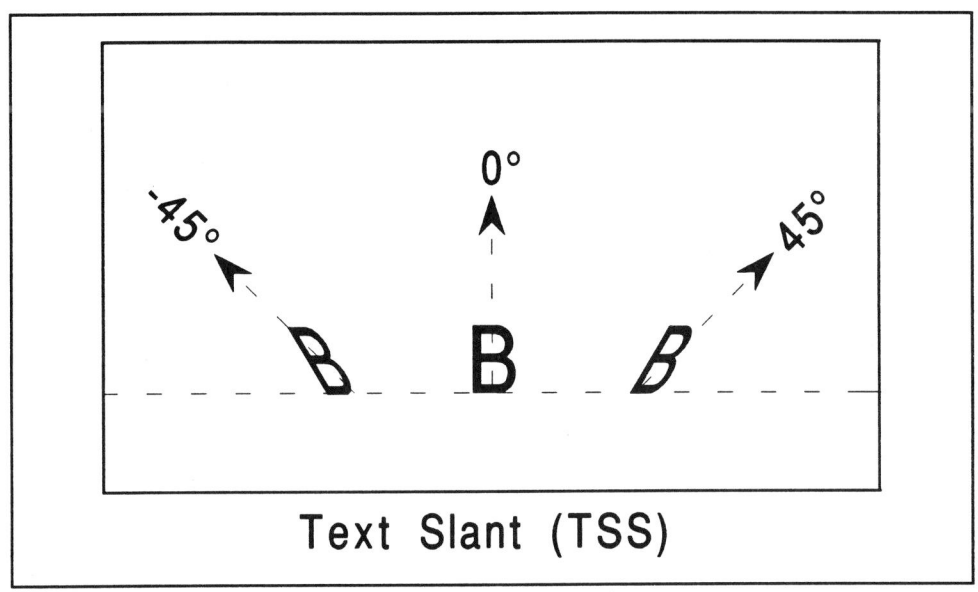

Figure 8.3 The effect of the Text Slant command.

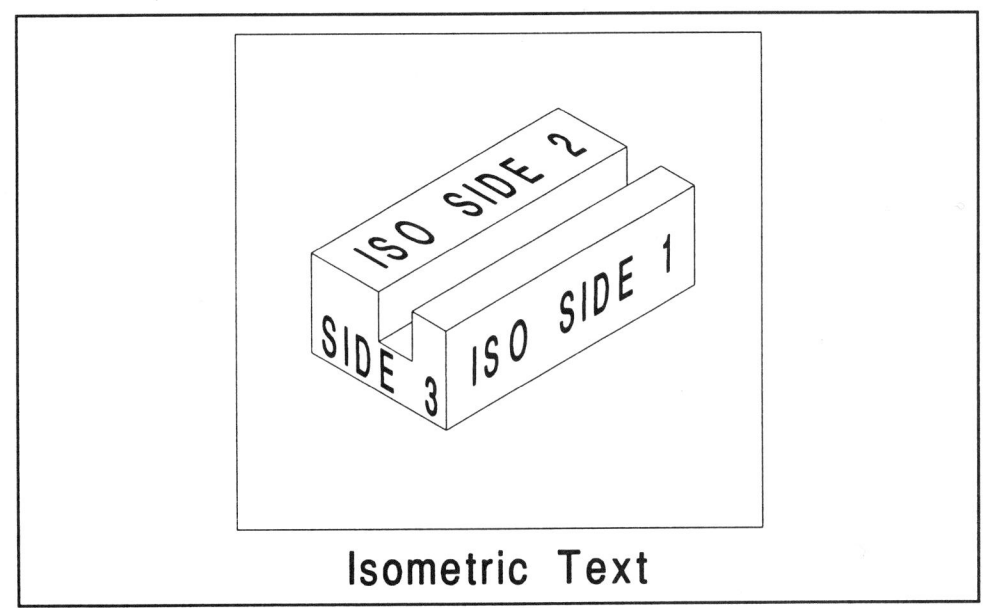

Figure 8.4 Using Text Slant and Rotation in isometric drawings.

Aspect. The Aspect feature controls the ration of the text's width to its height. Select the Aspect feature and at the prompt, enter a number value for the new aspect. An aspect of 2 doubles the width since it is a ratio of 2 to 1, width to height. An aspect of 0.5 cuts the width in half. The default aspect is 1.

To place text in your drawing that has 10 characters to the inch, the characters must be 0.1 inch wide. If you also don't want your text to look too blocky, you could set its height to 0.12 inch. Using the Aspect ratio formula of width/height (0.1/0.12), set your aspect ratio to 0.8333. This arrangement only works if you are using mono-spaced text. This means you are either using single-text characters (TP) or the Proportional feature is turned OFF. Figure 8.5 shows examples of text set to an Aspect ratio of 0.5, 1, and 2.

Rotation. With the Rotation feature, you can place text at any angle within a drawing. To set text rotation, enter the command code TS, then enter R. At the prompt, provide the number of degrees of rotation, from -360° to +360°, and press Enter. As with other rotation commands, the 0° default position is along the positive X-axis, horizontal and to the right. All text added after you set this command is displayed at the chosen angle. Text that was already placed in a drawing can later be rotated with the Rotate (RO) command. Figure 8.6 shows sample text placed at different angles.

```
Aspect = .5    ABCDEFGHIJ 1234567890
Aspect = 1           ABCDEFGH
Aspect   =   2
```

Text Aspect (TSA)

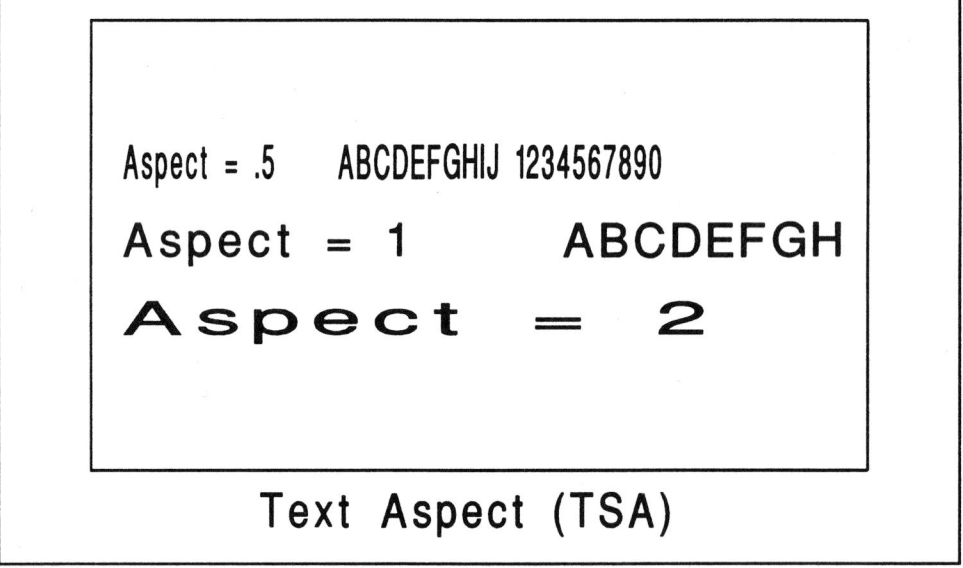

Figure 8.5 The effect of changing the Text Aspect.

Color. Select the color for text with the Color option. Either enter the number of the desired color, or select it from the color bar displayed on the sidebar menu. The Text Color prompt is also one of the options of the Color Settings (CS) command.

The Color feature does not change or affect the color of text already existing in the drawing. As with other color commands, your screen choices are limited to those available for your particular graphics display.

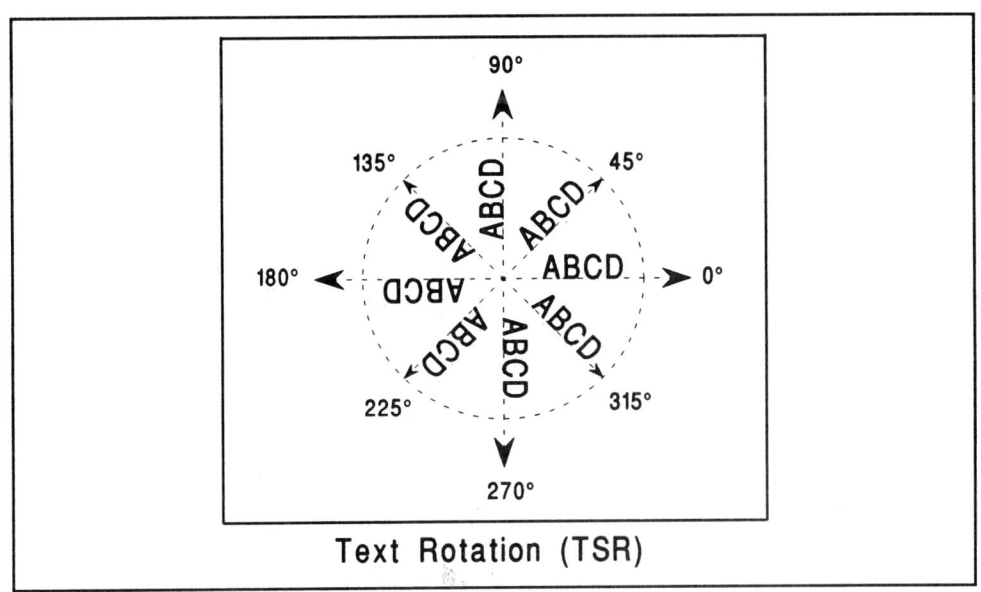

Figure 8.6 The effect of setting Rotation with Text Settings.

You can change text color even if you do not have a color adapter for your monitor. If you have a monochrome monitor, but a multi-pen plotter or color printer, you could set several color selections for your text and display them in a plot.

sPacing. The sPacing feature controls all the spacing characteristics of text. This feature contains three options: between Character, between Lines, and Proportional.

between Character. The between Character feature sets the actual space between the characters in text lines. This setting has *no* effect on characters placed with the Text Place (TP) command. Before this command will work with a Text Line (TL), the Proportional setting must be ON. At a setting of 20%, there is a space of one-fifth the width of a letter between the letters. If the spacing is set to a negative value, the text will be placed forward facing, but from right to left. Different fonts require a different minimum amount of negative spacing so characters will not overlap each other. For example, the MAIN font should be set to at least -150% to keep from overlapping. Figure 8.7 shows text characters spaced at 20%, 50%, 100%, and -150%.

between Line. The between Line feature sets the actual space between the lines of text in text lines. This setting has *no* effect on characters placed with the Text Place (TP) command. The value entered is a percent of text size. A setting of 150%, gives you a spacing of one and one-half the height of a text character between the lines. This spacing is measured from the reference point of the first line to the reference point of the second.

8-10 ■ Chapter 8: Adding Text

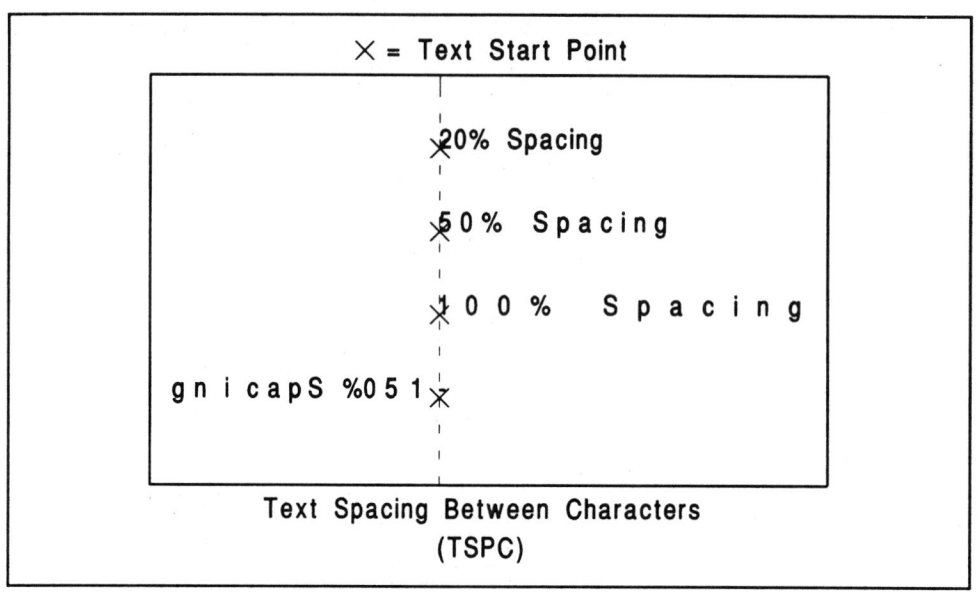

```
                    X = Text Start Point
                         
                        X20% Spacing
                        
                        X50%  Spacing
                        
                        X100%   S p a c i n g
                        
             g n i c a p S  %0 5 1 X
                        
              Text Spacing Between Characters
                            (TSPC)
```

Figure 8.7 Changing the Between Character Spacing with Text Settings.

A setting of 100% would leave you with virtually no room between text lines. Any setting less than 100% causes the text lines to overlap. 150% is a commonly used setting. Figure 8.8 shows text lines spaced at 100%, 150%, and 300%.

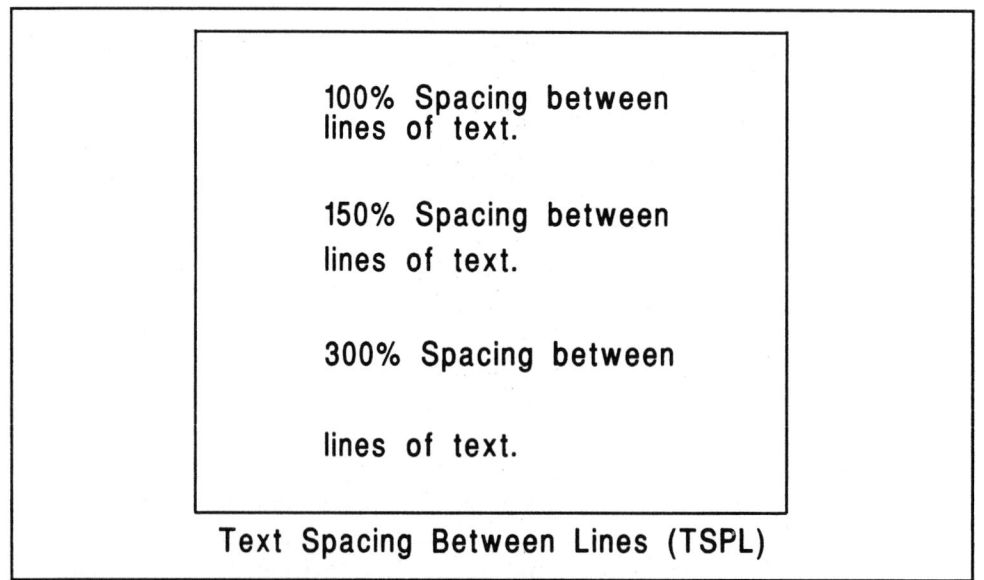

```
          100% Spacing between
          lines of text.

          150% Spacing between
          lines of text.

          300% Spacing between

          lines of text.

          Text Spacing Between Lines (TSPL)
```

Figure 8.8 The effect of changing the Between Line Spacing.

Proportional. The Proportional feature is a toggle which turns proportional spacing ON or OFF. This setting has no effect on characters placed with the Text Place (TP) command. When Proportional Spacing is OFF, the letter *i* takes up as much space as the letter *w*. This is called mono-spacing. When it is ON, the distance between characters is determined by the between-character percentage and the width of the characters, so *i* takes up less space than *w*. (See Figure 8.9.)

> **TIP:** Most of the AutoCAD fonts are proportional, which can cause problems when transferring drawings using these fonts to other CAD programs through DXF (Drawing eXchange Format.) It is usually best to use one font for proportional text and a separate font for monospaced text, such as in a table.

```
            Proportional Text is ON
            111222333 AAAIIIEEE




     Proportional   Text   is   OFF
     1 1 1 2 2 2 3 3 3   A A A I I I E E E


            Proportional Text (TSPP)
```

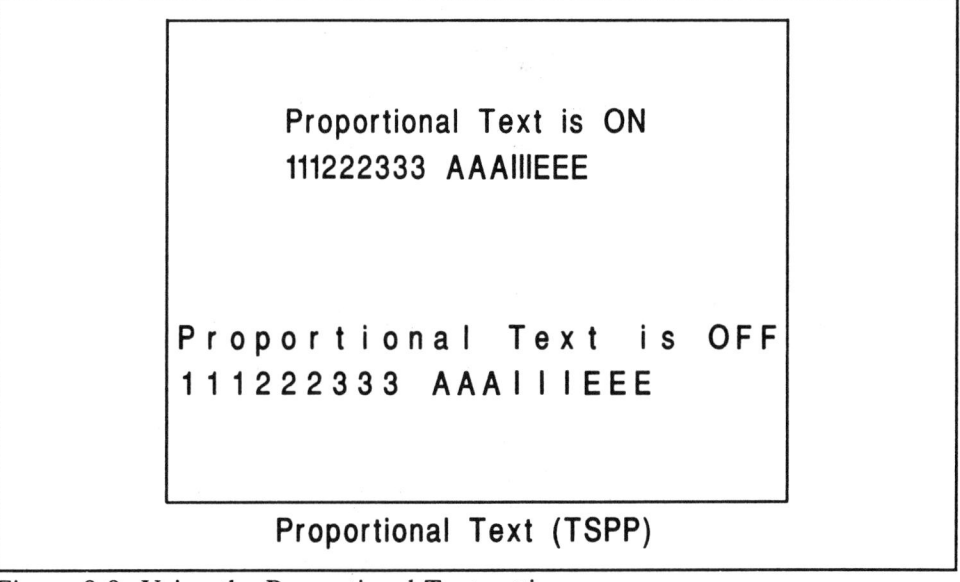

Figure 8.9 Using the Proportional Text setting.

ENTERING AND EDITING TEXT

Now that you have determined the various features of your text's appearance, you are ready to add text to drawings. This section will describe commands for entering groups of text, and commands for inserting, deleting, and replacing letters of text. Before you use these new commands, be sure to set the desired text features described in the preceding section.

After you have modified the text settings, place text in your drawing using the Text Place (TP) or Text Line (TL) commands. Begin these commands with either the command code TP or TL. At the prompt, move your cursor to where you want to insert text and press Enter. Each text character, or text line, has its own reference point located in the lower left corner of the character or line. When you select the point where the text is to be placed, you are actually choosing the character or line's reference point. You must also select this reference point whenever identifying letters for editing with the text commands discussed in this chapter, or with the EDIT commands discussed in other chapters. Begin typing your text, using basic word processing strategies. Use the arrow keys to maneuver the cursor, Enter to move to the beginning of the next line, and Backspace or Delete to remove letters.

Text Place (TP)

When using the Text Place (TP) command as described above, you see the characters displayed on-screen as they are typed in. If the Reference Points (PR) toggle is ON, you will also see the individual reference point at the lower left-hand corner of each text character. (See Figure 8.10.)

.a.b.c.A.B.C.1.2.3

Text Place (TP)

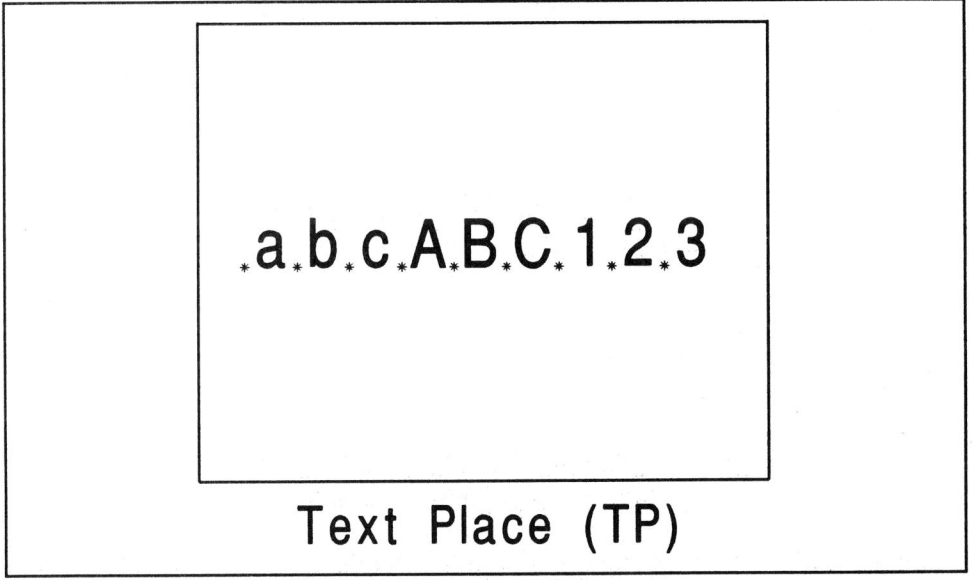

Figure 8.10 Placing individual characters with Text Place.

Text Line (TL)

When using the Text Line (TL) command, as described earlier, a box will appear as you begin to type. The actual characters are visible on the command line as you type. The box signifies the position and length of the characters entered. (See Figure 8.11.) If you click the first button on your mouse, you can reposition the box. This must be done *before* pressing Enter to approve the text line. The Escape key places the box back in its original position.

Chapter 8: Adding Text ■ 8-13

> **TIP:** The text settings, color, size, rotation, and spacing, can be set on-the-fly, while the box is still attached to the cursor for repositioning.

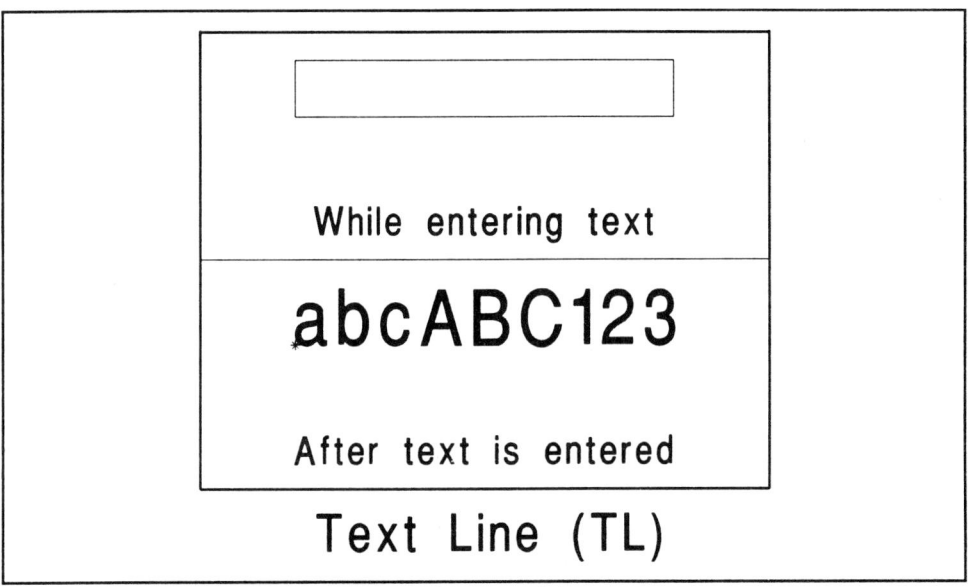

```
            ┌─────────────┐
            │             │
            └─────────────┘

           While entering text
           ───────────────────
            abcABC123
           ───────────────────
           After text is entered

           Text Line (TL)
```

Figure 8.11 Placing lines of text with Text Line.

The following commands provide ways to edit, or change, individual text characters and lines after they have been placed in a drawing. You can insert new characters and delete and replace characters. In all cases, after you enter the command code, you must identify the existing text character or line to be edited. Position the cursor near the character or line's reference point, and click or snap to its reference point with the SC or NP command. Snapping usually ensures that CADD 6 selects the character you intended to change.

> **TIP:** Turn Reference Points (PR) ON to display the text line and character's reference points so they can be easily selected for editing or moving.

The first three commands discussed (Text Insert (TI), Text Delete (TD), and Text Replace (TR)) work primarily on text placed as single-characters with the Text Place (TP) command. The Text Edit (TE) command is used to edit text lines, and is discussed following the Text Place editing commands.

Text Insert (TI)

If you are not a perfect typist, you will appreciate Text Insert (TI), the command for inserting a letter into a pre-existing set of text characters. To use Text Insert (TI), enter the command code TI. You will be prompted for the "Point to insert location." You must identify the reference point of the existing text character where you want to place the new character. Place your cursor at the character's reference point which will become the location of the new character. Click or snap, and a space opens up for a new character. Type in the new text character. The Text Insert (TI) command duplicates the settings of the modified text, so the inserted character has features (color, slant, size, and so on) identical to the original text line.

> **TIP:** If you use the Text Insert (TI) command on a text line, the text within the line is surrounded by the boundary box that appeared when initially placing the text. The editing takes place on the command line. The boundary box can be relocated by clicking the first button on your pointing device. This was discussed in the section on Text Line (TL).

Text Delete (TD)

Delete characters from existing text with the Text Delete (TD) command. To delete characters, enter the command code TD. At the prompt, move your cursor to the reference point of the letter to delete. All letters forward of the deleted character automatically adjust their position to fill the void in the line of text.

This command works like the Text Edit (TE) command when used on a text line.

Text Replace (TX)

Instead of adding or deleting letters, it is sometimes easier to replace letters with the Text Replace (TX) command. To begin Text Replace (TX), type the command TX. At the prompt, move your cursor to the reference point of the character to be replaced. Type in the new characters, and you will see the old characters replaced on the screen. When you finish replacing characters, press Esc to end the Text Replace (TX) process. The new text duplicates the settings of the existing text.

This command works like the Text Edit (TE) command when used on a text line.

The next three commands, Text Append (TA), Text Change (TG), and Text Edit (TE), work *only* on text placed as lines with the Text Line (TL) command.

Text Append (TA)

The Text Append (TA) command automatically calculates the position of a new text line below the selected text line (string.) At this point, you enter new text as you would when using the Text Line (TL) command. The new text duplicates the settings of the existing text.

Text Change (TG)

This command is used *strictly* on text lines placed with the Text Line (TL) command, and has no affect on text characters placed with the Text Place (TP) command. This command is used to change the font, justification, between character spacing, proportion, slant, and Aspect of existing text lines.

The Text Change (TG) command is executed by typing TG. You will be prompted with a selection set to choose the text lines to be changed. Once the appropriate text is selected, you can change any or all of the settings for font, justification, between character spacing, proportion, slant, and Aspect. When the desired changes are made, press Enter and the program automatically modifies the selected text.

Text Edit (TE)

This command is used *strictly* for text lines placed with the Text Line (TL) command, and has no affect on text characters placed with the Text Place (TP) command.

If you use the Text Edit (TE) command on a text line, the text within the line is surrounded by the boundary box that appeared when you initially placed the text. Type in new text or make changes to the existing text. Press Enter to complete the command. The boundary box can be relocated by clicking the first button on your mouse, as discussed in the section on Text Line (TL).

CREATING AND EDITING TEXT FONTS

Your text font options are not necessarily limited to the fonts provided with CADD 6. The Font Create (WT) command gives you the ability to design and create new characters by drawing them in CADD 6, as long as you use the primitive entity set: Lines, Circles, Arcs, Ellipses, Curves, and Points. Text characters and components, or hatches, cannot be used in a font unless they are previously exploded to their root entities. Fills cannot be used under any circumstances.

The new characters you create do not have to be letters. A font is just a series of symbols that have been assigned, or matched up with, the keys on the keyboard. When you type a certain key, CADD 6 knows to place the symbol assigned to that key. Consequently, you can create a font that is really a library of symbols to be entered in drawings with the Text Place (TP) or Text Line (TL) command. For example, you could create a font of foreign language characters. (Fonts of Greek characters and mathematical symbols are already a part of the CADD 6 font selection.)

Before you create a new text font, you must first choose a name for the font. Using the Text Settings (TS) command, select Font and enter the name of your new font (up to eight characters.) When you are asked whether this is a new font, answer yes. Don't enter the name of an existing CADD 6 font unless you are sure you want to change or modify an existing font. Once you have named the new font, begin defining characters.

These are some guidelines to follow when creating new fonts:

Use curves rather than arcs or circles, because only curves can be slanted at extreme angles without distortion with the Slant feature. However, the text characters take up more memory when curves are used instead of arcs and circles.

Pay attention to the size and proportion of the characters. This helps ensure that the character set (font) functions properly. Before creating new characters, you may want to set up a grid or particular reference box in which to create the characters. This ensures uniformity among the characters in your font.

When creating a new font, you can only use the upper and lower case alphanumeric keys. In other words, you can use the keyboard keys as they are, or you can select Shift and a keyboard key. If you need more keys than you can get with the standard keys and shifted standard keys, you can use numbers pertaining to the ASCII extended-character set. When creating a text character, instead of selecting a standard keyboard key, hold down the ALT key and type in a number (*from the keypad, not from the numbers above the alphabet keys*) between 128 and 255. All the numbers up to 200 are available, but some numbers between 200 and 255 do not work. CADD 6 reserves some of these ASCII characters for it's own use.

Draw your new character using the available Draw and Editing commands. When you are satisfied with the character's design and placement, enter the command code WT (Font Create.) Place a window around the character you just created. Next, you well be prompted to enter the character to be defined. Type in the letter you want to define from the keyboard. You do *not* need to press Enter. Next, will be prompted to enter the lower left corner of the character for a reference point. This completes the process of defining a letter.

CHAPTER SUMMARY

This chapter described the basic features of text and the commands for defining the appearance of text in your drawing. Text, in CADD 6 drawings, can be in the form of individual characters or text lines. The commands discussed explain how to create, enter, and manipulate text characters and text lines in a drawing. Not many drawings are complete without text of some kind. Once you become familiar with the text features in CADD 6, you will find that placing and manipulating text is fast and easy.

CHAPTER 9

Using Symbols

USING THE COMPONENTS AND ATTRIBUTES MENUS

This chapter will introduce you to *Components*, the name CADD 6 uses for symbols that are created by grouping objects together. Any entities drawn in CADD 6 can be grouped together into a component and assigned a name. The component can then be saved to disk and called up later for use in other drawings. You can create individual components of office furnishings, like desks and chairs, and never have to draw those symbols again. You simply load the desired desk and chair components from disk and place them into any of your drawings.

Although components may be created from many entities, CADD 6 treats each component as a single object when editing your drawing. When a component is created, you assign it a *Reference Point*, or handle that is later used to select the component for editing. This makes it possible to use any of the selection set editing commands with components, such as Move (MV), Copy (CO), and Scale (SZ). To select a component for any of these commands, choose the Object option (press O), then identify the desired component by clicking on its reference point.

Since a component is assigned a unique name when it is created, you can call it up from disk and use it in other drawings. In other words, once you create a symbol as a component, you never have to draw that symbol again. Simply load it from disk each time you need to use it. You can also place a component multiple times in the same drawing without reloading it from disk, which saves time and space in your drawing.

Components used for particular drawing applications can be grouped together into libraries, commonly called *symbol libraries*. A symbol library, for CADD 6, is simply a group of components commonly used in one drawing application. For example, an architect might create libraries of framing symbols, foundation symbols, plumbing fixtures, furnishings, or landscaping symbols. A civil engineer might use a library of surveying and mapping symbols. Electronic engineers may want libraries for electronic schematics, printed circuit board layout, microprocessors, and electronic packaging components.

You do not always have to create symbols, as there are many symbol libraries available for purchase from Autodesk Retail Products or from "third party developers." These libraries usually contain symbols, as well as custom menus to simplify symbol selection. The quality of symbol libraries varies widely, with each one costing between $25 and $200. Such libraries usually contain between 50 and 500 items. If you decide to purchase a library, be assured that you can always customize it by adding other components, modifying existing components, and modifying or creating custom video menus to simplify symbol selection. (Instructions for creating custom menus are included in Chapter 15.) To find out more about libraries you can purchase, contact your dealer or Autodesk Retail Products.

To introduce the use of components (symbols) and attributes (symbol information), this chapter examines the following commands:

COMPONENTS

Component Place (CP)
Component Create (CC)
Component Create Window (CW)

Component Scale (CZ)
Component Rotation (CR)
Component Explode (CE)
Component Replace (CN)
Component Remove (CX)

Component Image (CI)
Component Snap (GC)
Explode Destination Layer (XY)

Save Component (SAC)
Load Component (LOC)
Component Dump (CD)

ATTRIBUTES

Attribute Create (AC)

Attribute Attach (AT)
Attribute Detach (DE)

Attribute Edit (AE)

Load Attribute (LOT)
Save Attribute (SAT)
Export Attribute (XA)

Attribute Settings (AS)

A tutorial at the end of this chapter applies many of the Component and Attribute commands. The tutorial leads you to create some components and place them in a simple electronic schematic drawing. Schematic drawings are an excellent application for the use of grids, therefore, several of the Constraint commands for grids are also illustrated.

CREATING AND SAVING COMPONENTS

Component Create (CC)

To create a symbol from one entity, a group of objects, or an entire drawing, use the Component Create (CC) command. Creating a component has six basic steps, each of which are discussed in detail below:

1. Draw the symbol using the usual DRAW and EDIT commands
2. Type CC to execute the Component Create (CC) command
3. Select the objects to make into the component
4. Enter a name to use for identifying the component
5. Identify a reference point for the new component
6. Decide whether to replace the original entities with the new component

When you finish drawing a symbol, you are then ready to create it as a component. Begin by typing in the Component Create (CC) command. Use the selection menu to identify all objects to be included as part of the component. If the symbol was created as an individual drawing, you can select the entire drawing. If many symbols were created together on a drawing, pick individual objects, use a selection window, or use filters to identify the objects to be included in this component.

You will then be prompted to enter a name for the new component. This name is normally also used as the component's file name when you save it to disk. Be sure to specify a name that will allow you to readily identify the component later.

The next step is to specify the component's reference point. Move your cursor to the desired point and press Enter, or click with your pointing device. You usually want to

> **TIP:** Be sure to check which items are highlighted *prior* to accepting the selection set to create the component. If the objects that make up the new component were drawn on multiple layers, you may want to turn ON the All Layers Edit (AL) mode (see Chapter 12 for more information on layers.) By doing this you will know that your component includes everything on the display, regardless of the object's layer.

> **TIP:** Although a component's name can actually have up to 12 characters, DOS recognizes and uses only the first eight for the component's file name when it is saved. For this reason, it is highly recommended that you use a maximum of eight characters for component names. Using more than eight characters can lead to a great deal of confusion when you later try to load the component from disk.

use a snap command to exactly locate the reference point, perhaps on an endpoint of one object included in the component.

The location of the reference point is very important, as it is used to identify and place the component. When you place the component in a drawing, you specify where the reference point is to be located. The component is drawn relative to that point. You want to choose a point that is obvious and convenient. You should also consider whether you will later need to snap to the reference point, for example, to connect lines to it. If you are designing a set of similar components, you may want to create a few with the reference point at different locations, and then practice placing them in a drawing. The best location for the reference point quickly becomes obvious.

When constructing a library of similar symbols, try to use a consistent point on each component for the reference point, such as the center of round components, or the lower left corner of rectangular components. Setting consistent reference points as you develop a set of components makes them much easier to work with later. The electronic schematic symbols you create in the tutorial, later in this chapter, all have their reference points on a left endpoint, to allow them to be placed on a 0.05" X 0.05" grid. This ensures accurate placement of all symbols, and makes it easy to snap connection lines between them.

The final option in the Component Create (CC) command is to choose between the following:

1. Click on <RET> (or press Enter) to complete the command
2. Press R to replace the original entities with the new component

If you have created any attributes prior to executing Component Create (CC), a third option appears allowing you to attach an attribute by pressing A.

If you press Enter to complete the command, the definition of the new component is loaded into the drawing, but it is not placed anywhere in the drawing. Alternatively, you can choose to *Replace* (press R) the individual entities that were used to create the component with the actual component. This results in the component being created and placed in the drawing with a single command (CC).

If you wish to attach an attribute to the component at this time, select the A option, and choose the desired attribute from the sidebar menu. This will cause the attribute to become a part of the component definition, and every time that component is placed in a drawing, the attribute is placed with it.

Figure 9.1 shows how to create a component with Component Create (CC).

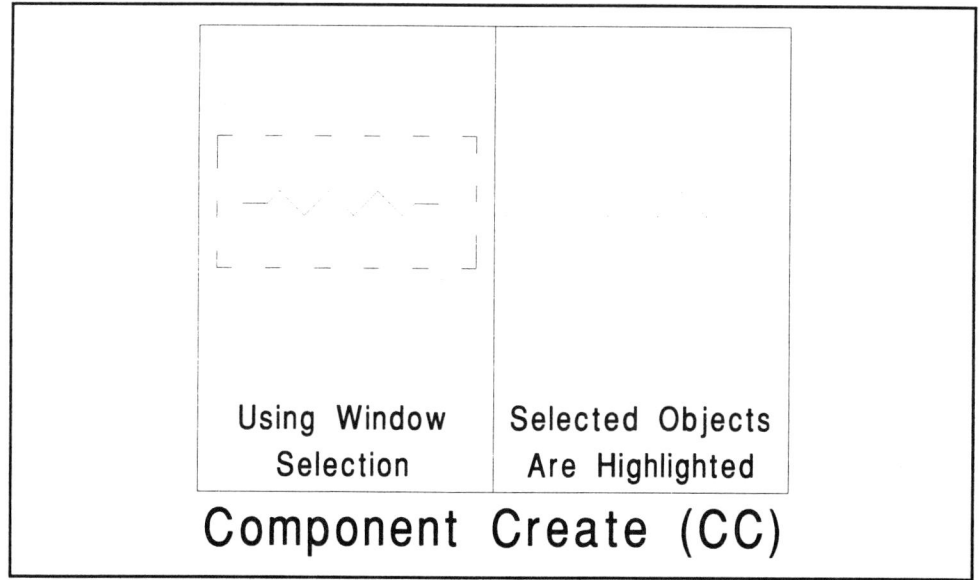

Figure 9.1 Selecting existing objects to Create a Component.

CADD 6 does not allow you to create two components, in one drawing, with an identical name. This commonly happens if you want to explode a component, modify it, and re-create it with the old name. If you try to create a component with the same name as another component, CADD 6 prompts:

Component: (Name) already defined!

At this prompt you can either repeat the command, entering a different name, or use the Component Remove (CX) command to remove the definition of the other component from the drawing. Then repeat the Component Create (CC) command with the desired component name.

You should understand that the Component Create (CC) command creates the component so it can *only* be used in the drawing in which it was created. In fact, if you create components, but do not place them anywhere in the drawing, they are lost when you quit that drawing. If you want to save the component to a disk file so it can be loaded into other drawings, you should use the Save Component (SAC) command, discussed later in this chapter.

Component Create Window (CW)

You can shortcut the selection process for creating components by using the window command, Component Create Window (CW). This is similar to the selection process used in the commands Window Copy (WC) and Window Rotate (WR).

Draw your symbol normally, and use Zoom commands as necessary to make sure the entire symbol is displayed on the screen. When you enclose the symbol in a selection window, there is no chance to add other objects to it.

Type CW to execute the Component Create Window (CW) command. At the prompt, place the selection window on your screen so that your symbol is completely inside of it. The command is then completed just like the Component Create (CC) command. When prompted, enter the component name and specify a reference point.

> **TIP:** If the objects that make up the new component were drawn on multiple layers, you may want to turn ON the All Layers Edit (AL) mode. Then you will know that your component includes everything on the display, regardless of the objects' layer locations.

The final option in the Component Create Window (CW) command is to choose between the following:

Click on <RET> (or use the Enter key) to Complete the command
Press R to Replace the original entities with the new component

If you press Enter to complete the command, the definition of the new component is loaded into the drawing, but it is not placed anywhere in the drawing. Alternatively, you can choose to *Replace* the individual entities that were used to create the component with the actual component. This results in the component being created and placed in the drawing with a single command (CW).

As for Component Create (CC), the Component Create Window (CW) command creates the component so it can *only* be used in the drawing in which it was created. Use the Save Component (SAC) command, discussed next, to save the component to a disk file so it can be loaded into other drawings.

Save Component (SAC)

Use Save Component (SAC) to save your previously created component to a disk file so it can be called into other drawings later. Refer to Chapter 13 for more information on the Save (SA) command. To save a component, enter the command code for Save (SA), then select the C option for Component. At the prompt, select the name of a previously created component from the sidebar menu. The file name, complete with the default DOS path name, should then be displayed. The default path is assumed unless you specifically enter a path name with the file name. Press Enter again to save the component in a file with this name.

If you want to save the component to a different location, such as a floppy disk or a different subdirectory, enter that path when you enter the component file name. When you save a component, CADD 6 automatically assigns the file extension .CMP to the file name, to differentiate them from regular drawing files. You do not have to type in the .CMP extension when you specify a component file name.

> **TIP:** You can save the component with a file name that is different from the name it was given upon creation. However, CADD 6 still only recognizes the original name, which can cause confusion when you later try to load that component. To keep things simple, it is strongly recommended that you use the same name.

Component Dump (CD)

Component Dump (CD) is an extension of the Save Component (SAC) command. The Component Dump command allows you to save all components in a drawing with one command, without individually selecting each component. To use Component Dump (CD), enter the command code CD. CADD 6 displays the default path and file name to be used for saving the first component. The default path is whatever the File Paths (FP) is currently set to. The file name is the name by which the component was created. Press Enter to accept this default name, or type in a new file name (with path if desired) for this particular component and press Enter. The first component is saved, and the suggested file name for the next component is displayed.

CADD 6 continues to prompt for the file name of each successive component in your drawing until they have all been saved to disk. This command can save a great deal of time if you want to create a library of symbols. Create them all (or as many as practical) in a single drawing, then use Component Dump (CD) to quickly save them all to disk. This way you do not have to execute the Save (SA) command and select each symbol individually.

USING COMPONENTS IN YOUR DRAWINGS

Load Component (LOC)

The Load Component (LOC) command loads a component from disk into your drawing, making it available for placement later. Use this command anytime you want components to be made available for faster placement, but do not want to place them yet. To load a component, enter the command code LO, then select option C for Component (the Load command is also explained in Chapter 13). At the prompt, select the desired component from the sidebar menu, which lists all components in the default directory. Alternatively, you can enter the path and the name of the component from the keyboard. The specified component is then loaded into the drawing, but does not show up anywhere on the drawing screen.

Once the component is loaded, you can use the Component Place (CP) command, or choose the component from the component list in order to place it in the drawing.

If you want to load a component from a directory other than the default component directory, you must enter the correct path as part of the component name so CADD 6 knows where to find it. You can also change the default component path using the File Paths (FP) command. If the component is not found in the default path, or in the path specified, CADD 6 will print the following message, with the file and path name:

Component Not Found: (file and path)

You should try the command again and make sure to enter the file and path name correctly, including the drive designation (A:, C:, etc.).

Component Place (CP)

When you are ready to place a component in your drawing, use Component Place (CP). To place a component, begin by entering the CP command code. You will then be prompted to:

Select a Component From the Side Menu >

You can select from the list of loaded components (if any), or enter the name of a component that has been saved to disk. The next prompt will ask where you want to place the component. Move your cursor to where you want the component's reference point in the drawing, and click to select the desired point. The component is then inserted.

As you place components in a drawing with the CP command (or Load them with LOC), CADD 6 automatically builds a list of names of all the components. Whenever you execute CP, you can select "Look on Disk" from the sidebar menu. This causes CADD 6 to print a list of all components in the default directory on the sidebar menu. You can then select any component from this list to simultaneously load from disk and place in the drawing. (See Figure 9.2.)

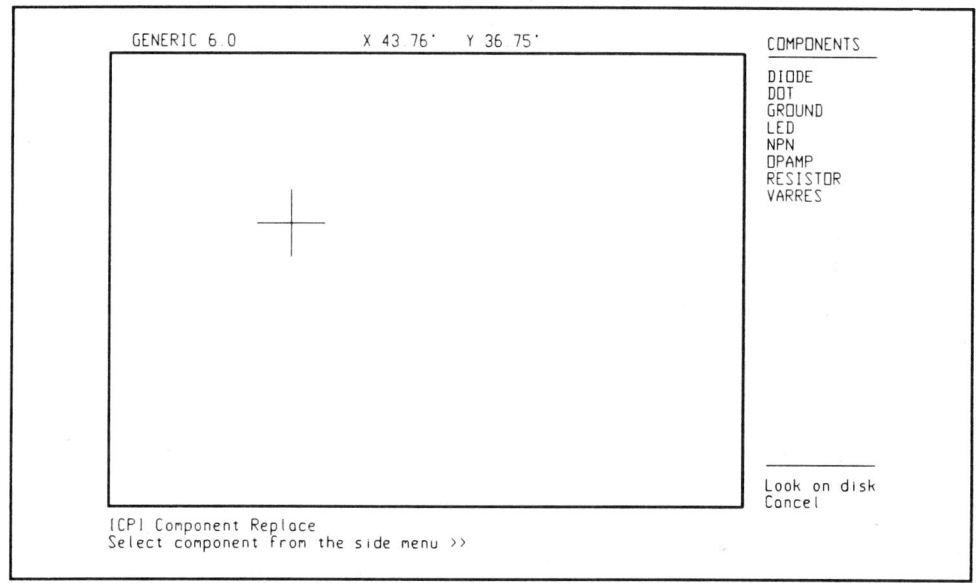

```
GENERIC 6.0           X 43.76'   Y 36.75'          COMPONENTS
                                                   DIODE
                                                   DOT
                                                   GROUND
                                                   LED
                                                   NPN
                                                   OPAMP
                                                   RESISTOR
                                                   VARRES




                          +




                                                   Look on disk
                                                   Cancel
[CP] Component Replace
Select component from the side menu >>
```

Figure 9.2 The list of existing Components.

CADD 6 has an Object Drag (OD) command which toggles the display of a "ghost image" of the component being placed. (See Chapter 7.) With this toggle set to ON, you see a ghost image of the component being placed, at the current scale and rotation. As you move your cursor around, the component image moves with it, allowing you to see when the component is perfectly placed, and if the scale and rotation factors are correct. (See Figure 9.3.)

Each component is placed at particular scale and rotation factors which are specified with the Component Scale (CZ) and Component Rotate (CR) commands. You can define factors prior to executing the CP command, or change them on-the-fly, when prompted to enter the component placement location. Once the ghost image of the component being placed is shown on the screen, if you don't like the scale or rotation of the component, change it by typing CZ or CR. Both of these commands are explained in detail later in this chapter.

If you mistakenly selected the wrong component name, you can abort the CP command by pressing Esc. Remember, once the component placement is complete, you can use any of the regular editing commands to move, rotate, scale, or erase the component.

Use the Erase Last (EL) command as a shortcut to erase the previously placed component.

```
+

Dragging a Component
```

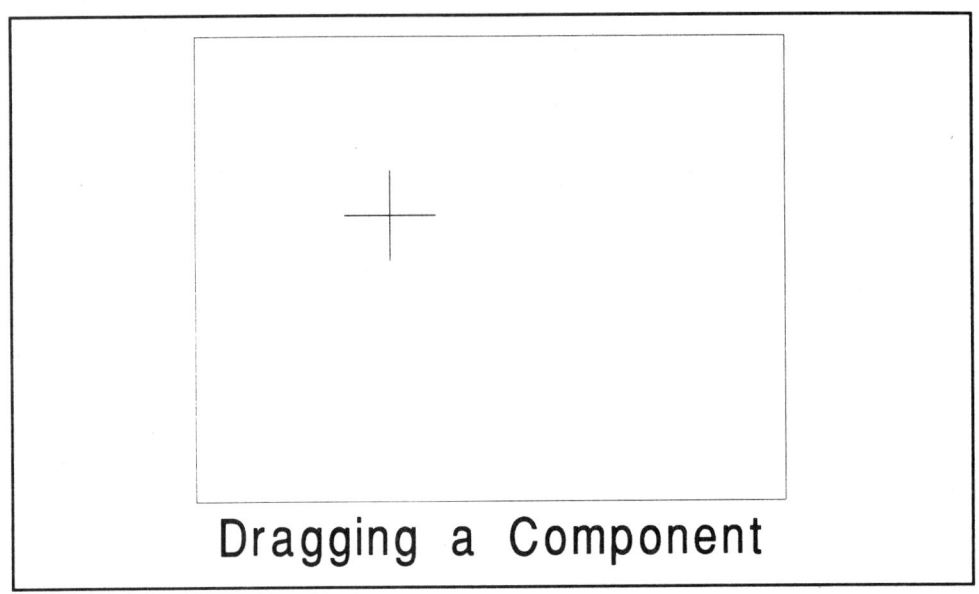

Figure 9.3 Using Object Drag for visual feedback.

Insertion Point (IP)

Normally, when a component is placed, you specify a point in the drawing that is to be the location of the reference point for that component. The reference point is placed, and the component is located relative to the reference point. Often the reference point is not in the most convenient place to use for locating the component. In this case, CADD 6 gives you the option of temporarily selecting another insertion point to use for placing the component.

After you execute the Component Place (CP) command and identify a component, CADD 6 prompts you to select the point in the drawing where the component should be placed. The component is shown as a "ghost image" on the screen, attached to your cursor at the component's reference point. You are then able to see if the reference point is at an acceptable insertion point, or if you need to use some other point. This is usually the case if you need to snap the component exactly onto an existing component, or entity, in your drawing.

When CADD 6 prompts for the placement point, type IP instead of identifying a point. This executes the Insertion Point (IP) command, which allows you to temporarily place the component, then re-attach the cursor to the new insertion point. When prompted, select any point in the drawing for the temporary placement point. The component image is detached from the cursor, and you are prompted to identify the new insertion point. Use a snap command to select an exact insertion point on the component, or simply click on a point. The component image is then re-attached to the cursor at the new point, and you can continue the Component Place command normally.

This command does not alter the actual location of the component's reference point. It simply allows you to temporarily use some other point for inserting the component. The next time you select that component for an editing operation, such as Move (MV) or Copy (CO), you will want to identify it by its reference point, not the temporary insertion point.

Component Explode (CE)

When you create a component, CADD 6 treats that component as one entity, even if it was made from many different lines, circles, curves, text, etc. As long as the component is in tact, you can no longer modify the individual entities that compose it. The only way to edit the composition of a component is to first *explode* it back to the primitive entities from which it was created. Once a component is exploded, you can use any of the regular editing commands to modify or add to the original entities.

To explode a component, type the command code CE to execute the Component Explode command. At the prompt, select the component to be exploded by clicking somewhere within its boundary. The component is then redrawn on the screen to signify it has reverted back to its original entities.

This command explodes and redraws *only* the individual component you select. It does not have any affect on other components, or other placements of that component. To explode multiple components with one command, use the Explode (EX) command with the Object (O) or Window (W) option to choose the components. (See Chapter 14.)

Explode Destination Layer (XY)

If you use multiple layers in your drawings that have components, you want to control what layer components revert to when they are exploded. This is specified with the Explode Destination Layer (XY) command.

Prior to executing the Component Explode (CE) command, type in XY to control the Explode Destination Layer (XY) setting. You are then prompted to choose one of the following layer options:

   O to explode back to their Original layers
   C to explode to the layer selected as Current
   P to explode to the layer on which the component was Placed

Once XY is set, the next component that is exploded is placed on the selected layer or layers. If the component was originally created on multiple layers, you can choose to have it revert back to those layers with the O option, or have all the entities moved to the Current (C) or Placement (P) layer.

Component Image (CI)

You can combine the functions of Component Place (CP) and Component Explode (CE) with the Component Image (CI) command. Use this command to place a component as the individual entities that make it up, rather than as an actual component. With this toggle ON, every component is placed as an exploded image, consisting of individual entities.

Component Image (CI) is a toggle that can either be ON or OFF. To change the toggle setting, type in the command code CI. If it is set to ON, all components placed thereafter are placed as exploded images. If CI is OFF, they are placed normally.

Once a component has been exploded, or has been placed in the drawing as an image, *none* of the other component commands (such as Component Replace (CN) and Component Remove (CX)) affect it. CADD 6 no longer treats it as a component, but as any other group of individual entities in the drawing.

Component Replace (CN)

With Component Replace (CN) you can replace one component in your drawing with another component, at particular locations which you select. This command allows you to use a selection set to choose specific placements of a component, or all placements, that are to be replaced with a new component. Component Replace (CN) operates like the search and replace commands in many word processing programs, where you can choose which words to replace, or specify a global replacement.

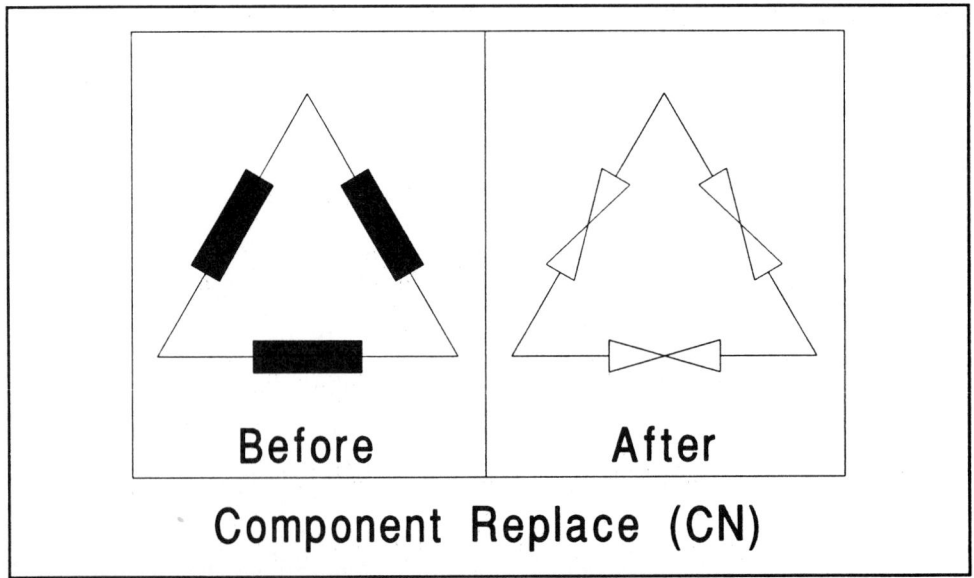

Figure 9.4 Replacing one Component with another.

To use this command, enter the command code CN, followed by the name of the component to be replaced. Select the component name from the sidebar menu, or enter it from the keyboard. You will then be prompted for the name of the new component. If you want to replace the old component *everywhere* it occurs in the drawing, press the Enter key to complete the command. To replace specific placements of a component, type S to indicate you want to make a selection, then use the regular selection process to choose the components to replace. New components are placed at the scale and rotation of the replaced components.

Component Replace (CN) is commonly used to update a design that uses one type of a component by replacing it with a new one. Perhaps a home floor plan drawing incorporated all wood frame windows, which you now want to replace with aluminum ones. Use Component Replace (CN) for each unique wood window component to replace it with the appropriate new aluminum one. The results of a Component Replace (CN) command are illustrated in Figure 9.4.

> **TIP:** The Component Replace (CN) command does *not* affect any components that were placed with Component Image (CI) toggled ON, or any components that were exploded after placement.

Component Replace (CN) works just as well on nested components. A nested component is created with another component as one of the objects that make it up. For example, draw a kitchen sink and turn it into a component. Next, draw a faucet and turn it into a component as well. Place the faucet component on the sink component, and create a third component from this combination. This is a nested component. Create a different faucet style and turn it into a component. Use the Component Replace (CN) command to replace the original faucet in the nested component with the new faucet component.

Component Remove (CX)

To remove *all* placements of a component from your drawing, use the Component Remove (CX) command. This is even more drastic than erasing components throughout the drawing, since Component Remove also *unloads* the definition of the component, removing it from the sidebar menu. To completely remove a component, type in the command code CX. At the prompt, enter the name of the component to be removed, or select it from the sidebar menu. CADD 6 warns:

   The component (name) will no longer exist!
   Remove the component? (Y/N) >

When the warning is displayed, press N to abort and return to your drawing, or press Y if you really want to remove the component.

Use the Component Remove (CX) command with caution, because it removes all placements of a specified component from the drawing file. This command also unloads the component definition from the drawing, so it can no longer be picked from the sidebar menu. To place that component later, it must be loaded from disk again. Do *not* use this command if you need the component somewhere else in your drawing. In that case, erase the undesired components with the Erase (ER) command instead of using Component Remove (CX).

Like Component Replace (CN), Component Remove does *not* affect components that have been exploded or placed in the drawing as images with CI toggled ON. Component Remove (CX) affects only components in the drawing currently displayed in CADD 6; it does *not* remove any components that have been saved to disk.

Component Scale (CZ)

Components, like all objects in CADD 6, can be scaled independently in the *X* and *Y* directions. Once a component is placed in a drawing, you can use the Scale (SZ) command to change its scale. However, if you know that components must have a particular scale, it would be nice to place them that way directly rather than having to change them later.

This is exactly the purpose of the Component Scale (CZ) command. To preset the scale of components before they are placed, use Component Scale. This command only affects components placed after CZ is executed. Use Component Scale to specify the scale values for each component to be placed. Suppose that you are placing components into a schematic drawing, for example, and all the symbols are to be half the size they were originally drawn. Set the CZ values for *X* and *Y* to 2, and all the components placed after that will be at the desired scale.

To preset the scale of *all* components to be placed in a drawing, enter the CZ command code. At the prompt, provide new *X* and *Y* scale factors. As with all scale commands (WZ and DZ), set *X* and *Y* to 2 to double the components' size. Setting both scales to 0.5 cuts the components' sizes in half. To place the mirror image of a component (around a vertical or horizontal line), enter negative values for *X*, *Y*, or both. Preset scale values stay in effect in a drawing until you change them. Some examples of components placed at various scales are shown in Figure 9.5.

You can use Component Scale (CZ) to define scale factors on-the-fly while executing Component Place (CP). This can be done when CADD 6 prompts you to enter the component placement location. Once the ghost image of the component being placed is shown on the screen, you are able to see the scale and rotation of the component. If you don't like what you see, change it by typing CZ and entering the correct value.

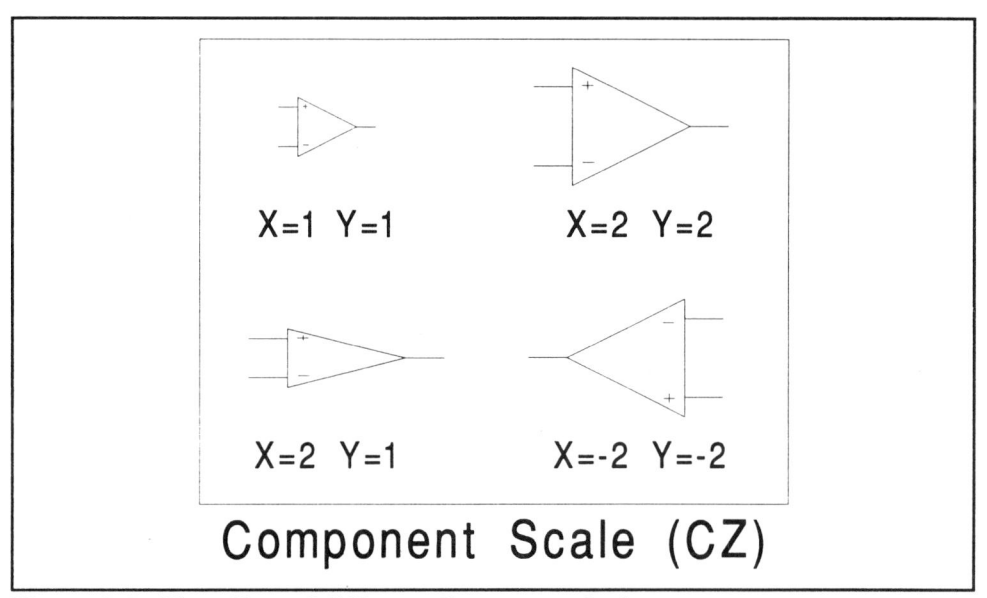

Figure 9.5 The effect of different Component Scales.

Component Rotate (CR)

Like Component Scale (CZ), Component Rotate (CR) presets a rotation value that is applied to all components placed from then on. To preset an angle for the component rotation, enter the CR command code. At the prompt, provide a rotation value and press Enter. The rotation factor stays constant in your drawing until you change it. Figure 9.6 shows examples of rotated components. If you want to rotate components after they are placed, use the Rotate (RO) command.

As with all rotation commands (RO and WR), the component rotation value can be specified as positive (counterclockwise) or negative (clockwise) 360°, where a zero angle is along the positive X-axis.

You can use Component Rotate (CR) to define a rotation angle on-the-fly, just as with Component Scale (CZ). This is done while executing the Component Place (CP) command when CADD 6 prompts you to enter the component placement location. Once the ghost image of the component being placed is shown on the screen, you are able to see the rotation of the component. If you don't like what you see, change it by typing CR and entering the correct angle.

Component Snaps (GC)

Component Snaps (GC) is a toggle command that allows snapping to any construction points of the entities used to create the component. With Component Snaps (GC) OFF, you can *only* snap to the reference point of a component. With this toggle set to ON, you can snap to most internal construction points as well.

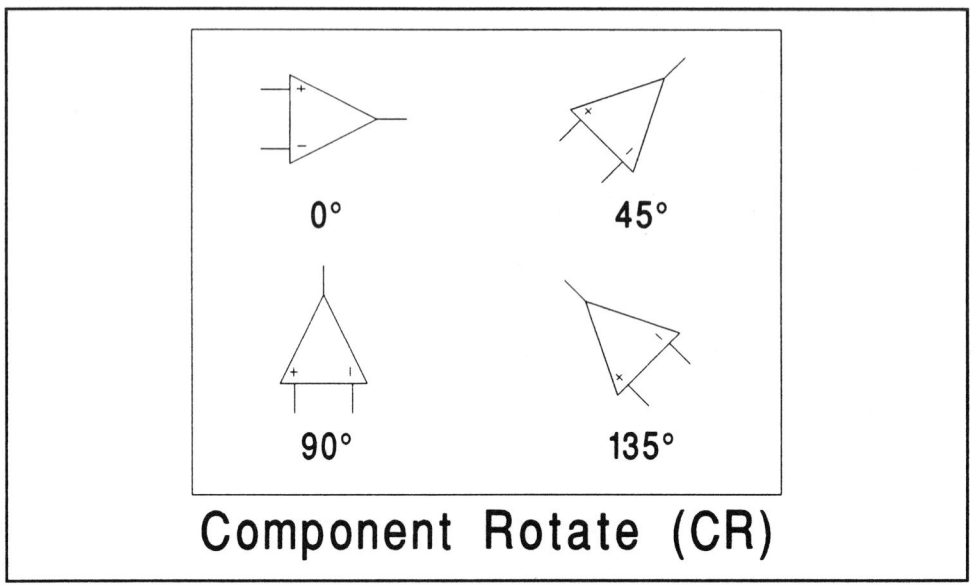

Figure 9.6 Using the Component Rotate command.

> **TIP:** Each component has its own X- and Y-axes which are rotated with it. This is important to remember if you scale a component that has already been rotated. The *X* and *Y* scale values are relative to the component's axes, rather than the normal drawing axes.
>
> For example, suppose you set Component Rotate (CR) to 90 and place a component. It will be placed so its X-axis is pointing up toward the top of the screen and its Y-axis is horizontal, 90° to the normal drawing axes. Then, set the Component Scale (CZ) with the *X* scale factor 2 and the *Y* scale factor 1. Place another component, and it will be twice as large in the *vertical direction*, since that is the component's X-axis (even though you might expect the vertical direction to be the Y- axis)!

This is a particularly useful command when you try to place components that attach to each other end-to-end. If you create a series of symbols with reference points on the left side you would normally not be able to attach any entities exactly to a point on their right side. But, with GC set to ON, you can use snap commands to place the left-hand reference point of one component exactly on a right-hand construction point of another one. This is illustrated with the electronic schematic symbols in the tutorial at the end of this chapter.

INTRODUCTION TO ATTRIBUTES

Many times it is not enough to just show a picture of a symbol in a drawing. You also want to include information such as the model number, cost, or dimensions of the object. For this purpose, CADD 6 has *attributes* which are used to attach text (nongraphical) information to any of the components in a drawing. An attribute can be used to attach up to 128 pieces of data to any component. This data includes a label and a default value. This data can later be extracted for use in the BOM (Bill of Materials), parts list, or inventory statement.

Once an attribute has been defined, you can use it in one of two ways: attached to any component that has already been placed in the drawing, or by *pre-attaching* it when the component itself is created. If you want an attribute to be associated with a particular component every time that component is used, pre-attach the attribute when you create the component. Alternatively, you can also add attributes to any other components, later in the drawing process, with the Attribute Attach (AT) command.

Once attributes are placed in a drawing, they can be displayed on the screen or hidden from view, as desired. When you attach a particular attribute, you can define whether it is normally displayed or not. The display status of individual attributes can also be overridden if you choose to display or hide *all* attributes in your drawing.

The Attribute commands are located on a sub-menu of the Components menu.

Attribute Create (AC)

Use Attribute Create (AC) to define attributes that will be attached to components. Type in AC to begin creating an attribute. CADD 6 first prompts you to enter the name of the attribute. You can enter any name, up to eight characters long. This name will probably be used later to save the attribute to a disk file, so be sure to use characters that are acceptable for DOS file names.

You will then be prompted to begin entering the field information, starting with the first field name or label. Each attribute can have up to 128 fields, with each field consisting of a *label* and a *default value*. CADD 6 will continue asking you for these pairs of data until you select to stop, or 128 pairs are entered. You can enter up to 80 alphanumeric characters for both the field label and the default value. The field label is how you identify the contents of the field. The default value is a value typically associated with that field, or it can be left blank by pressing Enter. You will be able to change the default value for each attribute placement later, if necessary. Examples of some fields might be:

LABEL:	DEFAULT VALUE:
Model No:	AR943-S
Cost:	$325.95
Vendor:	Jones Manufacturing
Address:	805 So. Main
City, State:	Portland, OR 97103

You can also attach fields from a previously defined attribute directly onto one currently being created. To do this, type an @ sign and the name of the existing attribute when you are prompted to enter any field label. You can then continue to add more fields or finish the command.

When you finish entering the field data for this attribute, press the F10 function key and the attribute is created. To abort the command at any time, you can press Esc.

This command is similar to Component Create (CC), because it creates the attribute definition but does not place it anywhere in your drawing. At this point, the attribute can *only* be used in the drawing in which it was created. In fact, if you create attributes, but do not place them anywhere in the drawing, they will be lost when you quit that drawing. If you want to copy the attribute to a disk file so it can be loaded into other drawings, you have to use the Save Attribute (SAT) command.

> **TIP:** Like components, an attribute's name can actually have up to 12 characters, but DOS only recognizes and uses the first eight for the file name when is saved. For this reason, it is highly recommended that you use a maximum of eight characters for all attribute names. Using more than eight characters can lead to a great deal of confusion when you later try to select an attribute from those stored on disk.

Save Attribute (SAT)

Use Save Attribute (SAT) to save your previously created attribute to a disk file so it can be called into other drawings later. To save an attribute, enter the command code SA for Save (SA), then select the T option for aTtribute. At the prompt, select one of the previously created attributes from the sidebar menu. The file name, complete with the default DOS path name, should then be displayed. The default path for components is assumed unless you specifically enter a path name with the file name. Press Enter to save the attribute with this name to a file.

If you want to save the attribute to a different location, such as a floppy disk or a different subdirectory, enter that path when you enter the attribute file name. When you save an attribute, CADD 6 automatically assigns the file extension .ATB to the file name to differentiate it from other types of files. You do not have to type in the .ATB extension when you specify an attribute file name.

> **TIP:** You can actually save the attribute with a file name different from the attribute name it was given upon creation. However, CADD 6.0 still only recognizes the original name, which can cause confusion when you later try to load that attribute. To keep things simple, it is strongly recommended that you use the same name.

Load Attribute (LOT)

The Load Attribute (LOT) command loads an attribute from disk into your drawing, making it available for placement later. Use this command anytime you want attributes to be made available for faster placement, but do not want to attach them yet. To load an attribute, first enter the command code LO, then select option T for aTtribute. At the prompt, select the desired attribute from the sidebar menu, which lists all attributes in the default component directory. Alternatively, you can enter the path and the name of the attribute from the keyboard. The specified attribute is then loaded into the drawing, but does not show up anywhere on the drawing screen.

Once the attribute is loaded, you can use the Attribute Attach (AT) command. Choose the attribute from the attribute list to attach it to any component in the drawing.

Attributes are normally stored in the directory specified as the default for components. If you want to load an attribute from a directory (other than the default component directory), you must enter the correct path as part of the attribute name so CADD 6 knows where to find it. You can also change the default component/attribute path with the File Paths (FP) command. If the attribute is not found in the default path, or in the path specified, CADD 6 will print the following message, with the file and path name:

Attribute Not Found: (file and path)

Try the command again, and make sure to enter the file and path name correctly, including the drive designation (A:, C:, etc.).

Attribute Attach (AT)

Once an attribute has been created (with AC), it is ready to be attached to an existing component. This can be accomplished with the Attribute Attach (AT) command. The exact functioning of this command is dependent on the status of the Attribute Settings (AS), specifically the Placement setting. For more information, refer to the description of that command later in this chapter.

Type AT to execute the Attribute Attach (AT) command. When prompted, click on the desired component to select it. Next, you will be asked to select the particular attribute to attach from the sidebar menu. This menu lists the names of all attributes that have been created or loaded into the drawing from disk. You can also type in the attribute name, if you prefer.

When an attribute is attached, the field information is placed in one of two ways. The method employed depends on the Placement option, defined with the Attribute Settings (AS) command:

1. If Placement is set to "Edit Fields," you will be prompted to enter each new field value (replacing each default value.)

2. If Placement is set to "Use Default Values," the default values for each field are placed, without prompting you for a change.

If the first option is in effect, the next prompt will show the first field label and its default value. Use the back arrow or Delete key to edit the value, or you can add characters directly to the end of the default value. Press Enter to complete editing of the value and accept it. If you want to accept the default value without making any changes, simply press Enter when you are first prompted. The next field label and default value will then be shown, until all fields have been edited or accepted.

When the second placement option is in effect, CADD 6 skips the field editing prompts, and leaves the default values as originally defined. This does not have to be the final field value, however, as you can change the field values and the field labels later with the Attribute Edit (AE) command.

For either placement option, the next prompt is to choose the default display status for the attribute. This defines a default condition, meaning it controls whether or not the attribute is displayed if another command does not override it. The display choices are:

O for display default of ON (displayed)
F for display default of OFF (hidden from view)

Either default display can be overridden with the Attribute Display (AD) command. For example, even if an attribute has a default display status of ON, its attribute is still hidden from view when the Attribute Display (AD) command is set to OFF.

The final prompt of the command allows you to specify the placement location for the attribute. CADD 6 displays a box on the screen representing the size and shape of the attribute characters, which allows you to see how best to fit it into your drawing. Remember (after all these prompts), that you are attaching the attribute to a particular component, so you probably want to place it near that component. Move your cursor to position the attribute as desired, then click with your pointing device. Use a snap command to pick an exact point, or press Enter.

When the command is completed, the attribute fields will be shown on the screen (assuming the display mode is ON) at the specified location. If desired, you can attach another attribute to the same component. If you do not like the attribute's location, you can change it later with the Move Object (MVO) command, and it still stays attached to the component. (To do this, be sure to select the attribute by clicking on the *text*, not the component.) Prior to selecting the attribute's placement point you can also change the size or alignment by using Attribute Settings (AS) on-the-fly. When prompted for the placement point, type in the command code instead, and follow the prompts. The box representing the attribute shape will be updated for the new parameters.

Attributes can also be *pre-attached* to components when they are created with the Component Create (CC) command. As a result, each time that component is placed in a drawing, the attribute is automatically placed with it.

The exact appearance of any attribute placed in your drawing depends on several parameters, specifically Font, Color, and Size. Some of these settings apply only to attributes placed *after* the setting is changed, and do not have any affect on attributes already in your drawing. For this reason, you should establish the desired parameters *before* attaching many attributes that will have to be changed later.

If you explode (with CE or EX) a component that has an attribute attached to it, the attribute is also exploded into text lines. Each field becomes a separate line that can be edited with Text Edit (TE). CADD 6 no longer recognizes the text as an attribute.

Attribute Detach (DE)

Use the Attribute Detach (DE) command to detach an attribute from an individual component. This erases a particular placement of the attribute, while other placements and the attribute definition are not changed.

To execute the command, type in the command code DE. At the prompt, use your pointing device to select the attribute you want to detach. It's a good idea to click on the attribute text, rather than on the component or its reference point which may make it harder for CADD 6 to find the correct attribute.

Attribute Edit (AE)

The definition of any existing Attribute can be modified by using the Attribute Edit (AE) command to change the field label and/or the default field value. You can also use Attribute Edit (AE) to change the field value in any attribute placed in a drawing with the Attribute Attach (AT) command, or as part of a component.

Edit an attribute definition, or value, by typing AE to start the command. CADD 6 will prompt you to choose between editing a Definition (D), or editing a Placement (P).

To Edit a Definition. Editing an attribute definition affects every placement of that attribute in the drawing. It does not change the disk file for that attribute, unless you specifically save the edited attribute.

You will first be prompted to select the attribute to edit. Select it from the sidebar menu, or enter the desired attribute's name. CADD 6 then lists each field label and default value consecutively for you to modify. Make the desired changes, or press Enter to accept the new information. You can use the PgDn key to skip to the next field, or use PgUp to move backward to any previous field.

When you finish editing all the desired fields, press the F10 function key to complete the command. The screen will be updated to show the changed attribute definitions. All field labels are changed to the new labels, and any default field values that were changed are updated. Attributes that have a field value other than the default value are not changed by editing the definition. Figure 9.7 shows a drawing containing attributes, before and after the attribute definition was edited.

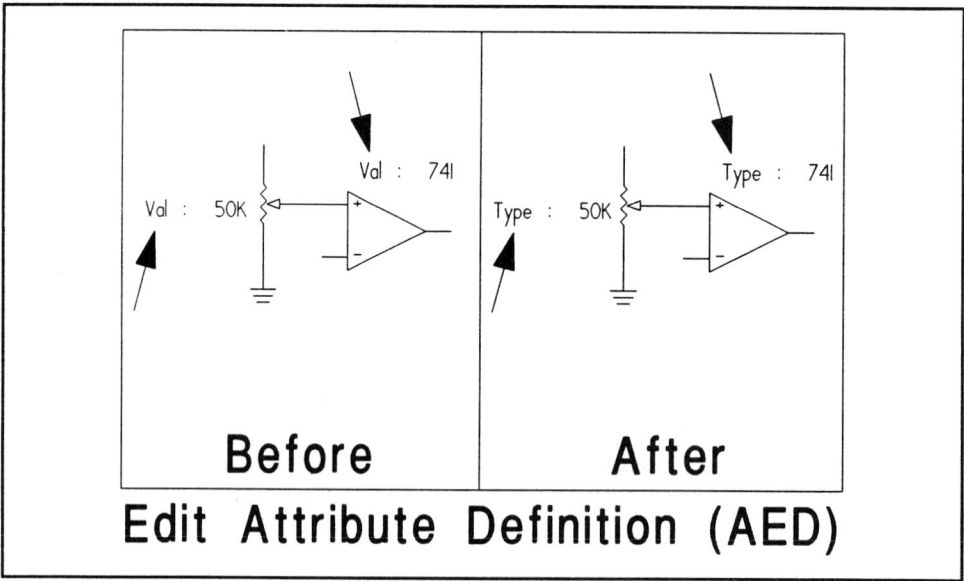

Figure 9.7 Changing attributes by Editing Definitions.

If you want to abort an attribute editing session at any time, press Esc to cancel any changes that were made, and return to the Attribute Edit option line.

To Edit a Placement. Selecting the option to edit a placement allows you to modify one specific placement of an attribute in the drawing. You will first be prompted to select the individual attribute you want to edit. Use your pointing device to click on the desired attribute. Next, select one of these options:

    F to change the field values
    D to change the default display option
    L to change the attribute label display option

If you choose option F, the field values are printed consecutively, allowing you to modify each value. If you do not want to make a change, press Enter to skip to the next field. Press the F10 function key to accept all the changes made to the field values.

To modify the default display status of the attribute, select the D option. If the current default display is ON, you can turn it OFF, and vice versa. When you have the desired display status, press Enter to complete the command, or press F to edit the field values. The modifications to the selected attribute will be shown on the screen when the Attribute Edit (AE) is completed. An example of editing an attribute placement and attribute definition is shown in Figure 9.8.

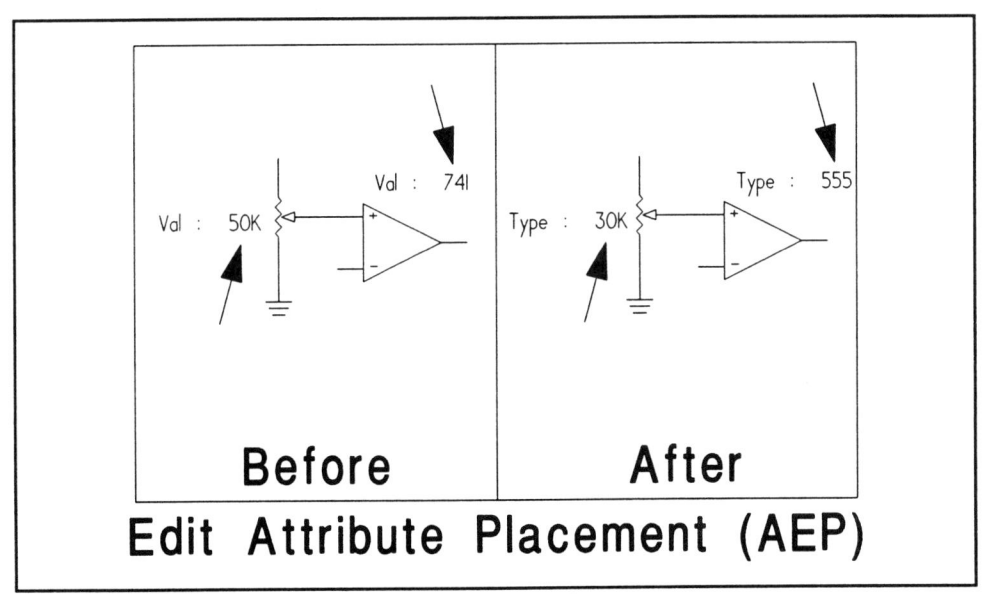

Figure 9.8 Changing one specific Attribute Placement.

If you choose L, you can change the attribute label setting to ON or OFF. If the Label option, contained in the Attribute Settings (AS) command, is set to Default, the field labels are displayed if Label is set to ON. When Label is turned OFF, only the field information is displayed. If the Label option is set to either ON or OFF (not Default) within the Attribute Settings (AS) command, turning Label ON or OFF from the

Attribute Edit (AE) command will not affect the display. The following is an example of attribute Labels ON and OFF:

Label (ON)
Model No: AR943-S
Cost: $325.95
Vendor: Jones Manufacturing
Address: 805 So. Main
City, State: Portland, OR 97103

Label (OFF)
AR943-S
$325.95
Jones Manufacturing
805 So. Main
Portland, OR 97103

Attribute Settings (AS)

This command is used to set the attribute's Font, Size, Color, Direction, and other settings for display and placement. The Attribute Settings (AS) command is executed by typing AS. You will be prompted with a selection set. The following is an explanation of the attribute settings commands.

Font. Use this feature to select and load one of the fonts included with CADD 6. A font is a typeface, or a group of characters assigned to the keys on the keyboard. They may be letters in a particular style or some other kind of characters.

Select Font, type the name of the font style you want to load, and press Enter to complete the selection. You can also select a font from the list of fonts which appears on the sidebar menu. Note that you may have to specify the font's correct file path if it is located somewhere other than the default file path.

The selected font is loaded automatically when it's selected. Depending on the complexity of the font, this process may take a few seconds.

> **TIP:** If you enter a font name that is not defined, you are asked whether this is a new font. Answer NO if you did not mean to make this selection. Answer YES if you are going to create a new font. Before trying to create a font, be sure to refer to the discussion of the Font Create (WT) command, described in Chapter 8.

siZe. Set the height of the attribute with the siZe feature. Make sure you set the height of your attribute appropriately. If you are working in a 50-foot area, 1-inch high text is barely visible. To change the attribute height, use the siZe feature. At the prompt, type in the new height and press Enter. As with other values you entered, the unit associated with the height (inches, centimeters, etc.) is the default unit, unless you specify something different (by adding a foot mark ('), for example.)

Color. Select the color of attributes with the Color feature. Either enter the number of the desired color, or select a color from the color bar displayed on the sidebar menu. The attribute Color prompt is also nested within the color selection prompts of Color Settings (CS). The Color feature does not change or affect the color of attributes already existing in the drawing. You can still change the attribute color even if you do not have a color adapter for your monitor. If you have a monochrome monitor, but a multi-pen plotter or color printer, you can set color selections in your attribute and have them displayed when they are plotted. As with other color selections, your screen choices are limited to those available with your particular graphics display.

dIsplay. The setting chosen for dIsplay determines whether all attributes (labels and values) in the drawing are turned ON and displayed, or turned OFF and hidden from view. Either of these options will override the default display setting defined for each individual attribute when it is attached (See Attribute Attach, AT.)

Select one of the three display options at the bottom of the screen by pressing:

    O for ON to dIsplay all attributes
    F for OFF to hide all attributes from view
    D for DEFAULT to turn each attribute ON or OFF, according to its default display settings

If you select the Off option, you may have to use Redraw (RD) to refresh the screen and hide all remnants of the attributes. You will probably use this option often to print the drawing with no attributes, or turn the attributes back On when you need to use the information contained in them.

Label. The setting chosen for Label determines whether all attribute Labels in the drawing are turned ON and displayed, or turned OFF and hidden from view. Either of these options will override the default display setting defined for each individual attribute when it is attached (See Attribute Attach, AT). The Label feature is overridden by the dIsplay feature. If dIsplay is OFF, and Label is ON, the attributes remain invisible.

Select one of the three display options at the bottom of the screen by pressing:

O for ON to display Labels if dIsplay is turned ON
F for OFF to hide all Labels from view if dIsplay is turned ON
D for DEFAULT turns each Label ON or OFF, according to its default settings

at Placement. The at Placement feature has two settings:

Edit fields   Default

When the at Placement option is set to "Edit fields," CADD 6 prompts for the field values whenever you place (attach) an attribute, or if a component with an attribute is placed in your drawing. If at Placement is set to "Default," attributes are automatically placed with their default field values. (Remember that you can always change the default field values after placement with Attribute Edit, (AE).)

Direction. The Direction option controls the rotation angle used to place attributes in your drawing. If you choose a direction of *Horizontal*, all attributes placed following this command are drawn with horizontal text. Selecting the *Aligned* direction causes all attributes to be drawn at the angle currently specified by the Component Rotate (CR) factor. See Figure 9.9 for an example of aligned attributes. If CR is set to 45°, when you place a component, it will be placed at that angle. If you then attach an attribute to the component, the attribute is will also be drawn at an angle of 45°.

Auto placement. The Auto placement option is a toggle that controls the placement location of any attributes pre-attached to a component. When a component is placed with a pre-attached attribute, the attribute can be located in one of two ways:

1. If Auto placement is set to ON, the attribute will automatically be located in the position where it was first placed during Component Create (CC), relative to the component itself.

2. If Auto placement is OFF, CADD 6 will prompt you to place the attribute once the component has been placed. If the attribute has more than one attribute attached, you will be prompted for the location of each.

All of the Attribute Settings (AS) affect how an attribute is placed in a drawing. For this reason, you may want to check that the settings are correct before attaching any attributes or bringing in a component that already has an attribute.

Export Attribute (XA)

Now that you know how to create attributes and manipulate them, the next step is extracting the data for use outside of CADD 6. Once you have a drawing containing attributes, you can use the Export Attribute (XA) command to save that attribute information to a disk file. This file can then be read into other programs, like a spreadsheet for analysis, or a word processor for creating a report.

Chapter 9: Using Symbols ■ 9-27

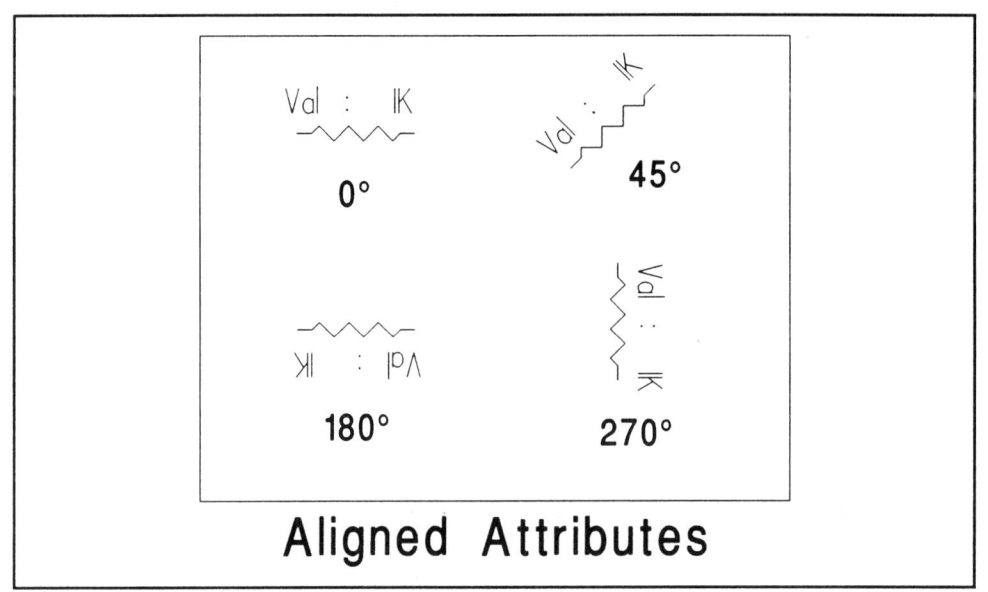

Figure 9.9 Changing the Attribute Direction.

Type XA to execute the Export Attribute command. You will be prompted with the standard selection menu. Choose the D option to export all the attributes in the drawing, or use other options to select specific attributes and use filters, as required. When you have finished defining the selection set, press Enter to return to the Export command.

The next prompt will ask which format you want to use for the export file. You can select from these choices:

A for ASCII (.ASC)
R for Lotus Row layout (.WK1)
L for Lotus Column layout (.WK1)

If you choose to save the file in one of the Lotus formats, the data file is formatted so that it can be loaded into Lotus 1-2-3, or any spreadsheet which accepts Lotus files (most spreadsheet programs.)

A file saved in ASCII can be read into any editor or program which accepts ASCII files (even CADD 6). For each attribute placement, the data file lists four lines of information:

/100 then the name of the component it is attached to
/200 then the name of the attribute
/300 then the name of each field, separated by commas
/400 then the value assigned to each field, separated by commas

Chapter 9: Using Symbols

In each line of the export file, the data (the actual name or value) is enclosed in quotes and separated by commas.

To complete the Attribute Export (XA) command you will be prompted to enter the file name for the data file. Type in the desired name with a path, if desired. If no path is given, CADD 6 will assume you want to save the file in the \CADD6 directory.

Figure 9.10 shows the drawing to be constructed in the tutorial which follows. The ASCII file is extracted from this drawing looks like:

/100,"RESISTOR"
/200,"VALUE"
/300,"VAL"
/400,"100k"
/100,"RESISTOR"
/200,"VALUE"
/300,"VAL"
/400,"1K"
/100,"RESISTOR"
/200,"VALUE"
/300,"VAL"
/400,"10K"
/100,"RESISTOR"
/200,"VALUE"
/300,"VAL"
/400,"1K"
/100,"NPN"
/200,"VALUE"
/300,"VAL"
/400,"2N2222"
/100,"DIODE"
/200,"VALUE"
/300,"VAL"
/400,"1N914"
/100,"OPAMP"
/200,"VALUE"
/300,"VAL"
/400,"741"

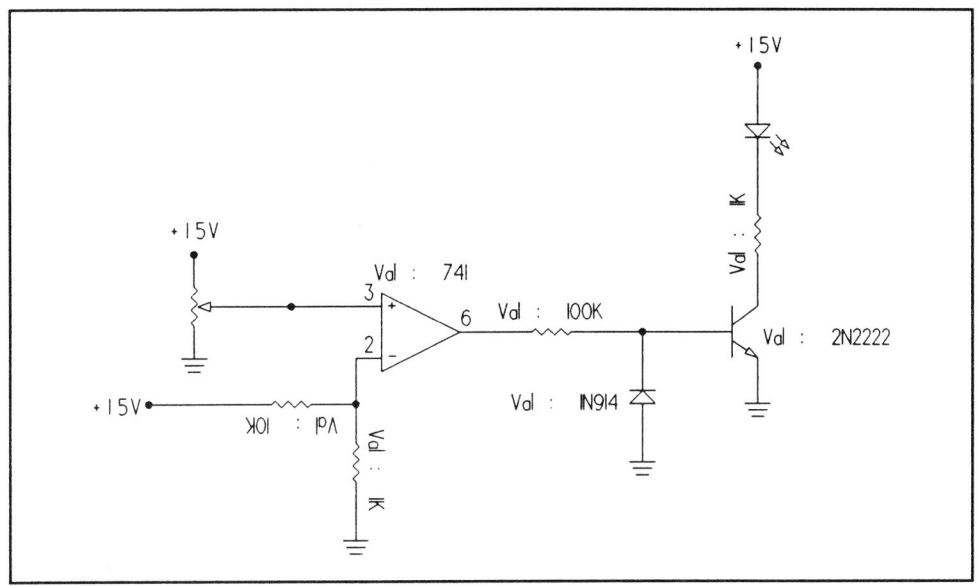

Figure 9.10 The completed Schematic Tutorial drawing.

ELECTRONIC SCHEMATIC TUTORIAL

During this tutorial, you will create the electronic schematic drawing shown in Figure 9.10, complete with attributes. Symbols are placed at various Component Scales (CZ) and Component Rotate (CR) angles. You will also attach attributes representing resistance and other values for the symbols.

Don't worry if you are not familiar with electronic schematics and components. You can still create the drawing from the illustrations and step-by-step instructions given. If you do not know what a resistor or operational amplifier looks like, just copy the symbols exactly as you see them in the figures. Even if your final components do not look exactly like the ones in the figures, you can still construct the schematic drawing and learn how to handle components and attributes.

Creating the Components and Attributes

You will first create all the components and attributes to be used in the schematic drawing. The symbols are drawn on a grid size of 0.025" X 0.025". The schematic drawing will then be created by snapping the symbols and lines onto grid points. This allows the symbols and lines to be snapped together accurately, without the extra step of using a snap command.

Step-by-step instructions are given for drawing the resistor component in Figure 9.11.

Start by setting the appropriate parameters that affect the drawing:

9-30 ■ Chapter 9: Using Symbols

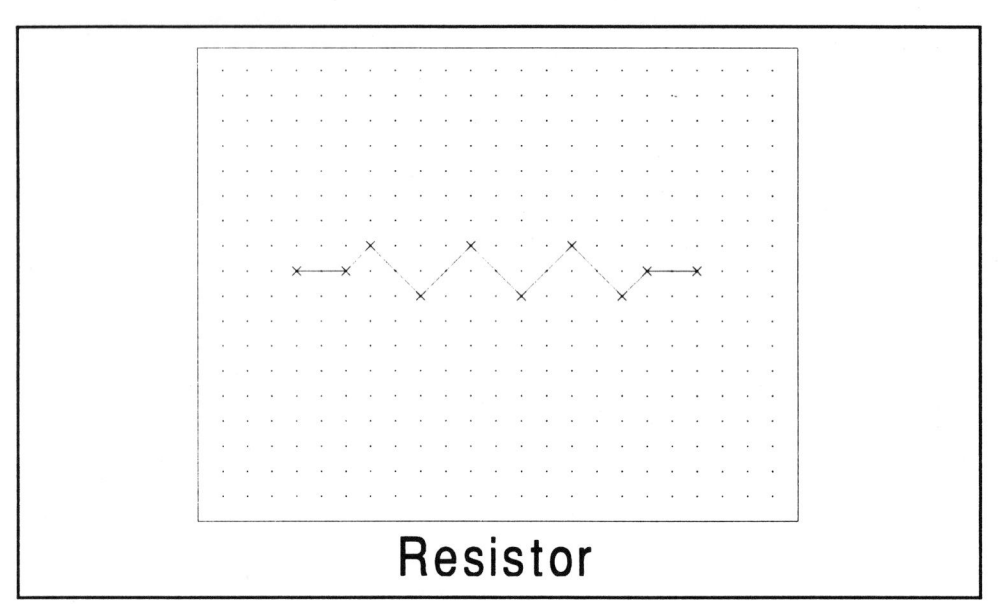

Figure 9.11 Drawing the Resistor Symbol.

    Type: GS to set the Grid Size
    Type: .025 (and press Enter) for both the X and Y Grid sizes
    Type: SG to turn ON the Snap Grid

This is a toggle. If it was originally ON, entering SG turns it OFF, and vice versa. Enter SG as necessary to make sure it is ON.

    Type: AS (for Attribute Settings)
    Type: Z (for size)
    Type: .12" (and press Enter) for the Attribute Size
    Press Enter to finish the Attribute Settings command

    Type: CS (for Color Settings) and select L for Line Color
    Pick color number 15 to use for drawing the components
    Select the A option for Attributes
    Pick color number 13 for the Attribute Color
    Press Enter to finish the Color Settings command

Zoom the display up to a small area, which is more appropriate for drawing a small symbol:

    Type: ZM (for Zoom Value)
    Type: .1 (and press Enter) for the Value
    Click on a point near the center of the screen for the "new center"

Chapter 9: Using Symbols ■ 9-31

Next, draw the lines:

    Click on a grid point near the left side of the screen
    Move the cursor two grid points (0.05") to the right
    Click (or press Enter) to complete the line

    Type: OR (for Ortho) and make sure that Ortho mode is OFF
    Move one grid point to the right and one point up
    Click to place the next point, as shown in Figure 9.12

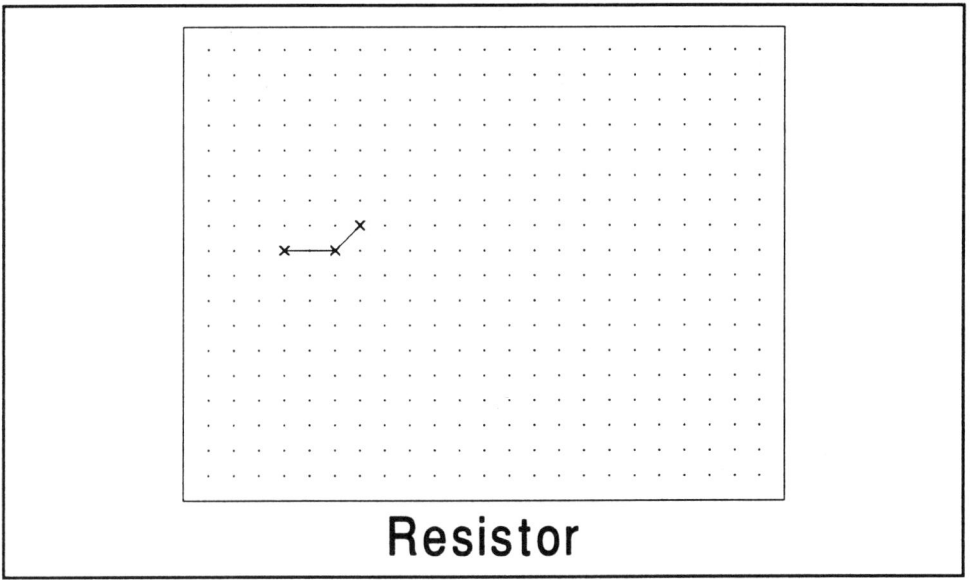

Figure 9.12 Drawing lines of the Resistor between grid points.

    Move two points to the right and two points down
    Click to place the point

    Move two points to the right again, and two points up
    Click to place the point

Repeat the previous procedure until your drawing looks like the resistor in Figure 9.11. Once the symbol is drawn, you are ready to create the attribute that becomes part of the resistor component. First, save your resistor drawing:

    Type: SA (for Save) then D (for Drawing)
    For the drawing name, type: RESISTOR (and press Enter)

    Type: AC (for Attribute Create)
    Type: VALUE (and press Enter) for the Attribute Name

9-32 ■ Chapter 9: Using Symbols

This is the name you will use to identify the attribute throughout this tutorial.

    Type: Val (and press Enter) for the first label
    Type: 1K (and press Enter) for the default value

This value of 1K is used as the field value unless you specifically change it.

    Press the F10 function key.

This completes the Attribute Create (AC) command. Be aware that pressing Enter does not complete the command, but simply skips to the next field.

Now, save the attribute so it is available for use in other drawings.

    Type: SA (for Save) then T (for aTtribute) to save the attribute to disk
    Select VALUE from the sidebar menu for the Attribute Name
    Press Enter to accept the default path and file name shown

Next, create a component from the resistor symbol, with the attribute attached.

    Type: CC (for Component Create)
    Select: W (for Window)
    Place a selection window around the entire resistor
    Press Enter to accept the selection
    Type: RESISTOR (and press Enter) for the Component Name

    For the reference point, use SC (Snap Closest Point) to snap exactly onto the left-most point of the resistor

Next, three options will be shown on the bottom of the screen.

    Select A to attach an Attribute
    Click on VALUE from the sidebar menu for the Attribute Name
    For the default display option select O for ON
    Select O for On at the Display Attribute Label prompt

This causes the attribute and label to be displayed, unless the dIsplay setting in Attribute Settings (AS) is toggled OFF.

Next, you must choose a location for the attribute. The attribute text is represented on the screen with a box.

    Move the box around until it is approximately centered over the symbol (See Figure 9.13)
    Click to select the Placement Point

Chapter 9: Using Symbols ■ 9-33

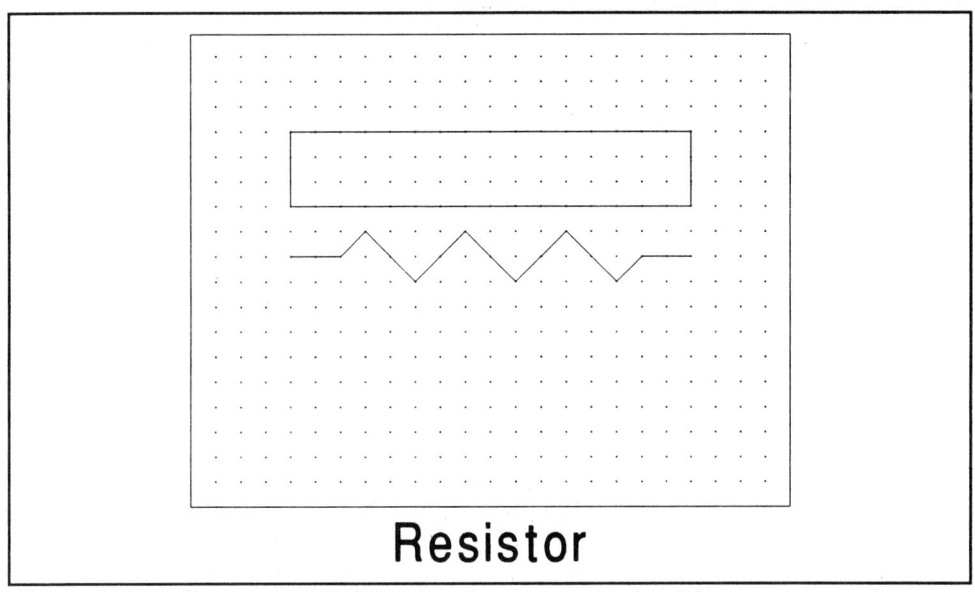

[Figure: Resistor symbol with box above zigzag, labeled "Resistor"]

Figure 9.13 Choosing a location for the resistor's Attribute.

Use your own judgement here, since the exact placement point is not important.

    At the next prompt select R to Replace
    Type: 1K (and press Enter) for the attribute VALUE field
    Place the attribute over the resistor, as before

This will cause the original objects to be replaced with the component. The attribute is then drawn in place of the box. The component is now created, as shown in Figure 9.14. The final step is to save the component to disk so it can be used in another drawing later.

    Type: SA (for Save), then select C (for Component)
    Select RESISTOR for the component name
    Press Enter to accept the default path

Your resistor component is now saved. Continue with this method to draw the remaining symbols, shown in the following figures:

Figure 9.15 DIODE	Figure 9.16 DOT
Figure 9.17 LED	Figure 9.18 NPN (transistor)
Figure 9.19 OPAMP (operational amplifier)	Figure 9.20 GROUND
Figure 9.21 VARRES (variable resistor)	

9-34 ■ Chapter 9: Using Symbols

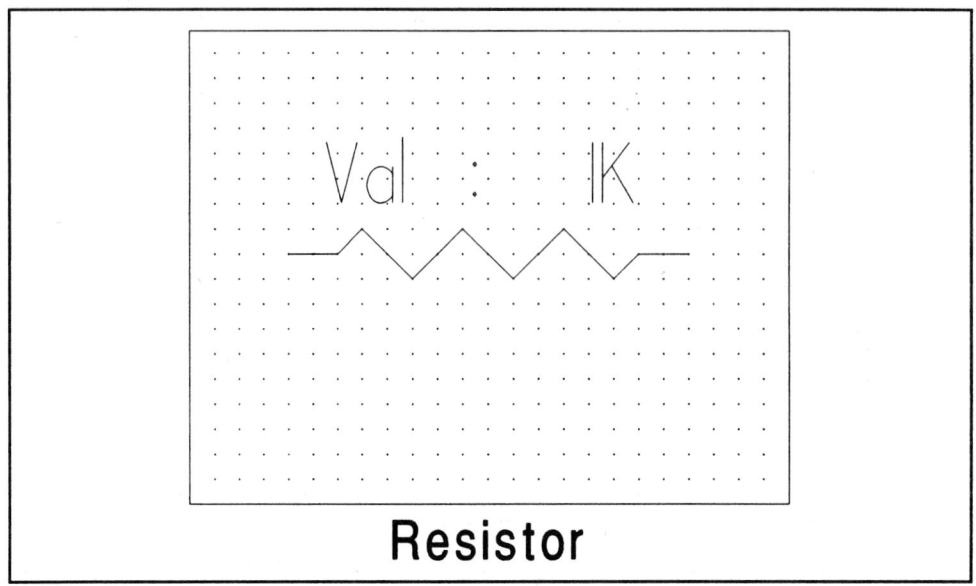

Figure 9.14 The resistor symbol with Attribute.

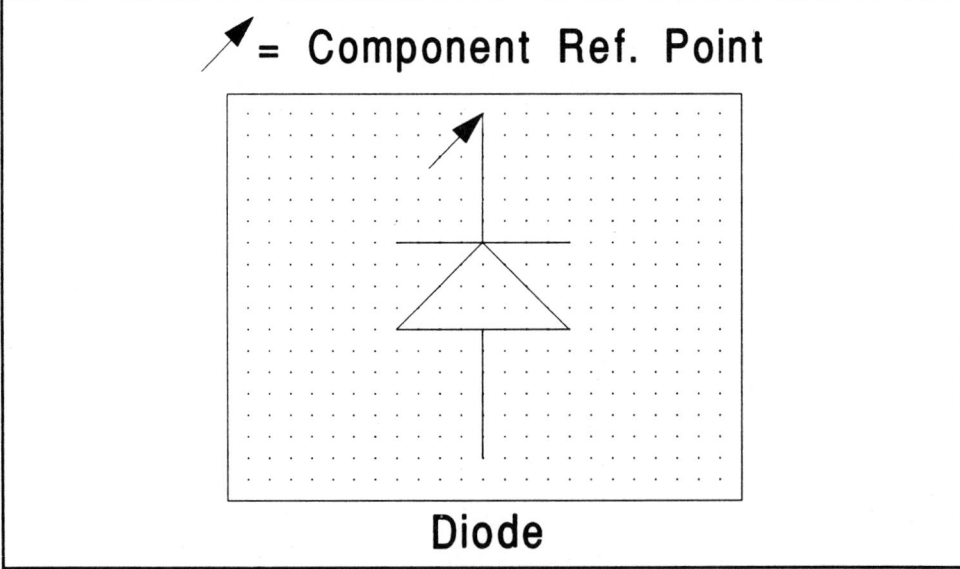

Figure 9.15 The size and shape of the Diode Component.

Chapter 9: Using Symbols ■ 9-35

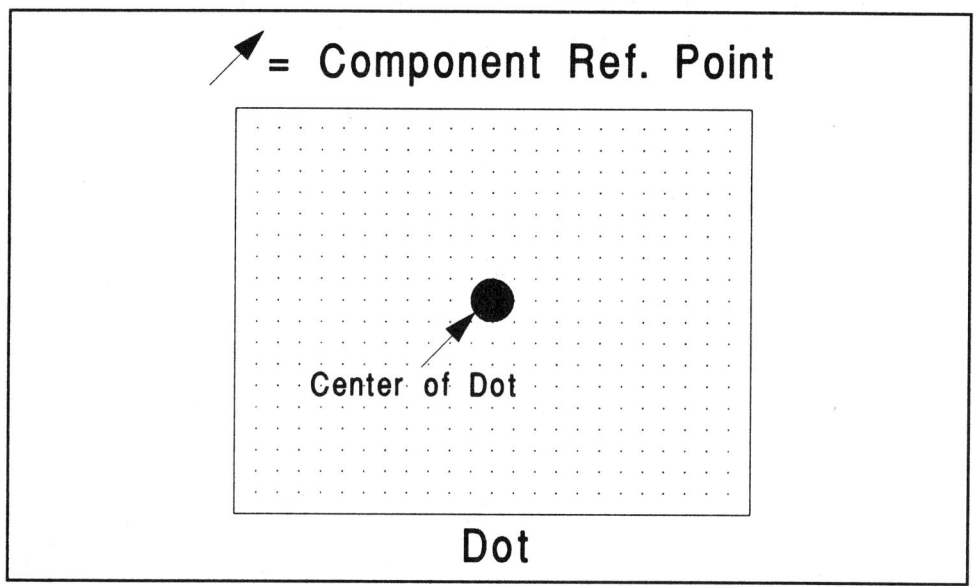

Figure 9.16 The connection Dot Component.

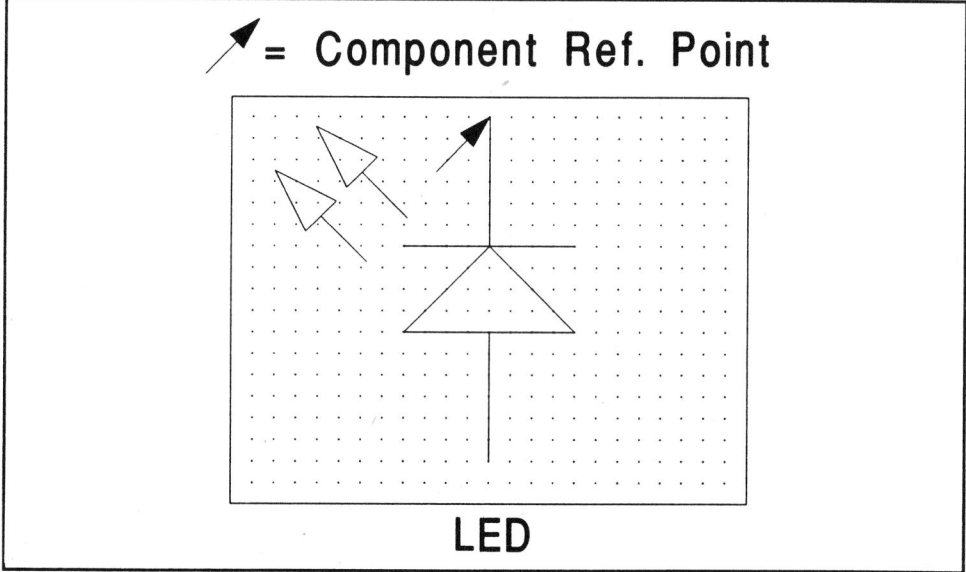

Figure 9.17 The size and shape of the LED Component.

9-36 ■ Chapter 9: Using Symbols

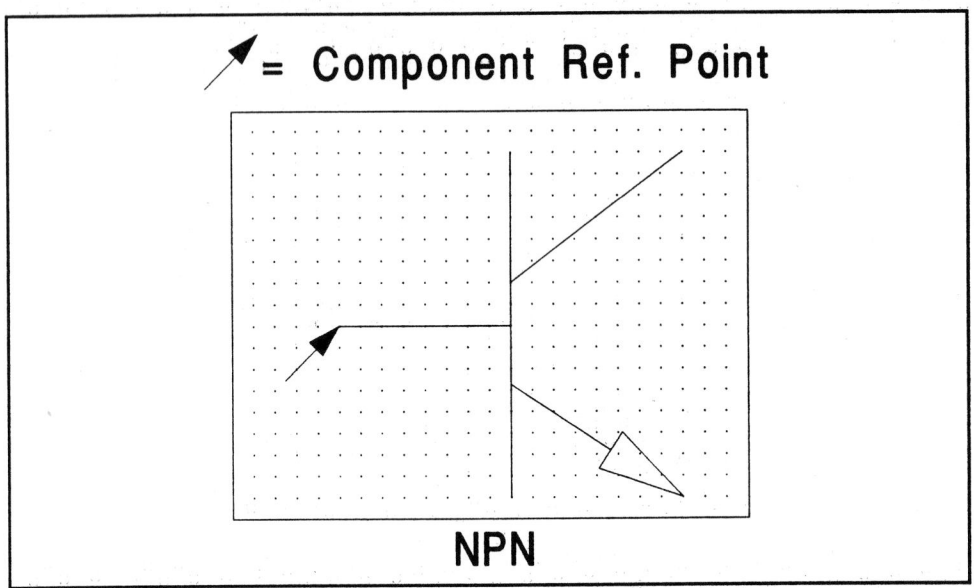

Figure 9.18 The size and shape of the Transistor (NPN) Component.

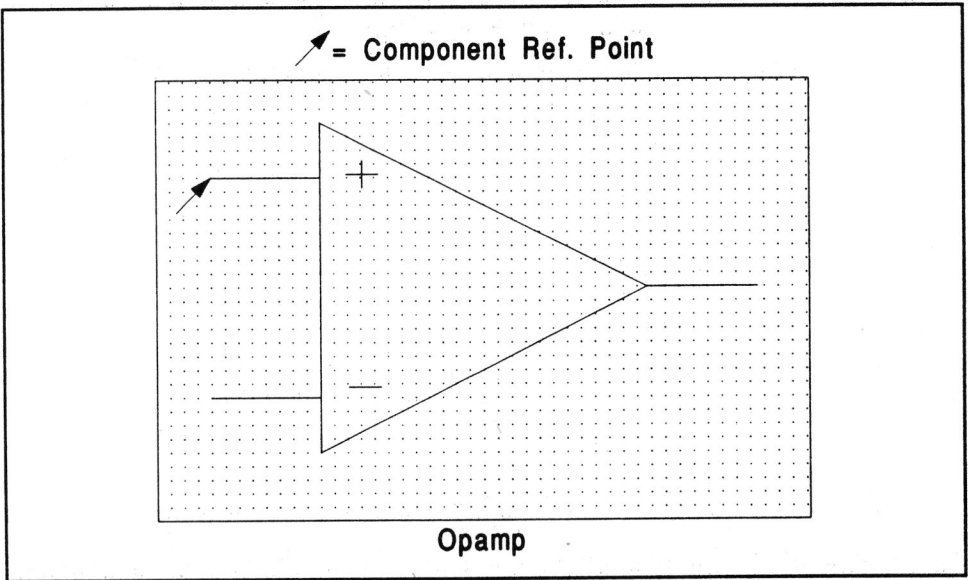

Figure 9.19 The size and shape of the Operational Amplifier Component.

To draw these components you must apply many of the commands introduced in all the earlier chapters. When drawing the arrows at an angle, like those shown in Figures 9.17 and 9.18, be sure to turn Snap Grid (SG) OFF. You can either draw each symbol as an individual drawing, or draw them all on one drawing, then save them as individual symbols.

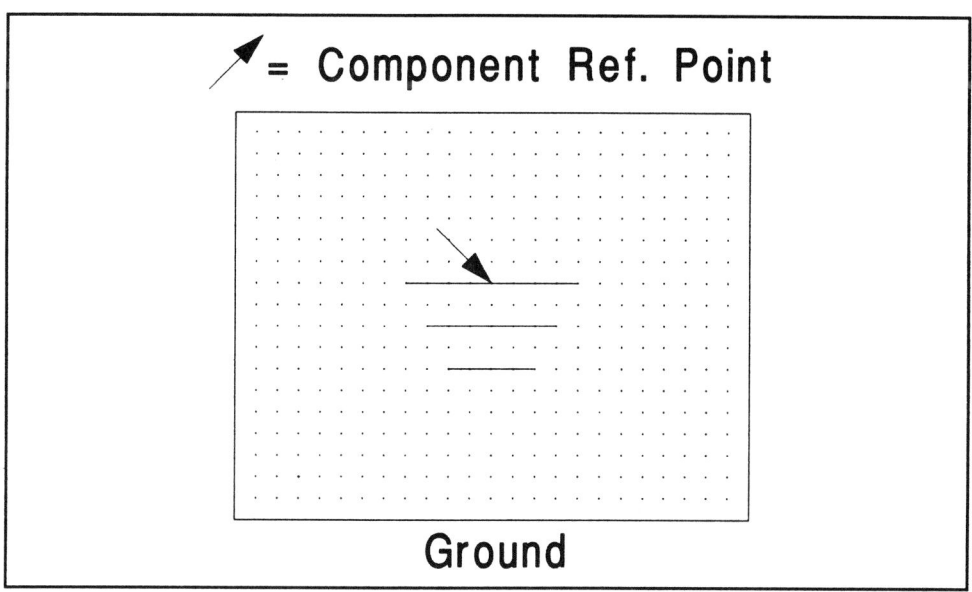

Figure 9.20 The size and shape of the Ground Component.

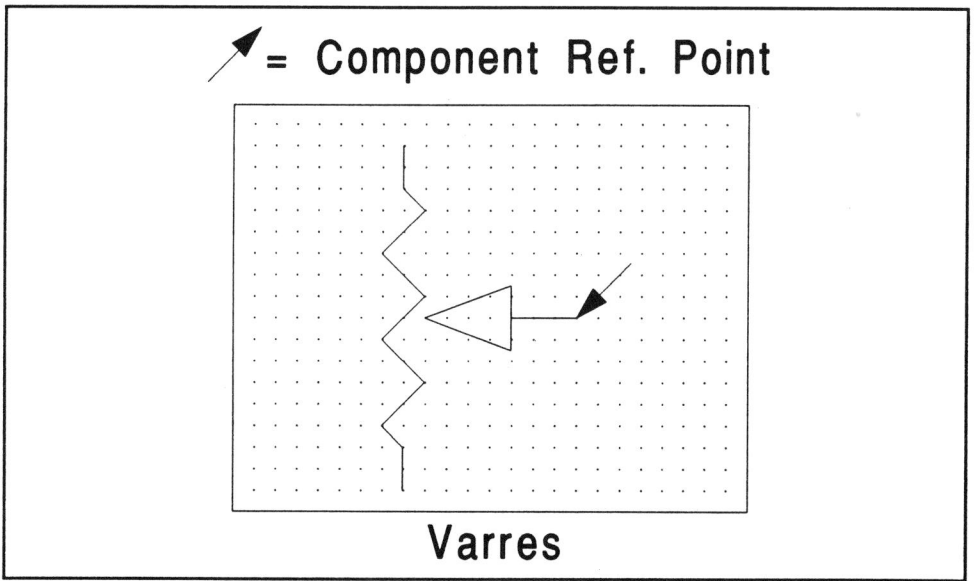

Figure 9.21 The size and shape of the Variable Resistor.

Use the Component Create (CC) command to create a component from each symbol, with the names shown on the figures
Save each component to disk using the Save Component (SAC) command

Note that only the first resistor drawing has an attribute pre-attached. Attributes are attached to the other components *after* they are placed in the schematic drawing.

Chapter 9: Using Symbols

> **TIP:** To create the connection dot, use one of the Fill commands covered in Chapter 10. If you haven't been through that chapter yet, try reading up on the Window Fill (WF) command. It can be used to easily fill the connection dot circle.

Creating the Schematic Drawing

Now that all the components have been created, you are ready to put them together to draw the schematic. You are not instructed during the tutorial to save your drawing, however you may want to do so periodically. This protects you from losing any information in case you have to finish the tutorial at a later time.

Start the drawing by setting up some initial parameters:

    Type: CZ (for Component Scale)
    Type: 1.0 (and press Enter) for both the *X* and *Y* scale factors

If CADD 6 displays that they are already at 1.0, press Enter to accept the values.

    Type: CR (for Component Rotate)
    Type: 0 (and press Enter) for a Rotation Angle of degrees, or press Enter if 0° is shown as the default

    Type: AS (for Attribute Settings) and set these options:

        at Placement - Edit fields
        Direction - Aligned
        Auto placement - OFF
        Font - Select the font ENGINEER from the sidebar menu
        siZe - Type: .12 (and press Enter)

    Type: TS (for Text Settings), then select:

        Font - Select the font ENGINEER from the sidebar menu
        siZe - Type: .12 (and press Enter)

    Type: CS (for Color Settings), and select:

        L for Line Color - Pick color number 11
        A for Attributes - Pick color number 13
        T for Text - Pick color number 14

Chapter 9: Using Symbols ■ 9-39

The components have already been drawn with color 15. They remain in this color, regardless of the other color settings.

>Type: GS (for Grid Size)
>Type: .05 (and press Enter) for both the *X* and *Y* values
>Type: SG to turn the snap grid ON

The first symbol to be placed is the operational amplifier, shown in Figure 9.19.

>Type: CP (for Component Place)
>Select the symbol named OPAMP from the sidebar menu
>Select a placement point by snapping to a grid point somewhere near the center of your screen

Starting at the right-hand point of the opamp:

>Draw a horizontal line approximately 0.3" long (count over 6 grid points)

This gives you enough room to attach the next symbol and place any required text. Now insert the resistor.

>Type: CP and select the symbol named RESISTOR
>Insert the resistor symbol by snapping it onto the right end of the horizontal line

This end point is on a grid point, so you do not have to use a snap command this time. Since the resistor symbol was created with an attribute attached, you will be prompted to enter the field values.

>Type: 100k (and press Enter) for the field name "Value" (the resistance value)
>Select a placement location for the attribute somewhere above, but near the resistor

Your drawing should now look like Figure 9.22.

>Draw a horizontal line, approximately 1" long, from the right end of the resistor
>Type: CP and select the DOT connection symbol
>Place the component near the midpoint of the line

Be sure you place all connection dots on grid points so other lines and symbols can be connected to them accurately.

>Draw a vertical line approximately 0.5" long from the connection dot, towards the bottom of your screen
>Type: CP and select the DIODE symbol
>Place the component on the lower end of the vertical line

9-40 ■ Chapter 9: Using Symbols

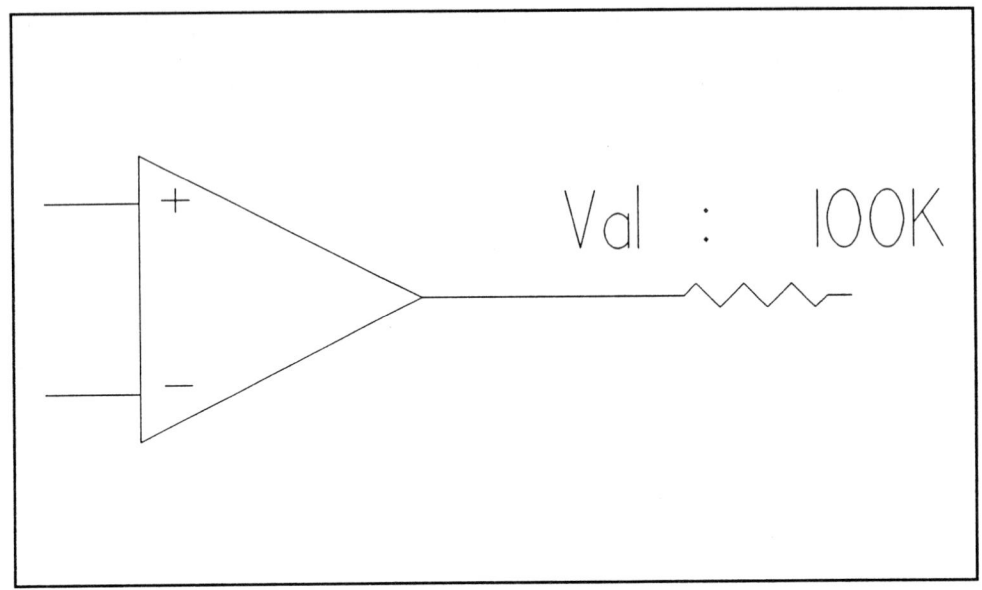

Figure 9.22 Placing the Resistor and its Attribute.

Your schematic should now look like the one in Figure 9.23.

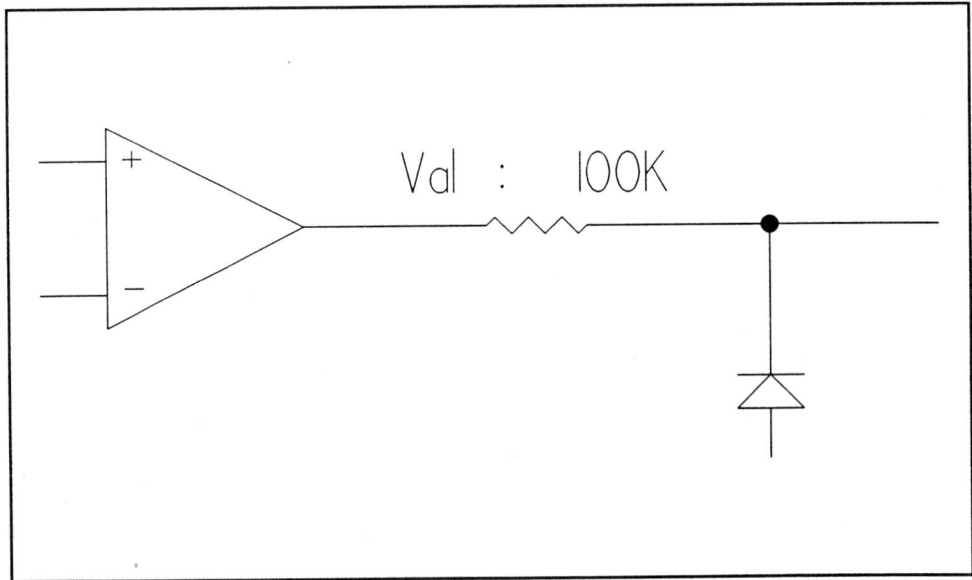

Figure 9.23 Adding the Diode Component.

Draw a short, vertical line downward from the diode
Type: CP and select the GROUND symbol
Place it at the endpoint of the line

Type: CP and select the NPN transistor symbol
Place it at the end of the line that was extended from the resistor
Accept all default values to place the symbol as shown in Figure 9.24

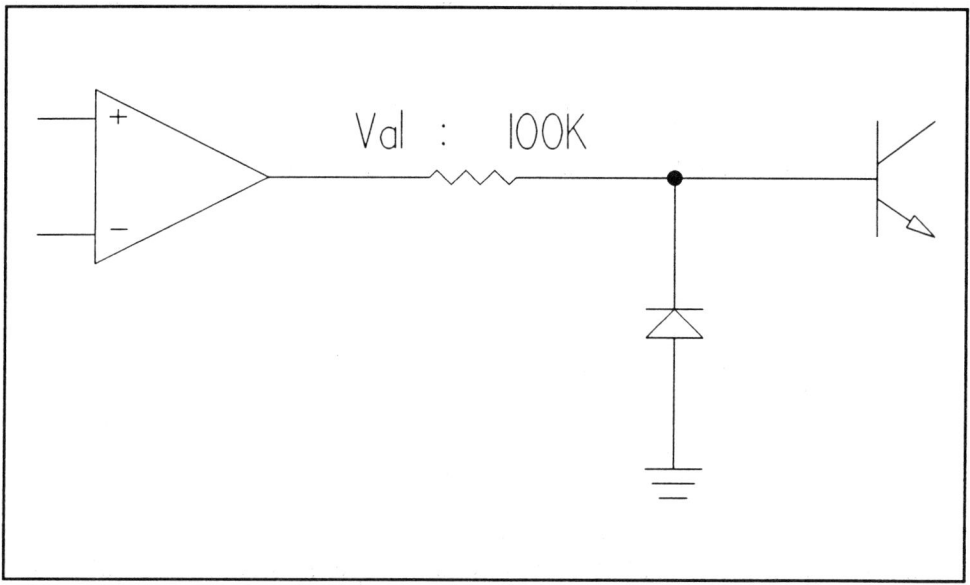

Figure 9.24 Placing the Transistor Component.

Extend a short, vertical line downward from the arrow of the transistor
Place a GROUND symbol at the end of the line

Draw a short, vertical line upward from the side of the transistor, opposite the ground
Type: CP and select another RESISTOR symbol

When the ghost image of the resistor is drawn on the screen, you are able to see that the component rotation is incorrect for this location. Remember that you can change the Component Rotation angle on-the-fly in the CP command. Prior to selecting the symbol placement point:

Type: CR (for Component Rotate)
At the prompt, enter a new component rotation of 90°
Click to place the resistor at the end of the vertical line

Since the resistor symbol was created with an attribute attached, you will be prompted to enter the field values.

Press Enter to accept the default resistance value of 1k
Place the attribute to the left of the symbol, as shown in Figure 9.25

9-42 ■ Chapter 9: Using Symbols

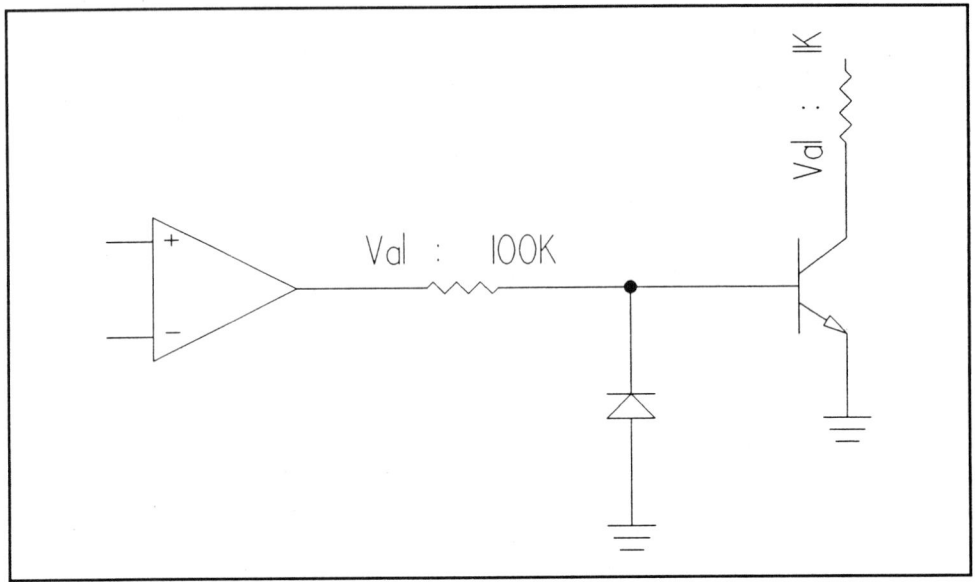

Figure 9.25 Placing the second Resistor and Attribute.

    Draw a short line upward from the top of the resistor
    Place the symbol named LED (Light Emitting Diode) at the end point of this line

Prior to specifying the placement point, use CR to adjust the rotation angle.

    Extend a short line upward from the LED
    Place a connection DOT symbol at the end of the line

This finishes this section of the circuit. Figure 9.26 shows the drawing as it has been completed so far.

Repeat the above procedures to insert the remaining symbols and connections to the left of the opamp. You need to place connection points, ground symbols, a variable resistor, and two resistors. Remember to enter the resistance values for the field values of the attributes, and place them as shown in Figure 9.27.

Now you are ready to attach other attributes to the symbols.

    Type: AT (for Attribute Attach)
    Click on the OPAMP to select it
    Select the attribute named VALUE from the sidebar menu
    Type: 741 (and press Enter) at the prompt for Field "Val"
    Set Display Attribute to ON
    Set Display Label to ON
    Specify a placement location above the symbol

Chapter 9: Using Symbols ■ 9-43

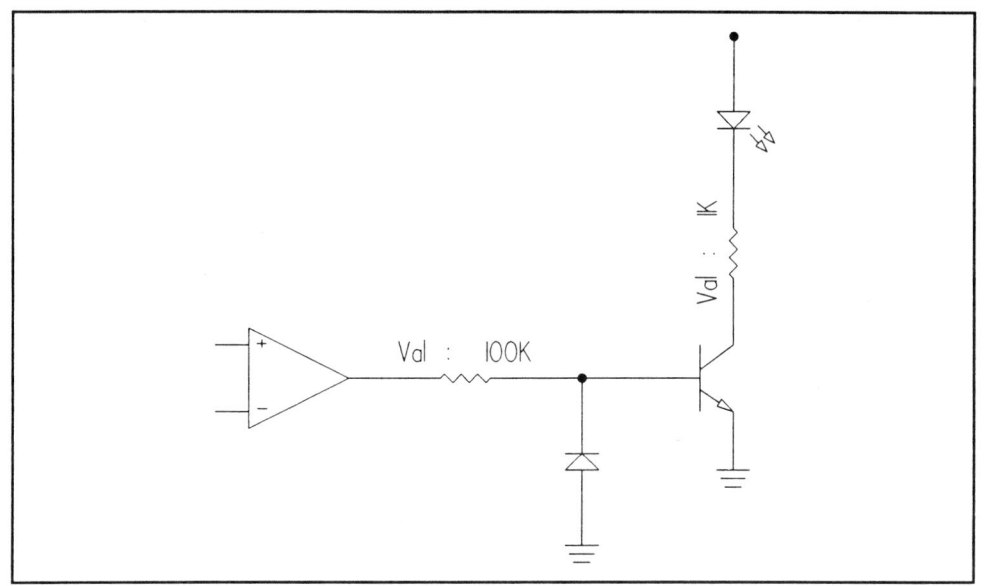

Figure 9.26 Placing the LED and connection dot.

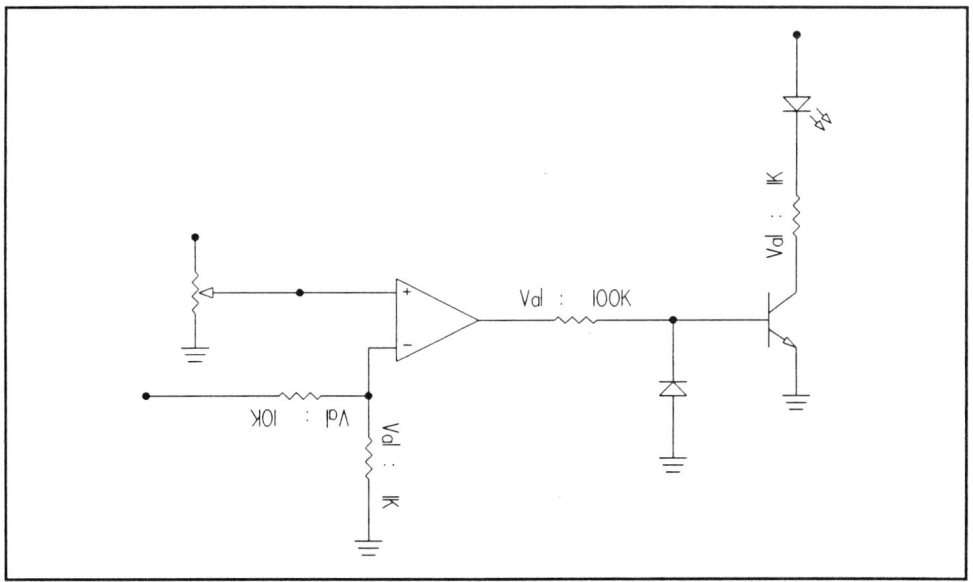

Figure 9.27 Completing Placement of the Components.

Repeat these steps to attach the VALUE attribute to the DIODE and NPN transistor symbols. Enter the values and placement locations shown in Figure 9.28.

Complete the diagram by adding the rest of the text (other than the attributes) shown in Figure 9.29. (See Chapter 8 for more information on placing Text in a drawing.)

9-44 ■ Chapter 9: Using Symbols

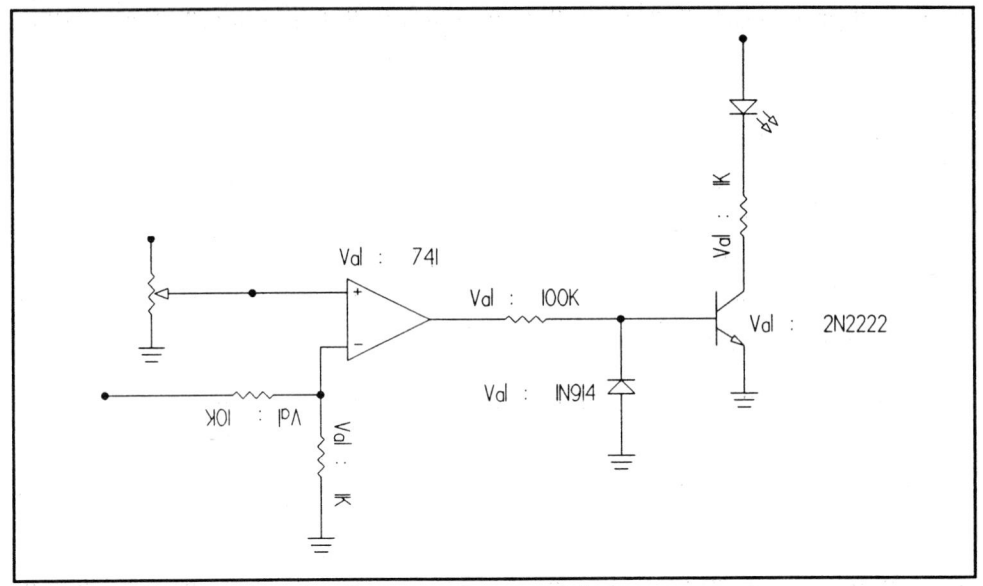

Figure 9.28 Attaching Attributes to the remaining components.

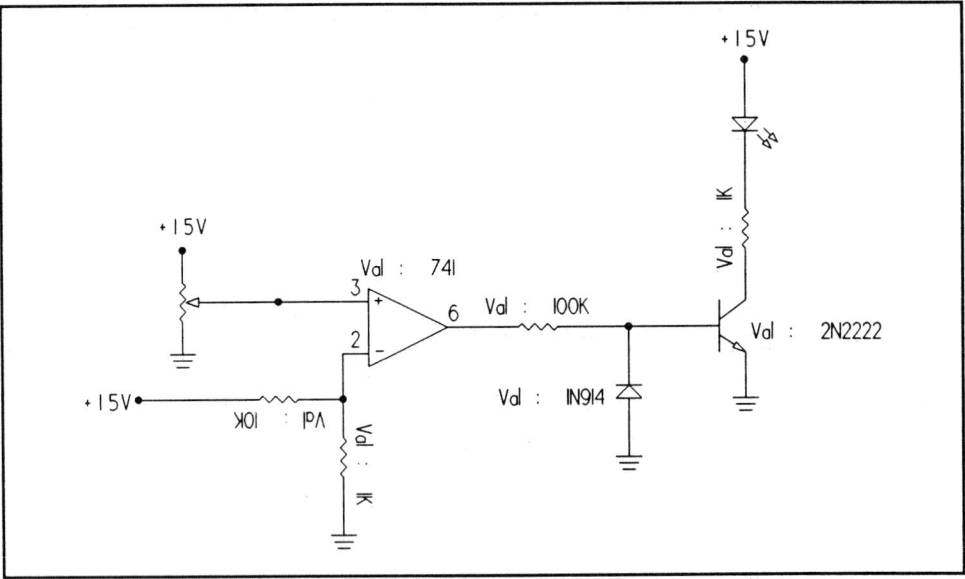

Figure 9.29 Adding the remaining text to the drawing.

Your schematic drawing should now have all the information shown in Figure 9.29. Your drawing probably looks somewhat different, depending on where you placed text and how long your connection lines are.

Before completing this tutorial, you may want to experiment with the attributes placed in the drawing.

Chapter 9: Using Symbols ■ 9-45

> Type: AS (for Attribute Settings)
> Select I for dIsplay and set the display mode to OFF
> Press Enter to finish the Attribute Settings command

The attributes will be erased from the display. Repeat the command, but enter ON, to turn the attribute display back ON. Next, select L for Label and turn the attribute label OFF. The attribute information will remain, but the "VAL:" label will not be present. This feature helps clean up the drawing considerably. Press Escape to exit the Attribute Settings (AS) command.

> Edit an attribute by typing AE (for Attribute Edit)
> Select D to edit a Definition
> When prompted to identify which attribute to edit, select VALUE from the sidebar menu
> Type: TYPE (and press Enter) for the new name of the field label "Val"
> Press the backspace key to erase the 1K value and press Enter
> Press the F10 function key to complete the command
> Type: AS then L for Label and turn the attribute Labels ON
> Type: RD to Redraw the screen and show the updated field labels

Next, you can export the attribute information to an ASCII file and look at the format of this data. To export the attribute data:

> Type: XA (for Export Attribute)
> Choose the D option to export all attributes in the drawing
> Press Enter to finish the Export Attribute command
> Select A for ASCII when prompted for the export file format
> Type: ELECATTS (and press Enter) for the name of the export file

Note the directory that CADD 6 uses to save the file because you will load it from there shortly.

Normally, you would now exit CADD 6 and use your text editor to read the export file and manipulate the data. Since we have no way of knowing what particular editor you have, in this tutorial you will load the ASCII file back into CADD 6.

> Type: ZO (for Zoom Out) to make more room on your screen
> Type: LA (for LOAD ASCII)

CADD 6 does not list the file you just exported as an ASCII file since it was saved with the file extension .ASC. You can get around this by typing in the whole file name *with* the file extension. At the prompt for an ASCII file:

> Use the Backspace key to correct the directory name
> Type: ELECATTS.ASC (and press Enter) for the file name

CADD 6 draws a box on the screen representing the size and shape of the attribute information for you to place in your drawing (See Chapter 13 for more information on the LOAD ASCII (LA) command). Once the attribute file is loaded into CADD 6, you can use the normal text editing commands to change it.

This completes the Component and Attribute Tutorial. Components and attributes are a very powerful feature of CADD 6, and you should take more time to investigate how you can put them to good use.

CHAPTER SUMMARY

Components are pre-drawn symbols that are named and saved to disk so they can be available for use in other drawings. By creating libraries of components for your drawing applications, you can save a great deal of time by never having to draw those symbols again. You will also be sure that symbols are always drawn and scaled consistently in your drawings. Attributes are used to attach text information to components that can then be displayed, or not, and exported to a disk file.

This chapter described commands found on both the Components and Attributes menus, which allow you to create and manipulate components and attributes. Many of these same commands were applied while creating the electronic schematic drawing, which contains several components with attributes.

CHAPTER 10

Hatching and Filling

USING THE HATCH/FILL MENU

You can fill areas with a color or add pre-defined patterns within specified boundaries of your drawings. CADD 6 refers to solid colors as *fills*, and pre-defined patterns as *hatches*. Several hatch patterns are available and can be inserted at any scale and rotation angle. If you are using a color video display, you can draw your hatches and fills in any of the available colors.

Use fills to make your drawings stand out more by "painting" or shading areas with color. This process is similar to the process of "rendering," which an architect uses to make drawings of a building look more realistic and interesting.

Included with CADD 6 are 50 different pre-defined hatch patterns. You can create your own as well. These patterns range from a standard crosshatch pattern, used for differentiating areas of a mechanical part drawing, to standard symbols (as defined by the American National Standards Institute, ANSI) for grass, earth, bricks, and insulation. There are other miscellaneous hatch patterns available such as stars, diamonds, lattice, cedar shakes, and herring bone.

Separate commands are used for drawing hatches and fills, but the methods are basically the same. Once drawn, a hatch or fill is identified by a single reference point, just like that of a component, text character, or text line. The hatch or fill can be moved or erased by selecting the reference point. This chapter will discuss all of the commands on the HATCH/FILL menu.

HATCH/FILL

Window Hatch	WH
Object Hatch	OH
Fitted Hatch	FH
Boundary Hatch	BH
Hatch Settings	HS
Window Fill	WF
Object Fill	OF
Fitted Fill	FF
Boundary Fill	BF
Fill Color	FC

HATCHING AND SELECTING BOUNDARIES

For all the hatch and fill methods, you must somehow identify the boundary of the area to be affected. The kinds of entities that can make up this boundary are limited. Except for the Window Fill (WF) command, any area within a closed boundary (with no gaps) created with drawing primitives can be filled. A list of the boundary entities accepted by the different commands are included in the explanations below.

Remember that rectangles, polygons, and construction ellipses are constructed from lines or arcs. Therefore, these entities are acceptable boundaries.

Window Hatch (WH)

Window Hatch (WH) is the easiest hatch command to use, but it is also the least flexible. With this command, you can draw a pattern in any closed or connected area that can be enclosed in a window. This closed area can be made up of lines, arcs, circles, and bezier curves. Placing a window around an area causes CADD 6 to determine what object boundaries are found within it. When CADD 6 determines that it has found a valid boundary, it begins hatching within that boundary, using your selected pattern in your selected scale and rotation.

Begin the Window Hatch (WH) command with the command code WH. You will be prompted to place a selection window around the area to be hatched, just as you did for the various EDITS commands discussed in Chapter 5. Move the cursor below and to the left of the objects you want to hatch, in order to enclose them in your window. Click to place the first corner of the window. Then move your cursor above and across the objects and click again. Any closed boundary within the window will be hatched.

TIP: If CADD 6.0 finds a legitimate boundary within another boundary (an island), it fills all but the island area. (See Figure 10.1.) A legitimate boundary area within another boundary can be made up of any entities, as long as they all either overlap or adjoin. You must explode components to use them as islands. If you want to leave an unhatched area in the center of a hatched area, make sure that all of the lines or arcs in the unhatched section adjoin each other. If you want the inner area hatched also, leave breaks in the boundary of the inner area. By doing this, you may no longer be able to see the boundary of the inner area. It may appear completely hatched, as if the inner boundary doesn't exist.

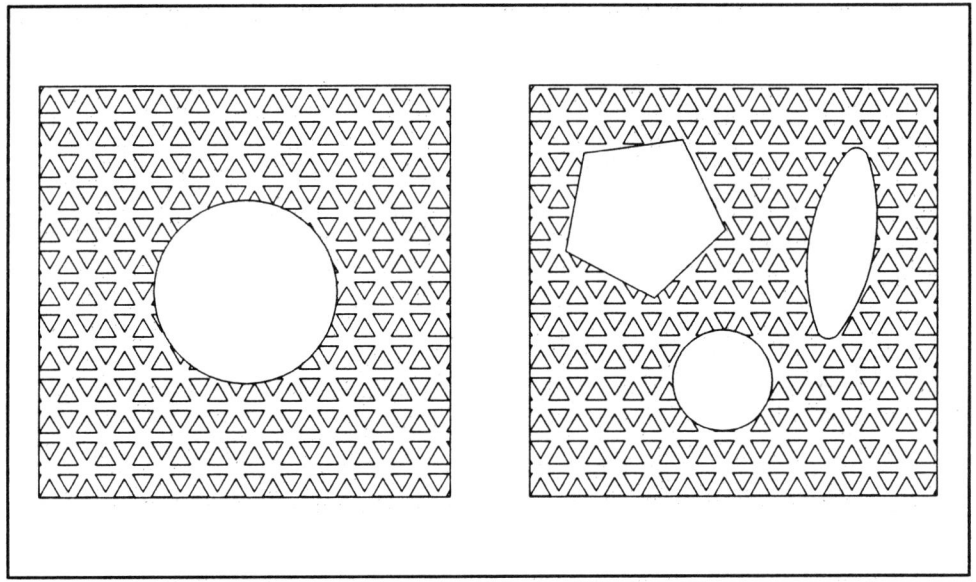

Figure 10.1 Hatching around islands with the Window Hatch command.

Object Hatch (OH)

The Object Hatch (OH) command identifies the boundaries of an object and fills in a pattern within them. The Object Hatch (OH) command works only on boundaries made up of lines, arcs, and circles. To use this command effectively, define your boundaries clearly by selecting several points on the object to be hatched. The word "object" in this case does not refer to a single entity or primitive (a line or arc, for example.) Rather, "object" refers to a group of primitives that are connected together to form an object with a closed boundary, such as a rectangle. The ends of consecutive entities on the boundary must meet precisely at a single point. This command does not find islands, so it hatches the entire area inside your preset boundaries. It ignores all lines, arcs, or objects other than the ones selected to define the boundary. If you do not want to hatch an inner area or island, you also need to mark the inner area with points on its boundaries.

Use the command code OH to start Object Hatch (OH). At the prompt, move your cursor to an entity located on the boundary, and press Enter to select that part of the boundary. Continue to identify boundary entities until the area to be hatched is clearly defined. When you finish, use the Pen Up (PU) command. The area is hatched with whatever pattern, scale, and rotation you previously defined. (See Figure 10.2.) Try to select points near the center of each line or arc you want to identify. If you select endpoints or intersection points, CADD 6 may not select the entity you intended. Also, do not identify objects more than once, as doing so can lead to unpredictable results.

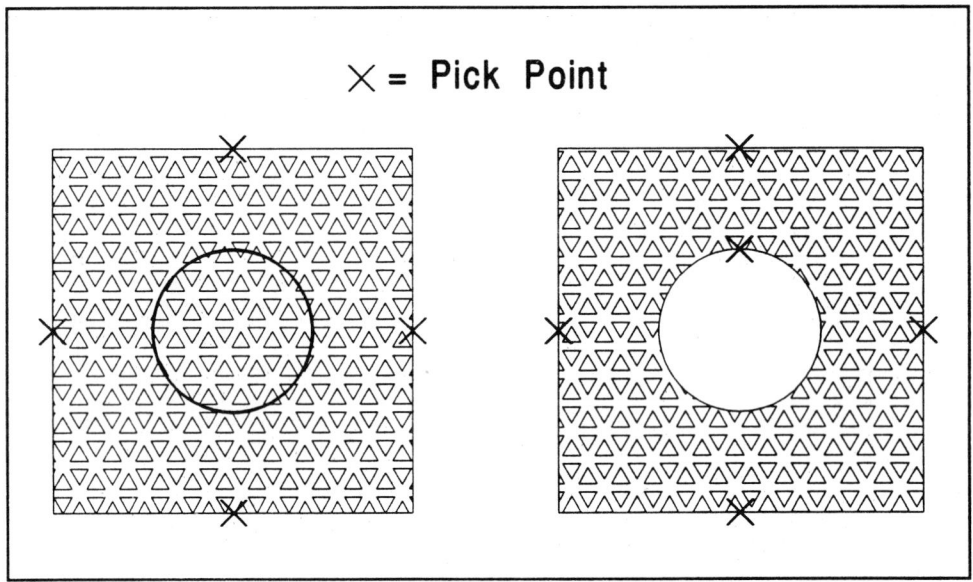

Figure 10.2 Using Object Hatch (OH) with and without an Island.

Fitted Hatch (FH)

With the Fitted Hatch (FH) command, you can fill areas that are irregularly shaped. Areas are filled based on preset boundaries, similar to the Object Hatch (OH) method. Fitted Hatch (FH), however, is much more predictable when you are working with areas of irregular shapes, or with boundary lines that do not end neatly at one another. This command works with lines and arcs, but not with circles. If you want to hatch circles, first convert them to two arcs.

Use the command code FH to start Fitted Hatch. At the prompt, move your cursor to an entity to be identified on the boundary and press Enter. Then, moving consecutively around the boundary, select all the other bounding entities to define the area to be hatched. When you enter Pen Up (PU), the area is hatched.

Figure 10.3 shows an example of using this command. With this method, all entities on the boundary must be connected. You cannot "pick up" the cursor and move it to another boundary as you can with Object Hatch (OH). Therefore, Fitted Hatch (FH) cannot be used with islands.

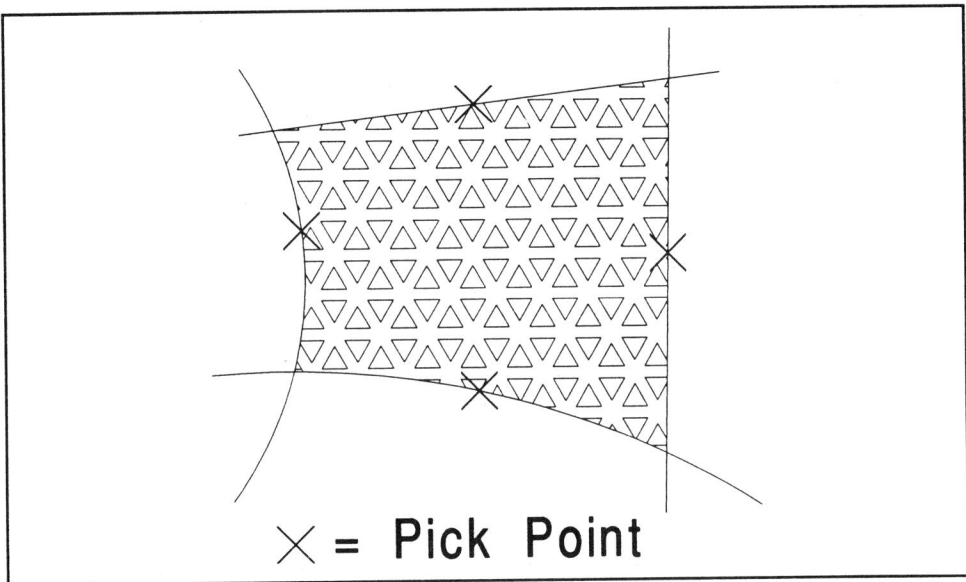

Figure 10.3 Using Fitted Hatch (FH) for Irregular shapes.

Boundary Hatch (BH)

The Boundary Hatch (BH) command is used to define a straight line boundary and hatch it at the same time. This command creates its own boundary, you do not have to use this command on existing lines. You can, however, trace an existing boundary, snapping to the endpoints with the NP command.

To execute a Boundary Hatch (BH), type BH. You will be asked to select points to form the boundary. If you select a point in error, press the Ctrl and Backspace keys simultaneously to de-select it. Each time you press the Ctrl-Backspace, one more boundary endpoint is de-selected. Enter PU when you have completed the boundary. Any openings are automatically closed by the program. For example, if you created a rectangular boundary, but didn't close off one end, CADD 6 hatches the shape as a rectangle, closing off the open end automatically. At least three points must be selected for the boundary to be hatched. (See Figure 10.4.)

Before executing a hatch command, you need to define parameters for how the hatch looks. These parameters should be defined before you actually place a hatch pattern (unless you use all the default values CADD 6 is preset for). The next section will examine the settings you can choose.

10-6 ■ Chapter 10: Hatching and Filling

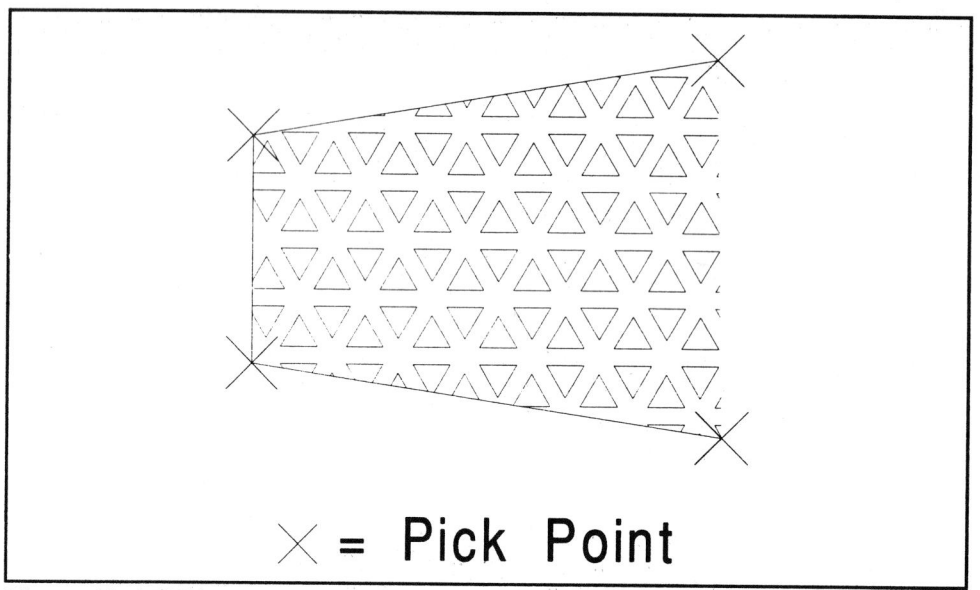

Figure 10.4 Using Boundary Hatch (BH).

SELECTING, CHANGING, AND DISPLAYING HATCH PATTERNS

To control the hatch's patterns, scale, rotation, color, and boundary display, use the Hatch Settings (HS) command. Any hatch options changed with this command affect only hatches created *after* the change. Any existing hatch patterns are unaffected.

> **TIP:** The Boundary (ON/OFF) setting affects all hatch patterns in the drawing. This setting is merely a display feature, the boundaries can be turned ON and OFF with this command.

Hatch Settings (HS)

The Hatch Settings (HS) command contains six options used to set hatch variables. These options are: Pattern, Scale, Rotation, Color, Display, and Boundary.

Pattern. To choose a hatch pattern, select the Pattern option with your pointing device, then type in the name of the pattern and press Enter, or select a pattern name from the compiled list on the sidebar menu. Pictures of the 50 patterns included in the program can be found in Appendix B of the CADD 6 Reference Guide. Figure 10.5, the "Hatch Wheel," shows examples of these hatch patterns. The numbers on the Hatch Wheel correspond to the list of hatch patterns printed below the figure.

Scale. The Scale option affects the size of the hatch patterns. This scale controls the actual distance between the lines that make up the hatch pattern. If you are hatching a very small object, you want an appropriately small hatch scale for it to look the way you want. To set the scale in your drawings, select the Scale option with your pointing device, or Enter S for Scale. (See Figure 10.6.)

Rotate. The Rotate selection sets the rotation of the hatch pattern in your drawing. The default setting is 0. The rotation can be any positive or negative number from -360° to 360°. To select a new hatch rotation, select Rotation with your pointing device, or Enter R. At the prompt, type the number of degrees of rotation and press Enter to complete your selection. As with other rotation commands, 0 degrees is along the positive x-axis (horizontal and to the right), and positive angles are counterclockwise from there. (See Figure 10.7.)

Color. The Color selection sets a color for the display of your hatch pattern on the screen. This command is intended for use only with color monitors. Your choices for settings are related to the color capabilities of your video graphics board. The selection possibilities are from 0 to 255. To use this selection, click on Color with your pointing device, or Enter C for Color. Answer the prompt by selecting a number from 0 to 255 and then press Enter.

10-8 ■ Chapter 10: Hatching and Filling

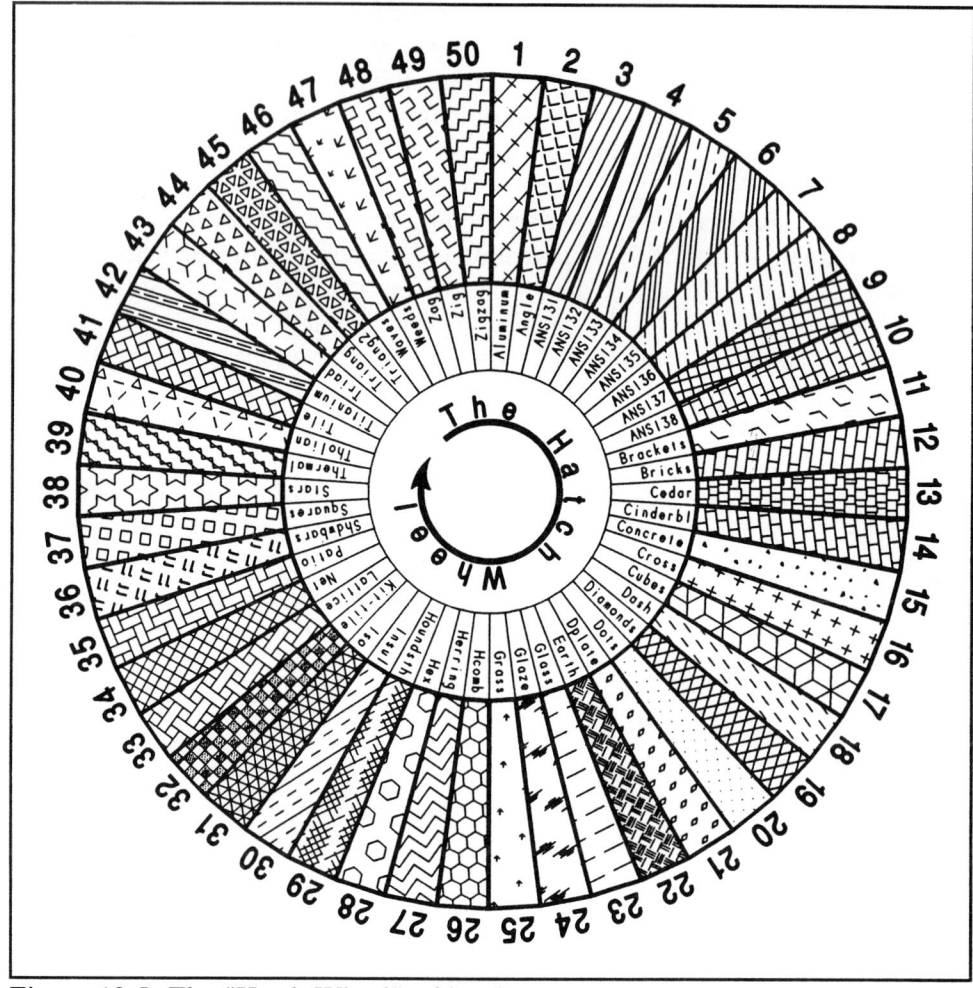

Figure 10.5 The "Hatch Wheel" of hatch patterns.

1 ALUMINUM	2 ANGLE	3 ANSI31	4 ANSI32
5 ANSI33	6 ANSI34	7 ANSI35	8 ANSI36
9 ANSI37	10 ANSI38	11 BRACKETS	12 BRICKS
13 CEDAR	14 CINDERBL	15 CONCRETE	16 CROSS
17 CUBES	18 DASH	19 DIAMOND	20 DOTS
21 DPLATE	22 EARTH	23 GLASS	24 GLAZE
25 GRASS	26 HCOMB	27 HERRING	28 HEX
29 HOUNDSTH	30 INSUL	31 ISO	32 KIT-TILE
33 LATTICE	34 NET	35 PATIO	36 SHDWBARS
37 SQUARES	38 STARS	39 THERMAL	40 THOLIAN
41 TILE	42 TITANIUM	43 TRIAD	44 TRIANG
45 TRIANG2	46 WAVES	47 WEEDS	48 ZAG
49 ZIG	50 ZIGZAG		

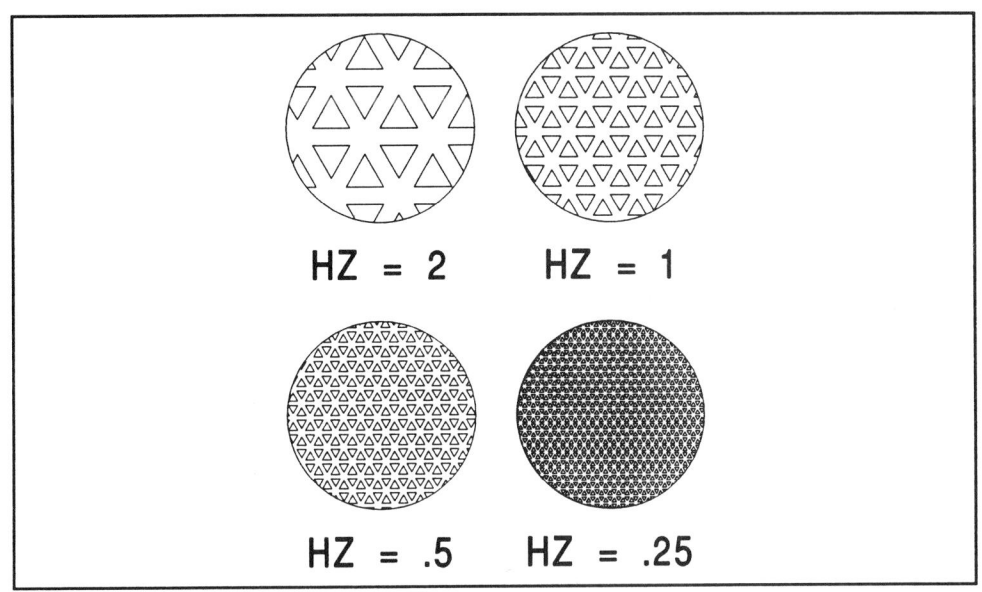

Figure 10.6 The effect of Hatch Settings Scale (HS).

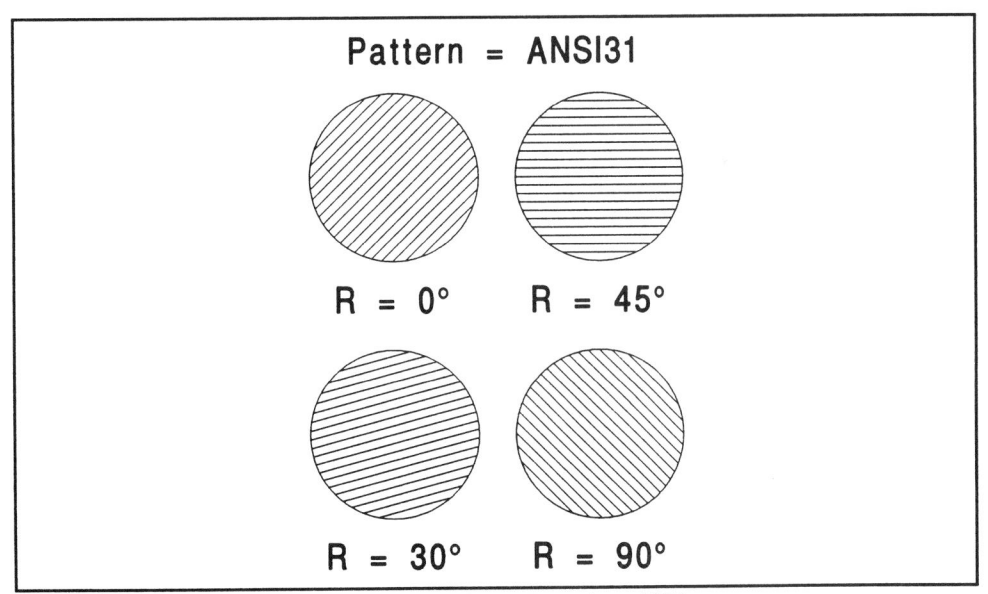

Figure 10.7 The effect of Hatch Settings Rotation (HS).

Display. The Display selection toggles ON or OFF the display of your hatch patterns on the video screen. With this toggle turned OFF, hatch patterns are not drawn on the screen, which can save a great deal of time on zooms and redraws. Click on Display with your pointing device, or Enter D for Display to turn this toggle ON or OFF. Redraw (RD) the screen to see the effect of turning the Display option ON or OFF.

Boundary. The Boundary selection toggles ON or OFF the display of hatch boundaries. The hatch pattern is still visible, but the hatch boundary is not displayed. If you create a hatch with the Boundary Hatch (BH) command (without tracing over an existing boundary) and toggle the Boundary display to OFF, the hatch appears without any boundary.

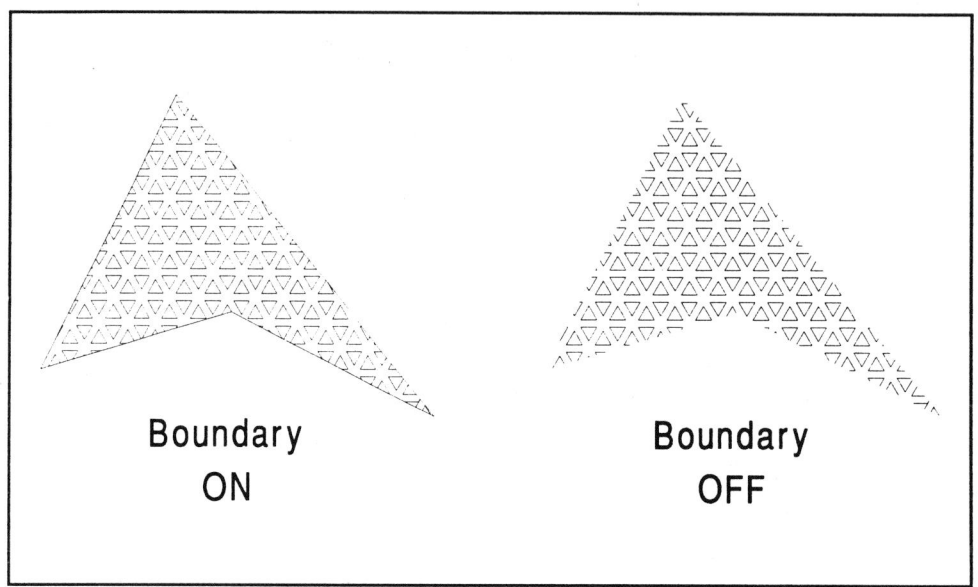

Figure 10.8 Displaying the Hatch Boundary with Hatch Settings (HS).

CHOOSING AND DISPLAYING FILLS

So far you have only looked at hatches, but fill commands work the same way. You identify an object or boundary to fill just as you do with hatches. The same boundary requirements needed for hatches must be met for fills. Just as for Object Hatch (OH), the Object Fill (OF) command works only with lines, arcs, and circles.

Fill Color (FC)

To set the screen color of fills, use the Fill Color (FC) command. Depending on your color graphics adapter, you have choices of 0 to 255 colors, with 1 as the default setting. To select a fill color, use the command code FC. At the prompt, enter the number of your selection and press Enter.

Turn the fills display ON or OFF with the toggle selection found in the Fast Redraw (FA) options. With the display OFF, you save time on zooms and redraws. To turn this toggle ON or OFF, use the command code FA and Enter F for Fills.

Chapter 10: Hatching and Filling ■ 10-11

IDENTIFYING BOUNDARIES FOR FILLS

Window Fill (WF)

Similar to Window Hatch (WH), Window Fill (WF) sets a boundary area enclosed by a window, but Window Fill (WF) fills in the area with a solid color. (See Figure 10.9.) Window Fill (WF) does *not* fill in a defined boundary area inside another boundary area (an island). Begin this command with the command code WF. Place a window to encompass the area you want filled and press Enter. The color of the fill depends on your previous selection of the fill color parameter.

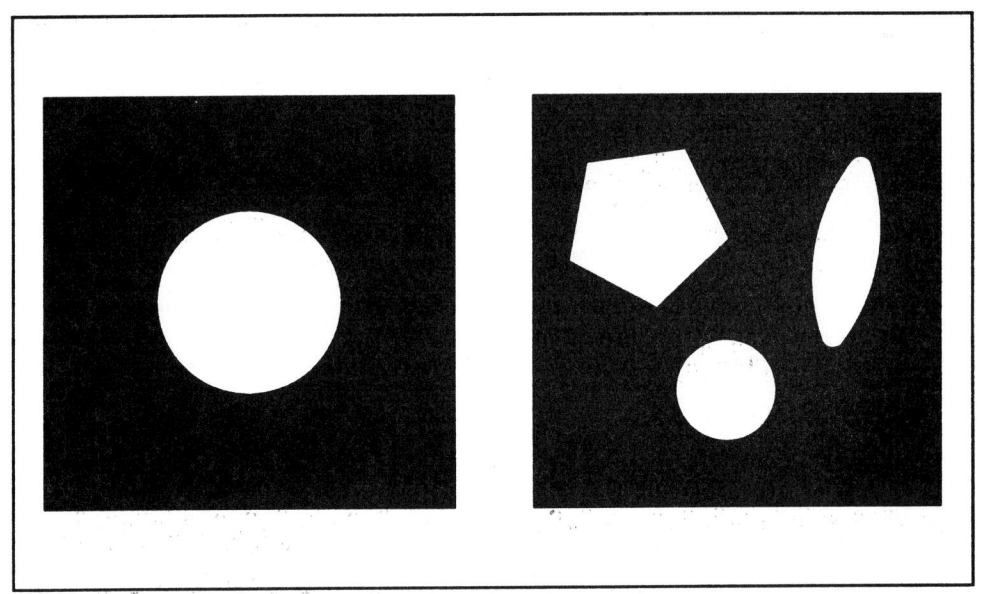

Figure 10.9 Using the Window Fill (WF) command.

Object Fill (OF)

The Object Fill (OF) command sets area boundaries similar to Object Hatch (OH), but fills them with a solid color. Object Fill (OF) interprets a boundary inside another boundary as an island. Rules for hatching also apply to setting boundaries, and to choosing attached lines or entities for constructing islands.

Use the command code OF to begin the Object Fill (OF) command. At the prompt, move your cursor to an entity. Set a boundary point on the entity by clicking on it or pressing Enter. Continue to set points on the area boundary until you have defined the area completely. When you have completed your selections, use the Pen Up (PU) command and the area will be filled. (See Figure 10.10.)

Fitted Fill (FF)

Choose the Fitted Fill (FF) command when the object or boundary area is irregularly shaped or entities are disjointed. Do *not* use this command with islands.

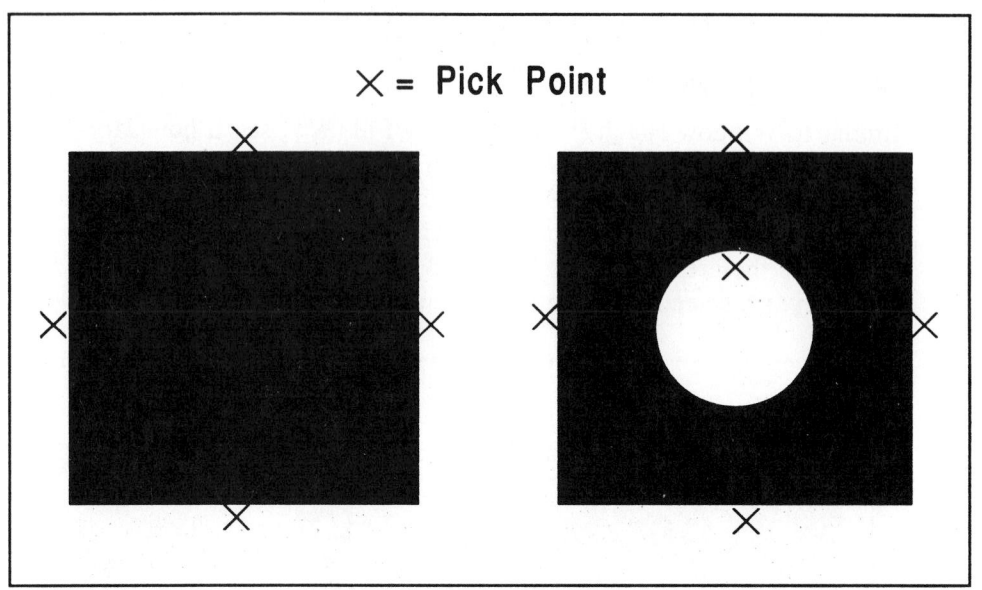

Figure 10.10 Object Fill (OF) with and without an island.

Start the Fitted Fill (FF) command with the command code FF. At the prompt, define the area boundary by moving your cursor consecutively to points you want to set and clicking for each selection. When all of the boundary is defined, use the Pen Up (PU) command and the area will be filled. (See Figure 10.11.) As with hatches, try to identify points near the center of the boundary objects, and do not identify boundary objects more than once.

Boundary Fill (BF)

The Boundary Fill (BF) command, like Boundary Hatch (BH), is used to define a straight line boundary and fill (instead of a hatch) at the same time. This command creates its own boundary; you do not have to use it with existing lines. You can, however, trace an existing boundary, snapping to the endpoints with the NP command.

To execute a Boundary Fill (BF), type BF. You will be asked to select points to form the boundary. If you select a point in error, press the Ctrl and Backspace keys simultaneously to de-select it. Each time you press the Ctrl-Backspace keys, one more boundary endpoint is de-selected. Enter PU when you have completed the boundary. Any openings will be automatically closed by CADD 6. For example, if you created a rectangular boundary, but did not close off one end, CADD 6 fills the shape as a rectangle, closing off the open end automatically. At least six points must be selected for the boundary to be filled. (See Figure 10.12.)

Now that you know how to hatch and fill areas, try using the commands in combination. You can hatch on top of a fill, but not the other way around. A fill

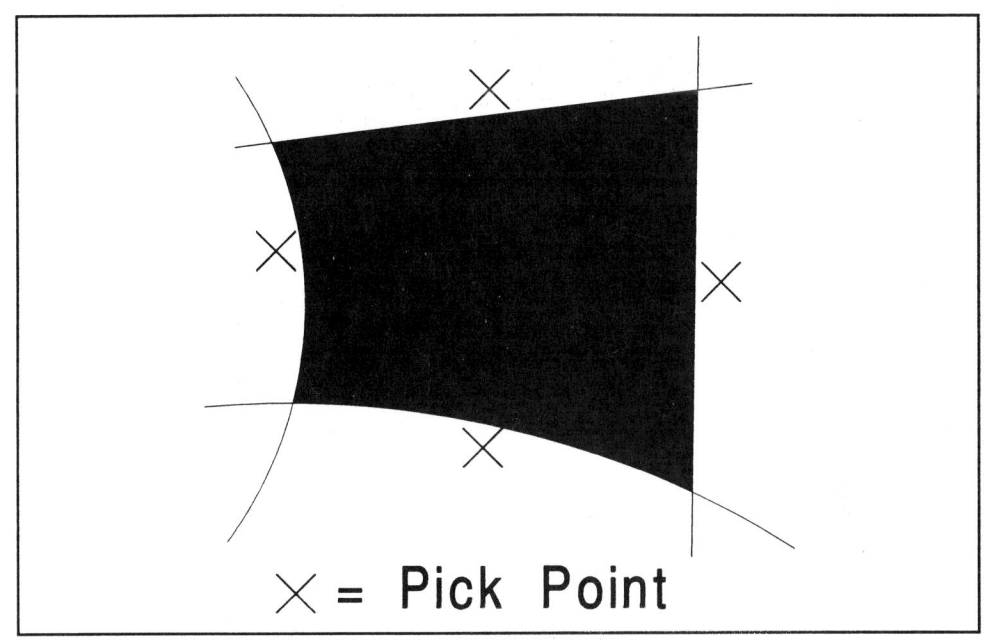

Figure 10.11 Using Fitted Fill (FF) for irregular shapes.

"paints" over the hatch pattern when it draws on the screen. However, if you use a multi-color plotter to plot the area (and you have chosen different colors for the hatch and the fill), both show up on the output.

Since so many variables are involved with drawing hatches and fills, you sometimes do not get the result you expect. In this case, remember to use the Erase Last (EL) command. It applies to hatches and fills the same as it applies to other entities.

Both hatches and fills have a reference point that CADD 6 defines. After you find where this reference point is, you can use it to select the hatch or fill similar to any other entity for move, copy, rotate, erase, and scale commands. You can actually move the pattern of fill away from its boundary, or erase the boundary independently of the hatch or fill. The trick is in finding the reference point. Turn the Reference Points (PR) toggle ON and search for the reference point's identifying asterisk. The reference point will be on one corner of the boundary.

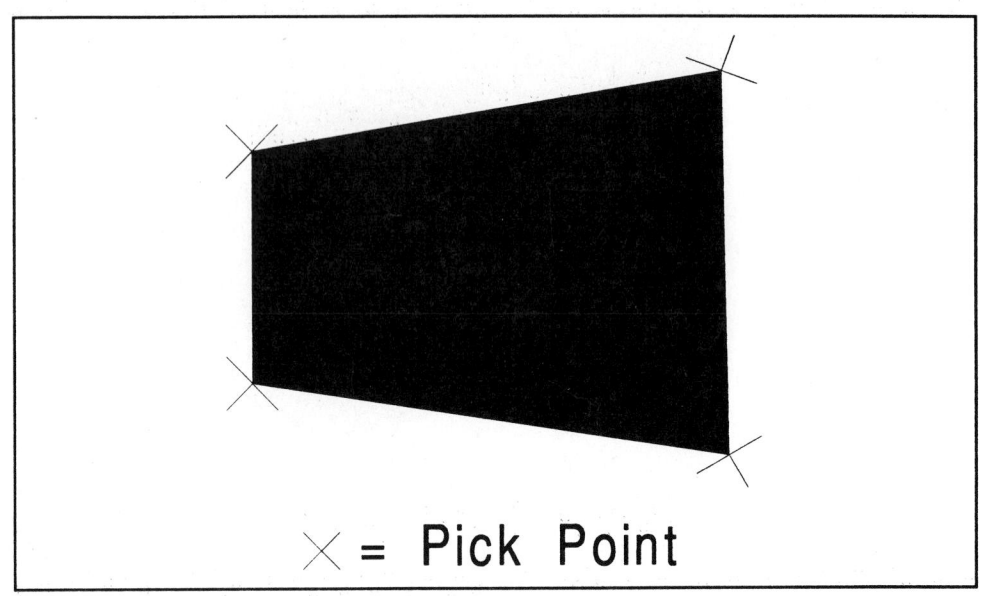

Figure 10.12 Using Boundary Fill (BF).

CHAPTER SUMMARY

In this chapter, you learned about ways to fill in areas with hatch patterns or colors (called fills.) You can select the area to be hatched or filled with a selection window, or by identifying the objects that make up the boundary of the area. CADD 6 also has commands for defining the color, scale, rotation angle, and hatch pattern.

Although CADD 6 separates the commands for working with fills and hatches, they are parallel commands and are used similarly.

CHAPTER 11

Dimensioning

USING THE DIMENSIONS MENU

In this chapter, you will learn to use dimensioning commands to place dimensions in your drawings. You will also set dimensioning variables that control the look and style of the dimension, such as the orientation of the dimension, the type of dimension pointer, and the size of dimensioning text. At the end of this chapter is a quick tutorial that uses some of the dimensioning commands discussed in this chapter.

Often, CADD 6 drawings are used as actual construction plans for building or manufacturing purposes. As construction plans, these drawings must contain all the information about the size and dimensions of the parts in order to be built accurately. There are standard ways of showing dimensions, especially with engineering and architectural drawings. The dimensioning features in Generic CADD 6 make it easier for you to insert dimensions that are accurate and professional looking.

CADD 6 dimensioning is especially powerful because it is *associative*. The dimensions you draw are actually associated with particular objects in your drawing, so if you change the size of those objects, the dimensions are automatically updated to reflect the changes. This can save you a tremendous amount of time when editing drawings, since CADD 6 will modify many of the dimensions for you.

Dimensioning in CADD 6 is sometimes referred to as *automatic dimensioning*. This term does not mean that you just identify the part to be dimensioned and then CADD 6 does the rest. Unfortunately, too many variables are involved for that to be possible. Automatic dimensioning means that you specify the format and look of the dimension and select two points to which the dimension applies. CADD 6 will then draw in the dimension, calculate the distance between the two points, and place the correct value as part of the dimension. CADD 6 prints the dimension value as whatever distance apart the points were drawn when the drawing was created, another reason you should always draw at full-scale. If you draw a 10-foot wall in CADD 6 at full-scale, when you dimension the wall, CADD 6 shows the length as 10 feet. However, if you draw the same wall at half-scale, CADD 6 thinks it is only 5 feet long and will dimension it as such.

This chapter covers all the commands on the DIMENSIONS menu, as follows:

DIMENSIONS

Linear Dimension (LX)
    Horizontal
    Vertical
    Aligned
    At an Angle

Dimension Mode (UM)
Proximity Fixed (PF)

Angular Dimension (AX)
Radial Dimension (RX)
Diameter Dimension (IX)
Dimension Leader (LE)
Shoulder Length (LL)

Dimension Move (UV)
Dimension Change (UG)
Dimension Settings (US)

Most dimensions consist of three parts: the extension lines that extend to the part being dimensioned, the dimension line that is placed between two extension lines, and the text (or lettering) which normally is the value of the dimension. (See Figure 11.1.) The extension offset is the distance between an object and the beginning of its extension lines.

CHOOSING DIMENSIONING VARIABLES

Each dimension consists of extension and dimension lines, arrow heads, and text. In any one drawing, you may want dimensions at different orientations (horizontal, vertical, or at an angle), in different modes (individual, cumulative, or partitioned), on multiple layers, or in different colors.

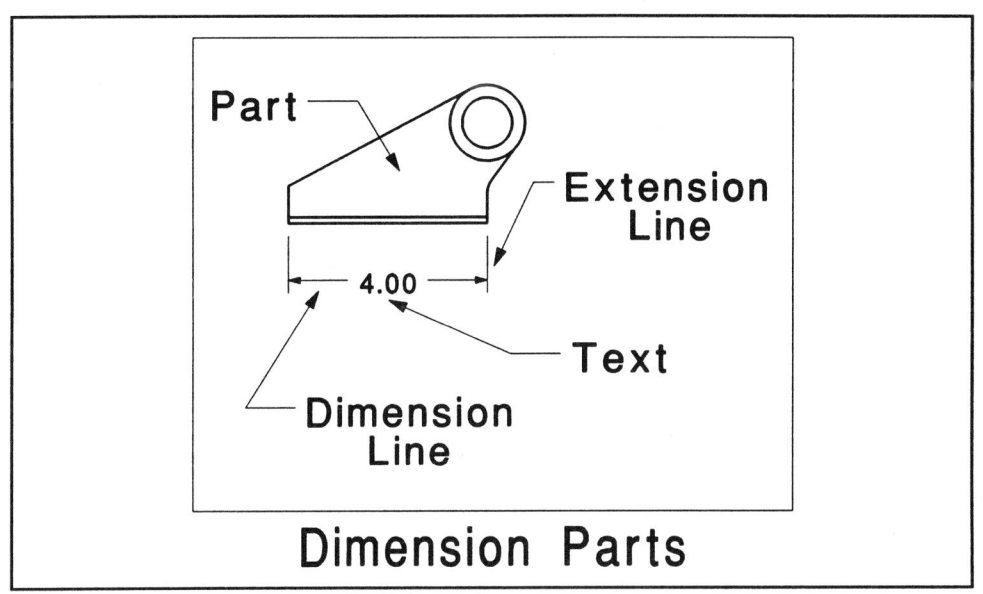

Figure 11.1 Components of a Dimension.

To make all of these variations possible, CADD 6 has a set of commands for setting dimensioning variables. These variables determine the look of your dimensions. Each of these variables affects only the dimensions placed in the drawing *after* the variable is set. These variables do not change any dimensions that already exist in the drawing.

The dimension variable features are found within the Dimension Settings (US) command. Use this command to change any element of the dimension line.

Dimension Settings (US)

When the Dimension Settings (US) command is entered, the following options are offered: Text, Extensions, Arrows, Dim line, Font, Layer, and Color. Additional options are available for each of the Text, Extensions, Arrows, and Dim line settings. In this section, each option and its variables are discussed.

Text. When the Text option is selected, the following options are offered to modify dimension text: Placement, Direction, Centered, siZe, Offset, Tolerance, and displaY. The following is an explanation of the dimension Text features.

Placement. The Letter Placement option is a toggle setting which sets the text placement within or above the dimension line. If you choose In-line placement, the dimension lines are broken in the center and the text is placed in the open space. If you choose Above-line placement, the text is drawn above the dimension line.

Direction. The Letter Direction option is a toggle setting which controls the direction in which dimensioning text is oriented. Dimension text can be placed horizontally or aligned with the object being dimensioned. The orientation of the text is defined independently from the dimension direction. Text can always be placed horizontally or aligned (at the same angle) with the dimension lines. On engineering drawings, placing text horizontally is common, even if the dimension lines are vertical or aligned. Architectural drawings, on the other hand, usually have aligned text in dimensions.

Centered. The Centering option is a toggle setting which controls whether the text is centered in or centered above the dimension line. (Whether the text is in the line or above it is determined by the Placement setting.) If the Centering option is OFF, you can move the text along the dimension line (in the line or above it), manually choosing its position.

siZe. The command Text Size, Dimension (TZD) is a three-letter command for setting the height of dimensioning text. When choosing a value for the letter size, you may want to consider whether your drawing will be printed out at some scale. If you want the lettering on your printed drawing to be 1" high, for example, and the drawing is to be printed at 1/4 scale, you should choose a letter size of 4". When the drawing is reduced at printing time, the lettering will be the correct size.

Offset. The In-line offset option controls the space between the text and the dimension line when Placement is set to In-line. The Above-line offset option controls the distance from the dimension text to the dimension line when Placement is set to Above-line.

Tolerance. The Tolerance option, when selected, prompts you with the following options: None, Max/min, Stacked variance, Fixed variance, and mUltiplier. Tolerance settings affect how your dimensions appear in the drawing. The following is an explanation of the Tolerance options. (See Figure 11.2.)

None. If you select the option None, your dimensions are displayed with a single dimension line.

Max/min. If you select the Max/min option you will be prompted to enter the lower tolerance. Next, you will be prompted to enter the upper tolerance. The final prompt will ask you to enter in the decimal precision between 0 and 6 of the dimension. In the Max/min tolerance format, the top number equals the dimension value plus the upper tolerance. The bottom number equals the dimension value minus the lower tolerance.

Stacked variance. Select this option and you will be prompted to enter the lower tolerance. Next, you will be prompted to enter the upper tolerance. The last prompt asks you to enter in the decimal precision between 0 and 6 of the dimension. Note, you do not have to enter the plus and minus signs associated with this type of tolerance format. CADD 6 does this automatically. In the Stacked variance format, the dimension is followed by whatever upper and lower tolerances you enter.

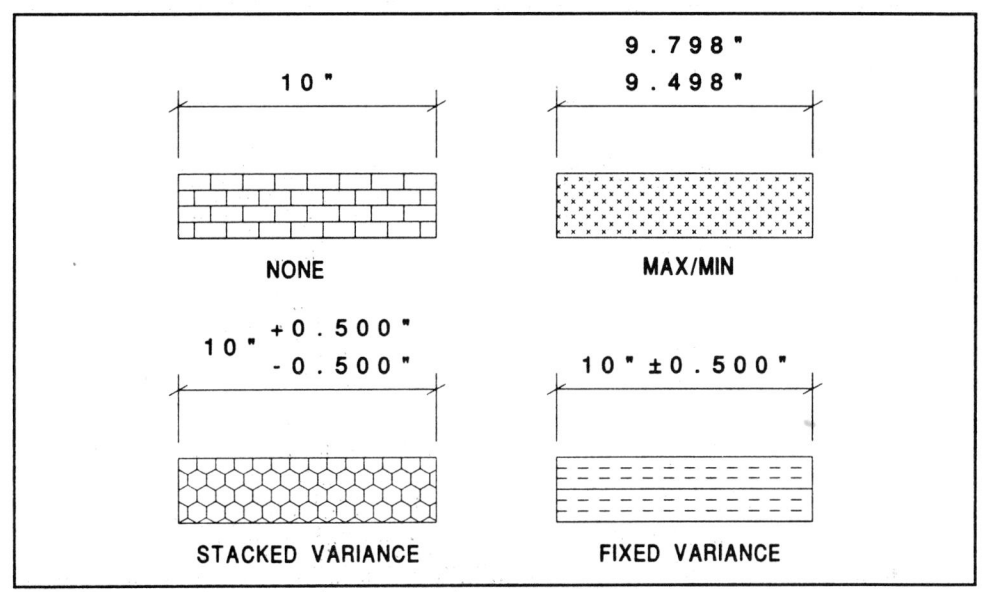

Figure 11.2 Dimension tolerance options.

Fixed variance. If you select the option Fixed variance, you will be prompted to enter a value for tolerance. Next, you will be prompted to enter in the decimal precision between 0 and 6 of the dimension. Note that you do not have to enter the plus/minus sign associated with this type of tolerance format. CADD 6 does this automatically. In the Fixed variance format, the dimension is followed by whatever tolerance you enter.

mUltiplier. The mUltiplier feature changes the factor by which the dimension value is displayed. For example, a portion of a drawing you are working on is too small or finely detailed, in comparison to the rest of the drawing, to dimension. If it were dimensioned, it would be too small or too close together to be readable. You could copy this particular section of drawing, scale it up to a workable size, and detail it separately from the rest of the drawing. If the detail drawing is scaled-up 5X, then your dimensioning would come out 5 times too large. In this case, set the mUltiplier to 0.2 (1/5) and then dimension the drawing. This will cause the dimensions to come out correctly relative to the actual size of the drawing.

displaY. The displaY feature is a toggle command that allows you to turn the dimension text On or Off in the drawing. The text display feature only affects dimensions placed *after* changes were made to this option. Any dimensions placed before changes were made to the display option will not be affected.

Extensions. The Extensions feature is used to control the offset, length above and below, stretch, and display status of extension lines. Refer to Figure 11.3 throughout this section. The Extensions feature will prompt you with the following options: Offset, length Above, length Below, Stretch, display 1, and display 2.

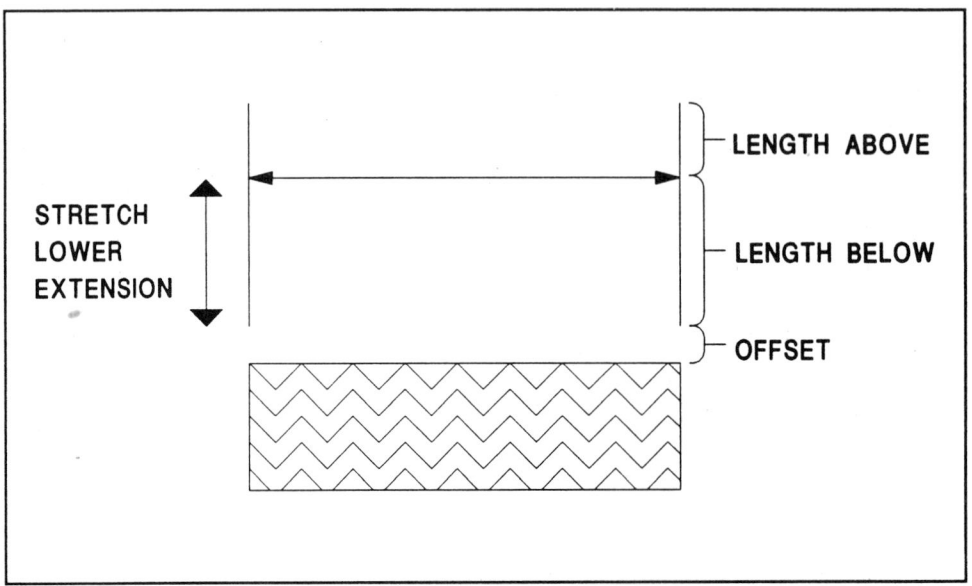

Figure 11.3 Options for Dimension Extensions.

The Extension feature only affects dimensions placed *after* changes were made to this feature. Any dimensions placed before changes were made to the Extensions feature will not be affected.

The effects of the Extension options work together with several other variables, including Proximity Fixed (PF), to create different styles of dimensioning.

The following is an explanation of the options found under the Extensions feature:

Offset. The Offset option sets the distance between the end of the extension line and the object being dimensioned. Extension lines are usually drawn slightly offset from the point being dimensioned so they are not confused with lines that define the object itself. This distance is always a constant, regardless of the state of Proximity Fixed (PF) or the Stretch feature.

length Above and length Below. The length Above and length Below option sets the length of the extension lines for your dimension display. The length Above option sets the length of the extension line above the dimension line, and the length Below sets the length of the extension line below the dimension line.

Stretch. With the toggle option Stretch, you can extend an extension line so that it reaches an object being dimensioned, only stopping short by the Offset value. With this

Chapter 11: Dimensioning ■ 11-7

toggle OFF, the extension line length is always a fixed-size set with the length Above and length Below command.

display 1 and display 2. The display 1 and display 2 options are toggles that allow you to turn either extension line's display On or Off. The extension line display features only affect dimensions placed *after* changes were made to these options. Any dimensions placed before changes were made to these options will not be affected.

Arrows. The Arrows option is used to control dimensioning and leader arrow settings. When the Arrow feature is selected, you will be prompted with the following options: Type, Angle, Length, lOcation, display 1, and display 2.

This command only affects dimensions placed *after* changes were made to the Arrow settings. Any dimensions placed before changes were made to this command will not be affected. The following is an explanation of the Arrow features:

Type. There are seven different arrow types: normal Closed, normal Open, normal Filled, Notched, circle Unfilled, circle fIlled, and Slash. (See Figure 11.4.)

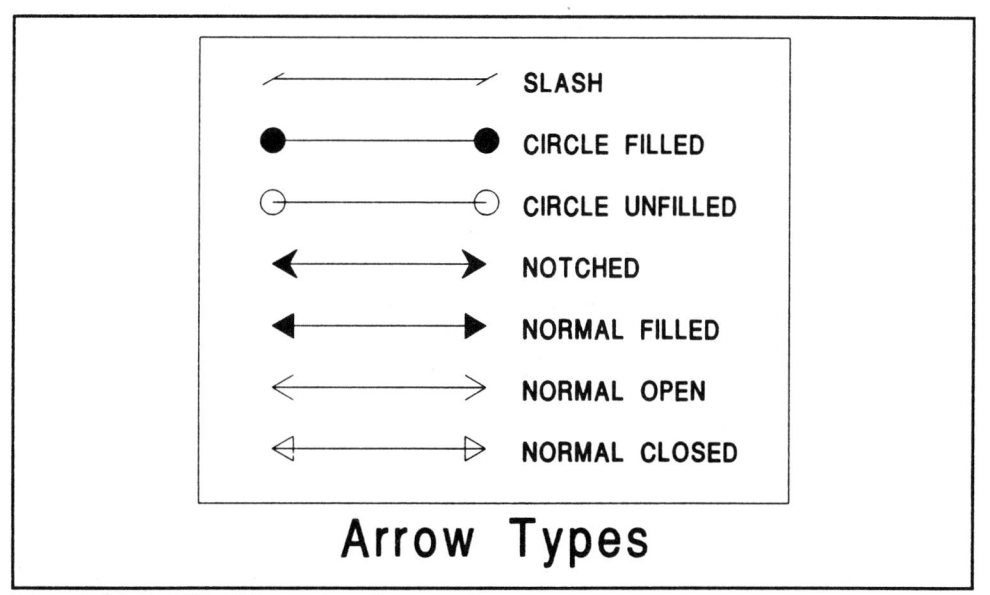

Figure 11.4 The Dimension Arrow types.

Angle. The Angle option lets you set the angle of the arrow head. This angle is measured between the dimension line and the arrow head line on either side of the dimension line. If you set the angle to 15°, the arrow head would be displayed with a total angle of 30°. This angle is calculated as 15° from each side of the dimension line.

Length. This option lets you establish the length of the arrow heads used in your dimensions. The length is measured from the arrow head tip to its other end, parallel to the dimension line.

lOcation. The lOcation option is a toggle which determines whether the arrow is inside, pointing outward, or outside, pointing inward.

display 1 and display 2. The display 1 and display 2 options are toggles that allow you to turn the display of either arrow ON or OFF. The arrow display settings only affect dimensions placed *after* changes were made to these options. Any dimensions placed before changes were made to these display options will not be affected.

Dim line. The Dim line options determine the direction and position of dimension lines in your drawing.

Proximity fixed. With the Proximity fixed feature, you can define the location of the dimension line in relation to the object being dimensioned. With Proximity Fixed toggled OFF, CADD 6 calculates the location to include the extension lines and their offset from the object. With Proximity fixed toggled ON, the dimension lines are always at a constant distance from the part (the proximity to the part is fixed.)

> **TIP:** The Extension settings can affect the function of the Proximity Fixed command. With Proximity fixed ON, the dimension lines are placed at a constant distance away from the part, which equals the value set for the Extension length variables plus the extension offset variable. With Proximity fixed OFF, the user specifies how far away from the part the dimension line is placed, overriding the Extension length settings.

In any case, when you place dimensions, CADD 6 prompts for a point that shows where to locate the dimension line. If Proximity fixed is OFF, the dimension line is placed at the distance defined by that point. If Proximity fixed is ON, the locating point is used to define which side of the part the dimension is drawn on, and the distance is always fixed at the Extension Lengths and Offset values.

directioN. The directioN options determine the direction of the next dimension(s) placed. At the prompt, choose from Aligned, Vertical, Horizontal, or At An Angle. The following is an explanation of the different dimension directions:

> *Aligned.* An Aligned dimension is aligned with the object being dimensioned. Aligned can be horizontal, vertical, or at an angle, depending on the orientation of

the part. (See Figure 11.5.) Dimensions placed in the Aligned mode measure the direct distance between the two dimension points selected.

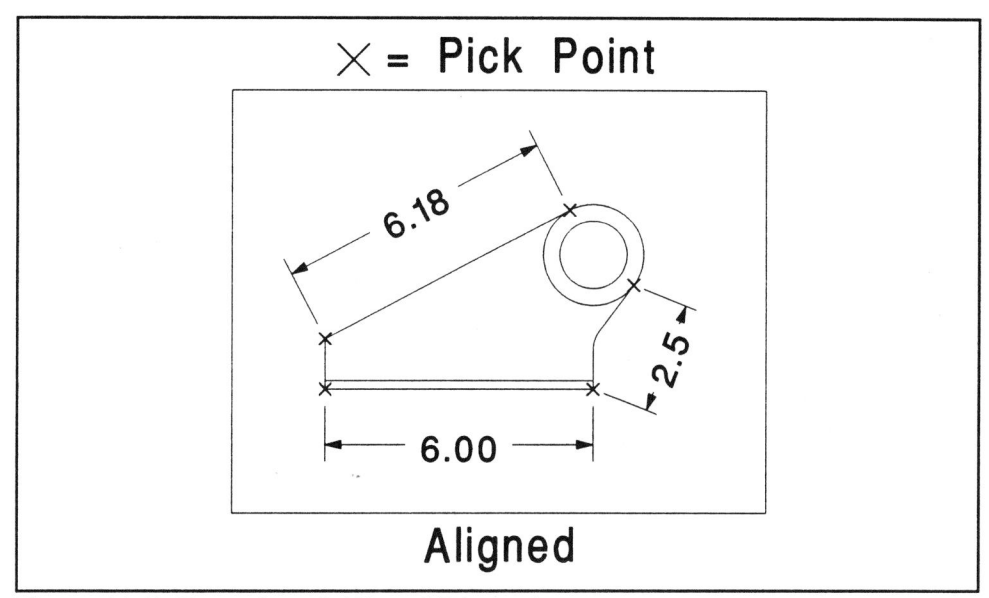

Figure 11.5 Examples of Aligned Dimensions.

Vertical and Horizontal. The Vertical and Horizontal dimension settings force dimension lines to be perfectly horizontal or vertical. (See Figure 11.6.) Dimensions set to Vertical mode measure the distance along the vertical, or Y-axis. Dimensions placed in the Horizontal mode measure the distance along the horizontal, or X-axis.

at an anglE. At an anglE prompts you for an angle to which to align the dimension. Linear dimensions placed afterwards are placed at that angle. The distance measured is the length of the line projected onto an imaginary line passing through the first point of that angle. (See Figure 11.7.)

Display. The Display option allows you to turn OFF the dimension line in the dimension display. The dimension line display feature only affects dimensions placed *after* changes were made to this option. Any dimensions placed before changes were made to the display option are not affected.

Font. Select the font to use for your dimensioning text with the Font option. At the prompt, enter the name of the font you want to use, or select it with your pointing device from the list of fonts on the sidebar menu.

11-10 ■ Chapter 11: Dimensioning

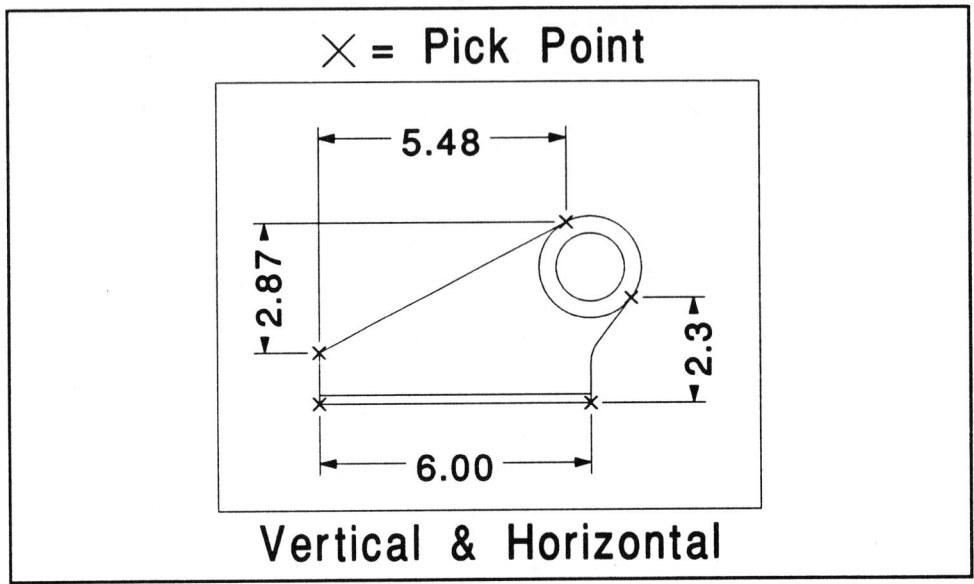

Figure 11.6 Vertical and Horizontal dimensions.

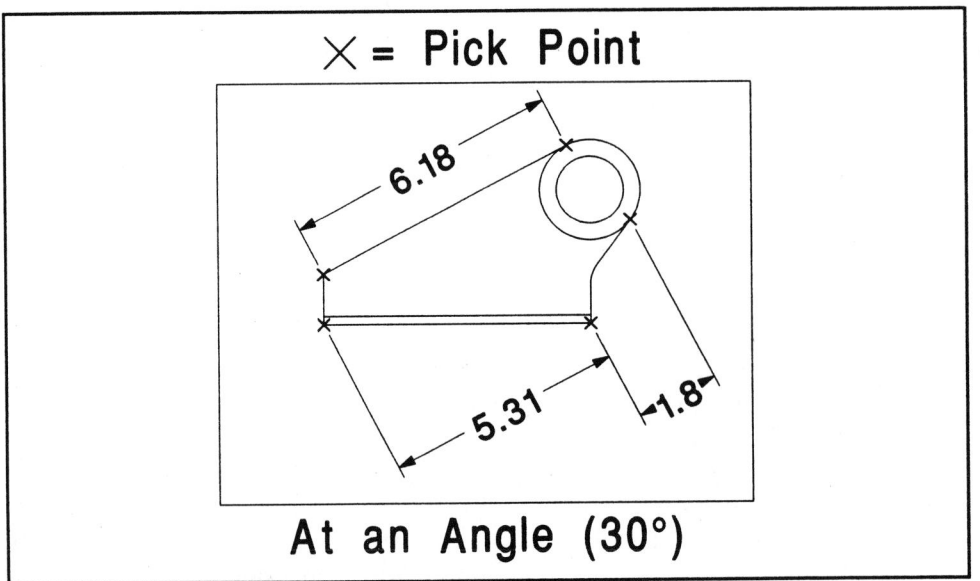

Figure 11.7 Dimensions at a Specified Angle.

Layer. The Layer option lets you select a particular layer on which to place all of your new dimensions. Often, you may want to set the dimension layer to a layer that is different from the one where the part is located. Doing so makes it easier for you to select and edit the dimensions later, and to plot out the drawing without showing all the dimensions. To set the dimension layer to a different layer, turn ON the All Layers Edit (AL) command before using the Layer option. Once a dimension layer is set,

CADD 6 automatically changes the current layer to the dimension layer whenever you use the dimension features. If All Layers (AL) is OFF, you can only snap to objects already on the dimension layer.

To choose a layer, enter the command code UY for Dimension Layer. At the prompt, enter the number of the layer (from 0 to 255) on which you want to place your dimension. This command only affects dimensions placed *after* it is executed. Dimension Layer does not affect existing dimensions.

Color. The Color option lets you select the color of dimensions added to the drawing. Putting dimensions in a different color helps you visually separate them from other lines and text in your drawing. If you have a color monitor, you can select a color from the color bar displayed in the menu area.

Dimension Mode (UM)

With the Dimension Mode (UM) command, you can select between three modes of dimensioning: Single, Partitioned, or Cumulative mode. (See Figure 11.8.)

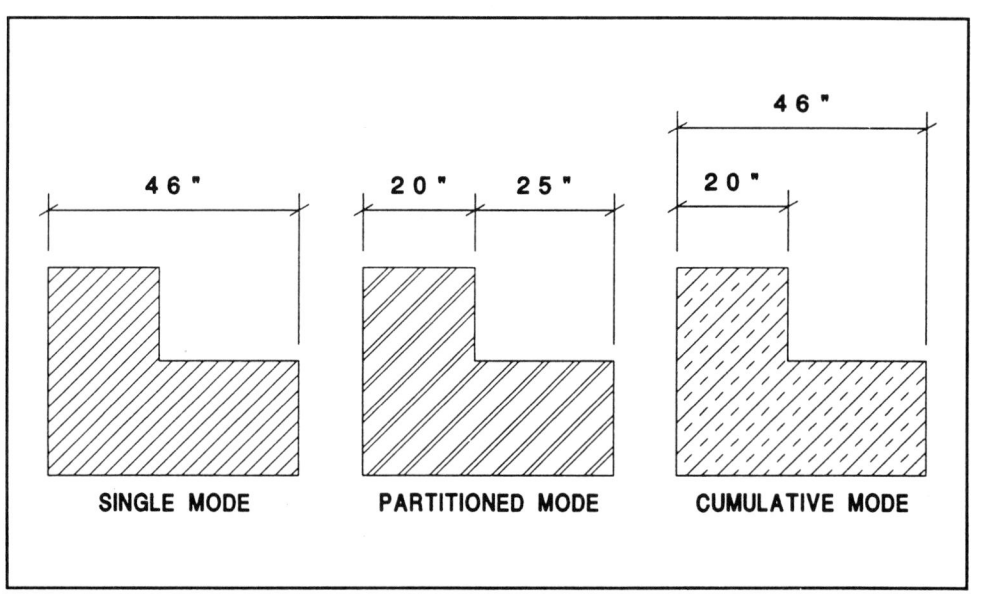

Figure 11.8 CADD 6.0's three Dimension Modes.

The following is an explanation of the different dimensioning modes:

Single. Individual (or Single) mode is the mode for entering individual dimensions that are not necessarily related or do not share extension lines. With this mode, you always have to identify two points, and the dimension is placed between them.

Partitioned. Partitioned mode is used for stringing several dimensions together consecutively. With this method, the second point chosen for placing a dimension can be used as the first point for the next dimension you place.

Cumulative. Cumulative display mode lets you use the first point of a dimension as the first point for multiple dimensions. Each dimension uses the same first point, but is offset from any previous dimension line so that no lines overlap. This method is commonly used on engineering drawings where there are several dimensions all referenced to one point or base line.

To use Dimension Mode (UM), enter the command code UM, or select the Dimension Mode (UM) command from the menu. Select one of the three options at the prompt. After your selection is complete, new dimensions will be drawn in the selected mode until a new mode is chosen.

Proximity Fixed (PF)

Refer to the previous explanation of Proximity fixed, found under the Dimension Settings - Dim Line feature discussed earlier in this chapter.

PLACING DIMENSIONS IN A DRAWING

All the preceding commands control the use and display of dimension lines. You can change these variables when you begin dimensioning a drawing in CADD 6, to determine the style of dimensioning you want and the size of the objects being dimensioned. The dimensioning variables can also be changed on-the-fly, in the middle of a dimension command.

The next section will describe commands for placing dimensions and settings that control where dimensions are placed in relation to the part. This includes the length of the extension lines and how far they are offset from the part.

Linear Dimension (LX)

Place linear dimension lines in a drawing with the Linear Dimension (LX) command, or select Horizontal, Vertical, Aligned, or At an Angle from the DIMENSIONS menu. (See Figure 11.9.) The direction of the dimension can be set to Horizontal, Vertical, Aligned, or At an Angle from the Dimension Settings (US) feature, under the Dim line option. Once this command is turned ON, you must press Esc to stop placing dimensions. Regardless of which dimensioning variables you have selected, the Linear Dimension (LX) command works basically the same way. You are *always* prompted to select the points being dimensioned, and then to select where to place the dimension line and text. CADD 6 calculates the dimension value based on the location of the selected points. To ensure accuracy, use snap commands to select dimension points.

```
            X = Pick Point

         |◄──── 12' ────►|
         X               X


         Linear Dimension (LX)
```

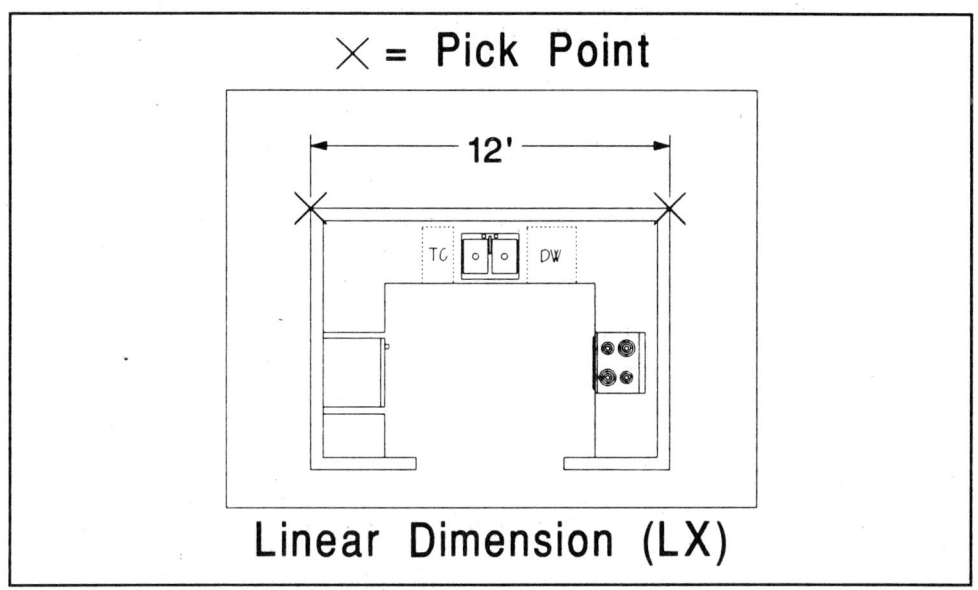

Figure 11.9 Placing a Linear Dimension.

To place a linear dimension:

> Type: LX (for Linear Dimension)
> At the prompt, move your cursor to the first point you are dimensioning
> Use a snap to select the point exactly
> Move your cursor to the second point to be dimensioned
> Select the second point with a snap command

Next, select a point for the dimension location. You will see the dimension text and lines rubberbanding from the selected points. Before you select the last point for the dimension location, change any dimensioning variables and view the changes before committing to the final position. At this point, the calculated value is displayed on the command line.

> Edit the dimension value or press Enter to accept it
> Press Esc to finish the Dimension command

> **TIP:** You can add more text to your dimension at the command line. If you want to replace or change the currently displayed text, backspace over the "#" sign on the command line, and enter a new value. The "#" sign signifies the calculated dimension value.

Angular Dimension (AX)

Use the Angular Dimension (AX) command to create angular dimensions. (See Figure 11.10.) The same 3-point method is used to dimension an angle as is used to measure or show one.

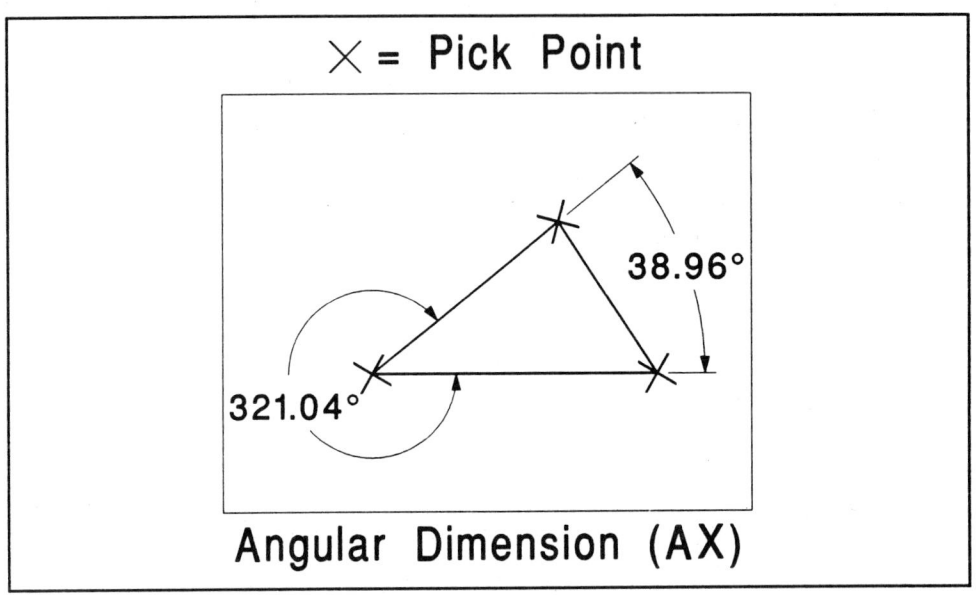

Figure 11.10 Placing an Angular Dimension.

```
Type: AX (for Angular Dimension)
Snap to select the center point of the angle you wish to dimension
Snap to select a point on the first ray of the angle
Snap to select a point on the second ray of the angle
```

Be sure to use snaps, as that is the only way to accurately dimension any angle made by existing objects in your drawing.

The last prompt will ask for the dimension location. As with the Linear Dimension command, you can rubberband the dimension on-screen and change dimensioning variables on-the-fly until you are satisfied with its appearance and location.

> **TIP:** You can place the dimension location on either side of the center point of the angle. For example, the dimension for the corner of a square could either be 90 degrees or 270 degrees.

Once the location has been specified, the dimension value will be displayed on the command line.

Edit the dimension value or press Enter to accept it

Once you have selected a value, the dimension will be placed in your drawing.

Radial Dimension (RX)

The Radial Dimension (RX) command is used to dimension arcs or circles. (See Figure 11.11.) Dimension Mode (UM), Extension settings (USE), and Proximity Fixed (PF) have no affect on this command.

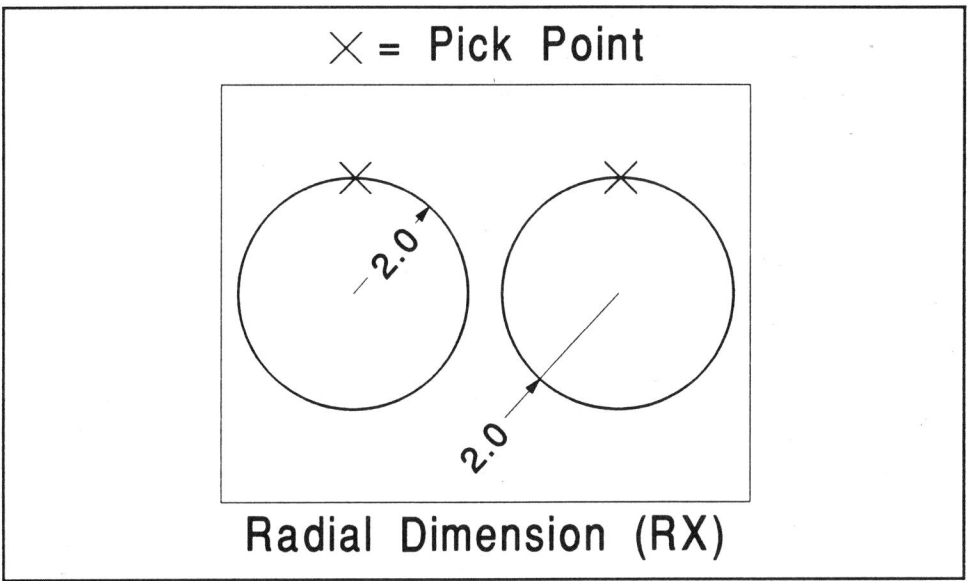

Figure 11.11 Placing Radial Dimensions.

To execute this command:

Type: RX (for Radial Dimension)
Click to select the arc or circle to radial dimension

The dimension value will be displayed on the command line.

Edit the value as needed, or press Enter to accept it

The last prompt will ask where to position the dimension. As with the Linear Dimension command, you can rubberband the dimension on-screen and change dimensioning variables on-the-fly until you are satisfied with its appearance and location.

Diameter Dimension (IX)

The Diameter Dimension (IX) command is used to dimension arcs or circles. (See Figure 11.12.) Dimension Mode (UM), Extension settings (USE), and Proximity Fixed (PF) have no affect on this command.

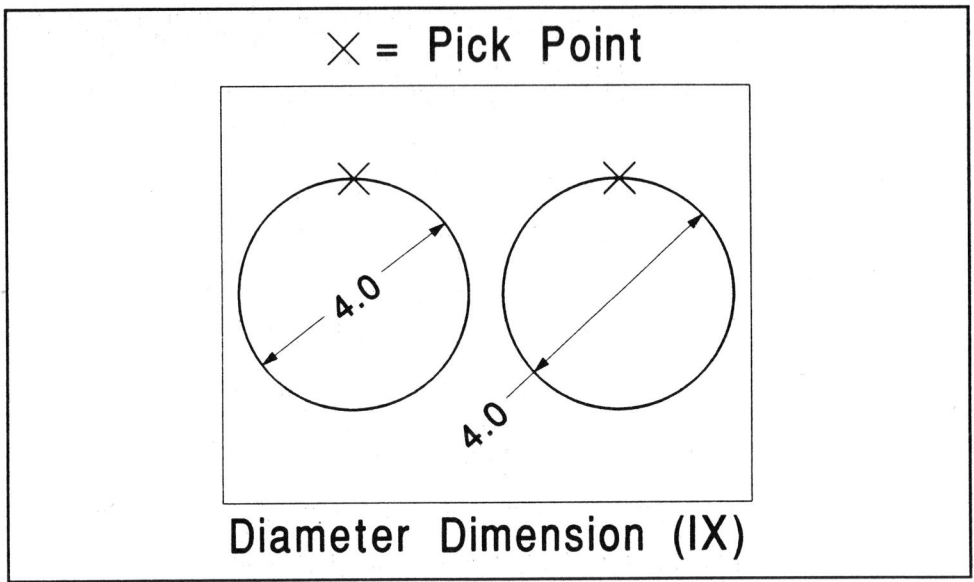

Figure 11.12 Placing Diameter Dimensions.

> Type: IX (for Diameter Dimension)
> Click to select the arc or circle to diameter dimension

The dimension will be displayed at the bottom of the screen.

> Edit the value as needed, or press Enter to accept the value shown

The last prompt will ask where the dimension is to be placed. As with the Linear Dimension command, you can rubberband the dimension on-screen and change dimensioning variables until you are satisfied with its appearance and location.

> **TIP:** The text position in a Diameter Dimension (IX) can be inside or outside the boundary of the circle. When you're prompted for the line's position, the dimension line and text move dynamically with the cursor. When the correct position is selected, Click with your mouse to select it.

Dimension Leader (LE)

The Dimension Leader (LE) is used to place an arrow at a specified point followed by a line, shoulder, and text on the other end. (See Figure 11.13) Use a Leader to point out a specific area of your drawing, assigning text pertinent to that area. To execute the Dimension Leader command:

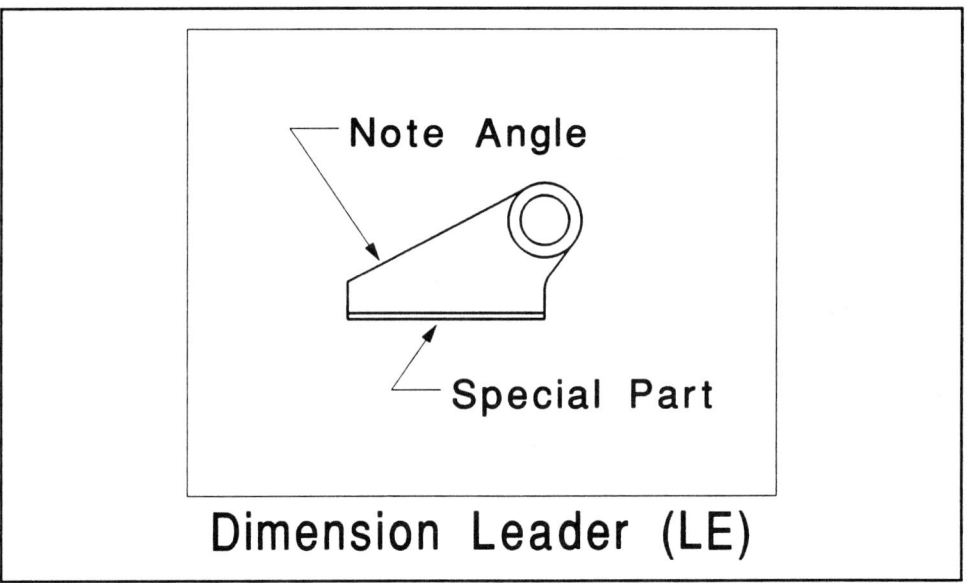

Figure 11.13 Using the Dimension Leader command.

```
Type:  LE (for Dimension Leader)
Type the text for the leader and press Enter
Click to select the leader's starting point
Click to select the leader's terminal point
```

The starting point is where you want the leader arrow to point. The terminal point is where the leader's shoulder and text begin. The last prompt will ask you to indicate the shoulder's direction. Move your cursor, and notice the shoulder and text boundary box flip to the left or right. The text and shoulder are always placed horizontally.

```
Position the text on the desired side of the leader
Click or press Enter to place it
```

> **TIP:** The arrow's appearance in a leader is determined by the Arrow settings (USA) feature.

Shoulder Length (LL)

The Shoulder Length (LL) command controls the length of the horizontal straight line drawn at the end of a dimension leader. (A leader is an arrow line used as a pointer, followed by a text note.) To use this command, enter the command code LL. At the prompt, accept the default by pressing Enter, or provide a new value.

Dimension Move (UV)

The Dimension Move (UV) command lets you reposition the placement of the dimension text in relation to the dimension line in previously placed dimensions. This command also changes the placement of the dimension line.

> **TIP:** The Dimension Move (UV) command does not move the dimension away from the points initially selected to dimension. If you wish to move the dimension away from these points, use the Move (MV) command.

To execute the Dimension Move (UV) command, type UV or select this command from the DIMENSIONS menu. You will be prompted to enter a point on the dimension you want to move. The point depends on the type of dimension you are moving.

The following is a description of the various options used to select points to move different dimension types:

Linear. With Linear dimensions, you have two choices: you can either select and move the text, or you can select and move the dimension line. (See Figure 11.14.)

Angular. With Angular dimensions, you have two choices. You can select the dimension text and move it within the dimension arc. The other option is to select the dimension arc and change its distance from the vertex of the angle. (See Figure 11.15.)

The dimension value will not change unless you move to the opposite side of the vertex currently selected. Depending on which side you move, the angle either increases or decreases. (See Figure 11.16.)

Radial and Diameter. With Radial and Diameter dimensions, you have one option. Select any point on the dimension. This allows you to reposition the text and dimension line. (See Figure 11.17.)

Leader. With the Leader, you have one option. Select any point on the leader. You are then able to reposition the leader, the shoulder, and the text. The arrow head will change its orientation, but remain fixed at the point at which it was initially placed. (See Figure 11.18.)

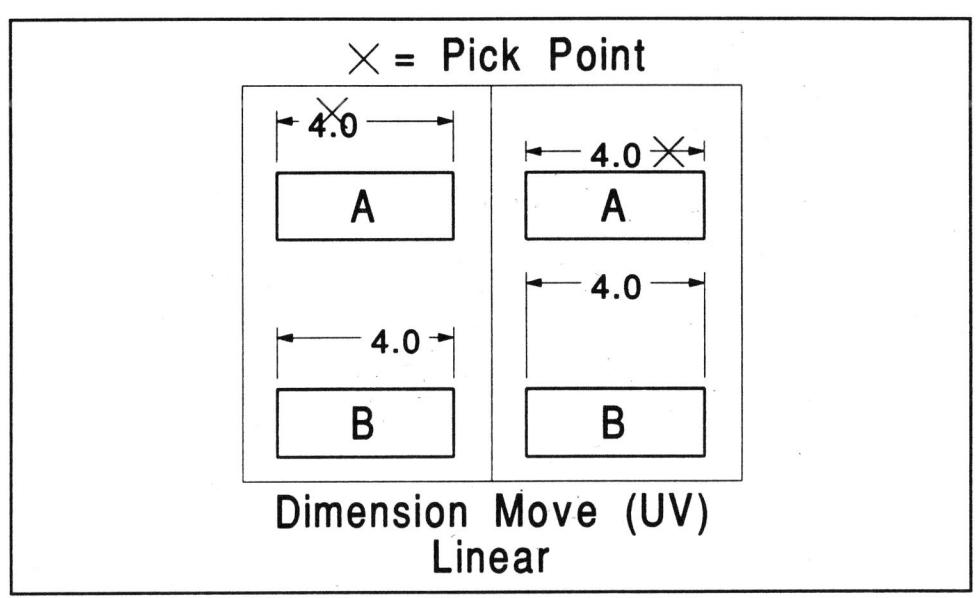

Figure 11.14 Repositioning text with Dimension Move.

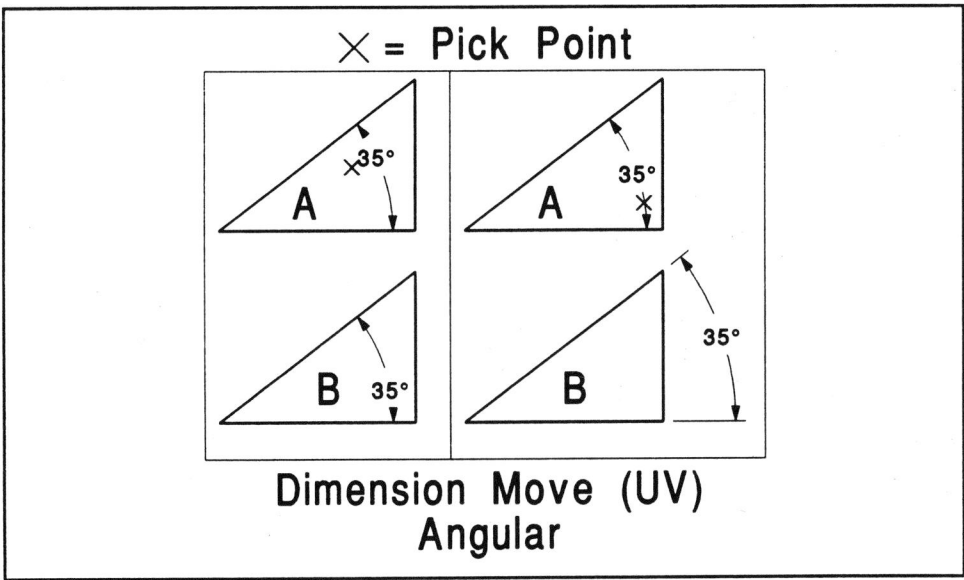

Figure 11.15 Repositioning text in Angular Dimensions.

11-20 ■ Chapter 11: Dimensioning

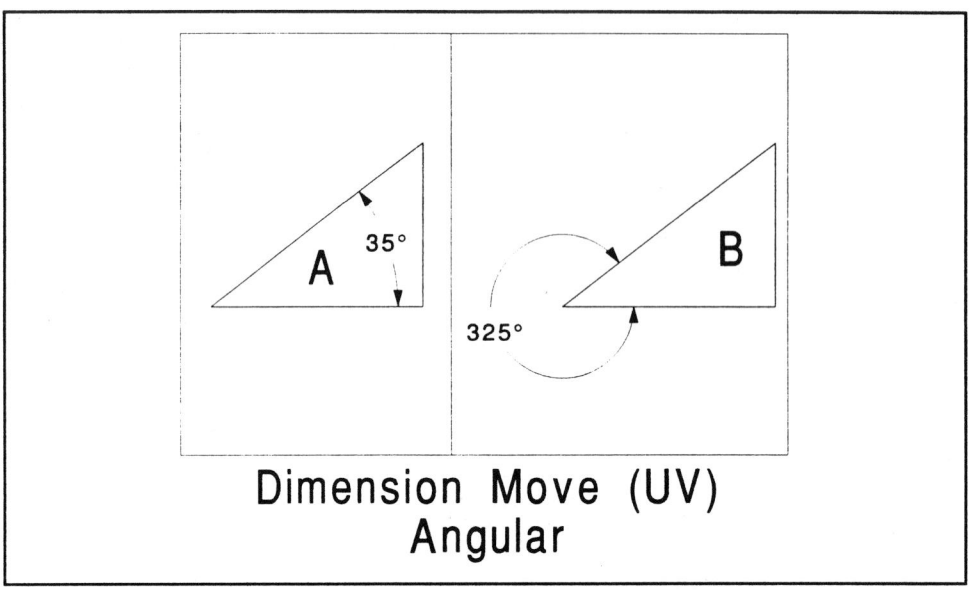

Figure 11.16 Changing the angle value with Dimension Move.

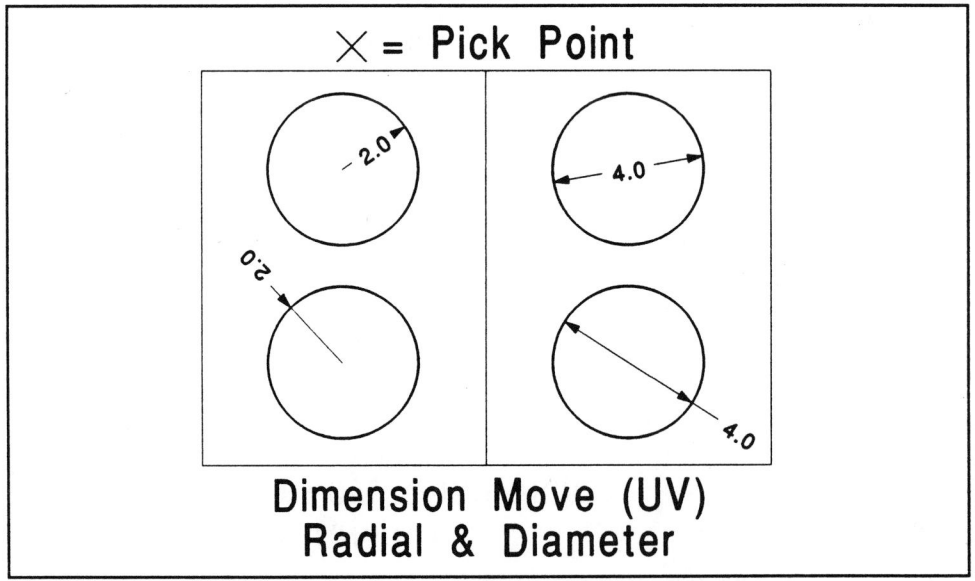

Figure 11.17 Moving text for Radial and Diameter Dimensions.

```
                    X = Pick Point
```

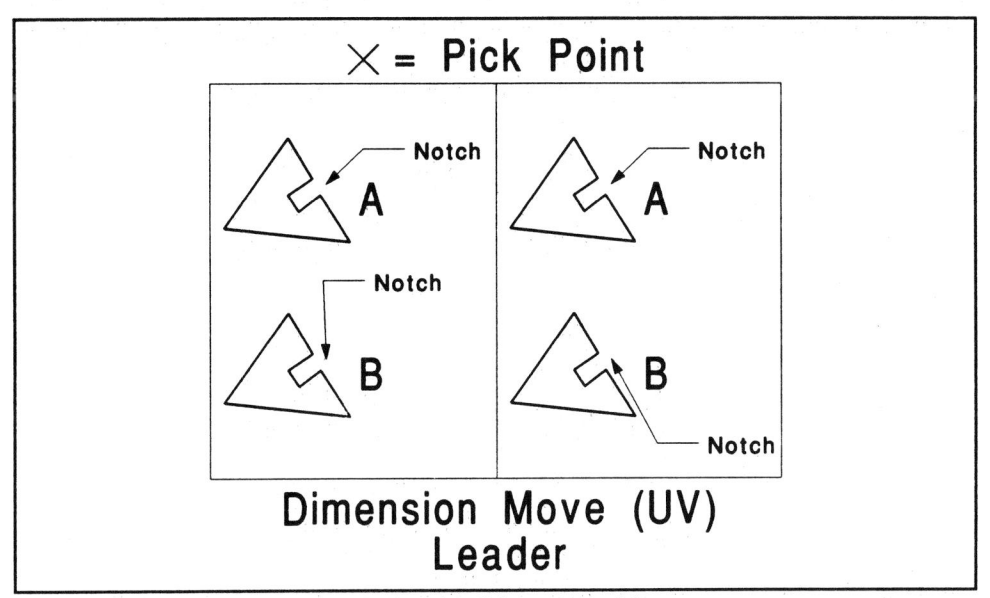

Figure 11.18 Changing Leaders with Dimension Move.

Dimension Change (UG)

The Dimension Change (UG) command allows you to change almost any part of an existing dimension. With this command, you can modify existing dimension arrows, dimension lines, extension lines, and dimension text. Execute the Dimension Change (UG) command, then click on the part of the dimension you wish to change. You will be prompted with the options that pertain to the dimension part selected.

Once a change has been made and entered, the following message will appear on the command line:

<RET> Change current - S for selection

If you press Enter <RET>, only the initial dimension selected is changed. If you select "S," you will be prompted with a selection set which allows you to select any other, or all dimensions in the drawing to receive the same change.

The following is the set of options available when using the Dimension Change (UG) command:

Arrows. Click on the arrow to be changed. The following arrow setting options are available:

11-22 ■ Chapter 11: Dimensioning

Type	Choose from seven arrow head types - normal closed, normal open, normal filled, notched, circle unfilled, circle filled, and slash
Angle	Enter a new arrow head angle
Length	Enter a new arrow head length
lOcation	Change the arrows to be on the inside or the outside of the dimension line
display 1	Change the display of arrow 1 to ON or OFF
display 2	Change the display of arrow 2 to ON or OFF

Both arrows will be affected by the changes made with this command, except for the display 1 and display 2 options. These options let you choose to display the arrow heads independently.

Dimension Lines. Click on the dimension line to change, then choose one of these options:

Proximity	Change from proximity fixed ON or OFF
directioN	Choose from aligned, horizontal, vertical, or at an angle
Display	Change the dimension line display to ON or OFF

Dimension Text. Click to pick the dimension text to change, then choose one of the following text setting options:

Edit	Change the dimension text
Format	Change the format of angular dimensions (degrees or Deg/Min/Sec), linear dimensions (decimal or fractions), decimal value (from 0 to 6), display of leading zeros (ON/OFF), display of units (ON/OFF), or fractional value (denominator or 2, 4, 8, 16, 32, or 64)
sPacing	Change the between-character spacing, between-line spacing, and proportional spacing (on/OFF)
Settings	Choose between Placement, Direction, Centered, siZe, Offsets, Tolerance, or dIsplay, just as for the Dimension Settings (US) command
Units	Choose between Inches, Feet/inches, feeT, Millimeters, Centimeters, or meterS

Extension Lines. Click to select the extension lines to change, then choose from the following options:

Offset	Change the extension line offset
length Above	Change the length of the extension line above the arrow
length Below	Change the length of the extension line below the arrow

Stretch	Change whether the length of the extension line is fixed
display 1	Change the display of extension line 1
display 2	Change the display of extension line 2

DIMENSIONING TUTORIAL

In this section, you will create one view of a mechanical part and dimension it. First, you will set your dimensioning variables. Then you will create the actual drawing of the part to dimension and last, you will dimension the part using commands on CADD 6's DIMENSIONS menu.

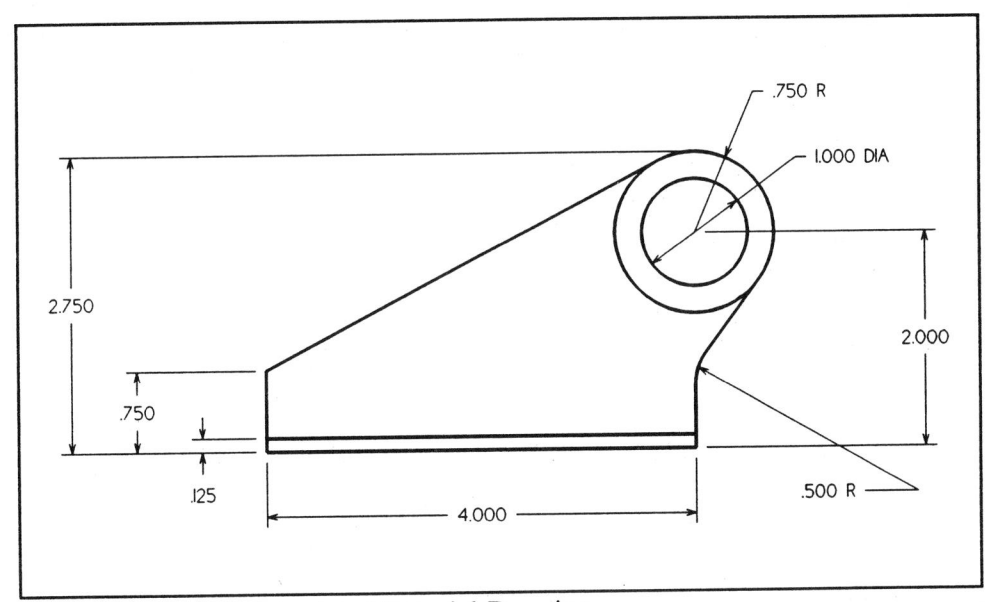

Figure 11.19 The completed Tutorial Drawing.

Part I — Setting Up Initial Dimensioning Variables

During the course of dimensioning, you always find that some variables need to be changed on-the-fly. No matter how thorough you are in pre-setting dimensioning variables, count on making changes as you dimension. CADD 6 is excellent at providing visual feedback, so take advantage of it when dimensioning.

In this tutorial, two and three-letter command codes are used to execute the necessary commands. Feel free to follow along, using the menu to execute the selected commands if you prefer. A combination of command codes and menu selections is ultimately the most productive method of command selection in CADD 6.

Type: US (for Dimension Settings)

Many of these commands, like Proximity fixed and Text ON, are toggles. If the command line reads OFF, selecting it turns it ON, and vice versa. Set the dimension options as listed below:

Text:

> Placement = In-line
> Direction = Horizontal
> Centered = ON
> Size = .12
> Offsets
> > In-line offset = .1
> > Above offset = .25

Extensions:

> Offset = .1
> length Above = .1
> length Below = .5
> Stretch = OFF

Arrows:

> Type = normal-Open
> Angle = 15
> Length = .1
> lOcation = Inside
> display 1 = ON
> display 2 = ON

Dim line:

> Proximity fixed = ON
> directioN = Aligned
> display = ON

Font:

> Select "Engineer" from the list of fonts on the sidebar menu

Alternatively, you can enter the font name at the command line.

Numeric Display Format:

Type: NF to set Numeric Display Format options

This command is found on the DISPLAY menu. Set the numeric format options as listed below:

Linear = Decimal
Decimal value = 3
leading Zeros = OFF
Show Units = OFF

Part II — Creating the Drawing to Dimension

Now you are ready to draw the mechanical part. If you completed the earlier tutorials, you are familiar with the basic DRAW and EDIT commands. The drawing steps are given here without further instructions:

Type: MR (for Manual Entry Relative)
Click a point on the screen to start drawing
Type: 4,0 (and press Enter)
Type: 0,.75 (and press Enter)
Type: C2
Type: 0,1.25 (and press Enter)
Type: 0,.5 (and press Enter)
Type: C2
Snap (NP) to the center of the last circle drawn
Type: 0,.75 (and press Enter)
Type: ZA (for Zoom All) to see the entire drawing

Your drawing should now look like Figure 11.20, with the exception of the labeled points.

Type: OR as required to turn Ortho Mode OFF
Snap NP to point A (Figure 11.20)
Type: ST (for Snap Tangent)
Click to the circle at point B (Figure 11.20)
Press Esc to finish drawing lines
Type: FR (Fillet Radius)
Type: .5 (and press Enter)
Type: FI (for Fillet) and select the two lines at the intersection of point A in Figure 11.20

To round off the corner at intersection point A:

Snap NP to point C (Figure 11.20)
Type: 0,.75 (and press Enter)
Type: ST (for Snap Tangent) and click on the circle at point D (Figure 11.20)

11-26 ■ Chapter 11: Dimensioning

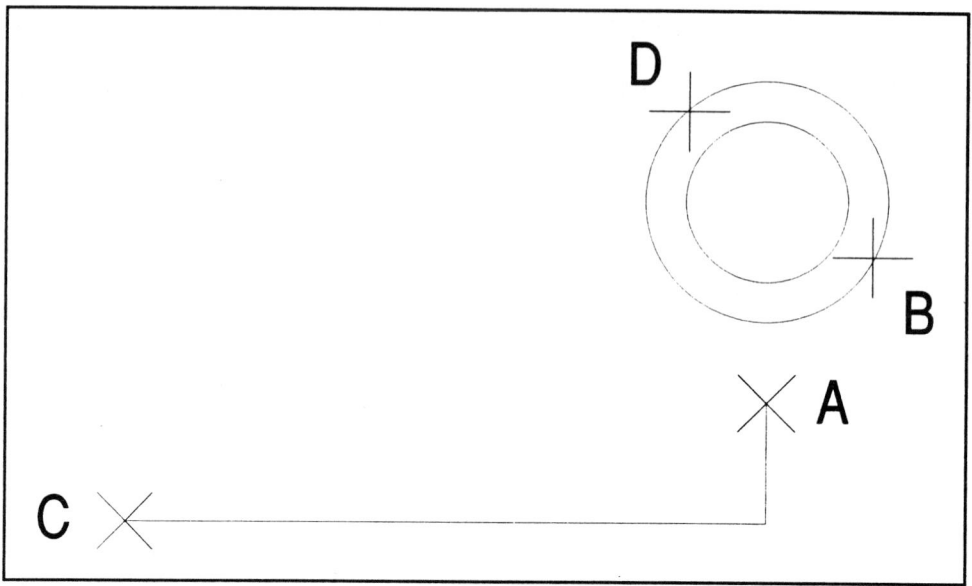

Figure 11.20 Constructing the Mechanical Part.

    Press Esc to finish drawing lines
    Snap NP to point C (Figure 11.20)
    Type: LI (for Line)
    Type: 0,.125 (and press Enter)
    Type: 4,0 (and press Enter)
    Press Esc to finish drawing lines

Figure 11.21 shows the completed drawing. The next step is to dimension it.

Part III - Dimensioning The Drawing

In this section, you will insert the dimensions. The initial dimension variables were already set in Part I. You may want to update the drawing Environment (EN) with the new settings for use in later drawings.

Refer to Figure 11.22 for the point selections in the following tutorial.

    Type: LX (for Linear Dimension)
    Snap NP to point A and then to point B

The command line should show a value of 4.000 for the dimension text.

    Press Enter to accept the value

Move the cursor until the dimension text is located below the part, as shown in Figure 11.23.

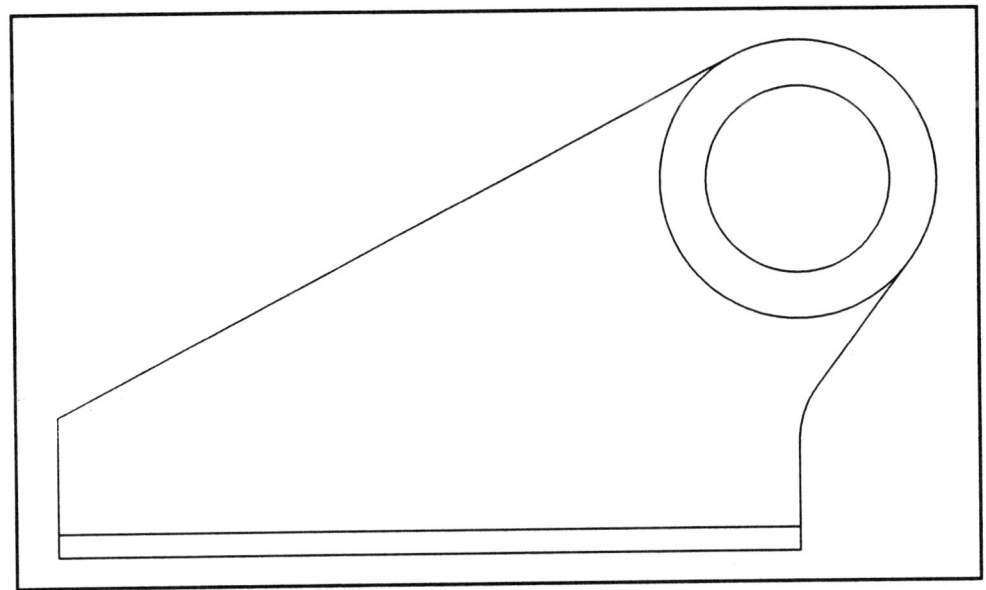

Figure 11.21 The Completed Mechanical Part.

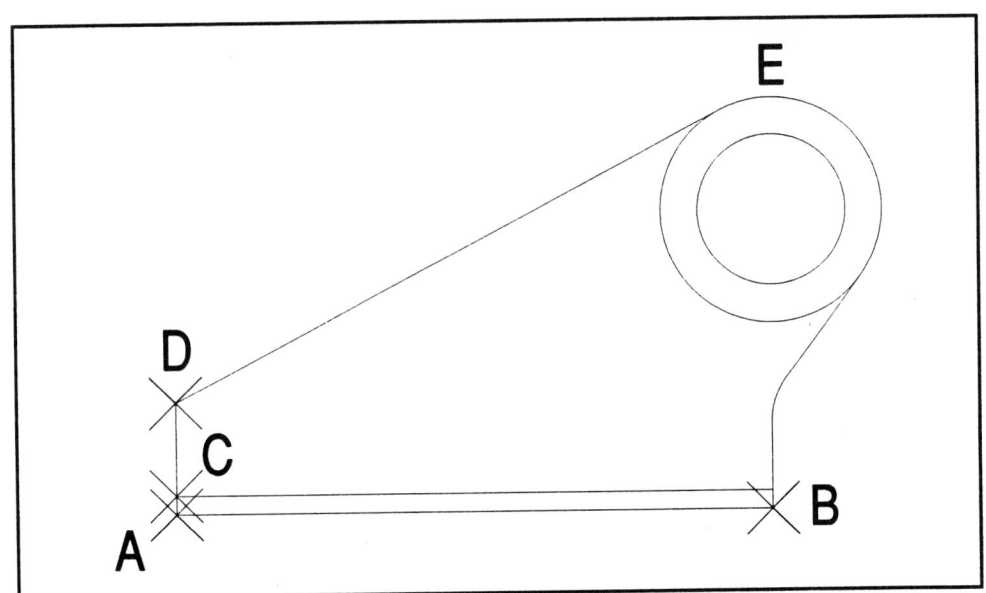

Figure 11.22 Reference points used to Construct the Dimensions.

Press Enter, or click to freeze the dimension
Type: UM (for Dimension Mode) then type C to select Cumulative dimensioning
Type: USE (for Dimension Settings, Extensions)
Type: S to flip the Stretch toggle ON
Press Enter twice to finish the command
Type: PF (for Proximity fixed) to toggle Proximity fixed (PF) OFF

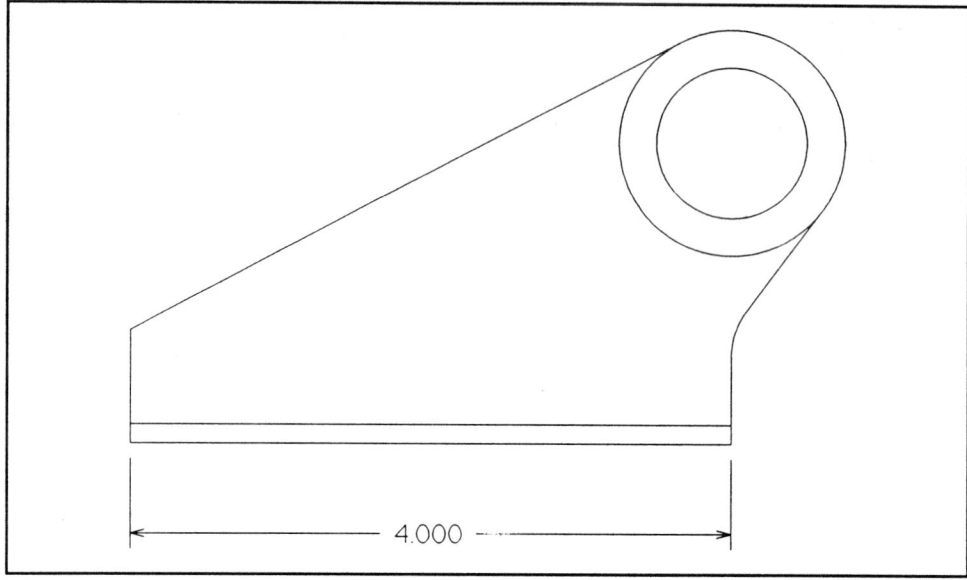

Figure 11.23 Placing the first Linear Dimension.

    Type: LX (for Linear Dimension)
    Snap NP to points A and C

You should notice that the dimension does not fit very well in this small section. You can change it by adjusting some dimension variables on-the-fly.

    Type: UST (for Dimension Settings, Text)
    Type: C to toggle the Centered option OFF
    Press Enter twice

Now the text boundary box moves about the dimension lines, but the arrows are still cramped between the lines.

    Type: USA (for Dimension Settings, Arrow)
    Type: O to toggle the arrow location outside the dimension lines
    Press Enter twice
    Place the text boundary box just below the bottom dimension arrow
    Press Enter to accept the .125 value at the prompt
    Type: USA (for Dimension Settings, Arrow)
    Type: O to toggle the arrow location back to the inside of the dimension lines
    Press Enter twice
    Snap NP to point D (See Figure 11.23.)
    Press Enter to accept the .750 value at the prompt
    Snap NP to point E (See Figure 11.23.)
    Press Enter to accept the 2.75 value at the prompt

Chapter 11: Dimensioning ■ 11-29

    Press Escape to abort cumulative dimensioning
    Type ZA (for Zoom All)

You should now be able to see the entire drawing. It should resemble Figure 11.24.

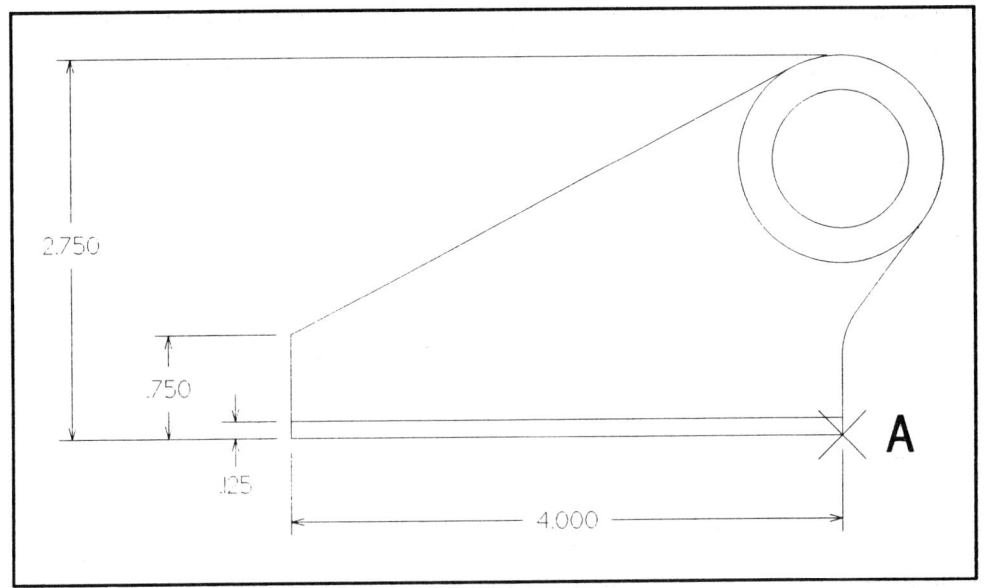

Figure 11.24 Placing Dimensions on the Left Side of the part.

    Type: UM (for Dimension Mode) and select S for Single mode
    Type: LX (for Linear Dimension)
    Snap NP to point B (Figure 11.23), then to the center of the hole at point E
    Press Enter to accept the 2.000 value

You should be able to move the dimension dynamically to the right or left. You will notice that the text boundary box moves freely.

    Type: UST (Dimension Settings, Text)
    Type: C to turn the Centered toggle ON
    Move the cursor to the right to pull the dimension that way
    Press Enter, or click to freeze the dimension

    Type: IX (for Diameter Dimension)
    Click on the inner circle
    At the "#" prompt for dimension value, press the spacebar once
    Type: DIA (and press Enter)
    Freeze the dimension in the position shown in Figure 11.26

11-30 ■ Chapter 11: Dimensioning

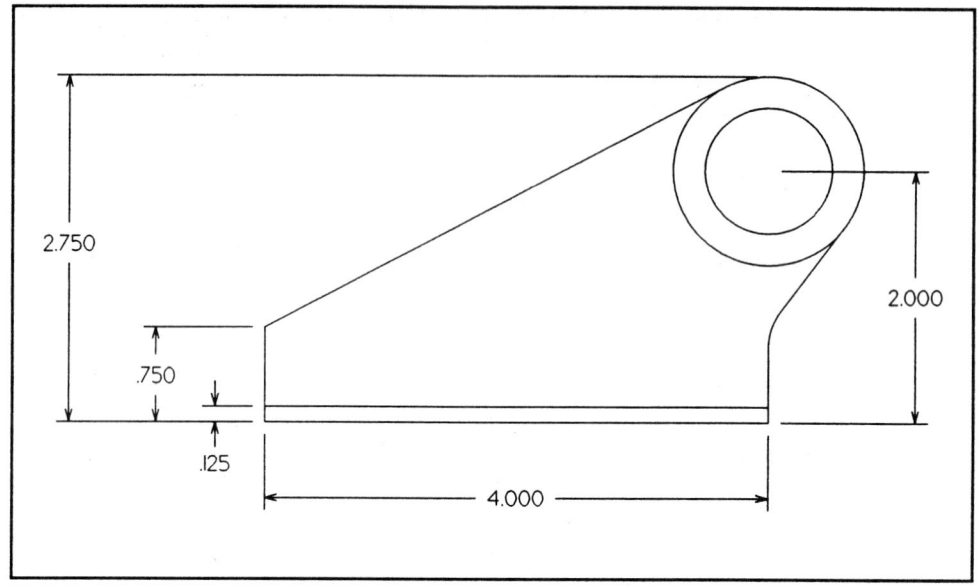

Figure 11.25 Dimensioning to the Center of the Circle.

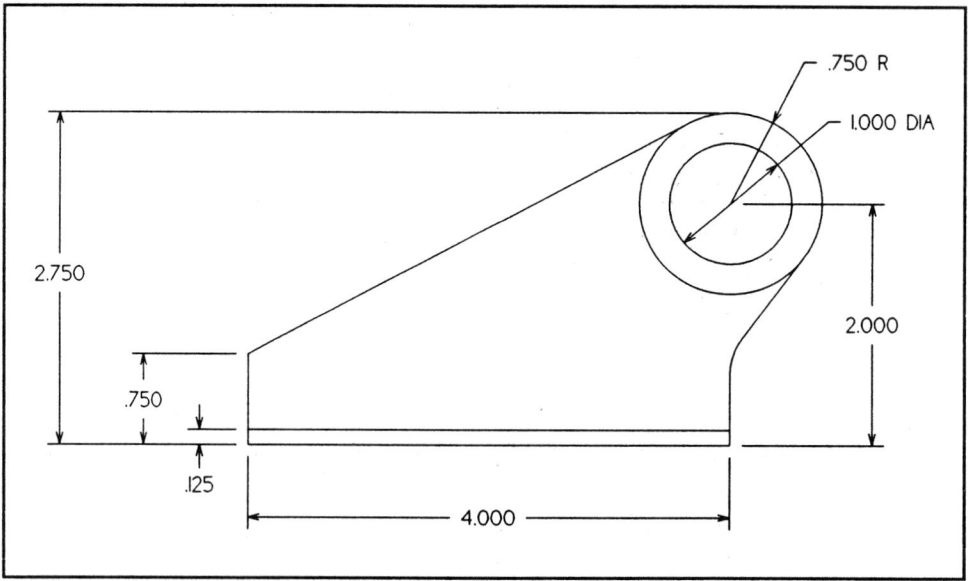

Figure 11.26 Placing the Radial and Diameter Dimensions.

    Type: RX (for Radial Dimension)
    Click to the outer circle at point E
    At the "#" prompt for dimension value, press the spacebar
    Type: R (and press Enter)
    Position the dimension, as shown in Figure 11.26

The last item to place in the drawing is a leader to label the .500 inch fillet you created earlier.

> Type: **LE** (for Leader)
> Type: **.500 R** (and press Enter)

This is the text to be placed with the arrow.

> Snap **NP** near the fillet, as shown in Figure 11.27

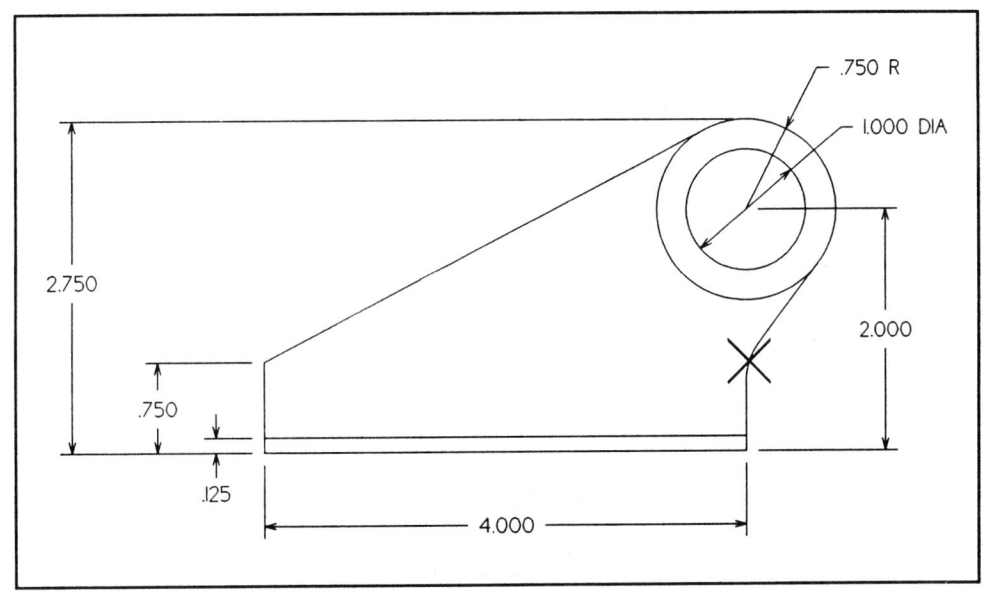

Figure 11.27 Snap Point for the Leader.

Before positioning the leader, adjust its shoulder length as follows:

> Type: **LL** (for Shoulder Length)
> Type: **.5** (and press Enter)
> Position and place the leader (as in Figure 11.28)

If the entire drawing is not shown on the screen:

> Type: **ZA** (for Zoom All) to view the final drawing

CHAPTER SUMMARY

After you become more familiar with the dimension commands, dimensioning your drawing is a snap. However, using the powerful and flexible dimensioning features requires setting quite a few variables. All of the variables are located on the menu, so

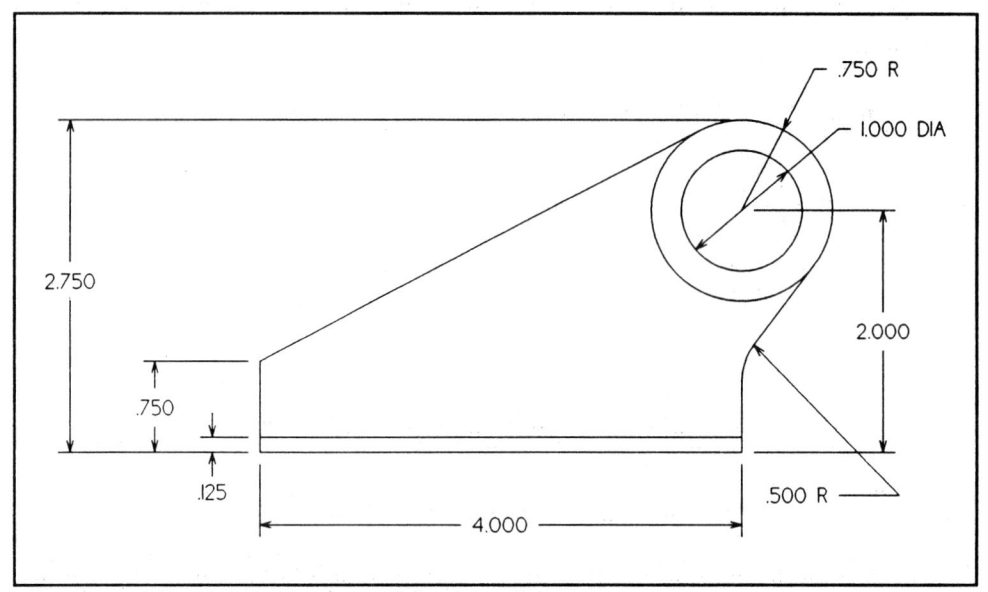

Figure 11.28 The final Dimensioned Drawing.

you do not have to memorize the two-character command codes. When initially setting dimensioning variables, it is a good idea to work your way down the compiled list of dimension settings, found in the Dimension Settings (US) command. These variables give you complete control over the dimension mode, direction, text size, text font and placement, arrow size and type, color, layer, and so on.

SAMPLE EXERCISES

Use the commands you have learned thus far to complete the following sample exercises. Use the dimensions shown to draw the parts to full-scale. At this time, you may also want to add dimensions to the sample exercises you completed in Chapters 4, 5, 6, and 7.

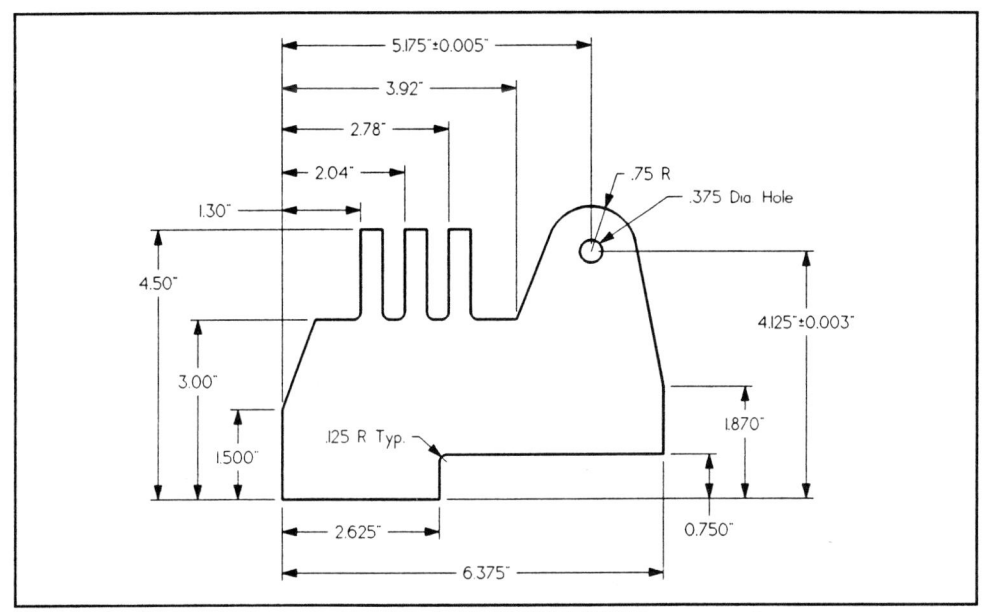

Figure 11.29 Sample exercise for the DIMENSION commands.

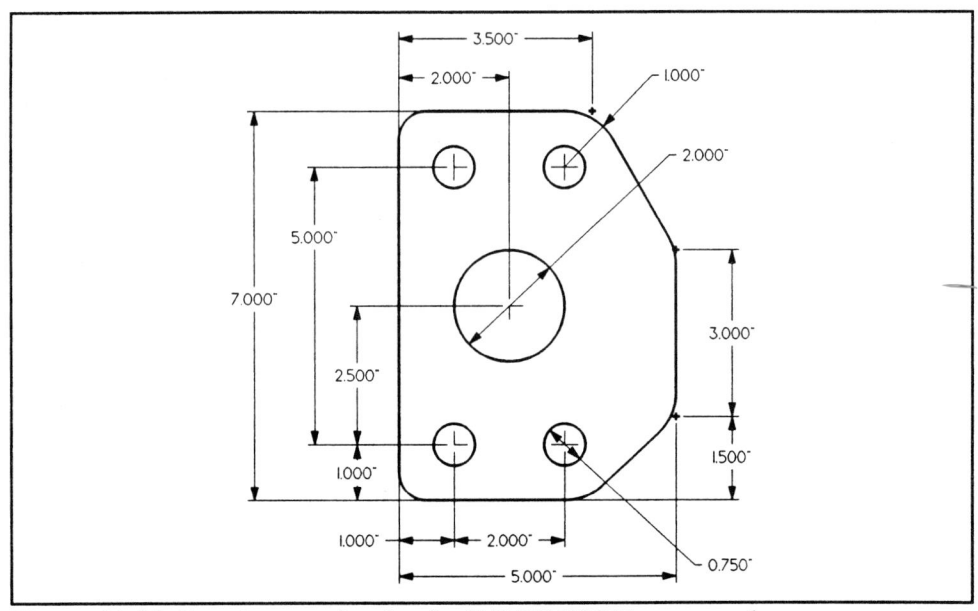

Figure 11.30 Sample exercise for the DIMENSION commands.

11-34 ■ Chapter 11: Dimensioning

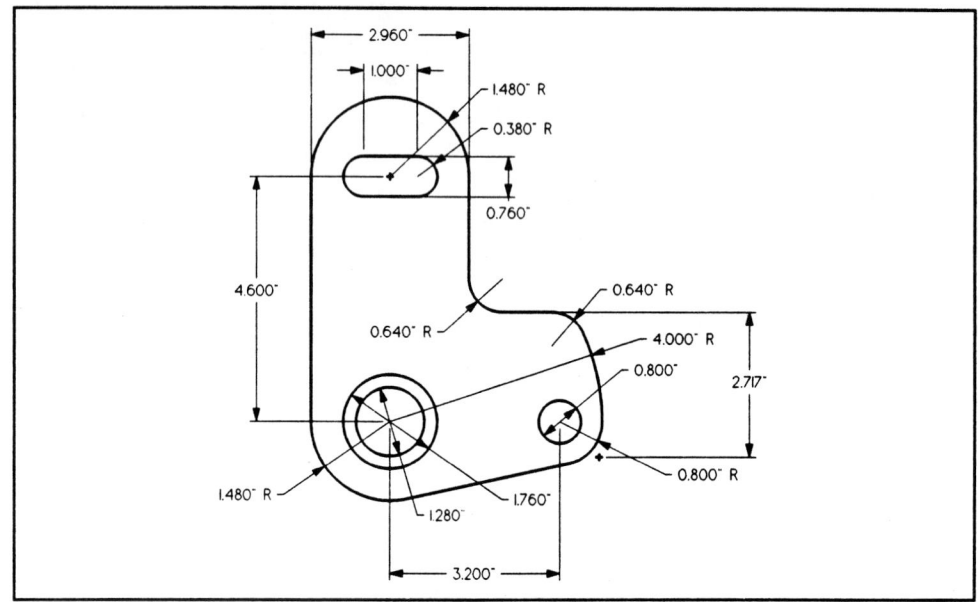

Figure 11.31 Sample exercise for the DIMENSION commands.

CHAPTER 12

Organizing

USING THE LAYERS MENU AND NAMED VIEWS

Generic CADD 6 is a very powerful program that can be used to produce large and complex drawings. As your drawings become larger, you may soon find that you are becoming less productive. You spend more time picking out just the right entities for editing, and even zooming around the drawing becomes slow and tedious. Do not be too concerned, however, because there are capabilities built into CADD 6 that help you organize your drawing so your level of productivity stays high.

One common way of organizing your drawings is to use *Layers* to separate or group similar objects together. For example, you may want to put all objects that come from the same vendor on one layer, such as all the doors and windows in a floor plan. Once objects are separated by layer, they can be selected easily for editing with commands that use selection sets like Move (MV) and Copy (CO). You can also choose to print any combination of layers, and save individual layers to disk for use in other drawings.

Working on a large, detailed drawing may require you to execute many Zoom and Pan commands to move between the various detailed sections. Each time you want to edit a small section, you may have to execute a Zoom All (ZA), then a Zoom Window (ZW), and that can take a great deal of time. To solve this problem, CADD 6 allows you to organize your drawing into different views and assign a name to each of them. You can then zoom from anywhere in your drawing directly to any named view, which saves valuable time. The Named View commands are found on the ZOOMS menu.

The commands included here to help organize your drawings are:

LAYERS

All Layers Edit (AL)
Set Current Layer (YC)
Layer Display (YD)
Layer Name (YN)
Layer Hide (YH)

Layer Erase (YE)
Layer Rotate (YR)
Layer Scale (YZ)
Layer Change (YG)

Dimension Layer (UL)

Layer Load (YL)
Layer Save (YS)

ZOOMS

Name View (NV)
Zoom View (ZV)
Delete Named View (NX)

INTRODUCTION TO LAYERS

Complex drawings can be organized into smaller pieces by separating similar objects onto *layers*. Use layers to divide the whole drawing into different parts, such as groups of related entities, text, title blocks, and dimensions. You can specify to work with one or more layers displayed on the screen at a time. A layer can also function as a template, which allows you to snap to entities located on it without actually modifying any of the entities on that layer.

With the layer commands, you can create the electronic equivalent of overlay sheets with separate sets of details for alternative drawing displays. Layers give you a way to organize your drawing so certain information can be displayed or not, as needed. Layers function like tracing paper that can be overlaid on a drawing or removed. CADD 6 provides 256 different layers, numbered from 0 to 255, and you can also assign alphanumeric names to any or all of the layers. As you work, you can instruct CADD 6 as to which layer to draw on, or you can move existing entities to different layers. You can then choose to display any combination of these layers.

If you think of layers as stacks of see-through overlay sheets, the current layer is the sheet you select to draw on. You can flip through the whole stack and select any one sheet to draw on, but you can only draw on one sheet at a time. The current layer must always be displayed, but any of the other layers can be *hidden* or turned OFF, as if those overlays were pulled out of the stack. The entities on those layers are not displayed on the screen, and no editing you do will affect anything on those layers. The information is not lost, however, only hidden from view. You can choose to re-display all of the layers at any time.

The Layer commands do not prompt the user to define a selection set, because they always affect *all* entities on the selected layer. If you need to edit only particular objects on a layer, use the editing commands with selection sets, such as MV (Move), CO (Copy), RO (Rotate), SZ (Scale), and so on. You can then select individual entities, or use a filter to define your selection set.

Note that almost all of the layer commands have a two-letter code that begins with the letter Y. This may not seem very easy to remember mnemonically, but unfortunately the letters L and A are used for other commands. Don't worry, will you soon become accustomed to associating Y with layers!

After all of the layer commands have been described, a short tutorial is included to illustrate their use. You will continue working with the KITCHEN drawing that you created in Chapters 2 through 6. In this tutorial you will learn how to organize the drawing into layers, and hide/display particular layers to create a new perspective of your drawing.

Layer Selection Methods

CADD 6 uses a *Point and Click* method of selecting layers. Whenever you are prompted to select a layer (for displaying, hiding, rotating, saving, etc.), a list of the layers is shown on the side of the screen in place of the normal CADD 6 menu. The layers on the list are marked to show which layer is the "Current Layer," which layers are displayed, and which layers have data or entities drawn on them. This layer list is shown in Figure 12.1, and is discussed further in the tutorial at the end of this chapter.

Use your pointing device to click on the type of list you want from the bottom of the menu. You can toggle between a "Long List" which displays all 256 layers (on multiple pages), or a "Short List" which only lists the layers that are current, have data, or have previously been named (See Layer Name, YN).

If the layer list is too long to fit on one screen (this is always the case for the Long List), use the PgUp or PgDn keys, or click on the "More..." item at the bottom of the menu. This will allow you to advance through each page of the layer list.

For all of the following commands (except All Layers Edit, AL) you have to select a layer. CADD 6 will prompt:

>   Select Layer From Sidebar menu > >

12-4 ■ Chapter 12: Organizing

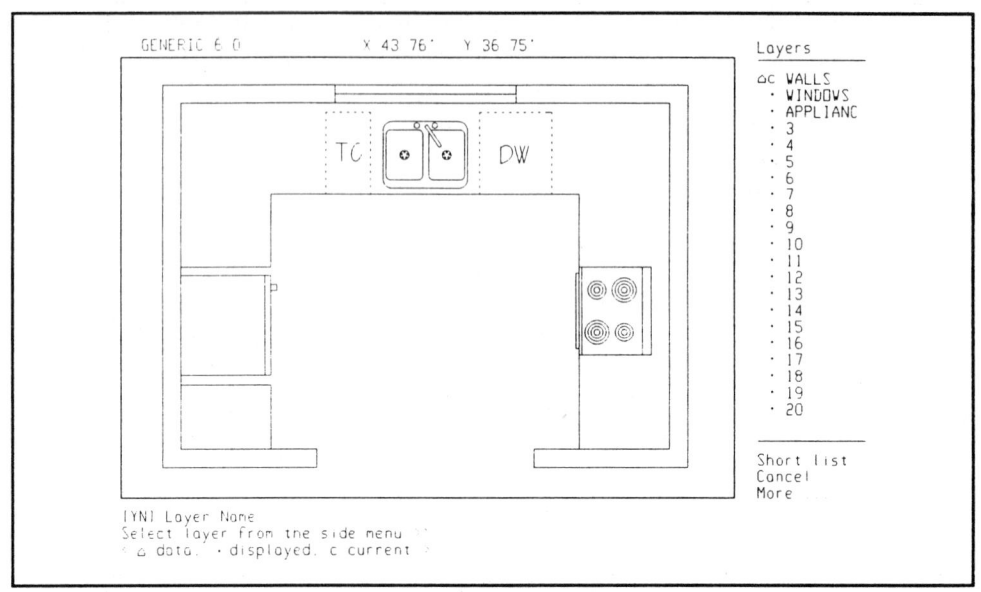

Figure 12.1 The Layer Listing on the sidebar menu.

You can respond to this prompt by using your pointing device to click on the desired layer shown on the layer list, by entering the desired layer's number from the keyboard, or by entering the layer's name (if it was assigned a name.) All layer selections can be made by one of these three methods.

All Layers Edit (AL)

This command is a toggle command that turns ON or OFF the editing of all layers that are displayed. With All Layers Edit (AL) turned ON, any editing you do affects all objects you can see on the screen, regardless of which layer they are on. For example, if you use Erase (ER) with the Window option to select several objects on the screen, all objects in the window are erased from every layer. If All Layers Edit (AL) were turned OFF, only the objects on the current layer would be erased, even though objects on other (non-current) layers were within the selection window.

This command is helpful when you need some to display some layers for visual reference, but you do not want those objects to be affected by editing. Perhaps you have digitized a map in CADD 6, and you want to replace a series of short, straight lines with a smooth curve. You could place the digitized drawing on layer 1 and set the Current Layer (YC) to layer 0. Then turn OFF All Layers Edit (AL). You construct the curve by tracing over the lines on the digitized drawing, then you can edit the new curve without the old lines getting in the way. When finished, switch to Layer 1 and erase the old lines.

Remember that you can also tell CADD 6 that you want to snap to points or objects on layers that are not available for editing with the All Layer Snap (SY) command (see Chapter 5 for more information on Snaps.)

Set Current Layer (YC)

Since you can only draw on one layer at a time (even though many layers may be displayed), you must specify the layer on which you want to draw. This layer is called the *Current Layer*, and it is specified with the "Set Current Layer" (YC) command. When you start a new drawing, the current layer is automatically set to layer 0 (unless you start from a template drawing whose environment has a different current layer). The name or number of the current layer is displayed on the screen status line in the format LAYER:10, where 10 would be the current layer.

To change the current layer, enter the command code YC. You will be prompted to specify a layer from the sidebar menu. Choose the desired layer from the sidebar menu, or type in the name or number of the layer. You can select any of the 256 layers to be the Current Layer. When the status line is re-displayed, the new current layer will be shown there.

Once you set a current layer, everything you draw is automatically placed on that layer. This is how you use Set Current Layer (YC) to organize your drawing onto layers as you create it. For example, if you want all of the walls of a floor plan to be on a layer called WALLS, use YC to select WALLS as the current layer and *then* draw the walls. To place doors and windows on a layer called DOORS, use YC to make DOORS the current layer and then draw the doors and windows on it. If you do not always have the foresight to initially draw everything on the correct layer, don't worry, you can always use the Change (CG) command to move objects to different layers later!

Layer Display (YD)

The Layer Display (YD) command is used to control which layers are currently displayed on your screen. This has the opposite effect of the Layer Hide (YH) command, which causes layers *not* to be displayed. When you first start a drawing in CADD 6, all layers are displayed, so you have to hide some layers before Layer Display (YD) has any effect. You should also note that the Current Layer must always be displayed.

To change which layers are displayed, enter the command code YD. CADD 6 will then prompt you to select which layer to display. Choose the desired layer from the sidebar menu, or type in the name or number of the layer. You can select any individual layer, or click the word "All" on the sidebar menu to display all layers. CADD 6 redraws the screen with the selected layers displayed, and allows you to continue selecting other layers to display. You can then select another layer, or press Enter to exit the YD command and return to the CADD 6 command line.

Layer Name (YN)

CADD 6 always assigns a layer number to each of its 256 layers, but you have the option of also giving each layer a unique alphanumeric name. This is a great help when organizing your drawings, since you can assign layer names that relate to the particular objects on each layer.

To name a layer, type in YN for Layer Name. CADD 6 will prompt you to select the layer to be named from the sidebar menu, or you can enter the desired layer's number. Next you will be prompted to type in the layer's name, using no more than eight characters. Be sure to enter names that you will recognize later, such as WALLS, ELECTRIC, or WINDOWS for architectural drawings. Type in the desired name and press Enter. You will be returned to the CADD 6 command line. If you want to name another layer, press the Space Bar to execute YN again, and repeat the process for the next layer.

If you create many drawings of the same type, try to develop a list of layer names that you can use for all of them. Then make a template drawing with the Environment Save (EN) command that has the layers already named, so you can save yourself the trouble of naming layers every time you start a new drawing.

All of the layers that are named show up on the "Short List" of layers, even if they do not have any data on them. They appear on the list in their original numerical order. CADD 6 still recognizes their layer number, as well as their assigned name, so you can select layers either way.

Layer Hide (YH)

With the Layer Hide (YH) command, you can hide layers to prevent them from being displayed on the screen. Hiding a layer is analogous to pulling that overlay sheet out of the stack. The information on that layer is not lost, it is just invisible until it is later redisplayed with the Layer Display (YD) command. The current layer can never be hidden; it must always be displayed. However, you can select any combination of the other 255 layers to be hidden.

To hide a layer, enter YH for Layer Hide. CADD 6 will then prompt you to select the layer to be hidden. Choose the desired layer from the sidebar menu, or type in the name or number of the layer. You can select any individual layer, or click the word "All" on the sidebar menu to hide all layers except the current one. CADD 6 redraws the screen with the selected layers hidden, and allows you to continue by selecting another layer to hide. You can then select another layer, or press Enter to exit the YH command and return to the command line.

If layers are hidden, they are not displayed on the screen, nor do they show up on a print or plot. However, all layers are always saved as part of the drawing when you save the drawing to disk.

Layer Erase (YX)

To erase everything from a particular layer, use the Layer Erase (YX) command. Enter the command code YX, and then specify the desired layer from the sidebar menu or by typing its name. As with all the Erase commands, you can always recover an erased layer with Unerase (UE) or Undo (OO), at least until you use Pack Data (PD), or exit the drawing.

Layer Rotate (YR)

The Layer Rotate (YR) command is similar to the command Window Rotate (WR). Layer Rotate (YR) causes *all* objects on a particular layer to be rotated around a specified axis point, by a specified angle.

Start the Layer Rotate command by entering YR, then select the name of the layer to be rotated from the sidebar menu. You will be prompted to identify an axis point about which the layer will be rotated. Use your pointing device to click on the desired point, use a snap, or enter coordinates to identify the rotation axis. Next you will be prompted to enter the number of degrees (positive or negative) to rotate the layer. After this angle is entered, the layer is rotated as was defined. Remember that with all rotation commands, 0° is along the positive X-axis, and positive angles cause a counter-clockwise rotation.

Layer Rotate (YR) allows you to rotate every entity on an individual layer, but what if you want to rotate more than one layer (and less than all of them)? First use the Layer Hide (YH) command to hide all of the layers you do not want to rotate. Then use the Window Rotate (WR) command to rotate all entities on the layers still displayed. This results in all but the hidden layers being rotated.

Layer Re-scale (YZ)

As you edit your drawing, you may also want to change the size of all objects on a particular layer. This is often used after you load a drawing onto a particular layer and then discover that it was drawn to a different scale than your current drawing.

The Layer Re-scale (YZ) command exists for this purpose. To use the command, enter YZ, then type the name of the layer to be scaled, or select it from the sidebar menu. You will then be prompted to enter the scale reference point. This is the point that remains in a constant location, while everything on the layer is scaled relative to it.

Next, CADD 6 will prompt for the X and Y re-scale factors as follows:

```
Enter New X Scale (1.0) >
Enter New Y Scale (1.0) >
```

As with all scale commands, entering fractional X and Y values reduce the size of objects on the layer. A scale factor of 2 doubles the size, but 0.5 cuts it in half. If you enter X and Y scale factors that are not equal, you distort the proportions of the original objects.

Layer Change (YG)

With the Layer Change (YG) command, you can change the properties of *all* objects on a particular layer. You can select to change the line width, type, color, or layer of the entities on the selected layer. For example, you could change all entities to color 10 and move them to a new layer with this command. Be aware that *all* changes affect *all* entities on the layer. If you need to further limit the selection of entities to be changed, use the Change (CG) command that prompts for a selection set and filters.

Begin the Layer Change command with the command code YG. At the first prompt, select the layer you want to change by typing in its name or using the sidebar menu. All further choices made with this command affect *only* objects on the layer just selected. Next, the status line lists a menu of the properties you can change for the selected items:

    Y for Layer
    C for Color
    T for Linetype
    W for Width

If you choose C for Color, then select color 10, you instruct CADD 6 to change all entities on the selected layer to Color 10, regardless of what color they were before. You can select to change one or all of the properties shown on the menu. If you select L to change the layer, the change command moves all the entities to the new layer. When you are finished making changes, press Enter to execute the command.

Layer Dimension (UL)

You can select a particular layer to be used for all dimensions with the Layer Dimension (UL) command. Enter UL and you will be prompted to select the layer for dimensions. Type in the layer name or select a layer from the sidebar menu. Following this command, all dimensions are placed on the specified layer. Any dimensions placed *before* the UL command was invoked are not changed, they stay on whatever layer UL was set to at the time they were drawn.

To help organize your drawings, it is usually a good idea to put all dimensions on a unique layer. This helps separate dimensions later for editing or hiding. You may want to set up all your drawings with a layer named DIMENS, or something else that you can readily identify as the layer containing dimensions.

Layer Load (YL)

With the Layer Load (YL) command, you can load any drawing previously saved to disk onto a particular layer of the drawing, on which you are currently working. Even if the drawing being loaded was created with different layers, all entities are placed on the one, specified layer of the current drawing.

To use Layer Load, enter the command code YL. At the prompt, enter the name of the designation layer where the new drawing is to be loaded, or select it from the sidebar menu. Next you are asked to identify the drawing to load onto the selected layer. Select the file name from the sidebar menu or type in the drawing name. Remember to specify a drive letter and directory if the drawing is not in the default location. The outline of the drawing is shown on the screen as a *Bounding Box*. Use your pointing device to move the box around the screen and position it where desired, or simply press Enter to accept the default placement at the origin of the current drawing. Of course, you also can select the insert origin by using a snap command, or manually entering coordinates. This process is very similar to that used for the Load Drawing (LOD) command.

The Layer Load (YL) command is especially useful for constructing a new drawing by using portions of other existing drawings. Suppose that you have three existing drawings with detail views of a part, and you want to use them to create a new drawing. Start the new drawing, and then use Layer Load (YL) to load the first detail drawing onto an unused layer. This makes it easy to move the detail view into position and erase any unwanted objects. If desired, you can use Layer Change to move this view to a different layer. Repeat the same process to load the two remaining views and finish constructing the new drawing.

Layer Save (YS)

To save an individual layer to disk as a separate drawing, use Layer Save (YS). This is similar to the Save Drawing (SAD) command, except you specify only one layer to be saved, regardless of how many layers have data on them. When you develop a plan for a new office, for example, you may draw the floor layout and the electrical layout for power pole locations on separate layers. With Layer Save (YS), you can save the electrical layout layer to a separate file and give just this drawing to the electrical contractor.

To use Layer Save, type the command code YS. When prompted, select the layer you want to save from the sidebar menu or by typing in the layer name. Next, you will be prompted to enter a file name for the new drawing. You can press Enter to accept the current drawing name, or enter a different file name of up to eight characters. Be sure the name uses only characters that are acceptable for DOS file names. CADD 6 assumes you want to save the drawing to the current default path for drawing files, as established during Installation or with the File Paths command. If you want to save the layer to a different location, enter the complete path along with the file name.

When you use Layer Save, specify a drawing file name that is different from the name of the complete drawing with all layers. If you save a layer to the same file as the original drawing, it will overwrite the drawing file that contains all of the layers.

USING NAMED VIEWS (ZOOMS)

When you are working on a large drawing, you often need to zoom to a view of a specific area. With the Name View (NV) command, you can define and name specific views that you can zoom directly to with Zoom View (ZV).

Name View (NV)

The first step in organizing a complex drawing into views is to consider what areas of the drawing you most likely want to zoom-in on to add information or make editing changes. These areas could be detail views of parts, connections, specific rooms of a floor plan, or notes.

To help you zoom directly to any of these specific views, you define them with the Name View command. First use Zoom Window (ZW), or any of the zoom commands to make sure the desired view is displayed on the screen exactly as you want it to appear. Type NV to execute Name View and CADD 6 will prompt:

    Enter View Name >

Type in the view name, up to 12 characters in length, and press Enter. Be sure to use some name that you will recognize later as being identified with the contents of the view. The current view is saved under the specified name. At a later time, you can use Zoom View (ZV) to return directly to the display of the view you named.

Zoom View (ZV)

Use the Zoom View (ZV) command to restore the display of a view that was previously created with the Name View (NV) command. Create named views for the sections of the drawing you often have to edit, then use Zoom View (ZV) to move directly between these views. This can save you from doing a Zoom All (ZA) and a Zoom Window (ZW) each time before you can edit another area of the drawing.

To zoom to any named view, type ZV. CADD 6 will then prompt you to select the desired view from the sidebar menu, or you can type in the view name. The screen is redrawn with the named view displayed.

Delete Named View (NX)

This command is used to delete named views that were previously named but are no longer needed in the drawing. To execute the command, type NX, and CADD 6 asks you to select the view to be deleted from the sidebar menu of view names. Use your pointing device to click on the view to delete. You will then be prompted to identify another view to delete. When you are finished deleting views, press the ESC key or click on the word "Cancel" at the bottom of the menu to abort the command and return to the CADD 6 command line.

KITCHEN TUTORIAL FOR LAYERS AND NAMED VIEWS

Next, you will organize the KITCHEN drawing (drawn in Chapters 3 - 5) into layers and named views. This drawing is so simple it really does not need this kind of organization, but you can still see how these concepts are applied. You will then know how to apply layers and named views to the complex drawings you create as you become more proficient with CADD 6.

To begin the tutorial, load the kitchen drawing:

> Type LOD and select the drawing named KITCHEN
> Press Enter to accept the origin for the insertion point

Next, assign names to three different layers so it is easy to tell which entities belong on which layers.

> Type: YN (for Layer Name)
> Select layer number 0 from the sidebar menu, or type 0 and press Enter
> Type: WALLS (and press Enter) as the new layer name

This layer can now be referred to either as layer number 0, or as the layer named WALLS. (See Figure 12.1.)

When you are returned to the CADD 6 command line:

> Press the space bar to repeat the last command (YN)
> Click on the sidebar menu to select layer number 1
> Type: WINDOWS (and press Enter) as the layer name for layer 1
> Repeat the YN command and change the name of layer 2 to APPLIANC

Each time you add a new layer name it shows up on the layer sidebar menu. You can check this by typing in YD for Layer Display. The layer menu shows that all layers are displayed, including the named layers: WALLS, WINDOWS, and APPLIANC. Only the WALLS layer has data on it at this time. The WALLS layer (layer 0) is also the current layer.

> Type: YD (for Layer Display)
> Click on the phrase "Short List" at the bottom of the menu

This changes the menu so it only lists the named layers and the layers that have data. If any numbered layers had data on them, they would be displayed on the short list. (See Figure 12.2.) Click on "Cancel," at the bottom of the menu, to return to the CADD 6 command line.

12-12 ■ Chapter 12: Organizing

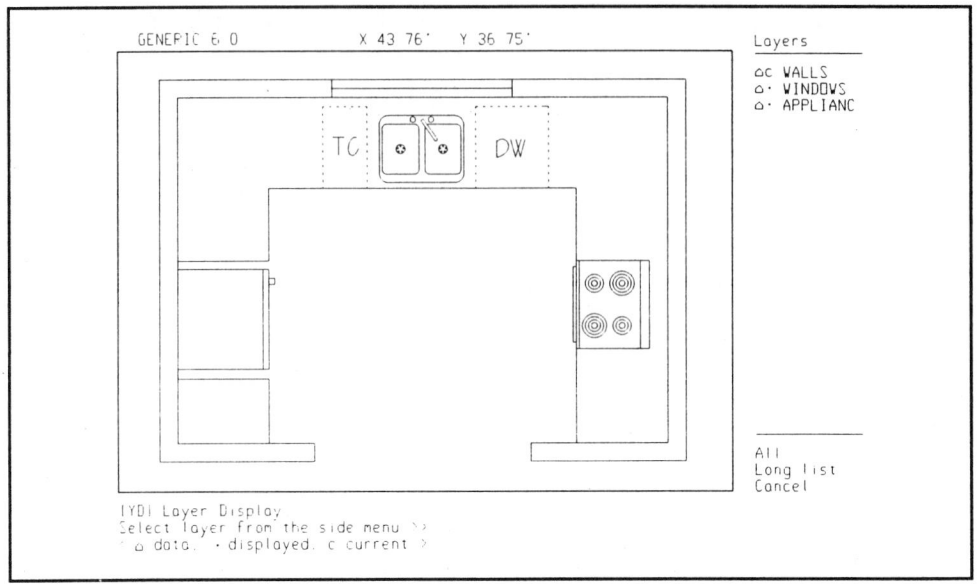

Figure 12.2 The Layer List for the Kitchen Tutorial.

The next steps show how to use the Change command to move particular entities in the drawing to the named layers. You will change the window to the layer called WINDOW, and the appliances and sink to the layer called APPLIANC. Selection filters are ideal for choosing the objects to change.

>
> Type: CG (for Change)
> Select F for Filter
> Select A for All, to filter All entity types
> Select [Ret] or press Enter to accept the option
> Select C for Color, the characteristic to filter
> Type: 14 (and press Enter) for the color of the entities to filter
> Select [Ret] or press Enter to accept the option
> Select D for Drawing, to select entities in the entire drawing
> Select [RET] or press Enter to accept the option
> Select Y for Layer, to change the objects to a new layer
> Type: WINDOWS (and press Enter) for the new layer name, or select WINDOWS from the sidebar menu

At this point the window (which was drawn with color 14) should be highlighted as part of the selection set. In other words, these options tell CADD 6 to change *all entities of color 14*, throughout the entire drawing, to the layer named WINDOWS. Since this is the result you want, press Enter or select [RET] to complete the command. The window is redrawn, signifying that it has been changed to the new layer. Since all layers are displayed, there are no other changes on the screen.

Chapter 12: Organizing ■ 12-13

>Repeat the Change command to move the appliances and fixtures to the APPLIANC layer

Select the same options as used above, except specify the "characteristic to change" as Color 15, and the layer to "change to" as layer APPLIANC.

The walls and countertops were already on layer WALLS, so they do not need to be changed. Now you can choose to hide or display any combination of the three layers.

>Type: YH (for Layer Hide) and click on the word ALL at the bottom of the sidebar menu
>Press Enter to return to the command line prompt

This turns OFF the display of all layers except the current layer, WALLS. The window, appliances and sink should have disappeared. You may want to do a Redraw (RD) at this time to clean up the screen display so it looks like Figure 12.3. Now, display the window again:

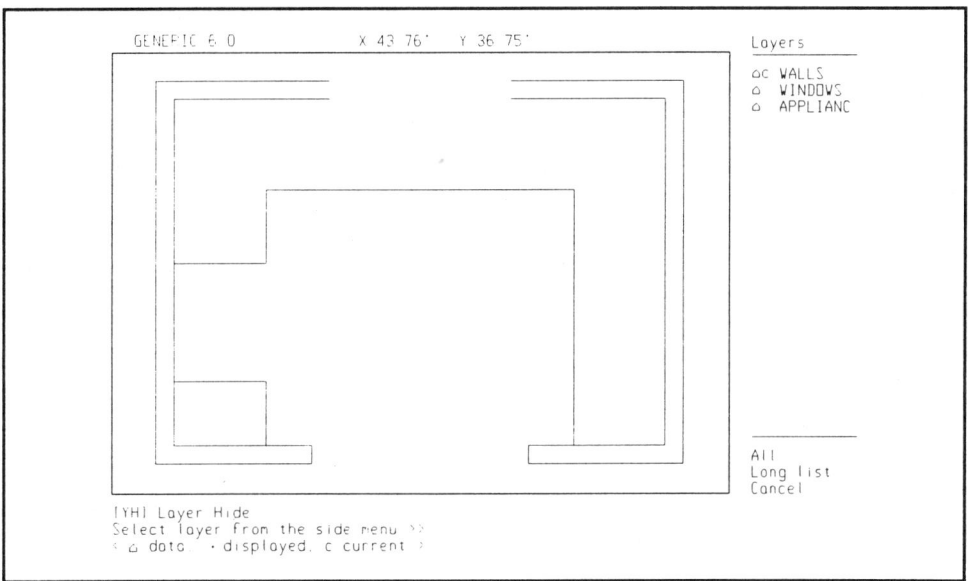

Figure 12.3 Hiding the WINDOWS and APPLIANC layers.

>Type: YD (for Layer Display)
>Select the layer name WINDOWS from the sidebar menu

The window is again displayed on the screen. (See Figure 12.4.)

>Repeat the YD command to display the layer APPLIANC

Your drawing should look just like it did when you first loaded it into CADD 6. However, the entities are now located on three separate layers. You can choose to

12-14 ■ Chapter 12: Organizing

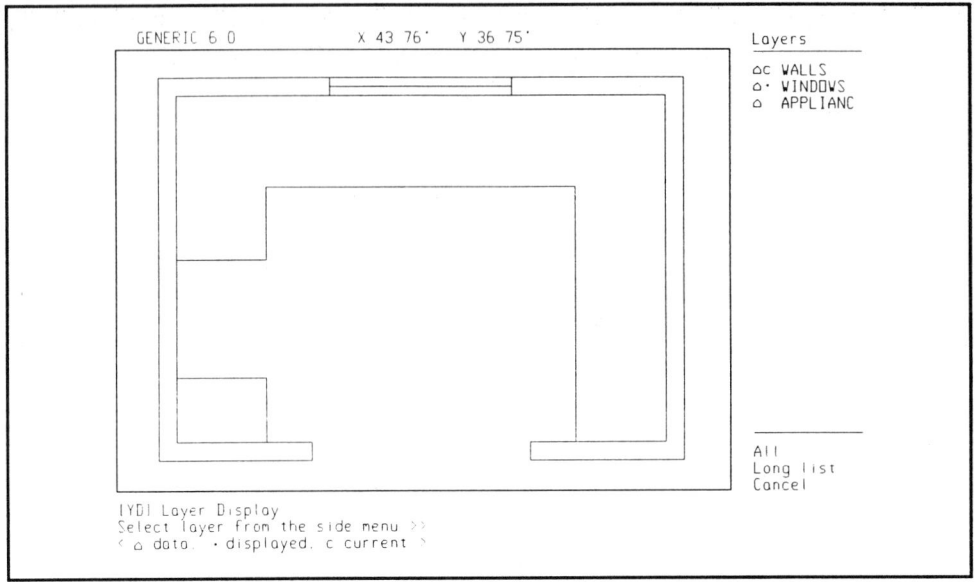

Figure 12.4 The APPLIANC layer hidden.

display or plot any combination of the three layers. Next, you will define and assign names to three different views of the drawing. Make the first view of the entire drawing, as it is currently displayed:

>   Type: NV (for Name View)
>   Type: ALL (and press Enter) for the View Name

Create other views of the sink area and the range:

>   Type: ZW (for Zoom Window) and enclose the sink in the selection window

The display is redrawn so that the sink covers most of the screen, as shown in Figure 12.5. This is the view you want to save as a Named View.

>   Type: NV (for Name View)
>   Type: SINK (and press Enter) for the View Name
>   Type: ZV (for Zoom View)
>   Select the view named ALL from the sidebar menu

This redraws the first view you created which was of the entire drawing:

>   Type: ZW (for Zoom Window) and draw a window around the range (shown in Figure 12.6)
>   Type: NV (for Named View)
>   Type: RANGE (and press Enter) for the view name
>   Type: ZV (for Zoom View) and select the view named SINK from the sidebar menu

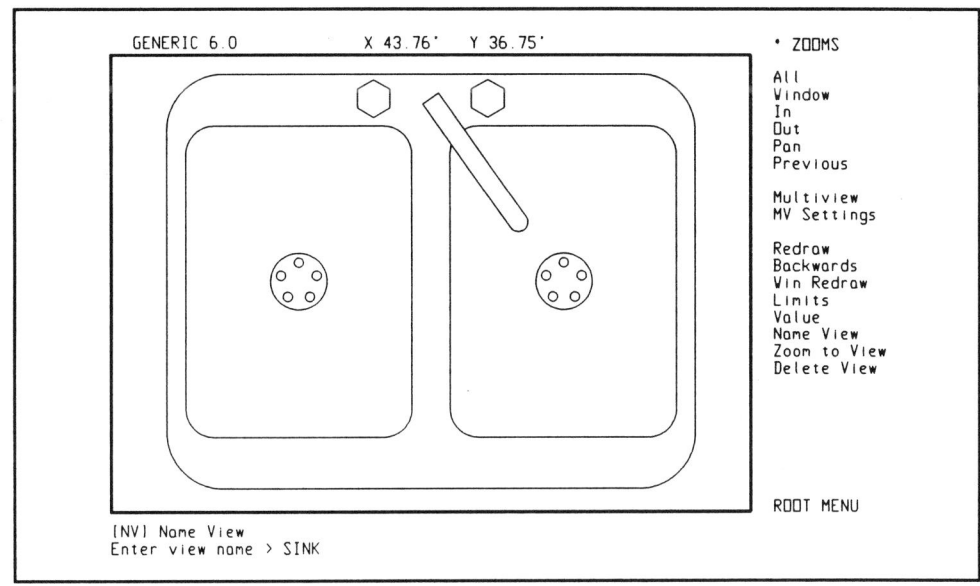

Figure 12.5 Creating a Named View of the sink.

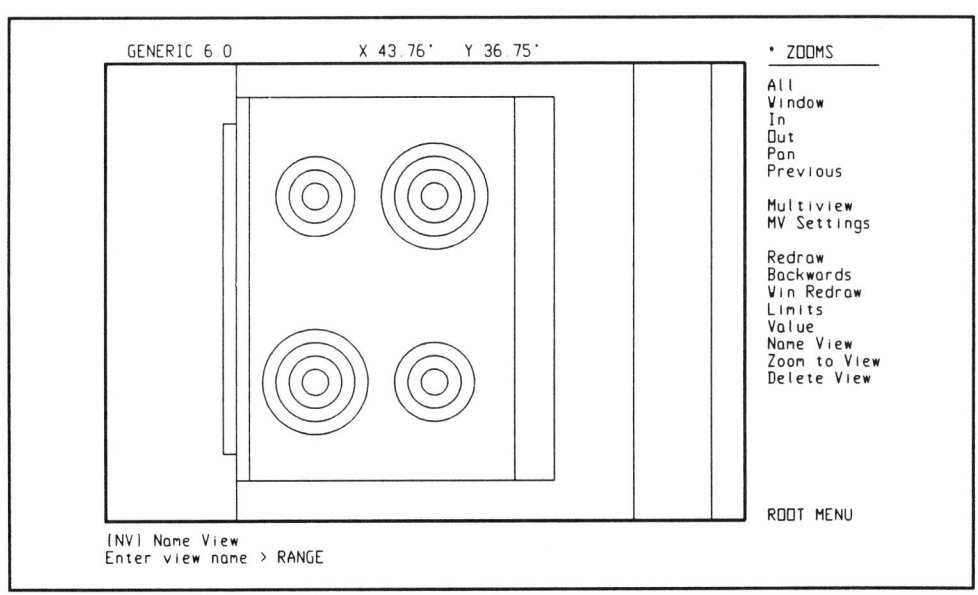

Figure 12.6 Creating a Named View of the range.

The screen is redrawn with the SINK view restored. Once views have been named, you can continue to use the Zoom View (ZV) command to move quickly between them. You may notice that the views are listed on the sidebar menu in alphabetical order, not in the order they were created.

The first view you named, the ALL view, is really not necessary since it results in the same view as the ZOOM ALL (ZA) command. Use the Named View Delete (NX) command to eliminate unnecessary views:

Type: NX (for View Delete)
Select the view named ALL from the sidebar menu

That view is removed from the list. You can continue to select views to delete from the list. When finished:

Press the ESC key or click on "CANCEL" at the bottom of the menu

This completes the Layer and Named View tutorial. You may want to save your drawing to save the layers and views you created here. Many of the examples presented here may seem unnecessary for this simple drawing, but try to imagine applying these concepts to a more complicated drawing like a complete floor plan with electrical plans, dimensions, notes, title block, etc. Using layers and named views, you can make even the most complex drawing easier and faster to work with.

CHAPTER SUMMARY

This chapter showed you some ways of organizing large and complex drawings that may otherwise be unwieldy and tedious to work with. To help divide your drawings into workable pieces, CADD 6 provides 256 layers and user-defined named views.

Named Layers are used for separating drawings into groups of similar entities for easier editing selection. Layers are also useful for creating special drawings for subcontractors and vendors. CADD 6 has menu-driven layer management which lets you name, display, hide, rotate, erase, scale, load, and save Layers with just a couple of mouse clicks.

Named Views are also a handy tool for organizing large drawings into sections that can be zoomed to quickly. By defining views of the detailed areas of a drawing, you can virtually eliminate the need to perform more than one zoom command between editing commands.

CHAPTER 13

Input and Output

USING THE FILE AND CONVERT MENUS

This chapter will introduce the FILE and CONVERT menus, which contain the commands for loading, saving, and printing CADD 6 drawings, and for converting drawings to other formats like DXF, HPGL, ASCII, or Image files. The FILE menu also contains commands used to remove unnecessary information from your drawing's database. You will also learn how to create drawing environments to save you the trouble of re-setting drawing parameters whenever you start a new drawing.

The following commands are covered in this chapter:

FILE

Print Manager
Plot/Print/PostScript (DP)
Selection Plot (PL)
Environment Save (EN)
Pack Data (PD)
Definition Unload (DU)

Selection Drawing Save (SV)
Drawing Rename (DN)
Drawing Remove (DX)
Load (LO)
Save (SA)
File Paths (FP)
Quit (QU)

CONVERT
AutoCAD Drawing In (LOA)

DXFIN (LOX)
DXFOUT (SAX)

Exchange Setup (XG)

HPGL to GCD
Load ASCII (LA)

USING THE FILE COMMANDS

Print Manager (Print Mgr)

The Print Manager is a new printing utility that was introduced in CADD 6.1. It allows you to select files and set them up to print or plot unattended, in batch mode. When you select Print Mgr from the FILE menu, the following four menu options appear:

   Select GCDs
   Prt Cfg
   Print
   Job Delete

Before you select the drawings you wish to print with Print Manager, be sure that the Drawing Plot options (discussed later in this chapter) have been set correctly. You can do this from the Output Menu that appears when you type DP, or by selecting Prt Cfg from the Print Manager menu.

Select GCDs. Select GCDs allows you to select a variety of drawings to print immediately, or to save as a print job to print later. A print job consists of one or more drawings which can be printed while unattended. More than one print job can be created, and more than one print job can be selected for unattended printing.

Pick Select GCDs from the menu. The first prompt is:

   PRINT SETUP
   You must first setup the Print Options before selecting drawings to print.
   Hit ESC to exit and Setup or ENTER to Continue

If you press ENTER the prompt is:

   Drawing Selection Menu
   Options: Fast Selection   Detail Selection

Next, choose whether you want to use the Fast Selection or Detail Selection to select the drawings to be printed. If you select *Fast Selection*, all the drawings are automatically printed to be Fit Full, Centered, and non-Rotated. The *Detail Selection* allows you to specify these settings for each drawing.

If you choose Detail Selection, you will be prompted to select the desired drawings from sidebar menu. You press the Escape (Esc) key to complete the selection.

You then have the option of entering a scale and a rotation for the drawing. If you do not want to enter a specific scale, you can select the Fit Full option, just as described for the Print/Plot/Postscript command. If you select Yes for the rotation, the drawing will be rotated 90° and printed with a Landscape orientation. A No response leaves it with a Portrait orientation. Choosing the Automatic rotation option allows CADD 6.1 to decide the orientation of the drawing.

Once you have specified any relevant settings, you can choose more drawings to print or press ESC to finish the Select GCDs process.

When you have finished the selection process, the following prompt will be displayed:

> Do you want to print Now or Save all settings to print later?

If you decide to save it for future printing, you will be prompted to enter a file name to assign to the print job. The job information is then saved so it can be recalled and printed automatically later. Should you type in an existing job name, you will need to choose whether to overwrite the existing job or rename the current job.

Use the Print option to print jobs that you have saved whenever you are ready.

Prt Cfg. This is the Print Configuration option. It brings up the standard Output Menu that is used by the Drawing Plot command. All the options on the Output Menu are described for the Plot/Print/Postscript (DP) command.

Each print job can have different print options. For example, one job could be set up for a printer on LPT2, another for a plotter on COM2, a third for a network printer on LPT1, and a fourth to create a Postscript print file. When you print all four jobs, the Print Manager will switch print options for each job. Note: You cannot use different print options for each drawing in a print job. If this is necessary, put each drawing in a different print job.

13-4 ■ Chapter 13: Input and Output

> **TIP:** When using Print Manager, you cannot set different resolutions for each drawing in a print job; neither can you print multiple print jobs at different resolutions. If this is necessary, print one job and then reset the printer resolution before printing the second job.
>
> Just as for resolution, you also cannot assign different page sizes to each drawing in a print job.

Print. This option allows you to select one or more print jobs to begin printing. Once you have confirmed the proper directory, you will be prompted to choose the job or jobs to print from the sidebar listing. Press ESC when you are finished selecting jobs.

When you finish selecting jobs to print, the follow prompt will be displayed:

PRINT CONFIRMATION
Options: Start Printing   Set Timer   Cancel

Start Printing. This option starts printing all jobs. It opens the first job and prints all the drawings in it, according to the settings you have specified. It continues with the next job until all the defined jobs are printed.

Set Timer. This option allows you to set a time for printing to begin. This option is ideal to use for a network printer, since you can schedule your jobs to print when there is less traffic on the printer. Note, however, that you cannot use your computer until the jobs are printed, so you would normally set the timer to print during a break or after you leave for the day.

When you choose Set Timer, you will be prompted for the time to begin printing. You must enter the time in the format of hour:minutes, including either am or pm. For example, you could enter 2:45am or 10:20pm.

> **TIP:** Be sure to set the time on your computer to the proper time, otherwise the timer will not function properly.

Job Delete. This option deletes print jobs that have been saved to your hard disk drive. When you select Job Delete, you will be prompted to select the jobs from the sidebar menu. Press the Escape (Esc) key to finish selecting files.

Troubleshooting. If your drawings do not print, check this list of possibilities:

1) Determine whether it is Print Manager, or one of the drawings that is the problem. To do this, try printing some of the drawings individually with Drawing Plot (DP) command.

2) Check whether the font path is set properly. If a particular font is used in a drawing, but Print Manager cannot locate it, the drawing will not load or print properly.

3) Check whether the printer has paper, is online, and is connected to the designated port.

If Print Manager does not print, or if it stops in the middle of a job:

1) Make sure that the file PRNTMGR.MCR is in the same directory as CADD6.MNU. The files JOBREM.EXE and PRTMGR.EXE should also be in that directory.

2) Increase the setting for FILES in your CONFIG.SYS file.

3) Be sure that you are *not* running CADD 6 from Microsoft Windows or any other shell programs. This will interfere with Print Manager.

Plot/Print/Postscript (DP)

You will frequently want to send your drawings to a plotter or printer to make hard copies. This is accomplished with the DP command, which gives the option of sending your drawing to a plotter, printer, PostScript device, or a plot file. It displays the Output Menu as shown in Figure 13.1. From this menu you select the output device, I/O port, page size, drawing view, scale, number of copies, and other options.

The first time you try to print or plot, each option on the menu is set to the default values that come with CADD 6. You change all the options related to your particular output device the first time you use it, and then these options become the new defaults. Prior to printing your first drawing, make sure you have entered information for at least the following options, preferably in this order:

Option 1 - Tells CADD 6 what kind of device to use
Option 4 - Configures CADD 6 for your particular device
Option 2 - Tells CADD 6 to which port your device is attached

Other options that affect an individual drawing may have to be set prior to each plot or print, including view type and page setup. Once all the options are set correctly, select Option 7 to actually start plotting or printing the drawing.

13-6 ■ Chapter 13: Input and Output

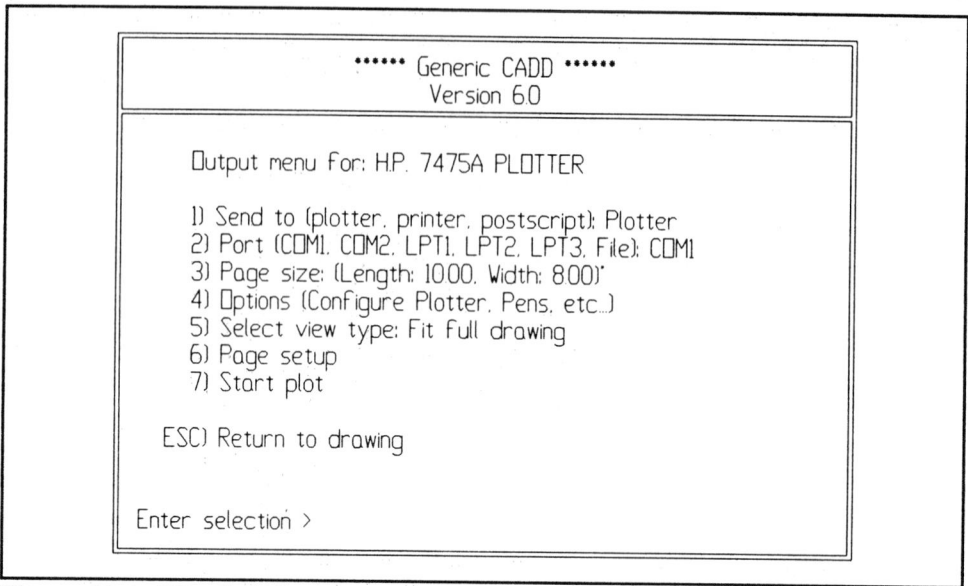

```
****** Generic CADD ******
         Version 6.0

Output menu for: H.P. 7475A PLOTTER

  1) Send to (plotter, printer, postscript): Plotter
  2) Port (COM1, COM2, LPT1, LPT2, LPT3, File): COM1
  3) Page size: (Length: 10.00, Width: 8.00)"
  4) Options (Configure Plotter, Pens, etc...)
  5) Select view type: Fit Full drawing
  6) Page setup
  7) Start plot

  ESC) Return to drawing

Enter selection >
```

Figure 13.1 The CADD 6.0 Output Menu.

The Output Menu gives the following options:

1) Send To. This option determines which hardware device your drawing is output to. The choices are:

1) Plotter
2) Printer
3) PostScript

The first line of the Output Menu shows what output device CADD 6 is currently configured for. For example, Figure 13.1 shows it configured for an H.P. 7475A plotter. Select menu option 1 to switch to another device, a printer for example. Once a new device is selected you are returned to the Output Menu. The menu is updated to show the default settings for the new device. If your hardware system consists of both a printer and plotter, use this option to switch between the two devices. CADD 6 remembers the specific devices for which you configured (with Option 4), you simply have to tell it whether you want to use the printer or plotter at this particular time.

This option does *not* allow you to configure your CADD 6 program for a particular plotter or printer. Prior to creating your first print or plot, you must select Option 4 to tell CADD 6 which specific output device is part of your system.

CADD 6 supports several PostScript devices, color and monochrome. With a PostScript device, CADD 6 gives you the options (under Option 4 on the Output Menu) of varying the print's line width and grey scale.

2) Port. You must tell CADD 6 to which Input/Output port your printer or plotter is attached, or if you want to output your drawing to a *file*. The choices are:

1) COM1
2) COM2
3) LPT1
4) LPT2
5) LPT3
6) Disk File

If you do not know which port to select, you may want to refer to your computer system documentation for help. Keep in mind that most (not all) printers are *parallel* devices so they use the LPT ports. Most plotters are *serial,* so they use COM ports.

If you still don't know which port to select, you may have to use the trial and error method. Create a simple drawing in CADD 6, and enter DP to try the first trial print. Make sure all the other options on the Output Menu are correct, including selection of the proper printer, page size, and view type. Then choose Option 2 to select a port. If you are using a printer, try LPT1 first. If you have a plotter, try COM1. Next, select Option 7 to print the drawing. Unfortunately, you have to wait until CADD 6 finishes processing the entire drawing to see if any information is sent to your printer. If nothing at all is printed, try repeating the process until you find the right port. Go back to the Output menu and try LPT2, and so on, until you are able to print the drawing.

> **TIP:** If you select COM1 or COM2, you will be prompted to set baud rate, data bits, stop bit, and parity. In most cases, the default settings will work with your plotter. If your drawing doesn't plot correctly, check your plotter manual for the exact settings.

In some cases you may want to output your drawing to a file that can be interpreted by a printer or plotter, rather than directly to the device. Every plotter requires a special set of instructions to interpret a CADD 6 drawing. This option enables you to save these instructions in a file for later plotting. For example, if you want to hire a plotting service company, you could take them the plot files in whatever format their particular plotter uses (provided it is one of the plotters CADD 6 supports.) To do this, use Option 1 to specify "Send To: Plotter," use Option 4 to select the desired type of plotter, then use Option 2 to select "Port: Disk File." Then when you select Option 7 to "Start Plot," CADD 6 creates the file of plotter instructions.

If you choose to print or plot to a file, you will also be prompted for the complete path and file name of the data file. Since print/plot files can be very large, it is not recommended that you send it directly to a floppy drive. To copy your print files to a floppy disk later, you may have to archive (compress) them or use a backup routine to compress them.

13-8 ■ Chapter 13: Input and Output

> **TIP:** Some word processors accept plot files into their documents. This is helpful if you wish to create illustrations for a report, manual, or book. For example, all the illustrations in this book were saved in HPGL format (Hewlett-Packard Graphics Language) and imported into WordPerfect 5.1.

3) Page Size. This option allows you to select the length and width of the page on which you want to print or plot. Once you have selected a particular output device with Option 1 (and Option 4), CADD 6 determines the most widely used paper sizes for that device and lists them here. As an example, for the HP Laserjet printer you can select from predetermined page sizes of:

    1) Length: 10.000"   Width: 8.000"
    2) Length: 10.000"   Width: 13.500"
    3) User Selected Size

You also have the option of specifying a "User Selected Size" which is different from any of the above choices. Use this option to print on smaller sheets of paper, or to give a larger margin around your drawing than the predetermined sizes allow. If you choose to enter a User Selected Size, CADD 6 will then prompt you to "Enter Plot Length" and "Enter Plot Width."

The page size you select determines the size of the *plot frame*. CADD 6 tries to plot over that entire area without adding any margins. Since every output device has minimum margins required for operation, you must specify the page size to be somewhat smaller than the actual sheet of paper you are using. For example, if you are using a plotter, you must allow enough margin space for the gripper wheels that hold the paper. If each gripper wheel requires a half-inch, then enter a sheet size that is 1 inch smaller than the actual paper you use. You may want to check the user manual that came with your plotter or printer for information on minimum top and side margins.

4) Options. Use this option to create multiple copies of a plot (print), and to control settings that are specific to the type of output device you are using. The particular options that will appear on the Options Menu depend on whether you specified to send your drawing to a printer, plotter or PostScript device (Output Menu Option 1.)

Options: Printer. If the Output Menu shows that you are using a printer, the Options Menu lists two choices:

    1) Configure Printer
    2) Number of Copies

Configure Printer lets you tell CADD 6 which particular brand of printer you use. When you select Option 1, the Printer Options menu is erased, and this prompt is displayed at the bottom of the screen:

   Please Enter Path to *.TPR files > >

This is asking for the name of the drive and directory where the printer drivers are stored. If you followed the standard setup when you first installed CADD 6, the drivers are in C:\CADD6, so enter that path name here. If you instructed the Installation Program to place the drivers elsewhere, enter the path name where they can be found. If the correct path name is already displayed on the screen as a default, simply press the Enter key to accept it.

A large list of available printer manufacturers are displayed next. Enter the number corresponding to the manufacturer of your printer. This results in the displaying of a list of all the models from that manufacturer that CADD 6 supports. Enter the number beside your printer model to select it. This completes the configuration process and returns you to the Options Menu.

If your exact printer is not listed, consult your printer manual to determine if it emulates some other printer. You may also want to consult Autodesk Retail Products Technical Support Department, they are the experts in configuring CADD 6 for hardware.

Number of Copies allows you to specify the number of copies of the drawing to be printed. The default value is to print one copy. When you select this option, you can enter a number larger than one to print multiple copies of the drawing, all with the exact same settings and page set-up. Whenever multiple copies are specified, you are asked at the start of the printing process if you want to be prompted before each copy is printed. Answer Y, for yes, if you need time to load new paper into the printer prior to each copy.

Options: Plotter. Once you have selected to use a plotter you can then select from the following options:

   1) Configure New Plotter
   2) Plot Hardware Arcs & Circles
   3) Pen Settings
   4) Import Plotter Command File
   5) Number of Copies

Configure New Plotter lets you tell CADD 6 which model of plotter you use, just as for printers. When you select Option 1, the Plotter Options menu is erased and the following prompt is displayed:

Please Enter Path to PLOTTERS.TPL files >>

Enter the path where your drivers can be found, as previously discussed for printers. A list of all the available plotters is then displayed. Select your plotter from the list, or select a plotter that yours can emulate.

Plot Hardware Arcs and Circles lets you take advantage of special capabilities available on some plotters. Some plotters have commands built-in that speed up the plotting of arcs and circles. CADD 6 calls these "Hardware Arcs & Circles," since they are only available if your hardware (plotter) can generate them. Plotter Option 2 allows you to toggle Hardware Arcs ON if you have a plotter that uses HPGL (Hewlett-Packard Graphics Language) or DMPL (Digital Microprocessor Plotter Language from Houston Instruments). Although this saves plotting time, be aware that very large circles may become jagged, and DMPL sometimes places endpoints inaccurately due to rounding errors.

Pen Settings brings up another menu of Pen Settings with the following choices:

1) Pen Speed	50
2) Pen Width	0.300 mm
3) Number of Plotter Pens	6
4) Pen Sort by Color	ON
5) Prompt for Pen Change	ON

Pen Speed is initially set to a default value of 50. You can select a speed from 1 (slowest) to 50 (fastest) for this option. You may want to consult your plotter manual for recommended pen speeds. Generally, the finer and more consistent you want the lines in the drawing to be, the slower pen speed you should use. Use a higher speed for quick plots where lower quality is acceptable.

Finding the right speeds for your plotter is usually a trial and error process. If you are trying to produce a high quality plot, but you find lines with inconsistent thickness or places where the pen has skipped, try reducing the pen speed before you plot it again.

Pen Width is initially set at .300 mm, which is one of the most commonly available widths. This option tells the plotter how far to move the pens for each stroke when making filled areas and wide lines. If the specified Pen Width is larger than the actual width of the pens, your fills will have gaps. If the width is too narrow the pens wear out unnecessarily and the paper may become blotted. To specify a new value for Pen Width, enter the desired width in millimeters, then press Enter.

Number of Plotter Pens allows you to set the number of pens to be used to plot the drawing. Multiple pens are required whenever you want to plot drawing objects in different colors. Even with a single pen plotter you can still specify multiple pens, causing CADD 6 to stop and prompt you to change pens whenever it needs to draw objects of a different color.

With a multiple pen plotter, you place pens of different colors in the plotter that correspond to colors used in your drawing. For example, pen number 2 plots all objects of color 2, pen number 3, color 3, and so on. However, you can use many more colors in CADD 6 than your plotter has pens. When CADD 6 uses the highest numbered pen, the next color is drawn by pen 1. If your plotter has six pens, color 7 is drawn with pen 1, color 8 with pen 2, and so on. Alternatively, CADD 6 can prompt you to insert new pens for higher color values by setting Option 5, "Prompt for Pen Change."

> **TIP:** If you are plotting complex drawings in a single color, such as black, you can keep your pens from wearing out and maintain consistent line quality by using several pens of the same color. Create your drawing with multiple colors, then load several black pens into your plotter so that each pen is used only for a portion of the plot.

> **TIP:** Another trick for using multipen plotters is to use a thicker pen for drawing lines you want emphasized, such as borders, title blocks, and section lines. As you create drawings, make these lines with a separate color, not used for any other objects. Then, when setting up your plotter, insert a thicker pen in the location that is used to plot only that color. You may want to do the same for text and dimensioning, but use a color that corresponds to a finer pen. The plotter then changes to pens of the desired width when it comes to the appropriate color in the drawing.

Pen Sort By Color is a toggle that instructs CADD 6 to sort the plot according to color. This assures that all objects of color number 1 are plotted in sequence with pen 1, then pen 2 is selected to plot all objects of color 2, and so on. If you try to plot a multi-color drawing with Pen Sort OFF, objects are plotted in the order they were drawn, resulting in many more pen changes and longer plotting time.

Prompt for Pen Change is another toggle that causes CADD 6 to pause and prompt you to insert another pen each time it needs to plot objects of another color. Turn this toggle ON in order to plot drawings with more colors than your plotter has pens. If this toggle is set to OFF, CADD 6 uses only the pens currently available in the plotter. If there are multiple colors in the drawing, but only one pen, all objects are plotted with that one pen.

Import Plotter Command File is used to load or import a special set of instructions for your plotter. A Plotter Command File can include special initialization codes or a plot file that was created earlier. For example, you could have a logo or title block stored as plot file. Use this option to import the logo plot file and send it to the plotter first, then plot your current drawing over it. When you use this option, the plot file to be loaded must be in the same directory as CADD 6, or you must include a path name. Selecting this option brings a prompt for the name of the file you want loaded. Type the file name of the command file and press Enter. This option is a toggle, so if it is currently OFF, select it to turn it ON, and vice versa.

Number of Copies lets you specify the number of copies of the drawing to be plotted. The default value is to print one copy. Once you select this option, you can enter the number of copies of the drawing you want to plot with the exact same settings and page set-up. Whenever multiple copies are specified, you are asked at the start of the plotting process if you want to be prompted before each copy is plotted. Answer Y, for yes, if you need time to load new paper into the plotter prior to each copy.

Options: Postscript. The options available for PostScript devices include:

1) Default Line Width (0.00 - 25.0 pt)
2) Gray Scale for Filled Objects
3) Color PostScript
4) Number of Copies
5) Select View Type
6) Page Setup

Default Line Width is a value which CADD 6 uses to determine the actual width of the lines on paper. The width of the output lines is determined by this formula:

Output Line Width = (LW value) X (Default Line Width)

The "Default Line Width" and the "Output Line Width" are the widths of the lines measured in units of *points,* where one point is 1/72 of an inch. The LW value is the "Line Width" factor (command code LW) that was used to draw the entity in CADD 6. For example, if a line in your drawing has a Line Width factor of 4, and the Default Line Width is set to 0.25 points, the line is drawn on paper as 1 point in width (4 X 0.25 points.)

The Default Line Width is initially set to a value of 0.0 points. PostScript interprets this as drawing the thinnest line possible for the particular output device being used. If you are using a laser printer with 300 dpi resolution, it is probably best to accept this value. However, if you are using a very high resolution typesetting device, the thinnest lines may be too fine to be seen clearly. In this case, try setting the Default Line Width to 0.25 points.

Grey Scale for Filled Objects is used to vary the amount of black and white your PostScript device uses for fills. (If you are using a color device, all fills are printed in the drawing colors, so this option is disabled.) Use this option to change the degree of darkness from a value of 1.0 (the lightest) to 0.0 (the darkest).

You can also set the Default Line Width to "Variable." This causes CADD 6 to assign shades of grey to the various colors that can be used in your drawings. Objects drawn in color 1 (blue) are printed in the darkest shade of gray. Objects in other color numbers are a slightly lighter shade, up to color 15 which are printed as white.

Color Postscript, option 3, lets you configure for a Color PostScript printer. This causes your drawings to be printed in colors corresponding to the CADD 6 drawing colors. If you are printing on a black and white device, you usually want to have Color turned OFF. This means all objects in your drawings are printed in black except fills, which are printed in shades of grey (see Option 2.) If Color is turned ON, your black and white device prints all colored objects in shades of grey, according to how the "Grey Scale" Option is set.

Number of Copies lets you specify the number of copies of the drawing to print. The default value is to print one copy. Select this option and then enter the number of copies of the drawing to print with the exact same settings and page set-up. Whenever multiple copies are specified, you are asked at the start of the printing process if you want to be prompted before each copy is sent. Answer Y, for yes, if you need time to load new paper into the printer prior to each copy.

Select View Type. Select View Type lets you tell CADD 6 how to fit your drawing on the paper. You can choose to print the exact view of the drawing on your screen, fit the entire drawing on the paper, or specify a particular drawing scale. A menu of the view choices is shown. (Print and Plot are used interchangeably throughout this section, since all options apply to both). The options include:

1) Use current view
2) Fit full drawing
3) Specify scale & origin

Select *Use Current View* to print the drawing view that was displayed when you selected Drawing Plot (DP). The current view is placed at the plot origin and scaled as necessary to fit on the selected paper size.

If you want to fit the entire drawing onto the paper select *Fit Full Drawing*. This option causes CADD 6 to automatically scale the drawing to be as large as possible so that all of it fits on the paper.

Specify Scale & Origin tells CADD 6 that you will specify an exact scale and origin to use when plotting the drawing. At this point you do not actually specify the desired scale, you simply tell CADD 6 that you *want* to plot the drawing at a specified scale. Then you return to the Output Menu and choose Option 6, "Page Setup," to specify the exact details.

Page Setup. Page Setup allows you to view your drawing just as it is placed on the paper. You can then choose to modify the drawing position (plot origin), specify a drawing scale, rotate, fit, or center the drawing on the paper.

Before the drawing is displayed you will be prompted:

Fast Redraw ? (Y/N)

If you answer Y for yes, your drawing is displayed simply as a *Boundary Box* with an X in the middle, as shown in Figure 13.2. This is the same way a drawing is displayed when it is first loaded into CADD 6 with the LOD command. If your drawing is complex, and you are only interested in how the outer boundaries fit on the paper, pick Fast Redraw so you do not have to wait for the entire drawing to redraw. If you must see the drawing details to position it properly on the paper, answer N for No so that the complete drawing is displayed.

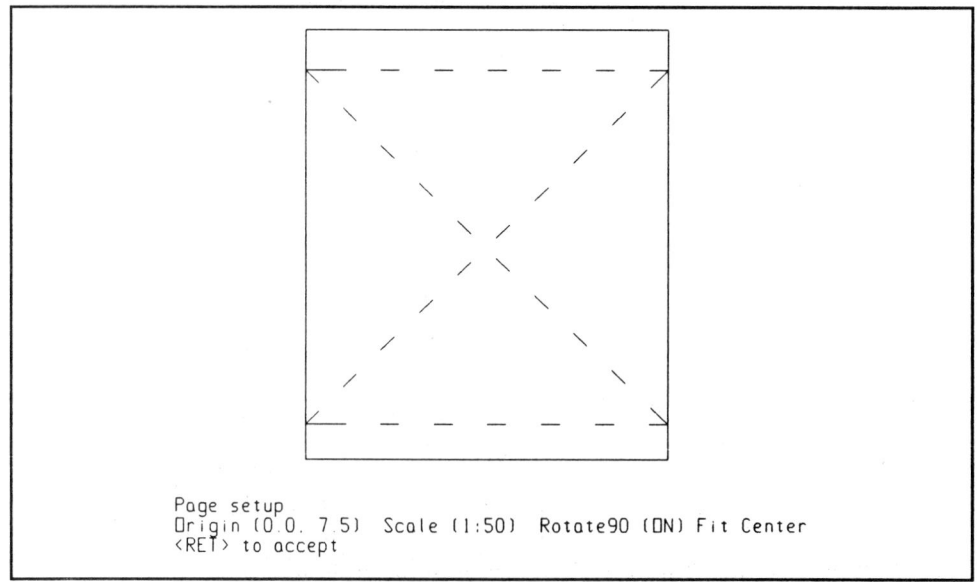

Figure 13.2 Page Setup with Fast Redraw.

The drawing is displayed inside a rectangle (shown with solid lines) that represents the paper size you selected. At this point it is obvious if you need to re-scale or re-position the drawing to create the desired plot. The next series of options allow you to make the necessary modifications. Figure 13.3 shows the Page Setup Options as they are printed along the bottom of the screen. To select one of the items, enter the letter in the name of the option that is highlighted.

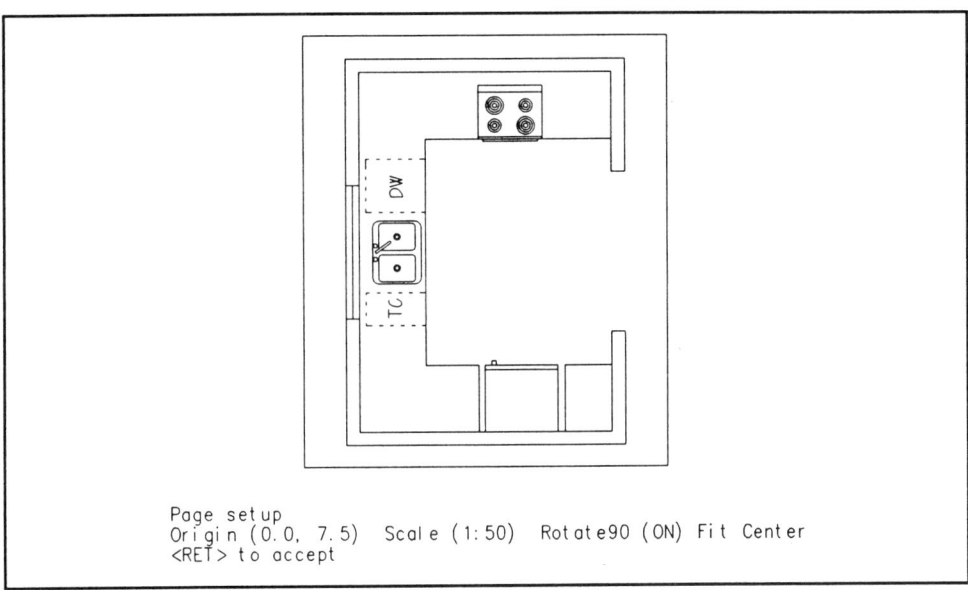

```
Page setup
Origin (0.0, 7.5)   Scale (1:50)   Rotate90 (ON)   Fit Center
<RET> to accept
```

Figure 13.3 The Page Setup options.

Origin. The Origin of a plot is the lower left hand corner of the paper, as shown by the rectangle on the screen. This option allows you to choose a new origin point, which results in the drawing being repositioned on the paper. If your drawing is not positioned properly within the border of the paper, or if you want it purposely off center, changing the origin gives this affect. Selecting option "O" to change the plot origin causes the paper boundary (shown by the rectangle) to be disconnected from the drawing. You can use your mouse to move the "paper" around the screen and position it exactly as desired. If you need to move the paper even farther than the screen allows, use the commands Zoom Out (ZO), Zoom In (ZI), or Pan (PA) to change the view of the drawing on the screen.

You can also use snaps or coordinates to specify the exact origin point in Absolute or Relative modes. If necessary, switch coordinate entry modes to Manual Entry Origin (MO) or Manual Entry Relative (MR). You may want to note that the origin coordinates shown on the Page Setup screen are in *Absolute Coordinates*, although the sign of the coordinates is the opposite of the corresponding point in your drawing.

When the paper is positioned as desired, click with your mouse (or press Enter) to finalize that position. The Page Setup Options, with the new origin coordinates, is then displayed.

Scale. Use this option to enter a specific scale for plotting your drawing. For some drawings it is only important that they fit on the paper, but many engineering and architectural drawings must be produced at a particular scale. If your drawing is physically large and it is drawn to real-world scale, you must scale it down in order to fit it on the paper. Although CADD 6 has a virtually unlimited size electronic drawing space, you still have to contend with the very real, very limited size of your printer or plotter paper.

To specify a scale, press S to select the Scale option. Then, enter the value in a format such that 1 unit on paper equals the number of units on the scaled drawing. For example, to plot your drawing at half size, specify the scale as 1 to 2. This makes 1" on paper equal to 2" on the drawing. To plot the drawing at a scale of 1/4" = 1 foot, specify the scale as 1 to 48 (0.25" to 12" is the same scale as 1" to 48").

Here are some examples of common scale factors you can use:

   1/2" = 1 foot is the same as a 1 to 24 scale.
   1/4" = 1 foot is the same as a 1 to 48 scale.
   1/8" = 1 foot is the same as a 1 to 96 scale.
   1/16" = 1 foot is the same as a 1 to 192 scale.
   1/32" = 1 foot is the same as a 1 to 384 scale.
   1/64" = 1 foot is the same as a 1 to 768 scale.

As a rule of thumb, plot out your drawing as large as you can for the paper you are using. If you do not want to specify a scale, CADD 6 has a function which automatically fits the drawing to the size of the paper selected.

Once you enter a scale, the screen display is updated to show your drawing at the new scale in relation to the paper. You can then use the Center or Origin options to reposition it before printing.

> **TIP:** If you're not sure at what scale to print your drawing, let CADD 6 help. Select Fit to make the drawing as large as possible for the current paper size. Read the Scale value after you Fit the drawing to paper, then enter a common scale value that's less so you can be sure the drawing fits within the boundary of the paper. For example, if you Fit the drawing and the Scale reads 1:43.52, then you might want to change the scale to 1:48.

Rotate90. The Rotate90 option is a toggle which causes the drawing to be rotated first 90 degrees clockwise, then back to its original position. This allows you to more appropriately fit some drawings on the paper.

Fit. This option re-sizes and repositions the drawing so that the whole thing fits on the paper. Using this option cancels any settings you entered previously for scale and origin.

Center. You often want to place your drawing in the center of the paper, with equal margins on left to right and top to bottom. Use this option to do so, especially if you have previously rotated the drawing with Rotate90 or changed the plot origin. This option does not change the pre-selected scale. If the drawing does not completely fit within the boundary of the paper, it is positioned so that the center point of the drawing is in the center of the paper. Remember that any parts of the drawing that do not fit within the paper boundary are not printed.

Start Plot. When you are satisfied that all the plotting variables have been set properly, you are ready to actually plot (or print) your drawing. Select Start Plot to send the drawing to your output device.

If you chose to plot multiple copies (Output Menu Option 4), you are asked if you want to be prompted to start each plot manually. Answer Y, for Yes, if you need to change the paper prior to each plot. If you want CADD 6 to automatically go from one copy to the next, answer N for No prompting.

When CADD 6 starts processing the plot, the bottom part of the screen shows the total number of buffers and lines, along with the line number being plotted. Do not be surprised if a high resolution print takes several minutes to process and print. Press any key if you need to interrupt a print. CADD 6 will ask:

    Press <Space Bar> To Continue Or <ESC> To Quit

If the interruption was accidental and you wish to continue plotting, press the space bar and everything continues normally. To abort the plot completely, press the Esc key. On plotters or printers with buffers, you have to wait for the buffer to empty before it stops, even after you press Esc.

Select Plot (PL)

The Select Plot (PL) command lets you apply a selection set to the Drawing Plot (DP) command. You can use the selection process to choose only specific items from the drawing to be plotted or printed.

Once you have selected all the desired objects, and they are highlighted on the screen, press Enter. This causes the Output Menu to be displayed on the screen so you can set all the required options to define the plot. Follow the previous instructions on the Drawing Plot (DP) command to set options and start your plot.

Upgrade Environment (EN)

As you create a drawing in CADD 6, you define many settings and parameters such as Color Settings (CS), Line Type (LT), Display Settings (DI), Font Select (FS), and Dimension Settings (US). The combination of all these settings is called the drawing *Environment*. Think of it as the environment you have established for creating that particular drawing. Each time you save your drawing to disk its environment is saved with it. When you load that drawing into CADD 6 later, the parameters are already set. You only have to make changes, rather than starting completely over.

You can use the Upgrade Environment (EN) command to create template drawings with pre-defined settings. For example, you could create one template drawing with dimension settings according to architectural standards (large, aligned text, large extension offsets, slash arrow types, etc.) and one for mechanical drawings (0.12" horizontal text, small offsets, filled arrows, etc.). Then use Drawing Load (DL) to load in the appropriate template environment prior to beginning either type of drawing. You may want to use Drawing Rename (DN) to immediately change the name of the new drawing so your template drawing does not get overwritten when you save the new drawing.

CADD 6 takes on the environment of the first drawing loaded when you start the program or after you execute Drawing Remove (DX). If you use Load (LOD) to bring another drawing into the current working drawing, the environment *is not* updated to match the new drawing. You should consider the first drawing you load to be the *master* drawing. It determines the master environment that you work in from then on. When you load in another drawing, it is incorporated into the master drawing so it does not affect the master environment.

Pack Data (PD)

When you erase objects from your drawing, CADD 6 keeps their definitions in memory so the Unerase (UE) and Undo (OO) commands can be used later to bring them back. If you do extensive editing on a drawing, the information stored for the Unerase (UE) and Undo (OO) commands can take up a great deal of memory. This can cause certain CADD 6 operations to be slowed down due to the amount of information that must be processed.

You can eliminate this problem by typing PD to execute the Pack Data (PD) command. Pack Data (PD) clears the memory of all erased objects and the record of past operations. This often causes CADD 6 to run faster since it no longer has to sort through all that information.

Definition Unload (DU)

This command produces results similar to Pack Data (PD) by clearing memory of unneeded information. While Pack Data (PD) clears memory across the board, Definition Unload (DU) allows you to select which items to eliminate.

> **TIP:** Be warned that once the memory is cleared with Pack Data (PD) you can no longer unerase objects or undo any earlier operations! CADD 6.0 does not have any memory of those previous operations.

Definition Unload (DU) is used to remove from memory the definitions of any fonts, components, hatch patterns, fills, and attributes that have been loaded but not used in the drawing. Having many unused definitions in memory can significantly slow down CADD 6's processing time. Font definitions are especially large and should be unloaded if they are not used.

To unload definitions, enter DU and select from the list of possible definitions:

T for Text (.FNT)
C for Components (.CMP)
H for Hatch Patterns (.HCH)
F for Fills
A for Attributes (.ATB)
L for All of the above

Beware that you can not use Undo (OO) or Unerase (UE) to reverse any commands executed prior to using DU.

Select Saved Drawing (SV)

This command combines the Save command (SA) with CADD 6's selection sets. Type in SV to execute Select Saved Drawing (SV) and display the selection menu. Then use the selection menu to choose only the specific items in the drawing you want to save.

Once you have selected all the desired objects, and they are highlighted on the screen, press Enter. You will then be prompted for a file name to use for saving the selected drawing objects. Type in the file name or press Enter to accept the default name shown. To specify a different path, type it in with the file name, or use the File Paths (FP) command prior to executing Save.

Drawing Rename (DN)

This command is used to change the name of the drawing you are currently working on. The name of the file on disk *is not* changed, so you have to save the drawing with the new name if you want it on disk.

Type DN to execute the command. You will then be prompted to enter the new file name. The file name can be up to eight characters in length. Remember that you can only use characters that are acceptable for DOS file names (do not use: . , * \ etc.).

Drawing Remove (DX)

If you want to completely remove your drawing, use the Drawing Remove (DX) command. This erases *everything* in the drawing and in memory (RAM) that relates to the drawing, including the unerase list. Don't worry, though. As long as the file was previously saved to disk, the drawing file is intact and can be re-loaded at any time.

To remove the drawing, type DX for Drawing Remove (DX) and CADD 6 will ask you to confirm that you really want to remove the drawing. If you do, type Y for Yes and it is cleared from memory. If you do not want to remove the drawing, answer N for No (if, for example, you forgot to save it first). You are then returned to the drawing as it was.

You will probably use this command often to switch between drawings without having to exit CADD 6. When you are finished working on one drawing, use the Save (SA) command to save it to disk, then type DX to erase the drawing completely and start on the next drawing.

Load (LO)

The Load (LO) command is used to load an existing drawing file into CADD 6, or to load various other types of files into your current drawing. Execute the command by typing LO, then you can choose to load one of eight types of files. To load a particular kind of file, press the letter that is highlighted on the screen:

D for Drawing file (.GCD)
C for Component file (.CMP)
B for Batch file (.MCR)
T for Attribute file (.ATB)
S for ASCII file (.DOC)
I for Image file (.GX2)
A for AutoCAD drawing (.DWG)
X for DXF files (.DXF)

Generally, all of the Load options require you to tell CADD 6 the name and path name of the particular file you wish to load. Whenever you are prompted for a file name, remember that you can either enter the name by typing it in from the keyboard, selecting it with your pointing device from the list of files displayed on the menu, or going to the File Selector to find and select the desired file or files. If you choose to enter file names from the keyboard, CADD 6 assumes the default path names are in effect. To specify a different path, use the File Paths (FP) command or enter the path name with the file name.

Drawing. Use this option to load any .GCD file that has been saved to disk into CADD 6 for editing, printing, etc. You can also use Load to merge a drawing from disk into the drawing on which you are currently working. For example, a drafter creating a mechanical installation drawing would load in the detail drawings of individual parts to prevent having to redraw them.

Enter LO for Load and select the D option to load a drawing. You are then prompted to enter the desired file name. Either type the file name with the correct path, or select the file name from the sidebar menu or the File Selector.

The drawing being loaded is first shown on the screen as a *Boundary Box*, a rectangle with an X through it. (See Figure 13.4.) Showing this box is a fast way for CADD 6 to represent the boundaries of the drawing, as the entire drawing fits within the box. Use your pointing device to move the box around the screen. This allows you to see how the drawing being loaded "fits" with your current drawing and how to position it properly.

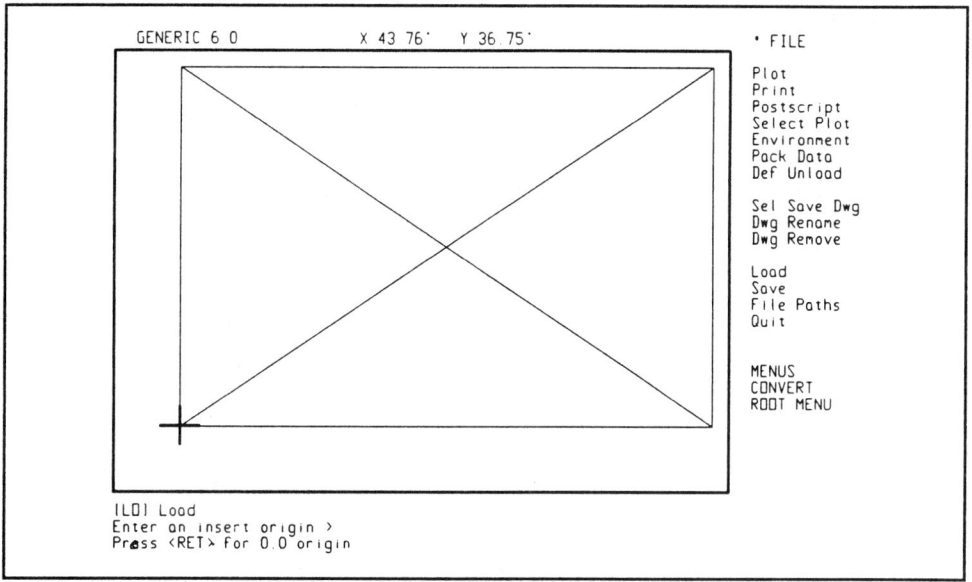

Figure 13.4 The boundary box used to show a drawing being loaded.

You are asked to identify an insertion point on the current drawing. The default insertion point is the origin of the current drawing. If you want the new drawing to be placed so that its origin is at the origin of the current drawing, press Enter to accept the default point. If you choose another insertion point, the new drawing is positioned so its lower left point (the corner of the boundary box) is placed at that point. You can also use snaps or manual coordinate entry to locate an exact insertion point on the current drawing. If necessary, use Zoom commands to change the view of the current drawing to help you locate the desired insertion point.

Once the insertion point is selected, the boundary box is erased and the new drawing is placed on the screen relative to the insertion point.

Component. Use this option to load a component file from disk into the current drawing. A component that is loaded with the LO command is not actually placed anywhere in the drawing, as it is with the Component Place (CP) command. Loaded components show up on the component list, and are available to be placed more quickly with the Component Place command since they do not first have to be called from disk.

To load a component, type LO for Load, then enter C to specify a component file. You will then be asked to identify the name of the component file. Either type in the file name, or select it from the menu or File Selector.

Batch file. Enter LO and then select B to load a batch file into your current drawing. Then enter the file name, or select it from the menu or File Selector.

A Batch file is a text file of CADD 6 commands that can be used to automate CADD 6 operations. Once a batch file is loaded, the commands it contains are automatically executed. Refer to Chapter 15, for more information on Batch files.

aTtribute. This option allows you to load an attribute from disk into your current drawing. When it is first loaded, the attribute is not associated with any particular component. Instead, it is available to be attached to any components with the Attribute Attach (AT) command. Refer to Chapter 8, for additional information on components and attributes.

To execute this option, type LO for Load, then T to specify an Attribute file. When prompted, enter the file name, or select the file from the menu or File Selector.

aScii. This option is used to load a file containing text in ASCII format and convert it to CADD 6 text lines. In other words, you could create a file in a text editor of all your standard drawing notes, save it in ASCII format, then load the file into your CADD 6 drawings. Once in CADD 6, the ASCII text becomes standard text lines and can be moved, edited, scaled, and so on.

Execute the LO command, then choose the S option to load an ASCII file. At the prompt for file name, either enter the name of the desired ASCII format file or select it from the menu. You will then be prompted to identify where you want to place the text in your drawing. The text is shown with a Boundary Box, similar to that used for loading a drawing. You can position the text by moving your pointing device and dragging the text into place. When you enter the insertion point, the text characters appear in the drawing.

As you move the text box around your drawing, you can also change the text font, size, justification, slant, aspect, rotation, color, and spacing with the Text Settings (TS) command on-the-fly. To find out more about text commands refer to Chapter 8.

This option of the Load command does exactly the same thing as the Load ASCII command (LA) on the TEXT menu.

Image. To load an Image file into CADD 6, execute the Load (LO) command, select the I option, then enter or select the appropriate image file name. This loads a screen image that has been previously created with the Save Image (SAI) command. The image is loaded exactly as it was saved. If the image was saved as only the drawing portion of the screen, then the drawing area is replaced by the image but the menu, coordinate display and status line are unaffected. Otherwise, the entire screen is updated to show the full image.

You should note that loading an image file does not affect your drawing in any way. The objects shown on the image do not replace your drawing and are not added to your drawing in any way. To restore your drawing screen to what it was before loading the image, simply do a Redraw (RD). Zoom commands also cause the image to be erased and your drawing restored.

This option is available only if your video driver (selected when you configured CADD 6) supports the Image capability.

AutoCAD drawing. Use this option to load AutoCAD drawings into CADD 6. AutoCAD drawings have a .DWG extension. Drawings created in earlier versions of Generic CADD have the .DWG extension as well. If you inadvertently select one of these older Generic CADD drawings, CADD 6 prompts you with an error message and asks you to press any key to abort the command.

Details of entity conversion between AutoCAD and CADD 6 are covered extensively in Appendix A of CADD 6's User Guide.

DXF. This option converts DXF (Drawing Exchange Format) files to CADD 6 .GCD files. The DXF format was popularized by AutoCAD and is supported by most CAD programs, as well as many desktop publishing, presentation graphics, and word processing programs. Details of DXF file conversion to CADD 6 are covered extensively in Appendix A of CADD 6's User Guide.

Save (SA)

The Save (SA) command is used to save files to disk for permanent storage. You can save the drawing file you are currently working on, or various other types of files you can create in CADD 6. Execute the command by typing SA, then select a letter to specify one of the seven types of files you can save. The options are:

D for Drawing file (.GCD)
C for Component file (.CMP)
B for Batch file (.MCR)

A for Attribute file (.ATB)
L for Level 3 drawing file (.DWG)
I for Image file (.GX2)
A for AutoCAD files (.DWG)
X for DXF files (.DXF)

All of the Save options require you to specify the file name to use for the particular file you wish to save. Whenever you are prompted for a file name, remember that you can either press Enter to accept the default name shown, or enter a different name by typing it in from the keyboard. CADD 6 automatically uses the default path names that were established during installation unless you specify new default paths with the File Paths (FP) command, or enter a path along with the file name.

Drawing. Select the Drawing option to save the drawing you are currently working on to disk, without exiting the program. CADD 6 then prompts you for the desired file name to use for saving the drawing. The name used to originally load or start the drawing is shown as the default, so press Enter to save it with this name. If you want to save the drawing with another name, enter it at the prompt, up to eight characters in length. You can only use characters that are acceptable for use in DOS file names (do not use: . , * \ etc.).

CADD 6 automatically adds the three letter file name extension .GCD to all the drawings you save. Unless you specify differently, the drawing is saved to the default path. To use a different path, enter it with the file name, or change it with the File Paths (FP) command before executing Save.

> **TIP:** Make a habit of saving your drawing every 10 or 15 minutes to avoid losing your work. Computer problems, power outages and other catastrophes can cause CADD 6.0 to stop dead and cause you to lose any work you did since the last time you saved your drawing. A habit of saving frequently guarantees that you never lose very much time.

When you enter a different drawing name to be used for saving a file, this does *not* change the name of your working drawing. The drawing you are working in retains its original name. This feature can be used to create several floor plan drawings that each have slight modifications. For example, create an initial drawing and save it as "Floor1." Then repeat the Save Drawing (SAD) command to save the same drawing as "Floor2" and "Floor3." When you are ready to edit each floor plan, use Load Drawing (LOD) to load them individually, make the modifications and re-save them.

CADD 6 always gives you a message before saving to an existing file and overwriting it. When you specify to save a drawing that already exists, CADD 6 prompts:

File exists, Overwrite or Rename old file to *.bak (O/R) ?

You can then choose to copy over the old file or rename the old file with a file extension of .BAK.

Component. This option saves a component to a disk file so that it can be loaded and placed in other drawings. Enter SA to Save and then select Components. You will then be prompted to enter a file name, with the name used to create the component shown as the default file name. You can enter another name, but this is not recommended and may make it confusing for you to load and use that component later. Press Enter to accept the default and make the file name the same as the component name.

The file is automatically saved to the default path with the extension .CMP so that it can be differentiated from regular drawing files. If you want to specify a different path, type it in with the file name or use the File Paths (FP) command prior to the Save.

Batch file. Select the Batch file option to save the current drawing as a batch file, a series of CADD 6 commands in ASCII. You are prompted to enter a file name, with the current drawing name given as the default. If you accept the default file name, CADD 6 automatically adds an extension of .MCR to signify that the file is a batch or macro file. For this reason, using the drawing name does not cause your drawing to be overwritten with the batch file. For more information about using Batch files refer to Chapter 15.

This command does exactly the same thing as the Save Batch (SB) command covered in Chapter 14.

Attribute. Use this option to save an attribute to a disk file so that it can be placed in other drawings. To save an attribute in your drawing, type SA then select Attributes. You will then be prompted to enter a file name with the name used to create the attribute shown as the default. While you can enter some other name, this is not recommended since CADD 6 still only recognizes the original attribute name once it is placed in a drawing. Press Enter to accept the default and make the file name the same as the attribute name. CADD 6 automatically adds the extension .ATB to all attributes so that they can be differentiated from other types of files.

Level 3 Drawing File. When CADD 6 drawings are saved to disk with the Save Drawing (SAD) command, they are not compatible with Generic CADD Level 3 (a previous version of Generic CADD.) The L option of the Save (SA) command allows you to save any CADD 6 file in a format that can be loaded into Level 3 and the early versions of the Generic 3D program.

Some objects used in CADD 6 are not available in Level 3, such as attributes, associative dimensions, and text lines. When saved as a Level 3 drawing, these objects are exploded into lines and text characters.

Like AutoCAD files, Level 3 files are saved with a .DWG extension. If you use this feature, be sure not to overwrite any of your AutoCAD .DWG files.

Image file. To save an Image file to disk, execute the Save (SA) command and then select the I option for Image. This saves a pixel image of everything on the screen which can be used for slide shows or previewing drawings. You are asked:

Save Full Screen Zoom Image? (Y/N) >

If you choose to save the entire screen, the image includes the drawing area, menu, and coordinate display. If you answer N for no, only the drawing area of the screen is saved.

Next you will be prompted to enter the file name to use for the image. Enter the desired file name and CADD 6 automatically appends the extension .GX2. If you want to specify a different path, type it in with the file name or use the File Paths (FP) command prior to executing Save.

This option is available *only* if your video driver (as selected when you configured CADD 6) supports the Image capability.

AutoCAD File. Select this option to save your CADD 6 drawing as an AutoCAD .DWG file. This feature is new in CADD 6.1. Together with the Load AutoCAD feature, this gives CADD 6.1 two-way compatibility with AutoCAD.

DXF. This option converts your CADD 6 drawing (.GCD) file into a DXF (Drawing Exchange Format) file. Details of DXF file conversion are covered extensively in Appendix A of CADD 6's User Guide.

File Paths (FP)

You are often prompted to give CADD 6 a file name, such as when you load and save drawings, components, batch files, etc. CADD 6 looks for certain types of files in certain locations on your hard disk, as specified by the DOS path names of the files (the particular disk drive partition and directory). If no file path is entered when you type in a file name, CADD 6 assumes that you want to use the default file paths. These default paths were established when you first installed CADD 6.

Once you are in CADD 6, you can change the default path names with the File Paths (FP) command. Enter FP and the following options are given for all types of files that CADD 6 uses:

G for Drawing files (.GCD)
C for Component files (.CMP)
F for Font files (.FNT)
B for Batch files (.MCR)
H for Hatch files (.HCH)
M for Menu files (.MNU)
S for Shell files (.COM or .EXE)
I for Miscellaneous files (.DOC or .TPR)
A for AutoCAD files (.DWG)
X for DXF files (.DXF)
L for Lock file path

Select the letter corresponding to the default path name you want to change. At the prompt, type in the new path and press Enter. From then on, during that drawing session, this newly entered path name is the default for that type of file. Make sure you enter the disk drive designation if it is a different drive (or partition) than where CADD 6 is located. If you load a file from a directory other than the default setting, that particular file path changes to the new directory path.

> **TIP:** To retain the file paths even if you load a file from another directory, set the Lock file path (L) selection to ON.

Quit (QU)

When you are ready to end your CADD 6 drawing session, use Enter QU to Quit. This command also gives you the chance to save your drawing to disk before you are returned to DOS.

When you enter QU to quit, CADD 6 will ask:

Save Current Drawing? (Y/N) >

If you do not want to save the drawing (perhaps you already saved it with the SA command), answer N for No. If you want to work on your drawing some more later, be sure to save it by entering Y for Yes. You will then be prompted to enter the file name to use for saving it. Press Enter to accept the default name shown, or type in a new file name. Remember that the default path for drawing files is automatically used unless you specifically enter another disk drive and directory with the file name.

CADD 6 gives you one more chance to change your mind before quitting by prompting:

Chapter 13: Input and Output

Quit Continue > >

Enter Q to quit CADD 6 and return to DOS. If you do not really want to quit, enter C to return to the drawing you were working on.

USING THE CONVERT COMMANDS

The CONVERT menu is accessed from the FILE menu. It contains commands for converting CADD 6 drawings to other formats, and importing files of other formats into CADD 6.

Drawing In (LOA)

Use this option to load AutoCAD drawings into CADD 6. Refer to the LOAD (LO) command using the AutoCAD option, described earlier in this chapter.

Dxfin (LOX)

This option converts DXF (Drawing Exchange Format) files to CADD 6 (.GCD) files. Details of DXF file conversion to CADD 6 are covered extensively in Appendix A of CADD 6's User Guide.

Dxfout (SAX)

This option converts CADD 6 (.GCD) files to DXF (Drawing Exchange Format) files. Details of DXF file conversion to CADD 6 are covered extensively in Appendix A of CADD 6's User Guide.

Exchange Setup (XG)

When the Exchange Setup (XG) command is selected, you automatically shell-out to the AutoConvert program where you set up all the DXF conversion parameters. Details of DXF file conversion to CADD 6 are covered extensively in Appendix A of CADD 6's User Guide.

HPGL to GCD

Use this command to convert HPGL files to CADD 6 (.GCD) files. HPGL files are formatted in the Hewlett-Packard Graphics Language commonly used by Hewlett-Packard plotters. The HPGL To GCD command allows you to bring files saved in this format into CADD 6.

> **TIP:** To create HPGL files, configure CADD 6.0 for one of the Hewlett-Packard plotters and select the Port: File option. Then start the plot normally and your drawing is saved to a file in HPGL format.

Load ASCII File (LA)

The Load ASCII (LA) command is used to load a file containing text in ASCII format and convert it to CADD 6 text lines. In other words, you can create a file in a text editor, save it as ASCII, then load that text into your CADD 6 drawing. Once in CADD 6, the ASCII text becomes standard CADD 6 text lines.

Before or after placing an ASCII file into your drawing, you can change the text font, size, justification, slant, aspect, rotation, color, and spacing with the Text Settings (TS) command. Changes to text settings can be made on-the-fly before choosing the location of the text. To find out more about text commands, refer to Chapter 8.

Once the command is executed you will be prompted to enter the name of the ASCII file. You can either type in the file name or select a file from the menu listing. ASCII files can also be loaded with the Load (LO) command by selecting the S option, as discussed previously.

CHAPTER SUMMARY

The most basic CADD 6 operations center around manipulating files, loading, saving, printing, and plotting. Many of the commands covered in this chapter will be used in every drawing session, so spend some time becoming familiar with them.

Producing hard copies of your drawings are covered in detail in the section on Drawing Plot\Print\Postscript (DP). This feature lets you easily take advantage of your output device to put your drawing on paper exactly the way you want it.

Other commands in the FILE menu can save your drawing environment to be used as a template drawing for future use. This increases productivity by minimizing drawing setup. Use features like Pack Data (PD) and Definition Unload (DU) to clear unwanted information from CADD 6's memory and optimize CADD 6's speed.

CHAPTER 14

Utility Commands

USING THE UTILITY MENU

This chapter will discuss the commands found on the UTILITIES video menu. Some of these commands have already been explained in the tutorials, so they will be discussed only briefly here.

These commands let you measure lengths, angles, and areas, explode complex objects, shell to DOS, and switch from the graphics mode to text mode to extract drawing data.

UTILITIES
Explode (EX)
Measure (ME)
Screen Flip (SF)
Object Information (OI)
Filter (EF)
Selection (SE)

Match (MH)
Shell Exe (SH)
View Fast Text (TV)
Set Limits (LS)
Drawing Origin (DO)
Save Batch (SB)
Selection Batch Save (BS)
Macro Assign (MA)

Bill of Materials (BI)
Shell to BOM

Explode (EX)

The Explode (EX) command is used to break up complex entities into the basic elements from which they were originally drawn. Explode (EX) offers a selection set for you to select the objects to explode. With the Explode (EX) command, you can break down components, dimensions, text lines, and text characters. The following list describes the entity to be exploded, and the objects that result from the explosion:

Entity	Result
Components	Individual objects that make up the component
Attributes	Text Lines
Dimensions	Lines, circles, text strings, and fills
Text Lines	Text characters
Text Characters	Lines, arcs, circles, and curves

> **Tip:** If you wish to fill the characters of a bold font, you can explode the font's individual text characters and then use the FILL commands to fill them in solid.

Measure (ME)

The Measure (ME) command allows you to extract distances, areas, and angles from your drawing. When using measure commands, be sure to use snap commands, like Snap Nearest Point (NP), to ensure that accurate measurements are taken.

To use the Measure command, type ME at the command line, or select Measure from the video menu. A list of the measurement method options is displayed, including Distance, Area, 2-point, and 3-point angles. Select one of these methods with your cursor, or type a D for Distance, A for Area, 2 for 2-point, or 3 for 3-point angles.

Distance. If you want to measure the distance between points, select D or Distance. You are first prompted to enter a starting point, then you are asked to select the next point on the line. While you are measuring a distance, notice a line rubberbanding between the cursor and the last point entered. This line is merely for reference, and does not remain in the drawing. Once the second point is selected, the distance between the two points are displayed on the command line. At this point, you can press the escape key or enter PU to complete the command, or you can continue measuring to additional points.

Chapter 14: Utility Commands ■ 14-3

> **TIP:** To select Pen Up, type PU and press Enter, or click on a blank spot on the video menu.

See Figure 14.1 for an example of using the Measure Distance feature.

Type: ME
Type: D (and press Enter)
Snap (NP) to point 1
Snap (NP) to point 2
Read the measurement displayed on the command line
Press the Escape key

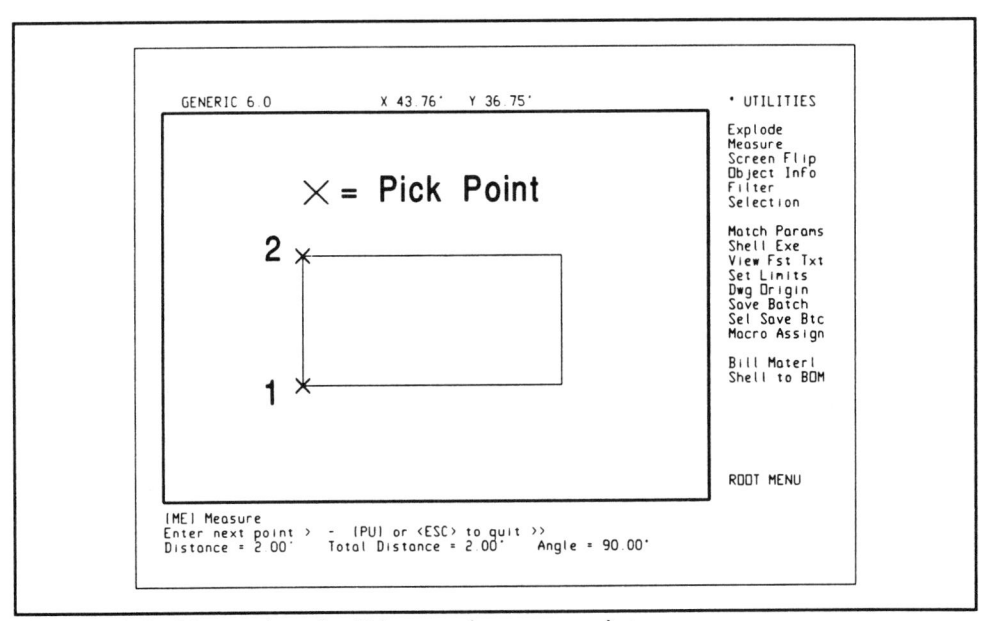

```
GENERIC 6.0          X 43.76'   Y 36.75'           * UTILITIES
                                                   Explode
                                                   Measure
                                                   Screen Flip
                                                   Object Info
                                                   Filter
            X = Pick Point                         Selection

                                                   Match Params
      2 X─────────────────────┐                    Shell_Exe
        │                     │                    View Fst Txt
        │                     │                    Set Limits
        │                     │                    Dwg Origin
        │                     │                    Save Batch
        │                     │                    Sel Save Btc
        │                     │                    Macro Assign
        │                     │
      1 X─────────────────────┘                    Bill Materl
                                                   Shell to BOM



                                                   ROOT MENU

[ME] Measure
Enter next point >  -  (PU) or <ESC> to quit >>
Distance = 2.00'    Total Distance = 2.00'   Angle = 90.00'
```

Figure 14.1 Measuring the Distance between points.

To continue measuring, such as determining the total perimeter of an area, simply snap to the next point and the next point after that. Each new distance is added to the total as you progress from point to point. The distance is updated on the display with each new point.

See Figure 14.2 for an example. Notice how the distance changes on the command line every time another point is selected.

14-4 ■ Chapter 14: Utility Commands

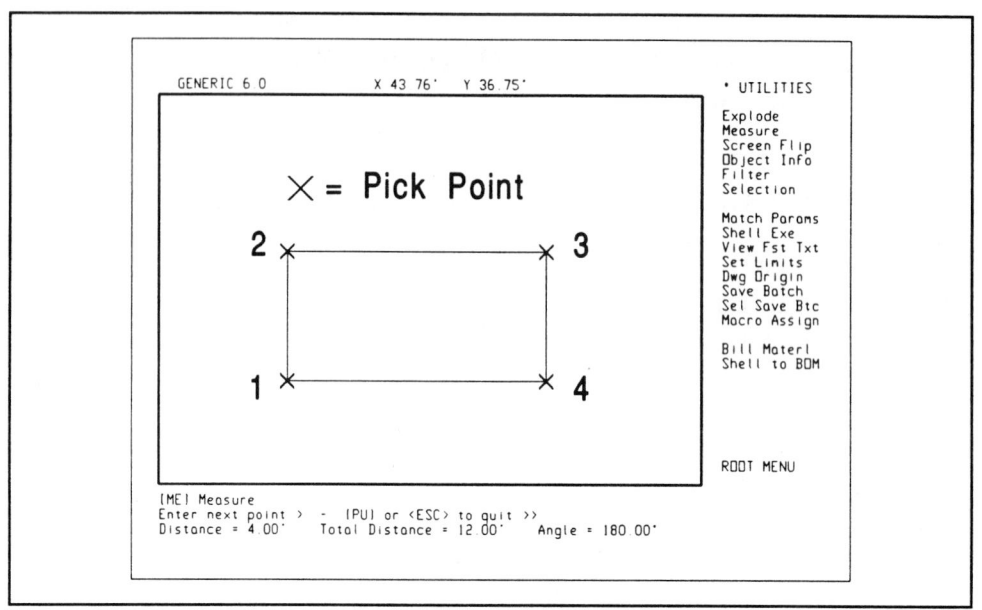

```
GENERIC 6.0          X 43.76'   Y 36.75'              • UTILITIES
                                                      Explode
                                                      Measure
                                                      Screen Flip
                                                      Object Info
              X = Pick Point                          Filter
                                                      Selection

        2 X────────────────X 3                        Match Parans
          │                │                          Shell Exe
          │                │                          View Fst Txt
          │                │                          Set Limits
          │                │                          Dwg Origin
          │                │                          Save Batch
          │                │                          Sel Save Btc
        1 X────────────────X 4                        Macro Assign

                                                      Bill Materl
                                                      Shell to BOM


                                                      ROOT MENU

[ME] Measure
Enter next point >  -  [PU] or <ESC> to quit >>
Distance = 4.00'    Total Distance = 12.00'   Angle = 180.00'
```

Figure 14.2 Measuring the Perimeter of an area.

    Type: ME
    Type: D (and press Enter)
    Snap (NP) to point 1
    Snap (NP) to point 2
    Snap (NP) to point 3
    Snap (NP) to point 4
    Snap (NP) to point 1
    Read the measurement displayed on the command line
    Press the Escape key

Area. This option lets you measure an area or a combination of areas. Measure Area prompts you to select points that define the boundary of the area to be measured. Type ME to bring up the Measure sub-menu. Type A or select Area with your cursor. Snap to the first point on the object in which you wish to calculate the area. (See Figure 14.3.) To measure the area of the rectangle in Figure 14.3, snap to point 1, then to points 2, 3, and 4. It is not necessary to snap back to point 1. CADD 6 calculates the area defined by the lines you selected, so it closes the boundary automatically. After snapping to point 4, press the Esc key, or enter PU. The area is displayed on the command line.

If you are measuring the area of a rectangle and select only three points, CADD 6 closes the boundary by connecting back to the first point. This means the calculated area is actually only half the rectangle. (See Figure 14.4.) Start the measure area command, and snap to points 1, 2, and 3. Press Esc or enter PU, CADD 6 calculates

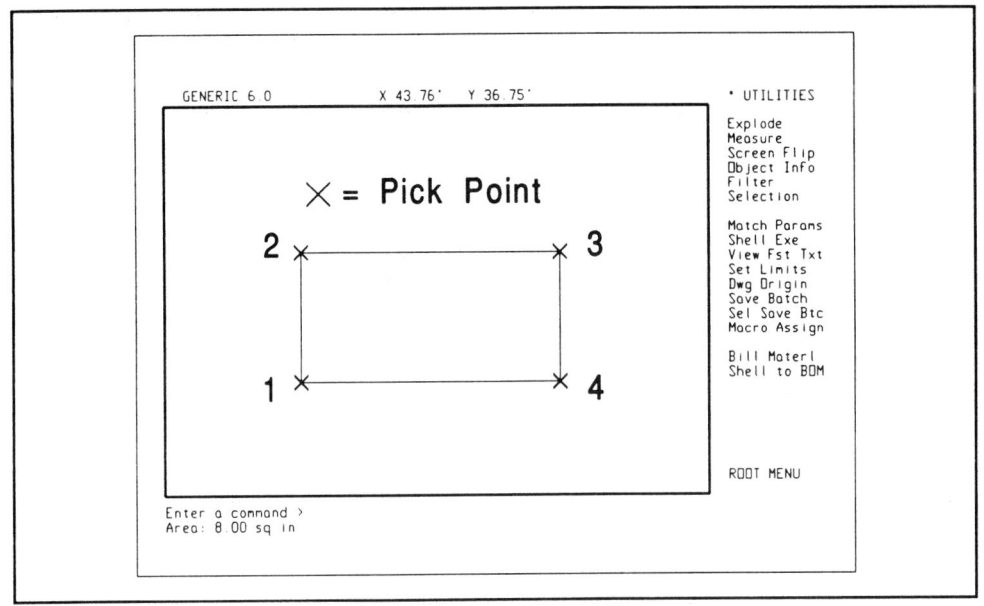

```
GENERIC 6.0        X 43.76'   Y 36.75'              • UTILITIES

                                                    Explode
                                                    Measure
                                                    Screen Flip
              X = Pick Point                        Object Info
                                                    Filter
         2 ×──────────────× 3                       Selection

           │              │                         Match Parans
           │              │                         Shell Exe
           │              │                         View Fst Txt
           │              │                         Set Limits
           │              │                         Dwg Origin
         1 ×──────────────× 4                       Save Batch
                                                    Sel Save Btc
                                                    Macro Assign

                                                    Bill Materl
                                                    Shell to BOM


                                                    ROOT MENU

Enter a command >
Area: 8.00 sq in
```

Figure 14.3 Using Measure to determine an area.

the area of the rectangle by assuming the third side is drawn between points 3 and 1. This triangle is half the area of the complete rectangle.

> **TIP:** CADD 6.0 needs at least two sides of an object to calculate an area. If you select only one side of an object and press Esc, or enter PU, the area is reported as 0.

The only way to calculate an area bounded by a curve or arc, is to approximate the curve or arc by specifying points along its boundary. The closer the distance between the points when approximating the arc or curve, the more accurate the measurement is. (See Figure 14.5.)

The areas of separate objects can be measured while also combining them to calculate the total area. For example, the total area of two rectangles can be calculated, combining their areas into one total. (See Figure 14.6.) Calculate the area for rectangle J using the ME command and selecting A for area. Snap to points 1, 2, 3, and 4. Enter PU. You are again prompted to enter the first point, just as you were with rectangle J. Now snap to points 1, 2, 3, and 4 of rectangle K. Press Esc to display the total area of both rectangles. Unlike calculating distance with the Area command (ME,A), entering PU lets you calculate the area of another object in the drawing. The escape key is the only way to complete the Measure Area command.

14-6 ■ Chapter 14: Utility Commands

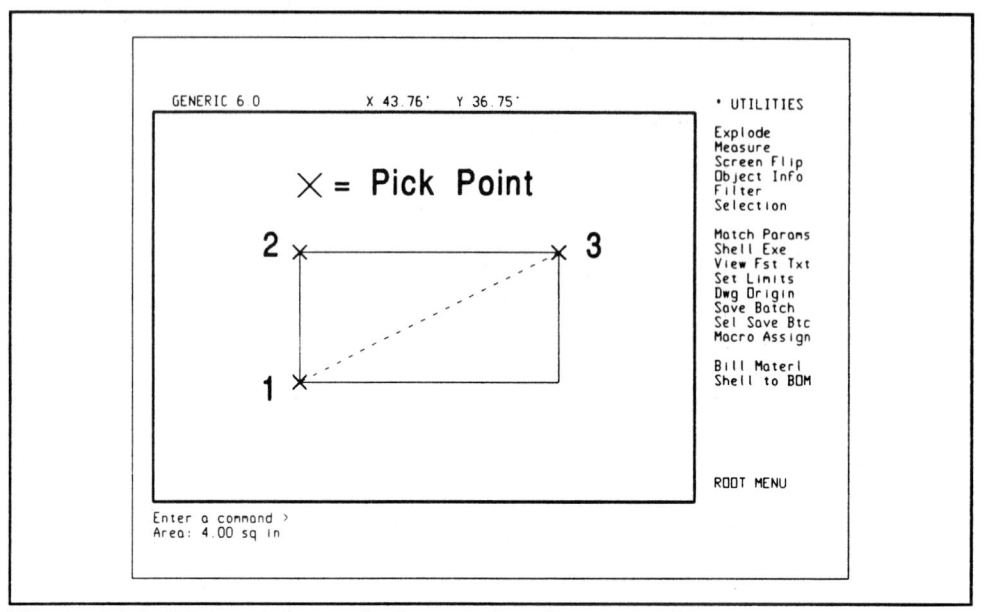

Figure 14.4 Measure Area, don't return to the start point.

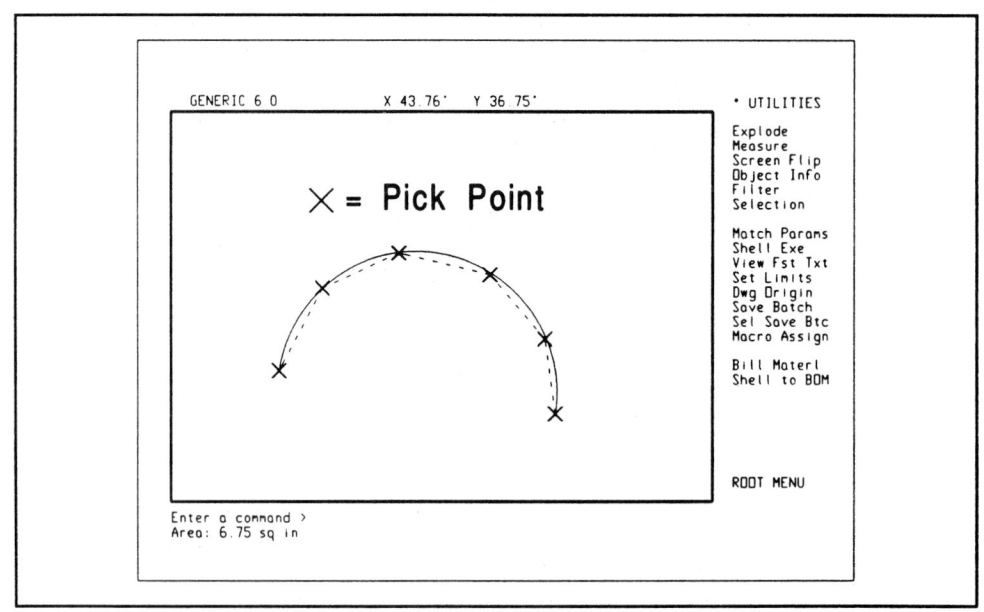

Figure 14.5 Measuring around an arc or curve.

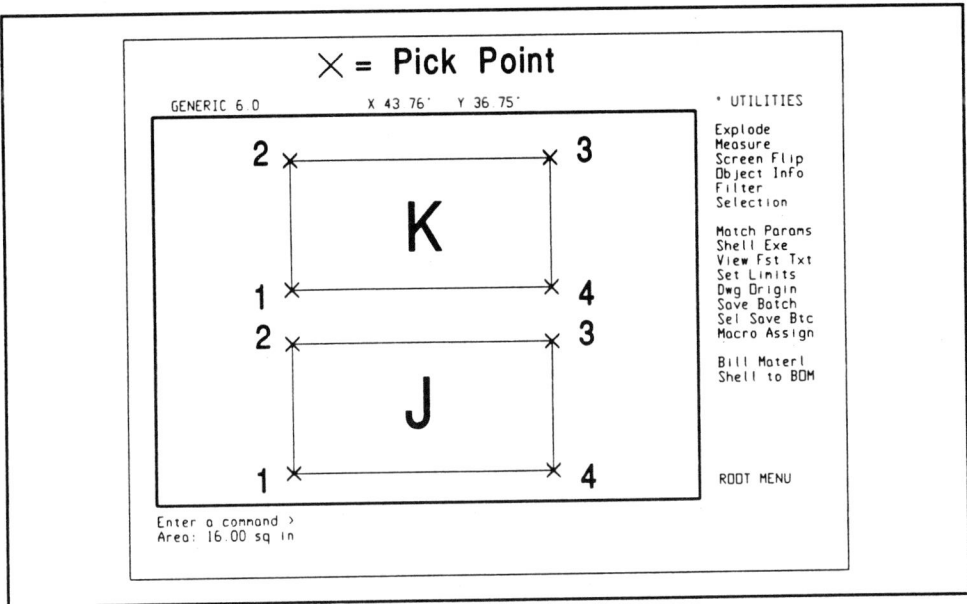

Figure 14.6 Measuring with the 2-Point Angle command.

2-Point Angle. There are two methods used to measure the angle of an object in CADD 6, the 2-point and 3-point method. To use the 2-point method, type ME and select 2-point or type 2. You are first prompted to identify the Base Point, then a point on the ray. The angle is measured counterclockwise from the horizontal to the line defined by the two points you selected. If your second point is placed directly above the first point, the resulting angle is 90°. Directly below results in an angle of 270°.

3-Point Angle. When you want to measure an angle defined by three points, type ME and 3, or select 3-point from the sub-menu. The angle is calculated based on two rays emanating from one point (the base of the angle). (See Figure 14.8.) This method of angle calculation is similar to the two-point method previously discussed, except you get to designate the 0 degree reference line. CADD 6 measures the angle counterclockwise from the first ray to the second ray. You will be prompted to enter the three points as follows:

1. Base of Angle - This is the point common to both rays
2. A point on the ray - The end point of the first ray
3. Next point - The end point of the second ray

You would get a value of 90° using the 3-point method of angle measurement if you placed a point (second point placed) directly to the right of the base point (first point placed), then placed a point (third point placed) directly above the base point (first point placed). (See Figure 14.9.) No matter how these three points are rotated on the screen, as long as it's together, the angle is calculated as 90°, as long as the first point

14-8 ■ Chapter 14: Utility Commands

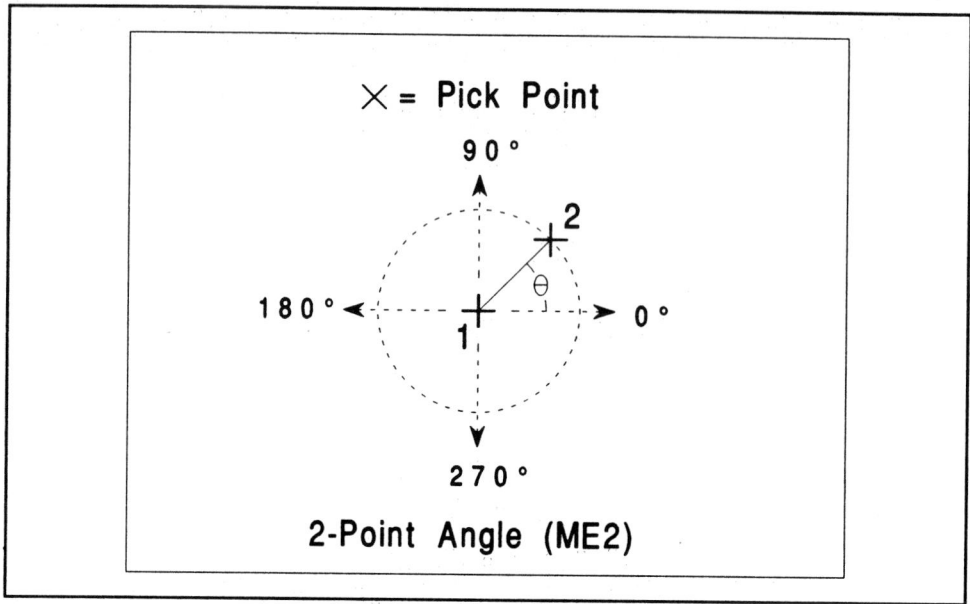

2-Point Angle (ME2)

× = Pick Point

Figure 14.7 Using Pen Up to calculate multiple areas.

3-Point Angle (ME3)

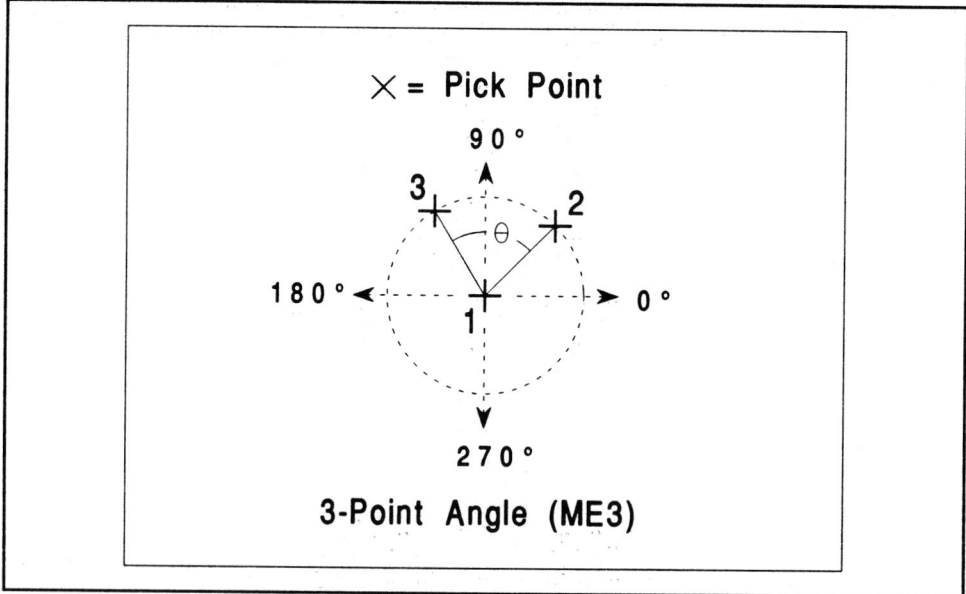

× = Pick Point

Figure 14.8 Measuring with the 3-Point Angle command.

selected is always the same. If you start by selecting points from the opposite direction, then the angle calculated equals 270°. Remember, the angle is calculated counter-clockwise from the first ray to the second ray.

```
                        X = Pick Point
                            90°
                     3      ↑      2
                      +   90°    +
              180° ←------+------→ 0°
                          1
                            ↓
                           270°
                    3-Point Angle (ME3)
```

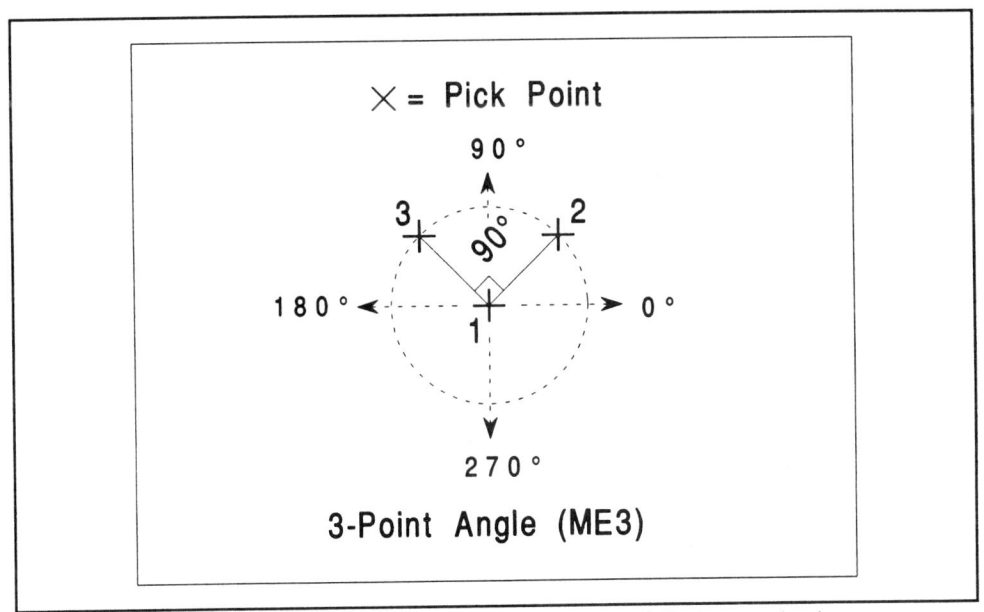

Figure 14.9 Measuring a 90 degree angle with the 3-Point method.

Screen Flip (SF)

The Screen Flip feature lets you leave the graphics screen and display a text mode screen where you have these options to choose from:

1) Display drawing status
2) List objects in drawing
3) Display assigned macros
4) File Selector
ESC) Return to drawing

> **TIP:** If you have a terminate-stay-resident (TSR) program that requires text mode, like a calendar or calculate, type SF to switch to text mode then you can pop up your TSR.

Select any of these options by entering the corresponding number from the keyboard, or selecting it with your mouse.

Figure 14.10 shows an example drawing used to explain the various Screen Flip (SF) functions.

14-10 ■ Chapter 14: Utility Commands

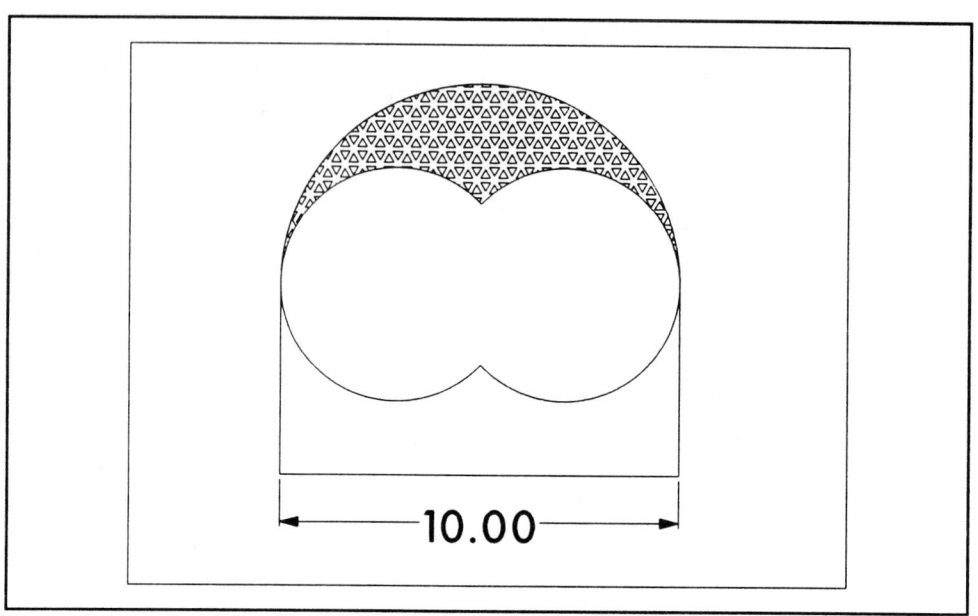

Figure 14.10 Example drawing used to illustrate Screen Flip.

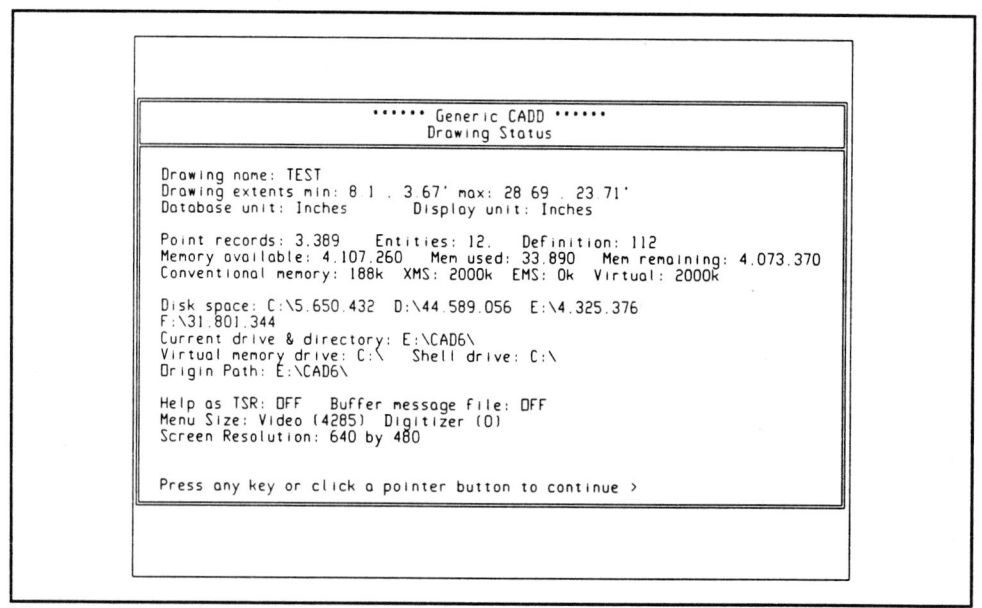

Figure 14.11 The Drawing Status screen of the Screen Flip command.

Display Drawing Status. If you want to read the status of your drawing, enter into Screen Flip (SF) and press 1 (Display Drawing Status). Information pertinent to the drawing is displayed on this screen, as shown in Figure 14.11. To leave this screen and return to the options screen, press Enter or Esc.

Drawing Extents. The meaning of some items on the Drawing Status screen may not be obvious to you, such as Drawing Extents. The extents of a drawing in CADD 6 are calculated relative to the drawing origin of CADD 6. If a rectangle is placed in MO (Manual Entry Relative to Origin) mode at 0,0 and extends 10" to the right, and 15" up, then the minimum extents equals 0,0 and the maximum extents equal 10,15.

> **TIP:** To find the drawing origin, type MO to get into the Manual Entry Origin mode. Next, type 0,0 and press Enter. The cursor moves to the drawing origin.

Point Records. Every object in your drawing has Point Records associated with it. If your entire drawing consists of one line, then the Point Records equal 3, because of the line's first point (1), second point (2), and the selection of line (3). The following is a list of some drawing primitives and their individual Point Record values:

Entity	Point Record
Point	2
Line	3
Circle	3
Arc	4
Curve	4
Bezier	5
Ellipse (True)	5
Ellipse (Constructed)	16

Entities. The Entities record simply lists the number of entities currently held in the drawing database. If you had a drawing which consisted of 1 circle, 1 line, and 1 arc, you would have 3 entities in the drawing.

Any entities previously erased, but not followed by a Pack Data (PD), are still included in the drawing status. If you had erased a circle, but did not perform the Pack Data (PD) feature, the Entities display still shows it in the record entities. To clear the memory of any extra items, you will need to Pack Data (PD) and perform a Definition Unload (DU).

Definitions. The Definitions record keeps a count of all defined entities in the drawing such as fonts, hatches, fills, and components. If a font is loaded, such as Gothic, you have 95 definitions displayed in drawing status in the Definitions record. There is one definition per text character. A hatch or fill also counts as one definition per hatched or filled item. Each component loaded counts as one definition. Multiple copies of the same component do not increase the definition count.

List Objects in Drawing. With this option, you can view a list of all the entities currently in the drawing. When you select this option, three choices appear on the screen:

1) View
2) Drawing
3) Selected list (Use the Selection command, SE, to create the list.)

The list includes the object's item number, description (name), line type, line width, color, and layer. If your drawing consists of two lines, (See Figure 14.12.), the first line is labeled as item 1. The second line is labeled as item 4. (See Figure 14.13) This is related to the Point Records display for entities, described earlier in this chapter under "Display Drawing Status". A line has a record of 3 points. These point records are considered items in the drawing list.

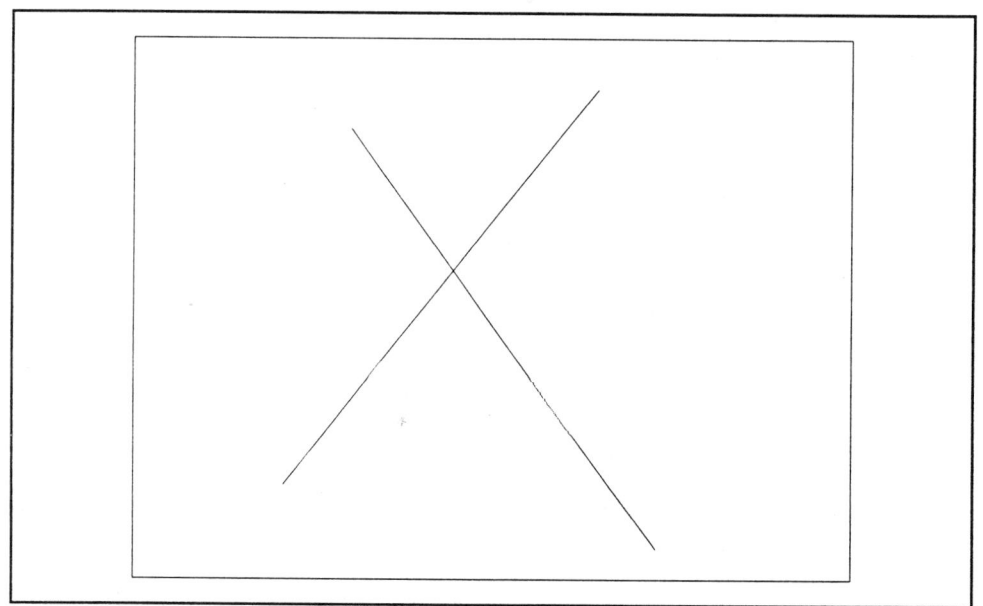

Figure 14.12 Example drawing to illustrate List Objects.

If there are more objects in the drawing than fit on the list, you can use page up and page down to move through the rest of the list. Make sure that All Layers Edit (AL) is ON to get a list of all the objects in the drawing. If All Layers Edit (AL) is OFF, only the objects in the current layer are listed.

View. If you press V, you will see a list of all the objects in the current view. For an object to be considered in the view, it must be entirely in the view. If you have a line in the view, but part of the line is off the screen, the line is not recognized as being in the view.

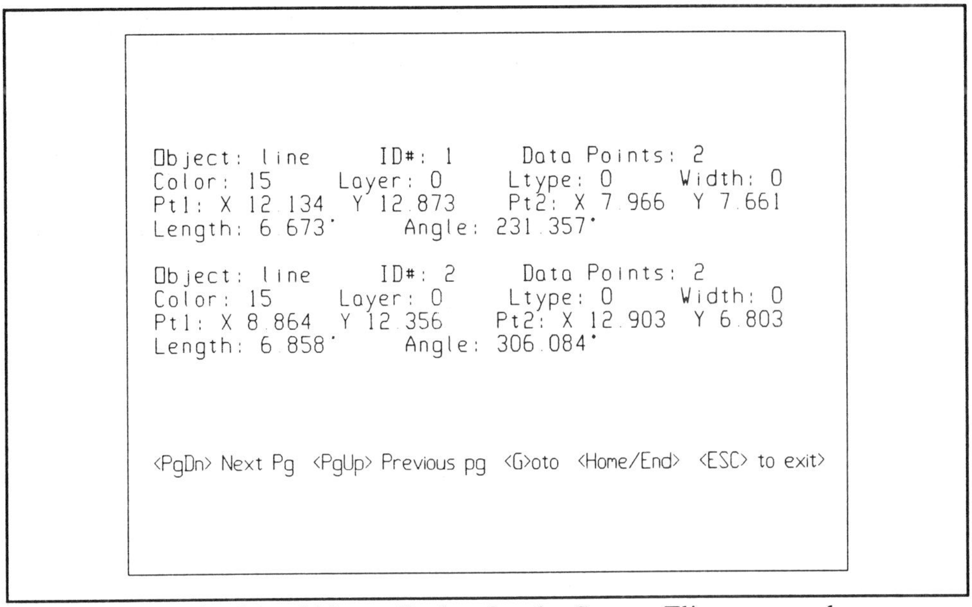

```
Object: line      ID#: 1      Data Points: 2
Color: 15      Layer: 0      Ltype: 0      Width: 0
Pt1: X 12.134  Y 12.873    Pt2: X 7.966  Y 7.661
Length: 6.673'     Angle: 231.357°

Object: line      ID#: 2      Data Points: 2
Color: 15      Layer: 0      Ltype: 0      Width: 0
Pt1: X 8.864   Y 12.356    Pt2: X 12.903 Y 6.803
Length: 6.858'     Angle: 306.084°



<PgDn> Next Pg  <PgUp> Previous pg  <G>oto  <Home/End>  <ESC> to exit>
```

Figure 14.13 The List Objects display for the Screen Flip command.

Drawing. Press D to list all the objects in the drawing.

Selected List. If you select entities within your drawing using the Selection (SE) command, you get a listing of the objects by selecting option S. If you execute a command using a selection set, and then "list the objects in a selected set," the result is a list of these objects selected during the command.

Display Assigned Macros. This option gives you a list of all the macros that you have assigned to function keys or pointer buttons. The first list is the macros assigned to the function keys as they are. If you type S, you see a list of the macros assigned to the Shift + function keys, A for the Alt + function keys, and C for the Ctrl + function keys. Press F to return to the initial function keys. Press P to view the macros assigned to the pointer buttons on your pointing device.

Not only does this selection display the macros currently assigned in CADD 6, but it allows you to assign and edit the macros as well. To enter or change macro information, press the key or combination of keys associated with the macro.

FILE SELECTOR

During any file loading procedure, notice the File Selector prompt located at the bottom of the video menu. (See Figure 14.14.) The File Selector is a full-screen file management utility where you can browse your hard disk or floppy disks in search of files. One advantage of the File Selector is the tree structure format it uses to view files. This is a more graphical representation of your CADD 6 file structure which allows easier selection.

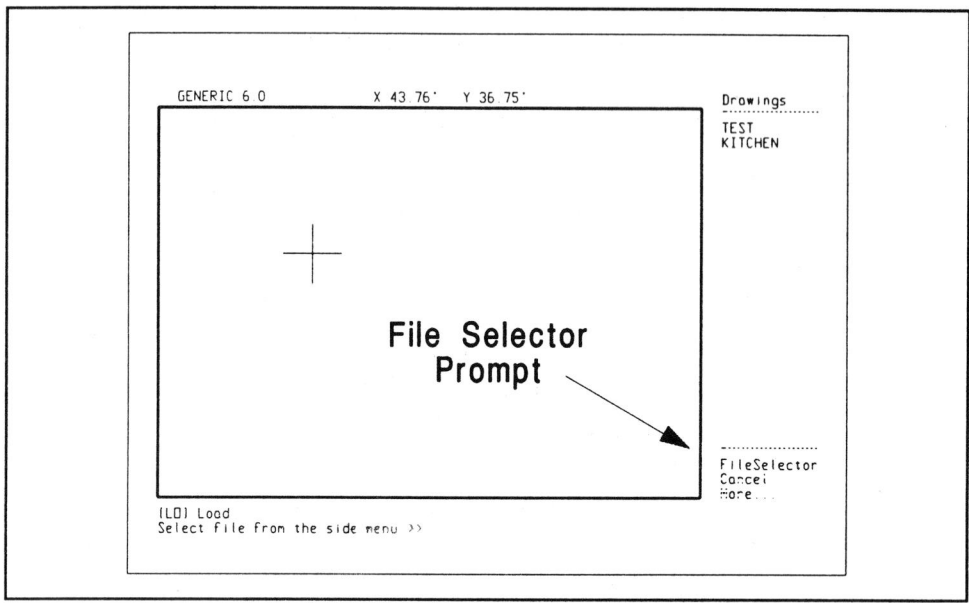

Figure 14.14 The File Selector prompt on the CADD 6.0 screen.

With the File Selector, you can search for a specific file by name and extension (such as FLORPLAN.GCD), or a wide range of files by their extensions:

Drawings (*.GCD)
Components (*.CMP)
Fonts (*.FNT)
Batch Files (*.MCR)
Hatches (*.HCH)
Menus (*.MNU)
Shell Files (*.EXE or *.COM)
Text Files (*.DOC or *.TPR)
Autocad Drawings (*.DWG)
DXF Files (*.DXF)

You can also review their size and creation date. With the Search option, you can search through the specified drive for any type of file. For instance, if your file specification is .GCD for drawings and you select the search command, CADD 6 finds the next directory with drawing files. Press search again and it searches until it finds another directory with drawing files.

Another advantage of using the File Selector is multiple file loading. In the case of components, more than one file is usually needed in the drawing. From the File Selector, the desired symbols can be tagged (marked with an arrow), and all the tagged files are loaded into CADD 6 at one time with the *Load* selection. Once the components are loaded into CADD 6, they are listed on the sidebar menu when the Component Place (CP) command is executed.

The File Selector program is a CADD 6 smart utility. The key features available in the File Selector depend upon the operation being performed at the time it's accessed. The following is a list of File Selector features available when accessed arbitrarily, when loading components and attributes, or when loading files other than components and attributes:

Arbitrarily:	Components and Attributes:	Other Files:
Rescan	Load	Delete
Search	Tag	Move
File Mask	Untag	Copy
Sort by	Tag All	Rename
File Info		Tag
New Drive		Untag
Help		Tag All
Exit		Mkdir
		RmDir

These functions are explained in detail under File Selector in the CADD 6 Reference Guide, as well as in the CADD 6 program's Online Help.

Object Information (OI)

The Object Information (OI) feature lists specific information about a selected object or objects. The information appears on a separate text screen when the object(s) are selected. The order objects are placed in CADD 6 determines the order in which they're displayed on the Object Information (OI) screen, if multiple objects are selected.

When Object Information (OI) is selected from the UTILITIES menu, you are prompted to select a single object in your drawing. If the 2-letter command (OI) is entered, you are prompted with a selection set, allowing you to select and list the information on multiple objects.

Specific information varies with the types of objects displayed. This information is displayed for all objects:

Object type
ID# (record number in CADD 6 database)
Number of data points
Color
Layer
Line type
Line width

The remaining information displayed depends upon the type of object. For instance, a 2-point Circle (C2) includes the following information after Line Width:

Location of the circle's center (*X* and *Y* coordinates)
Location of point 2 (*X* and *Y* coordinates)
Radius
Diameter
Circumference

For a Line, the information after Width includes:

Location of point 1 (*X* and *Y* coordinates)
Location of point 2 (*X* and *Y* coordinates)
Length
Angle

Entity Filter (EF)

For editing commands that do not have selection sets associated with them, such as Window Move (WM), use the Filter (EF) command to trap objects with specific characteristics for editing. First, use the Filter (EF) command to filter-out the entities to be influenced. An example might be all circles of color 12 and line width 3. Once the filter has been specified, type WM for Window Move (WM), and place a window around the entire drawing. The only entities that are affected by the Window Move (WM) command are the filtered entities enclosed by the window.

Selection (SE)

The Selection (SE) command by itself is passive, and can only select objects, not act upon them. The Selection (SE) command has the Filter (EF) command built into it, just as the EDIT commands which use a selection set. The combination of Selection (SE) with the Filter (EF) option lets you select a group of objects in a drawing based on their location, type, and characteristics.

Selection (SE) can be used to select specific entities to be used as a list when "Listing Objects In Drawing" with Screen Flip (SF). You can also select a group of objects, which can be used in a command with a selection prompt, when the Last Selection option is picked.

Match (MH)

The Match (MH) command is a real time-saver that lets you match the parameters of any object on the screen. You can match all the variable settings of text, dimensions, hatches, components, and basic entities.

To use the Match (MH) command, simply type MH or select Match (MH) from the menu, and select an object on the screen to match. CADD 6 sets all the appropriate settings. If you select a line, all the variables of that line are set to match that line. These variables include the line color, line width, line type, and the line's current layer setting. If you selected a component, the component's layer, scale, and rotation would be set to match the selected component. This command works just as well with text and dimension settings.

Shell Exe (SH)

During the drawing process, you may need to exit CADD 6 momentarily and go to another program or DOS. It can greatly hinder productivity to leave CADD 6 in the middle of a drawing and later try to pick up where you left off. With the Shell (SH) command you can exit CADD 6 to check system parameters, run other programs, copy files, or extract information from other sources in your system. Once the secondary task is completed, you can pick up where you left off with your CADD 6 drawing.

The Shell (SH) command unloads CADD 6 and your drawing from memory allowing room for another program to run.

Execute the Shell command by typing SH or selecting Shell from the menu. After executing the Shell command, select a file from the side-bar menu, the File Selector, or type the name of the file on the command line. You may have to specify the full path name of the file if it's in a different directory, or select a directory from the sidebar menu or File Selector.

> **TIP:** You should save your drawing before shelling-out of CADD 6.0 in case of a system crash. A crash could be caused by conflicting memory between CADD 6.0 and CADD 6.0 executed during the Shelling process. It's always a good idea to save your work periodically.

Once a file is selected, you will be prompted to enter the parameter. At this point, type in any appropriate parameter, such as the name of the file you want to use in CADD 6 to which you are shelling. When you exit the secondary program, you automatically return to CADD 6.

If you want to shell to a DOS prompt, select C:\COMMAND.COM as the file to run. To run a DOS batch file, select C:\COMMAND.COM as the file to run, and enter the name of the batch file as the parameter.

Fast Text View (TV)

This command works in conjunction with the Fast Text option in the Fast Redraw (FA) command. When the Fast Text option is selected, text converts to points on the screen during the first redraw. An individual text character is represented by a single point, and a string of text is represented by a single line. If you want to view the text currently represented by points, but you do not want to turn OFF the Fast Text mode, you can use the Fast Text View (TV) command.

To use the Fast Text View command, type TV or select View Fast Text (TV) from the menu. You will be prompted to place a window around the points or lines representing the text on your drawing screen that you wish to view. Once you've placed the window, the text becomes visible and stays visible until the next Redraw (RD) takes place.

This command is only temporary, and is used to help you modify existing text. Even in the Fast Text mode, text can be modified, you just can't see all the text characters on the screen. Make sure when placing the Fast Text View (TV) window, that the point or points to view are completely enclosed by the window. To view a string of text, enclose its reference point in a selection window. If Reference Points (PR) display is ON, you should see an asterisk (*) at one end of the line. This is the point the Fast Text View (TV) window should enclose. (See Figure 14.15.)

Set Limits (LS)

The Limits (LS) command is basically used to set the extents for the Zoom Limits (ZL) command. The limits are set relative to the drawing origin, usually to encompass the amount of area within which you intend to work. If you happen to be out of the main work area and wish to quickly view the drawing within the extents of the set limits, type ZL. If you wish to view everything in the entire drawing, type ZA (Zoom All).

The Limits (LS) command has no affect on anything in your drawing other than the Zoom Limits (ZL) command. If you think you are going to create a drawing that's 20' wide by 10' high, you might want to set your Limits to 22' by 12'. This gives you a small border around your drawing when you use the Zoom Limits (ZL) command.

To define limits, type LS or select Limits (LS) from the UTILITIES menu. You are first prompted for the height of the limits. This is the distance along the Y-axis. Type 12'. Next, you will be prompted for the width of the limits. This is the distance on the X-axis. In this case, type 22'. If you use the ZL (Zoom Limits) command to zoom-to the limits, you are able to draw a rectangle that is 10' high by 20' wide on the drawing screen and still be able to see it without any of the drawing going off the screen.

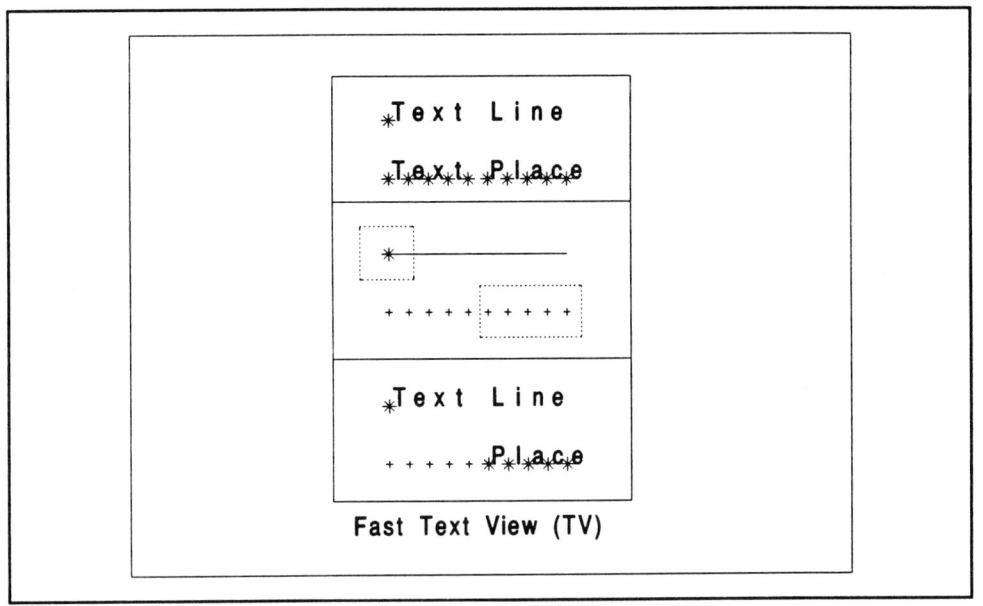

Figure 14.15 Selecting text in a Fast Text View window.

Drawing Origin (DO)

The Drawing Origin (DO) command is used to change the position of the coordinate origin point within the current drawing. To use this command, type DO or select Drawing Origin (DO) from the menu. When you type DO, you will see the message:

!! Warning !! This command cannot be UNDONE - continue? (Y/N)>>

Type Y to continue. The next prompt asks you to enter a new origin. Place a point elsewhere on the screen for the new origin. Use a snap command to place the new drawing origin on an existing point. You must realize that if you change the drawing origin's position, you will affect other variables. The Zoom Limits (ZL) command uses the origin as the lower-left corner of its extents. The screen centers for Named Views (NV) are also relative to the drawing origin. If you are currently in the Manual Entry Basepoint (MB) mode, you may not want to change the drawing origin, since it is relative to the drawing origin.

MACROS AND BATCH FILES

The creation of macros and batch files is covered in greater detail in Chapter 15. The following is a brief description of the commands: Save Batch (SB), Select Save Batch (BS), and Macro Assign (MA).

Save Batch (SB)

With the Save Batch (SB) command, you can save your current drawing to an ASCII batch file. This saves your drawing as a series of CADD 6 commands and definitions with locations and other pertinent variable settings. The batch file can be examined and modified with a text editor. A batch file is saved as a .MCR file, and can have information extracted from it by other software.

A batch file does not save hatches, fills, or unsaved components. The name of the component is saved in the batch file, but if the component has not been saved to disk, it will not be available when the batch file is run at a later time. Be sure to save your components before doing a Save Batch (SB).

To execute Save Batch (SB), either type SB or select Save Batch (SB) from the menu. A default name appears on the command line. This is usually the current drawing name. If you want to save the batch file under the default name, press Enter. If you want to save it under a different name, type in the new name. You may also have to type in the drive and directory to which to save the batch file. The .MCR file extension is automatically added to the batch file name.

Selection Batch Save (BS)

The Selection Batch Save (BS) command works in the same manner as the Save Batch (SB) command. The only difference between the two is the selection set prompt found, used for the Selection Batch Save (BS) command. This allows you to save specific sections and entity types to a batch file. Besides the selection set prompt, the Selection Batch Save (BS) command works identically to the Save Batch (SB) command. To use this command, either type BS or pick Selection Batch Save (BS) from the menu.

Macro Assign (MA)

The Macro Assign (MA) command lets you assign a macro to a function or pointing device button. A macro can be anything from a two-letter command to a total of 255 characters that combine several commands. The macro is executed by pressing the key to which the macro is assigned. By placing the NP (Snap Nearest Point) command on a button of your pointing device, you have created a macro. Using combinations of the two and three-letter commands, fairly complex macros can be created without exceeding the 255 character limit.

To assign a macro, either type MA or select Macro Assign (MA) from the menu. If a macro is currently present on the selected button or key, you will be prompted to edit that macro. Enter or edit the sequence of keystrokes you wish to assign to the key or button. Press Enter when you have completed the macro.

Macros can be assigned to 12 function keys, if available, including combinations of the function keys using the shift, alt, and ctrl keys in unison with the function keys. This gives a possible total of 48 macros assigned to function keys. A possible 14 macros can be assigned to your pointing device. You are given 16 choices, but do not forget, the first two buttons on your pointing device are reserved for pointing to the screen and menu and cannot have macros assigned to them.

Bill of Materials (Bl)

Select the Bill of Materials (BI) command to create a quick and simple Bill of Materials for insertion into the current drawing. The default Bill of Materials lists the names of the components in the drawing and quantity of each. This list is entered into the drawing as a component. The default BOM format can be changed from within the Bill of Materials program. Enter the BOM program by selecting Shell to BOM from the UTILITIES menu.

Shell to BOM. This feature does not have a corresponding two-letter command, it must be selected from the UTILITIES menu. This feature works the same as executing the SH (Shell) command, and entering BOM at the parameter prompt. (See the Shell command discussed earlier in this chapter.) The full BOM functionality is available when Shell to BOM is selected. When you quit the BOM program, you are returned to CADD 6.

For more extensive information of the BOM program, refer to the CADD 6's User Guide.

CHAPTER SUMMARY

The commands found on the UTILITIES menu allow you to go beyond the normal scope of a manually drafted drawing, giving you the power to extract and manipulate information from the drawing itself. These features go a long way to increase your drafting and design productivity. With the commands on the UTILITIES menu, you can speed up the drawing process as well as display information derived from the drawing in a usable format.

CHAPTER 15

Menus, Macros, and Batch Files

CUSTOMIZING CADD 6

The first section of this chapter will cover the rules used to create command sequences for macros, batch files, and slide shows. The last section will discuss creating video and digitizer menus. All menu commands will also be covered in this chapter.

Macros are a combination of CADD 6 commands that can be executed by a single action, either by selecting a function key or menu option, or by loading a batch file. The commands in the macro are executed exactly as they were entered, in the order they were entered.

Macros use combinations of CADD 6's two-letter commands along with some special macro programming commands and characters. There are three different methods of implementation: keyboard macros, menus, and batch files.

The three types of macros differ in how they are created, activated, and how much work they can do. Macros can contain anything you can enter into the program from the keyboard. All three macro types share certain command basics, but require different formats depending on the method used to activate them.

Keyboard Macros

Keyboard macros are created and edited within CADD 6. The commands that make up a keyboard macro are executed by pressing a pointing device button, a function key, or a combination of the Alt, Ctrl, or Shift key with a function key.

Keyboard macros can be assigned to the function keys by themselves or the function keys combined with the Shift, Alt, and Ctrl keys. In other words, one function key can have up to four macros assigned to it; 1) F1, 2) Shift+F1, 3) Alt+F1, and 4) Ctrl+F1. If you have 12 function keys, you could assign up to 48 macros to the function keys. Macros can also be assigned to buttons on your pointing device excluding buttons 1 and 2, since the first button is used to select points on the screen, and the second is used to make menu selections.

Keyboard macros are often used to assign commonly used commands to specific keys, such as snaps, toggles, and edit commands. They might be commands that are hard to remember or that lend themselves to a specific group. With the function keys, you could have four separate groups of commands, separated by the shift, alt, and ctrl keys. You might want to put all of the snap commands on the standard function keys, text commands on the shift+function keys, and component and attribute commands on the alt+function keys.

A keyboard macro must be on one line and have a maximum of 255 characters. All commands must be separated by a comma, and the macro must end with a semicolon. The program automatically places a semicolon at the end of a macro.

To assign a keyboard macro, either type MA (Macro Assign) or use the Screen Flip (SF) feature. To execute a macro, just press the function key or pointer button to which it is assigned.

An example of how a keyboard macro might look in CADD 6:

   MR,UN,I,GS,.5,.5,SG,++;

This macro turns the Manual Entry Relative (MR) mode on, sets Units (UN) to inches, the X and Y Grid Size (GS) to 0.5 inch, and forces the Snap Grid (SG) toggle on.

> **TIP:** Creating keyboard macros within CADD 6 is a great way to test macros out for later use in menus and batch files.

Menu Macros

Menu macros are accessed from the video or digitizer menus. CADD 6 menus are just ASCII files, created and edited in a word processor or text editor. A menu macro is executed by selecting an item from the video menu or a digitizer menu. Working with menus is covered more extensively later in this chapter, in the section on Video Menus.

Batch Files

A batch file is a *super macro* that can contain a long list of commands and macros. Every command in the batch file is executed, sequentially, when the batch is loaded. A menu macro can be created to load a batch file when selected.

Batch files are created using either a word processor or text editor, and must be saved as an ASCII file. Batch files can also be created from within CADD 6 by using the Save Batch (SB) or (SAB) command. CADD 6 saves the current drawing as a sequential list of commands and data, required to re-create the drawing if the batch file is loaded.

> **TIP:** Create a template drawing in CADD 6 and save it as a batch file. Modify the batch file in your text editor, adding user input items and variables. This turns the template into a parametric drawing, prompting for user input.

A batch file accepts an unlimited amount of command lines, allowing 255 characters per line. Each line must be followed by a semicolon. When executed, the program moves through each line sequentially until it reaches the end of the file. Commands do not have to be in one continuous line as with keyboard macros. For editing purposes, you may want to separate individual commands for more clarity.

Batch files must have the extension .MCR after the batch file name. CADD 6 only accepts .MCR files for batch files. To run a batch file, you need to use the Load (LO) command and select Batch file for the Load submenu. If a batch file has been incorporated into a menu, it can be selected from the menu.

An example of how a batch file might look in a text editor:

```
MR;
UN,I;
GS,.5,.5;
SG,++;
```

This batch file performs the same operations as the keyboard macro in the example above. It turns the Manual Entry Relative (MR) mode on, sets Units (UN) to inches, the Grid Size (GS) to 0.5 inches, and forces the Snap Grid (SG) toggle ON.

SPECIAL CHARACTERS USED IN MACROS AND BATCH FILES

There are special characters used in the creation of macros and batch files. This section lists these characters and gives examples of how to use them.

Comma (,)

The comma is used to separate commands, data, and special characters. The comma also acts as an Enter key. For example, create a macro that sets line, text color, and fill color using the Color Setting (CS) command.

>   CS,L,12,T,14,F,13!;

This sequence of commands automatically invokes the Color Setting (CS) command and sets the color of lines (L) to 12, text (T) to 14, and fills (F) to 13.

You can see that the comma separates the commands and it acts like the Enter key. If you manually typed CS, selected L, and entered 12, you would have to press the Enter key for the program to accept the 12.

Tilde (~)

The tilde prompts you to enter a single value or name. For example, you could use it to prompt for scale and rotation when calling up a component. You could construct a sequence of commands that first prompt you for the scale of the component, then the rotation, and then the component's name.

>   CZ,~,~,CR,~,CP,~;

The first operation in this sequence of commands is the command for Component Scale (CZ). This is followed by two tildes, used to prompt you to enter the values for the X- and Y-scale factors. After the last scale factor has been entered, you are prompted for the rotation of the component. After that, you are prompted for the name of the component and where you want it placed on the screen.

In place of the tilde characters, you could place preset values. If you always wanted the scale to be set to 1, you would change the command line to:

>   CZ,1,1,CR,~,CP,~;

At Sign (@)

The *at sign* prompts you to place a point either with the keyboard or your mouse. You might want to create a sequence of commands that move a selected entity 1 inch in the positive *X* direction.

>   OM,@,0,0,1,0;

This sequence of commands first invokes the Object Move (OM) command, which prompts you to select an object to move. The *at sign* allows you to point to and select the object. Normally, you are prompted for a reference point, but it is set to 0,0 in the macro. Then, the new location of the reference point is set to 1,0, which moves the object 1 inch horizontally to the right.

Pound Sign (#)

The pound sign acts like the Escape key. Some commands require you to press the Esc key to exit the command. Commands used to place text are a good example of this type of command. You can set up a sequence of commands that places your name in a location you specify. In this case, use the Text Line (TL) command.

    TL,@,YOUR NAME,#;

The first command TL, followed by the at sign prompts you to specify a point on your screen to start the line of text. Once this point is placed, the following text characters, YOUR NAME, are placed automatically. The text is followed by the pound sign which acts like the escape key and aborts the TL command.

Semicolon (;)

The semicolon is the *end of line* indicator. A semicolon must be placed at the end of any sequence of commands used to create a batch file or macro. Anything after the semicolon is ignored. To keep track of the type of macros or batch files you've created, you can enter remarks after the semicolon for future reference.

    MR,L1,0,0,1,0; Note: 1" Line from last point

Exclamation Point (!)

The exclamation point acts like the Enter key. When the command sequence runs into the exclamation point, it is the same as pressing the Enter key. One example of this could be creating a sequence of commands that types your name on the screen, spaces down two lines, and types in your company name.

    TL,@,YOUR NAME!!COMPANY,#;

The TL command and the @ sign prompt you for a point on the screen to begin the text. Once you pick a point, your name is typed in. The two exclamation points cause the text line to space down twice.

At this point, the name of your company is entered, followed by the pound sign which aborts the command.

Chapter 15: Menus, Macros and Batch Files

> **TIP:** Notice that there are no commas. A comma would be treated like the Enter key in this case, and would cause extra spaces between the text.

Forward Slash (/)

The forward slash deactivates special characters. If you wished your macro or batch file to automatically enter text that contained any of the special characters such as commas, exclamation points, and so on, you would need to use the forward slash just before the special character. If you want to use the forward slash itself, you must enter the forward slash twice: //.

Forces Toggle ON (++)

Any toggle command followed by a comma and ++ is turned ON, no matter what the current mode is of the toggle. Without this feature you could never be sure whether you were switching a toggle command ON or OFF.

OR,++;

This ensures that the Ortho Mode (OR) is ON.

Forces Toggle OFF (--)

If you can force a toggle ON, you will certainly want the ability to force a toggle OFF. This is done by following a toggle command with a comma and --.

OR,--;

This ensures that the Ortho Mode (OR) is OFF.

The force ON (++) and OFF (--) features only work with toggle commands. They have no effect anywhere else in the command sequence.

MORE ON BATCH FILES

Batch files and macros are very much alike, as you've seen in the previous section of this chapter. But because batch files can be created in or out of the program, they deserve more consideration.

In CADD 6, a batch file is just a list, or batch program, of CADD 6 commands that accomplish a particular task, such as setting up parameters or creating a drawing. You can generate batch files from within CADD 6 by using the Save Batch (SB) or Save (SAB) commands, or from outside CADD 6 by using any text editor or word processor. Batch files are primarily used for automating tasks such as setting up variables for dimensioning, or creating template drawings of borders and title blocks that are used frequently.

More experienced users create custom CADD 6 applications by using batch files. The batch file is actually a text version of the instructions CADD 6 needs to create a drawing. Since the instruction set can be created (and edited) from completely outside of CADD 6, you can take data from another source and turn it into a batch file that creates a drawing. For example, surveyor's notes could be used to create a batch file that draws the plot surveyed.

Trying to create a batch file from scratch in a word processor or text editor can be difficult the first time, because you have to be sure to enter every command in the proper format. To make it easier, CADD 6 can get you started. Begin by creating a drawing using many of the commands and options you use frequently and want to have in your batch file. In addition to saving this drawing as a .GCD file, also save it as a batch file with the Save Batch (SB) command. CADD 6 saves your file with a .MCR extension, which signifies that it is a batch file.

Once you have automatically created a batch file, you can exit CADD 6 and call up this file inside a word processor or text editor. All the commands in your drawing have been saved to an ASCII file. Modify this file to meet your needs, or repeat the process with a new drawing, saving it as a batch file.

Many people use .MCR files to pre-define a series of command settings. If you start each drawing by setting the same parameters, using a batch file saves you time. Once the batch file is created, you no longer have to enter each command individually. Here is a sample batch file of command options:

```
LS,25',25'; (limit screen size to 25 feet by 25 feet)
GS,.25,.25; (grid size 1/4 inch)
DI,Z,0,!; (cursor size, set to limits)
SG,++; (snap to grid)
TS,F,MAIN,!; (Text Settings, Font, MAIN)
```

You can also establish parameters for dimensioning variables, text options, line options (color, type, and width), and so on. Anything you do repetitively in many drawings should be automated with a batch file.

To load a batch file from within CADD 6, type LO (Load) and then type B to select Batch file. Enter the name of the batch file, or select the name from the sidebar menu. The sequence of commands in the batch file is executed in the program.

To load the batch file from DOS, start in your CADD 6 subdirectory, C:\CADD6 or wherever you installed CADD 6. From the DOS prompt,

Type: CADD dwgfile batchfile (and press Enter)

Where:

    CADD   - starts CADD 6
    dwgfile   - is the file name of the drawing to load; it does not have to be an existing drawing
    batchfile - is the file name of the batch file to load

For example, to start CADD 6, load a drawing named HOUSE, and run a batch file named SETUP, type:

CADD house setup (and press Enter)

If you wish to interrupt a macro or batch program that is running, press the Escape key. The control key (ctrl) and S key pressed simultaneously (CTRL-S) also interrupts batch programs. When a batch file is interrupted, you are given three options:

(A)   Abort - returns you to normal CADD 6 operation.

(P)   Pause - lets you break away from the batch file and allows you to perform normal CADD 6 operations. You must press CTRL-S to continue the batch file or abort it completely.

(C)   Continue - continues the batch file from where it was interrupted.

SLIDE SHOWS

CADD 6 lets you save any drawing as an *image* with the Save (SAI) command (provided you configured CADD 6 to have image capability for your video selection). An image is an exact copy of the screen in pixel format, similar to what a paint or draw program uses. In CADD 6, these images are saved to disk with the file extension .GX2. When you type in SA and select I to save an image, you are asked if you want to save the entire screen (Y/N). If you select Yes, the entire image on the screen is saved. If you select No, the graphics screen is displayed without the video menu, command and status line, or coordinate display. You can load images into CADD 6 with the Load (LO,I) command. The images are displayed on-screen, but you cannot modify or edit them with CADD 6 commands because they are not a true CADD 6 drawing.

Images can be thought of as slides taken of CADD 6 drawings. You can create a series of images to be put together in a slide show that is controlled with a CADD 6 batch file. When you finish saving some images, build a CADD 6 batch file in a word processor, or create a macro that links your slides in a format like the one that follows:

Macro:

    LO,I,SLIDE1,LO,I,SLIDE2,LO,I,SLIDE3;

Batch File:

    LO,I,SLIDE1;
    LO,I,SLIDE2;
    LO,I,SLIDE3;

To control the delay time between slides, use the Wait Batch (WB) command. The Wait Batch command should be placed after each slide that requires the specified delay. Any value used with the Wait Batch command is considered to be in seconds. The format for using the Wait Batch command is as follows:

    Slide Name,WB,nn

Where nn is the delay time, in seconds.

Using the previous slide show batch file and adding a 3-second delay time between slides, you end up with the following batch file:

    LO,I,SLIDE1,WB,3;
    LO,I,SLIDE2,WB,3;
    LO,I,SLIDE3;

The last line does not require a Wait Batch (WB) command. The last slide shown remains present until the screen is refreshed. The screen is refreshed by any of the Zoom commands or a Redraw (RD).

ADVANCED PROGRAMMING

CADD 6 provides programming commands that go beyond the previously discussed macro commands. These commands offer more power and control over the program, enabling you to tailor CADD 6 to a specific application. These features make use of variables and expressions, allow you to work with files on disk, control the flow of execution from one line to another, select and examine entities parametrically, issue and respond to prompts, and control the screen display.

Extensive documentation of these commands can be found in the CADD 6 Customization Guide.

Chapter 15: Menus, Macros and Batch Files

This section discusses the available math functions that can be use within CADD 6, like add, subtract, multiply, and divide. You can extract absolute values, natural logs, exponents, squares and square roots. Also included are trigonometric functions like sine, cosine, and tangent. These features can be used in the program directly to set variables, or in batch files and macros.

The variable $val is also covered in this section. With the use of this one variable, simple but powerful macros can be generated in CADD 6.

The chart below describes the math functions currently found in CADD 6, and shows how they are used:

DESCRIPTION	PROGRAM NOTATION
Addition	+
Subtraction	-
Multiplication	*
Division	/
Sine	$sin()
Cosine	$cos()
Tangent	$tan()
Arctangent	$atn()
Natural Exponential	$exp()
Natural Log	$ln()
Square	$sqr()
Square Root	$sqt()
System Numeric Variable	$val
System String Variable	$str

Algebraic Functions

To perform algebraic operations in the program, you first need a variable to use. Setting text size is a good example of setting a variable for a parameter, TZ (Text Size) in this case. This example uses math functions to set the text size.

Example: Your Text Size (TZ) is currently 0.12 inches. You now wish to enter text (3X) this size. Instead of calculating and entering this value yourself, let CADD 6 do it for you:

Type: TSZ (for Text Size)
Type: 3*.12 (and press Enter)

The value for Text Size (TSZ) changes to 0.36 and is displayed in brackets next to the Text heading.

Press Enter to accept the new value

Variables that require a numeric value can be defined with any of the listed math functions. You can define the fillet radius, rotation values, text settings, dimension settings, scale values, and so on. A string of functions can also be used to set variables. Take the last example for instance, to set the text size. At the prompt for text size:

Type: 5+10-3*2/6 (and press Enter)

To ensure that this complex statement is performed in the correct order, you could separate the functions by parentheses, as follows:

Type: (5+10-3)*(2/6) (and press Enter)

This equation changes your text height to 4.

Square and Square Root Functions. Any of the math functions in the previous list that end with parentheses, must use parentheses to enclose the variable. For example, if you wanted your text height to equal 4^2, you would use the square function at the text height prompt as follows:

$sqr(4)

This results in a text height of 16.

The next step is to use some of these functions in macros. For the next example, let's calculate the hypotenuse of a right triangle. The equation used to determine the length of the sides of a right triangle is:

$a^2 + b^2 = c^2$

where a and b are the legs of the triangle and c represents the hypotenuse. (See Figure 15.1.) Solving the equation for c, you end up with the equation:

c = square root of ($a^2 + b^2$)

In a macro, this equation could then be entered as:

$sqt($sqr(a)+$sqr(b))

Calculate the hypotenuse of a right triangle where a=4, and b=2 as follows:

$sqt($sqr(4)+$sqr(2))

This equation calculates 4.472 for the length of the hypotenuse.

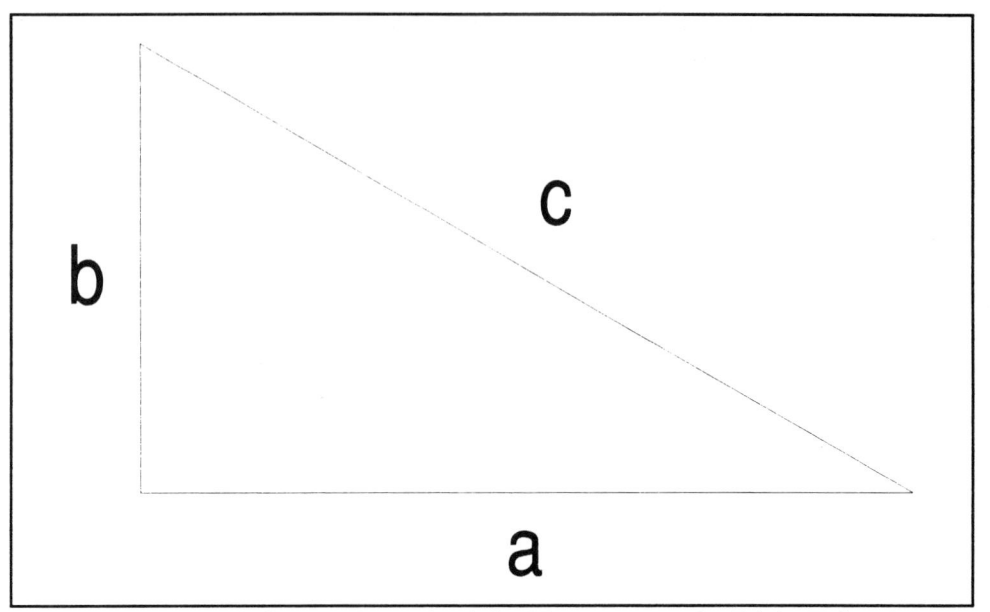

Figure 15.1 Calculating the Length of the Hypotenuse of a Right Triangle.

System Variable ($VAL)

To make the math features more interesting, we can use the system variable ($val). This variable takes on the value of the last variable set. The system variable can be extracted from program settings such as: Fillet Radius (FR), Component Rotate (CR), Shoulder Length (LL), and Component Scale (CZ). You can experiment to find other available variables if the need arises. The variables listed are enough to get you started.

You need a variable extraction feature to make your equations and macros work on a broader scale. It's OK to use math equations to set variables like text size, but you may want to place multiple points on the screen, like a sine wave, or rotate a component in multiples of 45 degrees before actually placing it.

In the information to follow, you extract and implement the current system variable in macros used to rotate components (on-the-fly) in 45 degree increments. You also learn how to create macros that scale components (on-the-fly) up and down and draw spirals and parabolas.

The system variable extracts the last variable entered into the program. If you've just completed setting the Component Rotation (CR) variable to 60, then the current system variable ($val) is 60. At this point, if you run any macros or equations using $val, the number 60 would be input everywhere $val was used. Run through the next examples on paper, and try them out in CADD 6 to get a better feel for how to take advantage of $val.

Using Manual Entry Modes with Macros

When running macros used to position points in a mathematically defined path, such as a parabolic curve or sine wave, be sure to set the drawing mode to MO, Manual Entry Offset Origin. These equations place points relative to a single origin. In MO mode, all point coordinates are defined relative to the screen origin, point 0,0 in the drawing. In order to see the screen origin, the Reference Point (PR) toggle must be on. The screen origin appears on the screen as an asterisk (*).

If you are in the MR mode (Manual Entry Offset Relative) while running a macro, each point is placed on the screen relative to the last point entered. This means the *reference point* changes with each new point entered. You should experiment with different drawing modes. Some macros may be easier to write for MR mode, while others are best in MO mode.

Example Macros

Automatic Component Rotate (45° Intervals). This example macro lets you select a component and rotate it in 45° intervals. The macro is then assigned to the F1 function key.

> Type: MA (for Macro Assign) to assign the macro to a function key
> Select F1 as the function key to assign the macro

Enter the following equation exactly as it's printed here:

> Type: CR,$val+45 (and press Enter)

TIP: CADD 6 automatically attaches a semicolon to the end of each macro line.

If you view the macro with the Screen Flip (SF) function, or edit that function key with the Macro Assign (MA) command, you see a statement that looks like this:

> CR,$val+45;

Every time you press the F1 function key, the Component Rotation (CR) variable is set to 45° plus the current value of the system variable. If the last system variable setting was the Component Rotation (CR) variable, preferably set at 0 for the initial setting, then the component's ghost image appears on the screen, attached to your cursor, at an angle of 0°. If you press the F1 key, the rotation of the component changes to 45°; press F1 again, and the rotation increments 45° to 90°. If the last CR value is 90° then the next is 135° and so on. By automatically setting a new rotation value, you automatically reset $val.

Component Scale (Step-Up by Increments Of 0.5). The following macro scales up a selected component by 50%.

>Type: MA (for Macro Assign) to assign the macro to a function key
>Select F2 as the function key to assign this macro

Enter the following equation, exactly as it's printed here:

>Type: CZ,$val+.5,$val (and press Enter)

Every time you press the F2 function key, the Component Scale (CZ) command adds 0.5 to the current scale value, increasing the size of the component by 50%. In this case, we're using CZ to set the $val variable. Notice, if you type CZ to set Component Scale, and enter the first value (X-axis scale factor), the second value (Y-axis scale factor) defaults to equal the first. So, in the macro equation, you increment the first value, but not the second, otherwise the second value would always be 0.5 greater than the first. This is a good example of how $val extracts the value of the last variable entered into the program. It can change during the course of the equation, depending on how the command receives data.

Set Component Scale (CZ) to an *X* value of 1 and *Y* value of 1. Bring in a component and its image is displayed at a scale factor of 1. Press the F2 key and watch the display. The component steps up in size by 50%. Press F2 again, and the component steps up in size again.

If you stepped the component up too far, you need to step it down somehow, so now you need to create a component scale step-down macro.

Component Scale (Step-Down by Increments Of 0.5). The following macro scales down a selected component by 50%.

>Type: MA (for Macro Assign)
>Select F3 as the function key to assign the macro
>Type: CZ,$val-.5,$val (and press Enter)

Every time you press the F3 function key, the Component Scale (CZ) command subtracts 0.5 from the current scale value. The only difference between this macro and the step-up macro is the -0.5 value in the equation.

With these three macros, the on-the-fly component rotate, step-up, and step-down macros, you used math functions to enhance the production power of CADD 6. The next set of macros use some simple math functions to help you place points on the screen in a spiral and parabolic fashion.

Drawing a Parabola. The parabolic shape symbolizes the path of objects in flight under the influence of gravity. This shape has also been used to design reflective surfaces such as automobile head lights and flashlights. A reflective parabolic surface reflects and directs light, making it a valuable and commonly used shape. The basic algebraic formula for a parabolic curve is:

$$x = y^2$$

As this formula sits, you end up with half a parabola about the Y-axis. (See Figure 15.2.) If you mirror the first section about the y axis, you create a complete parabola. (See Figure 15.3.)

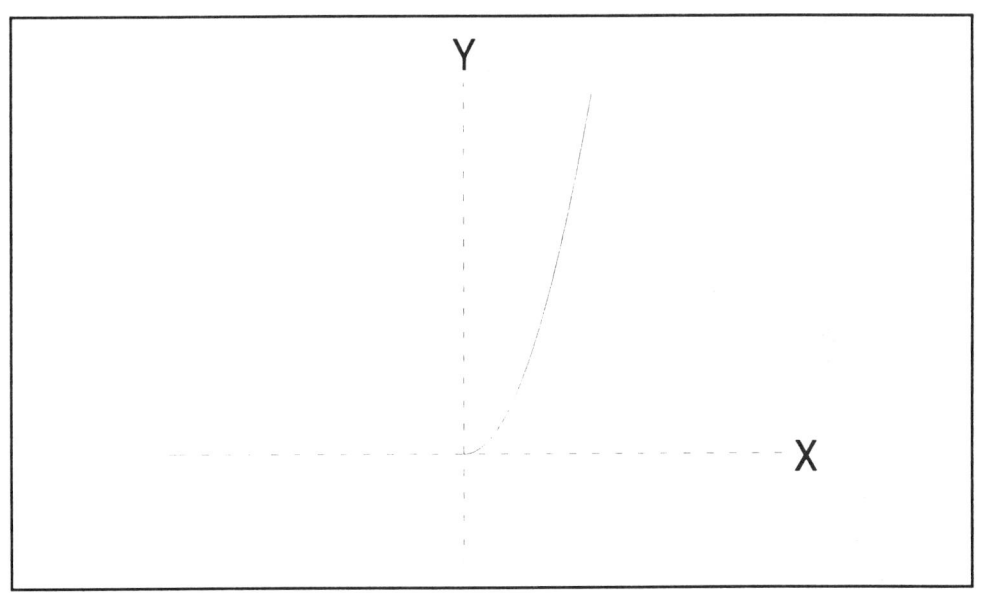

Figure 15.2 Drawing a Parabola in CADD 6.

Here is the macro that draws a parabola in CADD 6. Using the procedure described above, assign this macro to the F4 function key:

    P0,$val,$sqr($val),LL,$val+.05

By breaking down this equation into its elemental parts, you can get a better idea of how this macro works:

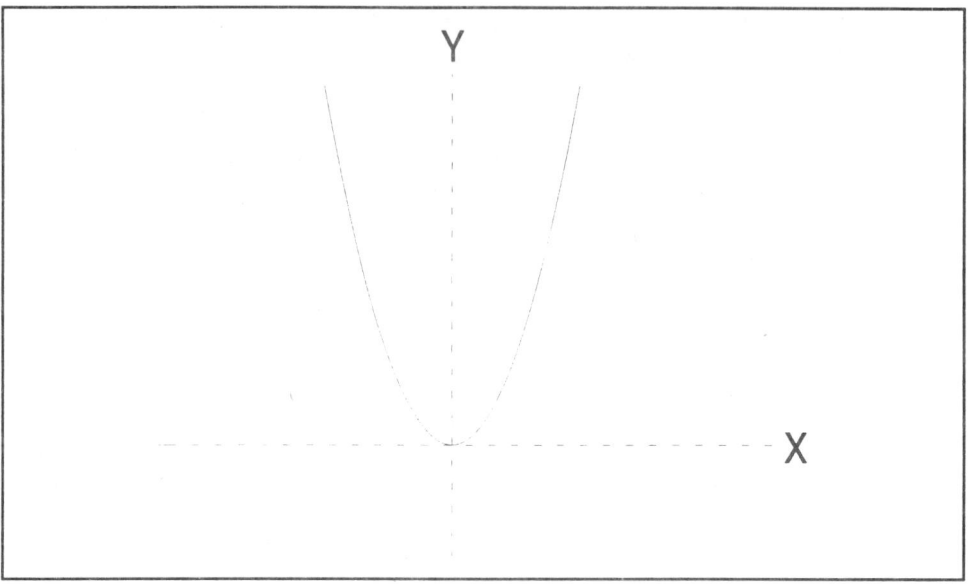

Figure 15.3 The complete Parabola.

PO - In any equation where the user is prompted to specify a point, it's a good idea to initially start out marking these positions on the screen with a Point (PO) command. Once you are confident the macro is working properly, try changing PO to other entities, such as the Bezier Curve (BV), Double Lines (L2), Rectangle (RE), 2-Point Circle (C2), or use an existing component.

Experiment with different entities and view your changes on screen. (See Figure 15.4.) If you want to try a component in this example, create a circle with a diameter of 0.1. Fill the circle with the Object Fill (OF) command. Create a component out of the filled circle with the reference point at the center of the circle. Name the component DOT. To use the component in place of a point, line, or curve, write the macro as follows:

    CP,dot,$val,$sqr($val),LL,$val+.05

$val, $sqr($val) - These values represent the X and Y coordinate values entered at the command line to place points on the screen. If the current $val equals 2, then the X coordinate equals 2, and the Y coordinate equals 4. If X equals 3, then Y equals 9 and so on.

LL - It probably seems odd to use the Shoulder Length command in this macro, but it was chosen because it solves these two problems:

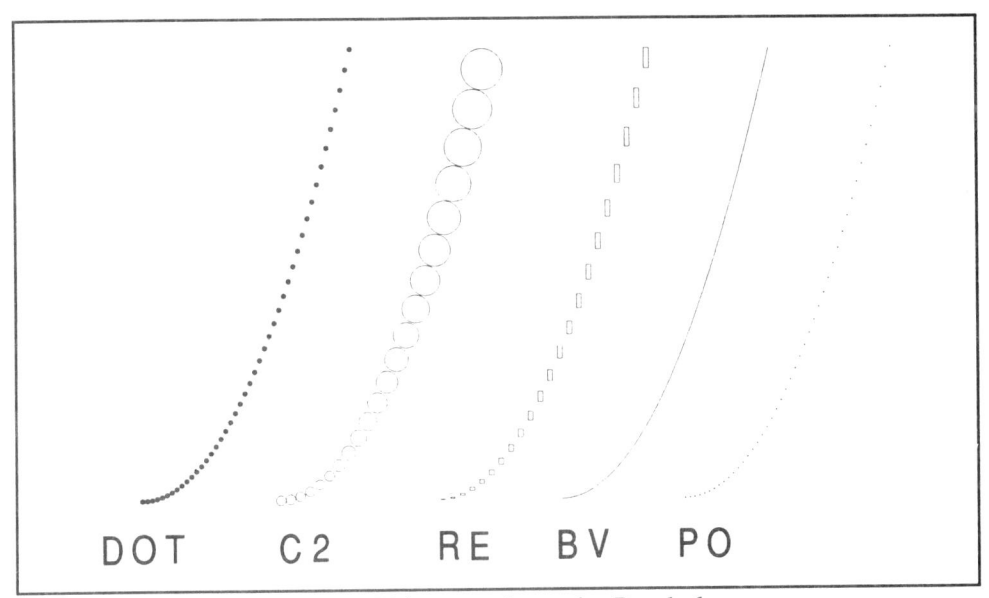

Figure 15.4 Using different Objects to draw the Parabola.

1) What variable setting do you use to set $val when you are not currently changing a variable, but simply placing points?

2) How do you keep changing or incrementing $val so the equation can be continually upgraded every time you run the macro, without inputting values manually?

To answer question 1, you want to use a variable that is not changed regularly by the tasks you are normally doing. The LL command code is used to set the Leader Length during the process of labeling. More than likely you won't be using this command often enough to have it get in your way during the operation of the macro.

Instead of LL, you could use something like the Component Rotate (CR) variable setting. The problem you may encounter with this variable is the numeric limit imposed in this command. When entering Component Rotate, you are prompted to specify a number between +360 and -360. If you run your macro and you pass 360, the variable resets itself and starts once again at 0, setting $val to 0. The macro repeats itself.

You could also use the Fillet Radius (FR) variable setting, but this is a command that could often be initially defined when a drawing is first being set up. You may find yourself using the Fillet (FL) command, and the fillet radius is wrong because it was changed by a macro. You need to experiment with different variables to find one that best suits your purposes.

$val+.05 - To answer question 2, you need to set up a function in the macro that increments the $val every time the macro is run. That's where $val+.05 comes into play. The value 0.05 is the amount to increment every time the macro is run. The smaller the increment, the more points are placed on the screen, and the more accurate the curve. Experiment with the curve by increasing and decreasing the increment value.

Circle and Spiral — Using Polar Coordinates. Now that you've seen an example of math functions using rectangular coordinates, it's time to look at an example using polar coordinates. Using polar coordinates specifying distances and bearings (angles), you can place points according to their distance and angle away from the screen origin (MO mode) or last point entered (MR mode).

Polar coordinates are entered into the program in the format:

> 3,<45

Where:

> 3 (distance)
> < (implies an angle follows)
> 45 (angle)

By specifying a constant distance, but incrementing the angle by a set number of degrees, points are placed on the screen in a circular fashion. By constantly incrementing (increasing) the angle and the distance, points are placed farther out from the origin, or last point, at every angle. This results in a spiral effect.

Compare the formula for a circular path with the formula for a spiral path:

> Circular Path (See Figure 15.5.):
> P0,10,<$val,LL,$val+15

> Spiral Path (See Figure 15.6.):
> P0,$val,<$val,LL,$val+15

In the examples above, LL provides the variable for $val. $val is incremented by a value of 15 every time the macro is run. The distance is constant for the circular path; in this case the radius is 10. The distance for the spiral path is determined by $val. The distance in this case increases in the same manner the angle increases. At a distance of 15, the angle equals 15°. At a distance of 30, the angle equals 30°. As this continues, the spiral takes shape on the screen. Change the amount $val is incremented, and notice that the smaller the increment, the more accurate the curve.

Figure 15.5 Drawing a Circle with Polar Coordinates.

Figure 15.6 Using polar coordinates to draw a spiral.

If you set up and run the spiral path macro, you find that the spiral repeats itself instead of continually increasing in size. Due to the way polar coordinates calculate angles, the macro repeats itself after one increment is placed past 360°. If the macro is incrementing by 15°, the macro places its last point at 375°. The next point placed is at the 30 degree point previously placed on the screen. If you are asking yourself why is the macro starting over at 30° instead of 15°?, take into consideration that the macro repeats itself at 375° which is equivalent to 15°. The next step is the second, or 30° increment.

> **TIP:** Before running these macros, make sure that LL is initially set to zero. The drawing mode should also be set to MO. These equations or macros can be assigned to a function key and operated as demonstrated earlier in this chapter.

Polar coordinates accept angles greater than 360° during normal program operation. During macro operation, one increment past 360° is allowed before the process is repeated, beginning at the second position. Follow the example above to verify the limitations.

Trigonometric Functions

Now you've seen that points can be placed on your screen using the math functions available and be creating macros in the form of math equations. The next set of functions to look at are the trigonometric functions. This next section will show you how to place points on your screen in sinusoidal form. Other trigonometric curves are discussed as well.

To create a sine wave, using rectangular coordinates (X, Y), you can follow the next formula:

PO,$val/90,$sin($val),LL,$val+15 (See Figure 15.7.)

Using this formula, you can determine that at the peak of the wave, 1 on the Y-axis, crosses 1 on the X-axis. By following the equation at 90° ($val = 90), it follows that 90/90 = 1, therefore X = 1, and sin(90) = 1, therefore Y = 1. This gives you a clean, recognizable sine wave on the screen.

For a more defined sine wave, change the increment value from 15 to a number like 5. Instead of using points to mark the position of the curve on the screen, try using a bezier curve, double line, 2-point circle, component, or rectangle. To use different entities, replace PO in the formula with either a BV, L2, C2, (CP, component name), or RE. (See Figure 15.8.) If you use L2 for this example, be sure to set the distance between the lines to 0.05 X 0.05 using the Double Line (DB) settings command. For another interesting effect, turn the solids setting ON. This toggle is also found in the Double Line settings.

Using the sine and cosine functions, you can create macros which plot points on the curves of various other trigonometric functions. Some of these curves include the

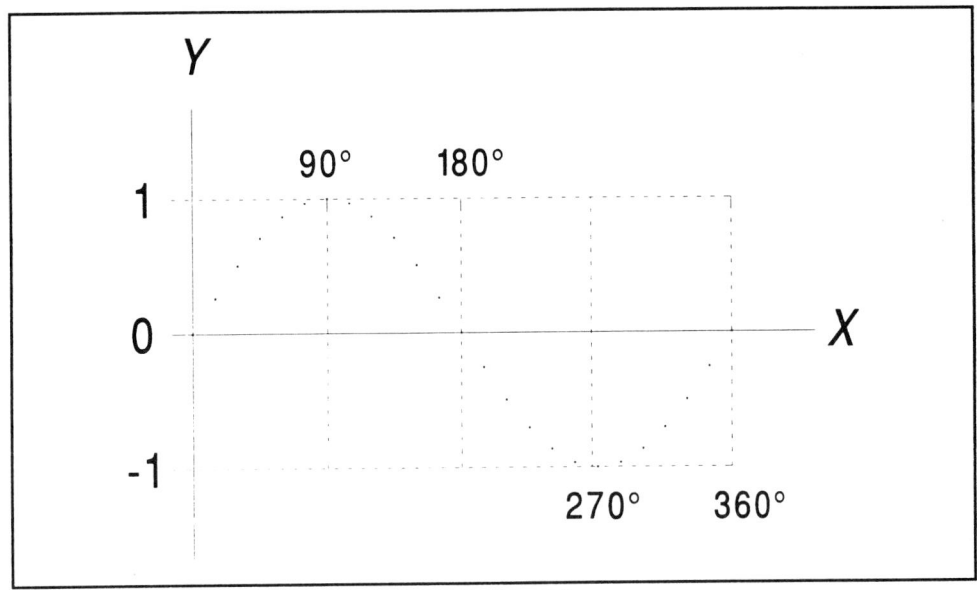

Figure 15.7 Using a macro to draw a Sine Wave.

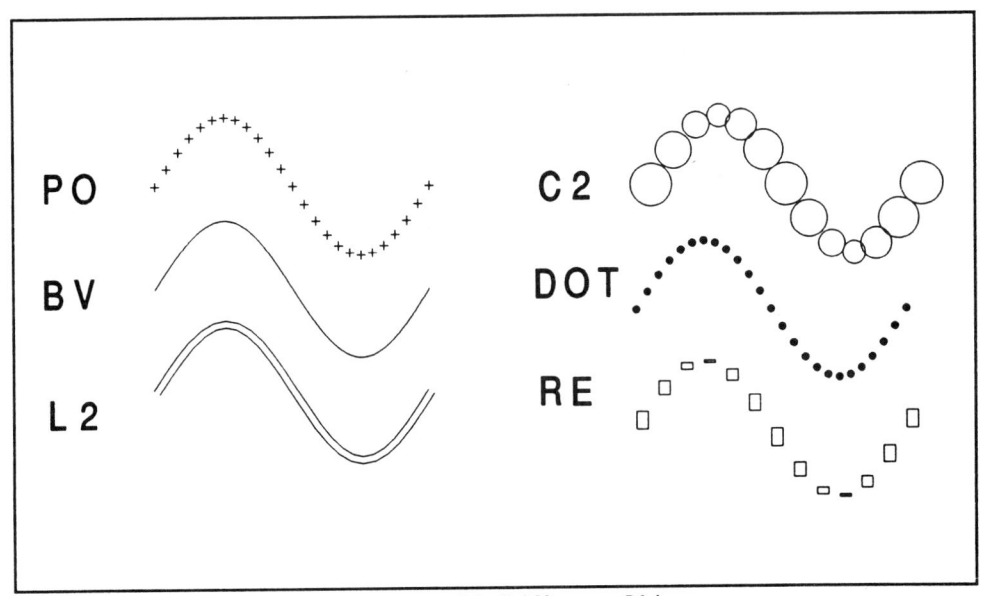

Figure 15.8 Drawing Sine Waves with Different Objects.

cosine, tangent, secant, and cosecant curves. Unlike the sine and cosine curves, the other trigonometric curves mentioned have limits. For example, the tangent curve can never reach 90°. At this point it is either infinite or undefined. You may cause the program to hang up or act oddly if you force it to a particular limit. The next figure shows the tangent and secant curves, both of which are restricted to certain limits. (See Figure 15.10.)

15-22 ■ Chapter 15: Menus, Macros and Batch Files

> **TIP:** Once again, make sure you're in the MO drawing mode, and LL is initially set to 0. If you're in the MR drawing mode while executing the sine wave macro, you get an ocean wave pattern as opposed to the sine wave. (See Figure 15.9.)

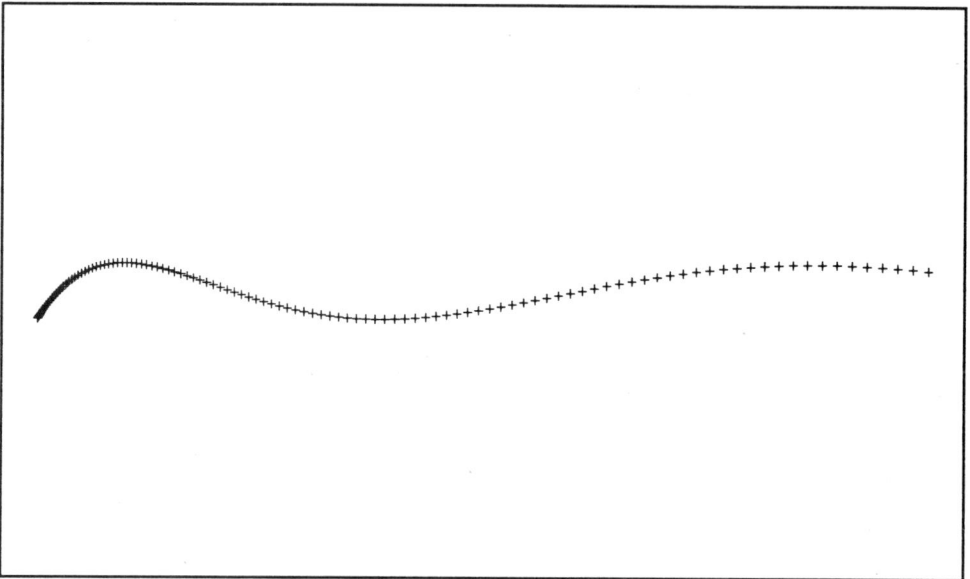

Figure 15.9 Executing the Sine Macro in MR mode.

CADD 6 provides a tangent function, but the secant of angles must be calculated as follows:

    Secant: sec(x) = 1/cos(x)

To use these in a macro, simply replace the sine function in the sine wave macro with the tangent or secant function. For better curve definition, decrease the increment from 15 to 5.

    Tangent Macro:
    P0,$val/90,$tan($val),LL,$val+5

    Secant Macro:
    P0,$val/90,(1/$cos($val)),LL,$val+5

If you have any problems running your macros, go back and check your equations. Make sure no commas, dollar signs, commands, or parenthesis are missing or are in the wrong place.

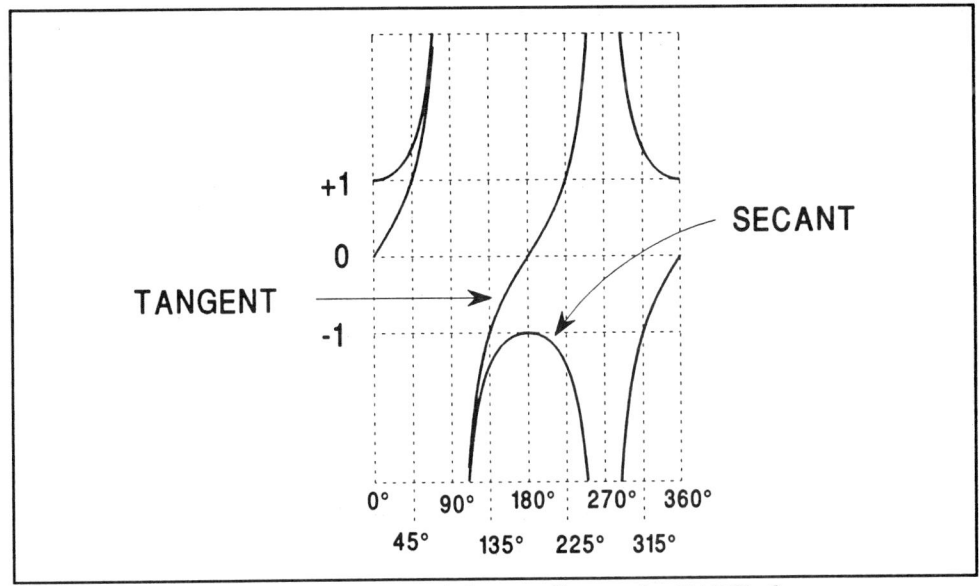

Figure 15.10 Drawing Tangent and Secant Curves in CADD 6.

Natural Log and the Exponential Function

Also included in the set of math features found in the program are the natural log and natural exponential functions. The symbol for the natural log function is **ln**; it must be typed in as **$ln()**. The symbol for the natural exponential function is e^x. In the program it must be input as **$exp()**. "e" is the inverse of the natural log and is an actual number. "e" is unique, irrational, and has the non-termination decimal expansion of 2.7182818....

Using the techniques described earlier in this chapter, you may want to graph the natural log (**$ln**) or exponential (**$exp**) functions. Whatever you may need to do, follow the guidelines laid out in this chapter to create and implement your math equations. Even if you just want to use CADD 6 as a calculator, these functions will come in handy. On the other hand, you may be converting a manually drafted drawing into CADD and need to calculate the angle of a line. You may be able to enter in trigonometric coordinates instead of solving the equation outside of CADD 6.

If you don't do anything else with these features but try them out, you'll get a lot of experience with the macro features. Working on methods like these to increase your productivity greatly improves your understanding of CADD 6's features and fundamentals.

The next section in this chapter will cover video and digitizer menus. The following is the list of commands found on the MENUS page of the video menu.

CREATING VIDEO MENUS

MENUS

----- Video -----

Load Video Menu (LV)
New Menu (VX)(LV)
Delete Video Menu (VX)
Display Video Menu (VM)

--- Digitizer ---

Load Digitizer Menu (LD)
Select Digitizer Menu (DM)

Drawing Align (DA)
Active Area (AA)

Trace Mode (TM)
Trace Scale (RZ)

The standard video menu in CADD 6 is called CADD6.MNU, and is a hierarchical listing of the commands in CADD 6. To execute a command, you simply select it from the menu. Also included is a menu called HELP6.MNU, which is similar to the CADD6.MNU, but also lists the two and three-letter command codes next to each command. There are three commands used in CADD 6 to control the video menus. They are found on the MENUS menu which can be selected from the FILE menu.

Load Video Menu (LV)
Delete Video Menu (VX)
Display Video Menu (VM)

Load Video Menu (LV) is the command used to load a video menu. Delete Video Menu (VX) is used to completely erase the menu currently active in the program. If you wish to erase the current menu and load another menu, such as the HELP6.MNU, follow this procedure:

        Type: VX (for Delete Video Menu)
        Type: LV (for Load Video Menu)
        Type: HELP6 (and press Enter)

The current menu is erased and the HELP6 video menu is installed. When typing in the name of a video menu, you do not need to add the .MNU extension. The program does this automatically.

Another command found on the MENU page is New Menu (VX)(LV). The New Menu (VX)(LV) command is a handy macro that has been added to the video menu. This macro performs the same function as the previous example. New Menu (VX)(LV) deletes the current video menu (VX), then executes the Load Video Menu (LV) command. When you select this macro, you are prompted to select a video menu to replace the current video menu.

Menu File Format

CADD 6 has its own set of rules for menu grammar or *syntax*. The menu included with CADD 6 contains multiple *pages*, or submenus, of similar commands. You should be familiar with this structure from working with the menu throughout earlier chapters of this book. When you start up CADD 6, you see the first page of the menu, which is the ROOT MENU. The ROOT MENU is just a listing of names of submenus included on the complete CADD 6 menu. At this time, you may want to start up CADD 6, and refer to the ROOT MENU as you continue with this section.

The Root Menu And Submenus

Look at the CADD 6 ROOT MENU to see examples of the first three rules of the menu format.

The first rule is that each submenu, or page of the menu, must start with a menu heading or title in the form:

    * HEADING

where HEADING represents the submenu name. (Include one space between the asterisk and the heading.) The ROOT MENU, for example, starts with the line:

    * ROOT MENU

The heading name can be a maximum of 10 characters in length, not including the asterisk and initial space. It can include spaces and most of the characters found on the keyboard. Do not use punctuation marks such as a comma, period, or semicolon, because these marks have special meanings when used on a menu.

The second rule of menu format is to reference the names of other submenus by putting a line on the menu such as:

    HEADING,**

where HEADING is the same submenu name that starts a new page of the menu. On the video screen, you see only the submenu name. The comma signals CADD 6 that all preceding characters (HEADING, in this case) are to be shown on the screen. The two asterisks (**) cause CADD 6 to search for the submenu page with the specified heading and display it.

As an example, selecting the menu item:

    DRAW,**

causes the submenu named DRAW to be displayed.

Knowing how to set up submenus is important so you can organize your menu into groups of similar commands. The DRAW submenu, for example, contains all commands for drawing primitives, such as points, lines, arcs, circles, and so on. Submenus like DRAW really contain the *meat* of the menu - the actual CADD 6 commands.

The third rule of menu formats is to use a comma to separate what is actually shown on-screen from the instructions CADD 6 is to execute. The format for placing commands in a menu item is:

    VIDEO NAME,XX;

where VIDEO NAME represents the name of the command that is displayed on the screen in CADD 6. This is the name you must recognize as being associated with the specific function. The video name can be a maximum of 12 characters in length, with the same restrictions as discussed previously for submenu names. A comma separates the video name from the actual two-character command, represented here by XX. This is the command that is executed when the menu item is selected. The command line must end with a semicolon.

Here is an example from the DRAW submenu:

    Rectangle,RE;

The word Rectangle is displayed on the menu screen. When you select this menu item, the command code RE is executed. This is the same two-character command code you enter from the keyboard to draw a rectangle. The menu just sends the code to CADD 6 for you.

Menu Page Command

The Menu Page command can be used to enhance your video menus and is used in the CADD6 and HELP6 menus. With this command, you can move to different menu

> **TIP:** The menu name you see on the screen does not instruct CADD 6 to execute a particular command. CADD 6 uses the two-character command code that appears after the comma. Thus, you can use any 12 characters for the name you select from the menu - whatever is the most intuitive to you. If you don't like the name Rectangle, for example, you can replace it with something else, like Box. Regardless of what shows on the screen, the command still causes the RE command code to be executed.

pages by specifying a number or a name. A submenu's page number may not always be obvious, but if a zero (0) is used, the menu moves to the last page selected. The following example shows how you could use PG in your video menus to move to the previous page:

   PREVIOUS,PG,0;

There are two rules to follow when using the PG command:

   1) Zero (0) always causes you to move to the previous menu page selected until it reaches the ROOT MENU page or Page 0. At this point, you can't move back any farther.

   2) Other pages are numbered in the order they appear in the menu file. In the CADD6 menu, for example, the DRAW menu is Page 1, the SNAPS menu is Page 2, and TRIMS is Page 3.

To experiment with the PG command while you are in CADD 6, type PG and enter a number. Notice what the current menu heading is, and execute PG again. If you enter 0 enough times, you will find yourself back at the ROOT MENU. You can also type PG and enter a name. For example, from the root menu, type PG and Enter TEXT. The video menu changes to the TEXT menu page.

Video Menu Macros

CADD 6 gives you the ability to create macros on menu command lines. A macro is simply a string of commands that you can execute by selecting a single menu item. In effect, you can create a new CADD 6 procedure that consists of any of the existing commands, give it a name, and place it as a menu item.

The video menu format for a macro command line is exactly the same as for a single command, except after the video name, you place all the additional two-character command codes that make up the macro, separated by commas. Macros also can include responses to any prompts that CADD 6 normally asks during the execution of a command, which brings up the next menu grammar rule:

Menu items that execute multiple commands (macros) can be a maximum of 255 characters in length, and each two-character command code or response to a prompt must be separated by commas. As with single command items, each macro menu item must end with a semicolon.

An example of a simple menu macro could be making the correct settings to draw a 4" filled wall.

  4" Wall,DB,L,2,!,R,2,!,S,++,L2;

The selection *4" Wall* is what you would see on your video menu. When this macro is selected, the first command activated is:

  Double Line Settings (DB in the macro)

From this command:

  Option L (Left offset) is set to 2 and entered (!)

Remember, the exclamation point (!) is the same as pressing Enter on your keyboard. From option L, the macro moves to the next setting:

  Option R (Right offset) is set to 2 and entered (!)

The last Double Line Setting (DB) is:

  Option S (Solid) which is toggled ON (++)

Remember, use ++ to force toggle commands ON, and -- to force toggle commands OFF. The macro then moves on to the command for drawing the Double Line (L2). From here, you are prompted to Enter the starting point of the double line. No matter what your current settings are, when the macro *4" Wall* is selected, you can be sure your wall will be 4 inch thick and solid.

Prompting for User Input

The CADD 6 menu structure also allows you to create menu items that pause during execution and prompt the user to supply information. This information can be the identification of a point on the drawing, or a value such as height or scale. By using the special characters for macros and batch files learned earlier in this chapter, you can create menu-selected macros that prompt you for information.

Suppose that you want to create a procedure for drawing a 12' X 18' room with its lower left corner located at some point specified by the user. The menu item for this procedure would be:

12x18 Room,RE,@,MR,12',18';

The @ symbol signifies that CADD 6 prompts you to provide the location of the first corner of the rectangle. The upper corner is then located relative to that first point.

Alternatively, suppose that the room is always located so that its lower left corner is at the drawing origin, and that the user is to provide the room dimensions. The menu item for this procedure would be:

Org Room,RE,MO,0,0,@;

This procedure places the program in Manual Entry Offset Origin (MO) mode, so the program interprets the coordinates 0,0 as the drawing origin. You are then prompted to enter the location of the second point needed to draw the rectangular room.

As an example of prompting for a single value, suppose that a macro is written to set up text parameters. You supply the name of the font to be loaded; the macro establishes text size, color, slant, and rotation. Here is the macro:

Text Setup,TS,Z,4,S,14,R,15,C,12,F,~,!;

TS activates the Text Settings (TS) command and sets these values:

   Z (siZe) = 4
   S (Slant) = 14
   R (Rotation) = 15
   C (Color) = 12
   F (Font)
   ~ (user input)

Modifying Menus

Now that you are familiar with the format of a video menu, you can try modifying your existing CADD 6 menu to customize it for yourself.

Before making any changes to the CADD6 menu, be sure to make a copy of it for future use. To do this using DOS, go to your CADD 6 directory and make a copy of the menu with the DOS COPY command. Type:

COPY CADD6.MNU MYMENU.MNU

With the initial menu safely saved, you can feel free to experiment with your custom menu file. If you get hopelessly lost or confused while modifying your menu, you can always return to the initial menu that came with your program.

To modify the menu, load it into your word processor or text editor. Make your changes according to the rules set earlier in this chapter. When you want to save the modified menu, be sure to save it as a text file, not in some proprietary word processing program format. (Refer to your word processor's manual for information on ASCII text files or non-document mode.) If your menu is saved as a text file, be sure the file extension is .MNU, or CADD 6 will not recognize it as a menu.

After the new menu is saved, load it into CADD 6 to test your changes. Start up CADD 6 and it automatically loads the original CADD6 menu. To load your new menu:

    Type: VX (for Video Menu Erase)
    Type: LV (for Load Video Menu)

At the prompt, give the name of your new menu. If the menu is not in the same directory as your CADD 6 program, you also must provide the correct path name so CADD 6 can find the file. After the menu is loaded, you can test the additions and changes you made.

Linking Menus

Because CADD 6 has macro capabilities, you can have an item on your menu that actually loads a different menu. As you become more proficient with CADD 6, you may want to develop several different menus for creating different types of drawings, or for using symbol libraries (symbol libraries are examined shortly). You can develop macros to link these libraries together by simply selecting the new menu name from the current menu.

Suppose that you have two different menus: CADD6.MNU and SYMBOLS.MNU. When you start up CADD 6, the program automatically loads the CADD6 menu. Insert a new menu line:

    SYMBOLS MENU,VX,LV,SYMBOLS;

When this item is selected, the current menu is erased and the SYMBOLS.MNU is loaded.

The SYMBOLS.MNU menu must be in the same directory as CADD 6 to function properly. To enable you to reload the original menu easily, place the following item in the SYMBOLS menu:

    CADD6 MENU,VX,LV,CADD6;

This procedure completes the link between the two menus.

Starting Batch Files from Video Menus

The procedure used to link menus can also be used to call-up individual batch files. Since one menu line is limited to 255 characters, you may find that you run out of room while creating a complex macro. A batch file can be of unlimited size, and can be called up by a macro placed in the video menu.

If you have a batch file, or groups of batch files that set variables in your program to meet different drawing requirements, you may want to call these up from your video menu. The next examples are menu lines, or macros, used to call-up batch files:

    Dim Set,LO,B,DIMSET;
    Ttle Blcks,LO,B,TBLOCK;

These command lines might be used to call-up large batch files used to set dimension variables or routines, to help you set up title blocks for various drawing types.

Symbol Library Menus

A common application for custom menus is to simplify the loading and placing of components from a symbol library. Most symbol libraries, available for purchase, include menus that list the name of each component. With this menu loaded, you simply select the desired component's name and the command to load the component from disk and place it in your drawing is executed. This process eliminates the need for you to type in the name (with correct spelling) of each component as you place it.

You will want an understanding of these menus to allow you to create one for your own libraries or modify any that you purchase. Usually the components are separated into groups that form submenus. Each menu item has the form:

    SYMBOL NAME,CP,FILE NAME;

where SYMBOL NAME is the name of the component displayed on-screen and FILE NAME is the name of the actual component file. You do not need to include the .CMP extension common to all component files. CADD 6 adds the extension automatically.

On some menus, the names used for SYMBOL NAME and FILE NAME will be the same. Sometimes, however, making the names different and taking advantage of the 12 characters available for menu item names will be more convenient.

Everything else about symbol library menus is exactly the same as with other video menus. You can include any CADD 6 commands and macros on the menu, along with the component-placing commands.

CREATING DIGITIZER MENUS

If you are using a digitizer as your pointing device in CADD 6, you can take advantage of this and create a personal digitizer template or overlay. A digitizer menu is a paper or plastic overlay that is placed on a digitizer tablet and lists or shows icons for the CADD 6 commands. You use a digitizer menu like a video menu by selecting commands from the digitizer instead of from the screen. A CADD 6 menu file is associated with the physical menu overlay. This file lists the commands in the order they appear on the overlay. When you click on a position on the overlay, that position is matched with a particular command in the menu file.

A digitizer menu overlay consists of a series of graphic blocks or squares, assigned in left-to-right rows, beginning at the top of your overlay. The menu file that matches the overlay must have the same number of lines as the overlay has command boxes. As with video menus, you can link menus or load batches of commands with a digitizer menu. In CADD 6, you can use up to 10 digitizer menus, individually, or all at the same time. Blank lines in your menus are treated the same as the Pen Up (PU), Escape (ES), or Escape (#) command in a video menu. (See Figure 15.11.)

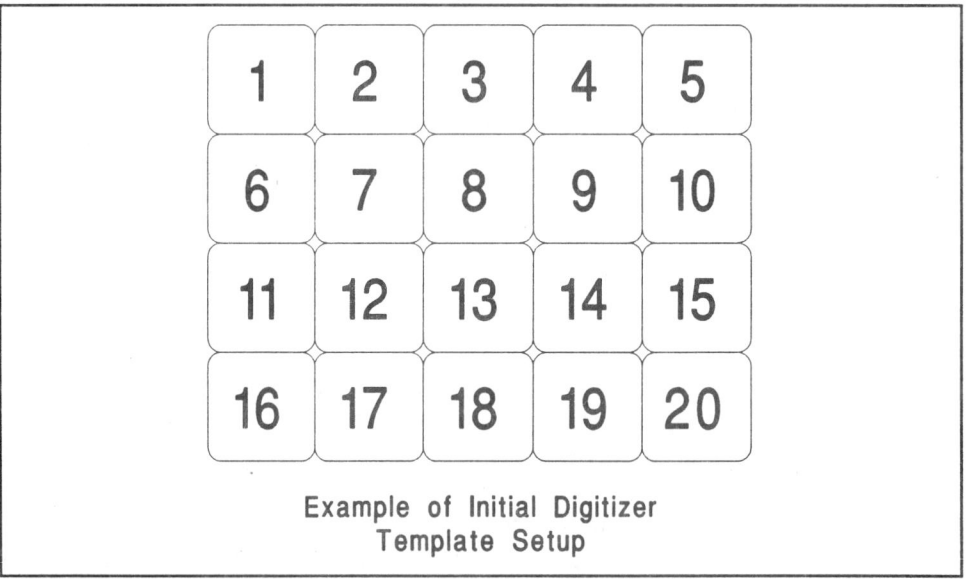

```
  +----+----+----+----+----+
  | 1  | 2  | 3  | 4  | 5  |
  +----+----+----+----+----+
  | 6  | 7  | 8  | 9  | 10 |
  +----+----+----+----+----+
  | 11 | 12 | 13 | 14 | 15 |
  +----+----+----+----+----+
  | 16 | 17 | 18 | 19 | 20 |
  +----+----+----+----+----+
      Example of Initial Digitizer
            Template Setup
```

Figure 15.11 A Digitizer Template setup.

Creating a Template Overlay

The first step is to create the actual physical menu overlay to place on your digitizer tablet. You may find it helpful to build a drawing in CADD 6 that depicts your digitizer menu and its selections. Use symbols, pictures, words, or whatever is easiest to recognize for representing the particular commands or procedures. If you define some areas of your menu for placing components, for example, you can put a simple picture of each component on the appropriate menu square.

Secure the template to the top of your digitizer pad. Remember, the overlay is just for visual reference so you'll know which line in the CADD 6 menu file will be executed when the corresponding picture on the digitizer is selected. (See Figure 15.12.)

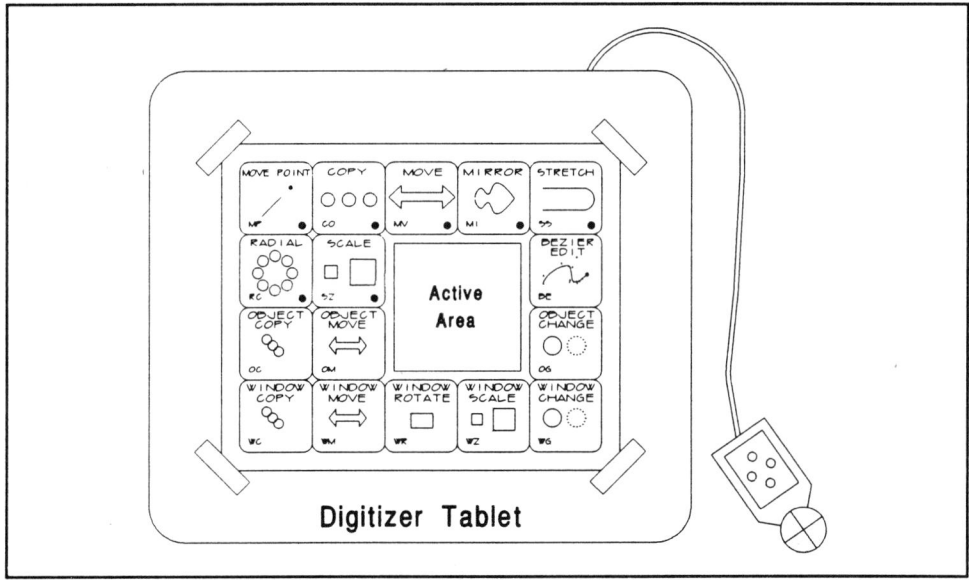

Figure 15.12 Using a Digitizer Tablet Overlay.

Creating the Digitizer .MNU File

Name your first digitizer menu DIGIT.MNU. Because digitizer menus have the same format as video menus, you can create it by copying the CADD6.MNU file to a file called DIGIT.MNU (use the DOS COPY command). Then edit DIGIT.MNU to delete any unused commands, add macros, add component-place commands, and so on.

This sample menu has been divided into four menus that can be activated individually or simultaneously. (See Figure 15.13.) Notice that a space is left open to define the active area of the digitizer, without impeding commands on the overlay. You must determine how you are going to initially break-up your menu. You can divide your menu into a maximum of 10 groups, or individual menus. When you define your menus, you are asked to point to the lower-left and upper-right of the overall boundary of the individual menu. You are then prompted to specify the number of horizontal and vertical squares in that menu. It is in these individually defined menus that the squares are numbered from left to right, top to bottom. The menus are labeled 1 through 10 in CADD 6. If menu 1 has 10 squares in it, then it relates directly to the first 10 command lines in the menu. Menu 2 begins with the menu command line number 11. Compare the following menu with Figure 15.12. It has been broken up to more easily see the divisions that occur on the overlay. These sections could have been saved individually as separate menu files.

```
1,MP; Move Point (MP)
2,CO; Copy (CO)
3,MV; Move (MV)
4,MI; Mirror (MI)
5,SS; Stretch (SS)
6,RC; Radial Copy (RC)
7,SZ; Scale (SZ)
8,OC; Object Copy (OC)
9,OM; Object Move (OM)
10,BE; Bezier Edit (BE)
11,OG; Object Change (OG)
12,WC; Window Copy (WC)
13,WM; Window Move (WM)
14,WR; Window Rotate (WR)
15,WZ; Window Scale (WZ)
16,WG; Window Change (WG)
```

Figure 15.13 A menu divided into Four Separate Areas.

You are allowed a total of 512 commands (and squares on your template). As stated earlier, each individual menu can be contained in its own file, or it can be listed one after another in the same file, as shown in the previous example. Any blank squares are considered a PU, ES, or (#) command. If the separate menus are also separate files, they are appended to each other when they're loaded. The menu files should be loaded in the same order they were initially set up.

The next section will cover the commands for creating and using digitizer menus:

Load Digitizer Menu (LD)
Select Digitizer Menu (DM)
Drawing Align (DA)
Active Area (AA)
Trace Mode (TM)
Trace Scale (RZ)

You configure CADD 6 to use a digitizer as a pointing device for any of these commands to function.

Load Digitizer Menu (LD)

Once you've created your digitizer menu and template, and have securely placed the template on your digitizer, you need to properly activate the menu from within CADD 6. Type LD, or select Load Digitizer Menu (LD) from the MENUS menu found under the FILE menu and enter the name of your menu. If your template is sectioned-off into separate menus, and you have created separate files for each of these menus, be sure to load them in the correct order. Remember, the menus are appended to one another in the order they are loaded.

Select Digitizer Menu (DM)

Type DM, or pick Select Digitizer Menu (DM) from the MENUS menu to setup and enable, or disable digitizer menus. DM can also be selected from the MENUS menu found on the DISPLAY menu. If you type DM, a submenu appears giving you the option to Enable/disable or Setup digitizer menus.

> Type: S to Setup your digitizer menu

TIP: When you enter DM, you are warned that your video menu will be turned OFF and you must confirm that you want to proceed. The same warning occurs if you try to load your video menu while using the digitizer menu.

You are first prompted for the menu number (1-10). Second, you are prompted for the location of the menu. Digitize the lower-left corner and upper-right corner of the menu. Third, you are asked to specify the number of horizontal and vertical boxes in the menu. Once this step is completed, you are asked whether or not you want to set up another menu. Answer Y for Yes, or N for No.

If you type E to Enable/disable your menus, you are prompted with a list of the menus currently active. By entering the number of a menu, you activate it (if it's not currently active and its number appears on the list). If it's number is currently listed, then entering the number deactivates it, and the number disappears from the list.

Once you've set up your digitizer menu, you select a command by positioning your cursor on the appropriate box and pressing the first button on the digitizer puck. This is unlike a mouse, where the second button is used to select items from the video menu.

The current digitizer setup is saved as a default setup in CADD 6. If you exit CADD 6 and return later, the digitizer is set up as it was when you last quit the program.

Drawing Align (DA)

The Drawing Align (DA) command lets you set up a paper drawing to be input into CADD by tracing it. It combines the functions of Trace Scale (RZ) and Trace Mode (TM) to compute a rotation angle and trace scale. The Drawing Align (DA) command can be selected either from the MENUS menu or by typing DA.

When you execute the DA command, the existing Trace Scale (RZ) is displayed with a prompt asking you:

> Is this the correct tracing scale? (Y/N)

If you answer Yes, CADD 6 immediately moves on to the next prompts required to calculate the rotation angle. If you answer No, you are prompted:

> Do you know the scale? (Y/N)

If you answer Yes, you may enter in the correct scale. If you answer No, you are prompted to provide information so CADD 6 can calculate the Trace Scale (RZ).

After you've answered the prompts for the Trace Scale (RZ), you are prompted:

> Enter any point on the screen, use the NP command

At this prompt, you want to snap to a point on the screen that relates to a point on the paper drawing. Next, you are prompted:

> Digitize the same point on the drawing

At this prompt, select a point on your paper drawing that relates to the point you previously selected on the screen. The next two prompts are a repeat of the last two prompts. CADD 6 uses the two points from the CADD 6 drawing and the paper drawing on the digitizer to calculate the Trace Scale (RZ) and the rotation angle. These values are displayed after you answer the last DA prompt.

Active Area (AA)

The Active Area of the digitizer must be set so it does not interfere with the commands on the digitizer template. The smaller this area, the less you have to move the puck in order to move the cursor across the screen. If it's too large, such as the entire pad, you find yourself moving your whole arm just to draw a line from one part of the screen to the other. If it's too small, the slightest movement causes the cursor to jump from one side to the other. You can think of this command as a *cursor sensitivity adjustment*.

Type AA, or select Active Area from the MENUS menu. Like the menu setup, you are prompted to digitize the lower-left corner and the upper-right corner of the active area. The active area can be changed at anytime while in CADD 6.

Trace Mode (TM)

Trace Mode (TM) toggles the program in and out of the trace mode. The trace mode allows a digitizer to be used to trace drawings of any scale. This command allows you to go back and forth between trace mode and the normal drawing mode without realigning the drawing on the digitizer. Select the Trace Mode command by typing TM, or selecting Trace Mode from the MENUS menu. If a drawing hasn't been aligned and the Trace Scale is set, go into Drawing Align. The Drawing Align (DA) command puts you into Trace Mode (TM) automatically after asking or calculating a Trace Scale (RZ) and rotation angle.

Trace Scale (RZ)

The Trace Scale (RZ) command is used to set the scale of a drawing that's already aligned. If the drawing isn't aligned, use the Drawing Align (DA) command. The Drawing Align command automatically transfers you to the Trace Scale command. Select Trace Scale (RZ) by typing RZ, or selecting Trace Scale from the MENUS menu. The Trace Scale (RZ) is effective only while you are in Trace Mode (TM).

CHAPTER SUMMARY

This chapter presented a few ideas about customizing CADD 6 with macros and batch files so it can do repetitive tasks for you. Macros can save you time and energy by automating much of your everyday work so you can devote time to more complex tasks. Macros let you link commands and data together so you can apply a command sequence all at once. You can even prompt the user to enter information for the macro to act upon. When creating macros, take a trial and error approach. Try creating some simple macros at first, then build on these to develop more sophisticated macros to further automate your CADD 6 tasks.

You also learned about modifying the CADD 6 video menu and creating your own video and digitizer menus. Customizing the CADD 6 menus can help you further automate repetitive tasks, and let you have ready access to your own macros and symbols.

APPENDIX A

Using Coordinates

COORDINATE SYSTEMS

This section will examine the coordinate systems used in CADD 6 (Cartesian and Polar). To use CADD 6 effectively, you need a good grasp of these coordinate systems and their associated drawing modes.

To be a productive CADD 6, user you need a good understanding of coordinate systems. Coordinate systems are used to identify the locations of points in two-dimensional space. The location of each point is specified by its horizontal and vertical position from some axis, or by giving a distance and bearing. Use of coordinates is necessary in CADD 6 to specify points in your drawing precisely. To do any work on a professional level, you must understand coordinate systems and their associated modes in CADD 6.

Using coordinates is much like locating points on a map that has letters across the top and numbers down one side. For example, a street might be identified at coordinates F4. You find that location by drawing an imaginary line down from column *F* and across from row *4*. The street is located at the intersection of this row and column.

CADD 6 programs use a similar concept to identify points with the Cartesian coordinate system. Figure A.1 shows the two-dimensional Cartesian coordinate system and associated nomenclature. Cartesian coordinates can be specified as rectangular or polar coordinates, as discussed in the following section.

A-2 ■ Appendix A: Using Coordinates

Cartesian Coordinate Axis

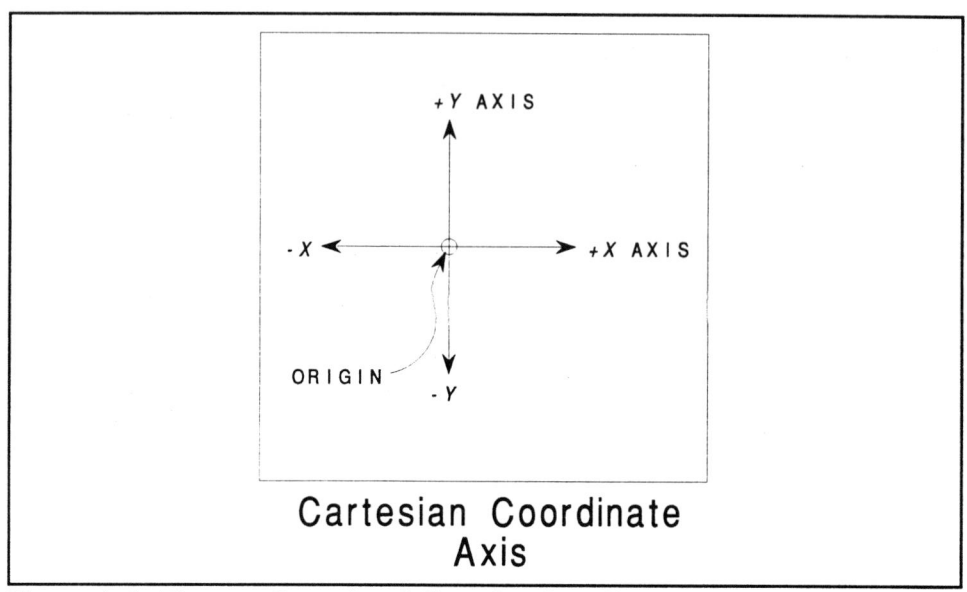

Figure A.1 The two-dimensional Cartesian Coordinate System.

Using Rectangular And Polar Coordinates

A two-dimensional Cartesian system is divided into four quadrants by the X and Y axes; two intersecting lines that are perpendicular to one another. The intersection of the X and Y axes is known as the *origin*. An *X coordinate* specifies a distance along the X-axis (usually horizontal), and a *Y coordinate* specifies a distance along the Y-axis (usually vertical). The origin or crossing of these two axes is indicated by coordinates 0,0. Each quadrant is described by specific positive or negative values for the X and Y coordinates. Figure A.2 shows the four quadrants.

To map out an object on your CADD 6 screen to an exact location, you specify a pair of X and Y coordinates. Each point in 2D space can be identified by one unique X coordinate value and one unique Y value.

For example, to draw a rectangle, you map out the points making up the rectangle's four corners. In CADD 6, you can create lines between these points automatically while mapping them out. Figures A.3 and A.4 show a rectangle mapped out with rectangular coordinates. These rectangles are identical to each other except for their locations relative to the X and Y axes.

Another way to specify points in the Cartesian system is with polar coordinates. Polar coordinates allow you to define a point by specifying the absolute distance from the origin (coordinates 0,0) to the point, and an angle from the horizontal axis to the point. Figure A.5 represents the polar coordinate form of locating a point relative to the horizontal and vertical axes.

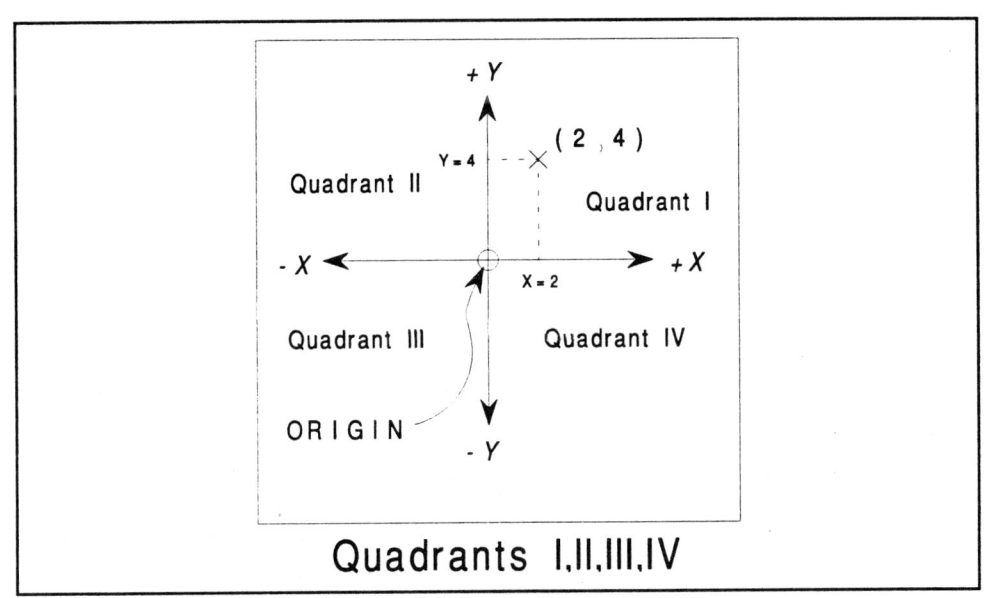

Figure A.2 The four quadrants of the coordinate system.

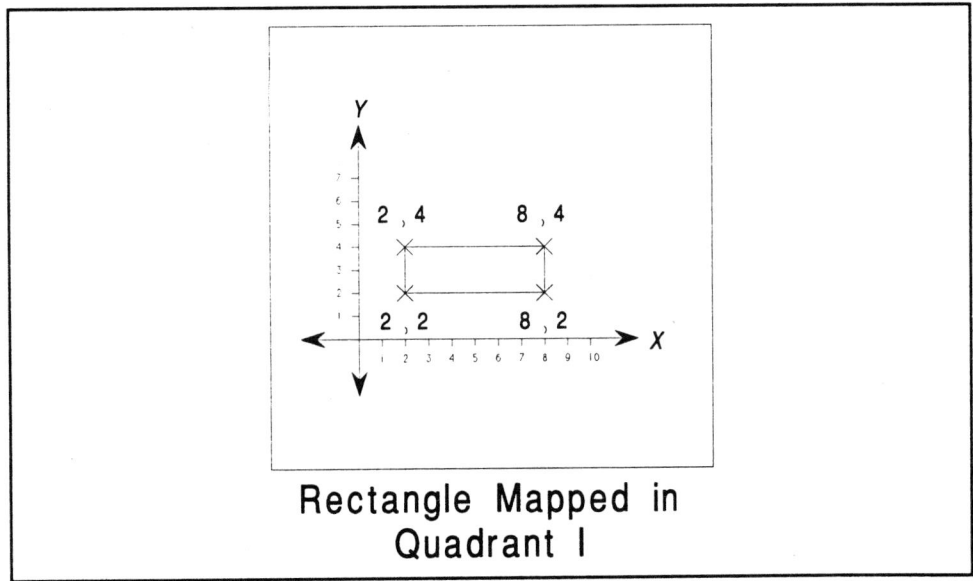

Figure A.3 A Rectangle mapped out in Quadrant I.

A-4 ■ Appendix A: Using Coordinates

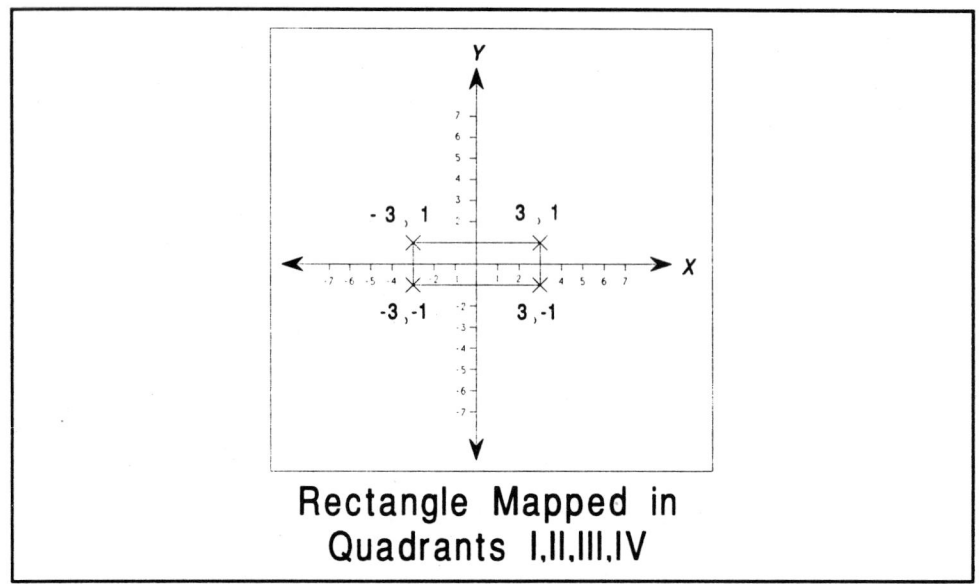

Figure A.4 A Rectangle with one corner in each Quadrant.

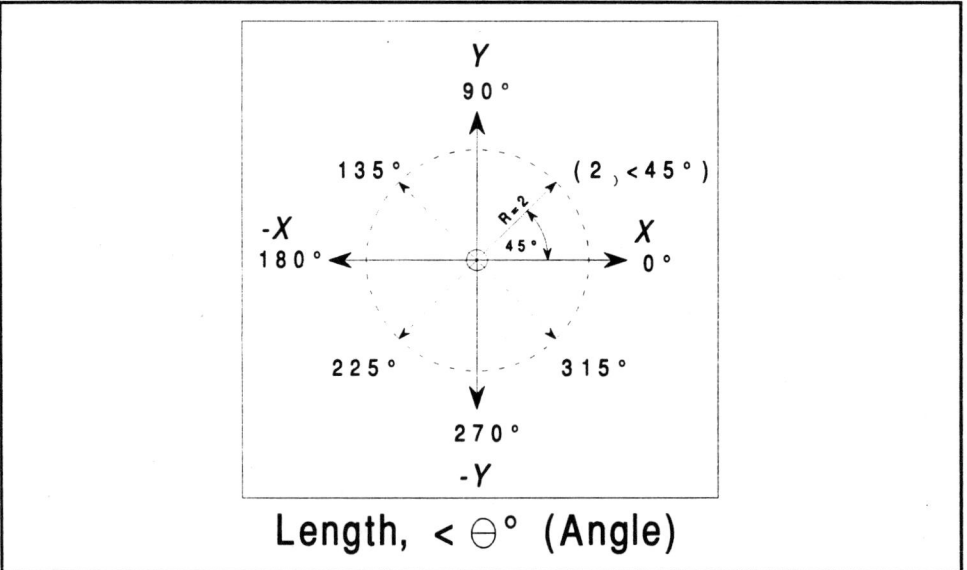

Figure A.5 Locating points with Polar Coordinates.

It is often more convenient to use rectangular coordinates, but sometimes polar coordinates can save you a great deal of time, especially when you're drawing objects at known angles from the X-axis. Figure A.6 shows the same rectangle from the previous example, but with polar coordinates rather than rectangular coordinates. Figure A.7 shows how you can calculate the angle and distance values in Figure A.6.

Appendix A: Using Coordinates ■ A-5

Using Polar Coordinates

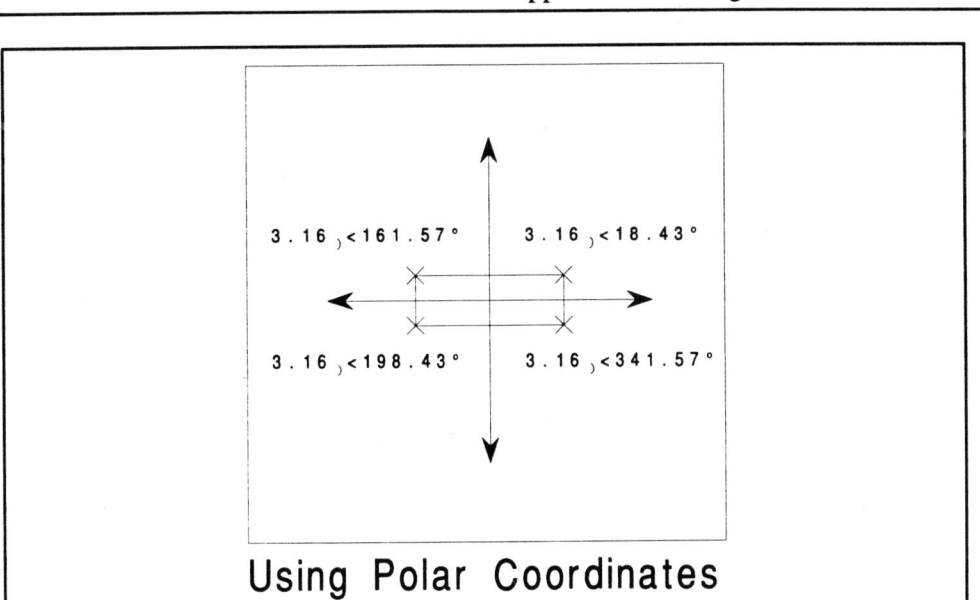

3.16) < 161.57°   3.16) < 18.43°

3.16) < 198.43°   3.16) < 341.57°

Figure A.6 The Previous Rectangle example with Polar Coordinates.

Calculating Angle and Distance

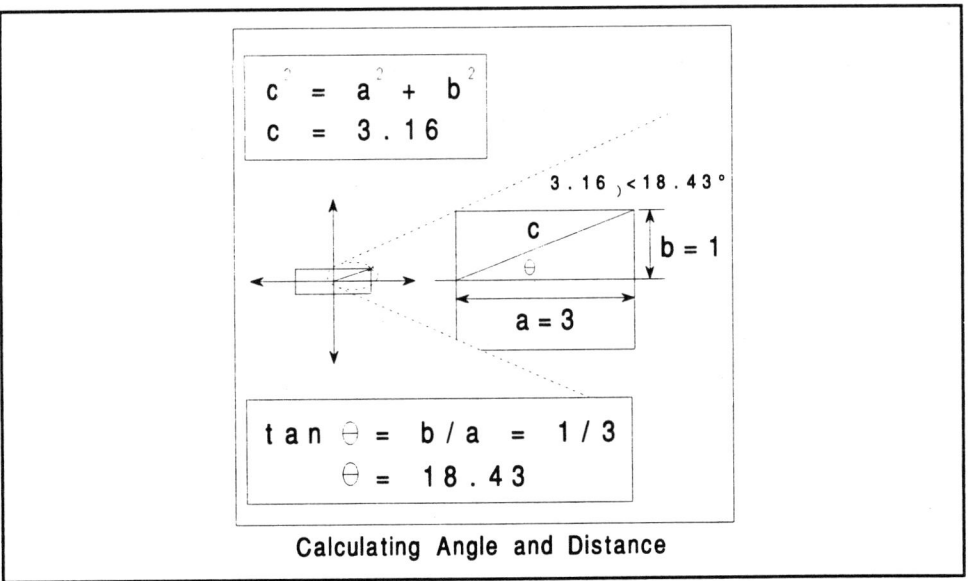

$c^2 = a^2 + b^2$
$c = 3.16$

3.16) < 18.43°

b = 1
a = 3

$\tan \theta = b/a = 1/3$
$\theta = 18.43$

Figure A.7 How to Calculate the Coordinates of the Rectangle in A.6.

Polar coordinate angles are always positive in the counterclockwise direction. If you want to use angles in a clockwise direction, just enter them as negative. In other words, -45° equals +315°, -90° equals +270°, -180° equals +180°, and so on.

Now that you have examined the basics of Cartesian coordinate systems (rectangular and polar), you are ready to see how they are used in CADD 6. First, however, let's examine how CADD 6 displays coordinate information on the screen.

The Drawing Origin, Coordinate Display, and Cursor

When working with coordinates and the different modes associated with them, you need to understand how CADD 6 displays the drawing origin, the coordinate values, and the cursor.

The drawing origin is the point located at the intersection of the X- and Y-axes. The origin point is represented by an asterisk (*) on the screen. The origin is located at the intersection of the *X* and *Y* axes. You cannot actually see the axes on the CADD 6 drawing screen, but rest assured that they are used to locate every point in your drawing. Use the crosshair cursor to help you visualize the X- and Y- axes. This may help you remember the positive and negative values in the different quadrants.

You may need to Zoom Out (ZO) to see the origin point, and you must make sure that Reference Points (PR) is set to ON.

When you start CADD 6, you see the first quadrant of the Cartesian system. The drawing origin is in the lower-left corner of the screen. You may first have to use the Zoom Back (ZB) command to actually see the origin point. You use ZOOM commands to change the display so you can look at, and draw in, the other quadrants.

The coordinates are displayed on the upper-left corner of your screen. As the cursor moves, the coordinate display simultaneously shows the current position of the cursor. If your cursor is resting on the origin, the coordinate display shows *X* 0 *Y* 0 (as long as coordinates are specified relative to the origin).

Now you're ready to work with coordinates in CADD 6. You do so by using one of the three drawing modes examined in the next section.

Using the Drawing Modes

CADD 6 gives you the opportunity to specify coordinates in various drawing modes:

Manual Entry Offset Origin (MO)
Manual Entry Offset Relative (MR)
Manual Entry Offset Base Point (MB)

The mode selected tells CADD 6 how to interpret the coordinates you enter from the keyboard. Each of these commands are found on the CONSTRAINTS menu.

The Manual Entry Offset Origin (MO) mode uses rectangular Cartesian coordinates. All coordinates entered in this mode are interpreted as being relative to the drawing origin. If you enter 0,0, the cursor moves to the drawing origin. Figure A.8 shows a rectangle drawn in the MO mode.

```
        0 , 1      1 , 1


        0 , 0      1 , 0

      Manual Entry Offset
          Origin (MO)
```

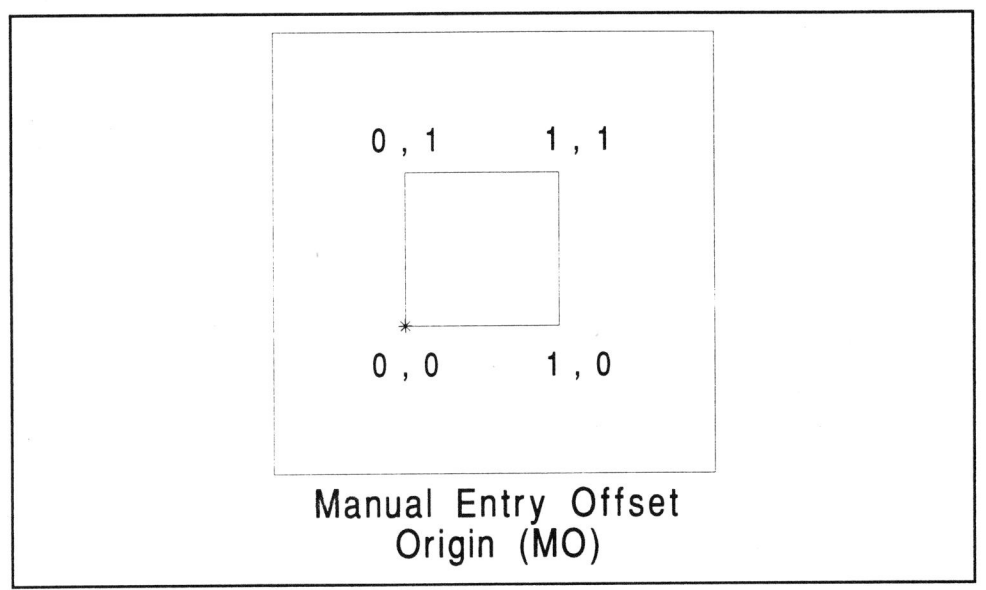

Figure A.8 A 1-Unit Square drawn in MO Mode.

The Manual Entry Offset Relative (MR) uses coordinates that are interpreted as being measured from the last point entered. The last point automatically becomes a temporary origin point, and coordinates are specified relative to that point. In this mode, you can draw connected lines by consecutively entering the coordinates of each endpoint as X and Y distances from the previous point. Compare the rectangle drawn in the MO mode with the same drawing done in the MR mode. (See Fig. A.9).

Notice that positive coordinates are interpreted as a direction along the positive X- or Y-axis and the opposite for negative coordinates. To draw the line from the upper-right corner to the lower one, for example, enter 0,-1. This setting tells CADD 6 to move in the negative Y direction one unit from the starting point.

The coordinates differ, depending on which direction you want to move. When following this diagram, remember that once a point is entered, it becomes 0,0. When you feel comfortable with this concept, you can enter coordinates quite rapidly with little or no calculation required.

The Manual Entry Offset Base Point (MB) causes coordinates to be interpreted as relative to a specified base point. You can specify a base point anywhere in your drawing. You can change the base point at any time without affecting the actual

```
                    0,1 ———→ 1,0
                    ↑              │
                    │              │
                    │              ↓
        0,0 START ←———  0,-1
        -1,0 END

        Manual Entry Offset
            Relative (MR)
```

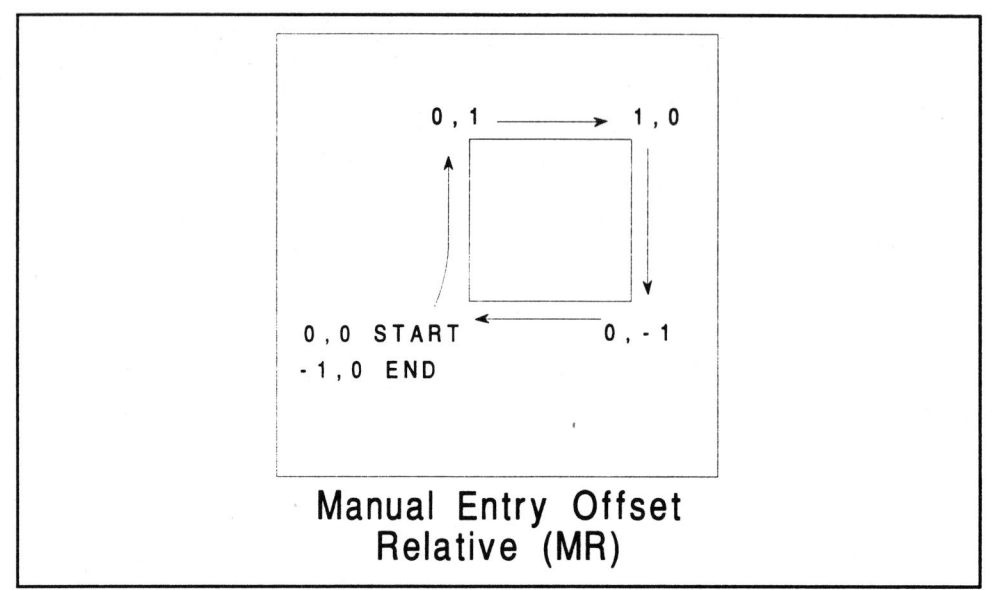

Figure A.9 A 1-Unit Square drawn MR Mode.

location of objects in the drawing. Compare a rectangle drawn in the MB mode that has a predetermined base point (shown in Figure A.10) with a rectangle drawn using the other two modes.

Specifying points with polar coordinates works the same as with rectangular coordinates. In CADD 6, the polar origin varies with the current drawing mode, just as with rectangular coordinates. In other words, polar coordinates are relative to the program's drawing origin in the MO mode, relative to the last point entered in the MR mode, and relative to the predetermined base point in the MB mode. Figures A.11, A.12, and A.13 show examples of a rectangle entered with polar coordinates in the different drawing modes. Remember that angles in polar coordinates are always measured from the positive X-axis and counterclockwise.

Changing the Coordinate Display

You can easily change the way coordinates are displayed on the drawing screen to show coordinates relative to the program origin, relative to the last point entered, or as polar. Regardless of what the display coordinates show, point placement is affected only by your current drawing mode: MO, MR, or MB. The drawing mode is not dependent on the type of coordinate display. The coordinate display is strictly for your reference and is not necessary to create drawings. Be sure to refer to the display often. It can be a big help while drawing.

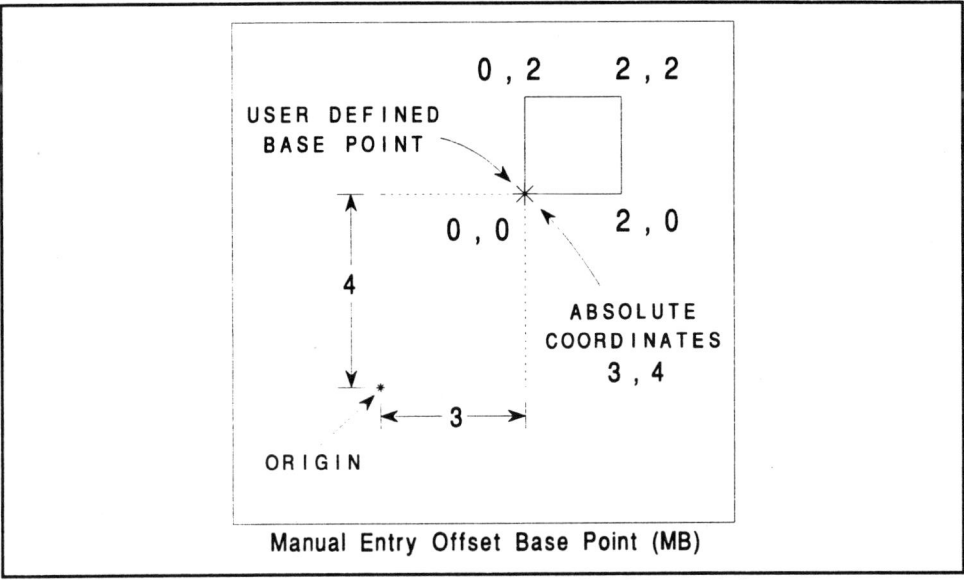

Figure A.10 Drawing a Square using a Pre-Defined Base Point.

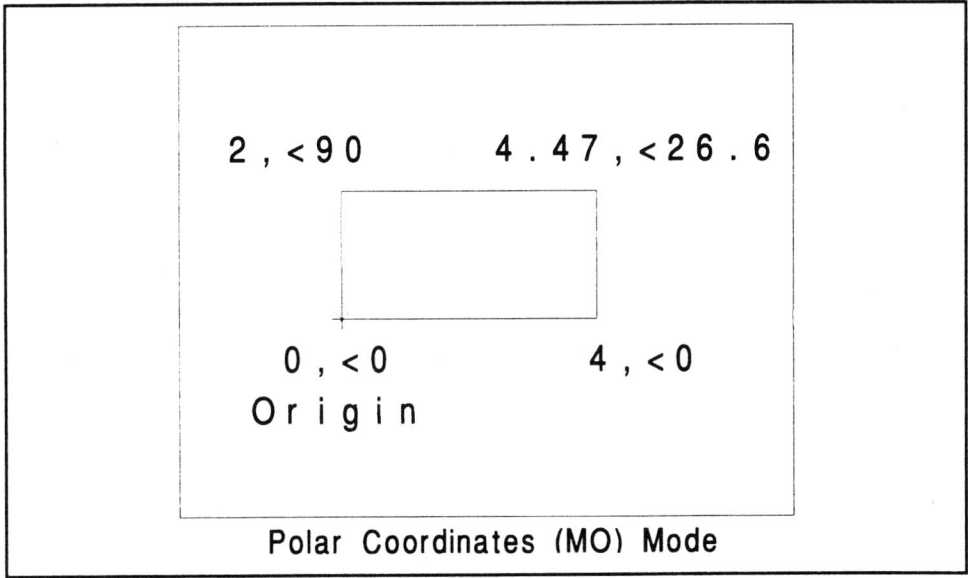

Figure A.11 Using Polar Coordinates with Manual Entry Offset.

Three common and useful coordinate display systems are:

1. Absolute coordinates, relative to the drawing origin
2. Delta coordinates, relative to the last point entered
3. Polar coordinates

A-10 ■ Appendix A: Using Coordinates

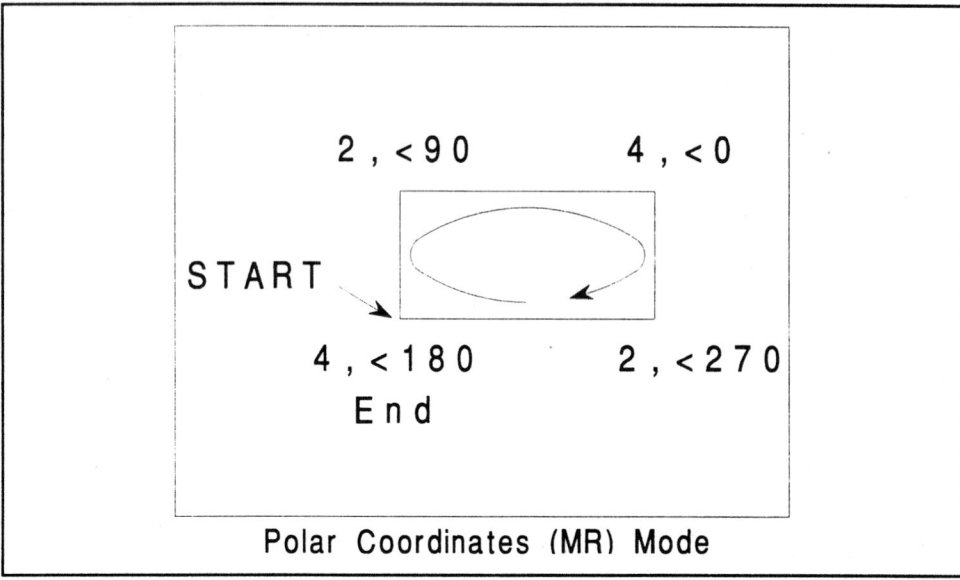

```
                2,<90            4,<0

        START
                4,<180           2,<270
                 End

        Polar Coordinates (MR) Mode
```

Figure A.12 Using Polar Coordinates with Manual Entry Relative.

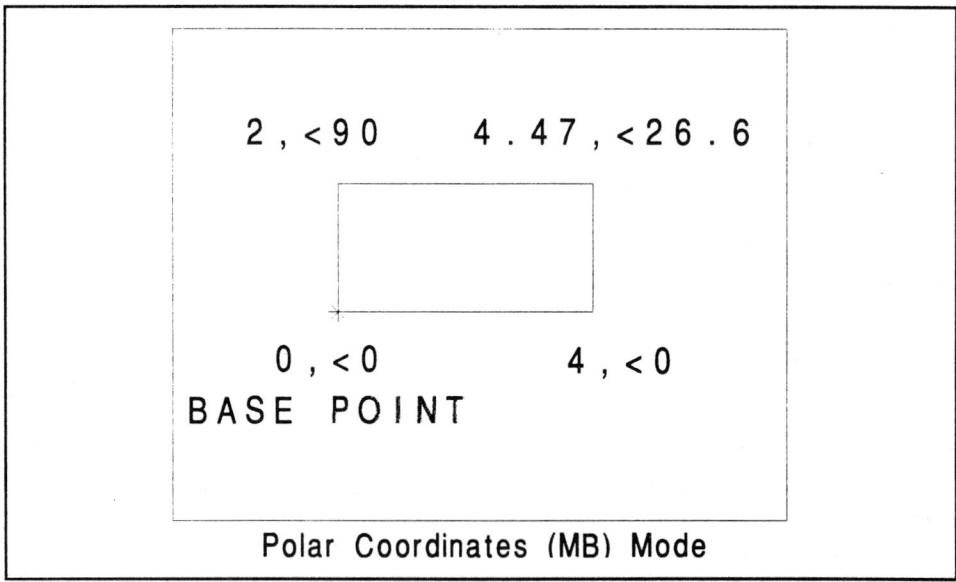

```
            2,<90      4.47,<26.6


            0,<0          4,<0
        BASE POINT


        Polar Coordinates (MB) Mode
```

Figure A.13 Using Polar Coordinates with Manual Entry Basepoint.

Absolute coordinates indicate the cursor's position relative to the program drawing origin, similar to Manual Entry Origin (MO) for entering points. As the cursor is moved around the drawing screen, the values for X and Y change.

Delta coordinates represent the cursor's position relative to the last point entered. Every time you press Enter to select a point, the display coordinates change to 0,0.

Polar coordinates are displayed only if delta coordinates are ON. The polar coordinates display actually shows a distance and an angle relative to the last point entered.

Using Polar Coordinates to Enter Bearings

A common drafting challenge is how to translate data in the form of distances and bearings into the coordinate information you need to create a CAD drawing. This type of information is typically used on plot maps and surveys. To create this kind of drawing, you simply apply what you already know about polar coordinates.

For example, given the information in Figure A.14, here is how you would draw the 100.25' line at a bearing of South 23° 10 minutes West:

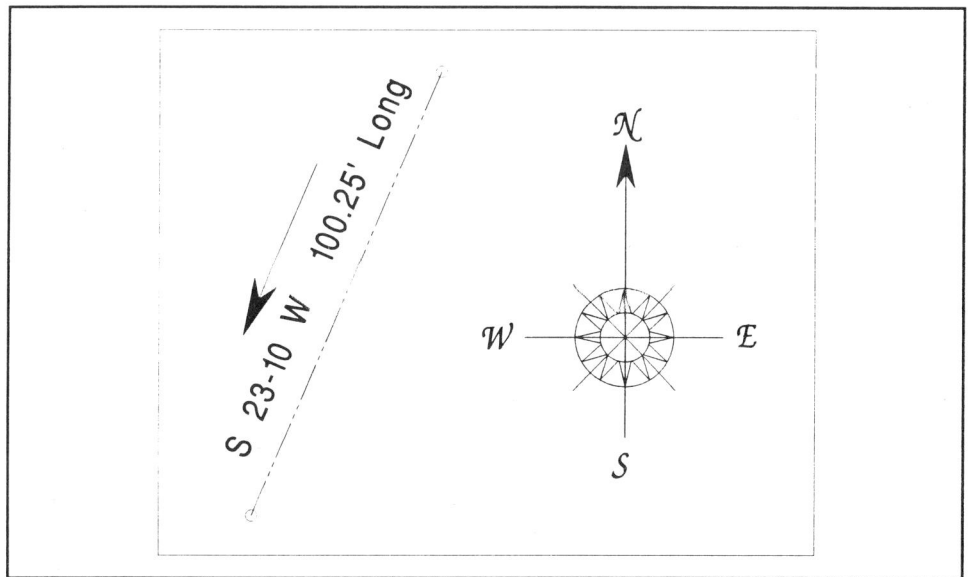

Figure A.14 Drawing a Property Line with Polar Coordinates.

```
Type:  MR (for Manual Entry Relative)
Click or snap to place the first endpoint of the line
Type:  100.25', < 270-23:10 (and press Enter)
```

If North is straight up in a CADD 6 drawing, it is at an angle of 90°. Remember that 0° is horizontal to the right, so it would be the same as straight East. That makes West the same as 180° and South 270°. To draw the line at South 23° 10 minutes West, you *subtract* 23:10 from 270°. The angle is subtracted from 270, since you must turn clockwise from South to get the desired angle.

SUMMARY

Practice is the only way to develop a good understanding of using coordinates in CADD 6. Experiment with the different systems for entering points and displaying coordinates in CADD 6. When working on an actual project, you may need to switch from one mode to another. This can make you more efficient, and help get the job done right.

APPENDIX B

Generic CADD 6.1 and AutoCAD

USING GENERIC CADD 6.1 AND AUTOCAD TOGETHER

For years, Generic CADD has included the ability to read and write .DXF files, which allows users to import from, and export to, AutoCAD and other Computer-Aided Design programs. Version 6.0 added the ability to read an AutoCAD drawing directly, in AutoCAD's native .DWG format, but you still could not save a drawing to the .DWG format. Version 6.1 now offers two-way compatibility, since it both *reads and writes* AutoCAD .DWG files directly.

This new feature makes CADD 6.1 and AutoCAD into a single, compatible CAD product line, making it possible for a company to more effectively use the products together. This feature makes operating multiple CAD stations more cost effective, allowing the more expensive AutoCAD to reside on fewer systems where its features are required, while multiple copies of Generic CADD are installed on additional systems.

The Same, Yet Different

Many CAD programs have similar functionality, and CADD 6.1 and AutoCAD are no exception. Their many similarities make them ideal partners in the workplace, but you must also be aware of their differences in order for the partnership to really work.

To use the programs together effectively, you should understand these two items:

Interface Similarities and the New AutoCAD-Style Menu. A special menu is included with CADD 6.1 that effectively allows Generic CADD to imitate AutoCAD's user interface. This AutoCAD-style menu is ideal for CADD 6.1 users who want to become familiar with AutoCAD, or for AutoCAD users who want to learn CADD 6.1. This menu contains only the AutoCAD commands that are most closely related to existing Generic CADD commands. It in no way represents the full set of AutoCAD commands. For example, the AutoCAD-style menu does not include any of AutoCAD's 3-D features.

The booklet titled "How to use Generic CADD with AutoCAD," included with CADD 6.1, explains this new menu and how to use it. It includes extensive tables that cross reference all the AutoCAD commands to the equivalent CADD 6.1 commands.

Drawing file translation. In order to effectively exchange drawings between the two programs, it is important to have a good understanding of how AutoCAD and Generic CADD are similar, and how they are different. There are some fundamental differences between the entities and settings used in the two programs. Before translating drawings, you should investigate the various options available for exchanging drawings between the products, including drawing entity correlation, and the relationship of fonts, layers, hatch patterns, and so on.

This topic is thoroughly discussed in the booklet titled "How to use Generic CADD with AutoCAD," which is included with CADD 6.1. This booklet also includes tables that show exactly how entities and settings are converted from one program to the other. For example, the table shows that AutoCAD's blocks are converted to Generic CADD's components, and vice versa.

Using The AutoCAD-Style Menu

While it is possible to create exactly the same 2D drawing in CADD 6.1 and in AutoCAD, you would normally use a very different method in each product. The basic CAD concepts are the same in the two products, but the actual methods of drawing, and the terminology used, are quite different. In other words, each product provides a different means to the same end.

For example, both AutoCAD and CADD 6.1 have commands for creating basic drawing entities, like lines, circles, arcs, and curves, and for editing drawings, like copy, move, rotate, and scale. They both use snaps, trims, and coordinate entry to accurately select and place points. However, in most cases the exact method needed to complete the operation, the terminology, and the command syntax is very different. For example, symbols are called "blocks" in AutoCAD and "components" in CADD 6.1.

Fortunately, AutoCAD users who wish to learn Generic CADD no longer have to be concerned about these differences. A special *ACAD Menu* is now included with CADD 6.1, that effectively imitates AutoCAD's user interface in Generic CADD. This menu includes all of the AutoCAD commands and settings that can be reproduced in Generic CADD, either with two-letter commands, or with macros.

To use the AutoCAD-style menu, go to the CADD 6.1 ROOT MENU and select:

ACAD MENU

This causes the AutoCAD-style menu to be loaded, and changes the cursor to an AutoCAD-style, full-screen cursor. Loading the AutoCAD menu also turns OFF CADD 6.1's Tandem Cursor mode. This setting is consistent with the AutoCAD standard of using the first mouse button to select menu items.

To change back to the standard CADD 6.1 menu, go to the root AUTOCAD menu and select:

CADD 6 MENU

When an item is selected from the ACAD Menu, the equivalent CADD 6.1 command is executed. For example, when you select CEN,RAD from the AutoCAD CIRCLE menu, the CADD 6.1 command C2, for a two-point circle, is executed. Due to a limited menu area in CADD 6.1, some of the items on the AutoCAD-style menu are abbreviated, so not all of the menu names look exactly alike.

CADD 6.1 also has some commands that do not have an equivalent in AutoCAD. These are shown on the menu in red. On the DRAW menu, for example, the FILL and CURVE commands are strictly available in CADD 6.1.

Using The Command Cross Reference Table

The CADD 6.1 booklet, "How to use Generic CADD with AutoCAD," includes a table of all the AutoCAD commands and the equivalent Generic CADD commands, along with any special notes about how to use them. The table includes the following helpful information about using the ACAD Menu:

- The AutoCAD menu name and command name.
- Any Generic CADD commands on the ACAD Menu that do not have an AutoCAD equivalent.
- The equivalent Generic CADD 6.1 two-letter command code and a description of the command.
- Any special notes about the command or how to execute it in Generic CADD 6.1.

Drawing File Translation

In order to exchange drawings and not lose critical data, you must clearly understand the differences between Generic CADD 6.1 and AutoCAD. For example, AutoCAD can create types of entities that do not have any counterpart in Generic CADD. If you use these entities in your AutoCAD drawings and then try to bring them into Generic CADD 6.1, some drawing information will be lost in the process. AutoCAD's three-dimensional (3D) objects are the best example of this. Since Generic CADD 6.1 is strictly a two-dimensional (2D) drawing product, any 3D objects in an AutoCAD drawing file cannot be imported into Generic CADD intact. The resulting Generic CADD drawing will contain only the current 2D view of the 3D objects.

Since CADD 6.1 and AutoCAD do not have exactly the same entities, drawing data must sometimes be translated into a different entity type that matches, as closely as possible, the original entity. In some cases this has little impact, as when translating CADD 6.1 components to AutoCAD blocks. In other cases, an entity cannot be translated at all, because there is no similar entity available. It is very important to understand this information in order to successfully translate drawings from one format to another.

The CADD 6.1 booklet, "How to use Generic CADD with AutoCAD," provides a file translation table that correlates AutoCAD entities and drawing settings in a .DWG file, to CADD 6.1 entities and settings in a .GCD file. Be sure to refer to the File Translation Table for specifics about how entities, settings, fonts, line types, and colors map from AutoCAD to CADD 6.1, and vice versa.

The following table summarizes some of the differences between the two programs:

AutoCAD entities and settings	Generic CADD entities and settings
3-Dimensional entities	Converts to a 2-Dimensional drawing according to the active AutoCAD viewport.
AME solid entities	Converts to a 2-Dimensional drawing, or not supported.
Color and linetype can be set for all entities on a particular layer.	Entity properties (i.e. color and linetype) are independent of layers, when converted, they become part of the entity definition.
Features 31 character layer names.	Features eight character layer names. AutoCAD layer names are truncated to eight characters, and a unique identifier is added.
Doesn't store units in the drawing, just displays them according to the current unit settings.	Displays units according to settings and also stores a default unit for the drawing database.
AutoCAD allows use of a scale factor during drawing creation.	Generic CADD doesn't use a scaling factor until the drawing is output to paper.
Entity selection and filters.	Entity selection is very similar. Filtering is available as a separate item on the selection menu.
Mode settings for snaps, dimensions, and entity placement allows repeating of commands.	Doesn't use modes, but uses the space bar to repeat the last command executed.
Uses a single-cursor mode — first mouse button is used to pick on the drawing screen and select items from the menu.	By default, uses a "tandem cursor" where the first button is used to pick on the drawing screen and the second button is used to select from the menu. Single cursor mode optional (used with AutoCAD-style menu).
Uses Ctrl-C to abort commands.	Uses Esc to abort commands.
Right mouse button repeats the last command executed.	By default, the right mouse button executes a Snap Nearpoint (NP) but it is programmable by the user.

Index

A
A2, 4-2, 4-5, 6-9, 15-11
A3, 4-2, 4-5, 6-9, B-6
AA, 15-24, 15-35, 15-37
Absolute coordinates, 13-15, A-11
AC, 9-2, 9-17, 9-19, 9-31, 9-32
ACAD Menu, B-1
Active View, 7-5
AE, 9-3, 9-21, 9-23, 9-24, 9-26, 9-45
AF, 6-13, 6-16, 6-17
AL, 5-17, 6-3, 9-4, 9-6, 11-10, 11-11, 12-2, 12-3, 12-4, 14-12
Aligned, 4-15, 8-6, 11-2, 11-4, 11-8, 11-22
All Layers Edit, 5-17, 6-3, 9-4, 9-6, 11-10, 12-2, 12-3, 12-4, 14-12
Angle measurement, 14-7
Angular Dimension, 11-2, 11-14
Arc, 4-2, 4-5, 5-18, 6-2, 6-5, 6-6, 6-9, 6-16, 7-15, 10-3, 10-4, 11-15, 14-5, 14-6, 14-11
ASCII, 8-2, 8-16, 9-27, 9-45, 13-20, 13-29, 14-20, 15-7, 15-30
Aspect, 8-7, 8-8, 13-22, 13-29
At an Angle, 9-26, 9-36, 11-2, 11-8, 11-9, 11-12, 11-22, 15-13
Attribute, 9-3, 9-17, 13-20, 13-22, 13-24, 13-25
Attribute Attach, 9-3, 9-17, 9-19, 9-20, 9-21, 9-25, 9-42, 13-22
Attribute Create, 9-2, 9-17, 9-31, 9-32
Attribute Display, 9-20, 9-45
AutoCAD, 8-3, 8-4, 8-11, 13-2, 13-20, 13-23, 13-24, 13-26, 13-27, 13-28, 14-14
    using with CADD, 6.1, B-1 to B-6
AutoConvert, 13-28
Autofillet, 4-11, 4-18, 6-13, 6-16, 6-17
AX, 11-2, 11-14

B
Basepoint, 7-11, 7-12, 14-19, A-10
BE, 4-8, 5-26
Bezier curves, 4-8, 4-11, 4-12, 5-25, 5-26, 10-2
BF, 10-2, 10-12, 10-14
BH, 10-2, 10-5, 10-6, 10-10, 10-12
BI, 14-2, 14-21

I-1

BOM program, 14-21
Boundary Fill, 10-2, 10-12, 10-14
Boundary Hatch, 10-2, 10-5, 10-6, 10-10, 10-12
Bounding box, 12-9
BR, 6-13, 7-2, 7-6
Break, 5-16, 5-23, 5-24
BS, 14-1, 14-19, 14-20, B-6
BV, 4-2, 4-7, 4-8, 15-16, 15-20, B-7
BW, 4-2, 4-8, B-7

C
C2, 2-6, 2-11, 4-2, 4-3, 4-4, 4-33, 4-34, 4-35, 6-9, 6-27, 11-25, 14-16, 15-11, 15-16, 15-20
C3, 4-2, 4-4, 6-9
CA, 6-13, 6-17, 6-18
CADD 6.1
    new features, 13-2, 13-26, B-1
Calculation
    angle, 14-7
    area, 14-7
    distance, 14-7
Cartesian coordinates, 3-23, 3-24, A-1, A-7
CC, 9-2, 9-3, 9-4, 9-5, 9-6, 9-7, 9-18, 9-21, 9-26, 9-32, 9-37
CD, 2-3, 9-2, 9-7, 9-8
CE, 6-13, 9-2, 9-11, 9-12, 9-21
Center construction, 2-20, 4-3
CF, 4-22, 4-23
CG, 5-2, 5-16, 12-5, 12-8, 12-12
CH, 6-13, 6-17, 6-18
Chamfer, 6-13, 6-17, 6-18, 6-19, 6-18
Change, 5-6, 5-9, 5-15, 5-17, 15-34
Change Object, 5-6
Changing
    default path names, 13-15, 13-26
    dimension settings, 11-19, 11-20, 13-15, 15-16
    text settings, 8-1, 8-8
CI, 3-9, 9-2, 9-12, 9-13, 9-14
Circles
    three-point, 4-2, 4-4, 6-9
    two-point, 2-6, 4-4, 4-33, 5-19
CM, 4-2, 4-16, B-7
CN, 9-2, 9-12, 9-13, 9-14, B-7
CO, 2-6, 2-12, 2-20, 3-9, 3-14, 5-2, 5-16, 9-1, 9-11, 12-1, 12-3, 15-34, B-7
Color
    dimensions, 7-10, 11-3, 11-11, 11-32
    drawing, 3-18, 7-1, 7-8, 7-10, 7-11
    text, 7-10, 8-2, 8-8, 8-9, 8-13, 8-14
Command line , 2-5
Commands
    editing, 2-3
    entering, 2-2, 2-3, 2-4, 2-5
    repeating previous, 3-9, 3-10
    two-character, 2-2, 2-3, 3-12, 3-13

Complex curves, 4-12
Component Create, 9-2, 9-3, 9-4, 9-5, 9-6, 9-7, 9-18, 9-21, 9-26, 9-32, 9-37
Component Dump, 9-2, 9-7, 9-8
Component Explode, 6-13, 9-2, 9-11, 9-12
Component Name, 9-6, 9-8, 9-9, 9-13, 9-32, 9-33, 13-25, 15-20
Component Place, 3-11, 3-15, 9-2, 9-8, 9-10, 9-11, 9-12, 9-14, 9-15, 9-39, 13-22, 14-15
Component Rotate, 9-9, 9-15, 9-16, 9-26, 9-29, 9-38, 9-41, 15-12, 15-13, 15-14, 15-17
Component Scale, 9-2, 9-9, 9-14, 9-15, 9-16, 9-38, 15-4, 15-12, 15-14
Component Snap, 6-11, 9-2, B-9
Components
 attributes, 9-1, 9-2, 9-3, 9-17, 9-18, 9-19, 9-21, 9-29
 creating, 9-2, 9-3, 9-4, 9-5, 9-6, 9-7
 modifying, 9-2, 9-11, 9-12
 retrieving, 9-1, 9-8 13-19
 saving, 9-1, 9-8, 13-22
 symbol libraries, 9-2, 15-31
 using existing, 9-1, 9-8
Configuration, 3-10, 6-2, 6-19, 7-4, 7-5, 13-3
Construction Points, 4-8, 4-17, 4-18, 5-21, 5-26, 6-2, 7-5, 7-8, 7-14, 9-15
Control points, 4-8, 5-25, 5-26
Conventions used, 2-1, 2-7
Conversion
 to AutoCAD .DWG, 13-23, 13-26, 13-28, B-1, B-5, B-6
 to DXF, 13-23, 13-26, 13-28, B-1
 to HPGL, 13-23, 13-26, 13-28
Coordinates
 about, 2-4, 3-23, 3-24, A-1 to A-12
 absolute, 7-11, 7-12, 15-13, A-1
 basepoint, 7-12
 Cartesian, 2-4, 3-3, A-1, A-7
 manual entry, 2-9, 4-17, 4-21, 7-11, 7-12, A-1 to A-8
 polar, A-5 to A-12
 relative, 2-9, 4-17, 4-21, 7-11, 15-13, A-1, A-2, A-3, A-4
Copy, 2-3, 2-6, 2-12, 2-20, 3-9, 3-14, 5-2, 5-3, 5-6, 5-15, 5-16, 9-1, 9-11, 15-34
Corners
 chamfered, 6-1, 6-16, 6-17
 filleted, 6-16, 6-17, 6-24, 6-25, 6-26
CP, 9-2, 9-8, 9-9, 9-10, 9-12, 9-14, 9-15, 9-39, 9-40, 9-41, 13-22, 14-15, 15-4, 15-16, 15-20, 15-31
CR, 9-2, 9-9, 9-15, 9-16, 9-26, 9-29, 9-38, 9-41, 9-42, 15-4, 15-12, 15-13, 15-17
CS, 3-18, 7-8, 7-10, 7-11, 8-8, 9-25, 9-30, 9-38, 13-18, 15-4
Current layer, 12-2, 12-3, 12-4, 12-5, 12-6, 12-11, 12-13
Cursor, 2-2, 2-3, 2-4
Curves
 Bezier, 4-6, 4-8, 5-25
 complex, 4-12
 drawing multiple, 4-11
Customizing
 CADD 6.0, 15-1, 15-37, 15-38
 menus, 15-1, 15-37, 15-38
CV, 4-2, 4-9
CW, 9-2, 9-6, 9-7, B-11

I-4 ■ Index

CX, 9-2, 9-5, 9-12, 9-13, 9-14, B-11
CZ, 3-14, 9-2, 9-9, 9-14, 9-15, 9-16, 9-29, 9-38, 15-4, 15-12, 15-14

D

DA, 15-24, 15-35, 15-36, 15-37
DB, 4-2, 4-9, 4-10, 4-18, 15-20, 15-28
DC, 4-17, 7-8, 7-11, 7-12
DE, 5-16, 5-19, 5-20, 9-3, 9-21, 10-5, 10-12
Default
    path for saving, 13-12, 13-24, 13-25, 13-26
    units, 7-8, 7-11
DG, 3-14, 5-2, 5-14
DI, 7-8, 7-13, 13-18, 15-7
Diameter dimension, 11-2, 11-16, 11-29
Digitizer, 2-2, 2-4, 3-9, 3-10, 6-2, 15-1, 15-2, 15-23, 15-24, 15-32, 15-33, 15-35, 15-36, 15-37, 15-38
Dimension Change, 11-2, 11-21
Dimension Mode, 11-2, 11-11, 11-12, 11-15, 11-16, 11-27, 11-29, 11-32, B-11
Dimension Settings, 11-2, 11-3, 11-12, 11-22, 11-23, 11-27, 11-28, 11-29, 11-32, 13-18
Dimensions
    angular, 11-14
    arrowheads, 11-7, 11-22
    cumulative mode, 11-12
    diameter, 11-16
    extension lines, 11-6, 11-7
    linear, 11-6, 11-7, 11-12
    modes, 11-11
    partitioned mode, 11-11
    Proximity Fixed, 11-8, 11-12
    radial, 11-14
    settings, 11-2, 11-3, 11-12, 11-14, 11-21
    single mode, 11-11
    text, 11-3, 11-4, 11-22
Direct distance, 3-21, 3-22, 4-20, 11-9, B-12
Display
    attributes, 9-25, 9-26
    construction points, 4-17, 5-21, 5-24, 6-2
    options, 7-13
    reference points, 5-21, 7-8, 7-14, 8-13
    standard points, 7-8, 7-14
Display Coordinates, 4-17, 7-11, 7-12, A-10, A-11, B-13
DM, 15-24, 15-35, B-13
DN, 3-14, 4-27, 13-1, 13-18, 13-19, B-13
Double lines
    distance between 4-2, 4-9, 4-10, 4-11, 4-18, 4-19, 15-16, B-13
    offsets, 4-2, 4-9, 4-10, 4-11, 4-18, 4-19, 15-16, B-13
    solid, 4-2, 4-9, 4-10, 4-11, 4-18, 4-19, 15-16, B-13
DP, 13-1, 13-2, 13-3, 13-5, 13-7, 13-13, 13-17, 13-29, B-13
DR, 5-2, 5-14, B-13
Drawing
    exchange format (DXF), 13-2, 13-28, B-1
    names, 13-23, 13-24, 13-25

Index ■ I-5

       opening, 13-2, 13-20, 13-21, 13-22, 13-23
       saving, 2-23, 13-24, 13-25
       scale, 1-2, 5-9, 5-13, 13-13
       screen, 2-4
Drawing Remove, 5-27, 13-1, 13-18, 13-20
DU, 5-27, 13-1, 13-18, 13-19, 13-29, 14-11
DWG extension, 13-23, 13-26, B-1, B-2, B-4
DX, 5-27, 13-1, 13-18, 13-20
DXF conversion, 13-28, B1
DXFIN, 13-2, 13-28
DXFOUT, 13-2, 13-28
DZ, 5-2, 5-9, 5-13, 9-14

E

Edit
       Bezier curves, 5-26, 5-27
       text, 8-12, 8-13, 8-14, 8-15
EF, 14-1, 14-16
EL, 4-18, 5-21, 9-10, 10-13
Ellipse, 4-2, 4-4, 4-6, 4-7, 4-6, 4-7, 5-13, 14-11
EN, 11-26, 12-6, 13-1, 13-18
Enter key, 2-2, 2-3, 3-8
Enter text
       characters, 8-2, 8-10, 8-11, 8-12
       lines, 15-6, 15-10, 15-27
Entity Filter, 5-7, 5-18, 14-16
EP, 4-2, 4-6
ER, 5-2, 5-16, 5-19, 9-14, 12-4
Erase, 4-36, 5-2, 5-16, 5-19, 5-27
Erase last, 3-20, 4-18, 5-21, 9-10, 10-13
Escape key, 2-5, 3-9
EX, 9-11, 9-21, 14-1, 14-2, 15-23
Explode, 3-2, 6-13, 9-2, 9-5, 9-11, 9-12, 9-21, 10-3, 14-1, 14-2, B-9, B-16
Extend, 6-13, 6-15, 6-20
Extension lines, 11-2, 11-5, 11-6, 11-8, 11-11, 11-12, 11-21, 11-22, B-12, B-16

F

FA, 7-8, 7-15, 10-10, 14-18
Fast Redraw, 7-8, 7-15, 10-10, 13-14, 14-18
FF, 10-2, 10-11, 10-12, 10-13
FH, 10-2, 10-4, 10-5
FI, 4-11, 6-13, 6-16, 6-17, 6-24, 6-25, 6-26, 11-25
Fields, 9-17, 9-18, 9-20, 9-21, 9-22, 9-26, 9-38
File
       loading, 13-2, 13-12
       saving, 2-22, 2-23, 13-23, 13-24, 13-25
File Selector, 13-20, 13-21, 13-22, 14-9, 14-13, 14-14, 14-15, 14-17
File translation
       to AutoCAD, B-4
       to DXF 13-28, B-1
Filled fonts, 8-4, B-16
Fillet, 6-13, 6-16, 6-17, 6-24, 6-25, 6-26

Fillet Radius, 6-13, 6-16, 6-17, 6-24, 6-25, 6-26
Fills, 10-1, 10-2, 10-4
    color, 10-10
Filtering
    de-selecting objects, 5-20
    selecting objects, 5-18, 5-19
Fitted Fill, 10-2, 10-11, 10-12, 10-13
Fitted Hatch, 10-2, 10-4, 10-5
Fonts
    AutoCAD, 8-3, 8-11
    changing, 8-3, 8-15
    default, 8-3
Format
    numeric, 7-12, 11-25
FP, 9-7, 9-8
FR, 6-13, 6-16, 6-17, 6-24, 6-26, 11-25, 15-12, 15-17

G

GC, 6-2, 6-11, 9-2, 9-15, 9-16
GCD extension, 4-26, 13-24
Generic 3D, 1-4, 13-25
GO, 4-15
GR, 4-2, 4-14, 4-15
Grids, 4-2, 4-15, 9-3
GS, 3-18, 4-2, 4-15, 9-30, 9-39, 15-2, 15-3, 15-7

H

Hatch patterns, 10-6, 10-7, 10-8, 10-9, 10-14, 13-19
Hatch Settings, 3-18, 10-2, 10-6, 10-9, 10-10
Hatching
    of objects, 10-1, 10-3
    within a boundary, 10-1, 10-7
    within a window, 10-2, 10-3
Hexagons, 4-3
HI, 2-6, 4-18, 7-8, 7-16, 7-17
Home key, 2-2, 3-9, 3-12
Horizontal dimension, 11-9
HS, 3-18, 10-2, 10-6, 10-9, 10-10

I

Individual Bezier Curve, 4-2, 4-8
Individual Line, 4-1, 4-3, 4-11
Insert key, 3-8
Insertion Point, 9-10, 9-11
Intersection Trim, 6-13, 6-18, 6-19
Isometric text, 8-6
IX, 11-2, 11-16, 11-29

J

Justification
    text, 2-21, 3-3, 3-19, 8-2, 8-6, 8-15, 13-22, 13-29

L

L1, 4-1, 4-3, 15-5
L2, 4-2, 4-9, 4-10, 4-11, 4-19, 15-16, 15-20, 15-28
Layer Display, 7-5, 7-16, 12-2, 12-5, 12-6, 12-11, 12-13
Layer Hide, 7-5, 7-16, 12-2, 12-5, 12-6, 12-7, 12-13
Layer Name, 12-2, 12-3, 12-6, 12-8, 12-9, 12-11, 12-12, 12-13
Layers
    about, 3-5, 12-2, 12-3, 12-4, 12-5, 12-6
    changing, 12-2, 12-3, 12-4, 12-5, 12-6, 12-8
    current, 12-2, 12-4, 12-5
    hiding, 12-6
    moving objects between, 12-12
    naming, 12-6, 12-12
LC, 4-17, 4-27, 4-29, 4-31, 6-22, 6-26, 7-8
LD, 15-24, 15-35
LE, 11-2, 11-17, 11-31
Leader, 11-2, 11-7, 11-17, 11-18, 11-31, 15-17
Letter direction
    aligned, 11-3
    dimensions, 11-3
    horizontal, 11-3
Letter placement
    above-line, 11-3
    dimensions, 11-3
    in-line, 11-3
LI 4-1, 4-3, 4-9, 4-11, 4-21, 4-22, 4-32, 4-36, 6-8, 11-26
Like, 3-13, 5-18
Line Type, 4-12, 4-28, 4-29, 4-30, 7-9, 7-10
Line Width, 7-8, 7-10
Linear Dimension, 11-2, 11-12, 11-13, 11-14, 11-15, 11-16, 11-26, 11-28, 11-29
Lines
    color, 7-8, 7-9, 7-10
    continuous, 2-7, 7-8
    double, 4-10, 4-11
    drawing multiple, 4-11, 4-12
    extending, 6-14, 6-16
    orthogonal, 4-12, 4-14
    parallel, 4-9, 4-10, 4-11
    patterns, 7-9
    trimming, 6-13, 6-14
    types, 7-9
    width, 7-9, 7-10
LL, 11-2, 11-18, 11-31, 15-12, 15-15
LO, 4-24, 6-21, 9-8, 9-19, 13-1, 13-20, 13-21, 13-22, 13-23
Load, 13-20, 13-21, 13-22, 13-23
LS, 7-6, 14-1, 14-18, 15-7
LT, 4-27, 4-28, 4-29, 4-30, 4-31, 7-8, 13-18
LV, 3-15, 15-24, 15-25, 15-30
LW, 7-8, 7-9, 13-12
LX, 11-2, 11-12, 11-13, 11-26, 11-28, 11-29
LZ, 4-17, 7-8, 7-9

M

MA, 14-1, 14-19, 14-20, 15-2, 15-13, 15-14
Macro Assign, 14-1, 14-19, 14-20, 15-2, 15-13, 15-14
Manual Entry Offset Basepoint, 7-12
Manual Entry Offset Origin, 7-11, 15-13, 15-29, A-7
Manual Entry Offset Relative, 2-6, 2-9, 4-17, 4-21, 6-21, 7-11, 15-13, A-7
Match Parameters, 8-2
MB, 7-12, 14-19, A-7, A-8, A-10
ME, 14-1, 14-2, 14-3, 14-4, 14-5, 14-7
Measure, 14-1, 14-2, 14-3, 14-4, 14-5, 14-4, 14-6, 14-5, 14-7
Measurement
    angles, 14-2, 14-3, 14-4, 14-5, 14-7
    area, 14-2, 14-3, 14-4, 14-5, 14-7
    distance, 14-2, 14-3, 14-4, 14-5, 14-7
Menu
    CADD6, 3-12, 3-15
    customizing, 15-24, 15-30
    HELP6, 3-15
    selecting from the, 2-2, 3-12
    video, 2-3, 2-4, 3-12, 3-15
MH, 8-2, 14-1, 14-17
MI, 5-16, 5-20, 5-22, 15-34
Mirror Copy, 5-10, 5-16, 5-20, 5-22
Mirror image, 5-10, 9-14
Mistakes, 2-3, 3-5, 3-20
MO, 7-11, 13-15, 14-11, 15-13, 15-18, 15-20, 15-21, 15-29, A-7, A-8, A-10, A-11
Mouse
    first button, 2-2, 2-4, 2-5, 2-7
    second button, 2-2, 2-4, 2-5, 2-7
    third button, 2-2, 2-4, 2-5, 2-7
Move, 2-16, 2-17, 5-2, 5-4, 5-8, 5-9
Move Point, 5-8, 5-20, 5-21, 15-34
Moving
    objects, 5-5, 5-8
    points, 5-9, 5-22, 15-34
MP, 5-8, 5-20, 5-21, 5-22, 15-34
MR, 2-6, 2-9, 3-20, 3-24, 4-17, 4-20, 4-21, 6-21, 7-11, 11-25, 13-15, 15-3, 15-5, 15-13, 15-18, 15-21, 15-29, A-7, A-10
MS, 4-2, 4-11
MT, 6-13, 6-19, 6-20
MU, 4-2, 4-11
MV, 2-6, 3-9, 3-13, 3-15, 5-2, 5-16, 9-1, 9-11, 11-18, 12-1, 12-3, 15-34
MX, 6-13, 6-20

N

Name View, 7-2, 12-2, 12-10, 12-14
Naming
    file, 12-6, 13-23, 13-24
    layers, 12-6, 12-11
    views, 12-3, 12-11, 12-12
Nested commands, 3-15, 3-16
NF, 7-8, 7-12, 11-25

NP, 3-10, 3-11, 4-20, 4-21, 6-1, 6-2
Numeric Display Format, 7-12, 11-24, 11-25
NV, 7-2, 12-2, 12-10, 12-14, 14-19
NX, 7-2, 12-2, 12-10, 12-16

O
OA, 4-2, 4-14
OB, 4-6, 5-16, 5-20, 5-23, 6-21, 6-29
Object Break, 4-6, 5-16, 5-20, 5-23, 5-24, 6-21, 6-29, 6-32
Object Change, 5-2, 5-4, 5-5, 5-6, 15-34
Object Fill, 10-2, 10-10, 10-11, 10-12, 15-16
Object Hatch, 10-2, 10-3, 10-4, 10-5, 10-10, 10-11
Object Move, 5-2, 5-4, 15-5, 15-34
Objects
    primitive, 1-3, 1-4, 4-1, 4-2
    selecting, 5-2, 5-16, 5-17, 5-18
OC, 5-1, 5-2, 5-6, 15-34
OD, 2-6, 2-14, 4-18, 5-3, 7-8, 7-14, 7-15, 9-9
OE, 4-36, 5-1, 5-2, 5-3
OF, 10-11
OG, 5-2, 5-4, 5-6, 15-34
OH, 10-2, 10-3, 10-4, 10-5, 10-10, 10-11
OI, 14-1, 14-15
OM, 5-2, 5-4, 15-4, 15-5, 15-34
Online help, 3-11, 14-15
OO, 2-7, 4-18, 5-16, 5-21, 5-27, 12-7, 13-18, 13-19
Overwriting, 13-25

P
PA, 7-1, 7-4, 13-15
Page
    size, 13-8
    width, 13-8
Pan, 7-1, 7-4, 12-1, 13-15
Parallel lines, 3-1, 4-9, 4-11, 6-1, 6-8, 6-16, 6-21
Path names
    changing the default, 13-20, 13-24, 13-26
PC, 4-8, 4-17, 7-8, 7-14
PD, 5-27, 12-7, 13-1, 13-18, 13-19, 13-18, 13-29, 14-11
Pen Up, 4-9, 4-26, 4-29, 4-30, 4-32, 6-21, 10-4, 10-11, 10-12, 14-3, 14-8, 15-32
Perpendicular lines, 6-1, 6-7
Pixels, 1-2
PL, 13-1, 13-17
Plot, 13-1, 13-3, 13-6, 13-7, 13-8, 13-9, 13-10, 13-11, 13-12, 13-13, 13-14, 13-15, 13-16, 13-17, 13-28, 13-29
Plotting
    entire drawing, 13-10, 13-11, 13-12, 13-14
    partial drawing, 13-10, 13-11
PO, 4-1, 4-2, 5-21, 7-15, 15-15, 15-16, 15-18, 15-20, 15-22
Point coordinates, 15-13
Points
    construction, 4-8, 4-17, 7-8, 7-14

I-10 ■ Index

        coordinates, 2-9, 3-24, 3-25, A-1 to A-12
           moving, 5-8, 5-21, 5-34
           reference, 5-21, 7-8, 7-14, 8-12, 8-13, 10-13, 14-8, 15-13
           standard, 4-1, 4-2, 4-3
Polar coordinates, 3-21, 3-22, 7-11, 7-12, 15-18, 15-19, 15-20, A-1 to A-12
Port, 13-5, 13-7, 13-28
Postscript, 8-3, 13-1, 13-3, 13-5, 13-6, 13-8, 13-12, 13-13, 13-29
PR, 5-21, 7-8, 7-14, 8-12, 8-13, 10-13, 14-18, 15-13, A-6
Precision, 11-4, 11-5
Primitive objects, 2-23, 3-2, 5-19, 5-21
Print, 13-1, 13-5 to 13-9
Print Manager, 13-1 to 13-5
Proximity Fixed, 11-2, 11-6, 11-8, 11-12, 11-15, 11-16, 11-22, 11-24, 11-27
PS, 7-8, 7-14

Q
QP, 6-2, 6-12, 6-13
QU, 13-1, 13-27
Quick Pick, 6-2, 6-12

R
Radial Copy, 5-16, 5-20, 5-23, 6-26, 6-28, 15-34
Radial Dimension, 11-2, 11-15, 11-30
RB, 4-1, 4-18, 7-8, 7-15
RC, 5-16, 5-20, 5-23, 6-26, 6-28, 15-34
RD, 4-19, 6-2, 7-2, 7-5, 7-6, 7-14, 7-16, 9-25, 9-45, 10-9, 12-13, 13-23, 14-18, 15-9
RE, 2-16, 4-1, 4-2, 4-3
Real-world scale, 13-16
Rectangle, 2-16, 4-1, 4-3
Redo, 2-7, 3-20, 5-16, 5-21, 5-27
Redraw, 4-19, 6-2, 7-2, 7-5, 7-6, 7-14, 7-16, 9-25, 9-45, 10-9, 12-13, 13-23, 14-18, 15-9
Reference Points, 5-21, 6-2, 7-1, 7-8, 7-14, 8-12, 8-13, 9-4, 9-16, 10-13, 11-27, 14-18, A-6
Regular Polygon
        center construction, 2-19, 4-2, 4-3
        side construction, 4-2, 4-3, 4-4
RM, 6-13, 6-14, 6-15, 6-19, 6-20
RO, 3-9, 5-2, 5-16, 6-29, 8-8, 9-15, 12-3
Root menu, 2-2, 2-4, 2-5, 2-7, 2-9, 2-10, 2-12, 2-15, 2-16, 2-19, 2-20, 2-21, 2-22, 3-11, 3-12, 15-25, 15-27
Rotate, 5-9, 5-14, 5-16, 8-8, 9-6, 9-9, 12-7
Rotating
        components, 9-9
        layers, 12-8
        objects, 5-9, 5-14, 5-16, 8-8, 9-6, 9-9, 12-7
        text, 8-8
RP, 2-6, 2-19, 4-2, 4-3, B-26
Rubberbanding, 2-8, 2-9, 2-10, 3-4, 4-1, 4-3, 4-6, 4-11, 4-18, 4-19, 4-23, 5-22, 7-4, 7-5, 7-8, 7-15, 11-13, 14-2
RX, 11-2, 11-15, 11-30
RZ, 15-24, 15-35, 15-36, 15-37

S

Index ■ I-11

SA, 2-6, 2-22, 4-26, 4-37, 6-32, 9-7, 9-8, 9-18, 9-31, 9-32, 9-33, 13-1, 13-19, 13-20, 13-23, 13-25, 13-26, 13-27, 15-8
Save
    components, 9-2, 9-7, 13-23, 13-25, 13-26
    drawing files, 2-23, 13-23, 13-24, 13-25
SB, 13-25, 14-1, 14-19, 14-20, 15-3, 15-6, 15-7
SC, 2-6, 2-10, 2-11, 2-14, 4-20, 4-21, 6-1, 6-2, 6-3, 6-12, 8-13, 9-32
Scale
    components, 9-14, 9-15
    hatch patterns, 10-7
    objects, 5-11, 5-12, 5-16
    print, 13-13, 13-16
    real world, 1-2, 1-3
    setting the, I-2, I-3, 1-2, 1-3, 13-13, 13-16
Screen Display, 7-4, 7-6, 7-8, 12-13, 13-16, 15-9
Screen Flip, 14-9, 14-10, 14-13, 14-16
SE, 14-1, 14-12, 14-13, 14-16
Select Plot, 13-17
Selection
    by crossing of window, 5-17, 5-16
    by drawing, 5-7
    by filter, 5-18, 5-19
    by layer 5-17, 5-18
    by object, 5-17, 5-18
    de-selecting, 5-20, 5-21
    window, 5-17
Set Current, 12-2, 12-5
Settings
    arrows, 11-7, 11-22
    color, 7-11, 7-12, 7-13
    dimensions, 11-3
    display, 7-13
    matching, 14-17
    text, 8-3
SF, 3-19, 14-1, 14-9, 14-10, 14-16, 15-2, 15-13
SG, 4-2, 4-15, 6-2, 6-11, 9-30, 9-36, 9-39, 15-2, 15-3, 15-7
SH, 14-1, 14-17, 14-21
Shell Exe, 14-1, 14-17
Shell to BOM, 14-2, 14-21
Shoulder Length, 11-2, 11-18, 11-31, 15-12, 15-16
SI, 6-2, 6-6, 6-7, 6-29
Side construction, 2-20, 4-3, 4-4
Sidebar menu, 2-4
SL, 6-2, 6-7, 6-8, 6-9
Slant, 8-6, 8-7
SM, 2-6, 2-17, 2-19, 3-13, 4-25, 4-26, 4-32, 6-1, 6-3, 6-21, 6-22, 6-29, B-30
SN, 6-2, 6-9, B-30
Snapping
    parallel, 6-2, 6-7
    perpendicular, 6-2, 6-7
    tangent, 6-10, 6-11

I-12 ■ Index

        to intersection, 3-17, 3-21, 6-4, 6-6, 6-10, 8-13, 9-15, 9-29, 9-39, 10-5, 10-12, 14-4, B-30
        to midpoint, 6-2, 6-6
        to nearest object, 6-1, 6-3
        to nearest point, 3-11, 4-20, 4-23, 6-1, 6-2
        to percentage, 6-1, 6-4, 6-5
Snaps, 2-9, 2-10, 3-11, 4-20, 6-1 to 6-11
SO, 6-2, 6-3
SP, 6-2, 6-7
Spacebar, 6-25, 11-29, 11-30
Spline curves, 4-11, 4-12
SR, 6-1, 6-3, 6-4, 6-5
SS, 5-2, 5-16, 5-20, 5-24, 15-34
ST, 6-2, 6-10, 6-11, 11-25
Standard Points, 6-2, 7-8, 7-14, 7-15, B-13
Status line, 5-5, 5-6, 5-15, 7-13, 12-5, 12-8, 13-23, 15-8
Stretch, 5-9, 5-10, 5-20, 5-24, 5-25
SV, 13-1, 13-19
SY, 6-2, 6-3, 12-5
Symbol Libraries, 9-1, 9-2, 15-30, 15-31
Symbols, 9-1, 9-2, 9-3, 15-30, 15-32, 15-38
SZ, 5-2, 5-16, 9-1, 9-14, 12-3, 15-34

T

TA, 8-1, 8-14
TD, 8-1, 8-13, 8-14
TE, 8-1, 8-13, 8-14, 8-15, 9-21
Text, 2-21, 8-1, 8-2, 8-3, 11-22
        aspect, 8-7
        color, 8-8
        dimension, 11-3
        editing, 8-13, 8-15, 8-16
        entering, 2-21, 8-1, 8-11, 8-12, 8-13
        font, 8-3, 8-4, 8-5
        justification, 8-6
        leader lines, 11-20, 11-21
        line appending, 8-14, 8-15
        proportional spacing, 8-10
        rotation, 8-8, 8-9
        settings, 8-2 to 8-11
        slant, 8-6
        spacing, 8-9, 8-10
Text Change, 8-14, 8-15
Text Delete, 8-13, 8-14
Text Edit, 8-13, 8-14, 8-15, 9-21
Text Insert, 8-13, 8-14
Text Replace, 8-13, 8-14
Text Settings, 2-6, 3-18, 3-19, 4-17, 8-1, 8-2, 8-3, 8-6, 8-9, 8-10, 8-11, 8-13, 8-15
TG, 8-1, 8-14, 8-15
TI, 8-1, 8-13, 8-14
TK, 3-22, 4-25, 4-26, 4-29, 4-30, 4-32, 6-21
TL, 2-6, 2-21, 4-28, 4-30, 7-15, 8-1, 8-2, 8-9, 8-11, 8-12, 8-14, 8-15, 15-5

TM, 15-24, 15-35, 15-36, 15-37
TO, 6-12
Toggles, 3-9, 3-19, 4-14, 4-18, 7-13, 7-14, 7-16, 9-9, 10-9, 10-10, 11-7, 11-8, 11-24, 15-2, 15-37
TP, 7-15, 8-1, 8-2, 8-4, 8-8, 8-9, 8-10, 8-11, 8-12, 8-13, 8-15
Tracking, 3-22, 3-23, 4-25, 4-26, 4-28, 4-29, 4-30, 4-32, 6-21
Trim, 6-1, 6-13, 6-14, 6-15, 6-16, 6-18, 6-19, 6-20
True ellipse, 4-6, 4-7
TS, 2-6, 2-21, 3-18, 4-17, 8-1, 8-2, 8-3, 8-5, 8-6, 8-8, 8-15, 9-38, 13-22, 13-29, 15-7, 15-29
TX, 8-1, 8-14
Typeface, 8-3, 9-24

U

UE, 4-18, 5-16, 5-21, 5-27, 12-7, 13-18, 13-19
UG, 11-2, 11-19, 11-21
UM, 11-2, 11-11, 11-12, 11-15, 11-16, 11-27, 11-29
UN, 4-17, 5-27, 7-8, 7-11, 8-4, 15-2, 15-3
Units
    of drawing database, 7-11
    of measurement, 4-17, 7-8, 7-11, 11-22
US, 11-2, 11-3, 11-12, 11-22, 11-23, 11-32, 13-18
Utilities
    File Selector, 14-15
    Macro Assign, 14-21
    Screen Flip, 14-9, 14-10
    Shell Exe, 14-17, 14-18
UU, 5-16, 5-21, 5-27
UV, 11-2, 11-18

V

Variables, 15-3, 15-7, 15-9, 15-10, 15-11, 15-12, 15-17, 15-31
Viewing drawings, 3-6
VM, 7-14, 15-24
VP, 7-1, 7-4
VX, 3-14, 3-15, 15-24, 15-25, 15-30

W

WC, 4-36, 5-1, 5-6, 9-6, 15-34
WD, 7-2, 7-6
WE, 2-2, 2-8, 2-12, 3-17, 5-1, 5-7, 5-27, 9-45, 15-12, 15-14
WF, 9-35, 10-2, 10-11
WG, 5-2, 5-6, 5-14, 15-34
WH, 10-2, 10-11
Window Fill, 9-35, 10-2, 10-11
Window Hatch, 10-2, 10-3, 10-2, 10-11
Window selection method, 3-19, 5-17, 6-29
WM, 4-25, 4-28, 4-30, 4-32, 5-2, 5-7, 14-16, 15-34
WordPerfect, 13-8
WR, 5-2, 5-9, 9-6, 9-15, 12-7, 15-34
WS, 5-2, 5-8
WT, 8-1, 8-5, 8-15, 8-16, 9-24
WZ, 5-2, 5-9, 5-13, 9-14, 15-34

X

XA, 9-3, 9-26, 9-27, 9-28, 9-45
XG, 13-2, 13-28
XT, 6-13, 6-15, 6-19, 6-20
XY, 9-2, 9-11

Y

Y coordinates, 2-4, 3-22, 7-11, 7-12, 14-16, A-2
YC, 4-17, 12-2, 12-4, 12-5
YD, 3-13, 7-5, 7-16, 12-2, 12-5, 12-6, 12-11, 12-13
YE, 12-2
YG, 12-2, 12-8
YH, 3-13, 7-5, 7-16, 12-2, 12-5, 12-6, 12-7, 12-13
YL, 12-2, 12-8, 12-9
YN, 12-2, 12-3, 12-6, 12-11
YR, 12-2, 12-7
YS, 12-2, 12-9
YZ, 12-2, 12-7

Z

ZA, 7-1, 7-2, 7-4, 7-5
ZI, 6-23, 6-26, 6-28, 7-1, 7-2, 13-15
ZL, 7-2, 7-5, 7-6, 14-18, 14-19
ZM, 7-2, 7-6, 7-7, 7-8, 9-30
ZO, 2-6, 4-15, 6-28, 6-29, 7-1, 7-2, 7-3, 9-45, 13-15, A-6
Zoom
    to fit screen, 7-1, 7-2, 7-3, 7-4, 7-5
    to named view, 12-11, 12-12
    to previous view, 7-4
Zoom All, 2-6, 7-1, 7-2, 7-4
Zoom In, 7-1, 7-2
Zoom Out, 7-1, 7-2
Zoom Previous, 7-1, 7-4
Zoom Value, 7-6, 7-7
Zoom View, 12-2, 12-10, 12-14, 12-15
Zoom Window, 7-1, 7-2
ZP, 7-1, 7-4, 7-5
ZV, 7-2, 7-5, 12-2, 12-10, 12-14, 12-15
ZW, 3-13, 3-15, 4-21, 4-33, 6-21, 6-29, 7-1, 7-2, 12-1, 12-10, 12-14

-Notes-

-Notes-

-Notes-

-Notes-

-Notes-

-Notes-

-Notes-

-Notes-

-Notes-

-Notes-